Romance Linguistics 2013

Romance Languages and Linguistic Theory (RLLT)

ISSN 1574-552X

The yearly 'Going Romance' meetings and the 'Linguistic Symposia on Romance Languages' feature research in formal linguistics of Romance languages, in the domains of syntax, morphology, phonology and semantics. Each volume brings together a peer-reviewed selection of papers that were presented at one of the meetings, aiming to provide a representation of the spread of topics at that conference, and of the variety of research carried out nowadays on Romance languages within theoretical linguistics.

For an overview of all books published in this series, please see
http://benjamins.com/catalog/rllt

Editor

Frank Drijkoningen
Utrecht University

Volume 9

Romance Linguistics 2013. Selected papers from the 43rd Linguistic Symposium on Romance Languages (LSRL), New York, 17–19 April, 2013
Edited by Christina Tortora, Marcel den Dikken, Ignacio L. Montoya and Teresa O'Neill

Romance Linguistics 2013

Selected papers from the 43rd Linguistic Symposium
on Romance Languages (LSRL),
New York, 17–19 April, 2013

Edited by

Christina Tortora
City University of New York (College of Staten Island
and The Graduate Center)

Marcel den Dikken
Eötvös Loránd University & Hungarian Academy of Sciences

Ignacio L. Montoya
City University of New York (The Graduate Center)

Teresa O'Neill
City University of New York (The Graduate Center)

John Benjamins Publishing Company

Amsterdam / Philadelphia

DOI 10.1075/rllt.9
Cataloging-in-Publication Data available from Library of Congress:
LCCN 2015033754 (PRINT) / 2015035623 (E-BOOK)

ISBN 978 90 272 0389 2   (HB)
ISBN 978 90 272 6768 9   (E-BOOK)

John Benjamins Publishing Company · https://benjamins.com

Table of contents

Introduction

Christina Tortora, Marcel den Dikken,
Ignacio L. Montoya & Teresa O'Neill

The forty-third meeting of the Linguistic Symposium on Romance Languages (LSRL43) took place April 17–19, 2013, at The Graduate Center in Manhattan, and was jointly organized by the College of Staten Island and The Graduate Center, two of the twenty-four colleges and professional schools that make up The City University of New York (CUNY). The organizers were very excited to host the first ever LSRL in New York City, and to do so with a particularly large installment: 167 abstracts were received, with 62 selected for presentation at the conference. In addition to these 62 peer-reviewed selections, the conference featured five keynote talks: two for the main session, by Ricardo Otheguy (The CUNY Graduate Center) and Lori Repetti (Stony Brook University), and three for our *Special Session on Romance Parsed Corpora*, by Anthony Kroch and Beatrice Santorini (University of Pennsylvania), Charlotte Galves (University of Campinas), and Ana Maria Martins (University of Lisbon). Following the conference, a rigorous review process led to the selection of 21 papers for this volume, which to our delight includes the two main-session invited papers by Otheguy and Repetti. Two of the invited papers from the Special Session (Kroch/Santorini and Galves) are being included in a companion volume, along with four other selections from LSRL43, to be published as a Special Issue of *Linguistic Variation* on Romance Parsed Corpora.

While every year the LSRL invites submissions on any aspect of Romance linguistics, previous selected LSRL proceedings have varied in terms of how the contributions are conceptualized, where sometimes the entire volume is organized around a particular theme, possibly related to a special area of inquiry highlighted at the conference itself. For this volume, the editors chose simple author-based alphabetical order for the organization of the contributions, but this should not detract from the fact that they cohere with one another in interesting ways that are worth noting. Indeed, these 21 papers naturally cluster around three different approaches to the study of language: first, because the *Special Session on Romance Parsed Corpora* inspired what we believe was an unusually large number of submissions incorporating corpus methods, there are several contributions in this volume which cohere as good examples of corpus-based approaches to formal analysis. Likewise, there is another set of contributions which take an experimental approach, and as such could be read as a group. And finally, as

DOI 10.1075/rllt.9.001int

has always been the case with LSRL, there is a good number of contributions which are most aptly characterized as straight formal analyses of issues in phonology, morpho-syntax, syntax, and semantics. Within this group, the themes addressed offer connections to one another, in terms of particular phenomena being treated, or in terms of the theoretical and analytical questions they bear on. Additionally, they provide connections to the corpus-based and experimental studies, precisely with respect to theory and formal analysis. Because of all of these connections, our discussion here of the contributions to this volume does not follow the order offered in the table of contents.

Let us begin by considering four papers which use corpora of historical Romance languages to support formal analyses of structural variation and change. In "Root gerunds in Old Romanian," **Gabriela Alboiu** and **Virginia Hill** examine the distribution of gerund clauses in both adjunct and root contexts in corpora of Old Romanian. They propose that the declarative force of root gerunds is licensed in Old Romanian — but not in Modern Romanian — by a null Assertion Operator in ForceP that allows the Fin-T complex to be valued pragmatically. Pragmatic valuation of Fin in Old Romanian is possible because verbs raise to T (but not beyond), so the features of Fin are not valued by the inflectional features of the verb. The authors further propose that since the evidence for the presence of the null operator in learner input was weak, it was lost, leading to the emergence of V+T-to-Fin, which valued Fin as irrealis, and led to the loss of root gerunds in Modern Romanian. Their proposal also makes the claim that declarative, indicative clauses can value their finiteness features contextually. This work also demonstrates how corpora can provide evidence supporting a particular formal analysis of a syntactic change.

A good complement to this paper is **Marie Labelle's** contribution on "Participle fronting and clause structure in Old and Middle French." Labelle examines stylistic fronting of participles in the *Modéliser le changement: les voies du français* (MCVF) parsed corpus of Old and Middle French (Martineau et al. 2010), comparing the construction to counterparts in other Romance languages and in Icelandic. The author presents a descriptive profile of participle fronting, arguing that although the majority of tokens appear to involve movement of V^0, participle fronting is actually always phrasal movement, often movement of a remnant VP. In addition, unlike what has been proposed for other languages, Labelle argues that participle fronting in Old and Middle French can target three different positions: (i) one IP-internal position below the subject, (ii) Spec, FinP (the only informationally unmarked position in the periphery), and, (iii) less commonly, Spec, FocP. Because participle fronting in French involves a phrase, and does not necessarily correspond to backgrounded or focused information, it is typologically distinct from participle fronting in the other languages under consideration.

Like Labelle, **Deborah Arteaga** and **Julia Herschensohn** also address syntactic change in French. Their paper on "Old French possessives and ellipsis" shows that in

Old French, ellipsis could occur with a wider variety of constructions than can occur in Modern French. Arteaga and Herschensohn argue that the source of this diachronic change was a convergence of phonological, morphological, and syntactic factors, using a minimalist approach and Distributed Morphology to model how these factors led to the change in ellipsis. One of the key differences between Old French and Modern French is that ellipsis of nouns in the former was possible with stress falling on the article. A change whereby stress was no longer possible on the article is related to, they argue, the change in the definite article itself, which became a clitic (which cannot license ellipsis) and a Phase Head. Another key factor that contributed to this change was the erosion of overt morphology from Old French to Modern French, which resulted in the loss of the overt two-case system. A consequence of the convergence of these factors is that Modern French possesses a system of noun ellipsis that is different from that of other Romance languages.

Another study which uses historical corpora to argue for structural change is "The generalization of preposition *para* via fusion and ensuing loss of compositionality," by **Joseph Bauman** and **Rena Torres Cacoullos**. This paper provides an account of the change in the uses of the preposition *para* in Spanish, where the authors argue that *para* has been on the increase over the years, gradually displacing *por*. Bauman and Torres Cacoullos support this claim through an examination of texts ranging from the 12th century through the 20th century. They note that in the earlier texts, there were more uses of *para* in the allative sense (i.e., in the spatial sense, as in *voy para el mar* 'I'm going to the beach'). However, through time, those uses have declined and the use of prepositions with infinitives in the purposive sense increased proportionately (e.g., as in *vinieron para comer* 'they came (in order) to eat'). This second sense in particular was formerly conveyed through *por*, which has been on the decrease overall through the years (though it should be noted that these are relative shifts, as both have co-existed — and continue to co-exist — in overlapping domains). This demonstrates a particular path of grammaticalization: allative > purposive. The authors also argue that there is evidence in support of the widely hypothesized idea that *para* developed from the coalescence of *por* and the particle *a*. Whereas early forms were decomposable into *por* + *a*, a loss of analyzability and compositionality is readily discernible in later texts. Bauman and Torres Cacoullos conclude that the development of *para* reflects not an abrupt change, as such a development is sometimes conceived, but rather a gradual process of change.

Like the above four corpus studies, **Ricardo Otheguy's** contribution also appeals to corpora to support his thesis, though the corpora appealed to are synchronic rather than historical. Otheguy's work also represents a departure from the typical contribution, in that it does not present a novel study on a particular linguistic phenomenon *per se*. Instead, in "The linguistic competence of second-generation bilinguals," Otheguy steps back and offers a novel problematization of the concepts of incomplete acquisition, target language, and linguistic competence. Critiquing various previous experimental studies of "heritage learners" of Spanish, Otheguy reminds us that our studies of the linguistic development of heritage speakers should not presuppose that there is some idealized target (possibly not even present in the learner's ambient input), which the learner fails to meet. He urges that as we pursue the study of heritage language development, we must remain mindful of at least two fundamental assumptions, namely, (i) that for all learners (not just heritage speakers), we understand "acquisition" to reflect individual development, with no expectations that the learner replicate the grammars of the speakers producing the ambient input, and (ii) that when we study learner production, it must be compared to what we are certain was in the learner's ambient input (and not to a linguistic variety which the learner had no access to in the first place). Assumption (i) (which holds for all learners) suggests that we avoid the adjective "incomplete" when framing the question of heritage language learning. Regarding (ii), Otheguy discusses, for example, previous studies on the use of the subjunctive in Spanish, many of which have purported to show that heritage learners have a comparatively infrequent use of this form (preferring the indicative in contexts where non-heritage speakers would use the subjunctive). Citing a corpus-based study by Bookhamer (2013), however, he argues that once one controls for the speakers who actually provide the input for the learners, the linguistic behavior of the learner actually reflects an output which is far more faithful to the ambient input than has otherwise been characterized in the literature (with differences found, not unexpectedly, in frequencies and also in categorical vs. variable behavior). In other words, while true that heritage speakers may use the subjunctive less than speakers of other Spanishes, this behavior is actually expected, given a close examination of the input for the heritage learners in question.

Otheguy's paper, which appeals to previous literature capitalizing on both corpus-based and experimental methods to study Spanish, provides a nice transition to another group of contributions, which cohere both in terms of their use of experimentation, and also in terms of the language of interest (Spanish). **Natalia Mazzaro, Alejandro Cuza**, and **Laura Colantoni**, who also take heritage speakers as their object of study, look at "Age effects and the discrimination of consonants and vowels." This paper compares the perception of certain consonantal and vocalic contrasts by native and heritage Spanish speakers, where the effects of language contact and cross-linguistic influence are in question (and where the difference between the participants lies in their exposure to English). The three groups considered are monolingual Spanish speakers (the control group), and two kinds of bilingual speakers, as the experimental groups. The bilingual speakers consist of (i) heritage speakers who were exposed to English early on and received formal education in English, and (ii) long-term immigrants who were exposed to English after puberty and received formal education in Spanish. (Recalling Otheguy's paper above: Mazzaro, Cuza, and Colantoni's control group consisted of recent arrivals to El Paso from Mexico, a background which aligns with that of the heritage speakers and long-term immigrants.) The specific phonological contrasts that were explored were Spanish voiced and voiceless stops in initial and medial position and mid and high vowels in stressed and unstressed syllables. Among the results of the study most relevant to the main hypotheses are (i) that monolingual controls performed significantly better than long-term immigrants, though there were no significant differences between advanced heritage speakers and long-term immigrants, and (ii) that in the domain of consonants, advanced heritage speakers performed similarly to monolingual controls with regard to labial contrasts, but similarly to long-term immigrants with regard to dorsal contrasts. From this, the authors conclude that there is no phonological-perceptual attrition in heritage speakers.

Related to bilingualism is the phenomenon of code-switching, which is addressed in **Raquel Fernández Fuertes, Juana Liceras,** and **Anahí Alba de la Fuente**'s paper on "Beyond the subject DP versus the subject pronoun divide in agreement switches." This contribution investigates subject-verb restrictions in English-Spanish code-switches; specifically, the authors explore two distinct syntactic factors which they predict to bear on acceptability judgments in code-switching bilinguals, namely: (i) the category of the subject (DP or pronoun), and (ii) the grammatical person (1st/2nd vs. 3rd) of pronominal subjects. The authors look at three different sets of speakers: simultaneous child bilinguals, subsequent child bilinguals, and subsequent adult bilinguals. Among the results emerging from this study is a preference for DP+V over pronoun+V sequences, for all groups in both languages. The authors attribute this to the absence of a PF Interface Condition violation with switches that involve DPs. Results from all three groups of participants also suggest that third-person pronoun switches are preferred over first- and second-person switches, and that this effect is stronger for Spanish than it is for English. The authors attribute these differences to Pesetsky and Torrego's (2001) double feature-checking mechanism and to Liceras et al.'s (2008) analogical criterion in agreement structures, which was formulated with regard to gender, but which can be extended to subject-verb agreement for the Spanish-dominant bilingual participants. Here, we see the potential of well-designed experiments to uncover contrasts which have been heretofore poorly understood or described, and likewise, for formal theory to make sense of experimental results, and provide explanations for syntactic phenomena which otherwise may have seemed unrelated. The reader might wish to read this paper back to back with the Ihsane and Sleeman contribution (discussed below), which also treats the question of the formal representation of gender agreement within DP.

Staying within the theme of experimental approaches to understanding contact phenomena, **John Lipski**'s contribution ("'Toned-up' Spanish: stress → pitch → tone(?) in Equatorial Guinea") explores the potential effects of contact with African languages that have lexical tone, and considers whether Equatorial Guinean

Spanish has experienced phonologization of Spanish pitch accents as lexical tones. To address this question, Lipski collected data from 20 speakers of Equatorial Guinean Spanish (balanced for gender and for language background, i.e., whether the speakers also spoke Fang or Bubi). A total of 80 utterances were selected from the free-conversation recordings of these speakers, and were compared to utterances from a group of speakers from Madrid. (Given the form of the data, incidentally, this work could also be characterized as a corpus study.) Among the data extracted from these utterances were the ratio of pitch accents produced on stressable syllables and the percentage of early-aligned prenuclear pitch accents. The results showed significant differences between the Spanish of the Madrid speakers and the Spanish of the Equatorial Guineans, such that Equatorial Guinean Spanish exhibited early-aligned pitch accents in lexically stressed syllables. Though such a prosodic pattern might be expected in citation forms for Madrid speakers, it is not characteristic of connected speech, as corroborated by the control group data. In their connected speech, Peninsular Spanish speakers reduce the correspondence between stress and pitch accent; that is, not all stressed syllables exhibit a higher pitch (even though stressed syllables are generally associated with higher pitch). In contrast, Equatorial Guineans exhibit much greater consistency in realizing higher pitch on stressed syllables in Spanish. Lipski proposes that this pattern is a result of the influence of Fang and Bubi, both languages with lexical tone (where pitch must be realized on each syllable). Under this hypothesis, then, it is not surprising that the Spanish of these speakers consistently realizes tone on every stressed syllable.

Lipski's paper is one of two in this volume which treat non-Indo-European language contact with Romance. In the second such paper, "French loanwords in Korean," **Haike Jacobs** looks at the Korean adaptation of French words ending in coronal voiceless stops. Jacobs provides an account for the fact that final /t/ in French is adapted into Korean either (i) as a tense or aspirated coronal plosive (e.g., /tʰ/) followed by vowel insertion, or (ii) as underlying /s/, which surfaces as [s] when followed by a vowel-initial suffix, and as [t] when not followed by such a suffix. The first process is interesting because Korean does not otherwise have vowel insertion after final consonants; the second process is interesting because Korean does have native words ending in surface [t] (though stem-final /t/ being replaced by /s/ is in fact attested). Jacobs challenges previous OT-accounts of these phenomena, which utilize lexical constraints and anti-faithfulness or anti-correspondence constraints. As an alternative, Jacobs proposes that lexical knowledge plays a role in determining the adaptation of loanwords. He models frequency and lexical knowledge using a markedness hierarchy which unifies the patterns for loanwords (from both French and English), and the native processes involving final coronal stops and /s/.

In contrast with the papers discussed up to this point (which use corpus-based and experimental methods and studies to treat the linguistic phenomena in question),

Jacobs' contribution stands out as one of several which we might characterize more as straight formal analysis of issues in phonology, morpho-syntax, syntax, and semantics. The remainder of papers we discuss in this introduction fall in this category. Consider for example **Tabea Ihsane** and **Petra Sleeman's** "Gender agreement with animate nouns in French," which treats mismatches between grammatical gender and semantic gender in French. These authors observe two puzzling sets of facts: first, in partitives, attributive adjectives modifying certain animate nouns may agree with the grammatical gender of the nouns or the semantic gender of their referents. Second, in some cases pronouns must match the grammatical gender of the animate noun antecedent, while in other cases, pronouns must match its semantic gender. The authors offer an account of these facts which takes gender features to come in two syntactic types, which are projected in two distinct positions in DP. Specifically, uninterpretable grammatical gender is located on N, while semantic gender is located on a dedicated functional head Gen(der); this latter feature is claimed to be present only in animate nouns. The authors show how the interpretability of the Gen feature, and its structural relation to both N and D, contribute to the range of mismatch effects observed in animate DPs. As noted earlier, the reader will find it interesting to compare Ihsane and Sleeman's proposal with the Fernández Fuertes et al. contribution, which treats Gender as an inherent N feature on D, and Gender Agreement as an inherent D feature on N (following the Liceras et al. 2008 analysis of Spanish DPs).

Lisa Reed's paper on the theory of control ("Some notes on *falloir, devoir*, and the theory of control") is also on French syntax, but in this case we are dealing with syntactic and semantic phenomena at the level of the clause. Reed presents a theory of control which treats PRO as a minimal pronoun, consisting of the feature matrix [+N, −expletive], and subject to a Bare Output Condition at LF that searches for an antecedent in the superordinate clause. This theory is used to account for some of the structures and interpretations associated with the modals *falloir* and *devoir*. These two modals exhibit a three-way ambiguity with respect to the category of their complement and the type of modal interpretation, so three distinct lexical entries are offered for each one. One of the entries for *falloir* and two of the entries for *devoir* are shown to interact with the Control Theory that Reed advances, such that the distribution of PRO is constrained by the selectional requirements of the modals and the presence of an external theta role associated with the verb in the complement clause. As noted below in the discussion of Castroviejo and Oltra-Massuet's paper, we suggest that those interested in modality read the Castroviejo & Oltra-Massuet and the Reed contributions together.

Keeping with the theme of null pronominals, in "On null objects and ellipses in Brazilian Portuguese," **Ruth Lopes** and **Sonia Cyrino** examine two different types of null object constructions in Brazilian Portuguese (BP), distinguishing between the structures produced by (i) Verb-Stranding Verb Phrase Ellipsis and (ii) Anaphoric

Null Object constructions. The authors argue that both structures in fact involve ellipsis: the former involves VP ellipsis, while the latter involves DP ellipsis. Similarities between the two ellipsis constructions are attributed to the fact that both are licensed only by a non-empty Asp head. Evidence for the ellipsis analysis of the Anaphoric Null Object construction comes from the structural parallelism requirement on the anaphoric null object and its antecedent, unexpected if the object is simply a *pro*. Since anaphoric null objects support both strict and sloppy identity readings, and fail to induce Principle C violations under reconstruction, the authors argue for an ellipsis derivation involving base-generated null phrase markers, following Fiengo and May (1994), rather than PF deletion. In reading this paper, the reader might find it interesting to circle back to Arteaga and Herschensohn's corpus-study of ellipsis in Old French DPs, where ellipsis can only be licensed by a non-clitic (or non-weak) element.

Again keeping with the theme of null pronominals and ellipsis, **Mary Kato's** paper offers a new analysis of "Affirmative polar replies in Brazilian Portuguese," comparing BP to European Portuguese (EP), Japanese, and Finnish. Affirmative replies may be simple, consisting only of the inflected verb, or complex, including a polar item *sim* 'yes'. Kato shows that since BP is not a true null subject language, an analysis restricting the availability of simple polar replies to languages with null subjects (and null objects) cannot be correct. The two varieties of Portuguese are compared to Japanese and Finnish, a null subject language and a partial null subject language, respectively, which both allow simple polar replies. Since the availability of different polar reply strategies does not hinge on the null subject parameter, Kato proposes instead that they involve ellipsis: the inflected verb raises to Foc, and the remnant clause moves to a presuppositional position (Spec,GroundP), where it is elided. As for complex polar replies, Kato uses a cartographic model of the left periphery to account for the distribution of the *sim* polar item with respect to the remnant clause in BP and EP. One remaining reply type in BP, where *sim* occurs above GroundP, patterns with Japanese in triggering a politeness interpretation.

Switching gears, **Lori Repetti's** paper on "The phonology of postverbal pronouns in Romance languages" provides a novel and multi-pronged approach to untangling the apparently complicated (and sometimes mysterious-seeming) cross-linguistic variation in stress patterns exhibited by Romance imperatives appearing with postverbal pronouns. As Repetti observes, in some varieties (or with some enclitics), enclisis on the imperative does not change the stress pattern of the verb, while in other varieties (and/or under certain structural conditions), enclisis can result in stress shifts, sometimes to the penultimate, sometimes to the antepenultimate, or sometimes to the final syllable. Many researchers have attempted phonological accounts for this behavior of imperatives with enclitics in the different Romance languages. Repetti argues, however, that no purely phonological analysis can account for the full range of available data. Capitalizing on an extensive database of imperative structures with clitics (which exists thanks to fieldwork done collaboratively with Francisco Ordóñez),

Repetti proposes that morpho-syntactic factors play an important role in the observed variation. Specifically, she posits that not all enclitics are actually clitics; instead, some are covert weak pronouns (hence the use of the term "postverbal pronoun" in the title, instead of "enclitic"). In contrast with clitics, Repetti argues that weak pronouns consist of a foot and can therefore be stressed. She further argues that the clitic–weak pronoun distinction bears on the prosodic structure of the imperative itself. The clitic–weak distinction thus gives rise to different prosodic structures in different languages, which in turn can account for the observed differences in the data.

Diego Pescarini's contribution, "The X^0 syntax of 'dative' clitics and the make-up of clitic combinations in Gallo-Romance," provides an interesting follow-up to the Repetti paper, as it looks in depth at the internal morpho-syntactic complexities of clitic clusters, in this case, third-person dative clitics in Gallo-Romance. Like the Rossi paper (discussed below), Pescarini uses data from a linguistic atlas (in this case, the *Atlas Linguistique de la France*). Taking into account the nature of the different clitic forms (etymological or non-etymological), and the different orders of the clitics, Pescarini uses the range of variation observed both diachronically and synchronically to support the hypothesis that clitic pronouns are not simple, but rather project a complex constituent, where the different morphological pieces of the clitics might instantiate different pieces of structure, either by being merged in dedicated positions, or moved to other positions within the structure.

Like Pescarini's paper, **Silvia Rossi's** contribution "From N to particle: Prepositionless *home* in the dialects of Northern Italy" also capitalizes on the concept of an articulated, fixed functional hierarchy, this time in the realm of PPs. Specifically, she examines the distribution of structures in Northern Italian dialects that have undergone preposition-drop with the equivalent of *casa* 'home'. Preposition-drop is relatively rare cross-linguistically, but, strikingly, when it does occur, it does so with *home*. Rossi claims that *home* in these preposition-drop structures constitutes a P (not an N), which can surface either as an adverb or as a particle. The paper integrates data and proposals from existing literature, as well as data from the *Atlante Sintattico d'Italia*. Her proposal, which incorporates the Split PP analysis (where the articulated PP structure contains a viewpoint modifier), draws from the facts of Borgomanerese, Old and Modern English, and Veneto dialects.

Continuing in the domain of Italian dialects, in "Marsican deixis and the nature of indexical syntax," **Mario Saltarelli** offers a close examination of deictic elements in a little-studied Abruzzese dialect of the Marsica region (specifically, the dialect of Pescasseroli), which he argues provide evidence to support the syntactic encoding of indexical elements in CP. Specifically, he takes the Speaker to be encoded as an operator in the higher functional field, binding a deictic variable in the vP. Marsican is like Latin in that deictic elements encode a three-term indexical context system of speaker (P1), hearer (P2), and −speaker/hearer (P3). Interestingly, with demonstratives, for example, only the first two can be optionally unstressed, e.g., (*quí*)*ste* 'this' (P1) and (*quí*)*sse* 'that'

(P2), vs. *quıse* 'that' (P3). He relates this contrast between P1 and P2 on the one hand, and P3 on the other, to other phenomena, such as the first/second vs. third person split in auxiliary selection, and the first/second vs. third person split in enclitic kinship genitives. A cross-linguistic comparison of the Marsican facts with a rich array of unrelated languages (such as Basque, Turkish, and Korean) provides support for his proposal regarding the syntactic instantiation of indexicality in the CP layer.

Continuing along the theme of the left periphery, in "Epistemic adverbs, the prosody-syntax interface, and the theory of phases," **Alessandra Giorgi** addresses the distribution of epistemic adverbs (such as 'probably') in Italian. The starting point of the analysis is Cinque's (1999) theory that there is an underlying common position of adverbs above IP, an analysis that is well suited for "normal" (or *flat*) intonation (and where it has been assumed that distinct surface orders must be the result of movement). Giorgi's contribution offers a detailed account for structures with other kinds of intonation, including parenthetical (or *comma*) intonation. In contrast with previous analyses of parentheticals, she proposes that even these adverbs are syntactically *integrated* (i.e., not adjoined). Appealing to the concept of phases, Giorgi's account expands on Cinque's analysis by proposing that the two phases, CP and v*P, both allow for a left periphery. She further argues that the parenthetical adverbs are generated in a left peripherical layer called KommaP (KP), where the head K is the feature [+comma]. The two basic positions of adverbs, therefore, are above IP (following Cinque and accounting for normal intonation), and above v*P, for parentheticals.

Moving closer to the realm of formal semantics, in "On capacities and their epistemic extensions" **Elena Castroviejo** and **Isabel Oltra-Massuet** take a close look at the modal expression *ser capaz* 'be able' in Spanish. They show that *ser capaz* is ambiguous between an abilitative reading and an epistemic reading, and propose that this ambiguity is structural (something that makes this work a nice companion piece to Reed's contribution, discussed above, which also treats modal ambiguity as structurally based). Specifically, they propose that the abilitative reading arises when the modal occupies a position below AspP, while the epistemic reading arises when the modal is above AspP. This syntactic treatment, in combination with a Kratzer (1991) style analysis of modals as quantification over worlds with respect to a modal base and an ordering source, accounts for interpretive differences between the two structures. *Ser capaz* itself is proposed to be a modal of slight possibility: it existentially quantifies over worlds where the capacity holds, which are non-stereotypical worlds.

The last two papers we discuss in this introduction treat adjectives. **Ion Giurgea's** paper on "Romanian *tough*-constructions and multi-headed constituents" examines the absence of agreement on adjectives in Romanian *tough*-constructions, which are otherwise similar to their counterparts in other Romance languages. Giurgea presents evidence that, contrary to previous analyses, *tough*-constructions in Romanian involve A-movement and adjectives (rather than adverbs), a proposal which would seem to make the absence of agreement on the alleged adjective puzzling. The absence of agreement is captured by treating the adjective as the internal head of the *tough*-construction, responsible for c-selecting the "supine clause," and treating the C-head of the supine clause as the external head of the construction, responsible for its label and external distribution. This analysis exploits a flexible label projection theory based on Citko's (2008) Project Goal, whereby the c-selected complement of the adjective projects its label up the tree. Finally, to account for the cross-linguistic distribution of non-agreeing *tough*-constructions, Giurgea proposes to restrict this labeling operation to languages which have no overt morphological distinction between the categories adjective and adverb. This reconceptualization of a particular lexical category is reminiscent of Rossi's contribution, where an element that was previously taken to be nominal is argued to actually be categorially a Preposition.

And last but by no means least, the paper by **Silvia Gumiel-Molina, Norberto Moreno-Quibén** and **Isabel Pérez-Jiménez** ("Depictive secondary predicates in Spanish and the relative/absolute distinction") examines the distribution of gradable adjectives as depictive secondary predicates, distinguishing between a relative and absolute interpretation, closely related to the individual-level vs. stage-level distinction. Gradable adjectives can serve as depictive secondary predicates only under the absolute/stage-level interpretation. The authors propose that their evaluation introduces a comparison class composed of stages of an individual that may vary across time, thereby requiring the *simultaneity condition* associated with depictive secondary predication to be met non-trivially. Relative/individual-level adjectives, on the other hand, are not evaluated with respect to stages, and therefore they are associated with an implicature of temporal persistence, so they satisfy the simultaneity condition trivially, making them pragmatically unsuitable as depictive secondary predicates.

As a transition to our Acknowledgments section below, we conclude with an expression of gratitude to the authors, for having contributed such a high-quality, interesting mix of novel studies. We believe that the 21 papers contained in this volume present to the reader a rich sample of the work that continues to be done in Romance linguistics today. In terms of formal linguistic theory, we are impressed by the range of research in the areas of semantics, syntax, morpho-syntax, and phonology, and by the rigor and clarity of the corpus-based and experimental works, and how they bear on important theoretical concerns of these core areas of linguistics. The editors wish to thank the authors for having provided us with the opportunity to associate our names with what we consider to be a fine example of the best of the LSRL tradition.

Acknowledgments

There are three different circumstances under which we need to acknowledge colleagues and collaborators, in the creation of this volume. First, it is important to note that this volume came into being during LSRL's transition from Benjamins' CILT series to its RLLT series. With respect to this transition, we have many people to thank for their assistance and patience. In particular we wish to acknowledge the leadership and guidance of both Haike Jacobs and Frank Drijkoningen (and the rest of the RLLT Editorial Board), and also the insight and expertise of Anke de Looper. We also wish to thank Konrad Koerner for his collaboration in the earlier stages of this book's development, and quite importantly, the authors (for their patience and enthusiasm as we moved to RLLT).

Second, beyond the context of this transition, we have many people to thank for help with the actual development of the volume. Again we wish to thank Frank Drijkoningen and Anke de Looper, and also Patricia Leplae for her guidance and constancy, especially during the proofing stage. We are also grateful to Julia Herschensohn, who remains a solid support for editors of LSRL volumes; we are all lucky to be able to rely on Julia's extensive experience with LSRL, and on her bottomless well of enthusiasm and goodwill. We also wish to thank Jason Smith and Tabea Ihsane, the editors of the selected proceedings of LSRL42, who provided great support as we together experienced the move to RLLT, in our capacity as the first two LSRL volumes to do so. And finally, most of all, we wish to thank the authors themselves for their wonderful contributions, and also the reviewers who devoted their time to providing invaluable feedback which helped to greatly improve this volume.

Finally, we would be being remiss if we did not also think back to 2013, and recognize that at the basis of a successful selected proceedings is a successful LSRL. For this we would like to thank a number of people. First and foremost, we thank William Fritz, President of the College of Staten Island, who gave thoughtful, compelling, and heartwarming opening remarks at the conference, which set a wonderful tone for the ensuing three days. We also thank Frances Blanchette, Michael Madden, Emily Wilson, and all the other CUNY students (both from CSI and The Graduate Center), who helped make the conference a success. In addition, we owe a debt of gratitude to the abstract reviewers, who read and commented on enormous quantities of abstracts, and who did so with great care and with an eye towards maintaining the consistently high quality of LSRL. And of course we cannot fail to mention William Mattiello, Chef and owner of *Via Emilia*, who created our wonderful conference dinner. Last but not least, we are grateful for the generous financial support which made the entire conference and subsequent proceedings possible. In particular, the *Special Session on Romance Parsed Corpora* was made possible by a grant from the National Science Foundation (#BCS-1256700) and a grant from the National Endowment for the Humanities Digital Humanities Start-Up program (#HD-51543). The main session was made possible through generous financial support from the College of Staten Island (Department of English; Office of the Dean of Humanities and Social Sciences; Office of the Provost/Senior Vice President for Academic Affairs; and Office of the President), and also through a generous grant from the CUNY Advanced Research Collaborative (ARC). For the ARC grant, we wish to thank Donald Robotham, for having taken out the time to understand the value of bringing the LSRL to the CUNY Graduate Center. We also wish to thank both Gita Martohardjono and Louise Lennihan, who put us in touch with Donald Robotham, and who also gave wonderful opening remarks at the conference.

References

Bookhamer, Kevin. 2013. *The Variable Grammar of the Spanish Subjunctive in Second-generation Bilinguals in New York City*. City University of New York, Ph.D. dissertation.
Cinque, Guglielmo. 1999. *Adverbs and Functional Heads*. Oxford: Oxford University Press.

Citko, Barbara. 2008. "Missing Labels." *Lingua* 118: 907–944. DOI: 10.1016/j.lingua.2008.01.001

Fiengo, Robert and Robert May. 1994. *Indices and Identity*. Cambridge, Mass: MIT Press.

Kratzer, Angelika. 1991. "Modality." In *Semantics: An International Handbook of Contemporary Research*. Ed. by Arnim von Stechow and Dieter Wunderlich, pp. 639–650. De Gruyter.

Liceras, Juana M., Raquel Fernández Fuertes, Susana Perales, Rocío Pérez-Tattam, and Kenton Todd Spradlin. 2008. "Gender and Gender Agreement in Bilingual Native and Non-native. Grammars: A View from Child and Adult Functional-lexical Mixings." *Lingua* 118: 827–851. DOI: 10.1016/j.lingua.2007.05.006

Martineau, France, Paul Hirschbühler, Anthony Kroch, and Yves Charles Morin. 2010. *Corpus MCVF (parsed corpus), Modéliser le changement: les voies du français*. Département de Français, Université d'Ottawa.

Pesetsky, David, and Esther Torrego. 2001. "T-to-C Movement: Causes and Consequences." In *Ken Hale: A life in language*, ed. by Micheal Kenstowicz, 355–426. MIT Press.

Root gerunds in Old Romanian

Gabriela Alboiu & Virginia Hill
York University / University of New Brunswick

Gerund verbs generate root clauses in Old Romanian (OR), but not in
Modern Romanian (MR). We argue that the root clause phenomenon arises
from the presence of a null Assertion Operator in OR, which has been lost
in MR. This Operator originates from the mapping of discourse features to
syntax, but involves a marked option for feature checking (i.e., pragmatic
versus syntactic), so it is easier for it to disappear in the process of language
acquisition.

1. Introduction

This paper focuses on gerund clauses in OR, which occur in both root and adjunct
configurations. We propose an account for these constructions and for the diachronic
change they undergo by combining the results of historical linguistic studies with formal tests and assessments.

The hypothesis is that a syntactic operation is at work that recovers declarative
clause typing and finiteness for root gerunds, in a way that makes them equivalent to
root indicative clauses. We argue that, in pre-recorded OR, root gerunds had V-to-
T but not higher, plus a null Assertion Operator in ForceP; crucially, the Assertion
Operator binds the Fin(ite)-T(ense) domain and allows it to be valued pragmatically, thus equating the properties of the gerund root clause with those of an indicative declarative clause. The weak evidence for the null operator, coupled with the
fact that pragmatic (versus syntactic) valuation is marked, triggered the eventual
loss of this operator, and changes in verb movement from V-to-T to V-to-C (specifically, V-to-Fin) with gerunds. The OR recorded documents we investigate show
some remnant V-to-T occurrences but are predominantly V-to-C, which is the new
default for gerunds. This change in verb movement coincides with a decrease in the
use of root gerunds. By comparison, in MR all gerunds systematically exhibit V-to-C
movement.

DOI 10.1075/rllt.9.01alb

2. Key data

A gerund form in OR consists of a verbal root to which we add the suffix *-ind(u)/-ând(u)*. For example, *mânca* 'to eat' > *mânc-ând* 'eating' (OR orthography in the corpus: *mîncînd*). This form is invariable and exclusively verbal, on par with its Latin ancestor (Miller 2000). Thus, the gerund is incompatible with determiners (e.g., **mâncândul* 'the eating') (Caragiu 1957; Edelstein 1972).

Historically, gerund clauses are adjuncts, by default, in all Romance languages, and this includes Romanian. However, the OR gerund can also generate declarative root clauses, in "out-of-the-blue" contexts; e.g., the lines in (1) stand by themselves, as a prelude to the chronicle.

(1)   *Traian* *întîiu,* *împăratul,*   **supuindu**   pre   *dahii./*   *Dragoş*
       Trajan first   emperor.the conquering DOM Dacians Dragos

       apoi *în* *moldoveni* **premenindu** *pre*   *vlahi./* *Martor* *este* *Troianul,*
       then   in Moldovans turning   DOM Vlachs witness is   Trojan.the

       şanţul *în* *ţara*   *noastră/ Şi* *Turnul* *Saverinului,*   *munteni,*
       ditch.the in country our   and tower.the Severin.the.GEN Vlachs

       în *ţara*   *voastră.*
       in country your

       'First, Trajan, the Emperor, conquered the Dacians. Then, Dragos
       turned some Vlachs into Moldavians. Witness is the Trojan ditch,
       in our country, and the Tower of Severinus, Wallachs, in your country.'
                                                                  (Costin 11)

In (1), the gerund is the only verb in each of the first two clauses. Each gerund displays its own lexical subject in Nominative (underlined). Oblique Cases have morphological marking in OR, and the subjects in (1) are not morphologically marked. This leaves either Nominative or Accusative structural Case as potential options for these lexical subjects. However, since the subjects in (1) are proper nouns with a [+human] feature which would trigger an obligatory Differential Object Marker (i.e., DOM *pe* or *pre*; Hill and Tasmowski 2008 a.o.) with Accusative Case, and these subjects do not display DOM, the Case on these DPs is Nominative. Moreover, there is no morphological marking for tense on the gerunds in (1): the past tense reading comes from the discourse context, since the subject matter concerns facts of ancient history, long before the time of the chronicle.

Root gerund clauses may be self-standing, as in (1), or they may occur in coordination with other root clauses, as in (2). Since the coordination in (2) relates the gerund to an indicative, they must have an equivalent syntactic status.

(2) *Apoi leşii,   vădzîndu aşè, au   început a scrie cu   bănat la*
     then Poles.the seeing   so   have started to write with anger to

     Vasilie vodă, iar Vasilie-vodă răspundzînd.
     Vasilie king   and Vasilie-king answering

     'Then the Poles, seeing this, started to write angrily to
     King Vasilie, and King Vasilie answered.'   (Neculce 114)

Note that, in (2), the root gerund licenses a lexical subject, which is different from the subject of the coordinated indicative. The tense reading of the gerund is achieved through a combination of the discourse context and the tense of the coordinated indicative verb.

The occurrence of root gerunds in OR, as in (1) and (2), begs explanation. Our hypothesis is that some syntactic operation is at work that recovers declarative clause typing and finiteness for root gerunds in a way that makes them equivalent to indicative clauses. In the rest of the paper, we investigate the syntax of gerund clauses, to see how this might be implemented.

3. Corpus

The data come from a corpus of *The Moldavian Chronicles* written directly in Romanian (from 1642 up to approximately 1750) by Ureche, Costin, Neculce, in this chronological order.[1] The combined texts amount to 259,536 words, generating 9,497 sentences. Quantifying the gerunds in these chronicles, Edelstein (1972: 128) found that the percentage of gerunds in relation to the total of verbal forms is 10%, which is double that of infinitives.

Edelstein (1972) does not differentiate the gerunds by clause type in her statistics. For us, that differentiation is paramount, since our focus is on a certain type of gerund clauses. In our corpus, we found 22 examples of root gerunds and over 100 occurrences of gerund clauses in adjunct position (adverbials and relatives).[2] These examples allow for assessments of word order and distribution of gerund verbs, because matrix and adjunct gerunds share most of their morpho-syntactic properties.

---

1. Traditional Romanian historical linguistics refers to the language of the16th–18th centuries as 'Old Romanian'. We maintain this label here, despite the fact that in Old Romance languages the qualification of '*old*' is confined to pre-medieval texts up to roughly the 13th century.

2. We stopped counting at 100, because this number is sufficient to show the disproportionate preference for gerunds as adjuncts.

4. Theoretical background

The analysis needs to assess the level of verb movement in gerund clauses and compare it with the location of indicative verbs, in similar contexts. For that, we use the cartographic representations, which allow for a precise appraisal in relation to the location of adverbs (Cinque 1999) and of the projections mapping the discourse features (i.e., Topic and Focus, as in Rizzi 1997, 2004).

In particular, the hierarchy of adverbs in Cinque (1999) in (3) helps to identify the position of the gerund verb and of its lexical subject.

(3) T_{past} 'once' > T_{future} 'then' > [$Asp_{habitual}$ 'usually' [$Asp_{repetitive\ I}$ 'again' [$Asp_{frequentativeI}$ 'often' [Asp .....[$Asp_{completiveII}$ 'tutto' > [**Voice** 'well']]]]]]

For the CP field we adopt the mapping in Rizzi (1997, 2004), shown in (4). This map allows us to test the constructions for constituent fronting to Topic and Focus, and for the availability of complementizers (in Force or Fin).

(4)   ForceP > TopP > FocusP$_{contrast}$ > (ModP) > FinP > TP

In addition, we use the reference points provided by the presence of negation and clitics. Unlike in English, where T is higher than Neg (Laka 1990), in Romance, the Neg head selects TP (Haegeman and Zanuttini 1996; Zanuttini 1997 a.o.), and this is also valid for Romanian (Alboiu 2002). Clitic pronouns are located in T in OR (Alboiu et al. 2014), which is also unexceptional for Romance languages (Kayne 1991). In OR, auxiliary verbs are also clitics (which is not typical for Romance languages), and they belong to the clitic cluster in T, together with clitic pronouns. Accordingly, in (5a) Neg selects a TP with proclitics on the (indicative) verb that moved to T. Data as in (5b), where the verb precedes the subject and the vP adverb *des* 'often', indicate V-to-T in OR.

(5)   a.   *Ce   împăratul Rîmului   alt   ajutoriu nu*
            but   king.the   Rome.the.GEN   other   help   not

        i-au   făgăduit.
        to.him-has   promised

        'But the Emperor of Rome has not promised him other help.'

                                                                    (Ureche 68)

        b.   *au   început a   strănuta Barnovschii-vodă des   și   tare*
            has   started   to   sneeze   Barnovsky-king   often   and   strongly
            'King Barnovsky started to sneeze often and strongly.'   (Neculce 113)

The triggers for verb movement within the hierarchies in (3) and (4) are justified through feature checking mechanisms. In particular, the [tense] feature of T is interpretable but not valued, and it probes a verb that has an uninterpretable [tense] feature, but an intrinsically (morphologically) specified tense value (Pesetsky and Torrego 2007). While this operation is unexceptional with indicative verbs, more needs to be said about OR gerund verbs that can occur in similar root contexts.

5. Distribution in the sentence

In this section we survey the distribution of OR gerunds in subordinate contexts and point out that gerund clauses are adjuncts (versus arguments). The conclusion is that gerunds are verbal in nature, unlike infinitives and supines, which have nominal properties and occur as arguments more productively.

5.1 Relative clauses

In this paper, we include the relatives in the class of adjuncts, on par with adverbial clauses. This classification is in line with analyses where relatives are defined as adjoined to NP or DP (Demirdache 1991 a.o.).

Gerund relative clauses may have a visible or a null relative phrase, as in (6a, b).

(6) a. *Înțelegîndu aceasta [boierii   [carii   fiindu pribegi în*
         finding.out this   boyars.the which.the being refugees in

         Țara   Leșască]] ce   s-au   lucrat   la Moldova,
         country.the Polish   what REFL-has worked   at Moldova,

         degrabŭ s-au   adunatu cu   toții   de au   sfătuit
         fast   REFL-have gathered with all.the DE have consulted

         în pripă.
         in hurry

         'Finding out what was maneuvered in Moldova, the boyars who
         were exiled in Poland assembled themselves promptly for immediate
         consultations.'   (Ureche 170)

     b. *Au și   prinsu [un omu$_j$ [viind$_j$ cu cărți$_k$ de la   Sibiiu*
         has also caught a man   coming   with letters of from Sibiu

         la comendatul   de Bistrița], [scriind$_k$ precum au
         to commander.the of Bistrita   writing   as   has

         bătut pre veziriul.]
         defeated Vizir.the

         'He also caught a man *who* was coming with letters from Sibiu to
         the commander at Bistrita, letters *in which* it was written that he
         had defeated the Vizir.'   (Neculce 328)

5.2   Adverbial clauses

The gerund is extensively used in non-selected contexts, for a variety of adverbial clauses (as it is in Romance languages in general). From a theoretical standpoint, adjuncts (and subject) clauses are phasal domains, as evidenced by the fact that they are islands to movement, among other things. Consequently, relative and adverbial OR gerund clauses are complete, fully fledged CP domains, as also confirmed by their empirical properties. Specifically, in OR, these constructions license Nominative (lexical or *pro*) subjects as in (7a, b). The subject may also be co-referent to an argument of the matrix clause, as in (7c), but this does not entail control, since at Spell-out the subject may lexicalize in the gerund instead of the matrix, as shown in (7d).

(7)   a.   [*Singur Ieremia-vodă fiindŭ în beserică la sfînta leturghie*],
           alone   Ieremia-king being in church at saint mass

           i-au   dat   ştire, cum oştile   lui Răzvan amu
           to.him-have given   news   that armies.the of   Razvan now

           să   vădŭ...
           REFL see

           'When King Ieremia was alone in church for Mass, they gave him news,
           that Razavan's army could now be seen...'   (Costin 16)

      b.   [*Acolo pro tocmindu-şi   oastea*] *ca   să   margă asupra*
           there   gathering-REFL army.the that SUBJ go   against

           lui Alexandru vodă Cornea, iată boierii   ţării
           him Alexandru king Cornea there boyars.the country.the.GEN

           Moldovei   prinseră de veste cum domniia ieste data lui
           Moldova.GEN caught   of news that throne.the is   given to

           Pătru vodă...
           Petru king

           'While he (i.e., King Peter) was hiring army there (i.e., in Brăila), to
           fight King Alexandru Cornea, the boyars of Moldova found out that
           the throne has been granted to King Peter...'   (Ureche 161)

      c.   *şi   au   iernatŭ de multe ori, [pro bătîndu-să uneori*
           and have wintered of many   times fighting-REFL sometime

           cu   sciţii   sau tătarii, uniori   cu   Bosna şi   cu
           with Scythes or   Tartars sometime with Bosna and with

           Rumele [şi   la perşi   trecîndŭ.]
           Rume   and to Persians crossing

           'and he has wintered many times, fighting sometimes against the
           Scythes or the Tartars, sometimes against Bosna and Rume, and
           crossing over to the Persians.'   (Ureche 67–68)

d. [...] *ce   l-au   îmbărbătat numai să   meargă la Poartă,*
    but him-have encouraged only   SUBJ go   to Porte

că apoi, **nemărgînd** *el, va   aduci perirea   țărîi*
for then not.going   he   will bring destruction.the country

și   boierimei.
and   boyars

'... but they strongly encouraged him to go to the Ottoman Porte, for
if he didn't, he'd cause the destruction of the country and the boyars.'

(Neculce 227)

To conclude, OR adjunct gerund clauses share important properties with root gerunds, because they are unselected, unrestricted in their distribution (i.e., they occur
pre- or post-verbally in relation to the matrix verb, or at long distance from the modified noun), and have the ability to license subjects (i.e., Nominative lexical subjects or
null pronouns). On par with root clauses, these are phasal CP domains.

6. The TAM system

In light of the above conclusions, it is theoretically desirable to surmise that matrix gerunds and adjunct gerunds have some similar morpho-syntactic properties and underlying structure, yet also diverge on some level, since MR preserved gerund adjuncts
(with identical properties as in OR) but not root gerunds. In this section, we show that
the syntactic similarity (i.e., phasal CP status) is corroborated by identical properties
in their TAM systems: the TAM values are unspecified.

6.1 Tense

Adjunct gerunds show independent values for the tense feature. For example, in (8)
the matrix verb is constantly in present perfect, but the reading on the gerund is past
in (8a), but future in (8b).

(8) a. *Mărs-au... la un sat   a   lui,* **avîndu** *și   curți   acolo.*
         gone-has to a   village of his having and   courts there
         'He went to one of his villages, because he had a house there.'

                                                                    (Neculce 69)

     b. *Apoi au vinit la Moldova cu   neguțitorie[...]* **lipindu-să**
         then has come   to Moldova with merchandise   attaching-REFL

         de curte, fiind și   Vasilie-vodă tot   de un neam.
         to court being and   Vasilie-king same of a   kin

         'Then he went to Moldova as a merchant, and will become
         attached to the court, since King Vasilie was his kin.'   (Neculce 119)

The two different tense values for the gerund in relation to the same matrix tense indicate that the tense reading is context-dependent (rather than structure-dependent). The same context-dependent reading for tense occurs in matrix gerunds:

(9)   *Duca-vodă* **gătindu**   *conace*   *și*   *poduri peste toate pîreile*
      Duca-king providing mansions and bridges over all   rivers.the

      cu   multă grijă, să   nu-i   afle   împărățiia vro pricină,
      with much care SUBJ not-him finds Empire   any blame

      să-șu   puie capu.
      SUBJ-REFL put   head

      'King Duca had provided mansions and bridges over all the rivers, with much care, so that the Empire would not find him any blame, and he would not risk his head.'   (Neculce 131)

In (9) the Turks had already entered the country, so King Duca's actions were finished prior to this event. The other verbs in (9) are in the present, and would have provided no clues for a past perfect interpretation of the gerund out of the relevant context.

6.2   Aspect

OR gerunds may have a progressive aspect, but they can also be perfective (10a), punctual (10b), or iterative (10c).

(10) a. *Muftiiul   s-ascunsese,   și   **găsindu-l,**   l-au   muncit...*
          priest.the REFL-hid.had and finding-him him-have worked
          'The elated priest had hid himself, but when they found him, they tortured him.'   (Neculce 167)

      b. *l-au   pus viziriul de au ședzut înaintea viziriului   pre*
          him-has put vizir.the DE has set   before   vizir.the.GEN on

          *măcat, și **n-au   fost avînd** meștei la   nădragi*
          carpet and not-has been having slippers with pants

          'the Vizir made him sit in front of him (the Vizir), on the carpet, and he didn't have slippers with his pants'   (Neculce 109)

      c. *Ș-au   mărsu la Ieși, dîrji și sămeți, **așteptînd** din*
          and-have gone   to Iassy strong and proud waiting   from

          ceas în ceas să   le   vie   cărți de la
          hour to hour SUBJ to.the come letters from

          Antohie vodă.
          Antohie King

          'And they went to Iassy, strong and proud, waiting hour on end, to receive letters from King Antohie.'   (Neculce 192)

6.3   Mood and modality

While the grammatical mood suffix -ind indicates the gerund paradigm in OR, this mood marker is not associated with a specific semantic modality. Thus, in adverbial clauses, the gerund is flexible for modal interpretation, and gets its value from the syntactic context. For example, the gerund is hypothetical in (11a) but *realis* in (11b).

(11)   a.   **Nedînd**   război   cazacilor,   să   le   închidză   hrana...
            not.giving   war   Cosacks.the.DAT   SUBJ   to.them   close   food.the

            ce   ar   hi   făcut   cu   tabăra   Timuş?
            what   would   be   done   with   camp.the   Timus

            'If he had not fought the Cosacks in order to cut their supply lines,
            what would Timus have done with his camp?'   (Costin 146)

       b.   Că   ei   **nefiind**   tocmiți   de   război,   nimica   de   arme
            because   they   not.being   prepared   for   war   nothing   of   weapons

            nu   s-au   apucatu
            not   REFL-have   taken

            'They did not arm themselves because they had not prepared
            themselves for war.'   (Ureche 93)

Root gerunds are different in this respect, insofar as the modality is always *realis*, as with root indicatives. Since -ind does not intrinsically bring a value for modality (as seen in (11)), something else must force the *realis* interpretation in root gerunds.

7.   Clause structure

The next step in our analysis is to determine the internal structure of the gerund clause, for which we use the theoretical tools presented in Section 3. First, we show that, by default, OR gerund clauses involve V-to-Fin. Then, we show that there are traces of V-to-T that can reasonably be attributed to systematic low verb movement in gerund clauses before the recorded times.

7.1   V-to-C

The first step is to show that the gerund moves out of the vP. This is tested with adverbs and with subjects in situ. In (12), *auzindu* 'hearing' is higher than the subject in situ, in Spec, vP (OR is a VSO language); whereas *avîndu* 'having' precedes the adverb *încă* 'still', which is high in the inflectional field (i.e., above Voice in (3) above).

(12)   *Aceste neaşedzări a   lui Ştefan-vodă* **auzindu** *doamna lui*
these   troubles   of of Stefan-king hearing lady.the of

Ieremie-vodă, **avîndu** *încă rămas un fecior copil mic,   anume*
Ieremia-king having still left   a son   child young namely

Bogdan-vodă,   au îndemnatu pre ginerii   săi, ...
Bogdan-king has persuaded DOM sons.in.law.the her

'King Ieremia's widow, finding out about King Stefan's attempts, and
still having a young son left [alive], that is, prince Bogdan, persuaded her
sons-in-law to...'   (Costin 35)

The same can be seen in root gerunds, as in (13), with the subject in situ.

(13)   *Pentru aceia,* **întrebîndu** *un împărat pre   un dascăl: cum ar*
for   that   asking   a king DOM a   teacher how would

fi **împăratu** *să hie   drag   tuturora?*
be king.the SUBJ be.3SG pleasant all.DAT.PL

'Therefore, a king asked a teacher: what would it take for a king to be loved
by everybody?'   (Costin 33)

Second, negation, enclitics and adverbs situated in T_{past} indicate that the gerund moves
out of TP. Gerund negation surfaces as the prefix *ne-*, instead of the free morpheme *nu*
'not' that occurs with other (finite or non-finite) verbs. This is valid for both root (14a)
and adjunct gerunds (14b).

(14)   a. *Decii Roman vodă* **neputîndu**   *să-şi   îngăduiască cu*
so   Roman king not.being.able SUBJ-REFL put.up   with

văru-său,   cu   Pătru, ficiorul lui Ştefan vodă, pentru domnie,
cousin-his with Petru son.the of Stefan king for   throne

că   cerea Roman să   omoară pe Pătru, de i-au   căutatu
that asked Roman SUBJ kill   DOM Petru DE him-has caused

a fugi lui Pătru vodă la unguri.
to run to Petru King to Hungarians

'Therefore, King Roman was not able to put up with his cousin,
Peter, King Stefan's son, in their co-reigning; that is why Roman was
asking to have Peter killed, and made Peter run to the Hungarians.'
                                                              (Ureche 84)

        b. *Şi* **neavîndu** *cu   nime   nici un război nicăiure în*
and not.having with nobody not one war   nowhere in

Ţara   Muntenească, au mărsu la Bucureşti
country.the Wallachia   has gone to Bucharest

'And not having any war with anyone, anywhere, he went to Bucharest.'
                                                              (Costin 21)

The affixal negation does not concern the properties of T (T must be present since the gerund occurs in root clauses), but, rather, is a by-product of the fact that the gerund verb moves out of T into C, and this movement would be blocked by the free morpheme *nu* 'not'. The intervener property of *nu* has been discussed in Rivero (1993) for Long Head Movement (LHM), which is a form of V-to-C.

T-to-C movement of gerunds is confirmed by the location of clitic pronouns (i.e., enclitics in (15)) and of post-verbal temporal adverbs, see *odată* 'once' in T_{past}, in (16).

(15) Şi <u>Ştefan vodă</u> tocmisă   puţini oameni preste lunca Bîrladului,ca
      and Stefan king organized few   men   over valley Birlad.the.GEN

      să-i   amăgească cu   buciune şi   cu   trîmbiţe, dîndu
      that SUBJ-them tease   with oboes   and with trombones giving

      semnu de războiŭ; atuncea <u>oastea</u>   <u>turcească</u> întorcîndu-să la
      sign   of   war   then   army.the Turks   turning-REFL   at

      glasul buciunelor   şi   împiedicîndu-i şi   <u>apa</u>   şi
      voice.the oboes.the.GEN and blocking-them   and water.the and

      <u>lunca</u>   şi   <u>negura</u> acoperindu-lu-i, tăindu lunca   şi
      valley.the and fog.the covering-them   cutting valley.the and

      sfărămîndu, ca   să   treacă la glasul   bucinilor.
      crushing   that SUBJ cross   to sound.the oboes.the.GEN

      'King Stefan organized a few men across the Bîrlad valley in order to tease
      them (the enemy) with oboes and trombones, by emitting the signs of war;
      then the Turkish army turned towards the sound of oboes, but the water
      delayed them, and the valley and the fog covered them when they were
      cutting through the valley and trampling it, trying to cross towards the
      sound of the oboes.'   (Ureche 100)

(16) <u>Ştefăniţă-vodă</u> vrînd   odată   să   scoată fumărit pe   ţară
      Stefanita-king wanting once   SUBJ   impose smoke.tax on country

      cîte şase orti de   casă, şi   înainte vreme era <u>obicei</u>   de da
      each six   units per house and before   time   was costume DE give

      numai cîte un   leu de casă, iar   <u>Toma vornicul</u> şi   cu
      only   each one leu per house and Toma judge.the   and with

      Iordachi, frate-său, <u>Cantacozineştii</u> nu-l   lăsa..., că
      Iordachi brother-his Cantacuzins.the   not-him let   for

      nu-i   bine.
      not-is good

      'King Stefanita wanted *at one time* to impose the smoke tax on the country,
      at six units per home, while in the old times the usual tax was only one
      leu per home, so judge Toma and his brother, Iordachi, the Cantacuzins,
      advised him not to do it, because it didn't look good.'   (Neculce 120)

We next identify the level of the CP field to which the gerund moves. In this respect, we work with the mapping in (4). ForceP may be occupied in gerund clauses, either by the complementizer *că* 'that', (17a), or by a relative phrase, (17b). Furthermore, there is material interfering between the gerund and the relative operator in (17b) indicating that the gerund verb does not target Force.

(17) a. **Că fiindu-i**   *nepot   şi-n   cinste   la   dînsul,*
          for being-him.DAT nephew and in honor   to   him

          îl   ştiè.
          him   knew.3SG

          'He knew him, for he was his nephew and in great esteem with him'
                                                                    (Neculce 179)

      b. *De care   lucru   cu   norocŭ* **semeţindu-să** Baiazitu,   *iară*
          of   which   thing with   luck   swelling-REFL Baiazid   again

          s-au   vîrtejitŭ   la   Tarigrad.
          REFL-has   stormed   to   Istanbul

          'For which reason being swollen of his luck, Baiazid stormed back to
          Istanbul'   (Ureche 129)

Moreover, constituents with Topic and contrastive Focus readings always precede the gerund verb, as shown in (18a, b).

(18) a. carii   [făr   nici o   grijă]   şi   [de primejdie ca
          which.the without no one worry and to danger   like

          aceia] **negîndindu-să,**
          that   not.thinking-REFL

          'who without worries and not thinking of a danger like that'
                                                                    (Ureche 190)

      b. *Şi   [de   acolo][multe]* **luund** *şi* **lipindu** *de ale noastre,*
          and from there many taking and sticking to of ours

          potrivindu vremea   şi   anii,   de   au   scris   acest letopiseţ.
          adjusting   time.the and years.the DE has written this   chronicle

          'And *from there MANY* (data) he took and added to ours, adjusting
          the periods and the years, so that he ended up writing this chronicle.'
                                                                    (Ureche 64)

In (18a), two coordinated constituents with contrastive topic reading follow the relative in Spec,ForceP. The root gerund in (18b) is preceded by an *aboutness* Topic *de acolo* 'from there', and the direct object *multe* 'many' fronted to contrastive Focus.

This word order indicates that V-to-C means V-to-Fin for the gerund. The same word order appears in MR, though MR does not support root gerunds.

7.2   V-to-T

The *Moldavian Chronicles* display a few gerund constructions that are an exception to the above word order rule: there are a few examples with the negation *nu* (instead of *ne-*); and some folk poems (ballads) display the possibility of proclitics with the gerunds.

The rare possibility of the gerund co-occurring with the free negative morpheme *nu* 'not' instead of the prefix *ne-*, as in (19), confirms that the gerund verb must have moved to T (not to C) in pre-recorded stages of the language, and that such rare examples are traces of this situation in OR.

(19)   *Ce* **nu** **lăsîndu** *in voia   căpăteniilor   de Ardeal* <u>*împăratul*</u>
        but not leaving at will.the captains.the.GEN of Ardeal emperor.the

        <u>*nemțescu*</u>, *au socotit   și   cu   sabiia   să-i   supuie, avîndu*
        German   has decided and with sword.the SUBJ-them repress having

        tocmeli cu   Bator.
        deals   with Bator

        'But the German Emperor, not leaving things at the will of Ardeal's captains, decided to repress them by sword, having arrangements with Bator.'

        (Costin 19)

The presence of this negation is possible only if the gerund verb stays in TP.

Outside of the *Moldavian Chronicles*, we find further traces of V-to-T in gerunds in folk poetry, as in (20). Although the ballad in (20) has been recorded in the 19th century, it reproduces a very old word order, fixed by the nature of the rhythm and rhyme, and transmitted orally from generation to generation.

(20)   *Cînd în tîrg   ca-n Tarigrad* **intrînd**,*/* <u>*Soarele*</u> **răsărind**, <u>*dughenele*</u>
        when in town as-in Istanbul entering sun.the rising   shops.the

        deschizînd.*/ Iar* <u>*cuconu mirele*</u>   *cu   ochi negri* <u>**le**</u>   *privind./*
        opening   and mister groom.the with eyes black them watching

        Si   cu   galbeni <u>**le**</u>   **cumpărînd**,*/ Fețisoarei dumitale*
        and with money them buying   face.DAT yours

        <u>**le**</u>   *potrivind.*
        them fitting

        'When he entered town as if in Istanbul, the sun was rising and the shops were opening. The groom watched them [the earrings] with black eyes and bought them, and fitted them to your face.'   (Gabinschi 2010: 83)

The relevance of (20) is that it displays proclitics to gerund verbs, which corroborates the conclusion drawn on the basis of the negation *nu* 'not' in the previous examples: there was a time in OR when the gerund verb stayed in T (i.e., adjacent to proclitics in T), and this configuration favored the use of gerunds in root clauses, because V-to-T with null CP is typical for root declaratives in the language (versus interrogatives or imperatives).

7.3   Summary

The data indicate two subsequent configurations for non-selected gerund clauses:

i.   Pre-recorded OR (i.e., before 16th century): gerund V-to-T
        The gerund is lower than Neg *nu* 'not', and displays clitc > V order. The gerund
        is higher than frequency adverbs and the subject in situ, hence outside of vP.
ii.   Recorded OR (i.e. mid-16th to end of 18th centuries):
        V-to-Fin and some V-to-T.
        In V-to-Fin, the gerund is higher than T_{past}, it has affixal negation, and it dis-
        plays V > clitic order. Concurrently, rare occurrences of V-to-T can be found,
        exhibiting the properties in (i).

Accordingly, OR represents a system in transition, undergoing a change in the gerund syntax, which becomes stabilized as V-to-Fin in MR. The stabilization of V-to-Fin in MR also coincides with the disappearance of root gerunds.

8.   Formalization

The analysis we develop in this section is that root gerund V-to-T is possible because of the mapping of an Assertion Operator in ForceP, in the spirit of Meinunger (2004). This operator values the clause-typing feature as declarative and, therefore, selects Fin with a *realis* modality, so, as with root indicatives, only V-to-T need apply. In the absence of the Assertion Operator, Fin is unvalued and triggers V-to-C so that the verb can check the modality feature of Fin. This movement, however, fails to value Fin as *realis*, hence the loss of the root gerund. This accounts for our previous observation, namely, that the loss of root gerunds coincides with the spread of V-to-Fin in these constructions.

8.1   Modality versus [mood]

In Rizzi's (1997, 2004) system, Fin is the head associated with finiteness and modal-ity. D'Alessandro and Ledgeway (2010) further refine this definition, by showing that Fin encodes semantic modality, whereas the grammatical [mood] feature is associated with T (versus Fin), since it belongs to the inflectional properties of the verb. Accord-ingly, the fact that the gerund verb has the inflectional mood mark *-ind* is irrelevant for the level of verb movement. In particular, following D'Alessandro and Ledgeway, [$_\text{T}$ GER-ind] would not automatically entail V-to-C. In general, when V-to-C takes place, it is triggered either by a clause typing probe (in Force) or by a feature in Fin (e.g., (i)realis, (non)-finite). The presence of grammatical mood, however, is of no consequence for the modality feature of Fin.

In configurations with root indicatives, T is by default [+finite] and [+tense], so Fin is [+finite]. For clause-typing, lack of an operator or any complementizer in root Force is taken by default to indicate a [declarative] value of this feature. Hence, the modality of Fin is valued as [+realis] under selection by [declarative] Force. If root gerunds are the counterpart of root indicatives, then we have to account for the following questions: (i) Why does the gerund verb in T count as [+finite], [+tense], when its form is invariable? and (ii) How is the [declarative] value of the clause typing feature achieved (which would predictably restrict the modality value of Fin to [realis])?

8.2   Underspecification

Since the gerund verb is unspecified for TAM, it has no inherent value to bring to T or to Fin. Further confirmation comes from its use in predicate cleft constructions, as in (21).

(21) ***Imblîndu*** *îmbla*   *şi*   *plînge.*
      wandering wanders and   cries
      'As for wandering, s/he wanders and cries.'   (*PS* apud Edelstein 1972: 81)

Predicate clefting fronts the V(P) for focus/topic purposes, with a copy of the V(P) in clause-internal position (Abels 2001; Roberts 2010: 198 a.o.). Importantly, while the clause-internal copy is fully inflected for TAM values, the fronted verb must be realized in a *default* form (see also Landau 2006). Therefore, (21) demonstrates that the OR gerund is an underspecified default form, which explains its plurifunctionality. Its underspecification does not, however, account for how the gerund acquires the various TAM values illustrated in Section 6.

8.3   Free variation and feature valuation

With respect to tense and aspect features (associated with T), Pesetsky and Torrego (2007) assume that interpretability and valuation are two distinct properties: both interpretable and uninterpretable features need to be valued. Thus, the [+tense] feature is interpretable but unvalued, and so acts as a probe targeting the finite lexical verb, which has an uninterpretable tense (uT). Tense valuation obtains from the intrinsic values on V (i.e. indicative inflectional endings), as in (22). We extend the same analysis to the [aspect] feature, since tense/aspect are generally clustered in the morphosyntactic mapping of OR/MR.

(22)   ...Tense ..... [v finite]   =>   ... Tense ...... [v finite]
           iT [ ] ..... uT + value   =>   ... iT [√] ..... uT̶ + value

With gerunds, the verb is not inflectionally specified for a Tense value, so is incapable of valuing iT [ ]. Hence, temporal deixis is acquired contextually, and valuation in (23) is pragmatic, not syntactic.[3]

(23)   ...Tense ..... [v]   =>   ... Tense ...... [v]
           iT [ ] ..... uT   =>   ... iT [√] ..... uT̶

The feature-checking system in (22) and (23) offers an explanation for temporal/aspectual deixis in both gerunds and indicatives, hence their free variation.

As for the speaker's choice between (22) and (23), we follow Adger and Smith (2005), who argue that intra-speaker variation follows from a system where competing syntactic derivations yield different Spell-Outs with identical semantics. Accordingly, we have to account for the fact that both the gerund and the indicative are propositional and have a *realis* interpretation (i.e. are identical in all of their semantic features).

8.4   The Assertion Operator

In semantics, Meinunger (2004) shows that root clauses are split between illocutionary force and propositional content. He argues that declaratives with indicative verbs have the illocutionary force realized through an Assertion Operator (Assert OP) in Spec,ForceP that takes the structured proposition as its argument. Hence, we infer that if an Assert OP is present in the semantic component of indicatives, it must be equally present in that of root gerunds.

Refining Meinunger's analysis, we suggest that root indicatives are parsed as declaratives by default (i.e. in the absence of any operator syntactically present in ForceP) since their Fin is intrinsically [+finite] and compatible with [+realis]. However, since gerunds are underspecified for all their TAM values, an Assert OP must obligatorily map to syntax in these cases. In other words, root gerunds need explicit declarative clause-typing, which can only be a consequence of merging the Assert OP in their Spec,ForceP, as in (24).

---

3.   Pragmatic valuation takes place in the semantic component when interpretable features (e.g., iT) do not receive a value upon feature-checking. This valuation is derived contextually, akin to situations of logophoric licensing of nominals (e.g., Landau 2013).

(24)

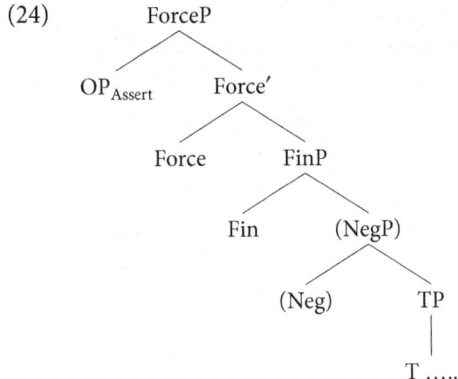

In (24) the Assert OP takes scope over Fin and T and, crucially, binds Fin as [+finite, +realis]. This explains the possibility of root gerunds with V-to-T, since T depends on Assert OP for its valuation.

Confirmation for the presence of Assert OP in (24) comes from the unavailability of gerunds in interrogatives: all the root gerunds we found are declaratives. This is predictable, since interrogatives need specific operators with propositional scope, whose merging in Force is blocked by the Assert OP.[4]

As for the change from V-to-T to V-to-Fin with root gerunds, we point out that the Assert OP is null, which weakens the evidence for its presence. Our inference is that *The Moldavian Chronicles* point to a system in transition, with the Assert OP present in some cases—specifically, with V-to-T—but not in others (i.e. V-to-Fin). Specifically, the 22 examples of root gerunds with V-to-Fin denote the absence of [+finite, +realis]-valuation by the Assert OP and a 'recuperating' mechanism of T-to-C raising. However, since $[_T$ GER] is not specified as [+finite, +realis], this system cannot be maintained and root gerunds are lost.

The situation in gerund adjuncts is somewhat different. Not all adjuncts would map an Assert OP even when this was available in the language. For instance, relative clauses contain a relative OP, which rules out an Assertion OP. Following Haegeman (2010: 307, and earlier work), adverbial clauses are of two types: 'central' adverbial clauses, whose function is "to structure the event expressed in the associated main clause" and 'peripheral' adverbial clauses, which provide a background proposition for the main clause event and are more root-like in that they have independent temporal deixis and illocutionary force. Central adjuncts are not propositional, so cannot have an Assert OP to begin with. Hence, the loss of this OP would not affect them. They

---

4.   Note that lower operators are not expected to interfere with the Assert OP, which explains the presence of operators in Spec,FocusP in OR gerunds, as in (18b). Unlike wh-phrases, focused constituents do not require specific clause-typing in Force.

continue to function in MR as they did in OR, by virtue of being associated with the speech act of the main clause. Peripheral adjuncts, on the other hand, do instantiate Force and require relevant anchoring. Following Haegeman (2010), who, in turn refers to Aboh's (2005) work on factives in Gungbe, this anchoring can be realized via an operator or via V-to-C. This explains why V-to-Fin/C generalizes with gerunds once the Assert OP is lost. However, unlike with root gerunds, which necessarily require a [+finite] specification, adjuncts have no such requirement, which explains the survival of gerund adjuncts into MR.

9. Conclusions

The key goal of this paper was to explain the possibility for gerund clauses in OR to occur in free variation with indicatives, either as root declaratives or under coordination (see (1) and (2)). The data showed that gerund clauses are overwhelmingly adjuncts (adverbial or relative). Tests of distribution and word order indicated that adjunct and root gerunds are phasal domains (i.e., CPs that license Nominative subjects), and have the same TAM properties (i.e., they are underspecified). For their internal structure, the tests showed that the older stages of OR had V-to-T, whereas the OR of the 16th century and later has primarily V-to-Fin in the same configurations.

The analysis we developed capitalized on the above observations and on the semantic equivalence between root gerunds and root indicatives. Following Meinunger (2004), we proposed that an Assertion Operator is mapped to syntax in root gerunds (though not in root indicatives). The Assertion OP scopes over the proposition and binds Fin-T, ensuring a [+finite, +realis] valuation.

The loss of root gerunds was derived from the presence of two mechanisms that could value the clause-type feature as declarative in OR: with a null OP and no operator (i.e. by default in indicatives). Since both instances lack overt phonological features, the language learner could easily mistake one for another. The consequence was V-to-Fin (instead of V-to-T), since the absence of the Assert OP in Spec,ForceP entailed failure to value the features of Fin. Thus, the stabilization of V-to-Fin in MR coincided with the complete loss of root gerunds, as these can no longer recover a [+finite] specification. However, phasal gerunds have been maintained as adjuncts in MR, with pragmatic tense valuation.

Corpus

Iordan, Iorgu. 1955. *Ion Neculce, Letopisețul Țării Moldovei*. Bucharest: Editura de Stat.
Panaitescu, Petre P. 1958. *Grigore Ureche, Letopisețul Țării Moldovei*. Bucharest: Editura de Stat.
Panaitescu, Petre P. 1979. *Miron Costin, Letopisețul Țării Moldovei*. Bucharest: Editura Minerva.

References

Abels, Klaus. 2001. "The Predicate Cleft Construction in Russian." *Formal Approaches to Slavic Linguistics 9*, ed. by Steven Franks and Michael Yadroff, 1–19. Bloomington, IN: Michigan Slavic Publications.

Aboh, Enoch. 2005. "Deriving Relative and Factive Constructions in Kwa." *Contributions to the Thirtieth Incontro di Grammatica Generativa,* ed. by Laura Brugè, Giuliana Giusti, Nicola Munaro, Walter Schweikert, and Giuseppina Turano, 265–285. Venezia: Libreria Editrice Cafoscarina.

Adger, David and Jennifer Smith. 2005. "Variation and the Minimalist Program." *Syntax and Variation: Reconciling the Biological and the Social,* ed. by Leonie Elise Alexandra Cornips and Karen P. Corrigan, 149–178. Amsterdam: John Benjamins. DOI: 10.1075/cilt.265.10adg

Alboiu, Gabriela. 2002. *The Features of Movement in Romanian.* Bucharest: EUB.

Alboiu, Gabriela, Virginia Hill and Ioanna Sitaridou. 2014. "Discourse driven V-to-Focus in Early Modern Romanian." *Natural Language & Linguistic Theory* (to appear). DOI: 10.1007/s11049-014-9270-8

Caragiu, Matilda. 1957. "Sintaxa gerunziului românesc." *Studii de gramatică* II. 61–89.

Cinque, Guglielmo. 1999. *Adverbs and Functional Heads. A cross-Linguistic Perspective.* New York: Oxford University Press.

D'Alessandro, Roberta and Adam Ledgeway. 2010. "At the C-T boundary: Investigating Abruzzese complementation." *Lingua* 120. 2040–2060. DOI: 10.1016/j.lingua.2010.02.003

Demirdache, Hamida. 1991. *Resumptive Chains in Restrictive Relatives, Appositives, and Dislocation Structures.* Ph.D. dissertation, MIT.

Edelstein, Frieda. 1972. *Sintaxa Gerunziului Românesc.* Bucharest: Editura Academiei.

Gabinschi, Marcu. 2010. *Formele Verbale Nepredicative Nonconjunctivale ale Limbii Române.* Chişinau: Institutul de filologie al AŞM.

Haegeman, Liliane. 2010. "Evidential Mood, Restructuring, and the Distribution of Functional Sembrare." *Mapping the Left Periphery,* ed. by Paola Benincà and Nicola Munaro, 297–327. Oxford: Oxford University Press.

Haegeman, Liliane and Raffaella Zanuttini. 1996. "Negative Concord in West Flemish." *Parameters and Functional Heads. Essays in Comparative Syntax,* ed. by Adriana Belletti, and Luigi Rizzi, 117–179. New York: Oxford University Press.

Hill, Virginia and Liliane Tasmowski. 2008. "Romanian Clitic Doubling: a View from Pragmatics-Semantics and Diachrony." *Clitic Doubling in the Balkan Languages,* ed. by Dalina Kallulli and Liliane Tasmowski, 133–163. Amsterdam: John Benjamins. DOI: 10.1075/la.130.10hil

Kayne, Richard. 1991. "Romance clitics, verb movement and PRO." *Linguistic Inquiry* 22.647–687.

Laka, Itziar. 1990. *Negation in Syntax.* Ph.D. dissertation, MIT.

Landau, Idan. 2006. "Chain Resolution in Hebrew VP-fronting." *Syntax* 9: 32–65. DOI: 10.1111/j.1467-9612.2006.00084.x

Landau, Idan. 2013. *Control in Generative Grammar: A Research companion.* Cambridge: Cambridge University Press. DOI: 10.1017/CBO9781139061858

Meinunger, André. 2004. "Verb Position, Verbal Mood and the Anchoring (Potential) of Sentences." *The Syntax and Semantics of the Left Periphery,* ed. by Horst Lohnstein and Susanne Trissler, 313–341. Berlin: Mouton de Gruyter.

Miller, Gary. 2000. "Gerund and gerundive in Latin." *Diachronica* XVII (2): 293–349. DOI: 10.1075/dia.17.2.03mil

Pesetsky, David and Esther Torrego. 2007. "The Syntax of Valuation and the Interpretability of Features." *Phrasal and Clausal Architecture: Syntactic Derivation and Interpretation*, ed. by Simin Karimi, Vida Samiian and Wendy K. Wilkins, 262–294. Amsterdam: John Benjamins. DOI: 10.1075/la.101.14pes

Rivero, Maria-Luiza. 1993. "Long Head Movement vs. V2 and null subjects in Old Romance." *Lingua* 89: 217–245. DOI: 10.1016/0024-3841(93)90053-Y

Rizzi, Luigi. 1997. "The fine structure of the left periphery." *Elements of Grammar*, ed. by Liliane Haegeman, 281–339. Dordrecht: Kluwer. DOI: 10.1007/978-94-011-5420-8_7

Rizzi, Luigi. 2004. "Locality and Left Periphery". *Structures and Beyond. The Cartography of Syntactic Structures*, vol. 3, ed. by Adriana Belletti, 223–251. New York: Oxford University Press.

Roberts, Ian. 2010. *Agreement and Head Movement: Clitics, Incorporation, and Defective Goals*. Cambridge, MA: The MIT Press. DOI: 10.7551/mitpress/9780262014304.001.0001

Zanuttini, Raffaella. 1997. *Negation and Clausal Structure: A Comparative Study of Romance Languages*. New York: Oxford University Press.

Old French possessives and ellipsis

Deborah Arteaga & Julia Herschensohn
University of Nevada / University of Washington

Sáez (2011), to account for Spanish definite articles in ellipsis contexts, such as *mi libro y el* [e] *de Juan* 'my book and that of John', proposes the Stress Condition on Remnants (SCR), which disallows unstressed syntactic elements to be anaphoric, while allowing definite articles to license empty categories. The focus of our paper is Old French (OF) possessive constructions and their elliptical expressions, such as *le mien livre* 'my book' and *le [e] de Jean* 'that of Jean'. OF had a more extensive inventory of possessive constructions than Modern French (MF): lexical genitives, prenominal possessives, and lexical and possessive ellipsis constructions. Adopting Arteaga & Herschensohn's (2010, 2013) proposal for lexical genitives, Sáez's (2011) SCR, and Lobeck's (1995) conditions on ellipsis, we argue that two major diachronic changes led to a difference in licensing of possessives from OF to MF: one, the erosion of morphological marking that led to a loss of the OF two case system, reducing feature strength to license ellipsis (Lobeck 1995), and two, the fact that definite articles became clitics and Phase Heads and thus became subject to the SCR as the prenominal nP domain (Carstens 2003) became a clitic zone prohibiting prenominal stressed possessives.

1. OF genitive constructions

1.1 Old French Case system

There are many syntactic and morphological differences between OF and MF. One of the most important differences is that OF had a case system, nominative (NOM) and oblique (OBL). The nominative encompassed both nominative and vocative in Latin; the oblique was used in all other instances:

(1) *A   cele   table   sistrent*
     at   that-F-SG-OBL table-F-SG-OBL sat.down-3PL

     li   frère
     the-M-PL-NOM brothers-M-PL-NOM

     'The brothers sat down at that table.'   (La Queste del Saint Graal 74 L24)

DOI 10.1075/rllt.9.02art

(2) *Par* **les**   *frères*   *qui a cele*
     by   the-M-PL-OBL brothers-M-PL-OBL who at that-F-SG-OBL

     table   *sistrent*
     table-F-SG-OBL sat-3PL

     'By the brothers who sat down at that table.'

                                          (La Queste del Saint Graal 74 L28)

In (1) above, the subject, *li frere*, is in the nominative case. The oblique would be *les frerès*, as in (2), which follows the preposition *par*.

1.2   Lexical genitive structures in OF

In OF, there were three lexical DP genitive structures (see Arteaga 1995, Delfitto and Paradisi 2009, and Arteaga and Herschensohn 2010, 2013), two of which have survived into MF (3)–(4), to wit:

(3) *La*   *suer*   *a mon*   *seigneur*
     the-F-SG-NOM sister-F-SG-NOM to my-M-SG-OBL lord-M-SG-OBL
     'My lord's sister'   (Dole 5041, Herslund 1980, 84)

(4) *le*   *cuer*   *de son*   *amy*
     the-M-SG-OBL heart-M-SG-OBL of his-M-SG-OBL friend-M-SG-OBL
     'His friend's heart'   (Palm 1977, 63)

In the above examples, the genitive is expressed by *à* 'to,' and *de*, 'of,' respectively. The possessors *mon seigneur* and *son amy* are in the oblique case, (nominative *mes sires, ses amis*) as they are objects of a preposition.

While *de* had the most widespread usage in OF genitive structures, the genitive with *à* was also more common than in MF. In MF, it is restricted to people, such as *le frère à mon ami* 'my friend's brother,' literally 'the brother to my friend,' but in OF, it could be used when the possessor was animate, not only a person, as in the example below:

(5) *Por la*   *teste*   *au*
     by   the-NOM-F-SG head-NOM-F-SG to-the-OBL-M-SG

     serpant   *felon*
     snake-OBL-M-SG traitorous-OBL-M-SG

     'By the head of the traitorous snake'   (Yvain 3378)

In OF, there is also one OF genitive structure that is no longer found in MF, namely the juxtaposition genitive (see inter alia, Arteaga and Herschensohn 2010, 2013 and Delfitto and Paradisi 2009). In the most common structure (6a), the possessor—

marked by oblique case—follows the possessed with no intervening preposition, but the possessor may also be prenominal (6b).[1]

(6)　　*la*　　　　　　*niece*　　　　　**le**　　　　　**duc**
　　　　the-F-SG-NOM niece-F-SG-NOM the-M-SG-OBL duke-M-SG-OBL
　　　　'The duke's niece'　　　　(La Chasteleine de Vergi 376 Foulet 1982, 14)

In MF, a preposition (*à* or *de*) would be obligatory before *le duc* in (6).

　　In OF, all three lexical genitive constructions in (3)–(6) allowed ellipsis, as in the following:

(7)　　*les*　　　　　　*armes*　　　　　*au*　　　　　*soudanc*　　　　*de*
　　　　the-F-PL-NOM weapons-F-PL-NOM to.the-M-SG-OBL sultan-M-SG-OBL of

　　　　H [...] les　　　　　*[e] au*　　　　　*soudanc*　　　　*de B*
　　　　H [...] the-F-PL-NOM [e] to.the-M-SG-OBL sultan-M-SG-OBL of B

　　　　'The weapons of the sultan of H and those of the Sultan of B' (Joinville)
　　　　(Gamillscheg 1957, 58) (cf. Modern French *celles du Soudanc de B.* 'those of the Sultan')

(8)　　*ne poursuite*　　　　*de compaignon*　　　　*se*　　　　*la*
　　　　no pursuit-F-SG-OBL of companion-M-SG-OBL except.for the-F-SG-OBL

　　　　[e] de Dieu
　　　　[e] of God-M-SG-OBL

　　　　'No pursuit of companion except for of God.' (cf. Modern French: *celle de Dieu* 'that one of God.') (Galeran de Bretagne, 4200–2) (Foulet 1982 §70)

(9)　　*defension*　　　　　*fors*　　*sol*　*la*　　　　*[e] Deu.*
　　　　protection-F-SG-OBL outside only the-F-SG-OBL [e] God-M-SG-OBL
　　　　'No protection other than God's.' (Livre des rois) (Anglade 1965, 149)
　　　　(cf. Modern French: *celle de Dieu* 'that one of God.'

In all three structures, the noun is the ellipsis site and the article may bear stress, unlike in MF. We will show that the reason for the loss of this structure is phonological, morphological, and syntactic. Indeed, we will argue that stress difference between OF and MF as well as the erosion of OF overt morphology are crucial factors that determine diachronic shifts in genitive ellipsis structures, as is the fact that the definite article heads a Phase. Before turning to possessive adjectives and pronouns, we describe the nature of French clitics and stressed forms.

1.　In this structure, two possibilities are found, the more common postposed possessor, but also the preposed possessor (see Arteaga and Herschensohn 2010).

We accept the three-way pronoun distinction of Cardinaletti and Starke (1999) that we extend to definite articles—strong, weak, and clitic pronouns—each of which has (from left to right) diminishing structure/content in terms of phonological independence, morphological features, syntactic mobility and semantic complexity. Essentially, Modern French has only strong and clitic pronouns. Modern French clitics cannot be stressed. For example, when they occur in phrase final stressed position in affirmative imperatives, the strong form must be used:

(10) a. *Ne te   lève   pas*
        not yourself get.up-2SG-imperative not
        'Don't get up!'

     b. *Lève-   toi!*
        get.up-2SG-imperative   yourself
        'Get up!'

(11) a. *Ne me   le   donne   pas*
        not to.me it-M-SG give-2SG-imperative not
        'Don't give it to me!'

     b. *Donne-   le-   moi!*
        give-2SG-imperative   it-M-SG to.me
        'Give it to me.'

Elision of vowels—the deletion of the vowel of a determiner or pronoun before another vowel (*le* + *âne* → *l'âne* 'the donkey')—is morpho-phonetically predictable, and not a vague case of reduction of function words. Not all function words undergo "reduction". Clitics behave in predictable patterns that are quite distinct and systematic, differing from strong pronouns in French. Many clitics are CV monosyllables with the schwa as the vowel (e.g. *le, me, se, te*); schwas are quite prone to deletion in informal speech. This optional stylistic deletion cannot be conflated with elision, the obligatory deletion of a vowel in a clitic in the environment preceding a vowel initial word. Definite articles in Modern French are also clitics. They cannot license ellipsis, so that the demonstrative article is used, as noted in examples (7)–(9) above.

1.3 Possessive adjectives and pronouns in OF: Morphology

OF evinced two prenominal possessive series, the former labeled as 'weak' by philologists, the other as 'strong.' The terms 'strong' and 'weak' were used to describe these possessives, because the vowel in the former, but not in the latter, underwent diphthongization. We will adopt this nomenclature, because it also describes their syntactic status.

The first series was declined as follows (Einhorn 1974, 35):

Table 1. Weak Possessives, OF

	1SG		2SG		3SG		1PL	2PL	3PL
	M	F	M	F	M	F	M/F	M/F	
NOM SG	mes	ma	tes	ta	ses	sa	nostre(s)	vostre(s)	lor
OBL SG	mon	ma	ton	ta	son	sa	nostre	vostre	lor
NOM PL	mi	mes	ti	tes	si	ses	nostre	vostre	lor
OBL PL	mes	mes	tes	tes	ses	ses	noz	voz	lor

As can be seen in Table 1 above, for the 1SG, 2SG, and 3SG persons, the masculine forms are fully declined whereas the feminine are only differentiated by singular vs. plural. The forms for the 1PL and the 2PL have only one form for both the feminine and the masculine, and the form for the 3PL was invariable.

OF examples of these possessive adjectives are as follows:

(12) *Il est munté sur **sun** destrier.*
he is-3SG mounted on his-M-SG-OBL horse-M-SG-OBL
'He mounted his horse.'   (Eliduc 283; Moignet 1988, 114).

(13) ***Mes** padre me desidret, si fait*
my-M-SG-NOM father-M-SG-NOM me wants-3SG so does-3SG

***ma** medre*
my-F-SG-NOM mother-F-SG-NOM

'My father wants me and so does my mother.'   (La vie de St. Alexis 206)

In (12)–(13) above, *sun* is in the oblique case (nominative *ses*) and *mes* is in the nominative case (oblique *mon*). Further, as we seen by the above examples, the weak forms of possessives in OF, like their counterparts in MF, were not accompanied by an article. Moreover, like their MF clitic counterparts, they could not stand alone, suggesting that they are already clitics in OF:

(14) ***Voz** oncles tient*
your-M-SG-NOM uncle-M-SG-NOM holds-3SG

***mon** pere a sage*
my-M-SG-OBL father-M-SG-OBL to wise-M-SG-OBL

'Your uncle considers my father wise.'
                (Le Vair palefroi 425) (Foulet 1982, 163)

(15) ****Voz** oncles tient mon [e]*
your-M-SG-NOM uncle-M-SG-NOM holds-3SG my-M-SG-OBL [e]

a sage
to wise-M-SG-OBL

'Your uncle considers mine (i.e., my uncle) wise.'

The utterance in (14) was attested in OF, but not that of the type in (15). There are other syntactic restrictions regarding the weak form of the possessives, namely that they must be adjacent to the noun or prenominal adjective, but allow no other intervening material. Importantly, they are always definite.

Note further that the first, second, and third person feminine singular can undergo ellipsis, as in the following:

(16) *m'*   *amie*
      my-F-SG-NOM friend-F-SG-NOM
      'my friend'   (Guillaume le Vinier XIX, 44) (Moignet 1988, 35)

(17) *t'*   *anme*
      your-F-SG-NOM soul-F-SG_NOM
      'your soul'   (Roland 2898) (Jensen 1990, 176)

(18) *s'*   *espee*
      his-F-SG-NOM sword F-SG-NOM
      'his sword'   (Roland 2089) (Ménard 1988, 35)

The examples from (16)–(18) are further evidence that the possessive adjectives in Old French were clitics.[2] In contrast, the morphology of the stressed version (called by philologists the "strong form") was as follows (Anglade 1965, 90–91):[3]

Table 2. First and Second Person Singular Strong Possessives

	1SG		2SG	
	M	**F**	**M**	**F**
NOM SG	li miens	la mienne/moie	li tiens/tuens	la tienne/toe
OBL SG	le mien	la mienne/moie	le tien/tuen	la tienne/toe
NOM PL	li mien	les miennes/moes	li tien/tuen	les tiennes/toies
OBL PL	les miens	les miennes/moies	les tiens/tuens	les tiennes/loes

---

2. MF uses the masculine singular form of the possessive instead of the elided form, which began to be used after the 13th century, according to philologists (i.e., *mon amie, ton âme, son épée.*)

3. Note that *mienne/moie,* etc. were dialectal variants.

Table 3. Third Person Strong Possessives

	3SG		3PL	
	M	**F**	**M**	**F**
NOM SG	li siens/suens	la sienne/soe	li lor/lour	la lor/lour
OBL SG	le sien/suen	la sienne/soe	le lor/lour	la lor/lour
NOM PL	li sien/suen	les siennes/soes	li lor/lour	les lor/lour
OBL PL	les siens/suens	les siennes/soes	les lor/lour	les lor/lour

Table 4. First and Second Person Plural Strong Possessives

	1PL		2PL	
	M	**F**	**M**	**F**
NOM SG	li nostre(s)	la nostre	li vostre(s)	la vostre
OBL SG	le nostre	la nostre	les vostres	la vostre
NOM PL	li nostre(s)	les nostres/noz/nos	li vostre(s)	les vostres/voz/vos
OBL PL	les nostres/noz/nos	les nostres/noz/nos	les vostres/voz/vos	les vostres/voz/vos

A determiner typically accompanies the strong forms; it may be a definite article (19), an indefinite article (20), or a demonstrative (21):

(19) *C'ost   grant   merveille   que*
      this-N-SG-NOM-is great-F-SG-NOM miracle-F-SG-NOM that
      li   miens   cuers   tant   duret!
      the-M-SG-NOM my-M-SG-NOM heart-M-SG-NOM so long lasts-3SG
      'It's a wonder that my heart lasts so long!   (Saint Alexis 445) (Jensen § 369)

(20) **un**   *sien   compere   en   apela.*
      one-M-SG-OBL his-M-SG-OBL friend-M-SG-OBL one called-3SG
      'They called one of his friends.'   (La male honte 16–17 Foulet 1982, 166)

(21) *Dist   Olivier: Par* **ceste**   *meie   barbe*
      said-3SG Oliver by this-F-SG-OBL my-F-SG-OBL beard-F-SG-OBL
      'Oliver said, "By this beard of mine'   (Roland 1719; Moignet 1988, 120)

Note further that philologists argue that it is the article, not the possessive, which is definite. This is in contrast to the weak forms, in which it is the possessive that carries the definite feature.

Importantly, for our purposes, the strong forms, as opposed to the weak forms, could license ellipsis:

(22)   *La*   *lor*   *terre*   *deis*   *[...] a*
       the-F-SG-OBL   their-F-SG-OBL   land-F-SG-OBL   must-2SG   to

       la   *nostre*   *[e]* joindre
       the-F-SG-OBL   our-F-SG-OBL   [e] to.join

       'You must join their land to ours'
                                       (Couronnement de Louis 77) (Jensen 1990, 179).

(23)   *Ses*   *cousins*   *estes*   *et*
       his-M-SG-NOM   cousin-M-SG-NOM   are-2PL   and

       li   *miens* [e]
       the-M-SG-NOM   mine-M-SG-NOM

       'You are his cousin and mine.'   (Huon de Bordeaux 2583) (Moignet)

Compare (22)–(23) above with the ungrammatical (15).

Spanish also evinces strong possessives type *el libro mío* (literally *the book mine*). However, in Spanish, such possessives must be postnominal (cf. **el mío libro*), which is an important difference between OF and Spanish; as in OF, the strong possessives must be prenominal. In other words, sequences like (23') are not attested (inter alia Moignet 1988; Ménard 1988; Jensen 1990; Arteaga 1995):

(23')   **li*   amis   miens
        the-M-SG-NOM   friend-M-SG-NOM   mine-M-SG-NOM (cf. *el amigo mío*)
        'My friend.'

To summarize, we have seen that OF had a series of possessive adjectives that were clitics, as well as a series that could license ellipsis. Both sets had to be prenominal.

2.   Theoretical framework

In this section, we first review relevant assumptions of minimalism and recent analyses of DP within this framework. We then discuss two earlier treatments of lexical OF genitives, Delfitto & Paradisi, (2009, henceforth D&P) and A&H, before considering the analysis of Arteaga (1995), who discusses strong and weak possessives.

2.1   The Minimalist framework

The cornerstone of Minimalism is the operation Merge: External Merge joining two syntactic objects, and Internal Merge moving a syntactic object within the domain of another one (Chomsky 2001, 2008); we follow D&P's interpretation of Merge.

Agree is an operation of matching features—for example, checking interpretable and uninterpretable features—that can be described as a probe-goal relationship (D&P 2009, 482) within the minimal Phase Head:

(24) a. Given an Agree relation A between probe P and goal G, morphophonological agreement between P and G is realized iff P and G are contained in the complement of the minimal Phase Head H.

   b. XP is the complement of a minimal Phase Head H iff there is no distinct phase head H' contained in XP whose complement YP contains P and G.

With respect to DPs, interpretable features are those with semantic content, such as gender or number on N or definiteness on determiners. Uninterpretable features, on the other hand, include case and [$u$def] on N and uninterpretable gender ([$u$gen]) and number ([$u$num]) on determiners or adjectives (Lin 2008). Interpretable features must persist through the derivation to enable interpretation, whereas uninterpretable features must be valued or the derivation crashes.

Adopting Pereltsvaig's (2007) defense of the universality of DP (cf. Abney 1987; Bernstein 1991; Mallén 1997), Lin (2008) claims that the syntactic structure for the nominal phrase DP is universal regardless of the presence of determiners in a given language. In his analysis, N can carry a [$u$def] feature to be matched and deleted by interpretable [def] on a determiner, which we also assume. We also adopt the nP shell approach advocated by Carstens (2000, 2003) for which functional features such as number or possessive constitute iterative nPs above the head noun. In Romance, N raises to higher positions (e.g., above the adjective), accommodating raising of the head noun or of nominal modifiers (e.g., Bernstein 1991; Longobardi 1994; Mallén 1997).

For the lexical genitive constructions, D&P (2009), propose a KP/PP that assigns oblique case to the possessor, with preposition (3)–(4) or without (9), (juxtaposition genitive), which can account for the oblique case assigned to the possessors in the JG, as well as those that follow *à* and *de*. A&H extend D&P's analysis of lexical genitives with respect to the [K] feature to account for both pre- and postnominal JGs.[4] A&H's proposal, unlike D&P's analysis—that initially situates the possessor prenominally, deriving postnominal possessor by head noun raising—uniformly situates the possessor postnominally in all constructions.

---

4. D&P do not discuss prenominal JGs. A&H propose a unified account exemplified in (i).

   (i)   [$_{DP}$ D [$_{nP}$ ... [$_{NP}$ N[$_{KP}$ [K/P [$_{DP}$ D [$_{nP}$ ... [$_{NP}$ N$_2$]]]]]]]]

Their derivation of the prepositional structures and the juxtaposition genitive is as follows; note that the genitive with *à* and with *de* have the same structure (25) (A & H 2013, 34):

(25)   *fille*   *ad un   comte*
       daughter-F-SG-NOM to a-M-SG-OBL count-M-SG-OBL
       'The Count's daughter.' (literally, 'The daughter to the Count.')

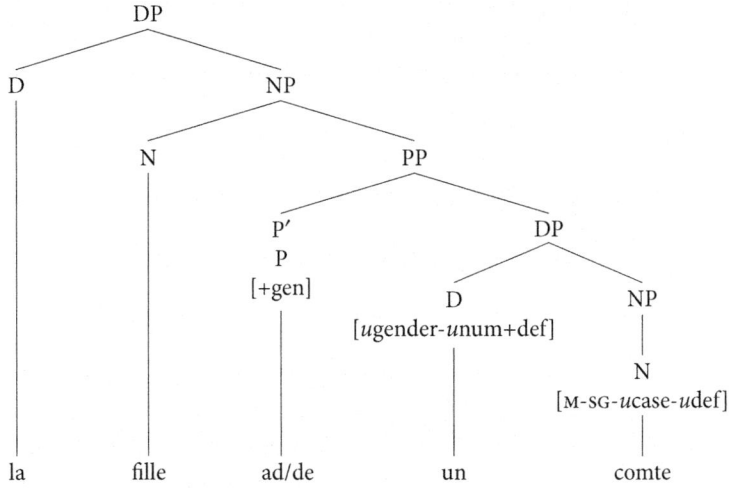

In (25) the uninterpretable features (number and gender) of the D are valued by the interpretable features (masculine singular) of the N, whereas the uninterpretable case feature of N is valued by the P *ad*.

(26)   *la   chambre   son   pere* (A & H 2013, 35)
       the-F-SG-NOM room-F-SG-NOM his-M-SG-OBL father-M-SG-OBL
       'The room of his father.' (literally, 'The room his father.')

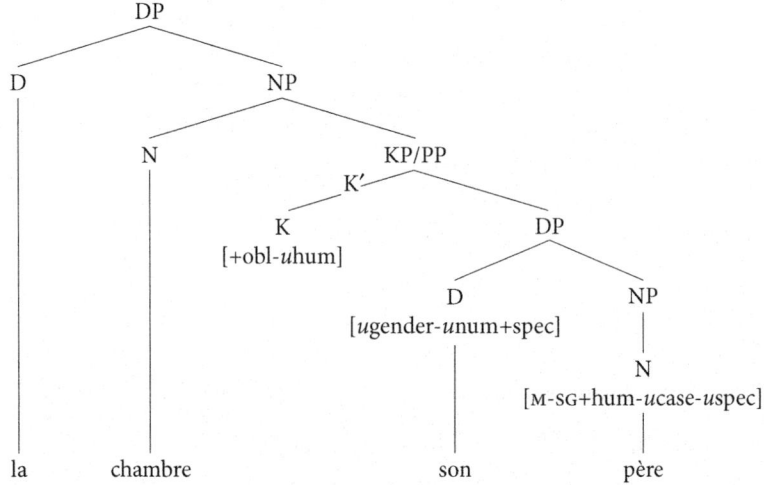

In (26) the uninterpretable features of the D (gen, num) are valued and deleted by the interpretable gender and number of *pere*, while its case feature values the noun's [*u*case]. Note that the uninterpretable K feature [*u*human] is valued by the possessor noun that is obligatorily human for the JG.

We next turn to previous analyses of ellipsis in possessive structures.

2.2   Arteaga (1995)

Arteaga discusses strong and weak possessives, and the fact that only the former can license ellipsis. She follows Picallo (1994), who makes a distinction between possessive adjectives ('weak possessives' in our terminology) and strong ones, arguing that in OF, the latter must front. Possessive adjectives and tonic pronouns preceded by 'de' are generated in the SPEC of NP.

2.3   Sáez

Sáez (2011, 156) discusses ellipsis in Modern Spanish, noting that while possessive adjectives cannot license ellipsis, the definite article can:

(27)   *No compraron vuestros   libros   de física,   sino*
        not bought-3PL your-M-PL books-M-PL of physics-F-SG Except

        nuestros   (*libros) de química.
        ours-M-PL (*books) of chemistry-F-SG

(28)   *... sino   los   de química.*
        except the-M-PL of chemistry-F-SG

In order to account for the above, he considers adopting Lobeck's (1995) ellipsis licensing requirements, summarized as the Strong Agreement Condition (29).

(29)   Strong Agreement Condition
        Ellipsis must be licensed by
        a.   a governing head
        b.   strong agreement (i.e., two or more overt morphological features)

Lobeck (1995, 131–134) notes that French licensers of ellipsis must carry two or more overt morphological features, such as number, gender, or case, all three of which are available in OF.

Noting that *nuestros* 'our' is also marked by strong agreement, and updating Lobeck's proposal within the Minimalist framework, he proposes the following Stress Condition on Remnants (henceforth SCR), which states that "Every ellipsis remnant must bear stress" (Sáez 2011, 159).

This proposal, he argues, follows Nissenbaum (2000), in claiming that it is Phase Complements and not Phase Heads that are the relevant structures for syntax, namely

(NP for the DP phase, and TP for the CP-Phase (Sáez 2010: 161). These units, in turn, are transferred to PHON as an economy principle (Chomsky 2008).

In order for the only the prenominal possessive adjective to be subject to the SCR, he proposes that Phase Heads are not subject to the SCR, so that the SCR is restricted, as follows (Sáez 2011, 161):

> (30)   The scope of the Stress Condition on Remnants is the Phase Head Comple-
> ment most recently transferred to PHON.

However, as pointed out by philologists for OF, Sáez notes that both the prenominal possessive adjective and the definite article in Spanish are unstressed, yet the definite article can license ellipsis but not the possessive adjectives.

In order for this revised SCR to apply only to definite articles, Sáez assumes that possessive adjectives are generated in the NP-PHC. Like Arteaga (1995), he follows Picallo 1994, although he proposes a simpler structure (31):

> (31) $[_{DP} [_{D} \textit{nuestros}_i] [_{GeP} \textbf{\textit{nuestros}}_i [_{NP} [_{N'} \textit{(libros)}]]]]$

In the derivation of the above, *nuestros* undergoes external merge, and its copy is deleted.[5]

3.   Current proposal

We briefly review three previous accounts of lexical genitives in OF (Arteaga 1995; D&P 2009; A&H 2010, 2013) that we will incorporate into our analysis.

3.1   Lexical Genitives

As we have seen, in ellipsis contexts, we find the same possibilities as in (7)–(9) above, repeated as (32)–(34) below, namely the possessor introduced by *à*, by *de*, and also the JG genitive:

> (32)   les   [armes]$_i$ au   soudanc   de
>   the-F-PL-NOM   weapons-F-PL-NOM   to.the-M-SG-OBL   sultan-M-SG-OBL   of
>   H [...] les   [e]   au   soudanc   de B
>   H [...] the-F-PL-NOM   [armes]$_i$ to.the-M-SG-OBL   sultan-M-SG-OBL   of   B
>   'The weapons of the sultan of H and those of the Sultan of B' (Joinville)
>   (Gamillscheg 1957, 58).

---

5.   One aspect of Sáez's proposal that is problematic is that he does not account for the fact that Spanish only allows ellipsis with the preposition 'de,' which, unlike OF, does not have to be possessive.

(33) *Et   le   suen   nom$_i$ et   le*
      and the-M-SG-OBL his-M-SG-OBL name-M-SG-OBL and the-M-SG-OBL

      [~~nom~~]$_i$ son   père
      [~~name~~] his-M-SG-OBL father-M-SG-OBL

      'His name and that of his father's.'   (Cligés 2975) (Togeby 1974, 53)

(34) *defension   fors   sol*
      protection-F-SG-OBL outside only

      la   [~~defension~~]$_i$ Deu.
      the-F-SG-OBL [~~defension~~]$_i$ God-M-SG-OBL

      'No protection other than God's.'   (Livre des rois) (Anglade 1965, 149)

Before addressing the ellipsis cases, we need to review analyses of the non-ellipsis jux-taposition genitives. D&P's (2009) analysis of OF genitive structures proposes a KP/PP assigning oblique case to the possessor and accounting for the oblique case of JG pos-sessors. A&H extend D&P's analysis of lexical genitives with respect to the [K] feature and uniformly situate the possessor postnominally in all constructions.

As for the lexical genitive constructions considered here, we propose that they license ellipsis through the definite article, which carries overt morphological features of gender-number-case (cf. *les* in (32), which agrees with *les armes*, *la* in (8) which agrees with *poursuite*, and *la* in (34), which agrees with *defension*) with the repeated noun copy deleted at spell-out [e].

In other words, in ellipsis contexts, all three gaps are licensed by the phi features and case of the antecedents and carried by the definite article. To use Sáez's terminol-ogy, the definite article in OF escapes the SCR because it is a Phase Head and it carries a sufficient number of overt features (gender, number, case) to meet Lobeck's Strong Agreement Condition.

(35) ... [$_{DP}$ [$_D$les [+*def*, ~~*unum, ugen, ucase*~~] [$_{NP}$ ~~armes~~ [~~*udef*~~, +*pl*, +*fem*, ~~*ucase*~~]
      [$_{PP}$ [a [$_{DP}$ [$_D$ le [$_{NP}$ soudanc]]]]]]]]]].

(36) ... [$_{DP}$ [$_D$ la [+*def*, ~~*unum, ugen, ucase*~~] [$_{NP}$ ~~poursuite~~ [~~*udef*~~, -*pl*, +*fem*, ~~*ucase*~~]
      [$_{PP}$ [de [$_{DP}$ [$_{NP}$ Dieu]]]]]]]]]].

(37) ... [$_{DP}$ [$_D$ la [+*def*, ~~*unum, ugen, ucase*~~] [$_{NP}$ ~~defension~~ [~~*udef*~~, -*pl*, +*fem*, ~~*ucase*~~]
      [$_{KP}$ [K-OBL [$_{DP}$ [$_{NP}$ Deu]]]]]]]]]].

The uninterpretable nominal features are checked and deleted within the DP: interpre-table [+PL], [+fem], [+def] value [*unum*], [*ugen*], [*udef*]; [*ucase*] which is checked is checked extra-DP by vP (OBL) or TP (NOM).

3.2   Weak possessive forms

In the case of weak possessives, we assume a Distributed Morphology approach (Halle and Marantz 1993; Harley and Noyer 1999; Harley and Ritter 2002) whereby the determiner feature bundle raises to D, valuing gender, number, case and possessive features along the way (cf. Bernstein 1991; Mallén 1997). We propose that the complement possessive nP of D hosting the possessive feature raises to merge to D where it values the [+def] feature and will eventually spell out as the weak possessive determiner (e.g., *sun*). In contrast to the stressed possessive in the nP shell, the unstressed possessive merges to D as do definite articles in MF. Unlike the strong possessive in OF, the weak possessive determiner is unstressed and has a [+def] feature.[6] Since it is unstressed and therefore subject to the SCR, it cannot serve in ellipsis contexts. Therefore, structures like (15) above are ungrammatical in OF:

(38)   a.   ... *[$_{DP}$ mon [*+poss, +def*, _unum_, _u_gen, ~~ucase~~] [$_{NP}$ e [_udef_, *-pl, -f*, _u_case]]. **mon [e]* 'my'

   b.   ... [$_{DP}$ [$_D$ mon [*+def*, ~~unum, ugen, ucase~~] [$_{nP-poss}$ ~~mon~~ [*+poss, udef,* ~~unum, ugen, ucase~~]
   [$_{NP}$ cousin [~~udef~~, *-pl, -f*, _u_case]]]]] *mon cousin* 'my cousin'

3.3   Strong possessive forms

In the spirit of Arteaga (1995) and updating her analysis to the Minimalist framework, we propose that the strong possessive is eventually, like the weak possessive, located in the prenominal poss nP projection. As we have seen above, philologists have proposed that in the strong possessive forms, it is the determiner (definite article, indefinite article, demonstrative) that is definite, not the possessive. Following Parodi (1994) for Catalan, Arteaga captures her insight by proposing that the unstressed possessive in OF carries a [+def] feature, but that the stressed does not.

   She further claims (cf. Picallo 1994), that strong possessives must front, accounting for the ungrammaticality of (19) with postposed strong possessive (**li amis miens*). We adopt this treatment of OF strong possessives that links them to their postnominal lexical genitive counterparts: these possessives originate in postnominal position and raise to prenominal position where the [*u*def] feature probes the determiner goal with the feature [def]. We further observe that the nP shell prenominal zone (Carstens 2003; D&P 2009; A&H 2010, 2013) in OF allows both clitic and stressed items, whose features and case are transparent.

   Unlike the weak possessive (+def) that is merged to D, the strong possessive has a [*u*def] feature that probes the determiner goal with an interpretable feature [±def]. This accounts for the fact that the strong possessives are prenominal and must be accompanied by an article. Note that this is quite distinct from MF, which does not allow prenominal strong possessives; the strong possessives in MF are only allowed in

---

6.   Both series did have the feature [specific] (cf. (16) above), but this is not relevant to our discussion.

ellipsis environments. Recall that in OF any D can be used with the strong possessive (15), (16) repeated here as (39) and (40):

(39) **un**   *sien*   *compere*   *en*   *apela.*
one-M-SG-OBL   his-M-SG-OBL   friend-M-SG-OBL   of them   called-3SG
'They called one of his friends.'   (La male honte 16–17 Foulet 1982, 166)

(40) *Dist Olivier: Par* **ceste**   *meie*   *barbe*
said Oliver   by   this-F-SG-OBL   my-F-SG-OBL   beard-F-SG-OBL
'By this beard of mine.'   (Roland 1719; Moignet 1988, 120)

The [*u*def] feature of the strong possessive can be valued by either positive or negative [def]. We further observe that the nP shell prenominal zone (Carstens 2003; D&P 2009; A&H 2010, 2013) in OF allows both clitic and stressed items, whose features and case are transparent.

In ellipsis cases, the null head nouns are licensed by the definite article, for morphological reasons and for syntactic ones. The definite article's features of case, gender, and number are the numerous overt morphological marks that constitute Lobeck's definition of strong agreement. Moreover, it is a Phase Head, and for these two reasons, it can license the null anaphor (A&H 2010, 2013). The nominal features carried by the anaphor and determiner value and delete uninterpretable features:

(41) ... [$_{DP}$ [$_D$ li [*+def, u̶n̶u̶m̶, u̶g̶e̶n̶, u̶c̶a̶s̶e̶*] [$_{nP\text{-poss}}$ miens [*+poss, u̶d̶e̶f̶, u̶n̶u̶m̶,*
u̶g̶e̶n̶, u̶c̶a̶s̶e̶][$_{NP}$ cousins [*u̶d̶e̶f̶, -pl, -f, u̶case̶*]]]]

U-nominal features are checked and deleted within the DP, except for case, which is checked by vP (OBL) or TP (NOM).

In summary, we propose a distinction between the feature bundle of weak possessives that must raise to D, carrying case, gender, number, possessive and eventually [+def] and that of strong possessives that carry case, gender, number, possessive and [*u*def]. All the ± interpretable features on the possessives either value or are valued by the counterparts on the head N. The former are subject to the SCR, as they are not Phase Heads. Our analysis further explains why elision is only possible in the genitive, as these structures were case-marked as genitives in OF.

3.4   Diachronic account of possessives

In the 13th century, a loss of final consonants led to morphophonological erosion. The loss of masculine final *-s* as the distinguishing feature of nominative, rendered the masculine paradigm undifferentiated, leading to the loss of the two-case system. The feminine paradigm (aside from a limited number of irregular nouns) never evinced the two cases.

Two converging morphophonological developments led to changes in the ellipsis options in Middle French. Reduction of the number of overt morphological features on the determiner resulted in an inadequate number for Lobeck's Strong Agreement Condition (plural articles are marked only for that one feature, number not gender) Sáez's SCR. This, in turn, meant that definite determiners could no longer license ellipsis through overt features.

Furthermore, morphophonological erosion led to a fixed word order in the DP: determiners all weakened to clitics, and they were no longer Phase Heads, and became subject to the SCR (as weak possessives had been in OF). Eventually the prenominal zone in French became almost exclusively clitic, which accounts for the loss of the stressed prenominal possessives by the 16th century; the OF strong possessives (which could act either as prenominal modifiers or as pronouns) took over the independent function of freestanding possessive pronouns accompanied by the definite article. In MF the prenominal zone allows adjectives, but they are semantically restricted and undergo sandhi variation in some cases.[7]

In summary, several complementary developments in the history of French contributed to the changes in licensing of ellipsis sites, phonological changes—loss of final consonants and loss of stress on definite articles—and morphological erosion leading to the loss of the two case system. Furthermore, the phonological weakening engendered cliticization of definite articles, rendering them incapable of licensing ellipsis sites due to the SCR, because they were no longer Phase Heads. Strong possessives eventually ceded the prenominal position only to the weak possessive, as clitics became the only prenominal option.[8] The convergence of morphological leveling and phonological loss of final consonants led to syntactic changes that have rendered MF's lack of N ellipsis quite distinct from other Romance languages.

References

Abney, Steven Paul. 1987. *The English Noun Phrase in its Sentential Aspect* (Doctoral Dissertation), MIT.

Anglade, Joseph. 1965. *Grammaire élémentaire de l'ancien français*. Paris: Armand Colin.

Arteaga, Deborah. 1995. "On Old French Genitive Constructions." In *Contemporary research in Romance linguistics*, ed. by John Amastae, Grant Goodall, Mario Montalbetti, and Marianne Phinney, 79–90. Amsterdam: John Benjamins. DOI: 10.1075/cilt.123.08art

---

7.   For example *le beau type* 'the handsome guy', but *le bel homme* 'the handsome man' (cf. *la belle femme* 'the beautiful woman').

8.   In MF, the prenominal zone—generally receptive to clitics does allow a limited set of nonclitic elements (e.g., adjectives, quantifiers).

Arteaga, Deborah, and Julia Herschensohn. 2013. "A Diachronic View of Old French Genitive Constructions." In *Research on Old French: The State of the Art*, ed. by Deborah Arteaga, 19–44. Dordrecht: Springer.

Arteaga, Deborah and J. Herschensohn. 2010. "A Phase-based Analysis of Old French Genitive Constructions." In *Romance Linguistics 2009*, ed. by Sonia Colina, Antxon Olarrea, and Ana Maria Carvalho, 285–300. Amsterdam/Philadelphia: John Benjamins. DOI: 10.1075/cilt.315.17art

Bernstein, Judy. 1991. "DPs in French and Walloon: Evidence for Parametric Variation in Nominal Head Movement." *Probus* 3: 101–126. DOI: 10.1515/prbs.1991.3.2.101

Cardinaletti, Anna, and Michal Starke 1999. "The Typology of Structural Deficiency: A Case Study of the Three Classes of Pronouns." In *Clitics in the Languages of Europe*, ed. by H. Van Riemsdijk, 145–233. Berlin: Mouton de Gruyter.

Carstens, Vicki. 2000. "Concord in Minimalist Theory." *Linguistic Inquiry* 31: 319–355. DOI: 10.1162/002438900554370

Carstens, Vicki. 2003. "Rethinking Complementizer Agreement: Agree with a Case-checked Goal." *Linguistic Inquiry* 34: 393–412. DOI: 10.1162/002438903322247533

Chomsky, Noam. 2001. "Derivation by Phase. In *Ken Hale: A Life in Language*," ed. by Michael Kenstowicz, 1–52. Cambridge MA: MIT Press.

Chomsky, Noam. 2008. "On Phases." In *Foundational Issues in Linguistic Theory*, ed. by Robert Freidin, Carlos Peregrín Otero, and Maria Luisa Zubizarreta, 133–166. Cambridge MA: MIT Press.

Delfitto, Denis and Paola Paradisi. 2009. "Towards a Diachronic Theory of Genitive Assignment in Romance." *Historical Syntax and Linguistic Theory*, 292–310. DOI: 10.1093/acprof:oso/9780199560547.003.0017

Einhorn, Elsabe. 1974. *Old French: A Concise Handbook*. Cambridge: Cambridge University Press.

Foulet, Lucien. 1982. *Petite syntaxe de l'ancien français*. Paris: Librairie Honoré Champion.

Gamillscheg, E. 1957. *Historische französiche Syntax*. Tübingen: Max Niewmeyer Verlag.

Halle, Morris and Alec Marantz. 1993. "Distributed Morphology and the Pieces of Inflection." In *The View from Building 20*, ed. by Kenneth Locke Hale, Samuel Jay Keyser, and Sylvain Bromberger, 53–110. Cambridge: MIT Press.

Harley, Heidi and Rolf Noyer. 1999. "State-of-the-article: Distributed Morphology." *Glot International*, 4(4): 3–9.

Harley, Heidi and Elizabeth Ritter. 2002. "Person and Number in Pronouns: A Feature Geometric Analysis." *Language* 78: 482–526. DOI: 10.1353/lan.2002.0158

Herslund, Michael. 1980. *Problèmes de syntaxe de l'ancien français. Compléments datifs et génitifs*. Uppsala: Akademisk Forlag.

Jensen, Frede. 1990. *Old French and Comparative Gallo-Romance Syntax*. Tubingen: Max Niemeyer Verlag. DOI: 10.1515/9783110938166

Lin, Yi-An. 2008. "A Probe-Goal Approach to Parametric Variation in English and Mandarin Chinese Nominal Phrases." In *Proceedings of the 20th North American Conference on Chinese Linguistics (NACCL-20)*, 775–784.

Lobeck, Anne C. 1995. *Ellipsis: Functional Heads, Licensing, and Identification*. New York/Oxford: Oxford University Press.

Longobardi, Giuseppe. 1994. "Reference and Proper Names: A Theory of N-movement in Syntax and Logical Form." *Linguistic Inquiry* 25: 609–665.

Mallén, Enrique. 1997. "A Minimalist Approach to Concord in Noun Phrases." *Theoretical Linguistics* 23: 49–77. DOI: 10.1515/thli.1997.23.1-2.49

Ménard, Philippe. 1988. *Syntaxe de l'ancien français*. Paris: Bordeaux Éditions Bière.

Moignet, Gérard. 1988. *Grammaire de l'ancien français*. Paris: Klincksieck.

Nussenbaum, Jonathan W. 2000. *Investigations of Covert Phrase Movement*. Ph.D. dissertation, MIT.

Palm, Lars. 1977. "La construction *li filz le rei* et les constructions concurrentes avec *à* et *de* étudiées dans des oeuvres littéraires de la second moitié du XIIe siècle et du premier quart du XIIIe siècle." Uppsala: Almqvist & Wiksell.

Peraltsvaig, Asya. 2007. "The Universality of DP: A View from Russian." *Studia Linguistica* 6: 59–94. DOI: 10.1111/j.1467-9582.2007.00129.x

Parodi, Claudia. 1994. "On Case and Agreement in Spanish and English NPs." In *Issues and Theory in Romance Linguistics*, ed. by Michael Lee Mazzola, 403–416. Georgetown: Georgetown University Press.

Picallo, M. Carme. 1994. "Catalan Possessive Pronouns." *Natural Language and Linguistic Theory* 12: 259–299. DOI: 10.1007/BF00993146

Sáez, Luis. 2011. "Peninsular Spanish Prenominal Possessives in Ellipsis Contexts: A Phase-based Account." In *Romance Linguistics 2010*, ed. by Julia Herschensohn, 155–175. Amsterdam/Philadelphia: John Benjamins. DOI: 10.1075/cilt.318.10sae

Old French texts consulted

Paris, Gaston. (Ed). 1924. *La vie de St. Alexis*. Paris: Ancienne Edouard Champion.

Pauphilet, Albert. (Ed). 1949. *La queste del Saint Graal*. Paris: Champion.

Walter, Philippe. (Ed) *Yvain, le chevalier au lion de Chrétien de Troyes*. Paris: Folio Classique.

The generalization of preposition *para* via fusion and ensuing loss of compositionality

Joseph Bauman & Rena Torres Cacoullos
Pennsylvania State University

This study traces two shifts in the distribution of the Spanish preposition *para* 'for, in order to': first, a drop in its allative uses and second, its replacement of the older preposition *por* 'for' with purposive infinitives. These distributional changes of the innovative *para*—across its own contexts of occurrence as well as in its variation with the older *por*—demonstrate the crosslinguistic allative-to-purposive grammaticalization path. Frequent co-occurrence of the source elements, *por* and *a*, foments their coalescence, reflected in changes in the orthographic/phonological form of the fused preposition as it loses structural analyzability. Semantic compositionality, whereby there was a discernable semantic contribution of the allative *a* component, is also lost as early prepositional objects designating persons decline. We find this account of the rise of *para*, based on gradual loss of analyzability and compositionality, to be compatible with the quantitative patterns and more insightful than an opaque and implicitly abrupt notion of reanalysis.

1. Introduction

In (1), from an Old Spanish text (the 14th c. *Zifar*), we observe variation between allative 'to' (1a) and purposive 'for, in order to' (1b) uses of the preposition *para*. In this paper we will see that the proportion of allative uses in [*para* + NP or adverb] occurrences declines on the one hand, and on the other, that the purposive infinitive construction, dominated by *por* for most of the history of Spanish, has become associated with *para*. This pair of changes indicates that the evolution of *para* is a case of the hypothesized cross-linguistic grammaticalization path depicted in (2).

(1) a. *fueron-se*   *para la*   *ribera de la   mar*
         go.PFV.3PL-REFL   to   ART.DEF.F.SG shore of the sea

     b. *para se   y- r*
         to   REFL go-INF [*Zifar*, 89]
         'they went to the shore to depart'

DOI 10.1075/rllt.9.03bau
© 2016 John Benjamins Publishing Company

(2)   Grammaticalization path:
      allative > purposive   (Heine and Kuteva 2002, 39)

We will show quantitative distributions to support our claim that the grammaticalization of *para*, which arises from the fusion of two earlier prepositions—*por* and *a*—involves loss of analyzability and compositionality.

The corpus compiled for this study comprises 17 texts, beginning with *El cantar de mio Cid* (1140–1207) and drawing on two prose texts for each subsequent century up to the 20th. From the 16th century onward, one of these is a peninsular (Spain) text and the other is a chronologically corresponding sample from the *Documentos Lingüísticos de la Nueva España* (New Spain/Mexico). For each century, approximately 1,000 tokens of *por* and *para* with a nominal or infinitive complement were extracted (that is, not extracted were tokens of *por* or *para* followed by the conjunction *que* and a finite verb). Note that counts for *para* include tokens of the form *pora* in the 12th and 13th century. Information on the sampling procedure and exclusions is given in Torres Cacoullos and Bauman (2014, 391–393).

Table 1 shows the texts, token counts, and frequency of *para* relative to *por* by century. Though not spectacular, there does seem to be an increase over time in the relative frequency of *para* on this overall measure. As we will see, superior measures are provided by patterns of co-occurrence with contextual elements, or relative frequencies in linguistic subcontexts.

2.   From allative origins to the decline of spatial uses

The uses of a preposition or the kinds of relations it signals may be classified as spatial, temporal or abstract (e.g., Delbeque 1996, 252). Applying this classification to tokens of *para* with something other than an infinitive complement, usually an NP, we examine here the spatial uses of the preposition. Table 2 shows the verbs modified by *para* in configurations comprised of [VERB + *para* + NP (or adverb)]. The most frequent verbs modified by a *para* phrase in such spatial uses are three verbs of directional motion—*ir* 'go', *venir* 'come', *tornar* 'return'. Furthermore, middle-marked *irse* is somewhat more frequent than unmarked *ir* in the earliest time period (at a ratio of 1.3 to 1, or 56 to 44 tokens). This does not reflect a general fact, since with the preposition *por* the opposite obtains, with *irse* ten times *less* frequent than *ir* (3 to 31 tokens). The preponderance of directional motion verbs, especially *se*-marked motion verbs (Maldonado 1999, 363–373), is consonant with an allative usage encoding movement to or towards a location.

Table 1. Texts by century, token counts (*para* and *por*) and frequency of *para* relative to *por*

Cent	Text*	N	% *para***
12th	*Cid*	370	17%
13th	*Calila*, pp. 91–181	406	17%
	GEI, pp. 5–122	563	
14th	*Zifar*, pp. 9–110	500	24%
	Lucanor, odd numbered *exempla*	572	
15th	*Corbacho*, pp. 67–104 (Primera parte, 1–17), pp. 145–183 (Segunda parte, 1–8)	511	21%
	Celestina, pp. 67–214	556	
16th	*LT*	348	30%
	DLNE 1535–1569, pp. 109–161 (docs. 17–36)	364	
17th	*Quijote II*, odd numbered chapters between 1 and 27	489	23%
	DLNE 1609–1640, pp. 240–347 (docs. 79–129)	495	
18th	*CN/Sí*	339	32%
	DLNE 1790–1810, pp. 611–709 (docs. 258–307)	495	
19th	*Regenta*, Chapters 16, 19, 22, 25	433	33%
	Bandidos, pp. 27–278 (Chapters 1–29)	503	
20th	*Madrid*, pp. 87–290 (transcripts 5–16)	630	32%
	México, pp. 11–172 (transcripts 1–13)	491	

*Editions are listed before the References.
**% *para* in each century combines data from the two texts. 12th- and 13th-century *para* counts include instances of *pora*. Counts of *pora—para* are, respectively, 63–1 in the *Cid*, 78–1 in *GEI*, 1–83 in *Calila*.

Table 2. Most frequent motion verbs modified by *para* and their proportion of the preposition's spatial uses

Century	*Ir*	*Irse*	*tornar(se)*	*venir(se)*	%
12th–14th	44	56	13	19	80% (132/164)
15th–16th	6	0	0	1	29% (7/24)
17th–20th	7	8	0	4	40% (19/47)

The grouping of the centuries in Table 2 into three time periods, namely 12th–14th, 15th–16th and 17th–20th, emerged once we considered each century separately. In the 12th–14th-century data, the three verbs of directional motion together constitute 80%

(132/164)—*ir(se)* alone close to two-thirds—of all spatial instances of *para*. Repeated co-occurrence with *ir(se)* is important for the evolution of *para*, in light of the proposal from typological studies that "in the presence of 'go'-verbs, allatives frequently take on a purposive reading" (Rice and Kabata 2007, 459) An example would be German *zu*, whose "allative use [ ] evolves into a purposive one" (Lehmann 2002, 6), as in (3) (intermediate stages not shown).

(3)   German *zu*: allative > purposive > subordinator of infinitive

(adapted from Lehmann 2002, 6)

   a.   *Der Prinz begab sich zur Königin*
         'The prince betook himself to the queen'

   b.   *Der Prinz begab sich zum Jagen*
         'The prince betook himself to hunting'

   c.   *Der Prinz entschied sich zu jagen*
         'The prince decided to hunt'

Formulations such as "take on a purposive reading" or "evolves into a purposive" do not mean an abrupt or even linear replacement of one use by another. We stress that from the earliest texts, allative and purposive uses coexist, as illustrated in (1) above. Rather, "semantic change [...] should be manifested in changing distribution and co-occurrence patterns" (Torres Cacoullos and Schwenter 2005, 357).

One measure is the distribution of *para* across its contexts of occurrence. We find that, while the proportion of temporal uses (e.g., *para mañana* 'for, by tomorrow') has remained steady at approximately 5% to 10% throughout the centuries, there is a notable shift in the proportion of spatial uses. The line marked with diamonds in Figure 1 shows the proportion of spatial uses of *para* by century (not counting occurrences with an infinitive complement). Even in the earliest texts *para* expresses spatial relations in (approximately) half (43%–52%) of its occurrences with an NP (or adverbial) object, that is, we do not find an initial period in which *para,* or its precursor *pora*, exclusively or even mostly had a spatial sense. Nevertheless, after the 14th century the proportion of spatial uses is no greater than 10%.

Comparison with *por* confirms that the decline of spatial uses is not a mere accident of genre or topic (for example, we would expect higher proportions of spatial uses in epics). The line marked with squares in Figure 1 shows the corresponding distribution of *por* tokens. In contradistinction to the decline of spatial uses with *para*, the stability of *por* in spatial uses is evident, with a proportion of approximately one-fifth (ranging from 10% to 30%).

In summary, the allative origins of *para* are indicated by co-occurrence with directional motion verbs, often *se* (middle)-marked, with spatial uses constituting approximately half of the preposition's tokens with a NP or adverbial complement.

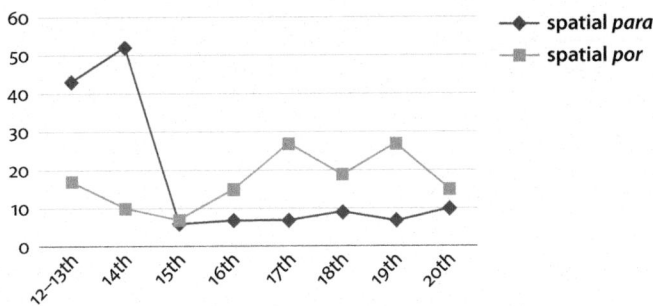

Figure 1. Proportion of spatial uses of *para*, compared with spatial uses of *por* (Ns *para*: 12–13th 75/173, 14th 89/170, 15th 7/120, 16th 8/115, 17th 9/122, 18th 12/134, 19th 9/122, 20th 26/261; Ns *por*: 12-13th 164/959, 14th 71/724, 15th 51/713, 16th 55/370, 17th 160/587, 18th 92/487, 19th 157/575, 20th 85/579.)

After the 14th century, *para* with a nominal complement appears mostly with non-spatial, abstract senses.[1]

3.   Generalization in purposive infinitive constructions

A second major quantitative change in co-occurrence patterns concerns infinitive complements. Here it is not distribution across contexts of occurrence that provides an enlightening measure, but variation with respect to the older preposition, *por*.

Table 3 depicts the frequency of *para* relative to *por* with an infinitive comple-ment. The two prepositions are fairly evenly distributed (~50%) in this context until the 17th century, after which the rate of *para* increases, such that it becomes two to five times greater than that of *por* (68%, 79% and 85% in the 18th, 19th and 20th centuries, respectively).

Figure 2 compares the increasing frequency of *para* relative to *por* overall (seen earlier in Table 1), in the line marked with squares, with that in the particular context of infinitives (Table 3), in the line marked with diamonds. It is clear that the frequency increase of the newer preposition has occurred disproportionally precisely in [+ infini-tive] constructions.

---

1.   The 14th century is when *para* definitively displaces *pora* (Riiho 1979, 232)

Table 3. Frequency of [*para* + infinitive] relative to [*por* + infinitive]

Century	% *para*: relative to *por* with an infinitive	N
12th–13th	41%	77/187
14th	53%	84/159
15th	46%	100/219
16th	46%	92/201
17th	41%	111/272
18th	**68%**	127/187
19th	**79%**	183/232
20th	**85%**	200/235

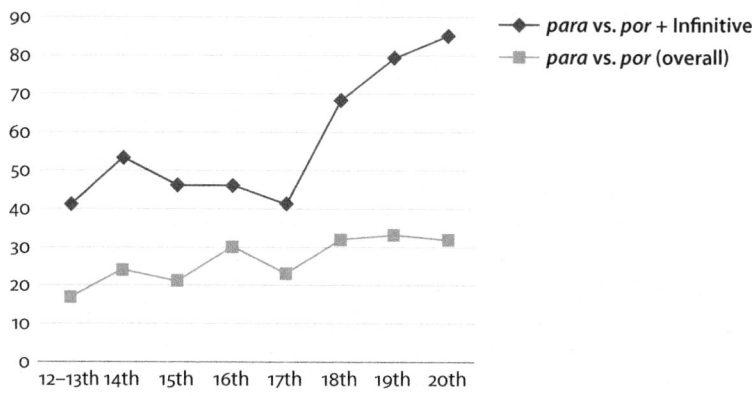

Figure 2. Increasing relative frequency of *para* vs. *por* overall (Table 1) and more striking increase in relative frequency of [*para* + infinitive] vs. [*por* + infinitive] (Table 3)

But is the displacement of *por* by *para* with infinitives a real linguistic change, or do the rate shifts merely reflect shifts in what is talked about or how it is talked about, that is, change in cultural context? (For such a scenario, see Myhill (1995) on American English modals.) In present-day Spanish, infinitive constructions with *por* mean something different from those with *para*, the former generally expressing cause (or reason) and the latter, purpose. For example, in (4a), with *por*, the subject felt guilty *because* he married off someone, whereas in (4b), with *para*, the subject needed money *in order to* retrieve his clothing. It is not inconceivable, then, that the increasing rate of *para* with infinitives reflects a shift toward more talk of purposes than of causes.

(4)   a.   [verb + ***por*** + infinitive] = cause (reason)
           *Se creía [...] culpable **por** <u>haber casado</u> a Tules* [19th c., *Bandidos*, 1.159]
           'He thought himself [...] guilty **for** <u>having married off</u> Tules'

b.   [verb + ***para*** + infinitive] = purpose
   *necesitaba diez pesos **para** sacar su ropa empeñada* [19th c., *Bandidos*, 1.154]
   'he needed money **in order to** <u>retrieve</u> his clothing that had been pawned'

To probe this issue, we look closely at cases where the prepositional phrase modifies a verb, i.e. at [verb + *por/para* + infinitive], since this is the locus of the generalization of [*para* + infinitive].[2] As a replicable measure, the purpose sense is operationalized in terms of the temporal reference of the situation: counted as having a purpose sense were cases in which the situation referred to by the infinitive is posterior to that of the main (finite) verb, as in (5). Figure 3 shows the distribution of *por* and *para* in *purposive* infinitive constructions in a sample of the texts. We see that in the 15th-century *Celestina* and 17th-century *Quijote*, purposive infinitive complements are evenly distributed between the two prepositions (50% (35/70) and 46% (28/61) for *para* in the two texts, respectively). That is, in Old and Golden Age Spanish, infinitives with *por* could, and robustly did, express purpose (as in (5)). In the 19th-century *Regenta* (Spain) and *Bandidos* (Mexico), however, the relative frequency of *para* in this same context is up to 90% (111/123). Thus, *para* has generalized in the purposive infinitive construction, largely replacing the older preposition, in support of genuine linguistic change.

(5)   [verb + ***por*** + infinitive] = purpose
   *También quiere a mí engañar como a mi amo **por** <u>ser</u> rica* [15th c., *Celestina*, 5.173]
   'She wants to trick me as well as my master **in order to** <u>become</u> rich'

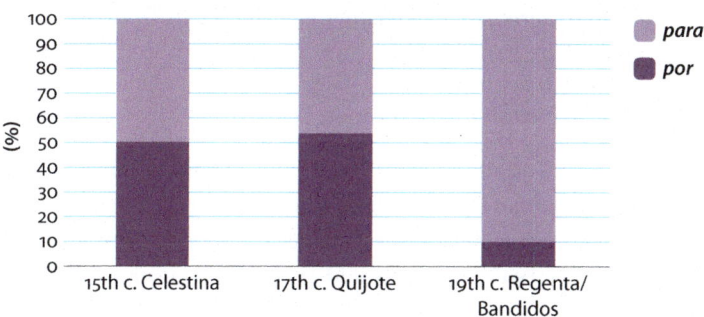

Figure 3. Rate of *para* relative to *por* with a purposive infinitive complement ([*para* + infinitive$_{purposive}$] vs. [*por* + infinitive$_{purposive}$])

---

2.   The proportion of tokens of [*para* + infinitive] modifying a nominal element is steady over time at approximately one-fourth, whereas for *por* it has remained at 5% or lower. Nouns recurring with a [*para* + infinitive] complement are *esfuerzo(s), facilidad, fuerza(s), licencia, motivo(s), tiempo, valor* and adjectives *aparejado, bueno, eficaz, hábil, mejor, necesario, suficiente, útil* , as in *sin <u>fuerzas</u> **para llamarle***'without strength to call him' [*Regenta*, 2.321].

Still, it might be argued that even in purposives there may be a meaning difference, such that purposive infinitive clauses with *por* express a nuance of "underlying
motive or incentive" that is absent from *para* (Bolinger 1945, 20).[3] How can we con-
front such a claim? The working hypothesis of the variationist method is that "within a
given locus of variability, or *variable context*, [....the] competing variants will occur at
greater or lesser rates depending on the features that constitute the context" (Poplack
2001, 405). If linguistic forms mean something different, they should be preferred
in different (sub)contexts. In other words, they should occur at higher or lower than
average rates in certain (sub)contexts (see also Aaron and Torres Cacoullos 2005, 615).

Therefore, we seek corroboration of the generalization of *para* in purposive infinitive constructions to the detriment of *por* indicated above in Figure 3 by comparing
the rates of the prepositions in two particular subcontexts that are compatible with
purposive meaning. One is [motion verb + *por/para* + infinitive], i.e. where *por* or
para with an infinitive complement modifies *acercarse* 'to approach', *andar* 'to walk',
correr 'to run', *descender* 'to descend', *dirigirse* 'to set off, go', *entrar* 'to enter', *huir* 'to
flee', *ir* 'to go', *llegar* 'to arrive', *moverse* 'to move', *salir* 'to leave', *seguir* 'to follow', *venir*
'to come', *volver* 'to return' and other intransitive motion verbs, as in (6). These verbs
favor use of [*por* + infinitive], with *para* at 32% (27/85) until the 17th century, after
which we observe a reversal, with *para* up to 90% (55/61).

(6)   variation in [motion verb + *por/para* + infinitive]
      a.   *quiero yr ala cort,* **por de mandar** *myos derechos*
            'I want to go to the court **in order to** demand my rights.' [*Cid*, 3079]

      b.   *dixo a su hermano que ella queria yr con él aquella noche* **para traer**
            aquello
            'she said to her brother that she wanted to go with him that night **in
            order to** recover that.' [Lucanor, Ej. 47]

A second subcontext providing evidence for genuine linguistic change is that in which
the subject NP has a human referent. If there is a meaning difference between [*por/
para* + infinitive] such that *por* expresses a nuance of "underlying motive or incentive"
(as claimed by Bolinger 1945, 20), we would expect human subjects to favor the use
of *por* and inanimate subjects to favor *para*, since inanimate subjects are incapable of
having motives or intentions. For example, with the inanimate subject 'fortune' in (8a),
the main verb is a stative (*es favorable* 'is favorable') and the usage is that of purpose in

---

3.   We take here the stance that the meaning(s) associated with a form are evident in its usage
(i.e. usage and meaning are directly linked in usage-based theory (Bybee 2010). That is to say
that the contexts in which a form appears, given frequent and sustained application to a given
usage, can effect a gradual but permanent change in the meaning(s) that are assumed to be
inherent to that form.

the sense of the utility of a thing. With human subjects (7), however, *para* would seem to express the purpose of an action with a sense of intention. Note that there would not appear to be a justification for considering the instance with *por* with a volitional human subject in (7a) as conveying more of a sense of underlying motive than the instance with *para* in (7b) (besides the circular argument that *por* itself has such a meaning).

(7) [human subject + verb + ***por/para***+ infinitive$_{purposive}$]

    a. *quiso turbarme **por** <u>oírme</u> decir otras docientas patochadas*
       [*Quijote* II, 7.680]
       '<u>he</u> tried to upset me **so as to** <u>hear</u> me say another two hundred follies'

    b. *quería vencerla, **para** <u>no padecer</u> tanto* [*Regenta*, 2.22]
       '<u>he</u> wanted to overcome it [his ambition], **so as to** <u>avoid suffering</u> so much'

(8) [inanimate subject + verb + ***por/para***+ infinitive$_{purposive}$]

    a. *para qué es la <u>fortuna</u> favorable y próspera sino **para** <u>servir</u> a la honrra*
       [*Celestina*, 2.130]
       'for what is <u>fortune</u> favorable and propitious if not **to** <u>serve</u> honor'

    b. *toda la <u>natura</u> se remiró **por** la <u>hazer</u> perfecta* [*Celestina*, 6.191]
       'all of <u>nature</u> exerted itself **to** <u>make</u> her [Melibea] perfect'

Figure 4 shows the distribution of *por* and *para* in purposive infinitive constructions with inanimate vs. human subjects (of the main verb). It does appear that inanimate subjects have always favored the choice of [*para* + infinitive] (top figure) (though Ns are low). However, while human subjects favor [*por* + infinitive] in the 15th-c. *Celestina* and 17th-c. *Quijote*, with *para* at 44% (48/110), the rate of *para* is 89% (102/114) in the 19th-c. *Regenta* and *Bandidos* (bottom figure). This reversal is a second measure of linguistic change: whereas in earlier times intentions of human subjects were expressed with *por,* now this function is served by *para*.

In summary, we first observed a reversal in the relative frequency of *por* and *para* in infinitive constructions overall (Figure 2). We then observed a parallel reversal more particularly with a *purposive* infinitive complement (counting as purposives those that are temporally posterior to the main verb) (Figure 3). Finally, we considered two replicable measures—the rate of *para* in infinitive constructions with motion main verbs and with human subjects—which again show a reversal of relative frequencies of *por* and *para* (Figure 4). The conclusion is that *para* has generalized as a purposive infinitive marker, as we may represent in (9).

(9) [VERB + *para* + infinitive]$_{purpose}$

Together with the decline of allative uses (Section 2), this is solid evidence for the postulated allative > purposive evolutionary path (exemplified from other languages in Heine and Kuteva 2002, 39–40). Such changes are often thought of as reanalysis (e.g.,

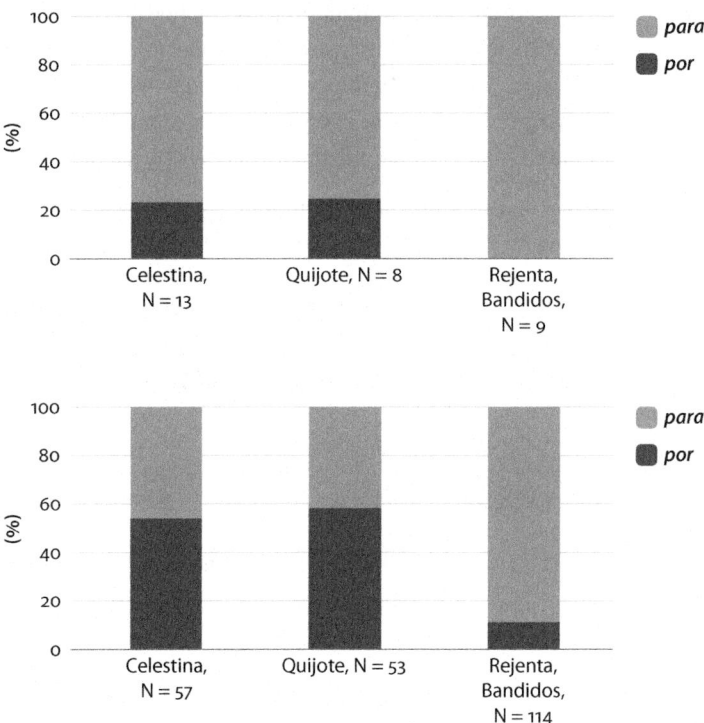

Figure 4. Rate of *para* relative to *por* with a purposive infinitive complement modifying a verb with an inanimate subject (top) or a human subject (bottom)

Campbell 1998, 284), which has been conceived as abrupt in language change. In the following section, we argue for an alternative view based on chunking and ensuing loss of analyzability and compositionality.

4.   Fusion and loss of internal analyzability: *Por + a > para*

It is widely hypothesized that *para* arises from fusion, or coalescence (Haspelmath 2011), of *por* (or its Latin antecedents PER and PRO (Riiho 1979, 13-28)) and *a(d)*. Evidence comes from 12th–13th-century examples in which *por* and *a* appear together in non-agglutinated form.[4] Example (10) illustrates variation between the non-agglutinated and the agglutinated form in the 13th-century *General Estoria, Primera parte* (*GEI*), in a near-identical context.

---

4.   30 tokens of *por + a* separated by a space (i.e. not agglutinated in the 600,000-word digital version of the *GEI* (Kasten, Nitti and Jonxis-Henkemans 1997).

(10)   *por* + *al* vs. *poral* variation
        diz q⟨ue⟩ agun bien es **por al** *om⟨n⟩e en no⟨n⟩ seer pecador. & maguer que*
        non es sa⟨n⟩cto. como diz q⟨ue⟩ es otrossi algo **poral** *om⟨n⟩e del qui non puede*
        seer Rey. [13th c., *GEI*, fol. 57v]
        'It is said that there is some good **for** man in not being a sinner even though
        he is not holy, as it is said that this is furthermore something **for** the man
        who cannot be king.'

The majority of the tokens of *por* + *a* separated by a space in the *GEI* occur with a noun
as the object of the preposition and with the definite article fused with *a* in *al*, as in
the first line in (10) above. That the construction which most resisted the fusion of *por*
and *a* is with the masculine definite article *el* is perhaps due to countervailing force of
the contraction of *el* to the preposition *a* (the contracted form *poral* persists into 17th-
century texts (Riiho 1979, 236)).

Nevertheless, we also find examples of non-agglutinated *por* + *a* in other contexts,
for example, with a pronoun, as in *por* **ami** 'for me' (12th c. *La Fazienda de Ultra-
mar* 13vA25, Ex.6, 7) (Dave McDougall, p.c.) or preceding an infinitive, as in *por a*
yr a Egipto 'to go to Egypt' (13th c. *GEI*,fol. 108v). Thus, although tokens with a space
between *por* and *a* are already a tiny minority, there are enough to suggest that scribes
utilized the non-agglutinated combination with some regularity in 13th-century texts.

Indeed, in 13th-century Spanish texts, there is a range of antecedent forms for
para. Most prominent is the agglutinated form *pora*, as illustrated in (11) and (12). The
relative frequency of *pora* with respect to *para* is reported to decrease precipitously
from 83% to 15% from the first to the second half of the 13th century (Riiho 1979, 232).
Other candidate antecedent forms are *pera* and *perad* (García de Diego 1951, 128).

(11)   Earlier form *pora*...
        a.   *Vansse* **pora** *San Pero* [12th c., *Cid*, v. 294]
              'They go **to** San Pedro'
        b.   *estas serien despues* **pora** *comer* **pora** *ell omne* [13th c., *GEI*, fol. 12v]
              'these would be then **for** man **to** eat'

(12)   ...in variation with *para*
        a.   **para** *Calatayuch quanto puede se va* [*Cid*, v. 774–775]
              '**to** Calatayud as soon as he can he goes'
        b.   *fuel aparta⟨n⟩do toda uia* **para** *si & alos suyos.* [13th c., *GEI*, fol. 5r] [5]
              'he divided it [the land] **for** himself and (to) his own'

However, we find inconsistency across and within editions of Old Spanish texts in
the realization of '*para*' and its variant forms. For example, in reproductions of the

---

5.   In ...*para si & alos suyos* [*GEI*, fol. 5r] (Example 12), *para* and *a* appear to compete in the
same context.

original manuscripts of the 13th-century *GEI* there already appear unequivocal tokens of *para* (13).

(13)   *para* in 13th-century original manuscript

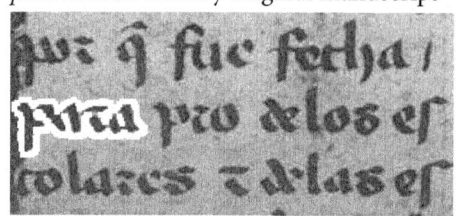

...*por q̃ fue fecha **para** pro delos escolares...*   [Solalinde 1930, 287]
'by which it was made for the good of the scholars'

In the same text, scribes also used the form depicted in (14). Here the preposition appears as an ambiguous abbreviation without the interior graphemes, displaying only the initial *p* and the final *a* (rather than representing loss of the second syllable (see Company 1994, 11)).

(14)   'para' in same 13th-century original manuscript

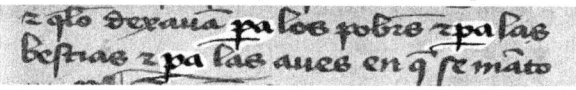

*et q̃lo dexauã **pa** los pobrē et **pa** las bestias et **pa** las aues...*
                                                    [Solalinde 1930, 424]
'...and that he left it for the poor and for the beasts and for the birds'

The abbreviation with a horizontal bar either crossing or connecting with the descender (the vertical line) of the *p*, depicted in (14) was a convention in the transcription of Latin *per* and *pro* (Cappelli 1899/1990, 257). In Cappelli's dictionary of abbreviations, the horizontal bar does not cross the descender in the abbreviation for *pro*, but merely connects with its left side. Thus, the abbreviations used for *per* more closely resemble the form of the *p* that is encountered in 13th-c. Spanish manuscripts, as in (14) above.

(15)   Abbreviations for *per:*   Abbreviations for *pro:*

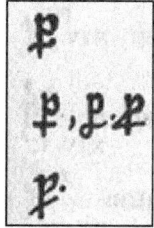   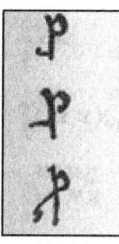   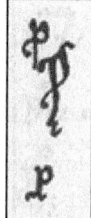

We find another example of this abbreviation, this time involving the adjective *perdonadas* (the adjectival form of the verb *perdonar* 'to pardon', which is unequivocally composed of the prefix *per-* and the root *donar* 'to give'), shown in (16). Nevertheless, this unambiguous abbreviation of *per-* using a *p* with a crossbar does not mean we must conclude that the examples of abbreviated *pa* necessarily represent *pera, pora,* or some other specific variant. Rather, it appears that this abbreviation was used to represent some vowel-/r/ combination, including the combinations of a vowel and /r/ in *pora, para,* and *per.*[6]

(16)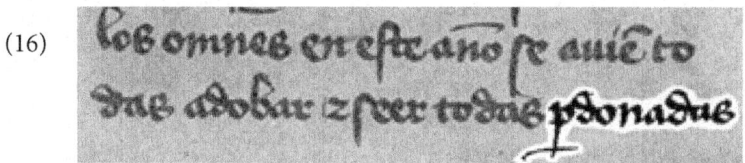

*los omnes en este año se auiē todas adobar et seer todas **pdonadas***
[Solalinde 1930, 424]
'the men in that year all had to dress and be pardoned'

It is clear, then, despite the vexing problem of manuscript editions and graphic conventions, that for a period of time non-agglutinated (*por a*) and agglutinated (*pora* but also *para*) orthographic variants were used contemporaneously. This orthographic evidence indicates that the combination of the prepositions *por* and *a* as independent elements may have persisted into early (13th-century) Spanish. Rather than a linear, consecutive evolution (*per/pro + ad > pora > para*), the coexistence of these forms in the same text indicates that the process of the fusion of the two (groups of) structural elements was not only gradual but also characterized by variation (cf. Weinreich, Labov and Herzog 1968).

The phonological course by which the first vowel in forms spelled *pera* and *pora* ultimately became /a/ in the modern *para* has been addressed by several scholars, appealing to various phonological processes, include lowering of the *e* in *pera* before a rhotic (e.g., García de Diego 1951, 128) and vocalic assimilation (e.g., Hanssen 1945, §726). Regardless of the exact course of events, the ultimate resolution of the variation between *pora* and *para* in the single modern form *para* is further evidence of the formal fusion of the erstwhile *per/pro* and *ad.* It is telling that as *para* wins out over *pora* by the end of the 14th century, the agglutinated form is already effectively unrecognizable (from both a phonological and an orthographic perspective) as consisting of two independent elements.

A requirement for the creation of a new unit is frequent co-occurrence of its erstwhile component parts.[7] From the perspective of a usage-based approach to grammatical forms, a mechanism for the creation of constituent structure is the chunking of

---

6.   Or even a consonant-vowel combination, in light of the frequent transposition of the *r* in Old Spanish (Corominas 1980–1991: see *por*).

7.   It could be argued that an additional requirement is the "semantic coherence" of the elements constituting the combination (Bybee 2010, 138). There has been discussion of the antecedent(s) of *por* (Latin *per* and/or *pro*), and their respective semantic contributions in

a sequence of morphemes that results from frequent repetition of the sequence (Bybee 2010, 34). In other words, "Items that are used together fuse together" per Bybee's Linear Fusion Hypothesis (Bybee 2002, 112). The hypothesis of chunking predicts that for the sequence *por* + *a* to result in a fused unit—whereas *por* in combination with other prepositions does not—the co-occurrence of *por* + *a* must be more frequent than other combinations.

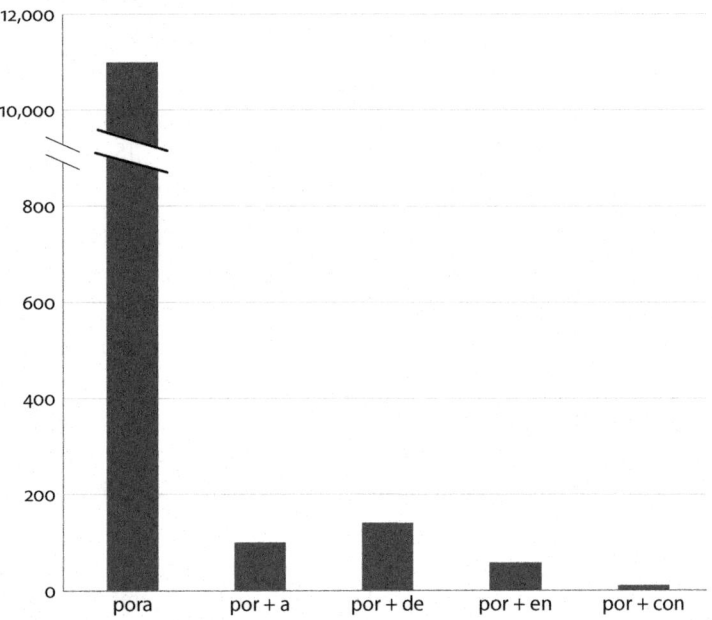

Figure 5. Token frequency of the sequence *por* + preposition (*Corpus del español* counts for 1200s)

Figure 5 shows the token frequency of *por* followed by another preposition for 13th-century texts drawn from the online corpus of Davies (2002-). For the purposes of tabulating co-occurrence of *por* + *a* vs. *por* + another preposition we count together *pora* ((already) agglutinated) and *por* + *a* (not-yet agglutinated), given the variation in this period between the agglutinated and non-agglutinated forms (example (10), above). When combined with the already orthographically fused *pora*—more than 10,000 tokens, compared with fewer than 200 cases of *por* + *de*—it is clear that the *por* + *a* sequence is indeed of high frequency compared to other sequences, as predicted

combination with *ad* (see Torres Cacoullos and Bauman 2014, §13.3 for a recent review). For an assessment of the semantic compositionality of *para*, see Section 5 below.

by the usage-based hypothesis of chunking with repetition. That this fusion was likely complete by the end of the 14th century is suggested by the disappearance of the *pora* variant. This leaves only *para*, a form no longer analyzable as a complex structure.

5.   Compositionality of *para*, and its loss

We saw (Section 2 above) that one change in the distribution of *para* was the quantitative decline of spatial uses after the 14th century. When we look more closely at those early spatial uses, we see that the change further involves the loss of a particular kind of spatial use. In the earliest texts we find examples in which the subject of the motion verb actually arrives at or reaches their destination. For example, in (17) below, *para* indicates the terminal point of the movement, a use that we associate with the preposition *a* in present-day Spanish. In (17a) the subject not only goes 'toward' the *posada* but actually reaches it, as verified by the fact that he speaks to the person there. In (17b) the subject came not 'toward', but 'to', Toledo.

(17)   [motion verb + *para* + NP] = to a location

    a.   *E el pleteo con ellos e fuese **para** la posada e dixole su muger commo auia pleteado con los marineros* [14th c., *Zifar*, 87]
        'And he argued with them and went **to** the inn and told his wife how he had argued with the seamen'

    b.   *et por ende vínose **para** Toledo para aprender de aquella sciença* [*Lucanor*, 94]
        'And therefore he came **to** Toledo to learn that science'

The endpoint of the motion may even be a person. Cases in which the object of *para* has a human referent are exemplified in (18). Again, in present-day Spanish we would not expect *para* in this context (but *a*).

(18)   [motion verb + *para* + NP$_{specific\ human}$]

    a.   *Venimos nós **para** ti que nos consejes* [13th c. *Calila*, 144]
        'We came **to** you so that you may advise us'

    b.   *E el moço se fue **para** su padre, e dixo la respuesta* [14th c. *Zifar*, 21]
        'And the boy went **to** his father and told him the answer'

    c.   *y assi me fuy **para** mi amo, que esperandome estaua.* [16th c. *LT*, 7]
        'and thus I went **to** my master, who was waiting for me'

Figure 6 shows the proportions of spatial uses of [*para* + NP] with prepositional objects that are persons, as in (18) above, as opposed to places (as in (17)). Object NPs with a human referent as the endpoint of motion constitute a full third, 35% (50/144), of spatial instances of *para* in 13th–14th century texts.

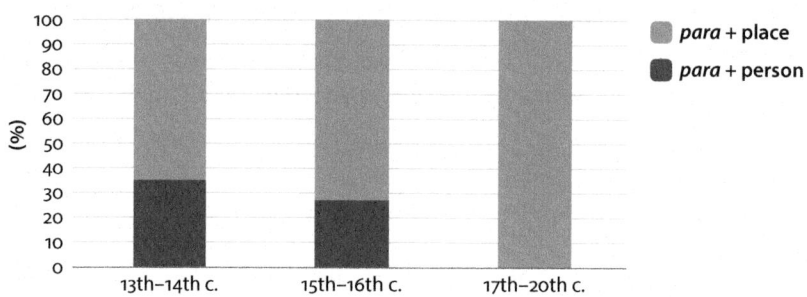

Figure 6. Spatial uses of [*para* + NP]: proportion of object NPs designating persons vs. places

In this motion-verb *para* construction with a destination that is a person, the human referent of the object appears as a personal pronoun (N = 20) or definite full NP (in which the determiner is a definite article (N = 16), possessive (N = 13), or demonstrative).[8] Furthermore, this NP with a human referent overwhelmingly appears in singular number (92%, 46/50, of 13th–14th c. tokens). From these nominal features we may infer that the referent is specific and individuated. This is precisely the kind of referent we would expect the preposition *a* to co-occur with, in accordance with its use as a dative marker (indirect objects tend to be human) and progressively also as an accusative marker for direct objects referring to persons (on the latter, see Company Company 2002).

We submit that this early *para* use with prepositional complements designating persons indicates that the semantic contribution of the preposition *a* was still discernible in the new preposition, that is, it constitutes evidence for a degree of compositionality in the beginnings of the new preposition (cf. Riiho 1979, 99). Following Bybee (2010, 44–45; see also Croft and Cruse 2004, 250–253; Langacker 1987, 292), compositionality is a semantic measure having to do with transparency of meaning, and refers to the degree to which the meaning of the whole is predictable from the meaning of the component parts (e.g. *hopeful* is more compositional than *awful*).[9] Figure 6 indicates that cases are still found in 15th–16th texts (4/15). But the [motion verb + *para* + NP$_{specific human}$] construction disappears from the corpus after the 16th c. (0/51). The disappearance of *para* object NPs with a human referent as the endpoint of motion may be taken as evidence that *a* no longer makes an independent semantic

---

8.   In *Calila*, we count as human the personified animals.

9.   In contrast with the semantic criterion of compositionality, *analyzability* is a morphosyntactic parameter, referring to the degree to which the internal structure and individual parts are recognizable; for example, while *pull strings* is not fully compositional because it has a metaphorical meaning, it is analyzable in that speakers are assumed to recognize an individual verb and its noun complement (Bybee 2010, 45).

contribution, thus demonstrating loss of compositionality, as *a* is completely absorbed into the new, chunked, preposition.

In summary, in addition to the presence of non-agglutinated *por* + *a* orthographic variants, another piece of evidence that *para* is the outcome of the fusion of two separate prepositions, one of which was *a*, comes from early compositionality of semantic content. We have shown how the semantic measure of compositionality can be operationalized in terms of the contexts of use of a linguistic form. In particular, we considered the kinds of object NPs with which *para* co-occurs in spatial relations. A robust [motion verb + *para* + NP$_{specific\ human}$] construction in early texts indicates early compositionality. The decline and disappearance of this construction indicates erosion of the semantic contribution of *a* as it is absorbed into the new preposition, and thus loss of compositionality of the whole.

6. Conclusion: Loss of analyzability and compositionality in grammaticalization

In tracking its generalization, we have seen two principal distribution shifts in the history of *para*, which is a newcomer among Spanish prepositions. First is the general decline of allative uses that is observed following the 14th century, after which the proportion of spatial uses of any kind fails to rise above one tenth of the occurrences of the preposition with a nominal (or adverb) complement. The second change, beginning in the 18th century, concerns infinitive complements, with which *para* replaces *por*, to become the majority variant for the expression of purpose. This pair of distributional changes provides a quantitative argument for allative-to-purposive evolution, a change that has been put forward as a cross-linguistic grammaticalization path (Heine and Kuteva 2002). Thus, change is observable both in the distribution of the newer preposition across its contexts of occurrence and in patterns of variation with respect to the older preposition.

The generalization of *para* as a purposive proceeds from the fusion of its erstwhile component parts. Support for the origin of *para* in the fusion of the sequence of *por* (< Latin *per* and/or *pro*) and *a* (< *ad*) comes from early analyzability and compositionality. Structural analyzability is indicated by instances, though rare, of non-agglutinated *por* + *a* in 13th-c. manuscripts. Semantic compositionality, which involves the independent semantic contribution of the preposition *a*, is discernable in an allative construction where the prepositional object designates a destination that is a person (rather than a location).

The new preposition is consolidated via subsequent loss of analyzability and compositionality. On the one hand, coalescence of the two prepositions is correlated with their frequent co-occurrence and is manifested in sound change in the new fused form. We take this as evidence for loss of analyzability. On the other hand, loss of compositionality is inferred from the decline and eventual disappearance of *para* objects designating a person.

In summary, allative > purposive grammaticalization of *para* proceeds via loss of morpho-syntactic analyzability, indicated by graphemic (and sound) change, and loss of semantic compositionality, operationalizable through co-occurrence patterns. In the loss of analyzability and compositionality the evolution of *para* is very similar to that of present-day complex prepositions such as Spanish *a pesar de* (Torres Cacoullos and Schwenter 2005; Torres Cacoullos 2006) and English in *spite of* (Beckner and Bybee 2009; Bybee 2010, 136–147). The conclusion is that what is often referred to as 'reanalysis' and conceived of as an abstract and abrupt change is the outcome of gradual processes of loss of analyzability and compositionality.

Corpus of texts (in chronological order, except for DLNE)

[*Cid*] Anonymous, *Cantar de mio Cid. Texto, gramática y vocabulario*, volume 3: *Texto*, paleographic edition of Ramón Menéndez Pidal. Madrid: Espasa Calpe, 1944–1945.

[*Calila*] Anonymous, *Calila e Dimna*, edition of Juan Manuel Cacho Blecua and María Jesús Lacarra. Madrid: Castalia, 1984.

[*GEI*] Alfonso X, *General estoria. Primera parte*, edition of Lloyd Kasten, John Nitti and Wilhelmina Jonxis-Henkemans, *The Electronic Texts and Concordances of the Prose Works of Alfonso X, El Sabio*. Madison: Hispanic Seminary of Medieval Studies, 1997.

[*Zifar*] Anonymous, El libro del cavallero Zifar, edition of Charles Ph. Wagner. Ann Arbor: University of Michigan Press, 1929.

[*Lucanor*] Don Juan Manuel, *El conde Lucanor o Libro de los enxiemplos del conde Lucanor et de Patronio*, edition of José Manuel Blecua. Madrid: Castalia, 1969/1971.

[*Corbacho*] Alfonso Martínez de Toledo, *Arcipreste de Talavera o Corbacho*, edition of Michael Gerli. Madrid: Cátedra, 1979/1992.

[*Celestina*] Fernando de Rojas, *La Celestina*, edition of Dorothy S. Severin. Madrid: Cátedra, 1993.

[*LT*] Anónimo, *Tri-linear edition of* Lazarillo de Tormes *of 1554 (Burgos, Alcalá de Henares, Amberes)*, edition of Joseph V. Ricapito. Madison: The Hispanic Seminary of Medieval Studies, 1987.

[*Quijote*] Miguel de Cervantes, *Don Quijote de la Mancha*, in *Obras completas*, volume 2, edition of Francisco Sevilla Arroyo and Antonio Rey Hazas. Madrid: Alianza Editorial-Centro de Estudios Cervantinos, 1996.

[*CN/Sí*] Leandro Fernández de Moratín, *La comedia nueva. El sí de las niñas*, edition of John Dowling and René Andioc. Madrid: Castalia, 1968.

[*Regenta*] Leopoldo Alas «Clarín», *La Regenta*, edition of Gonzalo Sobejano. Madrid: Castalia, 1981/1982.

[*Bandidos*] Manuel Payno, *Los bandidos de Río Frío*, in *Obras completas*, edition of Manuel Sol. México: Consejo Nacional para la Cultura y las Artes, 2000.

[*Madrid*] Manuel Esgueva y Margarita Cantarero (eds.), *El habla de la ciudad de Madrid: materiales para su estudio.* Madrid: Consejo Superior de Investigaciones Científicas, 1981.
[*México*] Juan M. Lope Blanch (coord.), *El habla de la ciudad de México. Materiales para su estudio.* México: Universidad Nacional Autónoma de México, 1971.
[*DLNE*] Concepción Company Company, *Documentos lingüísticos de la Nueva España. Altiplano central.* México: Universidad Nacional Autónoma de México, 1994.

References

Aaron, Jessi Elana, and Rena Torres Cacoullos. 2005. "Quantitative Measures of Subjectification: A Variationist Study of Spanish *salir(se)*." *Cognitive Linguistics* 16(4): 607–633. DOI: 10.1515/cogl.2005.16.4.607

Beckner, Clay, and Joan Bybee. 2009. "A Usage-based Account of Constituency and Reanalysis." *Language Learning* 59: 27–46. DOI: 10.1111/j.1467-9922.2009.00534.x

Bolinger, Dwight L. 1945. "Purpose with Por and Para." *Modern Language Journal* 28(1): 15–22. DOI: 10.2307/317177

Bybee, Joan L. 2002. "Sequentiality as the Basis of Constituent Structure." In *The Evolution of Language out of Pre-language*, ed. by T. Givón, and Bertram F. Malle, 109–134. Amsterdam: Benjamins. DOI: 10.1075/tsl.53.07byb

Bybee, Joan L. 2010. *Language, Usage and Cognition.* Cambridge: Cambridge University Press. DOI: 10.1017/CBO9780511750526

Campbell, Lyle 1998. *Historical Linguistics: An Introduction.* Cambridge, MA: MIT Press.

Cappelli, Adriano. 1889/1990. *Lexicon Abbreviaturarum: Dizionario di abbreviature latine ed italiane.* Sexta edición. Trento: Ulrico Hoepli Editore.

Company Company, Concepción. 2002. "Grammaticalization and Category Weakness." In *New Reflections on Grammaticalization*, ed. by Ilse Wischer and Gabriele Diewald, 201–215. Amsterdam: John Benjamins. DOI: 10.1075/tsl.49.14com

Company Company, Concepción. 1994. "Introducción", in *Documentos lingüísticos de la Nueva España*, Mexico: Universidad Nacional Autónoma de México, 1–19.

Corominas, Joan. 1980–1991. *Diccionario crítico-etimológico castellano e hispánico*, con la colaboración de José Antonio Pascual. Madrid: Gredos.

Croft, William and D. Alan Cruse. 2004. *Cognitive Linguistics.* Cambridge: Cambridge University Press. DOI: 10.1017/CBO9780511803864

Davies, Mark. 2002-. *Corpus del Español: 100 million words, 1200s-1900s.* Available online at http://www.corpusdelespanol.org.

García de Diego, Vicente. 1951. *Gramática histórica española.* Madrid: Gredos.

Hanssen, Federico. 1945. *Gramática histórica de la lengua castellana.* Buenos Aires: El Ateneo.

Haspelmath, Martin. 2011. "The Gradual Coalescence into 'Words' in Grammaticalization." In *The Oxford Handbook of Grammaticalization*, ed. by Bernd Heine and Heiko Narrog, 342–355. Oxford: Oxford University Press.

Heine, Benrd and Tania Kuteva. 2002. *World Lexicon of Grammaticalization.* Cambridge: Cambridge University Press. DOI: 10.1017/CBO9780511613463

Langacker, Ronald. 1987. *Foundations of Cognitive Grammar: Theoretical Prerequisites*, Vol 1. Stanford, CA: Stanford University Press.

Lehmann, Christian. 2002. "New Reflections on Grammaticalization and Lexicalization." In *New Reflections on Grammaticalization*, ed. by Ilse Wischer and Gabriele Diewald, 1–18. Amsterdam: John Benjamins. DOI: 10.1075/tsl.49.03leh

Maldonado, Ricardo. 1999. *A media voz: problemas conecptuales del clítico* se. México: Universidad Nacional Autónoma de México.

Myhill, John. 1995. "Change and Continuity in the Functions of the American English Modals." *Linguistics* 33(2): 157–211. DOI: 10.1515/ling.1995.33.2.157

Poplack, Shana. 2001. "Variability, Frequency and Productivity in the Irrealis Domain of French." In *Frequency and the Emergence of Linguistic Structure*, ed. by Joan Bybee and Paul Hopper, 405–428. Amsterdam: Benjamins. DOI: 10.1075/tsl.45.20pop

Rice, Sally and Kaori Kabata. 2007. "Crosslinguistic Grammaticalization Patterns of the allative." *Linguistic Typology* 11: 451–514. DOI: 10.1515/LINGTY.2007.031

Riiho, Timo. 1979. *Por y para. Estudio sobre los orígenes y la evolución de una oposición prepositiva iberorrománica*. Helsinki: Societas Scientiarum Fennica.

Solalinde, Antonio. 1930. *Alfonso el Sabio: General Estoria, primera parte*. Madrid: Centro de Estudios Históricos.

Torres Cacoullos, Rena. 2006. "Relative Frequency in the Grammaticization of Collocations: Nominal to Concessive *a pesar de*." In *Selected Proceedings of the* 8th *Hispanic Linguistics Symposium*, ed. by Timothy A. Face and Carol E. Klee, 37–49. Somerville: Cascadilla Proceedings Project.

Torres Cacoullos, Rena and Joseph Bauman. 2014. (in press). "Preposiciones III: Por, pora, para." *Sintaxis histórica de la lengua española*, part III: *Adverbios, preposiciones y conjunciones*, Concepción Company Company (director). Mexico: Fondo de Cultura Económica y Universidad Nacional Autónoma de México.

Torres Cacoullos, Rena and Scott A. Schwenter. 2005. "Towards an Operational Notion of Subjectification." In *Proceedings of the* 31st *Annual Meeting of the Berkeley Linguistics Society: General Session and Parasession on Prosodic Variation and Change*, ed. by Rebecca T. Cover and Yuni Kim, 347–358. Berkeley, CA: Berkeley Linguistics Society.

Weinreich, Uriel, William Labov, and Marvin Herzog. 1968. "Empirical Foundations for a Theory of Language Change. In *Directions for Historical Linguistics*, ed. by Winfred P. Lehmann and Yakov Malkiel, 95–195. Austin, TX: University of Texas Press.

On capacities and their epistemic extensions*

Elena Castroviejo & Isabel Oltra-Massuet

Instituto de Lengua, Literatura y Antropología (ILLA-CSIC) / Universitat Rovira i Virgili

The purpose of this paper is twofold; first, we aim to provide a series of tests that identify Spanish *ser capaz* 'be capable' (henceforth SC) as an ambiguous modal, just like English *must* or *can*. Specifically, we observe that SC has not only an abilitative flavor, but also an epistemic one. Second, we want to propose an analysis for SC that can account for this ambiguity and that is in accordance with current theories of modality such as Cinque (1999), Kratzer (1981, 1991), and Hacquard (2009, 2010). In a nutshell, we argue that SC can occupy two different positions, a low one below AspP, which corresponds to the abilitative interpretation, and a high one, above AspP, which translates as the epistemic reading. Concerning the semantics, we claim that SC denotes a slight possibility; i.e., the propositional argument is true in at least one world, but it is always true in the non-ordinary worlds.

1. Introduction

The main goal of this work is to propose an analysis that accounts for the semantic properties of the modal construction *ser capaz* 'be capable' in Spanish (henceforth SC). Specifically, our goal is twofold: first, to make a case for treating SC as a two-flavored modal, and, second, to incorporate its various epistemic and abilitative uses into the general syntactic and semantic theory of modality.

Our starting point is that SC does not mean *tener la capacidad* 'have the capacity'. Although for different reasons, this idea is also found in works like Thalberg (1972),

* This research has been partly supported by projects FFI2009-07114 (MICINN), FFI2012-34170 and FFI2010-22181-C03-01 (MINECO), and by the Ramón y Cajal program (RYC-2010-06070). We are grateful to two anonymous reviewers for their critic remarks, and to the audiences of the XLII Symposium of the Spanish Society of Linguistics (SEL) and the Linguistic Symposium on Romance Languages LSRL43 for their comments on a previous version of this work. We are also indebted to L. McNally for having provided us with English native judgments. Any remaining mistakes are our own responsibility.

DOI 10.1075/rllt.9.04cas

Piñón (2003) and Mari and Martin (2007). On the basis of examples like (1), they show that *be able* and *have the ability* are not synonyms.

(1)   a.   Brown was able to hit three bull's-eyes in a row.
      b.   Brown had the ability to hit three bull's-eyes in a row.

Note that (1a) does not entail (1b), because (1b) requires that Brown could repeat this performance if he wanted to, while (1a) can be accidental. Mari and Martin (2007) develop an account that distinguishes between so-called *generic abilities* vs. *action-dependent abilities*. In the present work we are not so much concerned about the notion of *ability*, but rather we delve into another ambiguity that SC exhibits, namely the one displayed in example (2).

(2)   a.   Hobbes fue capaz de traducir la obra completa de Homero a los 86 años.
           'Hobbes was capable of translating the complete works of Homer at 86.'
      b.   Mi hijo es capaz de haber resuelto el caso sin acudir a la policía.
           'My son is capable of having solved the case without going to the police.'

In a sentence like (2a), the modal SC has an abilitative interpretation: we refer to the capacity that Hobbes has to translate the complete works of Homer at the age of 86, which we consider a notable achievement. On the other hand, in (2b) a mother surmises that her son may have solved the case, which she regards as something unusual. That corresponds to the epistemic reading.

In this work we address the following questions:

i.   What are the empirical tests that distinguish between the abilitative and the epistemic use of SC?
ii.   Is this duality in meaning related to a structural difference?
iii. How can we describe such a duality in semantic terms?
iv.   What is the role of other criteria such as the aspect of *ser* 'to be', the aspect of the embedded VP or the agentive/animate status of the subject in determining the interpretation of SC?
v.   How do we incorporate to the analysis the 'unusual' component that is necessarily attributed to the proposition that appears in the complement position?

Before dealing with the data in Section 2, let us briefly anticipate our main proposal. We suggest a single lexical entry for SC as a modal with existential force; we derive its ambiguity on the basis of its syntactic position, above or below AspP (cf. Picallo 1990; Cinque 1999; Hacquard 2009, 2010), and on the basis of the content of its modal base, in compliance with Kratzer's model (Kratzer 1981, 1991). Whereas (2a) is a low modal and selects an abilitative modal base, (2b) has an epistemic modal base and the modal appears in a high position, above AspP.

2. The phenomenon: Data and background

2.1 The ambiguity

A good deal of the research on modality has centered on explaining why certain modal verbs show ambiguity between various interpretations. This is true for English *must*, which exhibits an epistemic (3a), as well as a deontic reading (3b), and Englih *can*, which can be deontic (4a), as well as circumstantial (4b).

(3) a. Your son must be late.
     b. Students must be on time.

(4) a. John cannot read these confidential reports.
     b. Palm trees can grow here.

As pointed out in Escandell (2004:296), the Spanish modal *deber* 'must' in (5) also admits two different readings: An epistemic reading, which refers to the conjectures and/or hypotheses that the speaker makes about the truth of the proposition, *Juan se va de vacaciones* 'Juan goes on vacation'; and a deontic interpretation that refers to the subject's duties, i.e., to Juan's obligations.

(5) Juan debe irse de vacaciones.
     'Juan must go on vacation.'

To the best of our knowledge, the ambiguity of the modal SC has not been analyzed in Spanish. Such ambiguity has no one-to-one equivalence with the corresponding English modals *be able* and *be capable*, as illustrated in (6). Even though we have not found any formal study on this or any other similar modal showing such diversity of use, *be capable* seems to behave like SC, whereas *be able* appears to be more restricted in its epistemic use, as the English judgments in (6b–c) suggest, as well as the contrast with the parallel Spanish sentences in (2c) and (7).

(6) *be able to/be capable of*
     a. Hobbes was {*able to translate/capable of translating*}
         Homer's collected works at the age of 86.   ABILITATIVE USE
     b. My son is {$^?$/*$able to have/$^?$/ ^{ok}capable of having*}
         solved (= may have solved) the case without going
         to the police.[1]   EPISTEMIC USE
     c. Belén Esteban is {*$able to write/^{ok}capable of writing*}
         novels if that helps her to appear on reality shows.   EPISTEMIC USE

---

1. There is variation among native speakers regarding the judgment of the two alternatives in (6b). There is, however, agreement in the strong preference for *be capable*.

(7)   Belén Esteban *es capaz* de escribir novelas si con eso consigue salir en los programas del corazón.
'Belén Esteban is capable of writing novels if that allows her to participate in romance shows.'

The existence of this double epistemic [EP] and abilitative [AB] interpretation of SC can be empirically tested. In what follows, we provide eight diagnostics that set these two interpretations apart.

First, only the abilitative reading exemplified in (2a) is compatible with the perfective aspect of 'ser capaz', (8).

(8)   a.   Hobbes *fue* capaz de traducir las obras completas de Homero. [AB]
'Hobbes was-PERF capable of translating Homer's collected works.'
b.   Mi hijo *fue* capaz de resolver el caso sin acudir a la policía. [AB]
'My son was-PERF capable of solving the case without going to the police.'

The use of imperfective aspect is possible, though, with SC, and can receive both epistemic and abilitative readings, as illustrated in (9). It is the context that will resolve the appropriate interpretation. Most importantly, for the epistemic reading, both the time of conjecture and the time where evidence is collected is the past (cf. von Fintel and Gillies 2007).

(9)   María era capaz de realizar cinco cosas a la vez.
'María was-IMPERF capable of doing five things at the same time.'
a.   In view of what I knew, it was possible that María did five things at the same time (for instance to prove herself). [EP]
b.   It was possible for María to do five things at the same time (for instance when she was young).[2] [AB]

Second, only the epistemic interpretation exemplified in (2b) above is compatible with perfective and progressive aspect of the embedded verb, (10).

(10)   a.   Este filósofo es capaz de *haber traducido/estar traduciendo* las obras completas de Homero. [EP]
'This philosopher is capable of having translated/being translating Homer's collected works.'

---

2.   From now on, we paraphrase the *epistemic* use in English as *It is possible that x Vs*, and the *abili*tative use as *It is possible for x to V* (cf. Mari 2011). Even if these paraphrases do not have the 'unusual' component mentioned in Section 1, they will be useful to tease apart the two modal flavors in English.

b.   Mi hijo es capaz de *haber resuelto/estar resolviendo* el caso sin acudir a la policía. [EP]
'Lit. My son is capable of having solved/being solving the case without going to the police.'[3]

Third, when SC appears in present, only the epistemic reading can license the temporal modifier *cualquier día de estos* 'one of these days', (11). As shown in (12), *cualquier día de estos* is compatible with the abilitative interpretation when SC is inflected for the future.

(11)   Este filósofo es capaz de traducir las obras completas de Homero cualquier día de estos.
  a.   'It is possible that this philosopher translates Homer's collected works one of these days.' [EP]
  b.   '#It is possible for this philosopher to translate Homer's collected works one of these days.' [AB]

(12)   Este filósofo será capaz de traducir las obras completas de Homero cualquier día de estos. [AB]
'It will be possible for this philosopher to translate Homer's collected works one of these days.'

Fourth, the abilitative modal imposes certain restrictions in that it requires the presence of an animate subject that has the ability attributed to it by the predicate. Thus, whereas (13) can only be interpreted epistemically, as in (13a), the sentence in (14) is ambiguous between both epistemic and abilitative readings.

(13)   Este libro es capaz de ser un éxito de ventas.
'This book is capable of being a best-seller.'
  a.   It is possible that this book ends up being a best-seller. [EP]
  b.   #It is possible for this book to end up being a best-seller. [AB]

(14)   Juan es capaz de cruzar el río a nado.
'Juan is capable of swimming across the river.'
  a.   It is possible that Juan swims across the river. [EP]
  b.   It is possible for Juan to swim across the river. [AB]

We have seen in the first test above that when the verbal aspect of the main verb is perfective, the only possible interpretation is the abilitative. Likewise, we have just shown that in the abilitative interpretation, the intervention or implication of an animate subject is required to predicate their abilities, which gives rise to contrasts such as the one in (15).

---

3.   A possible translation for the ungrammatical English progressive example could be something like, *being in the process of solving the case.*

(15)   a.   Juan fue capaz de cruzar el río a nado. [AB/*EP]
            'Juan was capable of swimming across the river.'

       b.   #El libro fue capaz de ser un éxito de ventas.
            'The book was capable of being a best-seller.'

The prediction is therefore that with verbs that do not involve the volitional action of a subject, the abilitative interpretation should be excluded. The impossibility of stative verbs in (16) and unaccusative verbs in (17) proves that this prediction is fully borne out.

(16)   a.   *Juan fue capaz de saber inglés.
            'Juan was-PERF capable of knowing English.'

       b.   *Juan fue capaz de necesitar ayuda.
            'Juan was-PERF capable of needing help.'

(17)   a.   *Juan fue capaz de caerse por las escaleras.
            'Juan was-PERF capable of falling off the stairs.'

       b.   *Mi madre fue capaz de preocuparse por mi tardanza.
            'My mother was-PERF capable of worrying about my delay.'

       c.   *El vestido fue capaz de arrugarse durante el viaje.
            'The dress was-PERF capable of wrinkling up during the trip.'

As further shown in (18)–(19), this type of predicates can only receive an epistemic reading. In all cases, the interpretation can be paraphrased as, *It is possible that p.*

(18)   a.   Juan es capaz de haber sabido inglés y no decirlo para no destacar.
            'It is possible that Juan knew English and did not say so to not stand out.'

       b.   Juan es capaz de necesitar ayuda y de no pedirla por timidez.
            'It is possible that Juan needs help and does not ask for it due to shyness.'

(19)   a.   Juan es capaz de caerse por las escaleras.
            'It is possible that Juan falls down the stairs.'

       b.   Mi madre es capaz de haberse preocupado por mi tardanza.
            'It is possible that my mother has worried about my delay.'

       c.   El vestido es capaz de haberse arrugado durante el viaje.
            'It is possible that the dress has wrinkled up during the trip.'

Fifth, epistemics accept expletives and passive complements, while abilitative modals select an animate subject argument, and cannot therefore license elements that appear in non-thematic positions (Picallo 1990:297). As we see in (20), the structure SC accepts meteorological verbs in complement position with an epistemic interpretation *puede que llueva/nieve* 'it may rain/snow'; on the other hand, they also license passive complements with inanimate subjects with the same epistemic reading, (21). Even though cases like (21) are rather uncommon, the very fact that they can be formed and that they can only receive an epistemic reading reinforces our classification.

(20) a. ¡Es capaz de llover esta tarde!⁴
          'It's capable of raining this evening!'

      b. El tiempo está tan loco que es capaz de nevar en primavera.
          'The weather is so crazy that it's capable of snowing in spring.'

(21) a. La franqueza de buena ley (la otra se confunde con la grosería)
          consiste, no en lanzar al rostro defectos irremediables, sino en
          amonestar blanda y piadosamente las faltas <u>capaces de ser corregidas.</u>
          (Ramón Cajal, *Charlas*) (NGRALE Section 25.5k)
          'True frankness (the other one is mistaken for rudeness) consists,
          not in hurling irreparable mistakes to one's face, but in delicately and
          kindly reproving those mistakes capable of being corrected.'

      b. Es preciso que lo haga de manera sencilla y convincente, <u>capaz de ser
          asimilada</u> por esos humildes campesinos y obreros. (Vargas Llosa,
          Verdad) (NGRALE Section 25.5k)
          'It is necessary that he does it in a simple and convincing way, capable of
          being understood by these humble farmers and working class people.'

Note that the incompatibility of perfective aspect with the epistemic reading can
explain the impossibility of these verbal forms with meteorological verbs, (22), or
inanimate passive complements, (23). The only possible reading with expletives and
passive complements would be the epistemic one, but the perfective aspect forces the
abilitative interpretation.

(22) a. *Ayer fue capaz de llover.
          'Yesterday it was capable of raining.'

      b. *El tiempo está tan loco que ha sido capaz de nevar en primavera.
          'The weather is so crazy that it has been capable of snowing in spring.'

(23) a. *Los errores fueron capaces de ser corregidos.
          'The mistakes were capable of being corrected.'

      b. *La respuesta fue capaz de ser identificada.⁵
          'The answer was capable of being identified.'

---

4. As pointed out by an anonymous reviewer, while these sentences are possible in Spanish,
their English counterparts with the adjective *capable* are ungrammatical, and would rather be
translated as, 'It may very well rain this evening.'

5. In cases like (23) above and others like (i), the NGRALE Section 26.5k recommends the
use of the adjective *susceptible* 'susceptible' instead of *capaz* 'capable'.

(i) una bomba capaz de ser detonada a distancia, una explicación capaz de ser
     comprendida por cualquiera
     'a bomb capable of being exploded by remote control, an explanation capable of
     being understood by anyone'

Note that the ungrammaticality of (23) stems from the use of *capaz* in a prescriptively disfavored
context with an aspectually perfective verb.

Sixth, in a scenario where the discourse participants observe how the relevant event is taking place, only the abilitative reading is available, because the epistemic interpretation is nonsensical (cf. Hackl's 1998:14 work on the different uses of the English modal *can*). For instance, in a situation where Juan is taking a bath in the river in winter and the participants are observing it, sentence (24), which would be ambiguous in another context, is infelicitous in its epistemic reading as a conjecture, but receives an ironic effect in its abilitative interpretation.

(24)   Situation: Everybody is looking at Juan bathing in the river.
       Juan es (realmente) capaz de bañarse en el río en invierno. [AB/#EP]
       'Juan is (really) capable of bathing in the river in winter.'

Seventh, in a scenario where the discourse participants have observed the completion of an event, the abilitative reading is ruled out as ungrammatical, and the epistemic reading is infelicitous (cf. Hackl 1998). For instance, sentence (25), with perfective aspect in the embedded verb, should receive an epistemic interpretation. In the situation described, where all participants know that the event has taken place, given that the epistemic reading is the only possible one, and cannot receive an abilitative interpretation, the sentence is anomalous.

(25)   Situation: Everybody knows that Juan has been bathing in the river.
       #Juan es capaz de haberse bañado en el río en invierno. [#EP/*AB]
       'Juan is capable of having bathed in the river in winter.'

To conclude the overview of the properties of the different uses of SC, we must mention a general and necessary characteristic of the proposition expressed in the complement position of SC. The proposition is always interpreted as something unusual. Hence, the sentences in (26) are felicitous only if they are uttered in a context where to blow one's nose or to fasten one's shoelaces can be interpreted as a notable achievement, for instance if Juan is a little child, or an adult that has suffered an accident that prevents him from doing actions that would be easy for an adult under normal conditions. In both cases, we would obtain an abilitative interpretation. Also the epistemic interpretation of SC requires a complement that refers to an unusual event, as depicted in (27).

(26)   a.   Juan es capaz de sonarse la nariz (él solo/ con solo tres añitos). [AB]
            'Juan is capable of blowing his nose (by himself/as a 3-year-old).'

       b.   Juan es capaz de atarse los cordones (él solo/ con solo tres añitos). [AB]
            'Juan is capable of fastening his shoelaces (by himself/as a 3-year-old).'

(27)   Juan es capaz de sonarse la nariz ruidosamente en medio de la
       conferencia. [EP]
       'Juan is capable of loudly blowing his nose in the middle of the talk.'

Note that the verb *poder* 'can' does not have such requirement, since we can say *Juan pudo sonarse la nariz antes de empezar la charla* 'Juan could blow his nose before start-ing the talk', where we can imagine that Juan is an adult that has no unusual abilities. If we uttered the same sentence but using SC (i.e., *Juan fue capaz de sonarse la nariz antes de empezar la charla* 'Juan was capable of blowing his nose before starting the talk'), we should imagine that Juan is disabled for some reason so that blowing his nose is a great achievement, or that he is a little child, as in (26a). Thus, the sentences in (28) can be interpreted as either deontic or abilitative depending on the context; those in (29) as epistemic or abilitative (and we could perhaps even find a deontic context, as well).

(28) a. Juan puede sonarse la nariz.
'Juan can blow his nose.'

b. Juan puede atarse los cordones.
'Juan can fasten his shoelaces.'

(29) a. Juan puede suspender el examen.
'Juan can fail the exam.'

b. Juan puede matarse en un accidente de coche.
'Juan can get killed in a car accident.'

For the abilitative interpretation of SC we require the presence of a complement that can be interpreted as an ability or an unusual capacity. Without discussing the details on the definition of capacity/ability, we observe that when, under normal circumstances, the interpretation of the complement SC cannot be abilitative, as in (30), the sentences are *a priori* infelicitous. It does not seem that under normal con-ditions *suspender un examen* 'to fail an exam' in (30a) can be considered as an abil-ity, skill, talent or capacity, as *aprobar un examen* 'to pass an exam' would be—even less the predicate *matarse en un accidente de coche* 'to get killed in a car accident' in (30b). Note that in both cases the use of the perfective forces the abilitative interpre-tation of the modal.

(30) a. #Juan fue capaz de suspender el examen.
'Juan was capable of failing the exam.'

b. #Juan fue capaz de matarse en un accidente de coche.
'Juan was capable of getting killed in a car accident.'

However, both sentences become fine and felicitous if they are supplied with an explicit context where the proposition can be interpreted as an unusual capacity, for instance, adding a clause that makes explicit a goal that one wants to achieve, as in (31).

(31) a. Juan fue capaz de suspender el examen para hacer enfadar a su madre.
'Juan was-PERF capable of failing the exam to annoy her mother.'

b. Juan fue capaz de matarse en accidente de coche para que su familia cobrara el seguro de vida.
    'Juan was-PERF capable of getting killed in a car accident in order for his family to be paid for his life insurance.'

Note that when using imperfective aspect, e.g., simple present, which does not force the abilitative interpretation, the sentences in (31) would be ambiguous between an epistemic reading, (32), and an abilitative reading, (33), depending on the context.

(32) a. (Conociéndole,) Juan es capaz de suspender el examen. [EP]
          '(Knowing him,) Juan is capable of failing the exam.'

      b. Juan es capaz de matarse en un accidente de coche (conduciendo a esa velocidad). [EP]
          'Juan is capable of getting himself killed in a car accident (if he drives at that speed).'

(33) a. Juan es capaz de suspender el examen (para hacer enfadar a su madre). [AB]
          'Juan is capable of failing the exam (to annoy his mother).'

      b. Juan es capaz de matarse en un accidente de coche (para que su familia cobre el seguro de vida). [AB]
          'Juan is capable of getting himself killed in a car accident in order for his family to be paid for his life insurance.'

Table 1 summarizes the properties that we have described for the two readings of SC ([EP] and [AB]). In subsection 3.2, we return to these data and explain how the proposed analysis accounts for them.

Table 1. Epistemic [EP] and abilitative [AB] uses of SC. Properties.

	Tests	
A	Perfective aspect	[EP] No/[AB] Ok (ex. (8)–(9))
B	Aspect of embedded verb	[EP] Ok/[AB] No (ex. (10))
C	License *cualquier día de estos*	[EP] Pres./[AB] Fut (ex. (11)–(12))
D	Selectional restrictions	[EP] No/[AB] Ok (ex. (13)–(19))
E	Expletives & passive complements	[EP] Ok/[AB] No (ex. (20)–(22))
F	Evidence of ongoing event	[EP] No/[AB] Ok (ex. (24))
G	Evidence that $p=1$	[EP] No/[AB] No (ex. (25))
H	'Unusual' proposition	[EP] Ok/[AB] Ok (ex. (26)–(31))

2.2   Modality in syntax and semantics

In modal logic, modality is expressed either as possibility ($\lozenge$) or as necessity ($\square$). The possibility of proposition p translates as the existence of a world where p holds. Necessity of p forces p to be true in all possible worlds. This is schematized in (34), where p is a proposition, M is a model, w is a world variable, and W is the set of all possible worlds in the model.

(34)   a. $[\![\lozenge p]\!]^{M,w0} = 1$ only if $\exists w' \in W$ $[\![p]\!]^{M,w'} = 1$ (existential force)

b. $[\![\square p]\!]^{M,w0} = 1$ only if $\forall w' \in W$ $[\![p]\!]^{M,w'} = 1$ (universal force)

(from Escandell Vidal 2004:295)

To translate the logic of modality into natural language, Kratzer (1981, 1991) incorporates the idea that modals are quantifiers with different force (existential vs. universal; she introduces more fine-grained subspecifications). She also introduces the notion of *conversational background* in order to account for the role context plays in the interpretation of modals, and to explain the different accessibility relations modals exhibit, notably epistemic, deontic, abilitative, etc. We know that languages tend to use the same modal to express a variety of accessibility relations. This triggers a great deal of ambiguity. In Kratzer's model, this ambiguity is derived through the choice of two types of conversational background, the modal base and the ordering source. The modal base $f(w)$ is the set of relevant worlds against which we verify the compatibility of p. For instance, it can be epistemic if it can be paraphrased as *in view of what we know*, or circumstantial if the paraphrase is *given the current circumstances*. The ordering source g establishes an ordering among the worlds such that there are worlds that are better than others. For instance, there are stereotypical ordering sources that state that the better worlds are those that are more normal (less surprising), and there are deontic ordering sources that choose as best worlds those that respect the rules. It is not always necessary that there be an ordering source, but when there is one, the proposition p verifies its compatibility with the intersection of the modal base and the ordering source.

Before we move on, we should acknowledge that abilitative modals have traditionally been difficult to fit in this model. Works such as Giannakidou (2001) and Giannakidou and Staraki (2013) defend the idea that abilitatives do not have existential but universal force. The reason for this is the existence of contrasts such as (35a) and (35b) concerning the actuality of the meaning conveyed by the complement of the modal.

(35)   a.   Juan ha podido cruzar el lago a nado.
'John was able to swim across the lake.'[AB]

b.   Puede que Juan haya cruzado el lago a nado.
'John might have swum across the lake.' [EP]

While (35a) entails that John managed to cross the lake, this is not the case for (35b). For the purposes of this paper, we will leave aside the debate on so-called *actuality entailments* (cf. Bhatt 1999; Hacquard 2006; Mari and Martin 2007) and will assume that abilitatives like *poder* 'can' or SC have the same force as their epistemic counterparts.

The research in the syntax of modals has focused on other aspects. The main claim is that, as already observed in Picallo (1990), from a syntactic point of view, modals occupy different positions.[6] Specifically, epistemics appear in a higher position than roots, which include both deontics and circumstantials.

Picallo shows that epistemic modals in Catalan cannot be preceded by auxiliaries.[7] See example (36), which is concerned with the Catalan epistemic modal *deure* 'must'.

(36)   *En Pere havia degut   venir.
        the Pere had   must-ppt come   (Picallo 1990: 288)

We observe that, in the case of SC, the presence of an auxiliary does not allow the epistemic reading. As we see in (37), in this case the sentences are not ungrammatical, but it seems as though the abilitative reading is the only possible one.

(37)   a.   Este filósofo ha sido capaz de traducir las obras completas de
            Homero. [AB]
            'This philosopher has been capable of translating the complete
            Homer's works.'

       b.   Mi hijo había sido capaz de resolver el caso sin acudir
            a la policía. [AB]
            'My son had been capable of solving the case without going to the
            police.'

On the other hand, according to Picallo (1990), when two modals co-occur, only the first one can obtain an epistemic interpretation, or in other words, the second modal in the sequence must have a root modal interpretation.

---

6.   Cf. Ross (1969), who was the first to propose a generative analysis in terms of *control-versus-raising*, where root modals (which were bi-argumental) stood opposite to epistemic modals (which were mono-argumental).

7.   Specifically, in a syntactic framework that precedes a highly articulated clausal structure, she argued that epistemic modals were located in INFL.

(38)   En Pere deu poder tocar el piano.
      'P. must + can play the piano.'   (Picallo 1990: 294)
    a.   'It must be the case that P. is able/allowed to play
        the piano.'   EP + ROOT
    b.   *'It must be the case that it is possible that P. would
        play the piano.'   EP + EP

(39)   En Jordi pot haver de venir. 'J. can + have to come.'   (Picallo 1990: 294)
    a.   'It is possible that J. is obliged/compelled to come.'   EP + ROOT
    b.   *'It is possible that it is necessary that J. come.'   EP + EP

If we apply this test to SC, the combination of the necessity epistemic modal *deber de* with SC should not admit the epistemic reading of SC but only the abilitative one. This prediction is borne out, as shown in (40).

(40)   Juan debe de ser capaz de tocar el piano.
      'J. must be capable of playing the piano.'
    a.   'It's almost certain that it is possible for J. to play the piano.' [EP + AB]
    b.   *'It's almost certain that it is possible that J. plays the piano.' [EP + EP]

Cinque (1999) proposes a hierarchy, which aims at being universal, which determines two possible projections for modals. Epistemics are located above Tense and Aspect, and roots are located between Aspect and VP, (41).

(41)   Universal hierarchy of functional projections according to Cinque (1999).
$$...MOD_{EPIST} > T > ASP > MOD_{ROOT} > VP$$

Later, Hacquard (2009, 2010) proposes to map Cinque's syntax with Kratzer's semantics. She takes from Kratzer the idea that modals are underspecified with respect to the accessibility relation; however, from Cinque, she adopts the idea that modals can occur in two different positions, so the duality of meanings is not resolved contextually, but rather, syntactically. That is, we only need one lexical entry for the two modals, and the choice of modal base relies on its syntactic position. Crucially, modal bases are relativized to events, which are treated as variables that need to be locally bound by the closest event binder (either aspect or the speech event binder λe_0). If the modal lies above TP, it is anchored to the speaker and the speech time event (e_0 in (42)). If the modal is just above VP, then it is anchored to the VP subject and the event time denoted by the VP (e_1 in (42)).

Hacquard further argues that speech events—but not VP events—have an associated *propositional content*, which provides the information state epistemic modals quantify over. By contrast, low modals do not have access to such a propositional content, so they obtain a root (i.e., circumstantial) interpretation. Thus, the different modal flavors (epistemic vs. root) emerge from the presence or absence of propositional content which is associated with the type of event.

(42)   Hacquard (2009, 2010)

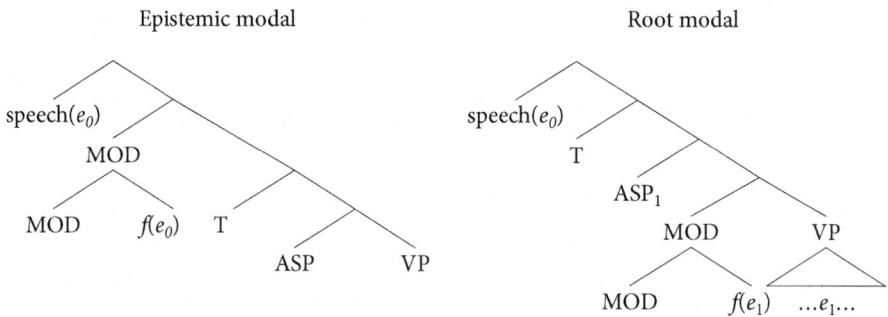

Epistemic modal   Root modal

The sentences in (43) and (44) from French in Hacquard (2010: 90) illustrate the predictions of this proposal.

(43)   Mary put prendre le train. 'Mary may have taken the train.'
   a. $[_{\text{ModP}}$ can $[_{\text{TP}}$ past $[_{\text{AspP}}$ perf$_1$ $[_{\text{VP}}$ Mary take the train e$_1$]]]]
   b.   There is a world w compatible with what is known in the actual world, such that there is a past event in w which is a train taking event by Mary.

In (43), the modal *can* takes scope over tense and perfective aspect. Hence, it is anchored to the speech time, while the VP event e$_1$ is located in the past and it is completed. The modal worlds evoked refer to the information compatible with what the speaker knows in the speech time.

    Consider now the alternative syntactic structure and interpretation of (44).

(44)   Mary put prendre le train.
        'Mary was able to take the train.'
   a. $[_{\text{TP}}$ past $[_{\text{AspP}}$ perf$_1$ $[_{\text{ModP}}$ can $[_{\text{VP}}$ Mary take the train e$_1$]]]]
   b.   There is a past event e$_1$ in the actual world, which in some world compatible with the circumstances in the actual world is a train taking event by Mary.

Here, the modal is below aspect and tense, so the modal worlds are relative to the aspect and tense of the VP event e$_1$. The worlds evoked are hence compatible with the circumstances in e$_1$.

    In what follows, we stick to this (probably idealized) research program, which allows us to establish a neat mapping between the syntax and the semantics and, more importantly, groups SC together with other better-known modals with respect to their dual interpretation.

3. Proposal

Based on the seminal works by Kratzer (1981, 1991), Hackl (1998), and Portner (2009), we propose a semantic analysis that accounts for the ambiguity that we have observed in SC. We assume that SC introduces a *slight possibility*, in Kratzer's terms. We adopt the essential tenets of Hacquard (2010), who attempts to map the typology of modals with the syntactic positions assigned by Cinque (1999), and we propose two positions for SC, a high one for the epistemic interpretation, and a low one for the abilitative interpretation.

3.1 Syntax and semantics

We propose that the force of SC corresponds to what Kratzer calls *slight possibility*, as described in (45).

> (45) *Slight possibility*   (Portner 2009: 69)
>   A proposition p is a slight possibility in w with respect to a modal base f and an ordering source g iff:
>   i. p is compatible with $f(w)$; and
>   ii. $\neg p$ is a necessity in w with respect to f and g.

If the force were simply possibility, we would not be able to easily tease apart the abilitative and epistemic readings of a verb like *poder* 'can' from the ones of SC. With (45) we want to convey that the proposition p is unusual, not standard. This is how we derive the intuition that it would be a notable achievement to translate Homer's works or to solve the case without telling the police. We believe the formula in (46) is general enough to account for both uses of SC.

> (46) $[\![SC]\!]^{e,f,g}(p) = 1$ iff $\exists w \in \cap f(e): p(w) = 1$ and $\forall w' \in \text{Best}_{g(e)}(\cap f(e)): p(w') = 0$

What (46) says is that SC combines with a proposition p and it turns out true iff there is a world w compatible with the intersection of f and g where p holds, and in all ordinary worlds w', p is not the case.[8]

   We propose the basic structure in (48) for an epistemic example of SC such as (47).

> (47)   Mi hijo es capaz de haber resuelto el caso. [EP]
>   'My son is capable of having solved the case.'

---

8.   As in Hacquard's work, the modal is relativized to an event, and so are the conversational backgrounds f and g.

(48)

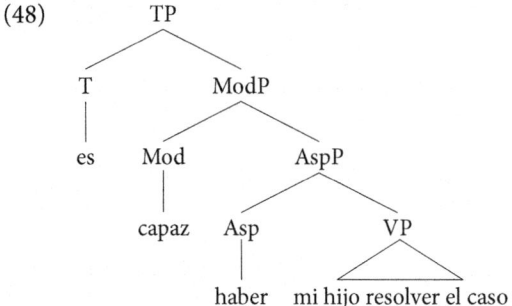

Note that we are essentially assuming Hacquard's ideas, but we depart from her in locating *capaz* below TP.[9] With this, we want to show that, unlike the English modals *may* or *might*, which are not inflected for tense, SC can occur in the present tense, but also in the past and the future, because *capaz* is preceded by the copula *ser* 'be'. What is crucial is that the epistemic use of SC occurs above AspP. This allows for an auxiliary to occur between the modal and VP, which is what forces the epistemic reading of the modal, as we have previously shown.

A possible paraphrase of the meaning of (47), implementing the formula proposed in (46), is as in (49).

(49)   There is a world *w* compatible with what the speaker knows at the speech event time such that there is a past event in *w* which is an event of the speaker's son solving the case (and in all the worlds *w'* compatible with what the speaker knows and which are most stereotypical, her son does not solve the case in *w'*).

If instead of *es capaz* 'is capable' we had *era capaz* 'was capable' or *será capaz* 'will be capable', T would be interpreted as the time in which the speaker makes the conjecture and has the evidence. For instance, (50).

(50)   a.   Mi hijo era capaz de haber resuelto el caso.
             'My son was capable of having solved the case'.

       b.   There is a world *w* compatible with what the speaker knew in a past event in the actual world such that there is a past event in *w* which is an event of her son solving the case (and in all worlds *w'* compatible with what the speaker knew and which are most stereotypical, her son does not solve the case in *w'*).

---

9.   As pointed out by an anonymous reviewer, we are treating SC as though it were a modal verb, but given that *capaz* is an adjective in a copular construction, a more fine-grained syntax should be provided. We leave this issue open for future research.

Regarding the root reading, we argue that we need an ordering source that ranks the worlds as the best ones if these are worlds in which the proper conditions for testing whether 'the subject can p' obtain (cf. Cross 1986). Pending further research on the lexical semantics of SC, this is how we encode the lexical information of SC and manage to generate some selection restrictions. Consider now example (51)–(52); the modal is low in the structure, below tense and aspect.

(51)   Hobbes fue capaz de traducir la obra de Homero. [AB]
        'Hobbes was capable of translating Homer's works.'

(52)

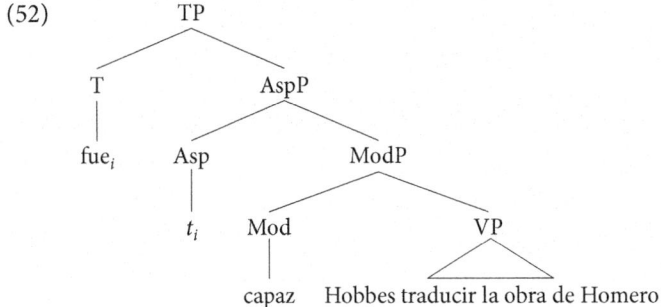

The paraphrase of (51), implementing the formula in (46), is shown in (53).

(53)   There is a past event in the actual world, which in some world w
        compatible with the circumstances at the VP event time in the actual
        world (i.e., the capacities of Hobbes, the VP subject) is an event of Hobbes
        translating Homer's works (and in all worlds w' compatible with the actual
        circumstances and which are most stereotypical, Hobbes does not translate
        Homer's works in w').

3.2   Accounting for the data

Let us now see how this proposal explains the various properties of SC observed in Section 2.1, which were summarized in Table 1 through labels A–H.

Regarding test A, we observed that if SC takes perfective aspect, then only the abilitative reading obtains. This contrast receives a syntactic explanation, since aspectually perfective forms such as *fue capaz* 'was-PERF capable' or *ha sido capaz* 'has been capable' force the position of the modal to be below AspP. Note in addition that perfective aspect on SC triggers an actuality entailment, which would be contradictory with the conjecture or prediction denoted by the epistemic use of the modal.

As for property B, in our analysis, root modals merge below aspect, so they do not admit an auxiliary between the modal and VP. The presence of auxiliary *haber* 'have' in Asp is interpreted as the completion of the event denoted by the VP. *Estar* 'be' + gerundive verb introduces the semantics of progressive aspect. It follows from our analysis that when there is no auxiliary between SC and the VP, the expression is in principle ambiguous, since two different syntactic structures are possible.

Concerning the possibility of licensing *cualquier día de estos* 'one of these days' (C), we argue that in the epistemic reading, the adverbial modifies the event denoted by the VP. The conjecture moment is the speech time, and the present on *es capaz* signals that the speaker knows how the VP subject is in the present time. Since the epistemic reading implies a prediction, when the VP denotes a realization or an achievement, the conjecture is projected towards the future. 'One of these days' just indicates that the event happens at some indeterminate point in the future, so there is no incompatibility. In view of what the speaker knows now, it is possible that at some moment in the future the event takes place. By contrast, in the abilitative reading there is simultaneity between the moment where the subject has the ability and the event that follows from this ability. 'One of these days' gives us the time in which the subject is capable of carrying out the specified event. Since this modifier refers to the future, only if SC is inflected for future tense can the sentence obtain a meaningful interpretation. There is an event that occurs in an indeterminate moment in the future in some world compatible with the circumstances (the subject's abilities) in the actual world which is an event of V-ing by the subject.

The reason why the epistemic reading is compatible either with expletives or with a subject of a passive (E) is that the subject the epistemic modal is relativized to is the speaker, who is the one evoking her information state to make the conjecture. In the case of the abilitative reading, the modal base contains the circumstances involved with the VP subject (i.e., her abilities). According to Hacquard, we expect that only root modals exhibit selectional restrictions. In this case, if the proposition p has to be compatible with a set of worlds where the proper conditions for testing whether 'the subject can p' obtain (i.e., whether the subject has abilities to realize actions), it follows that the subject must be agentive.

Properties F and G derive naturally from how epistemic readings are characterized (i.e., they refer to conjectures and predictions) and from the aforementioned incompatibility between perfective aspect and abilitative readings.

Lastly, we have suggested that the force assigned to SC is slight possibility. Such proposal means that not only does SC have existential quantification over worlds, but it also adds that in none of the ordinary worlds does the truth of p hold. Hence, we always interpret that translating Homer's works, writing a novel or swimming across the lake is a notable achievement or an unusual action for the subject.

4. Conclusions

There are two main aspects to the merits of this work. First, we have systematized a set of data that had not been considered in the modality literature, thus contributing new data into the modal semantics debates. We have shown that even though SC would at first sight be expected to be semantically equivalent to the expression 'have the capacity', it is in fact much more complex; not only because abilities may be of different sorts, but also because SC has both an abilitative and an epistemic reading. Moreover, we have accounted for these data within a widely acknowledged model of the syntax and semantics of modal expressions, which proposes that there are different syntactic positions for modals and that these positions relate to the anchoring of the subject and a time (speech vs. event). We have also followed standard practice in semantics in treating modals as quantifiers over worlds that take a proposition as an argument and are relativized to a modal base and an ordering source.

As mentioned at the onset, this work is also a first approach to a set of data that had previously not been studied in depth, which means that numerous questions remain to be addressed. In what follows, we suggest a brief list of remaining issues and open questions as a conclusion.

First, what do these data tell us about the notion of ability? We know that there are generic abilities and action-dependent abilities (Kenny 1975; Mari and Martin 2007). Does this distinction correlate in any way with our two readings? Are abilities and capacities the same? Related to this issue, how does SC pattern with respect to actuality entailments? Does aspect interact with SC in the same way as *poder* 'can' in this respect? Third, does the 'unusual' component yield a comparison between the actual subject and the same subject in normal worlds or else between the actual subject and other—more normal—subjects? How can this distinction be captured?[10] Fourth, what is the interaction between negation and SC? Could it be used as a diagnostic for the epistemic-abilitative distinction?

And a final related fact: when SC is negated, what is then denied, the capacity or also the unusual component? A further development on this issue may contribute an interesting comparison between the 'unusual' component and the unlikely/noteworthy component associated with *incluso* 'even' and its negative counterpart *ni siquiera* 'not even'.

---

10.   We thank an anonymous reviewer for pointing this question to us.

References

Bhatt, Rajesh. 1999. "Ability Modals and their Actuality Entailments." Proceedings of WCCFL 17. Ed. by Kimary N. Shahin, Susan Blake, and Eun-Sook Kim, 74–87.

Cinque, Guglielmo. 1999. Adverbs and Functional Heads: A Crosslinguistic Perspective. Oxford Studies in Comparative Syntax. Oxford and New York: Oxford University Press.

Cross, Charles B. 1986. "'Can' and the Logic of Ability." Philosophical Studies 50 (1): 53–64. DOI: 10.1007/BF00355160

Escandell Vidal, María Victoria. 2004. Fundamentos de Semántica Composicional. Ariel.

von Fintel, Kai and Anthony S. Gillies. 2007. "An Opinionated Guide to Epistemic Modality." In Oxford Studies in Epistemology, Vol. 2. Ed. by Tamar S. Gendler and John Hawthorne, 36–62. Oxford: Oxford University Press.

Giannakidou, Anastasia. 2001. The Meaning of Free Choice. Linguistics & Philosophy 24: 659–735. DOI: 10.1023/A:1012758115458

Giannakidou, Anastasia and Elena Staraki. 2013. "Ability, Action, and Causation: From Pure Ability to Force," In Genericity. Ed. by Alda Mari, Claire Beyssade and Fabio Del Prete. Oxford University Press.

Hackl, Martin. 1998. On the Semantics of Ability Attributions. Ms, MIT.

Hacquard, Valentine. 2006. Aspects of Modality. Ph.D. Thesis, MIT.

Hacquard, Valentine. 2009. "On the Interaction of Aspect and Modal Auxiliaries." Linguistics & Philosophy 32(3): 279–315. DOI: 10.1007/s10988-009-9061-6

Hacquard, Valentine. 2010. "On the Event Relativity of Modal Auxiliaries." Natural Language Semantics 18(1): 79–114. DOI: 10.1007/s11050-010-9056-4

Kenny, Angelika. 1975. Will, Freedom and Power. Oxford: Basic Blackwell.

Kratzer, Angelika. 1981. "The Notional Category of Modality." In Words, Worlds, and Contexts. Ed. by Hans-Jürgen Eikmeyer, Hannes Rieser, 38–74. Walter de Gruyter.

Kratzer, Angelica. 1991. "Modality." In Semantics: An International Handbook of Contemporary Research. Ed. by Arnim von Stechow and Dieter Wunderlich, pp. 639–650. De Gruyter.

Mari, Alda. 2011. Modalités et Temps: Des Modèles aux Données. Ms. Institut Jean Nicod (Habilitation à diriger des recherches).

Mari, Alda and Fabienne Martin. 2007. "Tense, Abilities and Actuality Entailment." In Proceedings of the Sixteenth Amsterdam Colloquium. Ed. by Maria Aloni, Paul Dekker und Floris Roelofsen, 151–156.

Picallo, M. Carme. 1990. "Modal verbs in Catalan." Natural Language & Linguistic Theory. 8(2): 285–312. DOI: 10.1007/BF00208525

Piñón, Christopher. 2003. "Being Able To." In Proceedings of WCCFL 22. Ed. by Gina Garding and Mimu Tsujimura, 384–397.

Portner, Paul. 2009. Modality. Oxford University Press.

RAE y Asociación de Academias de la Lengua Española. 2010. Nueva Gramática de la Lengua Española. Madrid: Espasa. [NGRALE].

Ross, John Robert. 1969. "Auxiliaries as Main Verbs." In Studies in Philosophical Linguistics Series I. Ed. by William Todd, 77–102.

Thalberg, Irving. 1972. Enigmas of Agency: Studies in the Philosophy of Human Action. London: Allen and Unwin.

Beyond the subject DP versus the subject pronoun divide in agreement switches*

Raquel Fernández Fuertes[1], Juana M. Liceras[3] &
Anahí Alba de la Fuente[2]
[1]Universidad de Valladolid / [2]Université de Montréal / [3]University of Ottawa and
Universidad Nebrija

Previous code-switching literature argues that no switch takes place between
a pronoun and a verb, while Determiner Phrases (DPs) do code-switch. This
paper uses code-switching acceptability judgment data elicited from three
groups of English–Spanish bilinguals (2L1 children, L2 English children and
L2 English adults) to test: (i) van Gelderen & MacSwan's (2008) PF disjunction
theorem intended to account for the DP/pronoun divide; and (ii) an agreement
version of the analogical criterion (Liceras et al. 2008) which is based on
Pesetsky & Torrego's (2001, 2007) double-feature valuation mechanism
intended to account for the different status of third person versus first and
second person pronominal subjects. We show that the PF disjunction theorem
is clearly rooted in the mind of the bilingual and that the Spanish dominant
bilinguals can 'relax' its requirements to value person agreement features as
predicted by the double-feature valuation mechanism.

1. Introduction

The main objective of this paper is to contribute to the characterization of SU(subject)–
V(verb) code-switching restrictions. Specifically, we aim at determining whether all
English–Spanish subject–verb switches are created equal; that is, whether the categorial nature of the subject (DP or pronoun, as in 1a–2a versus 1b–2b) or the grammatical person (first person, second person or third person pronominal subjects, as in

---

* This research has been funded by the Spanish Ministry of Science and Technology
[HUM2007-62213] and FEDER [DGICYT #BFF2002-00442], by the Faculty of Arts of the
University of Ottawa and the Social Sciences and Humanities Research Council of Canada
[SSHRC #410-2004-2034] and by the International Council for Canadian Studies and
Department of Foreign Affairs (International Education and Youth Division) [10-CEA-A].
We would also like to thank the International School in Valladolid (Spain) for their
collaboration.

DOI 10.1075/rllt.9.05fue
© 2016 John Benjamins Publishing Company

1b–2b versus 1c–2c) would make English–Spanish bilinguals perceive these switches differently:

(1) a. El niño *talks about dogs*   DP SU–V switch
         [The boy talks about dogs]

     b. Él *talks about dogs*   pronominal SU–V switch (3rd p.s.)
         [He talks about dogs]

     c. Yo *talk about dogs*   pronominal SU–V switch (1st p.s.)
         [I talk about dogs]

(2) a. *The boy* habla de los perros   DP SU–V switch
         [The boy talks about dogs]

     b. *He* habla de los perros   pronominal SU–V switch (3rd p.s.)
         [He talks about dogs]

     c. *I* hablo de los perros   pronominal SU–V switch (1st p.s)
         [I talk about dogs]

Previous research intended to characterize the categorial nature of the subject in SU–V switches (e.g. Gumperz 1976; Lipski 1978; Jake 1994; MacSwan 1999, 2000, 2005, 2009; van Gelderen and MacSwan 2008; Koronkiewicz 2012; MacSwan and Colina 2014) has shown that while DP subject–verb switches are both produced and accepted, subject pronoun–verb switches do not have the same status in the bilingual grammar (van Gelderen and MacSwan 2008). It has also been argued (MacSwan 1999, 2000) that production and acceptance of subject pronoun–verb switches by bilinguals varies. Specifically, while first and second person subject–verb switches may not occur, third person switches are considered to be well-formed, something that is attributed to a difference in the feature matrixes of the languages involved in code-switching.

In this paper, we discuss code-switching acceptability judgment data elicited from a group of child 2L1 (simultaneous Spanish L1–English heritage) bilinguals, a group of child English L2 (subsequent Spanish L1–English L2) bilinguals and a group of adult L2 (subsequent Spanish L1–English L2). We further investigate the categorial nature of the subject in subject–verb switches as well as the status of the three grammatical persons in pronominal subject–verb switches. We show that (i) there are significant differences between subject DPs and subject pronouns both in English and Spanish; (ii) there are significant differences between both English and Spanish third person standard position pronouns and first and second person standard position pronouns; (iii) Spanish third person standard position pronouns differ significantly from their English counterparts with respect to code-switching; (iv) Spanish third person standard position pronouns are closer to DPs than to their first and second person counterparts; and (v) differences between the data from 2L1 and

L2 bilinguals point to the fact that these groups do not perceive language properties in the same way when it comes to judging the acceptability of SU–V switches; more specifically, that the need to value person agreement features (i.e., the agreement version of the analogical criterion) is what guides these speakers' code-switching preferences. We analyze these results in light of linguistic proposals that place features and the way these are valued in the different languages as the locus of interlinguistic differences (Pesetsky and Torrego 2001, 2007; van Gelderen and MacSwan 2008; Liceras et al. 2008; Koronkiewicz 2012). Our specific aim is to provide an account of the issues that underlie code-switching preferences both across structure-types and across groups of participants.

This paper is organized as follows: Section 2 presents previous minimalist accounts on SU–V switches which lead us to formulate the research questions and hypotheses that appear in Section 3; a description of the participants and the task we used to elicit the data are shown in Section 4; Sections 5 and 6 include our results as well and the corresponding discussion; and our conclusions appear in Section 7.

2.   Minimalist accounts of SU–V switches

2.1   Subject category: DPs versus pronouns

More than three decades ago, researchers such as Timm (1975), Gumperz (1976) and Lipski (1978), among others, stated that while DPs code-switch, pronouns are unable to appear in code-switched structures. However, not all pronouns across languages had the same status and, in this respect, Jake (1994) differentiated 'grammatical' (English-like) subject pronouns from 'lexical' (French or Arabic) strong pronouns showing that it is only the former that cannot code-switch, as the acceptability of the examples in (3) reveals:

(3) a. *Moi* dxlt
         [I$_{French}$ [went-in]$_{Arabic}$]   (French/Moroccan Arabic)
     b. *Nta* tu vas travailler
         [You$_{Arabic}$ [you go work]$_{French}$]   (French/Moroccan Arabic)
     c. *Humaya* vergelijken de mentaliteit met de islam
         [They$_{Arabic}$ [compare the mentality with
         the islam]$_{Dutch}$]   (Dutch/Moroccan Arabic)

More recently, van Gelderen and MacSwan (2008), MacSwan (2009) and MacSwan and Colina (2014) have provided a Minimalist account of how the categorial nature of the subject determines the viability of subject–verb switches by bilingual speakers so that switching between the DP subject and the verb in (4) is a grammatical option while switching between the subject pronoun and the verb as in (5) is ungrammatical:

(4)   That teacher odia los exámenes
       [That teacher hates exams]

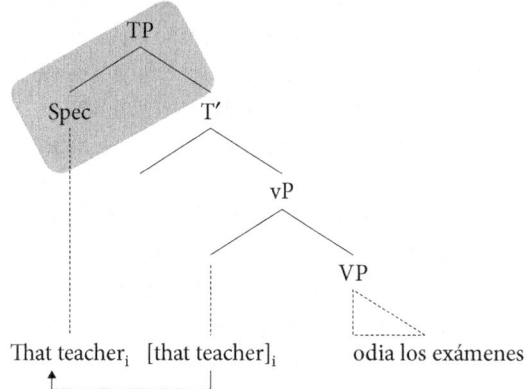

(5)   *She odia los exámenes
       [She hates exams]

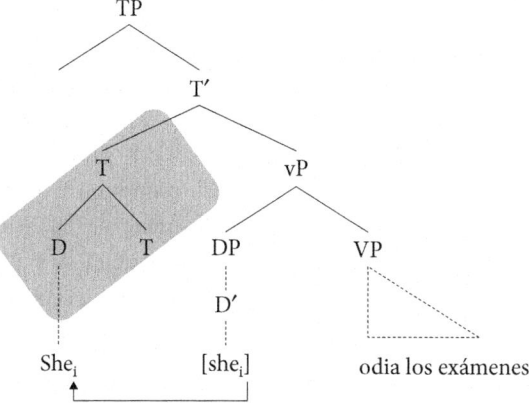

As shown in (4), lexical DPs check features in the Specifier of the Tense Phrase [Spec TP] while pronouns in (5) undergo D-to-T movement. Van Gelderen and MacSwan (2008) consider the switch in (5) to be ungrammatical because it results in a mixed-language complex head and so violates the P(honological) F(orm) Disjunction Theorem which rules out code-switching below X°. However, in the case of strong pronouns (Cardinaletti and Starke 1999) such as the French or Moroccan Arabic strong pronouns in (3) above, the PF Interface Condition would not be violated because, under van Gelderen and MacSwan's (2008) proposal, they would behave as DPs.

Van Gelderen and MacSwan's (2008) analysis treats Spanish pronouns like English pronouns and so they consider cases like (6a) and (6b) to be ill-formed:

(6) a. *Yo fight all the time
          [I fight all the time]   (Spanish subject pronoun + English verb)

     b. *They zeggen te veel
          [They say too much]   (English subject pronoun + Dutch verb)

However, this is not widely accepted and (at least some) Spanish pronouns are considered to be like French or Moroccan Arabic strong pronouns (Alexiadou and Anagnostopoulou 1988; Kato 1999, Koronkiewicz 2012). This means that not all Spanish pronouns may have the same status in the grammar. In this respect, Koronkiewicz (2012) calls for further refinement and an expansion of Cardinaletti and Starke's (1999) strong, weak, and clitic pronominal systems. His proposal is based on the different code-switching behavior attributed to standard subject position pronouns, as in (7), versus non-standard subject position pronouns (prosodically stressed, coordinated or modified), as in (8):

(7) ??? Ella hates exams
     [She hates exams]

(8) a. ELLA hates exams   prosodically stressed
          [SHE hates exams]

     b. Ella y Marsias hate exams   coordinated
          [She and Marsias hate exams]

     c. La de sintaxis hates exams   modified
          [Her _ of syntax hates exams]

Under Koronkiewicz's (2012) approach, only Spanish strong pronouns (8a) would have a different status in S–V switches, while Spanish weak pronouns (7) would yield ill-formed switches like those in (6). According to this distinction, we would expect the same code-switching differences between standard (weak) and non-standard (strong) position Spanish and English pronouns.

2.2   Pronoun type: 1st–2nd person versus 3rd person

Van Gelderen and MacSwan's (2008) proposal makes no prediction with respect to potential differences among Spanish first, second, and third person pronouns and so we would expect the same code-switching behavior for the three. In fact, they treat all switches between a Spanish subject pronoun and an English verb in the same way, as the examples in (9) show:

(9) a. *Yo fight all the time
          [I fight all the time]

     b. *Ellos fight all the time
          [They fight all the time]

    c.   *Ella* fights all the time
        [She fights all the time]   (van Gelderen and MacSwan 2008, 774)

However, they do refer to MacSwan (1999) who deals with the asymmetry in the switch between Spanish pronouns and Nahuatl verbs in that first and second person switches are ill-formed, (10a and 10b), while third person ones are well-formed, (10c):

(10)   a.   *Yo nikoas tlakemetl
          [I will buy clothes]

       b.   *Tu tikoas tlakemetl
           [You will buy clothes]

       c.   Él kikoas tlakemetl
           [He will buy clothes]   (van Gelderen and MacSwan 2008, 772)

They attribute this asymmetry to Nahuatl verb agreement affixes: since Nahuatl third person verbs have no agreement affixes, they do not enter into an agreement relation with T to check features and so no PF Interface Condition violation would occur, contrary to (5) above.

In order to account for the contrasting facts in (9) and (10) and to determine the code-switching status of Spanish–English pronominal SU–V switches, we propose to take as a point of departure Pesetsky and Torrego's (2001, 2007) double feature valuation mechanism concerning nominative case and agreement, as well as Liceras et al.'s (2008) double gender feature valuation mechanism for code-switching in concord structures captured in the so-called analogical criterion. Under Pesetsky and Torrego's (2001, 2007) proposal, nominative case is seen as an uninterpretable T feature on D and agreement as an uninterpretable D feature on T. Liceras et al. (2008) assume a parallel relation between inherent lexical Gender (Gen) and Gender Agreement (Φ), so that Gender is seen as an inherent N feature on D and Gender Agreement as an inherent D feature on N, as represented in (11):

(11)   DP

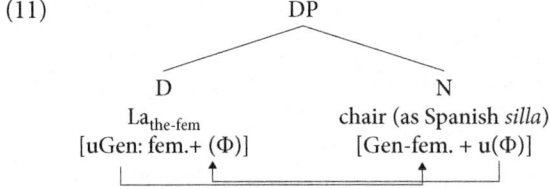

           D   N
        La$_{\text{the-fem}}$ chair (as Spanish *silla*)
      [uGen: fem.+ (Φ)]   [Gen-fem. + u(Φ)]

Liceras et al. (2008) have shown that the need to implement this double gender feature valuation mechanism underlies code-switching preferences in the case of concord structures such as those in (12) because simultaneous English–Spanish bilinguals and Spanish dominant bilinguals systematically reject clear-cut violations of the analogical criterion, as in (12b), where the Spanish feminine determiner occurs with an English noun whose corresponding Spanish translation is a masculine noun:[1]

(12) a. La house   [+analogical criterion]
          [The-fem. house: Spanish *casa*-fem.]

      b. La book   [-analogical criterion]
          [The-fem. book: Spanish *libro*-masc.]

We would like to propose that this code-switching formalization of Pesetsky and Torrego's (2001, 2007) double feature valuation mechanism could also be extended to SU–V switches. That is, parallel to the concord version of the analogical criterion in (12), SU–V switches could be formally analyzed on the basis of an agreement version of the analogical criterion. The relevant features are nominative case and person agreement, and their distribution, as in Pesetsky and Torrego's (2001, 2007) proposal, would be as follows: nominative case (NC) involves an uninterpretable Tense feature on D (i.e., subject bears uNC) which would receive an interpretation if it were part of T (i.e., verbal inflection, more specifically T, bears interpretable NC feature); agreement (Φ) involves an uninterpretable Φ-feature on T (i.e., T bears uΦ feature) which has no semantic interpretation as part of TP but would receive an interpretation if it were part of a nominal (i.e. subject bears interpretable Φ feature). This is spelled out below for English and Spanish non-switched and switched SU–V structures.

The examples in (13) and (14) show how the SU–V double feature valuation mechanism would take place in English and Spanish non-switched structures with standard position (i.e., weak) pronouns:

(13) a. Yo   le-o
          [I   read]

      b. Tú   lee-s
          [You   read]
          [uNC] [Φ]   [NC] [uΦ]

      c. Él   lee-Ø
          [He   reads]
          [uNC] [Φ]   [NC] [uΦ]

---

1. Examples like *el table* (the-masc table-fem in Spanish) could receive two interpretations. It could be an instance of [-analogical criterion], as in (12b), where the uninterpretable gender feature carried by the Spanish determiner is masculine (uGen: masc.). Alternatively it could be the so-called masculine by default option where the gender feature of the Spanish determiner is sub-specified. In this case gender feature matching is cancelled. The masculine determiner as a default form has been proposed in a number of studies on Spanish grammar (e.g., Roca 1989; Harris 1991) and on the acquisition of Spanish (e.g., Franceschina 2001; White et al. 2004; Liceras et al. 2006, 2008, 2012).

In Spanish first and second person SU–V structures, the uninterpretable nominative case feature ([uNC]) on the subject pronoun would be valued on the interpretable one present on the Spanish verb ([NC]); likewise, the uninterpretable person agreement feature on V would be valued on the interpretable one on the subject. This double feature valuation mechanism has a phonological realization. With regards to the third person (13c), it proceeds in the same way although no phonological realization appears, as marked by the lack of a person agreement marker in the Spanish verb.

In English, the valuation of the uninterpretable nominative case feature proceeds as in Spanish. In the case of first and second person SU–V structures, there is no phonological reflex of the valuation mechanism. In the third person, as in (14c), the -s marker appears in the English verb:

(14)   a.   I   read
       b.   You   read
            [uNC]   [NC]
       c.   He   read-S
            [uNC]   [NC]

In Spanish–English SU–V switches, the person agreement valuation mechanism would not be possible for first and second person switches, as in (15a) and (15b), because no such feature appears in the English verbs:

(15)   a.   Yo   read-ø
            [I   read]
       b.   Tú   read-ø
            [You   read]
            [Φ]
       c.   Él/ella   read-S
            [He/she   reads]
            [Φ]   [ ] // [uΦ]

For third person switches (15c), the -s marker in the English verb would allow the person agreement feature in the subject to be valued if the -s marker 'inherits' the corresponding feature that Spanish verbs overtly express in the agreement markers. This 'inheritance' is an instance of the analogical criterion in that English -s maker could be perceived as the locus of the uninterpretable person agreement feature (uF) that Spanish verbs have, as in (13a) and (13b). That is, the phonological realization in English third person verbs (the -s marker in 15c) could make bilinguals transfer into the English verb the person agreement feature Spanish verbs have in spite of the fact that it is precisely the third person the one that does not have a phonological realization (as in 13c versus 13a and 13b). This makes Spanish–English third person SU–V switches different from first and second persons where no such phonological realization on the English verb occurs. This mirrors the concord facts in (12a) where the English nouns are assigned a gender agreement feature as the English verb here is assigned a person agreement feature. We refer to this as the person agreement version of the analogical criterion as proposed by Liceras et al. (2008).

In English–Spanish SU–V switches, no valuation of the person agreement feature in the Spanish verb would be possible due to lack of this feature in the English subject pronouns, as in (16a) and (16b):

(16) a. I   le-o
          [I   read]

      b. You   lee-s
          [You   read]
                     [uΦ]

      c. He/she   lee-Ø
          [He/she   reads]
                     [uΦ]

The mechanisms depicted in (15) and (16) point to a possible asymmetry between first and second person pronouns and third person pronouns in SU–V switches. In the case of Spanish–English switches, the Spanish pronoun (15c) can value its agreement feature on the English verb (which is morphologically marked with an -*s*). This would imply that the need to use the agreement feature born by the Spanish pronoun into a feature valuation mechanism (to abide by what we propose as an SU–V version of the analogical criterion) supersedes the PF Interface Condition. In the case of English–Spanish switches, the fact that Spanish third person verbs lack an overt marker could make these switches less "offensive" than first and second person ones, where the agreement feature has a morphological correlate. We will capture these differences in our research questions below.

3. Research questions and hypotheses

The Minimalist account of SU–V switches presented above suggests two possible asymmetries in the case of English–Spanish SU–V switches: one concerning the categorical nature of the subject element (DP versus pronoun) and one concerning the grammatical person of the pronoun involved in pronominal SU–V switches (first, second or third person). In order to analyze whether these asymmetries are so perceived by bilingual speakers, the following research questions and their corresponding hypotheses have been formulated and will be then tested against experimental data:

1. Will the categorial nature of the subject be reflected in a difference between DP versus pronominal subject in SU–V agreement sequences in both English and Spanish? [Examples 4 versus 5 above].

Hypothesis #1. DP+V sequences will differ from standard pronoun+V ones because there is no PF Interface Condition violation, as proposed by van Gelderen and Mac-Swan (2008) and reformulated in MacSwan (2009) and MacSwan and Colina (2014). Also, since all pronouns considered are standard position pronouns in both languages, no distinction will appear between English pronouns and Spanish pronouns, as predicted by van Gelderen and MacSwan (2008) and Koronkiewicz (2012).

2. Will the need to value the person agreement feature (Φ) of Spanish third person pronouns on the verb be reflected in a difference between Spanish third person pronouns and English third person pronouns? [examples 15c versus 16c above].

Hypothesis #2. Spanish third person sequences will have a different status from English third person ones because the double feature valuation mechanism could take place if an uninterpretable feature is assigned to the English verb (relying on the -s affix) which would be valued on the Spanish third person subject pronoun, as suggested by the SU–V agreement version of the analogical criterion.

3. Will the need to value the person agreement features be reflected in a difference between Spanish third person pronouns versus Spanish first and second person pronouns? [examples 15a and 15b versus 15c].

Hypothesis #3. Spanish third person sequences will be different from Spanish first and second person ones if the presence of English -s leads to the assignment of the corresponding uninterpretable feature to the English verb so that the double feature valuation mechanism would take place.

4. Will the need to value the person features be reflected in a difference between English third person pronouns versus English first and second person pronouns? [examples 16a and 16b versus 16c].

Hypothesis #4. English third person sequences will be different from English first and second person ones if, even though no feature valuation applies in either case, the absence of this mechanism correlates with a sequence where the person agreement feature cannot be valued but does not have a morphological realization (Spanish third person verb) rather than with a sequence where this feature cannot be valued but does have a morphological realization (Spanish first and second person verb).

4.   Methodology

4.1   Participants

In order to address the research questions on English–Spanish SU–V switches above, we have tested two groups of bilingual children and one group of bilingual adults:

Table 1. Participants

| Group | Languages | | Mean age | Age range | # Participants |
	English	Spanish			
2L1	L1 (heritage)	L1	9,7	6–12	17
L2-children	L2 (immersion)	L1	10,9	10–13	18
L2-adults	L2	L1		20–30	27

The child participants were a group of L1 Spanish–L1 English heritage bilingual children living in Spain and a group of L1 Spanish–L2 English bilingual children studying English at an immersion school in Spain. The adult group consisted of L1 Spanish–L2 English bilinguals studying English at a Spanish university. None of the three groups are immersed in a code-switching community since in all three cases the language spoken in the community is only Spanish. In the case of the heritage group, English is restricted to the family context.

4.2   Data elicitation

We designed an acceptability judgment task in which the participants have to read a short dialogue related to a picture, as in Figure 1, and then rate the answer to the question by means of emoticon faces:

Figure 1. Sample experimental item

While adults completed a written version of the acceptability judgment task, children did an oral version of the same task.

The acceptability judgment task includes 66 short dialogues like the one in Figure 1 out of which 24 contain the experimental items (SU–V agreement switches), 24 are distractors, 10 are fillers and 8 are practice items.

The experimental items are divided into four different structures, illustrated in (17): 6 English standard position pronominal subject + Spanish verb (2 cases per grammatical person); 6 Spanish standard position pronominal subject + English verb (2 cases per grammatical person); 6 English DP subject + Spanish verb; and 6 Spanish DP subject + English verb:

(17) a. *I* quiero este vestido   EN standard position pronouns
[I want this dress]

     b. *She* lee un libro
[She reads a book]

     c. *Tú* cook every day   SP standard position pronouns
[You cook every day]

     d. *Él* runs many kilometers
[He runs many kilometers]

     e. *The boy* bebe agua   EN DPs
[The boy drinks water]

     f. *The lady* toca el violín
[The lady plays the violin]

     g. *El niño* paints landscapes   SP DPs
[The boy pains landscapes]

     h. *La señora* hugs her sister
[The lady hugs her sister]

Practice items include code-switches at different grammatical points, as in (18):

(18) a. *La jirafa está* near the trees   copula verb + PP
[The giraffe is near the trees]

     b. *Esto es un* fish*ito*   word-internal mixing
[This is a little fish; fish + Spanish diminutive -*ito*]

Fillers are deverbal compounds in English and Spanish, some of which are possible and some non-possible, as in (19):[2]

---

2. A reviewer wonders whether the incorporation of non-switched fillers could pose a methodological problem in that the non-switched structures could yield different results. In this respect, we would like to argue that there seems to be a consensus in that fillers, as opposed to distractors (which are also part of our study), involve a totally different structure from the one being tested. We chose as fillers non-switched deverbal compounds because they are an obvious and clear-cut different structure. As for results, possible compounds were rated

(19) a. Es un salvavidas
          [It's a lifesaver]

      b. *He is a fighter fire

Distractors are code-switched copulative structures (DP subject + adjectival predicate), as the ones in (20):

(20) a. *La mesa* is nice
          [The table is nice]

      b. *The table* es bonita
          [The table is nice]

5. Results

5.1 Child participants

The results obtained from the two groups of bilingual children appear in Figures 2 to 5.
In the case of the group of 2L1 (heritage) children, their preferences with regards to the
categorial nature of the subject appear in Figure 2:

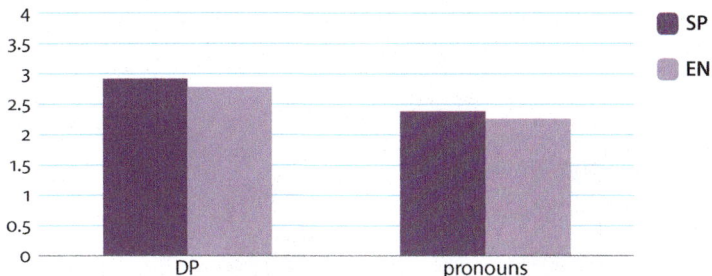

Figure 2. 2L1 children: DP versus pronoun SU–V switches

Participants prefer DP–V switches over pronoun–V switches in both Spanish
and English. The statistical analysis (ANOVA) shows that there is no main effect for

---

significantly higher than non-possible ones for both languages and, of course, the results were
more categorical than the ones obtained for code-switched sentences. This has always been
the case with grammaticality judgments involving code-switching because it is obvious that
prescriptive knowledge plays a role in experimental code-switching. However, what we have
systematically argued (e.g., Liceras et al. 2008) is that it is not the degree of categorical judgment that is obtained but the significant difference between expected versus non-expected
code-switches that is important.

language (F(1,10) = .411, *p* = .536) but there is a main effect for subject type (F(1,10) = 9.965, *p* = .010).

When comparing first and second person subject pronouns versus third person ones (Figure 3), 2L1 children show a preference for third person pronouns over first and second person ones in Spanish, although the differences do not reach significance (F(1,10) = 4.26, *p* = .062). No main effect for language appears (F(1,10) = .958, *p* = .873):

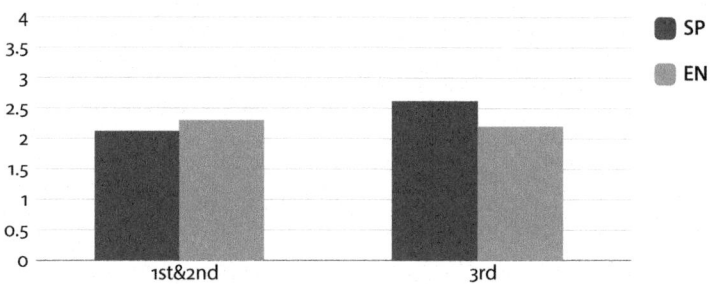

Figure 3. 2L1 children: 1st–2nd p. versus 3rd p. pronoun SU–V switches

The results corresponding to the L2 children are similar to the 2L1's with respect to the categorial nature of the subject, as shown in Figure 4:

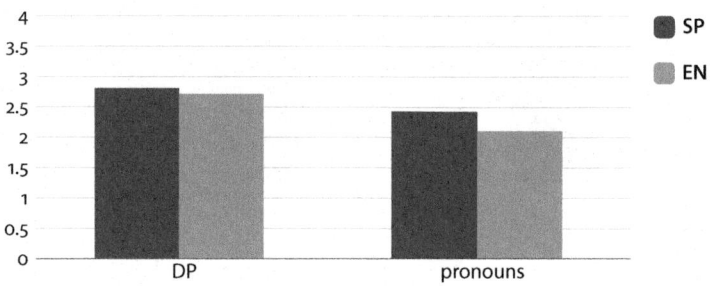

Figure 4. L2 children: DP versus pronoun SU–V switches

Participants prefer DP–V switches over pronoun–V switches in both Spanish and English. And although there is no main effect for language (F(1,17) = 3.746, *p* = .070), there is a main effect for subject type (F(1,17) = 52.626, *p* < .001).

In the case of the grammatical person in the pronoun switches L2 children prefer 3rd person Spanish pronouns over the other conditions, while in the case of English pronouns no difference between the three grammatical persons appears, as shown in (Figure 5):

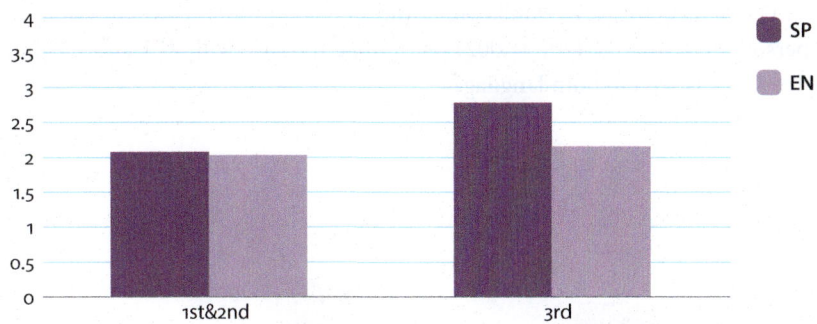

Figure 5. L2 children: 1st–2nd p. versus 3rd p. pronoun SU–V switches

The statistical analysis on the data in Figure 5 shows a main effect for language (F(1,17) = 9.736, p=.006) and a main effect for person (F(1,17) = 19.157, p<.001), attributed both to the overall preference for Spanish third person pronouns in these S–V switches.

These results point to the different status of DPs and pronouns in SU–V switches for both groups of children as well as to a preference for Spanish third person pronominal subject–V sequences. No significant differences are found between the two groups (2L1 and L2) in any condition.

5.2   Adult participants

The data from the group of L2 adult participants are displayed in Figures 6 and 7. As in the case of both groups of children, L2 adults prefer DP–V switches over pronoun–V switches in both Spanish and English (Figure 6), and again there is no main effect for language (F(1,26) = 0.573, p = .456) and a main effect for subject type appears (F(1,26) = 44.670, p < .001):

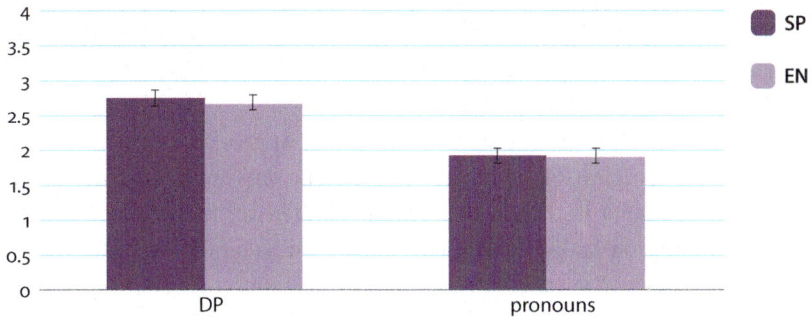

Figure 6. L2 adults: DP versus pronoun SU–V switches

As for person (Figure 7), L2 adults prefer third person pronoun switches (main effect for person: F(1,26) = 12.470, p=.002) but, unlike the case with 2L1 and L2 children, this tendency is seen in both languages:

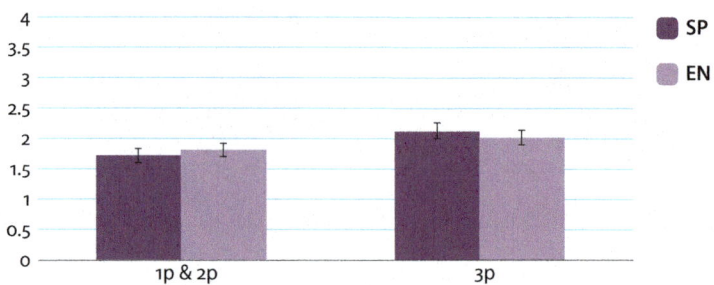

Figure 7. L2 adults: 1st–2nd p. versus 3rd p. pronoun SU–V switches

The adult participants behave like the two groups of child participants when comparing languages since they also favor Spanish third person pronouns (main effect for language: F(1,26) = 0.026, p=.873).

6.   Discussion

The results we have presented above allow us to address our initial research questions and hypotheses as follows.

With regard to our hypothesis #1, acceptability data from the three groups of participants reflect a preference for DP+V sequences over pronoun+V ones. In line with van Gelderen and MacSwan (2008), MacSwan (2009), and MacSwan and Colina (2014), this could be attributed to the lack of a PF Interface Condition violation in the case of switches involving DPs (Examples 4 and 5 above). This preference is seen in both English and Spanish so the status of the standard position pronouns in both languages seems to be perceived as similar by these bilingual speakers, as argued by Koronkiewicz (2012).

Hypothesis #2 addresses the status of third person pronoun switches in Spanish versus English (examples 15c versus 16c above). The data from the three groups of speakers analyzed point in the same direction: a preference for Spanish third person standard position pronoun switches versus English ones (significant in the case of the two groups of English L2 speakers). This points to the importance of the double feature checking mechanism, in the case of the Spanish dominant bilinguals, which parallels Liceras et al.'s (2008) findings with respect to the analogical criterion in concord structures.

This preference for the analogical criterion in agreement structures also shows in the different perception of the three grammatical persons that reflect a different perception of the valuation mechanisms present in each case. Namely, there is a difference between Spanish first and second person pronoun switches and third person ones (hypothesis #3). As for Spanish third person pronoun switches, the agreement version of the analogical criterion seem to hold for the three groups of speakers (both L2 speakers and 2L1 children) and with more strength in the L2 groups: L1 Spanish speakers assign an uninterpretable person agreement feature ($[u\Phi]$) to the English verb (relying on the -*s* affix) and value it on the Spanish third person interpretable counterpart ($[\Phi]$) in the Spanish pronoun (example 15c above).

The difference between English first and second person pronoun switches and third person ones (hypothesis #4) receives no confirmation in the results we have obtained since no distinction among the three grammatical persons appears. That is, a sequence where the person agreement feature cannot be valued but does not have a morphological realization (third person Spanish verb forms) is not preferred over a sequence where the person agreement feature cannot be valued but has a morphological realization (first and second person Spanish verb forms). In other words, in the case of English third person pronoun switches (example 16c above), neither the 2L1 nor the L2 speakers prefer the Spanish verb form that has no morphological marker (i.e., in the third person) and, consequently, does not require the implementation of the double feature checking mechanism.

Thus, following Liceras et al. (2008), we argue that, as it is the case with concord structures, with third person standard position pronouns, Pesetsky and Torrego's (2001, 2007) double feature valuation hypothesis leads Spanish dominant bilinguals' intuitions when judging code-switching structures.

7.   Conclusions

In this study we have used code-switching as a window to investigate how language is represented in the mind of the bilingual. We propose a formal account (i.e., the analogical criterion applied to agreement structures) as a framework to capture native speakers' intuitions independently of frequency of production. The acceptability judgment data indicate that the PF Interface Condition is clearly rooted in the mind of the bilingual. The data also show that bilinguals (more specifically Spanish dominant bilinguals) can 'relax' the requirements of the PF Interface Condition to value person agreement features (as it is the case with the analogical criterion in concord structures).

Our study has focused on two main issues regarding English–Spanish SU–V switches. With respect to subject type, SU–V switches involving DPs are perceived differently from standard position pronouns and are highly preferred over switches involving pronouns (as in van Gelderen & MacSwan 2008). Regarding pronoun type, the need to value formal features (Liceras et al. 2008) in SU–V switches makes Spanish–English bilinguals favor Spanish third person pronoun sequences. In this case, our findings point to a relaxation of the PF Interface Condition requirement in order to value person agreement features, that is, in order to implement the agreement version of the analogical criterion.

Even though subject pronoun–V switches may seldom occur in spontaneous production, we interpret these results as evidence that spontaneous production and experimental data elicited via acceptability judgments are not at odds but rather tap different cognitive abilities (contra Valdés Kroff et al. 2011). Valdés-Kroff et al.'s (2011) work is concerned with the auditory processing of gender in English–Spanish code-switched DPs by examining and comparing production (i.e., naturalistic) and comprehension data elicited via the eye-tracking methodology. They tested a group of code-switchers in the US and a group of non-code-switchers in Spain (although it is not clear whether these are L2 English speakers or English heritage speakers). In the US group, a preference for masculine as a default option appears and this is not seen in the Spanish group. They conclude that the gender of the article in code-switched DPs is processed differently by each group of participants and that only in the case of the US group, who are the ones exposed to the pattern attested in production data, comprehension data reflected the asymmetry found in production (i.e., that feminine gender is more restricted). This leads them to propose that in order to investigate code-switching, individuals who code-switch need to be investigated. In this respect, our acceptability judgment experiment accurately depicts how both the PF Interface Condition and the need to value formal features are rooted in the mind of the Spanish dominant English–Spanish bilinguals. However, the differences between balanced and non-balanced bilinguals (2L1 versus L1 Spanish–L2 English) point to the need to gather experimental data from code-switching communities to further explore how language is represented in the mind of these groups of bilinguals. What we would like to argue is that, as it is the case in the analysis of non-code-switched language, the analysis of data elicited via different techniques (e.g., naturalistic versus experimental, on-line versus off-line) as well as data gathered from different participant profiles (e.g., L2 versus L1, code-switchers versus non-code-switchers) could only but contribute to complete the picture (Gullberg, Indefrey and Muysken 2009). For instance, and concerning acceptability judgment data, results from formal and informal judgment collection methods (Sprouse, Schütze and Almeida 2013) have been shown to converge. However, it has also been shown that production and comprehension data may not converge (Jakubowicz et al. 1998; Jakubowicz and Roulet 2004, 2008).

References

Alexiadou, Artemis, and Elena Anagnostopoulou. 1998. "Parametrizing AGR: Word Order, V-movement and EPP-checking." *Natural Language and Linguistic Theory* 16. 491–539. DOI: 10.1023/A:1006090432389

Cardinaletti, Anna, and Michal Starke. 1999. "The Typology of Structural Deficiency: A Case Study of the Three Grammatical Classes." In *Clitics in the Languages of Europe*, ed. by H. van Riemsdijk, 145–233. Mouton de Gruyter.

Franceschina, Florencia. 2001. "Morphological or Syntactic Deficits in Near-native Speakers? An Assessment of Some Current Proposals." *Second Language Research* 17(3): 213–247. DOI: 10.1191/026765801680191497

Gullberg, Marianne, Peter Indefrey, and Pieter Muysken. 2009. "Research Techniques for the Study of Code-switching." In *The Cambridge Handbook of Linguistic Code-switching*, ed. by Barbara E. Bullock, and Almeida Jacqueline Toribio, 21–39. Cambridge University Press. DOI: 10.1017/CBO9780511576331.003

Gumperz, John J. 1976. "The Sociolinguistic Significance of Conversational Code-switching." *Papers on Language and Context: Working Papers* 46: 1–46.

Harris, James W. 1991. "The Exponence of Gender in Spanish." *Linguistic Inquiry* 22 (1): 27–62.

Jake, Janice L. 1994. "Intrasentential Code-switching and Pronouns: On the Cateogorial Status of Functional Elements." *Linguistics* 32: 271–298. DOI: 10.1515/ling.1994.32.2.271

Jakubowicz, Celia, and Leslie Roulet. 2004. "Do French-speaking Children with SLI Present a Selective Deficit on Tense?" In *Proceedings of the* 28th *Annual Boston Conference on Language Development*, ed. by Alejna Brugos, Linnea Micciulla, and Christine E. Smith, 256–266. Cascadilla Press.

Jakubowicz, Celia, and Leslie Roulet. 2008. "Narrow Syntax or Interface Deficit? Gender Agreement in French SLI." In *First language acquisition of morphology and syntax*, ed. by Pedro Guijarro-Fuentes, María Pilar Larrañaga, and John Clibbens. John Benjamins. DOI: 10.1075/lald.45

Jakubowicz, Celia, Lea Nash, Catherine Rigaut, and Christophe-Loic Gerard. 1998. "Determiners and Clitic Pronouns in French-speaking Children with SLI." *Language Acquisition* 7 (2–4): 113–160. DOI: 10.1207/s15327817la0702-4_3

Kato, Mary Aizawa. 1999. "Strong and Weak Pronominals and the Null Subject Parameter." *Probus* 11 (1): 1–38. DOI: 10.1515/prbs.1999.11.1.1

Koronkiewicz, Bryan. 2012. "Me, Myself y Yo: Pronoun Theories and Code-switching." Paper presented at the UIC Bilingualism Forum, Chicago, USA, October 2012.

Liceras, Juana M., Cristina Martinez, Rocío Perez-Tattam, Susana Perales, and R. Fernández Fuertes. 2006. "L2 Acquisition as a Process of Creolization: Insights from Child and Adult Code-mixing." In *L2 Acquisition and Creole Genesis*, ed. by Claire Lefebvre, Lydia White, and Christine Jourdan, 113–144. John Benjamins. DOI: 10.1075/lald.42.08lic

Liceras, Juana M., Raquel Fernández Fuertes, and Anahí Alba de la Fuente. 2012. "Overt Subjects and Copula Omission in the Spanish and the English Grammar of English–Spanish Bilinguals: On the Locus and Directionality of Interlinguistic Influence." *First Language* 32 (1–2): 88–115. DOI: 10.1177/0142723711403980

Liceras, Juana M., Raquel Fernández Fuertes, Susana Perales, Rocío Pérez-Tattam, and Kenton Todd Spradlin. 2008. "Gender and Gender Agreement in Bilingual Native and Non-native Grammars: A View from Child and Adult Functional-lexical Mixings." *Lingua* 118: 827–851. DOI: 10.1016/j.lingua.2007.05.006

Lipski, John. 1978. "Code-switching and the Problem of Bilingual Competence." In *Aspects of Bilingualism*, ed. by Michel Paradis. Hornbeam Press.

MacSwan, Jeff and Sonia Colina. 2014. "Some Consequences of Language Design: Codeswitching at the PF Interface." In *Grammatical theory and bilingual codeswitching*, ed. by Jeff MacSwan. MIT Press.

MacSwan, Jeff. 1999. *A Minimalist Approach to Intrasentential Code Switching*. Garland.

MacSwan, Jeff. 2000. "The Architecture of the Bilingual Language Faculty: Evidence from Intrasentential Code Switching". *Bilingualism: Language and Cognition* 3 (1): 37–54. DOI: 10.1017/S1366728900000122

MacSwan, Jeff. 2005. "Code-switching and Generative Grammar: A Critique of the MLF Model and Some Remarks on 'Modified Minimalism.'" *Bilingualism: Language and Cognition* 8 (1): 1–22. DOI: 10.1017/S1366728904002068

MacSwan, Jeff. 2009. "Generative Approaches to Codeswitching." In *The Cambridge Handbook of Linguistic Code-switching*, ed. by Barbara E. Bullock, and Almeida Jacqueline Toribio, 309–335. Cambridge University Press. DOI: 10.1017/CBO9780511576331.019

Pesetsky, David, and Esther Torrego. 2001. "T-to-C Movement: Causes and Consequences." In *Ken Hale: a life in language*, ed. by Micheal Kenstowicz, 355–426. MIT Press.

Pesetsky, David, and Esther Torrego. 2007. "The Syntax of Valuation and the Interpretability of Features." In *Phrasal and clausal architecture: syntactic derivation and interpretation*, ed. by Simin Karimi, Vida Samiian, and Wendy K. Wilkins, 262–294. John Benjamins. DOI: 10.1075/la.101.14pes

Roca, Iggy M. 1989. "The Organisation of Grammatical Gender." *Transactions of the Philological Society* 87: 1–32. DOI: 10.1111/j.1467-968X.1989.tb00617.x

Sprouse, Jon, Carson T. Schütze, and Diogo Almeida. 2013. "A Comparison of Informal and Formal Acceptability Judgments Using a Random Sample from Linguistic Inquiry 2001–2010." *Lingua* 134: 219–248. DOI: 10.1016/j.lingua.2013.07.002

Timm, Lenora A. 1975. "Spanish–English Code-switching: El porqué and How-not-to." *Romance Philology* 28: 473–482.

Valdés Kroff, Jorge, Paola Dussias, Chip Gerfen, Rosa Guzzardo Tamargo, Jason Gullifer, and Donna Coffman. 2011. "Using Experimental Methods to Investigate Spanish–English Code-switching: Eye-tracking as a Window into On-line Comprehension." Paper presented at the LSRL 41, Ottawa, Canada, May 2011.

van Gelderen, Elly, and Jeff MacSwan. 2008. "Interface Conditions and Code-switching: Pronouns, Lexical DPs, and Checking Theory." *Lingua* 118: 765–776. DOI: 10.1016/j.lingua.2007.05.003

White, Lydia, Elena Valenzuela, Martyna Kozlowska-MacGregor, and Yan-Kit Ingrid Leung. 2004. "Gender and Number Agreement in Nonnative Spanish." *Applied Psycholinguistics* 25 (1): 105–133. DOI: 10.1017/S0142716404001067

Epistemic adverbs, the prosody-syntax interface, and the theory of phases

Alessandra Giorgi

Dept. of Linguistics, Ca' Bembo

Epistemic adverbs in Italian (e.g., *probabilmente* 'probably') can appear in several positions. Cinque (1999) proposed that they always occupy the same position above IP and that the various orders are derived via movement of the other phrases around them. In this paper I consider contrasts between sentences where these adverbs are associated with a "normal intonation" and those where they are associated with a parenthetical (comma) intonation. To provide an account for the distribution of parenthetical adverbs, I appeal to Giorgi (2011, to appear). I consider parentheticals as syntactically *integrated* structures, rejecting adjunction and adopting the cartographic approach, based on Kayne's (1994) Linear Correspondence Axiom. As for the non-parenthetical occurrences, I propose that there are two basic positions for these adverbs, one for each phase: above v*P and above IP (Cinque's position). The existence of a low left periphery above v*P agrees has also been recently hypothesized for other phenomena in Old (Poletto, 2006 and to appear) and Modern Italian (Belletti, 2004).

1. Introduction

The existence of several possible positions for adverbs in a sentence is a long-standing issue in syntax. In some cases, the same adverb can occupy different positions without causing significant changes in the meaning. On other occasions, on the contrary, different positions give rise to different interpretations. Consider for instance the following Italian sentences:

(1) *Probabilmente Gianni vincerà la gara.*
     'Probably Gianni will win the race.'

(2) *Gianni probabilmente vincerà la gara.*
     'Gianni probably will win the race.'

DOI 10.1075/rllt.9.06gio

In these cases, *probabilmente* 'probably' can appear either before or after the subject without (significant) differences in the interpretation. In particular, in both cases the adverb has sentential scope. Consider however the following case:[1]

(3)   *Gianni ha mangiato probabilmente la torta.*
      'Gianni ate probably the cake.'

In example (3) the adverb only has local scope over the DP and cannot have sentential scope, meaning that Gianni ate something, which is *probably a cake*. Hence, in this case the location of the adverb in the sentence makes a difference with respect to the interpretation. Moreover, as I will better exemplify below, the kind of intonation associated to the adverb also affects the linear order and the interpretation of the adverb in the sentence.

Cinque (1999) proposed that the basic position of adverbs, when associated with the "normal" intonation, is unique and that the different orders are due to movement of other phrases around them. This solution had a big heuristic impact and proved greatly successful, in that it was shown to be theoretically and empirically adequate for a large set of data in many languages. However, in the light of more recent hypotheses about the structure of clauses and the properties of the interfaces, it can now be revisited to account for more fine-grained phenomena, taking into account prosodic properties as well.

The goal of this work is twofold: on one hand the empirical coverage of the theory of adverbs and clausal structure will be broadened, including an integrated view of parentheticals. On the other, it will provide an argument in favor of the existence of a low left periphery, above v*P, according to recent proposal of several scholars, among the others Poletto (2006 to appear).

I analyze here the distribution and properties of epistemic adverbs in Italian, when obtaining sentential scope, contrasting the "flat" with the "parenthetical" intonation, with and without negation. The conclusions might be generalized also to the other kinds of high sentential adverbs, such as evidentials—*allegedly*—and evaluatives—*fortunately*—and to other languages as well.[2]

This paper is organized as follows: In the second section I present the data, contrasting the *flat*—normal—intonation with the parenthetical one. In the third section I discuss a proposal for parenthetical adverbs, showing how that it can be independently

---

1.   For a discussion of this and similar cases, see also Tescari Neto (2013).

2.   As far as the cartographic approach is correct, the syntactic ordering of adverbs is universal, hence cross-linguistic differences are in principle not expected and the results achieved here might hold for other languages as well. However, there might be sources of variation not considered so far. In this paper, I will consider only Italian data and further cross-linguistic study would be required.

motivated on the basis of completely unrelated evidence. In the fourth, I consider the distribution of the adverbs with the non-parenthetical intonation and propose the existence of a second basic position, above the lower phase, v*P.

2.   Some data

2.1   The general hypothesis

In this section, I sketch a general outlining for an account of the parenthetical reading of IP adverbs, arguing in favor of an integrated view of parentheticals.

In order to account for the data in Section 4, I resort to the theory of phases, as discussed in Chomsky (2000, 2002). According to this theoretical framework, it is possible to identify two phases: CP and v*P. Interestingly, both projections have the property of being *propositional* (Chomsky 2000). Epistemic adverbs, together with evidential (*allegedly*) and evaluative (*fortunately*) ones, can be defined as *propositional adverbs* in that, by means of their presence, the speaker—or the superordinate subject for embedded contexts—qualifies the whole subsequent domain. I argue therefore that there are two basic positions for this kind of adverbs, one for each phase: one above v*P and a second above IP, in the domain of the C-layer, i.e., Cinque's position. In other words, I argue in favor of the existence of a *low* left-periphery.

This hypothesis accounts for some phenomena concerning the scope of negation and for the different properties found when these adverbs are used parenthetically. A very similar theoretical proposal has been independently argued for by Poletto (2006, to appear) in her account of word order phenomena in Old Italian.

2.2   The data

Let's consider now some relevant data. As noted by Cinque (1999), when giving a judgment, the native speaker must pay close attention to the kind of intonation associated with the adverb, because a slight change might be enough to considerably modify the distributional pattern of the adverb. The first example, concerns the distribution of the epistemic adverb *probabilmente* 'probably', when associated with the *flat* intonation in a simple transitive sentence:

(4)   *(probabilmente1) Gianni (probabilmente2) ha (probabilmente3) mangiato (probabilmente4 DP-scope only) la torta (*probabilmente5)*
(probably1) Gianni (probably2) has (probably3) eaten (probably4) the cake (probably5)

For simplicity, I associate here every position with a progressive number. The position of *probabilmente5* is ruled out, as discussed in Cinque (1999) and the one of *probabilmente4* has only local scope on *la torta* (the cake), as pointed out above.[3] Hence, in this case, the rightmost position available for *probabilmente*, retaining sentential scope, is *probabilmente3*, i.e., the one on the left of the participle.

Consider now what happens when the adverb is associated with the so-called *comma intonation*:[4]

(5)   *(probabilmente1,) Gianni (,probabilmente2,) ha (,probabilmente3,) mangiato (,probabilmente4,) la torta (,probabilmente5).*
      '(probably1,) Gianni (,probably2,) has (,probably3,) eaten (,probably4,) the cake (,probably5).'

In this case, all occurrences of the adverb are fully acceptable. Interestingly, *probabilmente* with the *comma intonation* always has sentential scope and cannot be forced in a local scope construction. In other words, the occurrence of *probabilmente4* can never have scope only on *la torta* (the cake).

At first sight, then, it seems that there are some constraints on the position of the adverb with the flat intonation, whereas none can be found with respect to the parenthetical, with the exception of the lack of local scope.

Consider now the following examples, contrasting the flat intonation—example (6)—and the comma one—example (7)—in sentences with sentential negation:

(6)   *(probabilmente1) Gianni (probabilmente2) non ha (#probabilmente3) mangiato (#probabilmente4) la torta (probabilmente5).*
      '(probably1) Gianni (probably2) NEG has (probably3) eaten (probably4) the cake (probably5).'

The meaning of the sentence with the adverb in position 1 or 2 is, as expected, the following: *what is probable is Gianni NOT eating the cake*, hence *probabilmente* has scope over negation. The interesting issue concerns the sentence with *probabilmente* in position 3. In this case the sentence is judged uninterpretable.[5] *Probabilmente4* is in general ruled out, even if some speakers seem able to assign it the NEG>prob reading, with local scope of the adverb over *the cake*. When the adverb occupies position 5, sentential negation is impossible, even if it can, marginally, i.e., not for all speakers,

---

3.   See however Tescari Neto (2013) for somewhat different judgments in Brazilian Portuguese.

4.   The *comma intonation* is the typical intonation usually associated with parentheticals and has been extensively studied by many scholars. In this paper, I do not have anything to add to the phonological theory concerning these phenomena and refer the reader to the literature on the topic. Among the very many others, see for instance Selkirk (2005).

5.   Speakers have a characteristic reaction: they first say that the example is more or less ok— i.e., anyway degraded with respect to positions 1 and 2, but not *ungrammatical*. When asked about its meaning they cannot tell, and say that the sentence is odd, or that it means nothing.

focus the adverb. Hence, 1 and 2 are the only positions truly compatible with sentential negation.[6]

Consider now the example with the parenthetical intonation:

(7) *(probabilmente1,) Gianni (,probabilmente2,) non ha (,probabilmente3,) mangiato (,probabilmente4,) la torta (,probabilmente5).*
'(probably1,) Gianni (,probably2,) NEG has (,probably3,) eaten (,probably4,) the cake (,probably5).'

All occurrences of the adverb are grammatical and they share the same interpretation: *probabilmente* has scope over negation and can never have a local scope.

Concluding this section, there is a contrast between examples (4) and (5), and examples (6) and (7) i.e., *probabilmente* with and without the comma intonation, in particular with respect to the occurrences in *probabilmente4* and *probabilmente5*, which are fully acceptable when parenthetical.

There is a contrast between examples (4) and (6) with respect to the scope of negation, in particular with respect to the non-availability of the position 3 in the sentence with negation.

In the following section, I consider the issue concerning the association of the adverb with the comma intonation.

3. Towards a syntax of the comma intonation

3.1 A proposal for parentheticals

As illustrated in the preceding section, the comma intonation makes all occurrences possible, with or without negation.

According to the analysis developed in Giorgi (2011, to appear), these parentheticals—together with several other types of parentheticals—are syntactically integrated and are generated in a position on the left of CP, in a layer called KommaP (KP), where the head K is the feature +comma, hypothesized among the others by Selkirk (2005). In what follows I will briefly summarize this points.[7]

---

6. I interviewed about 30 speakers. Most of them—about two thirds—are students of linguistics, some of them linguists, and some non-expert native speakers. Judgments were in general quite consistent and uniform.

7. I will not attempt to discuss here the complex characterization of the comma intonation, and I refer the reader to the existing literature, for instance the discussion in Dehé (2007 and 2009) and Döring (2007). Recall also that there is a huge and very interesting literature on parentheticals, which I will not be able to consider in this work. The issue is also especially interesting, because it is highly interdisciplinary, including considerations that go from syntax,

According to Selkirk (2005) a [+comma] feature is responsible for the *comma intonation* in a variety of structures: *as*-clauses, non-restrictive relatives, nominal appositives, etc. *Comma Phrases* are then mapped into *Intonational Phrases*. Selkirk mostly analyzes *as*-parentheticals, assuming for them the syntactic structure proposed by Potts (2005). Consider for instance the following example:

(8)   John, *as everybody knows*, likes to go to parties

As everybody knows, according to Selkirk, is a Comma Phrase, to be mapped into an Intonational Phrase.

From the syntactic point of view, supplements have been analyzed as syntactic units that are to some degree independent from the surrounding sentence. For some important properties, parentheticals can be legitimately analyzed as independent form their host. Consider for instance the following examples:[8]

(9)   She may have her parents with her, in which case where am I going to sleep?
          (from Huddleston and Pullum 2002; example quoted in Cinque 2007):

(10)   My friend, who God forbid you should ever meet,…
          (from Andrews 1975; example quoted in Cinque 2007)

(11)   The Romans, who arrived before one hundred AD, found a land of wooded hills
          (from Selkirk, 2005, ex. 5)

(12)   The Romans who arrived before one hundred AD found a land of wooded hills
          (from Selkirk, 2005, ex. 6)

Examples (9) and (10), as discussed in the cited references, show that parentheticals can be illocutionarily independent from their hosts—one being an interrogative embedded in an assertion, and the other being an exclamative—whereas this is never permitted in a subordination relation. Example (11) shows that the parenthetical might be false, while the sentence remains true. In this example an appositive, parenthetical, relative clause appears, contrasting with example (12), with a restrictive one. In the latter case, there must be a unique truth-value for the whole sentence.

On the other hand, in many cases the parenthetical seems deeply connected to their host, to the extent that several scholars have hypothesized a movement relation, for instance in Ross' (1973) *slifting* analysis, or in Emonds' (1973) hypothesis.[9]

---

to semantics and phonology. In the literature, the parenthetical is often called the *supplement*, and the sentence in which it is inserted is termed the *host*.

8.   For further details, cf. the discussion in Giorgi (to appear).

9.   In the same vein, for a different sort of parenthetical constructions, see also Reinhart (1983). For reasons of space, it is impossible to summarize here the relevant arguments

Two main accounts have been proposed in the literature so far: parentheticals are totally external to the syntactic structure of their host, as a sort of three-dimensional tree (cf. among the others Haegeman, 1991; Espinal 1991; Burton-Roberts 2006), or supplements are syntactically integrated and are adjoined to the host, for instance right-adjoined as in Potts (2002, 2005).

However, both views are problematic with respect to a linearization algorithm. The linearization issue concerning three-dimensional trees is self-apparent: such an algorithm would be extremely powerful and therefore not desirable. The right adjunction view, proposed for instance by Potts, is also to be rejected under the cartographic approach. Kayne (1994) excludes the possibility of an adjoined structure on the basis of the Linear Correspondence Axiom, according to which linear precedence reflects asymmetric c-command. This principle is the basic notion of the whole cartographic framework and in particular of Cinque's (1999, and subsequent works) syntactic analysis of the position of adverbials.[10]

On the basis of this consideration, Giorgi (2011, to appear) proposes that there is no adjunction. *Comma* is not just a feature, but a head, K, which projects a constituent. The host is its complement, in a structural sense—and therefore, there is a certain degree of 'permeability' between the host and the parenthetical, for instance, c-command relations can be computed across the tree, cf. Dehé and Kavalova (2007), and references there—but, importantly, there is no *subordination* relation, due to the nature of the head K, which is *not* a complementizer.

In other words, this proposal consists in an integrated view of parentheticals, where the relevant syntactic heads are prosodic ones, i.e., prosodic features, present in the Numeration, along with the other bundles of features. This approach might have several consequences with respect to the nature of the prosody-syntax interface that will not investigated here, for reasons of space.

3.2 Free Indirect Discourse (FID) and Quotation

In previous work, I worked out a proposal for the parentheticals introducing Free Indirect Discourse and quotations, and I will briefly summarize that discussion here. Consider the following example, featuring a FID case:[11]

---

concerning the typology of parentheticals. I refer the reader to Dehé and Kavalova (2007) and references cited there.

10. It should also be remembered that Kayne's (1994) Linear Correspondence Axiom is amply motivated on the basis of very rich independent evidence, hence worth of being taken seriously, independently of the cartographic approach.

11. Many scholars addressed the issues of FID and Quotation. On the analysis of the introducing predicate, see in particular Banfield (1982) and Guéron (2007). On the analysis of

(13)   The new ration did not start till tomorrow and he had only four cigarettes
left, *thought Winston*   (adapted, Orwell, *1984*, ch. 5)

The postponed introducing predicate *thought Winston* is a parenthetical and has
the function, as discussed in Giorgi (2011, to appear) of resetting the speaker's
temporal and spatial coordinates in the left-most complementizer position in the
C-layer of the host.[12] According to the proposal I sketched above, the comma features project a K constituent. As a result, the KP is projected on the left of the left
periphery, and all the possible orders are derived from this basic structure, as illustrated in (3):[13]

(14) $[_{KP}$ K [*thought Winston* $[_{KP}$ K [$_{CP}$ ..]]]]

Followed by re-merging of the whole CP in KP:

(15) $[_{KP}$ [$_{CP}$ ..]$_i$ K [*thought Winston* $[_{KP}$ K CP_i]]]

Analogously, in the following case:

(16)   The new ration, *thought Winston*, did not start till tomorrow and he had
only four cigarettes left,   (adapted, Orwell, *1984*, ch. 5)

FID itself, see among the others Doron (1991), Schlenker (2004) and Sharvit (2004). See also
Collins and Braningan (1997) for an analysis of *quotative inversion* in these contexts. Though
important, I will not pursue this issue in this work.

12.   The discussion of this issue is not the main topic of this paper, and therefore will not be
addressed here. I dubbed the left-most complementizer C-Speaker and it roughly corresponds
to Rizzi's (1997) Force. However, Rizzi collapses both the indicative and subjunctive complementizer in Force, whereas it can be argued that they do not occupy exactly the same position.
For an extended discussion, see Giorgi (2010). Hence, C-speaker refers only to the highest,
indicative complementizer.

13.   Note that on her work, Selkirk (2005, §2) points out: "Root sentences and supplements
form a natural class, in that *they both are comma phrases* [italics mine], and so [...] set off
by Intonational Phrase edges from what surrounds them." See Dehé (2009) for further discussion. The structure and derivation I propose here comply with Selkirk's observation.
According to Selkirk there are two *comma features* in the representation, and in my proposal there are two heads K. Each of them can be realized as a pause, as for instance in the
following example:

i.   The new ration, *thought Winston*, did not start till tomorrow and he had only four
cigarettes left.

If the parenthetical is in initial or final position, there is obviously no *phonological pause*
preceding or following the parenthetical respectively, but the abstract head K is always present,
as in Selkirk's proposal.

Followed by remerging of only a portion of the embedded structure:

(17) $[_{KP}$ [The new ration]$_i$ K [*thought Winston* $[_{KP}$ K $[_{IP}$ ~~The new ration~~ did not...]]]

The following example is a case of quotation:

(18) I will leave tomorrow, *said John*

The derivation is the same as above. The structure in (19) is the base generated one:

(19) $[_{KP}$ K [*said John* $[_{KP}$ K $[_{CP}$ ..]]]]

Followed by remerging of the CP:

(20) $[_{KP}$ $[_{CP}$ ..] K [*said John* $[_{KP}$ K ~~CP~~]]]

Note finally that these parentheticals cannot be embedded:

(21) **Luigi disse che Gianni, pensò Maria, sarebbe partito domani.*
      'Luigi said that Gianni, thought Maria, would leave tomorrow.'

We will show that in this respect, parenthetical *francamente* 'frankly' is similar to the un-embeddable parentheticals *thought Winston* and *said John*, as opposed to parenthetical *probabilmente* 'probably', which on the contrary can be embedded.

3.3 *Parenthetical* probabilmente

In this section I extend the proposal illustrated above to parenthetical *probabilmente*. According to this view, the adverb occupies the Spec position of a K projection, as in the following structure:

(22) $[_{KP}$ K $[_{KP}$ *probabilmente* K [Gianni (non) ha mangiato la torta]]
      'Probably Gianni (NEG) has eaten the cake.'

All parenthetical occurrences are derived from this basic structure, by means of remerging of a constituent in a still higher position. For instance, in example (23), the spec of the higher K is occupied by the subject:[14]

(23) [$_{KP}$ Gianni K $[_{KP}$ *probabilmente* K [~~Gianni~~ (non) ha mangiato la torta]]]
      'Gianni, probably, (NEG) has eaten the cake.'

---

14. The remerging presumably concerns only the phonological features, KP being a phonological constituent. The process might have much in common with ellipsis, but how this idea can be precisely captured is a topic for future research.

In these cases, a K also appears at the left of the adverb, hosting the remerged part. Furthermore, the whole clause might be remerged, giving rise to the order with *probabilmente* in position 5:

(24)   [~KP~ Gianni (non) ha mangiato la torta K [*probabilmente* [~KP~ K [G̶i̶a̶n̶n̶i̶ ̶(̶n̶o̶n̶)̶ ̶h̶a̶ ̶m̶a̶n̶g̶i̶a̶t̶o̶ ̶l̶a̶ ̶t̶o̶r̶t̶a̶]]]

Note that a Clitic Left Dislocated (CLLD) phrase can appear on the left of the parenthetical adverb, as in the following case: [15]

(25)   *Gianni, probabilmente, lo hai visto ieri*
       'Gianni, probably, you him-saw yesterday.'

In example (25) the dislocated phrase could either be in the Spec of KP, or in the left periphery in a position higher than the one occupied by the parenthetical. In Giorgi (forthcoming) I argue that these two possibilities can both occur, on the basis of independent evidence concerning CLLD, which I will not discuss here for reasons of space.

Note that it is not possible—or at least only very marginal—for a contrastive focus to intervene between the adverb and the topic, as in example (26):[16]

(26)   ?*Gianni, MARIO, probabilmente, lo ha visto ieri (non Paolo)
       'Gianni, MARIO, probably, (he) him-saw yesterday (not Paolo).'
       (Mario-FOC probably saw Gianni-CLLD)

In example (26) the topic cannot occupy a position in the left periphery higher than the one of the contrastive focus. The order Topic>Focus is otherwise possible, as in the following case:[17]

(27)   *Gianni, MARIO, lo ha visto ieri (non Paolo)*
       'Gianni, MARIO, (he) him-saw yesterday (not Paolo).'
       (Mario-FOC saw Gianni-CLLD)

Finally, a focus can appear on the other side of the adverb, i.e., between the adverb and the rest of the sentence as in (28):

---

15.   Note that this proposal is compatible with the analyses of CLLD as purely phonological movement, along the line of the base-generated approach by Cinque (1990).

16.   The sentence with only the adverb and the Focus is very marginal with the parenthetical intonation and it is much easier to associate it with the flat, non parenthetical, one:

(i)   MARIO, probabilmente incontrerai domani (non Paolo)
      MARIO, probably you will meet tomorrow (not Paolo)

17.   On the impossibility of the ordering Focus>Topic (CLLD), see Benincà and Poletto (2004), who argue, contra Rizzi, that real dislocated items cannot appear on the left of Focus. I fully endorse their discussion and conclusions.

(28)   *Gianni, probabilmente, MARIO lo ha visto ieri (non Paolo)*
       'Gianni, probably, MARIO (he) him-saw yesterday (not Paolo).'
       (Mario-FOC probably saw Gianni-CLLD)

These observations point to the conclusion that parenthetical *probabilmente* appears in the left periphery, in a position higher than contrastive Focus.[18]

Note that, since the structure in (21) is the only source for all parenthetical orders, parenthetical *probabilmente* never appears in the scope of negation, nor can it have a non-sentential scope.

Finally, this proposal provides a natural account for the so-called *backtracking phenomena*, which under most account constitute a problem for linearization algorithms.

It often happens that when using a parenthetical, the speaker repeats the same fragment both on the right and on the left of the parenthesis, as in the following examples:

(29)   But a different role ⟨,⟩ uh because **when we get to the time of Ezra**, as with
       the more classical Wellhausen uh hypothesis, **when we get to the time
       of Ezra** we have the further narrowing of the office of priest (ICE-GB:
       s1b-001, #9)   (from Dehé and Kavalova, 2007, p. 3)

(30)   But **I believe that if** at this stage, and it isn't too late because it's only
       what six months since your brother died, **I believe that if** you can bear…
       (DCPSE: DL-D08, #135)   (From Kavalova, 2007, p.160)

The proposal sketched above can easily account for these facts, by simply assuming that in these cases both copies, the one in the Spec of KP and the one on the right of the parenthetical, are spelled out.[19]

---

18.   This conclusion is compatible with Benincà and Poletto's (2004) analysis; see fn. 17.

19.   In the cases where the adverb occupies the position 3 in examples (4) above, it looks like the sequence on the left of the parenthetical is a non-constituent:

   i.   *Gianni ha, probabilmente, mangiato la torta.*
        'John has, probably, eaten the cake.'

Constituency can however be recovered by hypothesizing the following derivation: first the VP *eaten the cake* is moved in the left periphery of the host in the spec of a head F, and then remnant movement of the whole clause in KP takes place, in a way analogous to example (23) above:

   ii.   [$_{KP}$ Probabilmente K [$_{IP}$ Gianni ha [$_{VP}$ mangiato la torta]]
         'Probably Gianni has eaten the cake.'

   iii. [$_{KP}$ Probabilmente K [$_{FP}$ mangiato la torta F [Gianni ha ~~mangiato la torta~~]]

   iv.   [$_{KP}$ Gianni ha K [$_{KP}$ probabilmente [$_{KP}$ K [mangiato la torta ~~Gianni ha~~]]

3.4   Embedded contexts

The distribution of *probabilmente* in embedded contexts does not significantly differ from the one in main clauses:

(31)   *Mario mi ha detto che (,probabilmente1,) Gianni (,probabilmente2,) ha (,probabilmente3,) mangiato (,probabilmente4,) la torta (,probabilmente5).*
        'Mario told me that (,probably1,) Gianni (,probably2,) has (,probably3,) eaten (,probably4,) the cake (,probably5).'

(32)   *Mario mi ha detto che (,probabilmente1,) Gianni (,probabilmente2,) non ha (,probabilmente3,) mangiato (,probabilmente4,) la torta (,probabilmente5).*
        'Mario told me that (,probably1,) Gianni (,probably2,) NEG has (,probably3,) eaten (,probably4,) the cake (,probably5).

In embedded contexts, the epistemic state concerns the superordinate subject and *probabilmente* has scope only on the embedded clause. The structure we can hypothesize in these cases is therefore the following one:

(33)   ...that $[_{KP}$ K [*probabilmente* $[_{KP}$ K $[_{IP}$...]]]]

In this case, the parenthetical appears on the right of the complementizer and takes the IP as its complement.

Probabilmente is not exceptional in this behavior, since other sentential parentheticals exhibit the same one. Consider for instance *as-clauses* (see Potts 2002):

(34)   Alan claimed that cryptography is a blast, as you mentioned

(Potts 2002, ex.42)

(35)   Alan claimed that, as you mentioned, cryptography is a blast

(Potts 2002, ex.43)

Interestingly, Potts points out that sentence (34) is ambiguous, whereas (35) is not. This property can be accounted for by hypothesizing the following two structures, according to the theory sketched above:

(36) $[_{KP}$ K [*as* you mentioned $[_{KP}$ K [Alan claimed that cryptography is a blast]]]]

For reasons of space, I cannot provide here a more detailed discussion on the nature of the landing site of the moved VP and, more generally, about the properties of the derivation sketched in (i)–(iv). I refer the reader on future work on the topic.

The issue concerning the precise derivation is also relevant for sentence (30). However, whatever the derivation, note that in a representation where no spec position on the left of the parenthetical is available, the sentences with backtracking could not be possible at all. Therefore, the hypothesis discussed here seems more adequate with respect to these cases.

(37)   Alan claimed that [$_{KP}$ K [*as* you mentioned [$_{KP}$ K [cryptography is
       a blast]]]]

The structure in (36) can undergo the following derivation:

(38)   [$_{KP}$ Alan claimed that cryptography is a blast K [*as* you mentioned [$_{KP}$ K
       [~~Alan claimed that cryptography is a blast~~]]]]

This way, one of the two possible interpretations of example (33) is obtained, i.e., the
one in which what has been mentioned is the whole sentence. The structure in (36)
can stay as it is, yielding therefore the non-ambiguous interpretation of (34), or can
undergo the following derivation:

(39)   Alan claimed that [$_{KP}$ cryptography is a blast K [*as* you mentioned [$_{KP}$ K
       [~~cryptography is a blast~~]]]]

In this case, the second interpretation of (33) is obtained, the one according to which
you mentioned only that *cryptography is a blast*.[20]

Now we can check whether non-embeddable parenthetical adverbs exist, corresponding to non-embeddable sentential parentheticals, such as the *introducing
predicates* discussed above. A candidate is constituted by the class of so-called *viewpoint*—or pragmatic—adverbs, such as *frankly*. These adverbs, according to Cinque
(1999), occupy a higher position, preceding evidential, evaluative and epistemic
ones:

(40)   *Francamente, probabilmente Gianni ha vinto la gara.*
       'Frankly probably Gianni won the race.'

(41)   **Probabilmente francamente Gianni ha vinto la gara.*
       'Probably frankly Gianni won the race.'

These adverbs cannot be embedded:

(42)   **Gianni spera che francamente Mario vinca la gara.*
       'Gianni hope that frankly Mario will win the race.'

Probabilmente could shift and refer to the embedded subject, as illustrate above. *Francamente* cannot do it and is simply ruled out when not appearing at root level. This
adverb, at least in Italian, is only a root one and, coherently with this distributional
property, semantically does not contribute the speakers'—or subject's—opinion on the
proposition, as *probabilmente* or *fortunatamente* do, but qualifies the relation between

---

20.   For a more detailed discussion, see Giorgi (to appear).

the speaker and her audience, meaning *I am speaking* frankly *to you*. Hence, it is always *external* to the propositional content.[21]

4.   Non-parenthetical probabilmente

4.1   An account

In this section, I will propose an account for the distribution of non-parenthetical *probabilmente*, in particular with respect to the distribution observed with negation. Example (4) in fact contrasts with example (6) in the availability of *probabilmente3*, which turns out to be odd with negation.

As I briefly suggested above, I will assume here Chomsky's Minimalist framework (Chomsky 2000, 2001), according to which there are two *Phases*: CP and v*P. I propose that both of them admit of a left periphery, and that, therefore, there are two basic positions for these kind of adverbs, one for each phase: one above v*P and a second above IP, in the domain of the C-layer, i.e., Cinque's position.[22]

A similar hypothesis has been proposed by Poletto (2006, to appear), who claims that phases are built in a uniform way and that they share the formal properties of their functional projections.[23] In particular, Poletto considers in this light Topic and Focus projections in Old Italian, but the theoretical claim can—and presumably must—be generalized to the other projections hosted in the left periphery as well.

Here, I suggest extending this view to epistemic, evaluative, and evidential adverbs, i.e., those adverbs that express the point of view of the speaker on the content of the clause. As I said above, I maintain that *francamente* belongs to a different class, presumably always and only parenthetical. The hierarchy proposed by Cinque (1999) is the following:

(43)   …[evaluative [evidential [epistemic … IP

---

21.   We might wonder whether *francamente* is *always* parenthetical. In this sense, it is very similar to the predicates introducing FID and Quotations. Prosodically, it seems to be associated with a special contour, which cannot be integrated in the sentence, contrasting with the one of non-parenthetical *probabilmente*. Further interdisciplinary investigation is however required.

22.   A reviewer remarks that technically the phase is the CP, whereas the adverbs in question appear above IP and not above CP. However, the point relevant to this discussion is that the adverbs both in the case of the v*P and in the case of the IP, occupy a structural position on the left of the *external* (subject) argument, taking in their scope the propositional content. I thank the reviewer for this observation.

23.   See also Belletti (2004) and references cited there.

Moreoever, according to Zanuttini (1997), sentential negation is above T:[24]

(44)   AGR NEG T V

My proposal for epistemics—to be extended to the other left-peripheral adverbs—is therefore the following:

(45)   CP Epistemic1 IP NEG T Epistemic2 v*P

In the representation (45) the position of *Epistemic1* is above negation, whereas *Epistemic2* is below it, above the projections of v*.

According to this view, the properties of the non-parenthetical positions are accounted for as follows: positions 1 and 3 are the base-generated in the left periphery of the two phases. The ordering found with position 2—*Gianni probabilmente*—is derived (Cinque 1999) by means of movement of the subject to a higher position on the left of the adverb. Both positions are higher then sentential negation (Zanuttini 1997); hence in both cases *probabilmente* and *non* have sentential scope and *probabilmente* modifies the negated sentence. Position 3 is base-generated and is lower than negation. Therefore, when negation is not there, *probabilmente* retains sentential scope, but when NEG is realized a conflict arises: Negation has scope on *probabilmente*, due to its structural position, but *probabilmente* must have propositional scope, because the position right above v*P is a "propositional" position. On the other hand, negation is part of the propositional content, but *probabilmente* cannot have scope on it; hence a conflict arises. This state of things gives rise to the typical pattern of judgments described above. Simplifying, the sentence is perceived as grammatical, but not interpretable.

When occupying positions 4 and 5 *probabilmente* is in the scope of negation, but it is not generated in a "propositional" position; hence it can have only local scope, which in the case of position 5 is excluded. Therefore, there is no derivation available for them and these positions are available only with the parenthetical intonation.

4.2   Some exceptions

In certain cases, however, the adverb can appear in a position on the right of negation, without giving rise to ungrammaticality. The sentences in (46)—(49) below are in general judged better than those discussed in the previous section. The structures in question are copular sentences or sentences with the verb *have*, where *have* is not an aspectual auxiliary. I will not provide here a full discussion of these phenomena, but only give a few suggestions for further investigation.

---

24.   Here I will disregard the Agreement projection.

Consider for instance the following examples, both with epistemic and evaluative adverbs:[25]

(46)   (?)?*Gianni non è probabilmente stato felice a Parigi.*
       'Gianni NEG has probably been happy in Paris.'

(47)   (?)?*Gianni non ha probabilmente avuto occasione di telefonarle.*
       'Gianni NEG has probably had occasion to call her.'

(48)   (?)?*Gianni non è fortunatamente stato malato a Parigi.*
       'Gianni NEG has fortunately been sick in Paris.'

(49)   (?)?*Gianni non ha fortunatamente avuto occasione di telefonarle.*
       'Gianni NEG has fortunately had occasion to call her.'

In the examples above, the conflict arising from the simultaneous presence of the adverb and negation is much milder, even if not completely absent. Both *probabilmente/fortunatamente* and NEG can have sentential scope, even if for some speaker these sentences retain a significant degree of marginality. On the other hand, these examples are perfect when the adverb is associated to the comma intonation, as expected under to the analysis discussed above.

I follow here the proposal by Kayne (1993) according to which *have* doesn't differ from *be* and is obtained by means of incorporation of an empty P. Hence, *have* is identical to *be*, but for the incorporation of an abstract preposition. According to this view, (46)—(49) share the same syntax.

I suggest that in these cases the structure is impoverished with respect to the other cases, in that there is a small clause—a predicative structure—and not a complete verbal projection. The phasal nature of such a structure might differ with respect to v*P, permitting configurations not otherwise admitted. To account for the improved status of the sentences above, I propose therefore that in these cases only one position is available for IP adverbs, instead of two, and that is the higher one. According to this view, *probabilmente* and *fortunatamente* are generated in the IP position, as hypothesized by Cinque (1999), and consequently, they have sentential scope: the meaning of these sentences in fact, is that what is probable, or fortunate, is the *negative* eventuality. In the basic configuration, no conflict between the adverb and negation arises. The less than perfect status of these sentences might be due to the fact that linear order is reversed, negation preceding the adverb. The ordering in (46)–(49) is a derived one and is not perfectly natural for native speakers. The issue

---

25. Judgments vary. For some speakers the sentences are quite bad, for other ones they are considerably better than the ones discussed above. It seems to me that in any case, the issue is worth discussing.

concerning the phasal nature of predicative constructions is an important one, and deserves further attention.

5. Conclusions

In this paper I reviewed some phenomena concerning high IP adverbs, which according to Cinque (1999) are base generated in a position above the subject. Cinque (1999) already points out that the kind of intonation associated to these adverbs can affect their distribution. I considered here all the occurrences of these adverbs—when having sentential scope—in a simple transitive sentence, taking into account both the flat and the comma intonation. I proposed an account for the distribution of the adverb associated with the comma intonation, which is independently motivated by the analysis of other parenthetical structures. I also proposed an account for an unexpected contrast found with the non-parenthetical adverb in co-occurrence with negation. I proposed that there is an additional basic position available to these adverbs, above the v*P. This proposal agrees with recent results by Poletto (2006, to appear) and Belletti (2004), who investigated the properties of Focus and Topic and hypothesized the existence of a low left periphery. According to the view proposed here, such a low left periphery is not limited to dislocated phrases, but includes (sentential) adverbs as well.

References

Andrews, Avery Delano III. 1975. "Studies in the Syntax of Relative and Comparative Clauses." MIT Ph.D. Dissertation.

Burton-Roberts, Noel. 2006. "Parentheticals." In *Encyclopaedia of Language and Linguistics*, Vol. 9 (2nd edition), ed. by Keith Brown, 179–182. Amsterdam: Elsevier Science.
    DOI: 10.1016/B0-08-044854-2/02013-7

Banfield, Ann. 1982. *Unspeakable Sentences*. London: Routledge.

Belletti, Adriana. 2004. "Aspects of the Low IP Area." In *The Structure of CP and IP*, ed. by Luigi Rizzi, 16–51. New York: Oxford University Press.

Benincà, Paola, and Cecilia Poletto. 2004. "Topic, Focus and V2: Defining the CP Sublayers." In *The Structure of CP and IP*, ed. by Luigi Rizzi, 52–75. New York: Oxford University Press.

Cinque, Guglielmo. 1990. *Types of A-bar Dependencies*. LI Monograph. Cambridge MA: MIT Press.

Cinque, Guglielmo. 1999. *Adverbs and Functional Heads*. Oxford: Oxford University Press.

Chomsky, Noam. 2000. "Minimalist Inquiries: The Framework." In *Step by Step—Essays in Minimalist Syntax in Honor of Howard Lasnik*, ed. by Roger Martin, David Michaels, and Juan Uriagereka. Cambridge, MA: MIT Press.

Chomsky, Noam. 2002. Derivation by Phase. In *Ken Hale: A life in Language*, ed. by Michael Kenstowicz. Cambridge, MA: MIT Press.

Collins, Chris, and Paul Branigan. 1997. "Quotative Inversion." *Natural Language & Linguistic Theory* 15 (1): 1–41. DOI: 10.1023/A:1005722729974

Dehé, Nicole. 2007. "The Relation between Syntactic and Prosodic Parenthesis." In *Parentheticals*, ed. by Nicole Dehé, and Yordanka Kavalova, 261–284. Amsterdam/Philadelphia: John Benjamins. DOI: 10.1075/la.106.15deh

Dehé, Nicole, and Yadranka Kavalova (Eds.). 2007. *Parentheticals*. Amsterdam/Philadelphia: John Benjamins. DOI: 10.1075/la.106

Dehé, Nicole. 2009. "Clausal Parentheticals, Intonational Phrasing, and Prosodic Theory." *Journal of Linguistics* 45: 569–615. DOI: 10.1017/S002222670999003X

Döring, Sandra. 2007. "Quieter, Faster, Lower and Set off by Pauses?" In *Parentheticals*, ed. by Nicole Dehé, and Yordanka Kavalova, 285–307, Amsterdam/Philadelphia: John Benjamins. DOI: 10.1075/la.106.16dor

Doron, Edit. 1991. "Point of View as a Factor of Content." *Proceedings of SALT 11, Cornell University*: 51–64.

Emonds, Joe. 1973. "Parenthetical Clauses." In *You Take the High Node and I'll Take the Low Node*, ed. by Corum Claudia et al., 333–347. Chicago: Chicago Linguistic Society.

Espinal, Maria Teresa. 1991. "The Representation of Disjunct Constituents." *Language* 67 (4): 726–762. DOI: 10.2307/415075

Giorgi, Alessandra. 2010. *About the Speaker.*, Oxford: Oxford University Press.

Giorgi, Alessandra. 2011. "The Syntax of Commas: An Analysis of Two Types of Parentheticals." In *Universals and Variation,* ed. by Gao Ming-le. Beijing: Beijing University Press.

Giorgi, Alessandra. to appear. "Prosodic Signals as Syntactic Formatives in the Left Periphery." (http://ling.auf.net/lingbuzz/001625).

Guéron, Jacqueline. 2007. "Remarks on the Grammar of Unspeakable Sentences." Manuscript. University of Paris X.

Huddleston, Rodney, and Geoffrey Pullum. 2002. *The Cambridge Grammar of the English Language*. Cambridge University Press.

Kayne, Richard. 1993. "Toward a Modular Theory of Auxiliary Selection." *Lingua* 47: 3–31.

Kayne, Richard. 1994. *The Antisymmetry of Syntax*, LI Monograph. MIT Press.

Kavalova, Yodranka. 2007. *And* Parenthetical Clauses. In *Parentheticals*, ed. by Nicole Dehé, and Yordanka Kavalova, 145–172. Amsterdam/Philadelphia: John Benjamins. DOI: 10.1075/la.106.09kav

Haegeman, Liliane, 1991. "Parenthetical Adverbials: The radical Orphanage Approach." *Aspects of Modern English Linguistics: Papers presented to Masatomo Ukaji on his 60th birthday*: 232–254.

Poletto, Cecilia. 2006. "Parallel Phases: A Study on the High and Low Left Periphery of Old Italian." *Phases of Interpretation* 91: 261–294. DOI: 10.1515/9783110197723.4.261

Poletto, Cecilia. to appear. *Word Order in Old Italian*, Oxford: Oxford University Press. DOI: 10.1093/acprof:oso/9780199660247.001.0001

Potts, Christopher. 2002. "The Syntax and Semantics of as-parentheticals." *Natural Language and Linguistic Theory* 20(3): 623–689. DOI: 10.1023/A:1015892718818

Potts, Christopher. 2005. *The Logic of Conventional Implicatures*. Oxford: Oxford University Press.

Reinhart, Tanya. 1983. "Point of View in Language—The Use of Parentheticals." *Essays on Deixis*: 169–194.

Rizzi, Luigi. 1997. "The Fine Structure of the Left Periphery." In *Elements of Grammar*, ed. by Liliane Haegeman, 281–337. Dordrecht: Kluwer. DOI: 10.1007/978-94-011-5420-8_7

Ross, John. 1973. "Slifting." *The Formal Analysis of Natural Languages*: 133–169.

Schlenker, Philippe. 2004. "Context of Thought and Context of Utterance." *Mind and Language* 19: 279–304. DOI: 10.1111/j.1468-0017.2004.00259.x

Selkirk, Lisa. 2005. "Comments on intonational phrasing." In *Prosodies*, ed. by Sonia Frota, Marina Vigario, and Maria Joao Freitas, 11–58. Berlin: Mouton de Gruyter

Sharvit, Yael. 2004. "Free indirect discourse and de re pronouns." *Proceedings of Semantics and Linguistic Theory (SALT) 14, Cornell University*: 305–322.

Tescari Neto, Aquiles. 2013. "On Verb Movement in Brazilian Portuguese: A Cartographic Study." *Dissertation*, Ca' Foscari University of Venice

Zanuttini, Raffaella. 1997. *Negation and Clausal Structure*. New York: Oxford University Press.

Romanian *tough*-constructions and multi-headed constituents

Ion Giurgea

The "Iorgu Iordan - Alexandru Rosetti" Institute of Linguistics of the Romanian Academy, Bucharest

I propose an account for the absence of agreement on *tough*-words in Romanian *tough*- constructions (TCs). I argue that absence of agreement cannot be explained by an A-bar movement derivation, because Romanian TCs involve A-movement, the non-finite complement having passive properties. I also argue against an adverb analysis of Romanian *tough*-words and against a subject analysis of the clausal argument of the *tough*-word. I propose a novel analysis, which is supported by West Germanic data: non-agreeing TCs are multi-headed constituents, in which the adjective is the internal head, selecting the supine CP, and the supine C is the external head. Since the adjective is not the external head, it cannot take part in agreement relations involving the [Adjective+Supine] constituent. I provide a technical implementation of the notion of multi-headed constituents which relies on Citko's (2008) flexible label projection: in this case, it is the label of the complement that projects (an instance of Project-Goal). Finally, I discuss the correlation between the availability of multi-headed TCs and the morphological (in)distinctness between adjectives and adverbs.

1. Introduction: The problem of Romanian *Tough*- Constructions

Standard Romanian is unique among Romance languages in that it disallows agreement on the adjective in *tough*-constructions (TCs). As can be seen in (1), sequences *tough*-adjective + Supine can be used attributively with a noun interpreted as the object of the supine (see (1a)) as well as predicatively with a subject interpreted as the object of the supine (see (1b)), where verb agreement indicates that the preverbal DP is the grammatical subject), exactly like TCs in the other Romance languages and in English. However, the adjective in these constructions fails to agree with the head noun or subject, respectively:

(1) a. o teorie   greu   de înțeles   (Attributive TC)
         a theory(F) hard.MSG of understand.SUP
         'a theory hard to understand'

DOI 10.1075/rllt.9.07giu

    b. Aceste teorii   sunt greu   de înțeles.   (Predicative TC)
       these theories(F) are hard.MSG of understand.SUP
       'These theories are hard to understand.'

Instead, it shows a masculine singular form. This form can be analyzed as a morpho-logical default, used when the adjective's gender and number features remain unval-ued, being the form used when the adjective is the predicate of a sentence without a nominal subject, as can be seen in (2) (note that (2a) is the impersonal pattern of *tough-* adjectives):

(2) a. E greu   {să înțelegem   teoria   / de rezolvat
       is hard.MSG SBJV understand.1PL theory-the of solve.SUP

       atâtea   probleme}.
       so-many problems

       'It's hard {for us to understand the theory/to solve so many problems}.'

    b. [A vorbi   liber despre aceste subiecte] nu e ușor.
       to talk.INF freely about these   matters   not is easy.MSG
       'To talk offhandedly about these matters is not easy.'

In other Romance languages (see (3a-c)) as well as in some non-standard varieties of Romanian and in the older language (see (3d)), *tough*-adjectives do agree:

(3) a. teorie   difficili   da testare   (It.)

    b. théories difficiles   à   tester   (Fr.)

    c. teorías   difíciles   de probar   (Sp.)
       theories difficult.PL to test

    d. Pogor o   declară   rea și **imposibilă**   **de primit.**
       Pogor it(F) declared bad and impossible.FSG of receive.SUP
                   (XIXth century Ro.: Negruzzi, apud Pană-Dindelegan 1982)
       'Pogor declared it bad and impossible to accept.'

Given the fact that the [*tough*-A + Supine] constituent occupies an attributive position in (1a), and the copula does agree in (2b), the absence of agreement in (1) is surprising. In this paper I will concentrate on the analysis of this construction, which is the most challenging from a theoretical point of view. I will also present analyses of the agreeing pattern, insofar as the explanation for the absence of agreement in the other construc-tion implies a comparison with the 'normal', agreeing construction.

    Various solutions have been proposed for the problem of the lack of agreement, which I will revise in Section 2, where I will also show that each of these analyses has a number of problems. In Section 3 I will propose my own solution to the prob-lem, which combines insights from some of the previous analyses and uses a non-standard syntactic concept, that of multi-headed constituents. I will explain the lack of agreement by the fact that the verbal functional head selected by the adjective acts as the *external* head of the construction (the adjective being the *internal* head). In Section 4 I will discuss the theoretical aspects of this analysis, proposing an implementation of the idea which is based on the flexible label projection mechanism proposed by Citko (2008), a.o. In Section 5 I will discuss the correlation between the availability of multi-headed TCs and the morphologic (in)distinctness between adjectives and adverbs.

Before discussing the analyses, a few remarks are in order about the non-finite form used in Romanian TCs: this is the so-called "supine", a second infinitival form of Romanian, formally identical to the masculine singular of the past participle, preceded either by *de* 'of' or by prepositions.[1] The element *de* has acquired here the status of a low non-finite complementizer, similar to French *de, à* and Italian *di, a,* hence its analysis as C (Soare 2002; Hill 2002) or Fin (Giurgea and Soare 2010a). Given that in some contexts (in reduced relatives) the supine has modal properties (see Section 2.3 below), and Romanian has a similar modal particle for the subjunctive (*să*), another possible label of *de* is Mood (Giurgea and Soare 2007). Since a fine-grained analysis of Romanian supines is outside the scope of this paper, I will use here the label C—which is justified by the fact that *de* alternates with prepositions. Nevertheless, it should be stressed that this element behaves as a defective C, insofar as supine clauses, unlike other non-finite clauses in Romanian, do not license a subject (see Soare 2002) and do allow A-movement (as we will see in 2.1 below).[2]

2. Previous accounts and their problems

2.1 Dye (2006)

Building on the well-established correlation between A-movement and agreement, Dye (2006) proposes that agreeing TCs involve A-movement, whereas non-agreeing TCs involve A-bar movement.

For non-agreeing TCs, Dye assumes that the *tough*-A selects a CP, whose verb is in the active voice (represented as a TransP below a PredP; Dye adopts Bowers's 2002 analysis of voice). The object of the supine is a null operator undergoing A-bar movement inside this CP, to SpecCP. The subject of the TC is base-generated in a SpecPredP above the *tough*-A and is coindexed with the null operator:

(4) $[_{PredP}$ Subj$_i$ [Pred^0 $[_{VP}$ $[be$ $[_{AP}$ *easy* $[_{CP}$ Op$_i$ de $[_{PredP}$ V$_{Supine}$ $[_{TransP}$ t$_V$ $[_{VP}$ t$_V$ t$_{Op}$]]]]]]]]]

---

1.   This form does not directly continue the Latin supine, but originates in a verbal nominalization built with the same suffix as the past participle (see Soare 2002; Dragomirescu 2013); the nominal use is still productive today (see Cornilescu et al. 2013).

2.   For a few exceptions, see Pană-Dindelegan (2011), Dragomirescu (2013).

For agreeing TCs, she assumes that the *tough*-A selects a smaller projection (PredP), which lacks TransP (the supine thus being passive). The object of the supine, which, unlike in (4), is not case-licensed by the supine verb, raises to the supine's SpecPred, then to SpecAP and further up to SpecPredP, becoming the subject of the main clause:

(5) $[_{PredP}$ Subj$_i$ $[Pred^0$ $[_{VP}$ [be $[_{AP}$ t$_i$ [easy $[_{PredP}$ t$_i$ [de $[V_{Supine}$ t$_i$]]]]]]]]]

This account is confronted with serious problems. First, there is no evidence for A-bar movement in non-agreeing TCs, as opposed to agreeing TCs. As noticed by Soare (2002) and Giurgea and Soare (2007), in non-agreeing TCs the dependency must be stricly local, unlike in English TCs:

(6)   a.   *Această carte   e   greu   de convins   copiii
              this   book(F)   is   hard.MSG   of   convince.SUP   children-the

              s(-o)   citească
              SBJV(-it)   read.3

       b.   This book is hard to convince children to read.

Soare (2002) concludes that the supine in non-agreeing TCs is passive. This is supported by the fact that it allows *by*- phrases (as noticed by Giurgea and Soare 2007):

(7)   cărți   greu   de   înțeles   de   către   copii
       books   hard   of   understand.SUP   by   children

Dye gives two pieces of evidence in favor of A-bar movement in non-agreeing TCs. The first one involves a supine verb taking another supine as its complement:

(8)   Noțiuni de genul   acesta   vor   fi   dificil   de   început
       notions of kind-the   this   will   be   hard   of   begin.SUP

       de   abordat   (OK for Dye 2006)
       of   approach.SUP

First, notice that such examples are not fully acceptable (for me and other speakers I consulted) and I have been able to find only one example of this type on Google:

(9)   Ai   deschis   un subiect   interesant   și   deloc   ușor   de
       have.2SG   opened   a   subject   interesting   and   not-at-all   easy   of

       terminat   de   dezbătut.
       finish.SUP   of   discuss.SUP

       'You opened a subject that is interesting and not at all easy to finish debating upon.'
       (http://www.linkedin.com/groups/Atitudinea-sau-experienta-2260452.S.49801983)

More importantly, there is evidence that these constructions involve A-movement. First, notice that such a local relation is only possible if the low verb is also a supine. Moreover, the high verb must be *a verb that allows a long passive*. This construction, not fully grammatical in Romanian, is the easiest to get precisely with the verb *termina* 'finish', as shown by the following attested example:

(10) după ce Scriptura a fost terminată de scris
      after that Bible-the.F has been finished.FSG of write.SUP

(www.crestinortodox.ro/forum/)

This type of example has the same degree of acceptability as those in (8)–(9) (and the same sporadic occurrence on the Internet).

The second argument for A-bar movement offered by Dye is licensing of parasitic gaps. Here I strongly disagree with the author, finding the example totally unaccept-able (a judgment shared by the speakers I consulted):

(11) *Aceste formule sunt uşor de memorat fără (de)
       these formulae are easy of memorize.SUP without (of)

      a înţelege   (OK for Dye 2006)
      to understand

In conclusion, non-agreeing TCs appear to involve A-movement, the supine comple-ment having passive properties (see (7)). The locality constraints are the same as for the agreeing TCs of other Romance languages (see Canac-Marquis 1996 for French; Giurgea and Soare 2010b for French and Italian):

(12) *des livres difficiles à convaincre tes enfants de lire (Fr.)
       INDEF.PL books difficult.PL to convince your children to read

Secondly, it is not clear, under Dye's analysis in (4), how the thematic interpretation of the external argument is achieved. Dye assumes that this argument is somehow linked ("by some notion of predication coindexation") to the null operator in the adjective's complement. But what element in the structure guarantees the interpretative connec-tion between the subject and the null operator? I think the only possible candidate is the adjective, because this construction is lexically restricted to certain adjectives, and the clause hosting the null operator is selected by the adjective. SpecPred is not a thematic position *per se*. But this implies that the subject must be argumentally related to the adjective. Then we expect agreement, as we do for any external argument of an adjective.

Thirdly, in (4), the subject, although it sits in SpecPred, fails to trigger agreement on the adjective. But Pred(icate)Phrases have been introduced precisely for hosting the base (thematic) position of the external argument of adjectives in general (see Bowers 1993; Baker 2003), and predicative adjectives in Romanian do agree, like in the other Romance languages.

2.2   Giurgea and Soare (2007)

The two other analyses I discuss share the idea that Romanian TCs involve A-movement, as we have seen in Section 2.1 above.

Giurgea and Soare (2007) propose that in non-agreeing TC the clause is a subject, sitting in SpecPred:

(13) $[_{PredP}\ [_{SupineP}\ V\ Subject]\ [Pred\ AP]]$

By contrast, in agreeing TCs, the clause is a complement; the verb's object, which needs to raise for case-licensing, passes through SpecPred, whereby it triggers agreement:

(14) $[_{PredP}\ Subject\ [_{AP}\ A\ [_{InfinitiveP}\ V\ \text{Subject}]]]$

A potential problem of this analysis is that in non-agreeing TCs, the clause normally *follows* the adjective, so that obligatory extraposition of a clausal SpecPred must be assumed. This is indeed the normal order with clausal arguments of impersonal adjectives as in (15):

(15)   E   important   să   fim   devreme.
        is   important   SBJV be.1PL early
        'It's important that we be there early.'

Since the clause is the *external* argument of the adjective, it can be analyzed as occupying SpecPred (on the assumption that copular constructions uniformly involve a PredP complement). We thus have independent evidence for obligatory extraposition of clausal SpecPred.

But the analysis in (13) still faces problems: for predicative TCs, it is not clear why T probes the DP subject inside the subject clause, instead of showing a default 3sg form, like in other cases of clausal subjects—in other words, what is the difference between the impersonal construction in (16a) (and also (2) above) and the TC in (16b–c)?

(16)   a.   E   greu   de rezolvat   atâtea   probleme.
              is   hard.MSG of solve.SUP so-many problems
              'It's hard to solve so many problems.'

        b.   Sunt   greu de rezolvat   problemele.
              are.3PL hard of solve.SUP problems-the

        c.   Atâtea   probleme sunt   greu de rezolvat
              so-many problems are.3PL hard of solve.SUP

A possible answer is that the subject clause is phasal in (16a) and non-phasal in (16b–c). The non-finite projection in TCs would thus be transparent for Agree with T, leading to the licensing of the supine's (deep) object as a nominative subject. For attributive TCs, the role of T in promoting the object would be played by the head involved in relativization (Pred$_{+rel}$ according to Giurgea and Soare 2007).

The most problematic aspect of this analysis is the assumption that the finite clause is not c-selected in non-agreeing TCs, as opposed to agreeing TCs (where it is a complement). This leads us to expect non-agreeing TCs to be less dependent on the lexical choice of the adjective than agreeing TCs. But Romanian non-agreeing TCs show roughly *the same lexical restrictions* as their agreeing counterparts in other languages—as we can see in (17), not all adjectives that can take a clausal subject can appear in non-agreeing TCs:

(17)   a.   E amuzant   de citit   povestirile lui.
            is amusing.MSG of read.SUP stories-the his
            'It's amusing to read his stories.'

       b.   *Povestirile   lui sunt amuzant   de citit.
            stories(F)-the his are   amusing.MSG of read.SUP

       c.   E frumos   {să-ţi   respecţi   părinţii   / de spălat
            is beautiful SUBJ-you.DAT respect.2SG parents-the   of wash.SUP

            rufele   afară}.
            linen(PL)-the outside

            'It is proper to respect your parents/to wash the linen outside.'

       d.   *Părinţii   sunt frumos   de respectat.
            parents-the are   beautiful.MSG of respect.SUP

       d'. *Rufele   sunt frumos   de spălat   afară.
            linen(PL)   are   beautiful.MSG of wash.SUP outside

       e.   E plăcut   de făcut   focul   pe plajă.
            is pleasant of make.SUP fire.the on beach
            'It's pleasant to make the fire on the beach.'

       f.   *foc plăcut   de făcut
            fire pleasant of do.SUP

This strongly suggests c-selection by the adjective. But SpecPred is not c-selected.

Moreover, one may wonder why the derivation leading to non-agreeing TCs is not available in the other Romance languages.

2.3   Soare (2002), Soare and Dobrovie-Sorin (2002), Giurgea and Soare (2010a,b)

These studies adopt the traditional analysis (see, e.g., Pană-Dindelegan 1992), which takes the *tough* word in non-agreeing TCs to be an adverb (rather than an adjective). Indeed, adverbs in Romanian are usually homophonous with masculine singular adjective forms (this holds for all adjectives involved in TCs):

(18)   Cântă/scrie greu.
       sings/writes hard(.MSG)
       'S/he sings/writes with difficulty/hard.'

In this analysis, the *tough*-word is not the head selecting the supine, but a specifier of the verbal projection. Giurgea and Soare (2010a,b), analyzing *de* as Mood^0, place the *tough*-word in SpecMoodP:

(19) $[_{\text{PredP}}$ teorie [Pred^0 $[_{\text{MoodP}}$ greu $[[_{\text{Mood}}$ de][înțeles ~~teorie~~]]]]]

(Giurgea and Soare 2010a,b)

Since the *tough*-word is not the (lexical) head of the construction, this analysis predicts that supines should be able to function as adnominal modifiers and predicates in the absence of the *tough*-word. This prediction is borne out: *de*-supines can function as modal reduced relatives, with a deontic necessity or teleological possibility meaning (see Giurgea and Soare 2010b):

(20) a.   cărți de citit
         book of read.SUP
         'books to (be) read'

      a'   cărți   greu de citit
         books hard of read.SUP
         'books hard to read'

      b.   Cărțile   sunt de citit   (de către elevi)   până mâine.
         books-the are of read.SUP by   pupils   until tomorrow
         'The books are to be read (by the pupils) until tomorrow.'

      b'.   Cărțile   sunt greu de citit   (de către copii)
         books-the are hard of read.SUP by   children
         'The books are hard to read (for children).'

The passive character of both constructions is indicated by the agent-PPs in (20b–b').

   This analysis faces two problems: (i) Since in non-agreeing TCs *tough*-words do not take the clause either as an external or as an internal argument, the connection between the use of *tough*-words in TCs and their adjectival use in the impersonal construction (see (2)) is lost.

   (ii) We expect to find TCs built with adverbs in languages where adverbs do have distinct morphology, contrary to fact:

(21) a.   *livres facilement à lire   (Fr.)
      b.   *books easily to read/to be read

This casts some doubt on the analysis of *tough*-words in Romanian TCs as adverbs.

3.   Proposal: Non-agreeing TCs as multi-headed constituents

The solution I propose combines the account for the lack of agreement in the analysis 2.3, namely, the fact that the verbal functional head rather than the *tough*-word is the head of the construction, with the idea that the *tough*-word c-selects the adjective (dispensing thus with an adjective/adverb ambiguity of *tough*-words, as in Section 2.3, and with the idea that the clause is the external argument, problematic for the reasons exposed in Section 2.2 above).

These two apparently contradictory claims can be reconciled by using the notion of *multi-headed constituents*, i.e., constituents where a distinction can be made between an *internal* and an *external* head. The internal head is the word that c-selects a phrase as its complement, building the structure. The external head, a word different from the internal head, is the word that gives the entire constituent its label—it is called *external* because it behaves as a head in everything that concerns the distribution of the whole constituent, i.e., its *external* syntactic relations.

In our case, the adjective that c-selects the supine clause is the *internal* head. However, the whole [A+Supine] constituent takes the label of the complement (the label of the Supine complement projects). Thus, the functional head of the supine, for which I use the label C here, is the *external* head. The constituent [A + CP] is thus labeled CP.

This labeling is supported by the fact that TCs and modal reduced relatives show the same distribution, as we have seen in (20) above. Lack of agreement follows from the fact that agreement is an *external* relation of the [A+Supine] constituent, and the external head of this constituent is C.

Multi-headed constituents have been proposed on independent grounds, for other constructions. For instance, some modified cardinals are built by using prepositions, as illustrated in (22). The preposition takes the cardinal as its complement, behaving thus as an internal head (notice that in (22b) the preposition selects a coordination of cardinals). The whole constituent nevertheless shows the distribution of cardinals, and not that of (spatial) PPs. Thus, in (22) we see it occupy the position between a definite determiner and a noun, which is typical of cardinals and other nominal quantity expressions. Note also that the cardinal behaves as the head with respect to agreement—as can be seen in (22), cardinals that have inflection (such as *doi, două* 'two.M', 'two.F') agree with the head noun and the determiner:

(22) a. cele   [peste două] zile   (Rom.)
          the.FPL over two.F days(F)
          'the more than ten days'

      b. cele   [între   două   și   șase] luni
          the.FPL between three.F and six   months(F)

The cardinal can also appear inside the prepositional complement of a degree head, and still show the behavior of a head with respect to distribution of the entire constituent and agreement (notice that *doi* agrees, whereas the quantitative *mult* 'much', although the lexical head on which the comparative is built, does *not* agree—it does not show the M.PL form *mulți*):

(23)   cei   [mai   mult   [de doi]]   ani   (Rom.)
        the.ML   more   much   of   two.M   years(M)
        'the more than two years'

Another example, discussed in Van Riemsdijk (2006), is (24). Since English obeys the head-final constraint on prenominal modifiers, the adjective *obvious* must be considered the head of this construction. However, it is inside a PP selected by the adverb *far*. Using a multi-headed constituent analysis, *far* is to be treated as the internal head, and the adjective as the external head (such constituents indeed have the distribution of adjectives):

(24)   a [far [from obvious]] matter

Crucial evidence for the multi-headedness analysis of TCs is provided by German and Dutch.[3] In these languages, TCs can appear attributively in prenominal position, ending with the infinitive verb. Since prenominal modifiers obey the head-final constraint in these languages, the infinitive should be considered the (external) head of the constituent. Moreover, in German the infinitive also receives agreement (plus a -*d*- morpheme which is inserted between the infinitive ending and the agreement morpheme, making it look like the present participle, see (25a)):

(25)   a.   ein   [schwer   zu   lesen-d-es]   Buch (German)
              a   hard   to   read.INF-*d*-NSG.NOM/ACC   book(N)

        b.   Das   Buch   ist   schwer   zu   lesen
              the   book   is   hard   to   read.INF

(26)   een   [makkelijk   te   maken]   tentamen   (Dutch, Zwart 2012)
        a   easy   to   make.INF   test

Agreement clearly indicates that the infinitival verb is the external head of the constituent.

Like in Romanian, the non-finite form in TCs is the same as the one used in modal reduced relatives:

(27)   a.   ein   [zu   lesen-d-es]   Buch   (German)
              a   to   read.INF-*d*-NSG.NOM/ACC   book(N)
              'a book to read/to be read'

        b.   Das   Buch   ist   zu   lesen.
              the   book   is   to   read.INF
              'The book is to be read.'

---

3.   I am grateful to Petra Sleeman for having pointed out to me the Dutch construction.

The analysis proposed for Romanian extends thus to German and Dutch.

The derivation of Romanian TCs is schematized in (28), which I assume to be the common part of predicative and attributive TCs—a reduced relative, analyzable as a PredP (see Giurgea and Soare 2010a). The predicative and attributive constructions are derived according to whether this PredP is the complement of the copula (or embedded in other predicative environments), see (29a), or embedded into a relativization structure, for which I assume a nominalizing head (see Bhatt 2002; Giurgea and Soare 2010a), as in (29b):

(28) $[_{\text{PredP}} \text{DP} [\text{Pred}^0 [_{\text{CP}} \text{A} [_{\text{CP}} \text{de+V} [_{\text{SupP}} t_{\text{DP}} t_{\text{V}} [_{\text{vP}} t_{\text{V}} [_{\text{VP}} t_{\text{V}} t_{\text{DP}}]]]]]]]$

(29) a. Predicative TC (with copula):
$[_{\text{TP}} \text{DP} [\text{T}^0 [_{\text{vP}} \textit{be} [_{\text{PredP}} t_{\text{DP}} [\text{Pred}^0 [_{\text{CP}} \text{A} [_{\text{CP}} \text{de+V} [_{\text{SupP}} t_{\text{DP}} t_{\text{V}} [_{\text{vP}} t_{\text{V}} [_{\text{VP}} t_{\text{V}} t_{\text{DP}}]]]]]]]]]]]$

      b. Attributive TC:
$[_{\text{NomP}} \text{NP} [\text{Nom}^0 [_{\text{PredP}} t_{\text{NP}} [\text{Pred}^0 [_{\text{CP}} \text{A} [_{\text{CP}} \text{de+V} [_{\text{SupP}} t_{\text{NP}} t_{\text{V}} [_{\text{vP}} t_{\text{V}} [_{\text{VP}} t_{\text{V}} t_{\text{NP}}]]]]]]]]]]$

Regarding the structure in (28), the claims defended here are the following: (i) although the A selects the CP, the external head is the supine C, therefore the A+CP constituent is labeled CP; (ii) the entire CP domain is a reduced clause which doesn't case-license the object (see Section 2.1 above for the passive nature of the supine in TCs); the object raises to SpecPred for case-licensing reasons (possibly through an intermediate specifier position inside the clause, according to the preferred analysis of passivization).[4] It is a well-known property of reduced relatives that they involve an un-case-marked argument (see Bhatt 1999, who uses the term 'external argument'; in passive reduced relatives, this argument is, of course, the deep object).

Other details about the structure in (28) are not relevant for our topic and are represented for convenience—I made no choice about the inflectional head which bears the supine morphology, using the label Sup. Since in Romanian mood particles/low complementizers and auxiliaries always form a complex head with the verb (Dobrovie-Sorin 1994; Barbu 1999; Giurgea 2011), I represented the verb as raised to the C head *de* (with a non-standard order inside the complex head *de*+V).

Agreeing TCs that are based on a passive configuration—in non-standard varieties of Romanian as well as other Romance languages (see (3) above)—differ from the structures in (28)–(29) only in labeling, which in their case proceeds in the standard way (there is no relabeling): the A+CP constituent is labeled AP—the A is both the

---

4. For recent proposals on passivization, see Collins (2005), Roberts (2010), Bruening (2013), a.o.

external and the internal head of the construction. Therefore, it establishes an agreement relation with SpecPred. Since the raised object passes through SpecPred, the adjective establishes agreement with it.

The table in (30) below summarizes the comparison between the proposed account and the previous analyses. (The first five rows are requirements, showing why the proposed analysis is to be preferred over its predecessors; the sixth and seventh rows are predictions, therefore the 'no' in the respective columns is not to be taken as an argument against the analyses.)

(30)   Comparison between the proposed analysis and previous ones, discussed in Section 2

	Proposed analysis	Analysis 2.1	Analysis 2.2	Analysis 2.3
tough-words have the same category in all their uses	OK	OK	OK	*
tough- words *select* the clause in non-agreeing TCs (like in agreeing TCs)	OK	OK	*	*
TCs involve A-movement	OK	*	OK	OK
Lack of agreement	OK	*	OK	OK
Absence of TCs with marked adverbs (**eas-ily to do,*difficilement à faire*)	OK	OK	OK	*
predicts that TCs have the same distribution as modal reduced relatives	yes	no	no	yes
predicts that the *tough*-word in non-agreeing TCs have the same forms as adverbs	no	no	no	yes

4.   On the formal implementation of multi-headedness

The main problem of the account proposed in the previous section is the use of non-standard analytical tools. This section is devoted to a discussion of the theoretical aspects of my proposal.

Van Riemsdijk (2006) formalizes multi-headedness by the concept of *grafting*. Noticing that the minimalist notion of Merge leaves open the possibility of re-merging a syntactic object that is not the root, he proposes that in multi-headed constituents the external head is remerged into a different tree, as represented below:

(31)

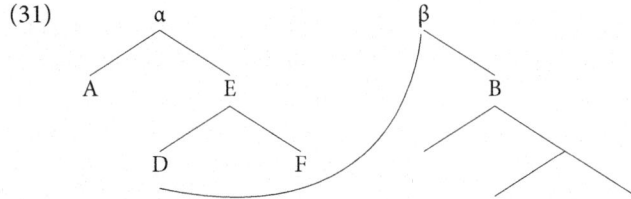

Citko (2005, 2011) uses the same mechanism, called *parallel Merge*, for the derivation of a variety of constructions:[5] ATB movement, *wh-* questions with conjoined pronouns, right node raising, gapping, free relatives, transparent free relatives, *wh*-amalgams, cleft amalgams., The operation can be represented as in (32), treating re-merging as sharing:

(32)

(Citko 2011, 121 (3))

Here, the constituent γ is shared between α and β. Applying the idea to multi-headed constituents, the head of γ would be the external head, and the head of α—the internal head.

The main problem of this proposal is how these structures are interpreted at the interfaces, in particular at the PF-interface, where a single string must be obtained from the two trees.[6] Note moreover that the constructions treated by this mechanism by Citko fall for the most part into two major types—(i) constructions involving coordination, where the trees which share a constituent are sub-trees of a single big tree (ATB movement, *wh*-questions with conjoined pronouns, right node raising, gapping), and (ii) constructions with a parenthetical interpretation (transparent free relatives, *wh-* amalgams, cleft amalgams). The solutions to the linearization problem envisaged by Citko (2011) mainly apply to type (i). In any case, TCs don't belong to either of these types; multi-headedness in TCs is correlated to a *lexical* property of *tough*-words, appearing in one of their c-selectional patterns.

---

5. Similar notions are Bobaljik and Brown's (1997) 'interarboreal movement' and Nunes's (2001, 2004) 'sideward movement'.

6. For other problems regarding van Riemsdijk's (2006) proposal, see Grosu (2010).

For these reasons, I adopt a different account of multi-headedness in TCs (which may extend to the other multi-headed constructions discussed in Section 3). I do not assume multidominance, but rather relabeling: multi-headedness appears when the label of a constituent is different from the label of the head whose selectional properties have built that constituent. The external head is the one that projects its label in this non-standard fashion (such as C in TCs, which is the head of A's complement).

As pointed out by Chomsky (2000), the assumption that the selector projects its label (i.e., the label of (α,β), where α is the selector, is necessarily (α)) is an axiom (it is non-derivable from any other principle). Since this observation was made, several studies have proposed to abandon this assumption in specific cases—for instance, allowing moved elements to project their label (Larson 1998; Donati 2006, a.o., for free relatives; Iatridou, Anagnostopoulou, and Izvorski 1999/2001, adopted by Bhatt 1999, for raising relatives—the claim is that the NP attracted to SpecCP projects its label). The most radical proposal was made by Citko (2008), who allows all possibilities of label projection: Project Probe (i.e., selector: the standard label projection), Project Goal (i.e., selectee; this includes both specifiers and complements), Project Both (used for extended projections and head movement), and Project None (suggested for the root node).[7] Notice that projection of the label of the complement is assumed to be possible, and is in fact used, in the form of Project Both (where the 'Goal' is the complement), to explain the percolation of the categorial feature of the lexical head in extended projections.

In our TCs, we have an instance of projection of the complement's label. Because this type of label projection is certainly more restricted than Project Probe, I propose to formalize it by using a special projection feature on the Probe—the default mechanism, used when there is no special projection feature, being Project Probe. This feature is a lexical feature associated to a given selectional feature. I call selectional features the features that trigger Merge of a complement or a specifier (see Bruening 2013).

I propose thus that *tough*-adjectives in Romanian have a c-selectional feature $[+de_{Sup}\text{-}CP]$ (where de_{Sup} is the complementizer *de* that selects the supine) associated to a [Project Goal] feature in TCs:[8]

---

7. In addition to Citko's examples of the various possibilities, a clear case where the label is projected from the specifier is coordination constructions: e.g., in [DP [& DP]], & is the internal head, but D(P) is the label of the whole constituent.

8. This specification is necessary because Romanian has other *de* complementizers, with different properties (supine *de* and infinitive *de* have the same origin—the preposition *de*—but there also exists an indicative *de*, of unclear etymology).

(33) $[_A$ *tough*$]^{+de\text{-}CP\ +\text{Project-Goal}}$ + $[_{CP}$ *de*-V$_{\text{Supine}}$ .....Object] $\rightarrow$ $[_{CP}$ [A] [*de*-V$_{\text{Supine}}$ .....Object]]

In the impersonal construction (see (2) in Section (1), *tough*-adjectives select for any irrealis clause (they can take supines, subjunctives or infinitives) and have no [Project Goal] feature.

A problem for this hypothesis is that *tough*- adjectives in TCs can combine with degree words:

(34)   probleme   [atât   de uşor de rezolvat]/ [mai uşor de rezolvat]
       problems   so-much of easy of solve.SUP more easy of solve.SUP
       'problems so easy to solve/easier to solve'

If such words involve a DegP (for which there is evidence in Romanian, see Corver 2000; Vişan 2004; Cornilescu and Giurgea 2013), it follows that the A+Supine constituent does not immediately become a CP, but can still behave as an adjective, being selected by Deg.

A solution to this problem is to assume that the [Project-Goal] feature becomes active only after the functional structure of the head is built. It is widely admitted that functional heads share some features of the lexical head (this idea is at the core of the notion of 'extended projection' proposed by Grimshaw 1991). In the flexible label projection theory, as we have seen, the concept of extended projection can be represented using Project Both—we would thus have a label {Deg,A} instead of Deg on the DegP. Let's assume that the [Project-Goal] feature of the A percolates to the Deg-level and triggers relabeling only after the functional domain of the internal head (i.e., the DegP) is completed. The labeling mechanism would work as follows:

(35) $[_{Deg}$ mai] + $[_A$ uşor $[_C$ de rezolvat]]$_{A\ (+CP+\ \text{Project-Goal})} \rightarrow$
       [mai $[[_A$ uşor $[_C$ de rezolvat]]$_{Deg+A\ (+CP+\ \text{Project-Goal})} \rightarrow [_{CP}$ mai $[[_A$ uşor $[_C$ de rezolvat]]

5.   Non-agreeing TCs and the Adj/Adv indistinctness

In discussing the analysis of *tough*-words as adverbs (Section 2.3), we noticed that in Romanian most adverbs do not have a distinctive morphology, showing the default form of adjectives instead (which is the masculine singular form). We have seen that, in spite of this fact, an analysis as adverbs is unlikely because in languages with overt adverbial marking (like Engl. -*ly*, Fr. -*ment*, It. -*mente* etc.), we never find such forms in TCs. Nevertheless, there seems to be a correlation between non-agreeing TCs (in languages which have adjectival agreement) and lack of adverbial morphology: not just in Romanian, but also in the Germanic languages discussed in the previous section, which also show relabeling in TCs, adverbs are usually not formally distinguished from adjectives:

(36) a. Er singt wunderbar/ schön   / schrecklich.   (German)
        he sings wonderful   beautiful   horrible
        'He sings/is singing wonderfully/beautifully/horribly.'

     b. Er ist wunderbar/ schön   / schrecklich.
        he is wonderful   beautiful   horrible
        'He is wonderful/beautiful/horrible.'

(37) Hij zingt/is prachtig.   (Dutch)
     he sings/is splendid
     'He sings splendidly/He is splendid.'

On the other hand, the other Romance languages, which use a suffix derived from Latin *mente* for adverbs, do not have non-agreeing TCs.

(38) a. *Ces   livres sont difficile /   difficilement à   lire   (Fr.)
     b. *Questi libri   sono difficile /   difficilmente da leggere   (It.)
     c. *Esos   libros son   difícil /   dificilmente   de leer
         these   books   are   difficult.SG / difficult-ly   to read

These data support the following generalization:

(39) TCs with relabeling are found in languages where adjectives and adverbs are not formally distinguished.

If this generalization proves to hold cross-linguistically, we should provide an explanation for it. What I would suggest is that *tough*-words, although merged as adjectives, must be *compatible* with the syntactic environment created by non-standard label projection, and in this environment, they come to occupy an adverbial position. Therefore, the construction is allowed only in languages which have items *underspecified* for the adjective/adverb distinction—items for which we should rather assume an 'archi-category' *a*.

   Since there are many semantic and distributional similarities between quality adjectives and adverbs (both are typically modifiers, with a poor functional structure—only the Degree projection—and often express properties which can be applied either to individuals or to events or states of affairs, see *a beautiful woman/a beautiful dance/She dances beautifully*; *This is a clever action/He cleverly did it*), and for those properties that can apply both to individuals and events there is a productive way of forming adjective-adverb pairs (even in languages where the two classes are morphologically distinct, see Fr. *-ment*, Engl. *-ly*, etc.), the hypothesis that languages where there is no overt morphological difference between the members of these pairs have an archi-category *a* instead of a zero derivational morpheme (for the adverb) does not seem unreasonable. Baker, in his book on lexical categories also argues that adjectives and adverbs are "essentially the same category" (Baker 2003, 151; see Section 4.5 of the book).

A possible objection against this hypothesis comes from agreement. Of course, even when there is no adverbial suffix, adjectives differ from adverbs by the fact that they can show agreeing forms. Adopting the current minimalist assumption that agreeing items come from the lexicon with unvalued features, one might say that adjectives are distinct from adverbs by possessing unvalued ϕ-features in their lexical entries. A full treatment of this objection would require a discussion of current theories of agreement, which cannot be addressed in the space of this paper. However, I think there is an answer to this objection which holds no matter which theory of agreement we choose. As we have seen in Section 1, items which are definitely adjectives can appear in environments where no value for their ϕ-features is provided (in predicate position of 'impersonal' clauses, e.g., when the subject is a clause, see (2) above).[9] This means that either adjectives can come without ϕ-features or that absence of valuation does not make the derivation crash (unvalued features do not create a problem at the PF-interface if the system has morphological defaults—underspecified vocabulary insertion rules in the Distributed Morphology framework). No matter which account is chosen, it is equally applicable to adverbs (*a* items in an adverbial use).

6. Conclusion

I have argued that the difference between Romanian TCs, where the *tough*-word does not agree, and agreeing TCs is not to be found in the argument structure—the clause is a complement of the adjective in both constructions—or in the type of movement (non-agreeing and agreeing TCs both rely on A-movement). I proposed that the lack of agreement is due to a non-standard label projection (or 'relabeling') by which the [A+CP] constituent receives the label CP instead of AP (a theoretical possibility for which Citko 2008 provided independent evidence). We thus obtain a 'multi-headed' constituent, in which the adjective is the internal head (selecting the clause) and the non-finite C is the external head. Since agreement is an *external* relation of the [A+Supine] constituent, the adjective does not take part in it. This type of TC has been shown to exist in German and Dutch. Since in these languages, like in Romanian,

---

9. It is unlikely that adjectives in impersonal constructions get their ϕ-features valued by an expletive subject in all instances: languages with overt expletives still have cases in which the clausal/verbal projection itself occupies the subject position, no expletive being present, e.g., Fr. *Se coucher tard est nuisible* 'REFL go-to-sleep.INF late is harmful'.

adverbs are normally indistinguishable from (the default form of) adjectives, I envisaged the possibility of a correlation between relabeling in TC and the existence of an 'archi'-category *a* comprising both adjectives and adverbs. This correlation may be explained by the fact that in the 'relabeled' constituent the adjective finds itself in an adverbial environment.

References

Baker, Mark. 2003. *Lexical Categories*. Cambridge University Press.
    DOI: 10.1017/CBO9780511615047
Bhatt, Rajesh. 1999. *Covert Modality in Non-Finite Contexts*. Ph.D. Diss., University of Pennsylvania.
Bhatt, Rajesh. 2002. "The Raising Analysis of Relative Clauses: Evidence from Adjectival Modification." *Natural Language Semantics* 10: 43–90. DOI: 10.1023/A:1015536226396
Bobaljik, Jonathan and Samuel Brown. 1997. "Interarboreal Operations: Head Movement and the Extension Requirement." *Linguistic Inquiry* 28: 345–356.
Bowers, John. 1993. "The Syntax of Predication." *Linguistic Inquiry* 24: 591–656.
Bruening, Benjamin. 2013. "By-Phrases in Passives and Nominals." *Syntax* 16(1): 1–41.
    DOI: 10.1111/j.1467-9612.2012.00171.x
Canac-Marquis, Réjean. 1996. "The Distribution of A and DEin *Tough* Constructions in French." In *Grammatical theory and Romance languages: Selected papers from the* 25th *Linguistics Symposium on Romance Languages*, ed. by Karen Zagona, 35–46. Amsterdam: John Benjamins. DOI: 10.1075/cilt.133.04can
Chomsky, Noam. 2000. "Minimalist Inquiries." In *Step by Step: Essays on Minimalist Syntax in Honor of Howard Lasnik,* ed. by Roger Martin, David Michaels, Juan Uriagereka, SamuelJay Keyser, 89–156. MIT Press, Cambridge, MA.
Citko, Barbara. 2005. "On the Nature of Merge: External Merge, Internal Merge, and Parallel Merge." *Linguistic Inquiry* 36: 475–497. DOI: 10.1162/002438905774464331
Citko, Barbara. 2008. "Missing Labels." *Lingua* 118: 907–944. DOI: 10.1016/j.lingua.2008.01.001
Citko, Barbara. 2011. "Multidominance." *Linguistic Minimalism*, ed. by Cedric Boeckx, 119–142. Oxford: Oxford University Press.
Corver, Norbert. 2000. "Degree Adverbs as Displaced Predicates." *Rivista di Linguistica*, 12: 1. 155–191.
Collins, Chris. 2005. "A Smuggling Approach to the Passive in English." *Syntax* 8: 81–120.
    DOI: 10.1111/j.1467-9612.2005.00076.x
Cornilescu, Alexandra and Ion Giurgea. 2013. "The Adjective." *A Reference Grammar of Romanian. I: The Noun Phrase*, ed. by Carmen Dobrovie-Sorin and Ion Giurgea, 355–530. Amsterdam & Philadelphia: John Benjamins. DOI: 10.1075/la.207.07cor
Cornilescu, Alexandra, Carmen Dobrovie-Sorin, Ion Giurgea, Elena Soare, and Camelia Stan. 2013. "Deverbal Nouns." *A Reference Grammar of Romanian. I: The Noun Phrase*, ed. by Carmen Dobrovie-Sorin and Ion Giurgea, 663–718. Amsterdam & Philadelphia: John Benjamins. DOI: 10.1075/la.207.11cor
Donati, Valentina. 2006. "On Wh-head Movement." In *Wh-Movement. Moving On*, ed. by Lisa Cheng and Norbert Corver, 21–46. MIT Press.

Dragomirescu, Adina. 2013. *Particularități sintactice ale limbii române în context romanic. Supinul.* Bucharest: Editura Muzeului Național al Literaturii Române.

Dye, Cristina. 2006. "A- and Ā-Movement in Romanian Supine Constructions." *Linguistic Inquiry* 37(4): 665–674. DOI: 10.1162/ling.2006.37.4.665

Giurgea, Ion. 2011. The Romanian Verbal Cluster and the Theory of Head Movement. In Julia Herschensohn ed. *Romance Linguistics 2010. Selected papers from the 40th Linguistic Symposium on Romance Languages (LSRL), Seattle, Washington, March 2010,* 271–286. Amsterdam, Philadelphia: John Benjamins. DOI: 10.1075/cilt.318.17giu

Giurgea, Ion and Elena Soare. 2007. "Tough Constructions and Raising Reduced Relatives." *Bucharest Working Papers in Linguistics,* IX.1: 124–136.

Giurgea, Ion and Elena Soare, 2010a. "Predication and the Nature of Non-Finite Relatives in Romance." In *Edges, Heads and Projections: Interface Properties,* ed. by Anna Maria Di Sciullo and Virginia Hill, 313–353. John Benjamins. DOI: 10.1075/la.156.12giu

Giurgea, Ion and Elena Soare. 2010b. "Modal Non-Finite Relatives in Romance." In *Modality and Mood in Romance: Modal interpretation, mood selection, and mood alternation,* ed. by Eva-Maria Remberger and Martin Becker, 67–94. De Gruyter.

Grosu, Alexander. 2010. "On the Pre-Theoretical Notion Phrasal Head." In *Edges, Heads and Projections,* ed. by Anna Maria Di Sciullo and Virginia Hill, 151–190. John Benjamins. DOI: 10.1075/la.156.11gro

Hill, Virginia. 2002. "The Gray Area of Supine Clauses." *Linguistics* 40: 495–517. DOI: 10.1515/ling.2002.021

Iatridou, Sabina, Elena Anagnostopoulou, and Roumyana Izvorski. 2001. "Observations About the Form and Meaning of the Perfect." In *Ken Hale: A Life in Language,* ed. by Kenstowicz, Michael, 189–238. Cambridge: MIT Press.

Larson, Richard. 1998. Free Relative Clauses and Missing P's: Reply to Grosu. Ms., Stony Brook University.

Nunes, Jairo. 2001. "Sideward Movement." *Linguistic Inquiry* 32: 303–344. DOI: 10.1162/00243890152001780

Nunes, Jairo. 2004. *Linearization of Chains and Sideward Movement.* Cambridge, MA: MIT Press.

Pană-Dindelegan, G. 1982. Structura sintactică nominal +adverb (sau adjectiv) + supin. *Limba Română,* 31: 5–13.

Pană-Dindelegan, G. 1992. *Sintaxă și semantică. Clase de cuvinte și forme gramaticale cu dublă natură.* Bucharest: Tipografia Universității din București.

Pană-Dindelegan, G. 2011. Din istoria supinului românesc. In *Limba română—ipostaze ale variației lingvistiice,* I, ed. by R. Zafiu, C. Ușurelu, H. Bogdan Oprea, 119–130. Bucharest: Editura Universității din București.

van Riemsdijk, Henk. 2006. "Grafts Follow from Merge." In *Phases of Interpretation,* Mara Frascarelli, 17–44. De Gruyter. DOI: 10.1515/9783110197723.2.17

Roberts, Ian. 2010. *Agreement and Head Movement: Clitics, Incorporation and Defective Goals.* Cambridge, MA: MIT Press. DOI: 10.7551/mitpress/9780262014304.001.0001

Soare, Elena. 2002. *Le supin roumain et la théorie des catégories mixtes.* Ph.D. dissertation, University of Paris 7.

Soare, Elena. and Carmen Dobrovie-Sorin. 2002. "The Romanian Supine and Adjectival Complementation. Tough Constructions." *Bucharest Working Papers in Linguistics* 4(1): 75–87.

Vişan, Ruxandra. 2004. "The Cât de/Cum...de Exclamative Patterns in Romanian." *Bucharest Working Papers in Linguistics*, 6: 1.

Zwart, Jan-Wouter. 2012. "Easy to (Re)analyse: Tough-Constructions in Minimalism." *Linguistics in the Netherlands 2012*, ed. by Elenbaas, Marion and Suzanne Aalberse, 147–158. Amsterdam, Philadelphia: John Benjamins. DOI: 10.1075/avt.29.12zwa

Depictive secondary predicates in Spanish and the relative/absolute distinction*

Silvia Gumiel-Molina, Norberto Moreno-Quibén &
Isabel Pérez-Jiménez
Universidad de Alcalá / Consejo Superior de Investigaciones Científicas /
Universidad de Alcalá and Consejo Superior de Investigaciones Científicas

This study accounts for the unacceptability of individual-level gradable adjectives as (depictive) secondary predicates on the basis of two factors: (a) the semantics of gradable adjectives—specifically the way their comparison classes are formed in the syntax, giving rise to the difference between relative/absolute adjectives; (b) the pragmatic *inference of temporal persistence* that characterizes IL predicates. Absolute adjectives are evaluated with respect to a comparison class composed of counterparts (stages) of an individual, so that the property they express must be interpreted as subject to variation. Therefore, the inference of temporal persistence which seems to be at the basis of the individual-level character of predicates does not arise, giving rise to the stage-level interpretation that absolute adjectives receive. The inference of temporal persistence arises by default in the case of relative adjectives since in the comparison class selected by these adjectives there are no stages (of an individual) instantiating different degrees of the property but just different individuals manifesting different degrees of it. The inference of temporal persistence associated with relative adjectives makes the *simultaneity constraint* required by secondary predication contexts (McNally 1994) trivial and uninformative. As a consequence, only absolute adjectives are allowed in this syntactic environment.

1. Introduction

The distinction between individual and stage-level predicates (IL, SL, henceforth)—implemented in different ways in the literature, and generally considered as a lexical property of predicates—has been taken to explain a wide variety of linguistic contrasts

* Authors are in alphabetical order. The research underlying this work has been partly supported by a grant to the projects SPYCE III-(FFI2012-31785) and COMPSYSIN-(FFI2012-32886) from the Spanish MINECO.

DOI 10.1075/rllt.9.08gum
© 2016 John Benjamins Publishing Company

in many languages. In Spanish, it has been taken to account for the distribution of predicates with the copulas *ser* ('be$_{SER}$') and *estar* ('be$_{ESTAR}$'). Nouns, DPs, and IL adjectives (for example, relational adjectives) combine with *ser*, (1a), while SL adjectives combine with *estar*; this is specifically the case of so-called 'perfective adjectives', morphologically connected with participles and expressing the final state of an event, (1b). *Alternating adjectives* combine with both copulas: this is the case of most qualifying gradable adjectives in Spanish, (1c). Alternating adjectives have received three kinds of analyses within lexicalist proposals that consider the IL/SL character of adjectives a lexical property: (a) they have been analyzed as basically IL adjectives that can be coerced into SL adjectives in certain syntactic contexts (like in copular sentences with *estar*) —this is the most widespread proposal in the literature; (b) they have been analyzed as neutral/unmarked with respect to the IL/SL characterization, with the syntactic context they are inserted in determining their aspectual characterization; (c) they have been analyzed as doubly-marked adjectives (IL and SL) in the lexicon.

(1)   a.   *Mi hijo {es/*está}   {(el) presidente/ vegetariano}.*
         my son is$_{\{SER/*ESTAR\}}$ the president vegetarian
         'My son is {the president/vegetarian}.'

      b.   *María {*es/está}   {enfadada/ enferma}.*
         María is$_{\{*SER/ESTAR\}}$ angry   ill
         'María is {angry/ill}.'

      c.   *Mi hijo {es/está}   {alto / delgado/ feliz,*
         my son is$_{\{SER/ESTAR\}}$ tall   thin   happy
         nervioso / valiente / ágil / fuerte}.
         excitable courageous agile strong
         'My son is {tall/thin/happy/excitable/courageous/agile/strong}.'

As illustrated in (2), the IL/SL distinction has also been taken to crucially account for the distribution of predicates in depictive secondary predication environments (an explicit definition of depictive secondary predicate will be given in Section 2). As generally claimed (see the references in Footnote 1), IL adjectives cannot appear as depictive secondary predicates. This is the behavior shown by qualifying alternating adjectives lexically classified as IL predicates (recall (1c) *alta* 'tall', *delgada* 'thin', etc.). On the contrary, adjectives lexically classified as stage-level (*enfadada* 'angry', *enferma* 'ill') can appear as depictive secondary predicates.[1] Nominal predicates and relational adjectives will be left aside in this paper.

---

1.   Secondary predicates have been commonly classified into two groups in the literature: *resultative predicates* (which do not exist in Romance languages) and *depictive predicates*. In Spanish, depictives can be subject-oriented, (i), and object-oriented, (ii).

(2)

	Individual-level predicate	Stage-level predicate
Depictive secondary predicates	*/# *María llegó alta* (lit. María arrived tall) */#*Ana leyó el libro delgada* (lit. Ana read the book thin)	*María llegó enfadada* (María arrived angry) *Ana leyó el libro enferma* (Ana read the book ill)

Following our proposal in Section 3 explaining the distribution of adjectives in copular sentences in Spanish (Gumiel-Molina, Moreno-Quibén, and Pérez-Jiménez' 2015), in this paper, we show that the behavior of qualifying gradable adjectives as depictive secondary predicates, e.g., (2), can be derived from their gradability properties, namely from the relative/absolute distinction (as defined in Toledo and Sassoon 2011; Sassoon 2013). We assume McNally's (1994) hypothesis that a pragmatic explanation in terms of an inference of temporal persistence associated with IL-predications can account for their ungrammaticality/unacceptability in secondary predication environments. Our claim is that the way in which the comparison class needed to evaluate the adjectival predication within the secondary predication clause is formed, giving rise to relative or absolute gradable adjectives, triggers the inference of temporal persistence for relative adjectives and crucially determines the judgments in (2). Under this viewpoint, we argue that the IL/SL distinction in the domain of secondary predication is connected (or even can be reduced) to the relative/absolute distinction, at least in the domain of gradable adjectives.

Moreover, we claim that gradable adjectives are not relative or absolute (IL or SL) *per se*, but they can be evaluated with respect to a comparison class comprising individuals or stages of individuals. The comparison class is introduced in the syntax by a specific functional node, so that adjectives are not marked as relative or absolute in the lexicon. Our proposal is that the paradigm in (2) derives from two facts: (a) the fact

---

(i)   a.   *Juan cocinó los pasteles cansado* / John baked the cakes tired.
    b.   *Juan llegó enfadado* / John arrived angry.
    c.   *Juan sonrió contento* / lit. John smiled happy (Intended: John smiled happily).

(ii)   *Pedro recogió rotos los juguetes* / Peter collected the toys broken.

In this paper, we focus on subject-oriented depictive secondary predicates. For a detailed description of these predicates in Spanish see Hernanz (1988), Demonte (1988, 1992), Bosque (1990), Leonetti and Escandell-Vidal (1991), Carrier and Randall (1992), Mallén (1991), Demonte and Masullo (1999), Ardid-Gumiel (2001).

In (2), we use # to indicate pragmatic/semantic ill-formedness. The examples doubly marked as */# have been generally judged as ungrammatical in the literature.

that the syntactic context in (2)—the secondary predication environment—requires an absolute interpretation of adjectives, and (b) the fact that it is difficult to obtain such an interpretation for some adjectives due to the specific dimension they express and how properties are conceived in the real world, as we will explain in Section 5.

The paper is organized as follows: in Section 2 we introduce depictive secondary predicates and also McNally's (1994) pragmatic account for the contrast in (2); in Section 3 we present the difference between relative and absolute gradable adjectives; in Section 4, we argue for the absolute character of gradable adjectives when they occur as secondary predicates; finally, in Sections 5 and 6, we analyze the reason why only absolute adjectives can be secondary predicates and also account for some odd cases of secondary predication (with stative verbs) in pragmatic terms.

2.   Depictive secondary predicates. The McNallyan turn

Depictive secondary predicates "express a state the referent of their controller is in at the time the state of affairs described by the main predicate holds" (Rosthein 1983; apud, McNally 1994, 3). In (3) (which is the structure assumed in McNally 1994 for secondary predication), the sentence expresses the simultaneity between the running time of the event (in a broad sense to include states) denoted by the secondary predicate *cansado* and the running time of the main predicate. Depictive secondary predicates are thus subject to a *simultaneity condition*.

(3)   Juan [$_{VP}$ [$_{V}'$ *llegó*   (*a su casa*)] [$_{AP=PREDP}$ *cansado*]].
       Juan   arrived   (to his home)   tired
       'Juan arrived home tired.'

Depictive secondary predicates are semantically combined with the main predication via the *Predicative Adjunct Rule*, (4), which gives rise to the simultaneity condition described above (McNally 1994; Rothstein 2011, a.o.).

(4)   Predicative Adjunct Rule (McNally 1994, 7)

$||[V' \; XP \, [PRED]_i \,]_{VP}||$(where i is the index of the controller)

$$= \left\{ <e, x> \;\middle|\; \begin{array}{c} \text{there is an e', e''} \le \text{e such that } \mathbf{V}'(e', x), \mathbf{XP}\,[\mathbf{PRED}]_i\,(e''), \\ \text{and } \tau(e) = \tau(e') = \tau(e'') \end{array} \right\}$$

A sentence like (3) will have the denotation in (5), once the entity argument has saturated the open positions of the main predicate and the adjunct. *Llegó cansado* describes an event with two coextensive parts, the one described by the main predicate, *to arrive*, and the one described by the secondary predicate, *tired*. What (5) amounts to is the assertion that the two eventualities hold simultaneously during a time span (the running time of the two events).

From the point of view of syntax, let us assume a multidimensional approach (based on Rapoport 1999; Gumiel 2008), where the subject of the sentence is both an argument in the main clause and in the secondary predicative phrase (PredP; Bowers 1993).

(5)
$$\left\{ e \middle| \begin{array}{c} \text{there is an } e', e'' \le e \text{ such that } \textbf{llegar}(e', j), \textbf{cansado}(e'', j), \\ \text{and } \tau(e) = \tau(e') = \tau(e'') \end{array} \right\}$$

(6)   T...

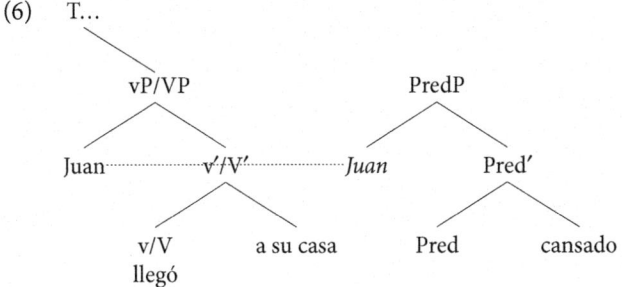

As claimed in the Introduction, and restricting the discussion to qualifying gradable adjectives, only stage-level predicates can occur as depictive secondary predicates, (7). Adjectives usually classified as being lexically individual-level predicates sound odd in this context, (8).

(7)   a.   *María llegó   a   su   casa   {cansada / sola / enfadada}.*
           María arrived to her house   tired   alone angry
           'María arrived home {tired/alone/angry}'

      b.   *María se examinó   {contenta / enferma}.*
           María took-the-exam   happy   ill
           'María took the exam {happy/ill}.'

      c.   *María leyó   el   poema {sobria / exhausta}.*
           María read the poem   sober   exhausted
           'María read the poem {sober /exhausted}.'

(8)   a.   */# *María llegó   a   su   casa   {cauta /   joven}.*
           María arrived to her house   cautious / young

      b.   */# *María se examinó   {alta / inteligente}.*
           María took-the-exam   tall / intelligent

      c.   */# *María leyó   el   poema {delgada / lista}.*
           María read the poem   thin   bright

The simultaneity condition makes no distinction between IL and SL predicates. There-fore, in and of itself it does not explain the reason why IL predicates sound bad in the context of secondary predication. To explain this fact, McNally appeals to a pragmatic explanation (see also Condoravdi 1992). She claims that the simultaneity condition must be relevant and informative, hence, non-trivially met. However, according to her, individual-level predicates trigger a pragmatic inference of temporal persistence, (9), which makes the simultaneity condition trivial.

(9)   "Individual-level predicates are associated with an inference of temporal persistence; stage-level predicates are not. The inference of temporal persis-tence in effect specifies the following: if an eventuality is going on at time t and you have no information that it is not going on at some later time t', then infer that it is going on at that later [and previous] time t' as well. Note that this is a default inference, surfacing only if there is no information to the contrary."   (McNally 1994, 9)

Given this inference of temporal persistence, the simultaneity condition is trivially met in many cases in out-of-the-blue contexts with IL adjectives, giving rise to infelicitous sentences such as those in (2) and (8). However, note that examples like (10), also containing alternating adjectives (recall the examples in (1c)) are grammatical and acceptable:[2]

(10)   a.   *María llegó   a   su   casa   alegre.*
            María arrived to her house happy
            'María arrived home happy.'

        b.   *María se examinó   ágil.*
            María took-the-exam agile
            'María took the physical exam being agile.'

        c.   *María leyó el   libro   feliz.*
            María read the book happy
            'María read the book happy.'

---

2.   McNally (1994) for English and Ardid-Gumiel (2001) for Spanish also claim that nouns and relational adjectives (both IL predicates) can occur as secondary predicates in sentences expressing transitions.

(i)   *Juan volvió   vegetariano de   la   India.*
       Juan came.back vegetarian   from the India
       'Juan came back from India being a vegetarian.'

We leave for further research a unified account of the behavior of both qualifying adjectives and relational adjectives as secondary predicates.

In those proposals where adjectives are lexically IL or SL, acceptable examples like these could be analyzed as examples containing stage-level adjectives, perhaps as a consequence of a coercion process triggered by the syntactic context; however, Escandell-Vidal and Leonetti (2002) claim that aspectual coercion cannot be triggered in the context of secondary predication, because this context lacks a syntactic trigger of the coercion process (contrary to what happens in copular sentences with *estar*, where the copula itself is the trigger of the aspectual coercion of IL adjectives, recall (1c)). Moreover, proposing a coercion process to explain the grammaticality of these examples leaves unexplained the ungrammaticality/oddness of the examples in (8).

In the following sections, we will recast McNally's proposal, leaving aside the hypothesis that adjectives are lexically individual or stage-level predicates, in order to explain the behavior of qualifying gradable adjectives as depictive secondary predicates. We will show that the crucial property at the core of the paradigm in (7) and (8) is the relative/absolute distinction, which is syntactically built up, to which we turn in the following section. The contrast between (8) and (10) will be explained in Section 5.

3. The relative/absolute distinction

We follow Toledo and Sassoon (2011) in proposing that all gradable adjectives require a standard of comparison established in relation to a comparison class to be interpreted.[3] The difference between relative and absolute adjectives is determined by the nature of the comparison class selected in each case. The comparison class of an adjective depends on the individual it is predicated of and can be established based on *variance between individuals* (relative adjectives) or based on *variance within the same individual* (absolute adjectives).

First, an adjective can be evaluated with respect to an extensional comparison class, C, composed of individuals sharing some property in the index of evaluation, (11), which defaults to a midpoint standard value. This variance between individuals defines relative adjectives, (12).

(11) $C=\{y: P(y)\} = \lambda y.P(y)$

---

3.   The point of view assumed here differs from the hypothesis argued for in Kennedy and McNally (2005), Kennedy (2007), and subsequent work, where it is proposed that the interpretation of absolute adjectives is based on a conventionally fixed standard dependent on the scalar structure of the adjective.

(12)   a.   *Juan es* [$_{AP}$ *alto para ser jugador de fútbol*].
       Juan is$_{SER}$ tall   for   be   player   of   soccer
       'Juan is tall for a soccer player.'

     b.   Comparison class for *alto para ser jugador de fútbol/tall for a soccer player*:
       C = {y | **jugador de futbol**(y) in w}

     c.   [[Juan es alto para ser jugador de fútbol]]^{w,t}=1 if the degree of Juan's height is equal to or greater than the standard degree of height of members of the class of soccer players as given by function M. (See (15) for a definition of this function.)

Second, adjectives may have a comparison class established within the same individual, (13). This comparison class defines absolute adjectives, (14). Absolute adjectives are evaluated with respect to a comparison class comprising counterparts of the subject. Counterparts are understood as stages of the subject manifesting different degrees of the property in question in different indices. One of these degrees is considered the standard value, which is therefore conceived by default as a class-maximal/minimal value. In the case of *lleno* 'full', the comparison class is composed of counterparts of the predicate argument, the restaurant in this particular case, as this argument is instantiated in different stages in every contextually salient typical world. The fact that the degrees of the property in question are manifested through stages of the subject has the consequence that the standard degree selected by M will count as maximal or minimal (within the comparison class).[4]

(13)   C = λs.∀w'[[w'Aw][x is R(ealized) as s at w' & {P(x)/x is related to P} at s in w']]

(14)   a.   *El restaurante está* [$_{AP}$ *lleno*].
       'The restaurant is$_{ESTAR}$ full.'

     b.   Comparison class for *lleno/full*: C = λs.∀w'[[w'Aw][x=the restaurant is R(ealized) as s at w' & {P(x)/x is related to P} at s in w']]

     c.   [[El restaurante está lleno C$_{pro}$]]^{w,t}=1 iff the degree of fullness of the restaurant is equal to the standard (maximal) degree of fullness of the restaurant as it would be typically instantiated (realized) as a stage s included in every normal world w'.

---

4.   In (13), w' ranges over world-time pairs; A is an accessibility relation that, given a world w, relates w to worlds w' which are normal or where all the things that normally hold do hold (Asher & Morreau 1995). The function in (13) returns the set of stages such that for every accessible typical world w', the individual x has a realization s, and x normally {manifests/is/is related to} P at s in w' (see Gumiel-Molina, Moreno-Quibén, and Pérez-Jiménez 2015).

We claim that being absolute or relative is *not* a *lexical* property of adjectives. Our proposal is that the relative/absolute interpretation of an adjective is syntactically linked to the degree morphology with which the adjective combines. The degree morpheme, *pos* in the positive form of the adjective, is syntactically generated as the head of the Deg(ree) node present in the extended projection of gradable adjectives (Corver 1991). *Pos* introduces the type of the comparison class (Kennedy 1999; Fults 2006), which is responsible of the categorization of adjectives as absolute or relative. Specifically, the comparison class acts as a second argument of the M function introduced by *pos*, (15).[5]

(15)

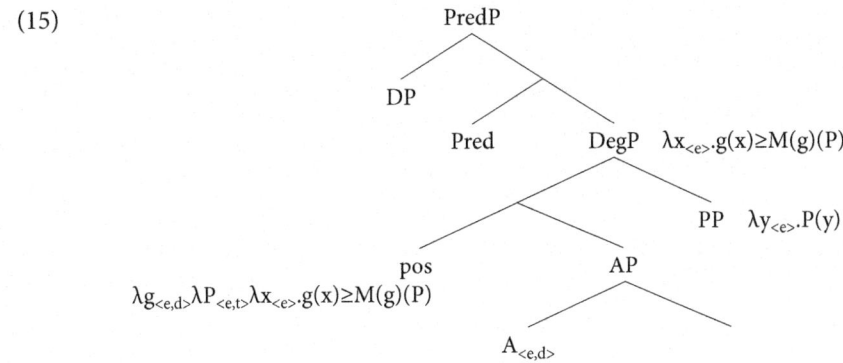

$$\text{PredP}$$

DP

Pred — DegP $\lambda x_{<e>}.g(x) \geq M(g)(P)$

PP $\lambda y_{<e>}.P(y)$

pos $\lambda g_{<e,d>}\lambda P_{<e,t>}\lambda x_{<e>}.g(x) \geq M(g)(P)$

AP

$A_{<e,d>}$

The function M sets the standard degree to which the reference degree (i.e. the degree assigned to the individual by the function) is compared, and can be regarded as a "function over gradable properties [g] and comparison class properties [P]" (Fults 2006, 134). The comparison class is normally instantiated by a PP headed by *for* in English or *para* in Spanish, but it can also be instantiated by a null pronoun C, as commonly assumed in the literature, recall (14c).

In Gumiel-Molina, Moreno-Quibén, and Pérez-Jiménez (2015), it is claimed that the relative/absolute distinction explains the distribution of gradable qualifying adjectives with copular verbs in Spanish. The copulas *ser* and *estar* combine with relative and absolute adjectives respectively (recall (1)). Relative and absolute adjectives behave differently in their combination with *for*-phrases. Relative adjectives (co-occurring with *ser*) are compatible with *for*-phrases that extensionally restrict the comparison

---

5. This proposal is compatible with McNally's (1994) proposal in (9) and the structure in (6). In (15) Pred introduces a predicate of events and individuals by which the predicate argument receives the thematic role of holder of a property. The PredP in (15) hooks to the VP/vP in the multidimensional structure of (6), which introduces the temporal trace or running time of an event.

class to objects that are members of the set defined by the nominal complement of the preposition *for*. *For*-phrases do co-occur with absolute adjectives (combining with *estar*) if the *for*-phrase references counterparts of the individual of which the adjective is predicated, (16) and (17).

(16) a. *Soy   bajo   para ser   jugador de baloncesto.*
         am$_{SER}$ short for   be$_{SER}$ player of basketball
         'I am short for being a basketball-player.'

      b. *#Estoy   bajo   para ser   jugador de baloncesto.*
         am$_{ESTAR}$ short for   be$_{SER}$ player of basketball

(17) a. *#Soy   delgada para ser   yo.*
         am$_{SER}$ thin   for   be$_{SER}$ I
         Intended: 'I'm thin for being me.'

      b. *Estoy   delgada para ser   yo.*
         am$_{ESTAR}$ thin   for   be$_{SER}$ I
         'I look thin for being me.'

In Gumiel-Molina, Moreno-Quibén, and Pérez-Jiménez (2015), it was also claimed that the relative/absolute distinction is not a lexical property of adjectives but is built up in the syntax by functional structure (*pos*—DegP; cf. Husband 2012, a.o.). This proposal allowed us to explain the fact that most qualifying gradable adjectives are variable-behavior adjectives that behave as relative or absolute adjectives, therefore combining with *ser* or with *estar* as it was shown in (1c), repeated here for convenience.[6]

(18) *Mi hijo {es/está}   {alto / delgado / feliz,*
      my son is$_{SER/ESTAR}$ tall   thin   happy
      nervioso / valiente /   ágil / fuerte}.
      excitable   courageous agile   strong
      'My son is {tall/thin/happy/excitable/courageous/agile/strong}.'

In *estar*-sentences, where absolute adjectives are found, the within-individual comparison class includes counterparts of the subject. Necessarily, then, there is a change regarding the degree to which the individual holds the property in different indices. Therefore, with absolute adjectives the inference of temporal persistence is not obtained. In other words, since the property contributed by the absolute adjective is evaluated with respect to stages of the subject, no inference of temporal persistence of

---

6. Cases of non-variability, namely *perfective adjectives* (recall (1b)), which derive from participles and combine with *estar*, and relational (non-gradable) adjectives, (1a), which are semantically modifiers of kinds (Boleda et al. 2012, among others), and combine with *ser*, receive an independent explanation. See Gumiel-Molina, Moreno-Quibén, and Pérez-Jiménez (2015).

the property with respect to the subject is available when the truth of the sentence is evaluated.

On the other hand, in *ser*-sentences, relative adjectives express the degree in which an entity has a specific property compared to other entities (between-individuals comparison class). These adjectives give rise to the inference of temporal persistence as a default inference, since in the domain of the discourse in which the sentence is evaluated, stages of the subject/property are not found, but only different individuals instantiating different degrees of the property in question.

The individual/stage distinction is thus conceived in the adjectival domain as a distinction related to the kind of elements that built up the comparison class needed to evaluate the adjectival predication.

4.   Absolute secondary predicates

If the IL/SL distinction can, thus, be remodeled for qualifying gradable adjectives as proposed in the previous section, and if we accept the generalization that only SL predicates can occur as depictive secondary predicates, we expect, then, that adjectives show an absolute behavior when they occur in this syntactic environment. Consider, on the one hand, the behavior of alternating gradable adjectives (recall (1c)) with *para/for*-adjuncts. In (19), the *for*-phrase induces the formation of a within-individual comparison class (absolute interpretation of the A) in (a), and a between-individuals comparison class (relative interpretation of the A) in (b). Accordingly, the examples are differently judged.

(19)   a.   *Juan   llegó*   [$_{AP}$ *ágil* [$_{PP}$ *para   ser   miércoles*]].
            Juan   arrived   agile   for   be$_{SER}$ Wednesday
            (Context: On Wednesdays, he takes care of his parents, and generally he is tired.)
            'Juan arrived agile for a Wednesday.'

      b.   *#Juan   llegó*   [$_{AP}$ *ágil* [$_{PP}$ *para   ser   bombero*]].
            Juan   arrived   agile   for   be$_{SER}$ fireman
            (Context: Juan is a firemen, so, he already has the properties firemen typically have, he is strong and agile.)
            Intended: 'Juan arrived agile for being a fireman.'

On the other hand, note that secondary predicates admit a continuation with the copula *estar*, expressing a generalization about how a given individual can be. A continuation with the copula *ser* is not possible. According to Toledo and Sassoon (2011) this inference is only triggered by absolute adjectives since only in these cases is the comparison class composed of counterparts—possible temporal stages of that same individual in actual but not present circumstances (namely, in the past), or in normal, although not actual, circumstances. A comparison to these counterparts validates inferences concerning how the individual can be.[7]

(20)   a.   *María llegó*   [$_{AP}$ *ágil*], *tan ágil como podía estar.*
             María arrived   agile, as   agile as   could be$_{ESTAR}$
             'Maria arrived agile, as agile as she could have been.'

       b.   #*María llegó*   [$_{AP}$ *ágil*], *tan ágil como podía ser.*
             María arrived   agile, as   agile as   could be$_{SER}$

(21)   a.   *María se examinó*   [$_{AP}$ *inquieta*],
             María took-the-exam   restless,

             tan inquieta como podía estar.
             as   restless as   could be$_{ESTAR}$
             'María took the exam restless, as restless as she could have been.'

       b.   #*María se examinó*   [$_{AP}$ *inquieta*],
             María took-the-exam   restless,

             tan inquieta como podía ser.
             as   restless as   could be$_{SER}$

Note also that it is a contradiction to assert that at the time that the situation described by the main predicate holds, the referent of the secondary predicate's controller is in the state described by the adjective, and immediately to deny that this latter state holds, (22a) and (23a). But it is not a contradiction to assert the coincidence in time of the state described by the main predication and the state expressed by the adjunct predicate, and subsequently deny that the same entity does not hold a property to the standard degree as given by the comparison class composed by other distinct individuals.

(22)   a.   #*María llegó*   [$_{AP}$ *ágil*], *aunque no estaba*   [$_{AP}$ *ágil*].
             María arrived   agile, although not was$_{ESTAR}$ agile

       b.   *María llegó*   [$_{AP}$ *ágil*], *aunque no era*   [$_{AP}$ *ágil*].
             María arrived   agile, although not was$_{SER}$ agile
             'María arrived agile, although she was not agile.'

---

7.   These inferences are also obtained in copular sentences with *estar*, where the adjectival complement is interpreted as absolute. The sentence *María está alta* (María is$_{ESTAR}$ tall) gives rise to the inference that *María está tan alta como puede estar* (María is$_{ESTAR}$ as tall as she can be$_{ESTAR}$). On the contrary, *María es alta* (María is$_{SER}$ tall) does not give rise to the inference that #*María es tan alta como puede ser* (María is$_{SER}$ as tall as she can be$_{SER}$).

(23) a. #*María se examinó*   [$_{AP}$ *inquieta*],
María took-the-exam   restless,

aunque no estaba   [$_{AP}$ *inquieta*].
although not was$_{ESTAR}$ restless

b. *María se examinó*   [$_{AP}$ *inquieta*],
María took-the-exam   restless,

aunque no era   [$_{AP}$ *inquieta*].
although not was$_{SER}$ restless

'María took the exam restless, although she was not restless.'

For the contradiction not to arise it is crucial that the adjectives are interpreted as absolute in the context of secondary predication and as relative in the context of the *ser* 'be$_{SER}$' predication. Therefore, in the previous examples the property expressed by *agile* or *restless* changes with respect to one individual, namely the referent of the subject of predication. The adjectives *agile* and *restless* select for within-individual comparison classes. Note that an example like the following, which is only possible in the context of *Alice in Wonderland*, means that Alicia's height changed. *Alta* 'tall' is necessarily interpreted in this context as an absolute adjective.

(24) *Alicia entró en la habitación alta y salió baja.*
Alicia went in-to the room   tall and came-out short
'Alicia went into the room tall and came out short.'

We conclude, thus, that adjectives are necessarily interpreted as absolute in the context of depictive secondary predication. At this point, two questions arise:

a. If all gradable adjectives can be interpreted as relative or absolute (i.e., if all qualifying gradable adjectives are *alternating adjectives,* except for *perfective adjectives*), why are the examples in (8) judged as degraded (ungrammatical/infelicitous)? (Recall the contrast between (8) and (10).)
b. Why can only absolute adjectives be secondary predicates?

We will try to answer these questions in the following sections.

5. The role of the dimension of the adjective

If any alternating gradable adjective can be built up in the syntax as relative or absolute, why is it so difficult for some adjectives, like *alto/tall, bajo/short, inteligente/intelligent,* to be construed as secondary predicates? Why are the examples in (8) judged as degraded (ungrammatical/infelicitous)? How can we explain the contrast between (8) and (10)?

We claim that this is a consequence of the specific dimension expressed by the adjectives involved, plus the simultaneity requirement imposed by the secondary predication context. Adjectives like *alto/tall* or *inteligente/intelligent* express properties with respect to which entities do not show rapid changes. The dimension of the adjective makes it difficult to compare different stages of the subject in a short span of time (as forced by the timespan associated with the main predication), a characteristic that seems to be necessary for the simultaneity condition to be satisfied. Only in severely constrained contexts, like (25) (which seem to be "magic contexts"), is it possible to compare the degrees of height of different stages of the subject in short spans of time.

(25)   *Alicia tomó la pócima mágica que la hacía cambiar*
        Alicia drank the potion magic that her made change

        de tamaño en unos segundos, así que se sentó a jugar al
        of size in some seconds, so that SE sat to play to.the

        ajedrez [$_{AP}$ *alta*] *y terminó la partida* [$_{AP}$ *bajita*].
        chess tall and finished the game short

        'As soon as Alice drank the magic potion, her size changed, so she started playing chess tall and end up playing short.'

6.   Why are secondary predicates absolute adjectives?

The crucial question to be answered now is why the absolute interpretation of the adjective is the one obtained in the context of secondary predication. Where does this constraint come from?

In previous approaches, the licensing of adjectives as secondary predicates is usually explained in terms of an identification requirement applying to the secondary predicate and the main verb. For example, Hernanz (1988) claims that secondary predicates are licensed via *thematic identification* with the main verb: only those adjectives encoding an eventive variable <e> (i.e., SL adjectives) can occur as secondary predicates since only in those cases can the eventive variable of the adjective and the eventive variable encoded by the main verb be thematically identified. Therefore, stative verbs are predicted not to license depictive secondary predicates:

(26)   #*Pedro sabe francés contento.*
        Pedro knows French happy
        Intended: 'Pedro knows French when he is happy.'

Similarly, Jiménez (2000) claims that adjectives have aspectual features that must match the aspectual features of the main verb (encoded in an ASP node). Only those adjectives with a [+perfective] feature (i.e., SL adjectives) can satisfy the aspectual feature of [+perfective] verbs. Any other combination of features will make the derivation crash. Therefore, only SL adjectives can be depictive secondary predicates, and only non-stative verbs can support them. We will come back to stative verbs in Section 6.

Within the proposal developed in this paper, the reason why only absolute adjectives appear as depictive secondary predicates is the following. When the main predicate of the clause is not stative, it introduces in the domain of discourse an event in which the entity argument/the subject is a participant. Hence, stages of the subject of predication are readily available and stand out in the discourse context favoring the compatibility with an adjectival comparison class that includes stages. In consequence, the absolute interpretation of alternating gradable adjectives acting as secondary predicates is favored. This is the case in (27), where alternating adjectives receive an absolute interpretation, as has been shown above.

(27) a. *María   llegó*   [_AP *alegre*].
          María   arrived   happy
          'María arrived happy.'

      b. *María   se examinó*   [_AP *fuerte*].
          María   took-the-exam   strong
          'María took the physical exam being strong.'

In these cases, the simultaneity condition governing the well-formedness of secondary predication structures is non-trivially met. Since the property contributed by the absolute adjective is evaluated with respect to stages of the subject, no inference of temporal persistence of the property with respect to the subject is available, and simultaneity is relevant and informative: there is a moment in the past in which María arrives and is happy simultaneously. The assertion that this particular temporal interval exists is not trivial from the point of view of information sharing.

A relative interpretation of alternating adjectives in this context is disfavored and, moreover, would give rise to a violation of the simultaneity constraint. Relative adjectives, expressing the degree in which an entity has a specific property compared to other entities (between-individuals comparison class), give rise to the inference of temporal persistence which makes the simultaneity constraint trivial, as claimed by McNally (1994) for IL predicates.

When the context (specifically the main verb) does not provide stages of the entity argument, the absolute interpretation of alternating adjectives acting as secondary predicates is very hard to get and the predication as a whole cannot receive a coherent interpretation. This is precisely what we find when the main predicate of the clause is a stative predicate. In this case secondary predication with alternating adjectives is generally odd.

(28) a. #*María   sabe   fránces* [_AP *ágil*].
          María   knows   French   agile
          Intended: 'María knows French (when she is) agile.'

b. #A María le   gustan los coches [$_{AP}$ *alta*].
    to María to-her like   the cars   tall
    Intended: 'María likes cars (when she is) tall.'

Stative predicates are spatiotemporally independent: the entities participating in these states will do so no matter what their spatiotemporal location happens to be (McNally 1998; Magri 2009). In this particular context, stages of the subject/entity argument do not stand out because the discourse is populated with entities and not with stages of the argument. The formation of within-individual comparison classes is disfavored and the adjective acting as a secondary predicate is interpreted as relative. In these cases, the simultaneity condition on the coextensive parts of the situation expressed by the main and secondary predication is trivially met, hence uninformative, and the whole sentence is infelicitous.

When the stative predicate combines with an absolute adjective whose comparison class is made up of stages that vary across a very short span of time and are spatiotemporally dependent (which is always the case with *perfective adjectives* like *sobrio/sober* or *dormido/asleep*, recall (1b)), the sentence greatly improves and the inference of temporal persistence associated to the main predicate is suspended (McNally 1994). In (29), we infer that María likes cars when and only when she is sober or that María loves Juan when and only when she is asleep. The stages comprising the within-individual comparison of the absolute perfective adjectives introduce into the discourse context a salient time that sets up a temporal limit to the temporal persistence associated with the main predication, whose effect is the cancellation of the inference. Then, the assertion of the simultaneity between the events is not trivial and it is not uninformative.

(29) a. A María [$_{VP}$ *le*   *gustan* *los* *coches*] [$_{AP}$ *sobria*].
          to María   to-her like   the   cars   sober
          'María likes the cars (when she is) sober.'

     b. *María* [$_{VP}$ *ama* *a* *Juan*] [$_{AP}$ *dormida*].
         María   loves to Juan   asleep
         'María loves John (when she is) asleep.'

The IL/SL distinction that has been proposed to explain the aforementioned differences in the context of secondary predication can thus be understood, in the domain of gradable adjectives, as a distinction related to the kind of elements that build up the comparison class needed to evaluate the adjectival property, together with the inference of temporal persistence.

Between-individual and within-individual comparison classes give rise to two different types of gradable adjectives, relative and absolute ones. If an adjective is evaluated with respect to a comparison class comprising counterparts of an individual, the property manifested by the counterparts of the individual in different indices must be interpreted as subject to variation. Therefore, the inference of temporal persistence which seems to be at the basis of the individual-level character of predicates (McNally

1994; Percus 1997; Magri 2009) does not arise, giving rise to the stage-level interpretation. On the other hand, the inference of temporal persistence arises as a default inference in the case of relative adjectives since in the comparison class selected by these adjectives there are no stages instantiating different degrees of the property but just individuals manifesting different degrees of it.

Moreover, it must be taken into account that secondary predication environments are subject to a general coherence constraint which, at this point, seems to us the only way to explain the contrast between (26) and (29), also exemplified in (30). The fact that adjectives like *contento* express psychological states, vs. adjectives like *borracho* (Marín 2001), could perhaps open a way to understand this contrast, a matter that we leave for further research.

(30)   a.   *#Juan teme las tormentas {contento/ nervioso}.*
             Juan fears the storms   happy   nervous

        b.   *Juan teme las tormentas {borracho/ sobrio}.*
             Juan fears the storms   drunk   sober
             'Juan fears storms when he is {drunk/sober}.'

7. Conclusions

In this paper, we claim that the IL/SL distinction is connected to the semantics of gradable adjectives via comparison class formation. Between-individuals and within-individual comparison classes give rise to two different types of gradable adjectives, relative and absolute ones. We thus argue for an extension of the explanatory value of the IL/SL distinction to the domain of gradability. Under this new point of view, we have argued that the IL/SL distinction in the domain of secondary predication can be connected to the relative/absolute distinction.

The hypothesis that we have put forward is that gradable adjectives that act as secondary predicates must be interpreted as absolute. Adjectives can be syntactically construed as absolute or relative, and a combination of semantic and pragmatic factors conspires to favor the absolute interpretation of the gradable adjective in the context of secondary predication.

References

Ardid-Gumiel, Ana. 2001. "The Syntax of Depictives. Subjects, Modes of Judgement and I–L/S-L Properties." *ZAS Working Papers in Linguistics* 26: 61–86.

Asher, Nicholas and Michael Morreau. 1995. "What Generic Sentences Mean." In *The Generic Book,* ed. by Gregory Carlson and Francis Jeffry Pelletier, 300–338. Chicago: University of Chicago Press.

Boleda, Gemma, Stefan Evert, Berit Gehrke, and Louise McNally. 2012. "Adjectives as Saturators vs. Modifiers: Statistical Evidence." In *Logic, Language and Meaning*, 18th *Amsterdam Colloquium, Amsterdam, The Netherlands, December 19-21, 2011, Revised Selected Papers,* ed. by Maria Aloni, Vadim Kimmelman, Floris Roelofsen, Galit Sassoon, Katrin Schulz, and Matthijs Westera, 112-121. Dordrecht: Springer.

Bosque, Ignacio. 1990. "Sobre el aspecto en los participios y los adjetivos." In *Tiempo y aspecto en español,* ed. by Ignacio Bosque, 177-210. Madrid: Cátedra.

Bowers, John. 1993. "The Syntax of Predication". *Linguistic Inquiry* 24 (4): 591-656.

Carrier, Jill and Janet H. Randall. 1992. "The Argument Structure and Syntactic Structure of Resultatives." *Linguistic Inquiry* 23: 173-234.

Condoravdi, Cleo. 1992. "Individual-level Predicates in Conditional Clauses." Talk given at the *LSA Annual Meeting,* Philadelphia, PA.

Corver, Norbert. 1991. "Evidence for DegP." *Proceedings of NELS* 21: 33-47. UMass, Amherst.

Demonte, Violeta and Pascual Masullo. 1999. "La predicación: complementos predicativos." In *Nueva gramática descriptiva de la lengua española,* ed. by Ignacio Bosque and Violeta Demonte, Chapter 38. Madrid: Espasa-Calpe.

Demonte, Violeta. 1988. "Remarks on Secondary Predicates: C-command, Extraction, and Reanalysis." *Linguistic Review* 6: 1-39. DOI: 10.1515/tlir.1987.6.1.1

Demonte, Violeta. 1992. "Temporal and Aspectual Constraints on Predicative APs." In *Current Studies in Spanish Linguistics,* ed. by Héctor Campos and Fernando Martínez-Gil, 165-200. Washington: Georgetown University Press.

Escandell-Vidal, M. Victoria and Manuel Leonetti. 2002. "Coercion and the Stage/Individual Distinction." In *From Words to Discourse. Trends in Spanish Semantics and Pragmatics,* ed. by Javier Gutiérrez Rexach, 159-180. Oxford: Elsevier.

Fults, Scott. 2006. *The Structure of Comparison: An Investigation of Gradable Adjectives.* Ph.D. Dissertation, University of Maryland.

Gumiel-Molina, Silvia. 2008. *Estructura argumental y predicación secundaria.* Alcalá de Henares: Servicio de publicaciones de la UAH.

Gumiel-Molina, Silvia, Norberto Moreno-Quibén, and Isabel Pérez-Jiménez. 2015. "Comparison classes and the relative/absolute distinction: A degree-based compositional account of the ser/estar alternation in Spanish". B. Gehrke & E. Castroviejo (Eds.), *Degree and manner modification across categories, special volume of Natural Language and Linguistic Theory.* DOI: 10.1007/s11049-015-9284-x

Hernanz, M. Lluïsa. 1988. "En torno a la sintaxis y la semántica de los complementos predicativos en español." *Estudis de Sintaxi, Estudi General* 8: 7-29.

Husband, Matthew. 2012. *On the Compositional Nature of States.* Amsterdam: John Benjamins. DOI: 10.1075/la.188

Jiménez, Ángel. 2000. "Minimalismo, aspecto y predicados secundarios." *Phiologia Hispalensis* 12: 161-170.

Kennedy, Christopher. 1999. *Projecting the Adjective: the Syntax and Semantics of Gradability and Comparison. Outstanding dissertations in Linguistics.* New York: Garland.

Kennedy, Christopher. 2007. "Vagueness and Grammar: the Semantics of Relative and Absolute Gradable Adjectives." *Linguistics and Philosophy* 30 (1): 1-45. DOI: 10.1007/s10988-006-9008-0

Kennedy, Cristopher and Louise McNally. 2005. "Scale Structure, Degree Modification, and the Semantics of Gradable Predicates." *Language* 81: 345-381. DOI: 10.1353/lan.2005.0071

Leonetti, Manuel and Victoria Escandell-Vidal. 1991. "Secondary Predication inside DPs." *University of Venice Working Papers in Linguistics* I/7: 1–35.

Magri, Giorgio. 2009. "A Theory of Individual-level Predicates Based on Blind Mandatory Scalar Implicatures." *Natural Language Semantics* 17 (3): 245–297. DOI: 10.1007/s11050-009-9042-x

Mallén, Enrique. 1991. "A Syntactic Analysis of Secondary Predication in Spanish." *Journal of Linguistics* 27: 375–403. DOI: 10.1017/S002222670001272X

Marín, Rafael. 2001. *El componente aspectual de la predicación*. Doctoral Dissertation, Universidad Autónoma de Barcelona.

McNally, Louise. 1994. "Adjunct Predicates and the Individual/Stage Distinction." *Proceedings of WCCFL* vol. 12: 561–576.

McNally, Louise. 1998. "Stativity and Theticity." In *Events and Grammar*, ed. by Susan Rothstein, 293–308. Dordrecht: Kluwer. DOI: 10.1007/978-94-011-3969-4_12

Percus, Orin J. 1997. *Aspects of A*. Ph.D. Dissertation, MIT.

Rapoport, Tova R. 1999. "Structure, Aspect and the Predicate." *Language* 75 (4): 653–677. DOI: 10.2307/417729

Rothstein, Susan. 1983. *The Syntactic Forms of Predication*. Ph.D. Dissertation, MIT.

Rothstein, Susan. 2011. "Secondary Predicates." In *Semantics: An International Handbook of Natural Language Meaning* (Vol. 2), ed. by Klaus von Heusinger, Claudia Mainborn, Paul Portner, 1142–1662. Berlin: Mouton de Gruyter.

Sassoon, Galit W. 2013. *Vagueness, Gradability and Typicality: the Interpretation of Adjective and Nouns*. Leiden-Boston: Brill. DOI: 10.1163/9789004248588

Toledo, Assaf and Galit W. Sassoon. 2011. "Absolute vs. Relative Adjectives—Variance Within vs. Between Individuals." *Proceedings of SALT* 21: 135–154.

Gender agreement with animate nouns in French[*]

Tabea Ihsane & Petra Sleeman
Département de Linguistique, Faculté des Lettres, Université de Genève /
Department of Linguistics, University of Amsterdam

Grammatical gender and semantic gender do not always go hand in hand. In French such mismatches can be observed outside the strict DP. To account for such phenomena and for gender more generally, we propose that gender is expressed in two positions within DP: on N as an uninterpretable feature accounting for grammatical gender and on the head of a Gender Phrase as a feature accounting for semantic gender. To account for the mismatches we discuss, we propose that the gender of the nouns involved is unspecified inside DP and that it can be specified in D later in the derivation.

We further show that inside the strict DP, grammatical gender agreement between Gen and NP is stricter than in the 'looser' DP (partitive), which is in turn stricter than the agreeing/referring relation with elements outside DP, reflecting Corbett's agreement hierarchy, to which we add a *partitive* position.

1. Introduction

French exhibits challenging gender phenomena with animate nouns such as *fille* 'girl', *garçon* 'boy', *professeur* 'professor', etc.: in some contexts, gender can be, must be, or cannot be overridden, as illustrated in (1), (2), and (3), respectively.[1,2]

---

[*] We are grateful to the reviewers for their fruitful comments and suggestions. We also thank Roberta d'Alessandro, Leston Buell, and Elisabeth Stark for their comments on an earlier version of this paper. All remaining errors are our own.

[1] The grammaticality judgments are mainly based on the intuitions of native speakers of French from Switzerland. Feminine forms of profession nouns are accepted to various degrees in French speaking countries. This may also lead to a different acceptance of feminine agreement in (2), especially with respect to agreement with the predicative adjective. (1)–(3) are our own, but similar examples can also be found on the Internet (i) or in the French database Frantext (ii):

(i)	*Mon*	*professeur était*	*très*	*gentille.*
	my.MASC	professor was	very	kind.FEM

DOI 10.1075/rllt.9.09ihs

(1) a. *Le   plus jeune/ La   plus   jeune de mes gentils*
the.MASC more young/ the.FEM more young of my sweet

enfants s'   appelle Nina.
children REFL is.called Nina

'The name of the youngest of my sweet children is Nina.'

b. *De tous   mes   professeurs, seul   le*
of all.MASC my   professors   only.MASC the.MASC

plus jeune / seule   la   plus   jeune – Mme Dupont
more young/ only.FEM the.FEM more young   Mrs Dupont

parle bien l'   anglais.
speaks well the English

'Of all my professors, only the youngest one—Mrs Dupont—speaks English well.'

(2) *Mon   ancien   professeur de français était toujours*
my.MASC former.MASC professor of French was always

contente   de mon travail. Elle vient de partir à la   retraite.
satisfied.FEM of my work   she just of leave in the retirement

'My former French teacher was always satisfied with my work.
She just retired.'

(3) a. *La   sentinelle arriva. Elle/*Il avait une longue barbe.*
the.FEM sentinel   arrived she/he had a   long   beard
'The sentinel arrived. He had a long beard.'

b. *J'ai vu un   léopard. Il/*Elle allaitait   ses   petits.*
I have seen a.MASC leopard he/she was.nursing his/her young
'I saw a leopard. She was nursing her young.'

In (1), both the masculine *(seul) le plus jeune* '(only) the youngest one' and the feminine *(seule) la plus jeune* are possible with *enfant* 'child' and *professeur* 'professor'. This is puzzling because both nouns are masculine, as shown by the

---

(ii) *Elle était la   plus jeune des   enfants vivants.*
she was the.FEM more young of.the children living.MASC
'She was the youngest one of the children who were still alive.'

2. To our judgment, in (3), there has to be gender sharing in a linguistic context. However, when pointing is involved, gender sharing is not necessary.

(i) *Voici la   sentinelle.   Il/Elle a   une longue barbe.*
here.is the sentinel.FEM he/she has a   long   beard
'Here is the sentinel. He has a long beard.'

agreement on *gentils* 'sweet' and *ancien* 'former', respectively, even though they refer to a female. (2) differs from (1) in that the predicative adjective *contente* 'satisfied. FEM' is feminine even though it corresponds to the masculine noun *professeur* (but see Note 1). In addition to the agreement facts just described, the gender phenomena that interest us in this paper concern reference: in the second part of (2), if the referent is a woman, a feminine pronoun has to be used to refer to the masculine noun *professeur*. In (3), in contrast, the feminine pronoun *elle* 'she' must be used to refer to the noun *sentinelle* 'sentinel', which is grammatically feminine but refers to a man.

These facts need be explained, especially since, in French, pronouns usually have the same gender as the nouns they replace (4), attributive adjectives agree in gender with the noun they modify (5), and predicative adjectives agree with the subject of the sentence (6).

(4) a. *Une belle fille est arrivée. Elle (*Il) s' est assise*
   a.FEM pretty girl is arrived she (he) REFL is seated.FEM
   *(*assis) au bar.*
   (seated.MASC) at.the bar
   'A pretty girl arrived. She sat down at the bar.'

   b. *Un grand garçon est arrivé. Il (*Elle) s' est assis*
   a.MASC tall boy is arrived he (she) REFL is seated.MASC
   *(*assise) au bar.*
   (seated.FEM) at.the bar
   'A tall boy arrived. He sat down at the bar.'

(5) a. *La plus intelligente (*Le plus intelligent) des filles*
   the most intelligent.FEM (the most intelligent.MASC) of.the girls
   vient d'arriver.
   just of arrive

   b. *Le plus intelligent (*La plus intelligente) des*
   the most intelligent.MASC (the most intelligent.FEM) of.the
   garçons vient d'arriver.
   boys just of arrive

(6) a. *La belle fille est intelligente (*intelligent).*
   the pretty girl is intelligent.FEM (intelligent.MASC)

   b. *Le grand garçon est intelligent (*intelligente).*
   the tall boy is intelligent.MASC (intelligent.FEM)

(4) shows that only a feminine pronoun, *elle* 'she', can refer to the feminine noun *fille* 'girl' and that only a masculine pronoun, *il* 'he', can replace the masculine noun *garçon*

'boy'. In (5), we can see that the adjectives *intelligente* 'intelligent.FEM' and *intelligent* 'intelligent.MASC' must have the same gender as *filles* 'girls' and *garçons* 'boys', respectively. This is also the case in (6).

Our goal in this paper is to account for the facts in (1)–(3), to explain the contrast between such examples and the ones in (4)–(6), and more generally to provide an analysis of gender that extends to all nominals, including inanimate ones. This implies focussing on the nouns involved (*enfant* 'child' vs. *fille/garçon* 'girl/boy') but also on the structures/contexts that allow the gender phenomena we are investigating.

Theoretical issues have to be dealt with as well. It must be determined whether gender is represented in the syntax of nominals or not. If it is, the questions as to what its nature is and where it is located need to be answered. Those questions have been widely debated in the literature in recent years. Some linguists associate gender with a specific projection like Gender Phrase (as proposed by Picallo 1991), whereas others do not (such as Ritter 1993).[3] For some, gender is rather uniform, whereas for others different aspects should be distinguished, such as morphological/grammatical gender and semantic/natural gender, i.e., sex. This of course depends on several factors, like the language examined or the theoretical framework adopted. In a Minimalist approach, for example, whether a gender feature is interpretable or not, and valued or not will have to be determined.

To solve the puzzles presented above, we develop an analysis in which grammatical and semantic/natural gender are distinguished, as they may interfere or conflict (cf. Atkinson 2015, following Kramer 2009), and in which the semantic gender of some nouns (like *enfant* 'child' and *professeur* 'professor' in (1) and (2)) receives a feature specification through semantic reference later in the derivation.

The paper is organized as follows. In Section 2, we describe the French gender paradigm and mention the different noun classes found in that language. Section 3 reports two accounts on which we will build our own analysis (Kramer's 2009 for Amharic and Atkinson's 2015 for French). In Section 4, we make our theoretical assumptions explicit, present our analysis for the gender mismatches we examine, and propose an account for gender that extends to all the classes of nouns identified in Section 2. Section 5 concludes the paper.

---

3. Ritter's (1993) arguments against Gender Phrase as a separate category are only based on some exceptional cases in languages different from French. Furthermore, the argumentation does not explicitly concern animate nouns, which are the main subject of our paper.

2.   The French paradigm

In Romance languages, both inanimate and animate nouns have gender distinctions, namely masculine and feminine. This includes French, on which this paper focuses. However, when it comes to gender, French inanimate and animate nouns have non-uniform characteristics. The gender of the former is completely arbitrary: *le mot,* for instance, is masculine whereas *la parole* is feminine, although both can mean 'the word'. The facts are more complex for animate nouns, as their grammatical gender and their semantic gender do not always match. For instance, the noun *sentinelle* 'sentinel' is feminine although it usually refers to a man.

As animacy is a crucial property of the nouns involved in the challenging examples presented in the introduction, this subsection concentrates on nouns with this feature; however, not all animates can be treated in the same way: *enfant* 'child' and *professeur* 'professor', for example, do not necessarily trigger grammatical agreement, at least not in contexts like (1), whereas *fille* 'girl' and *garçon* 'boy' in (5)–(6) do. In addition, nouns like *fille/garçon* and the pronoun replacing them must have the same gender, as in (4), whereas a word like *professeur* and the pronoun replacing it cannot share their gender feature in examples like (2). Those facts suggest that animate nouns in French belong to different categories, which can be described as follows:

a.   *Suppletive forms:* Nouns with unrelated morphological forms, used to refer to males and females. For such nouns, sex and gender conflate: *une fille* 'a girl' is feminine and female and *un garçon* 'a boy' is masculine and male; the same holds for *une jument* 'a mare' vs. *un étalon* 'a stallion'.

b.   *Stem change:* Sex differences are expressed by related forms, viz. stems with an alternating suffix. Sex and gender are not differentiated: *le directeur* 'the director (masc.)' is masculine and male and *la directrice* (fem.) feminine and female; the same holds for *un chat* 'a cat (masc.)' vs. *une chatte* 'a cat (fem.)'.

c.   *Fixed forms with article change:* Nouns which have the same form in the masculine and in the feminine. Gender/sex differences are expressed solely by alternating determiners: *un/une enfant* 'a child (masc./fem.)', *un/une secrétaire* 'a secretary (masc./fem.)'. This class includes nouns that were originally masculine and are used to designate professions: *un/une professeur* 'a professor, teacher (masc./fem.)'; *un/une mannequin* 'a fashion model (masc./fem.)'.[4]

---

4.   In addition to these forms, the French dictionary *Le Petit Robert* (Rey-Debove and Rey 2010) also mentions the variants *une professeure* and *une mannequine.*

d. *Forms with a fixed article:* Nouns with a fixed gender used to refer to both sexes. Their forms do not alternate in the feminine and in the masculine, and there is no article change: *la sentinelle* 'the sentinel', with a feminine determiner, can refer to both men and women. Gender and sex may differ. The same holds for feminine nouns like *la personne* 'the person' or *la victime* 'the victim'. Another example would be the masculine form *un léopard*, which can refer to male and female leopards.

e. *Default masculine forms:* Some nouns classified under (b) and (c) have a default use of the masculine form. This means that masculine forms are used to refer to both males and females: *le chat, un enfant, le professeur,* and *le mannequin.* For expository reasons, we group these nouns in an independent class.

The above classification sheds a new light on the examples discussed in the introduction. First, we realize that in French both grammatical and semantic gender play a role. Second, we can observe that the nouns that give rise to the gender mismatches in (1) (*enfant* 'child' and *professeur* 'professor') have default masculine forms, thus representing our class (e). Put differently, gender sharing outside the strict DP necessarily takes place with the nouns of class (a), (b), (c), and (d), but not with those of class (e) (cf. (3) for class (d), and (4)–(6) for class (a)).

The differences among the animate nouns described in this section have to be accounted for by a theory of gender. Whether current work on agreement in French achieves this or not will be discussed in the next section.

3.   Previous analyses

As both grammatical gender and semantic gender have to be considered to explain the French data, we limit our presentation of previous works on gender to two recent papers that make a distinction between the two, namely Kramer's (2009) and Atkinson's (2015). Only Atkinson's paper deals with gender in French, but since it builds on Kramer's work, we will also discuss Kramer (2009).

3.1   Kramer (2009)

Kramer studies the DP in Amharic, a language with two genders, masculine and feminine, indicated by agreement on, e.g., the definite marker (-*u*: 'the.MASC.SG' and -*wa* 'the.FEM.SG'), and in which inanimate nouns are generally masculine. The Amharic system for assigning gender to animate nouns relies heavily on natural gender, i.e., sex. If the natural gender of the referent is unknown, the nominal is masculine. This means that masculine is the default, except with certain animals that are feminine if their gender is unknown/irrelevant (Leslau 1995).

(7) a. *ayt'-wa*   b. *bäk'lo-wa*
mouse-DEF.FEM   mule-DEF.FEM
'the mouse'   'the mule'

If the natural gender of the referent for one of these animal nouns is known, natural gender overrides grammatical gender. This also holds for the default masculine nouns.

(8) *ayt'-u*
mouse-DEF.MASC
'the male mouse'

In order to capture the Amharic facts, Kramer proposes, in a Distributed Morphology approach, that both the root and *n* can have a gender feature: an uninterpretable feature on the root that represents grammatical gender and an interpretable feature on *n* that encodes natural gender. The latter comes in three flavours, [+fem], [–fem] or unspecified. The split analysis advocated can be represented as in (9):

(9)

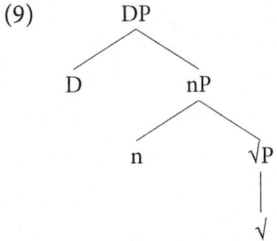

This system allows Kramer (2009: 130–132) to account for examples like (7) and (8) in the following way. Animate feminine roots like 'mouse' in (7) are [+fem], whereas masculine roots do not need a gender feature, masculine being the default. When the sex of the referent is unknown/irrelevant as in (7), *n* is unspecified, whereas when it is known, it can be [+fem] or [–fem] as in (8). Inanimate roots have an unspecified *n*. Masculine inanimate nouns do not have a gender feature on the root, masculine being the default; feminine inanimate nouns have a [+fem] feature on the root. As a consequence, it is the highest feature in the tree which is involved in agreement processes, with D, for instance. This means that when a noun is specified for sex with a feature [+/–fem] on *n*, it is this gender which is the agreeing element. Otherwise, when *n* lacks gender, the agreeing gender is the grammatical gender.

This searching process, e.g., by D, down the tree, can be captured by an Agree operation from a Minimalist perspective. In the standard versions of Agree (Chomsky 2000, 2001) uninterpretable features must be valued (or checked) and then deleted. This process has to take place before the derivation is sent to Logical Form (LF); otherwise, the derivation crashes. Valuation (checking) takes place via Agree.

However, Kramer observes that the mechanism proposed by Chomsky is problematic if it is to account for the Amharic facts. One reason is that this system implies that an uninterpretable feature is unvalued. This is because unvalued and uninterpretable features are collapsed in such a way that Agree leads to the valuation of an unvalued feature, and to the deletion of an uninterpretable one. But in Amharic, the gender of some feminine nouns (with a [+fem] feature on the root) is clearly uninterpretable *and* valued, suggesting that uninterpretability and lack of valuation do not necessarily go hand in hand. A second problem with the standard assumptions of the Minimalist framework is that the latter assumes that an uninterpretable feature must be checked by its interpretable counterpart. However, the grammatical gender feature, which is uninterpretable, does not always co-occur with an interpretable gender feature, as seen in the above discussion of Amharic. This is the case, for example, of inanimates, which lack sex features, and which therefore have an uninterpretable feature that should cause the derivation to crash, and also of animate nouns with only an (uninterpretable) feature on the root but no feature on *n*, such as the default forms of the nouns in (7).

To solve these problems Kramer adopts Pesetsky and Torrego's (2007) (henceforth P&T) version of Agree, in which both interpretable and uninterpretable features can be either valued or unvalued. This is possible because the arbitrary relationship between unvaluation and uninterpretability is eliminated in this approach. As a result, the valued uninterpretable gender feature on the root assumed by Kramer for Amharic is no longer offending. Furthermore, to acknowledge the existence of uninterpretable features with no interpretable counterpart, Kramer draws on Legate (2002), as in her system, "unvalued features are what must be dealt with via Agree before the derivation is sent to the interfaces, and uninterpretable features can simply be deleted in a global fashion on the way to the semantic component" (2009:143).

The aspects of P&T and Legate adopted by Kramer allow her to account for the Amharic gender facts. Nevertheless, there are some conceptual and empirical problems with Kramer's analysis. First, the structures of inanimate feminine nouns and of feminine nouns for which sex is unknown/irrelevant are identical, gender being only specified on the root. The same holds for inanimate masculine nouns and masculine nouns for which sex is unknown/irrelevant. This is counterintuitive, because animacy and semantic gender go together. In other words, the referents of animate nouns are specified for sex, in contrast to inanimates. This difference should thus be represented in an analysis that distinguishes between semantic and grammatical gender. Furthermore, in Kramer's analysis, the gender of the default feminine noun can be overridden by a male or female feature on *n* and genderless roots can be inserted under a [+fem] or [−fem] *n*. The feature on *n* is inherited by D. For the French nouns allowing gender mismatches, this analysis cannot be adopted, because these nouns do not change from a class (e) noun, i.e., default masculine, into a class (c) noun, i.e., the *le/la professeur* class, as the Amharic animal nouns with a feminine default gender seem to do. In the French gender mismatch cases, the whole DP expresses default grammatical gender agreement. Therefore, while for Kramer it is always the highest gender feature that

determines agreement, in our French examples both semantic and grammatical gender may play a role in agreement. Finally, the absence of a gender feature on masculine
roots is problematic for languages like French, where masculine is not the default for
inanimate nouns. This issue has been taken up by Atkinson (2015) whose analysis of
French nouns is reported in the next subsection.

3.2   Atkinson (2015)

Atkinson builds on Kramer's (2009) work and tries to account for agreement in the
French DP. Just like Kramer for Amharic, she assumes that gender in French should be
expressed in two positions:

i.   on the root as an uninterpretable feature accounting for grammatical gender
ii.   on the head of nP as an interpretable feature accounting for semantic gender

Let us see if (i) and (ii) allow Atkinson to account for the characteristics of the French
animate noun classes listed in Section 2. In her analysis, (i) holds for inanimate nouns
and for the animates in our class (d), that is, nouns like *la sentinelle* (fem.) 'the sentinel'. This means that for Atkinson a root cannot only be [+fem], but also [–fem] (see
(10) below), an option not available in Kramer's analysis. The reason for this assumption is that in French, masculine is not the default for inanimates, which contrasts
with Amharic. Postulating that French roots can be [+/–fem] addresses the empirical
problem mentioned at the end of the previous section. As for our class (e) nouns, it is
the default masculine on the root that determines agreement (grammatical gender).
(ii) applies to our noun classes (a) (suppletive forms), (b) (stem change by means of
alternating suffixes) and (c) (article change), i.e., to nouns like *la fille* 'the girl', *la chatte*
(fem.) 'the female cat', *une enfant* (fem.) 'a female child', respectively.
     The structures corresponding to Atkinson's proposals, before valuation of the
feature on D, are provided in (10) and (11):

(10)   a.   Inanimates: *le magasin* 'the store' (masc.)
       b.   Class (d): *la sentinelle* 'the sentinel'
       c.   Class (e): *le chat* 'the cat'

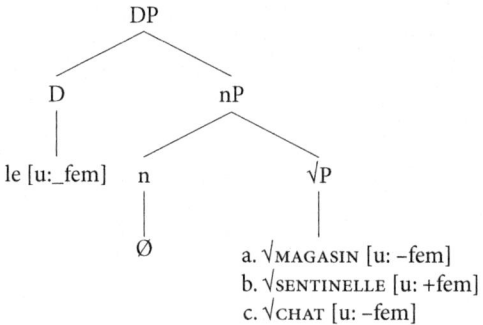

a. √MAGASIN [u: –fem]
b. √SENTINELLE [u: +fem]
c. √CHAT [u: –fem]

(11)   Classes (a), (b), (c): *le garçon* 'the boy' (masc.); *le chat* 'the male cat'; *le secrétaire* 'the male secretary'

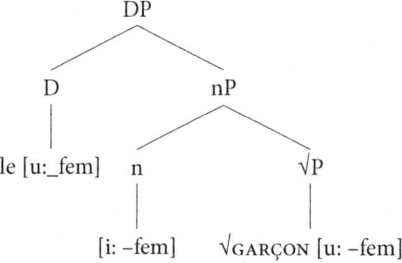

The crucial difference between (10) and (11) is that the latter contains a sex feature on *n*, in contrast to the former. This account, however, raises conceptual problems similar to the ones evoked for Kramer's work (see Section 3.1). It implies that some animate nouns (our classes d) (*la sentinelle*) and (e) (default masculine nouns)) have the same structure as inanimates and that some animates do not encode sex. Conflating our classes (d) and (e) as in (10) also predicts that these nouns pattern the same in contexts allowing gender mismatches, contrary to fact (recall (2) vs. (3)). Furthermore, Atkinson's analysis seems to be limited to local agreement within the strict DP (cf. Section 4.2). Yet, we have shown in the introduction to this paper that gender agreement outside the strict DP can differ from agreement inside the strict DP. Atkinson's analysis does not seem to extend to such cases. These issues are addressed in the next section.

4. Analysis

4.1 Theoretical assumptions

Following Harris (1991:36), we assume that grammatical gender of inanimates is purely a formal, grammatical feature and in the terminology of Chomsky (2000) that it is uninterpretable (cf. Zamparelli 2008). We further assume that DP-internal Agree relations value concord (Carstens 2000).

To account for the fact that in Romance languages, and in French in particular, grammatical gender does not always correspond to semantic gender for animate nouns, we build on Kramer's (2009) and Atkinson's (2015) works, presented in Section 3. *La sentinelle* (fem.) 'the sentinel' and *la victime* (fem.) 'the victim', which can both refer to men and women, illustrate this characteristic. This means that we adopt an analysis where gender is not expressed in a single position within DP (e.g., on the root as in Alexiadou 2004 or on *n* as in Lowenstamm 2008), but in two positions. As we do not explicitly adopt a Distributed Morphology analysis for our data, we will assume that these heads are N and Gen, the head of a Gender Phrase (GenP) (cf. Picallo 1991). These labels differ from the ones in Kramer (2009) and Atkinson (2015) in that NP replaces the root and GenP the nP. Although nothing hinges on the choice of these categories, we believe that postulating a GenP is justified as it encodes semantic gender, i.e., an interpretable feature (*une chatte* (fem.) 'a female cat'; *une enfant* (fem.) 'a female child'). NP, in contrast, encodes grammatical gender, which is uninterpretable (*le magasin* (masc.) 'the shop').

Our analysis also subsumes some aspects of Agree proposed in Pesetsky and Torrego (2007), and some in Legate (2002) discussed in Section 3. In a nutshell, following P&T we assume that valuation and interpretability are treated independently, in the sense that an uninterpretable feature is not necessarily unvalued. This contrasts with Chomsky's (2000, 2001) conception of Agree as it means that both interpretable and uninterpretable features can be valued or unvalued. As a consequence, P&T's version of Agree is a mechanism by which a probe with unvalued features searches down the tree for a matching valued feature (as in Chomsky 2001) but which does not require the goal to have an interpretable feature. This is important for our analysis, as the grammatical gender feature in French can serve as a goal, although it is uninterpretable. Also, Gen may contain an interpretable, but unvalued, feature. Furthermore, we adopt Legate's (2002) proposal that uninterpretable features can simply be deleted in a global fashion, and that Agree deals with unvalued features before the derivation is sent to the interfaces. We believe that the distinction between uninterpretable and interpretable features only plays a role at LF: interpretable features contribute to the interpretation; uninterpretable features do not.

Another difference between the Agree operation proposed by Chomsky and the one put forward by P&T is that in the latter there is a link between the instances of the feature involved, say F_1 and F_2, which is accessible to subsequent processes. In the former, in contrast, once Agree has taken place, the syntax can no longer relate F_1 and F_2, as there is no permanent connection between them. Agreement in P&T thus results in feature sharing (Frampton and Gutmann 2000), in the sense that the output of Agree is a single feature shared by two (or more) locations. The Agree mechanism that we adopt thus involves feature sharing. With these theoretical considerations in mind, let us turn to the gender mismatches presented in the introduction.

4.2   Analysis of the mismatches

We now return to the challenging data introduced in Section 1 ((1)–(3)). (1) and (2) involve nouns of our class (e), i.e., the default masculine nouns, and illustrate the gender mismatches we are interested in. They contrast with examples like (3) where no mismatch is possible. An analysis of (1)–(3) should explain why, in some cases, the gender feature on NP can be, must be, or cannot be overridden. In addition, it should account for the distinction between inanimate and animate nouns. This is particularly important for our classes (d) (the *la sentinelle* class) and (e) (the default masculine nouns), which have the same structure as inanimate nouns in Atkinson's work (recall

(10)). Another puzzle that has to be addressed is why in some cases gender *can* be overridden, whereas in others it *must* be.

As animacy is a crucial property of the nouns found in the examples we are examining, we will start our discussion with the distinction between inanimate and animate nominals. As the latter are specified for sex, we will assume that the two properties (animacy and sex) go hand in hand, even though this might be a simplification. What we suggest is that the difference between the nouns whose referent is animate and those whose referent is not is represented in their structure. More precisely, we propose that animates have a Gender projection, in contrast to inanimates. For the classes (a), (b), and (c), i.e., the suppletive forms (*garcon* 'boy'/*fille* 'girl'), the stem change forms (*directeur/directrice*), and the article change forms (*le/la professeur*), we partly adopt Atkinson's analysis presented in (11), the difference being that we replace nP by GenP and √P by NP. The noun has an uninterpretable [+fem] or [−fem] feature, which values the interpretable unvalued feature on Gen and, after feature sharing, the uninterpretable unvalued feature on D. The semantic gender of such nouns corresponds to their gender on NP as observed in Section 2: a noun which refers to a female is [+fem] and a noun which refers to a male is [−fem].

To deal with the specificities of our noun class (d), the *la sentinelle* class, we propose that the feature of Gen, which is generally interpretable because it contributes to the interpretation of the noun, is *uninterpretable* with this class of nouns: although the referent of such nouns is specified for sex, this information is not available.[5] To account for this fact, we suggest that their Gen feature is uninterpretable and unvalued (cf. Percus 2011 for Italian). It *becomes* valued when it receives the [+/−fem] value from N and shares it with the uninterpretable unvalued D. The structure of such nouns, after valuation, is given below:

(12)   (cf. (10b))

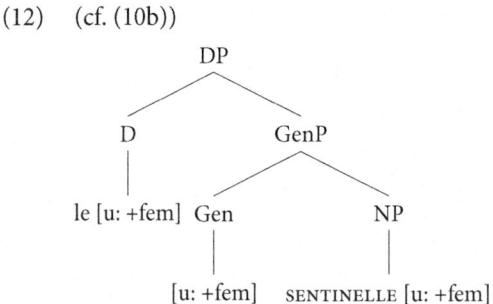

---

5.   Alexiadou (2004) does not allow gender to be expressed in a functional projection, because functional projections should have a semantic or syntactic function. In our approach Gen does express semantic gender, but in the case of class d) nouns, sex is not specified because it does not correspond to grammatical gender on the root.

In (12), the feature [+fem] of the noun *sentinelle* 'sentinel' has been passed onto Gen, and then onto D. This structure contains no information about the sex of the sentinel. This is why, in some cases, sex and grammatical gender may conflict. Our analysis allows us to account for (i) the similarities between *sentinelle*-like nouns and other animate nouns—the presence of a sex feature, as they are all animate, (ii) the difference between such nouns and inanimate nouns, which do not have a sex feature, and (iii) the difference between *sentinelle*-like nouns and nouns like *le garçon* 'the boy' and *la fille* 'the girl', for which sex and gender correspond. In sum, we assume that there is a difference between 'no sex', which is a property of inanimates, and 'no information about sex', which is a characteristic of *sentinelle*-like nouns, represented by the uninterpretable Gen we argue for.

As for nouns of class (e), the default masculine nouns, we suggest that they do not have a gender value: although GenP is present in their structure, signaling that we are dealing with an animate noun, gender is absent on the noun and the unvalued gender feature of the probes cannot be valued. According to Preminger (2011), Agree is obligatory, but its success is not guaranteed. A possible result of failed agreement is default morphology (Preminger 2009). This is what we propose for φ-incomplete nouns such as *professeur*: with class (e) nouns, Agree fails, but this does not lead to ungrammaticality. Rather, the unvalued features in DP are spelled out as default agreement at PF. It is the absence of a feature specification for gender that will allow sex to be specified later in the derivation and to override grammatical gender in partitive structures (1), in predicative contexts (2), and in contexts of reference (3). The absence of gender specification with class (e) nouns is thus an essential point of our account. In Atkinson's analysis of these nouns, gender on the noun is specified, viz. as masculine. This suggests that sex cannot be specified later and hence that her analysis cannot account for data like (1) and (2). Our analysis also implies that class (e) nouns and *sentinelle*-like nouns differ in that only the former are unspecified for gender (and therefore sex) and can hence be involved in the gender phenomena we are discussing. In our analysis, the class (d) nouns, the *la sentinelle* class, are specified for gender, which values the feature on Gen, but this feature on Gen is not interpretable for sex. In Atkinson's analysis both types of nouns are treated on a par and should therefore not differ in constructions like (1)–(2), contrary to fact. The tree we propose for class (e) nouns, which are masculine by default (because of Failed Agree), as it is sent as a phase to PF, is provided below:

(13)

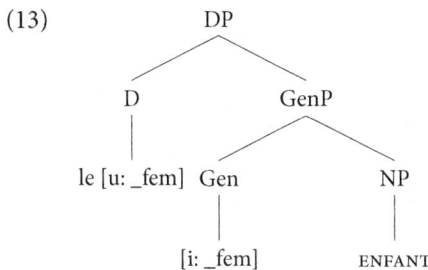

What we propose implies that polysemous words like *enfant* are listed twice in the lexicon depending on the information they encode: as nouns either specified for gender or not. However, as the two meanings are related (both specify ENFANT), they are in the same entry. Only nouns specified for gender (in)directly value the unvalued feature on D. When its value is [+fem], the article, for instance, is *la* 'the.FEM', and when it is [–fem] the article is *le* 'the.MASC'. As proposed above, when the noun is not specified for gender, the gender feature on D remains unvalued and is spelled out as default gender at PF. As the default gender in French is masculine, the article will be *le* 'the.MASC'.

The gender mismatches discussed in this paper only occur with class (e) nouns, which have a default masculine gender, interpreted as an unspecified gender on the noun. The DP with the unvalued features will be sent as a phase to PF, where the unvalued features on D and adjectives will be spelled out as default masculine. In a compositional view of phases, Hinzen (2012) argues that due to Transfer of the phase interior, the phase is reduced to its head and its left edge, both of which then belong to the next phase and are interpreted therein (cf. Chomsky's 2001 Phase Impenetrability Condition: PIC). At this point semantic agreement comes in: since valuation of the gender feature of the probing D has not taken place, the unspecified gender value of the head of the DP phase, D, can be provided with a specification. In line with Yatsu-shiro and Sauerland (2006) and others, we assume that the gender value is inserted in a high position within the DP, viz. in D. In the case of class (e) nouns like *professeur*, a feminine gender feature in D entails reference to a woman and a masculine gender feature in D entails reference to a man (cf. e.g., Corbett 2003). Specified D can serve as a goal for agreement with, e.g., a predicative adjective. Since the DP that has been sent to the Interfaces contains a GenP (linked to D via (failed) Agree), gender in D will be interpreted as a sex value.

In the gender phenomena we are investigating, the distance between the agreeing element and the noun also plays a role. The examples show that within the DP, local agreement takes place with the noun. Elements that are less local, however, do not necessarily agree or do not agree at all in grammatical gender. Whereas attributive adjectives agree in grammatical gender, partitive elements do not necessarily do so. Less local elements like pronouns do not syntactically agree in grammatical gender: the unspecified gender feature in D receives a feature corresponding to sex. This is summarized in (14).

(14)   Observations for class (e):

    i.   Within the strict DP: the D unspecified for gender <u>cannot</u> receive a semantic gender specification. Hence default masculine.

    ii.   In the 'looser' DP: the D unspecified for gender <u>can</u> receive a semantic gender specification: partitive constructions (1).

    iii.   Agreeing/referring elements outside DP: the D unspecified for gender <u>must</u> receive a semantic gender specification: predicates (but recall Note 1), pronouns (2).

That distance may play a role in gender agreement has also been observed by Corbett (1979, and later work). On the basis of Russian, English, French, German, and some other languages, and on the basis of various constructions, Corbett (1979) shows that whereas local relations favor grammatical agreement, less local relations favor semantic agreement. This is expressed in Corbett's (1979) agreement hierarchy:

(15)   Attributive—predicate—relative pronoun—personal pronoun

The hierarchy expresses that the distance between the element that determines agreement (the controller) and the agreeing element has an impact on the kind of agreement that takes place, namely grammatical vs. semantic agreement. Semantic agreement occurs more often in languages of the world if the agreeing element is a personal pronoun than if it is a relative pronoun. On the other hand, grammatical agreement is much more common if the agreeing element is an attribute than if it is a predicate. Corbett's agreement hierarchy is corroborated by the French data presented in this paper. The examples (1)–(2) show that whereas within the strict DP gender agreement may not be semantic, in the looser DP and outside the DP gender agreement may or must be semantic.

    (1) illustrates semantic gender agreement within partitive constructions: the semantic gender feature specifies the unvalued gender feature in D within the strict DP. The partitive agreement relation is not expressed in Corbett's hierarchy and could be added to it. Since in both examples the attribute grammatically agrees with the noun, partitive as an agreeing element should be lower in the hierarchy than the attributive position. Taking examples like (1) into consideration, we propose to refine (15) as (16):

(16)   Attributive—**partitive**—predicate—relative pronoun—personal pronoun

Whereas (15), refined as (16), just describes, in terms of locality, with which agreeing elements semantic agreement is more common, the hierarchy is also predicted in an account based on valuation, as proposed in this paper. We claim that an analysis of agreement in terms of valuation, i.e., feature sharing, can account for the hierarchy. Feature sharing through valuation only takes place within a phase (Chomsky 2001). If the strict DP is a phase, this explains why attributive agreement occupies the highest position in the hierarchy. In French, a semantic specification can only be added after the failure of Agree within the DP phase. In other words, in case of a failed Agree relation, specification of the unspecified gender feature in D is still possible. Notice that this means that the semantic feature is inserted after the valuation cycle within the strict or 'looser' DP, in order to serve as a goal for agreement relations in a second cycle of merge. This accounts for the fact that grammatical agreement takes place in earlier cycles and semantic agreement in later cycles of the derivation.

5. Conclusion

In this paper we have shown that with some default masculine nouns in French gender mismatches are possible. In partitive constructions, predicative APs or with pronouns the default masculine agreement can be overridden by semantic agreement.

To account for the gender phenomena discussed in this paper and building on Atkinson (2015), based on Kramer (2009), we have proposed that gender is expressed in two positions in DP: on NP as an uninterpretable feature accounting for grammatical gender and on the head of GenP as a feature accounting for semantic gender. We have proposed that only animate nouns have a GenP, in contrast to inanimate ones, and that the feature on Gen for the *sentinelle*-like nouns is uninterpretable, so that the feminine feature inherited from the noun is not necessarily interpreted as female. For default masculine nouns such as *professeur* and *mannequin*, we have claimed that gender is unspecified inside DP but that it can be specified in D through semantic reference serving as a goal in a second cycle of merge, accounting for gender mismatches outside the strict DP.

We have also shown that gender mismatches concern relations that are not strictly local. Inside the strict DP, grammatical gender agreement between Gen and NP is stricter than in the 'looser' DP, which is in turn stricter than the agreeing/referring relation with elements outside DP, reflecting Corbett's agreement hierarchy, to which we have added *partitive*. We have argued that an account in terms of valuation within the phase can nicely account for the locality restrictions.

References

Alexiadou, Artemis. 2004. "Inflection Class, Gender and DP-internal Structure." *Explorations in Nominal Inflection* ed. by Gereon Muller et al., 21–50. Berlin: Mouton.
DOI: 10.1515/9783110197501.21

Atkinson, Emily. 2015. "Gender Features on *n* & the Root: An account of gender in French." *Selected Proceedings of the LSRL 42* ed. by Jason Smith and Tabea Ihsane, 229–244. John Benjamins.

Carstens, Vicki. 2000. "Concord in Minimalist Theory." *Linguistic Inquiry* 31.319–355.
DOI: 10.1162/002438900554370

Chomsky, Noam. 2000. "Minimalist Inquiries: the Framework." *Step by Step: Essays on Minimalist Syntax in Honor of Howard Lasnik* ed. by Roger Martin, David Michaels and Juan Uriagereka, 89–155. Cambridge, MA: MIT Press.

Chomsky, Noam. 2001. "Derivation by Phase." *Ken Hale: A Life in Language* ed. by Michael Kenstowicz, 1–52. Cambridge, MA: MIT Press.

Corbett, Greville. 1979. "The Agreement Hierarchy." *Journal of Linguistics* 15.203–224. DOI: 10.1017/S0022226700016352

Corbett, Greville. 2003. "Agreement: Terms and Boundaries." *The Role of Agreement in Natural Language: TLS 5 Proceedings* ed. by William E. Griffin, 109–122. Texas Linguistics Forum, 53.

Frampton, John and Sam Gutmann. 2000. "Agreement is Feature Sharing." Ms. Northeastern University. Boston. http://www.math.neu.edu/ling/.

Harris, James. 1991. "The Exponence of Gender in Spanish." *Linguistic Inquiry* 22.27–62.

Hinzen, Wolfram. 2012. "Phases and Semantics." *Phases: Developing the Framework* ed. by Ángel J. Gallego, 309–342. Berlin & Boston: Walter de Gruyter.

Kramer, Ruth. 2009. *Definite Markers, Phi-features and Agreement: A Morphosyntactic Investigation of the Amharic DP*. Ph.D. dissertation, UC Santa Cruz.

Legate, Julie Anne. 2002. "Phases in 'beyond Explanatory Adequacy.'" Ms., MIT.

Leslau, Wolf. 1995. *Reference Grammar of Amharic*. Wiesbaden: Harrassowitz.

Lowenstamm, Jean. 2008. "On Little *n*, √, and Types of Nouns." *Sounds of Silence: Empty Elements in Syntax and Phonology* ed. by Jutta Hartmann, Veronika Hegedus and Henk van Riemsdijk 105–144. Amsterdam: Elsevier.

Percus, Orin. 2011. "Gender Features and Interpretation: A case study." *Morphology* 21.167–196. DOI: 10.1007/s11525-010-9157-2

Pesetsky, David and Esther Torrego. 2007. "The Syntax of Valuation and the Interpretability of Features." *Phrasal and Clausal Architecture: Syntactic Derivation and Interpretation* ed. by Simin Karimi, Vida Samiian and Wendy K. Wilkins, 262–294. Amsterdam: John Benjamins. DOI: 10.1075/la.101.14pes

Picallo, Carmen. 1991. "Nominals and Nominalizations in Catalan." *Probus* 3.279–316. DOI: 10.1515/prbs.1991.3.3.279

Preminger, Omer. 2009. "Breaking Agreements: Distinguishing Agreement and Clitic Doubling by their Failures." *Linguistic Inquiry* 40: 4.619–666. DOI: 10.1162/ling.2009.40.4.619

Preminger, Omer. 2011. *Agreement as a Fallible Operation*. Ph.D. dissertation, MIT.

Rey-Debove, Josette and Alain Rey. 2010. *Le Nouveau Petit Robert de la Langue Française*. Paris: Dictionnaires le Robert.

Ritter, Elisabeth. 1993. "Where's Gender?" *Linguistic Inquiry* 24: 3.795–803.

Yatsushiro, Kazuko and Uli Sauerland. 2006. "[Feminine] in a High Position." *Snippets* 13.11–12.

Zamparelli, Roberto. 2008. "On the Interpretability of φ-features." *The Bantu–Romance Connection* ed. by Cécile De Cat and Katherine Demuth, 167–199. Amsterdam: John Benjamins. DOI: 10.1075/la.131.11zam

French loanwords in Korean

Modeling lexical knowledge in OT

Haike Jacobs

Radboud University, Department of Romance languages and cultures

This paper discusses the Korean adaptation of French word-final coronal plosives. They are adapted, just as the English ones, with or without vowel insertion. In the latter case they are treated as ending in underlying /s/. Replacement of word-final coronal plosives by underlying /s/ is also active in the native phonology. We will critically discuss a number of previous proposals and argue that they are unable to describe the two aspects in a uniform way. We propose to model frequency and lexical knowledge in the form of a markedness hierarchy which accounts for both loanword adaptation of final coronal plosives as underlying /s/ and for the analogical pressure within the native phonology.

1. Introduction

French words ending in postvocalic coronal voiceless plosives are adapted in two different ways in Korean (cf. Kim 2010, Kim ms). Either the final [t] is replaced by a tense or aspirated coronal plosive followed by vowel insertion as in (1f), or the coronal plosive is adapted as an underlying /s/ which shows up as surface [s] when followed by a vowel-initial suffix, such as locative [-ɛ] or accusative [-il] as in (1d–e). If not followed by a vowel-initial suffix, that is, the citation form (Kang 2003), the underlying /s/ surfaces as [t]. The adaptation of French word-final postvocalic plosives as underlying /s/ is intriguing, given the fact that there are Korean words that end in surface [t], such as, for instance, [pat] 'field'. Korean has phonetic surface forms ending in [t], but no forms that end in [tʰ, tsʰ, or s]. These latter consonants do occur in underlying representations, but are modified by two regular phonological processes: CODA NEUTR(ALIZATION), as in (1a), by which only voiceless lenis plosives are allowed to occur in coda position, and STRIDENT NEUTR(ALIZATION), as in (1c), by which underlying strident consonants are turned into non-strident ones). Some examples are given in (1).

DOI 10.1075/rllt.9.10jac

(1)   *Korean and French word-final coronals*
    a)   UR: /patʰ/   [pa.tʰɛ] 'field LOC'   CODA NEUTR   [pat] 'field'
    b)   UR: /kot/   [kot] 'immediately'
    c)   UR: /os/   [o.si] 'clothes NOM'   STRIDENT NEUTR   [ot] 'clothes'
    d)   *omelette*   UR: /omil.lɛs/   [o.mil.lɛ.sil]   ACC   [o.mil.lɛt]
    e)   *croquette*   UR:/kʰilokʰɛs/   [kʰi.ɾo.kʰɛ.sil]   ACC   [kʰi.ɾo.kʰɛt]
    f)   *baguette*   UR:/pakɛtʰi/   [pa.kɛ.tʰélil]   ACC   [pa.kɛ.tʰi]

In Korean native phonology, there is no vowel insertion (*/patʰ/ →[pa.tʰi]), but there is coda neutralization (/patʰ/ →[pat] (1b)). Vowel insertion, however, can be observed in loanwords as in [pa.kɛ.tʰi] in (1f). Similarly, if Korean allows word-final coronal plosives as in (1a–c), why are the French word-final coronal plosives adapted with UR /s/ as in (1d–e)? Furthermore, importantly, the replacement of word-final postvocalic coronal plosives by underlying /s/ can be observed in native Korean phonology as well (cf. among others, Albright 2002; Davis and Kang 2006; Kang 2003), where next to locative [pa.tʰi] topic forms such as [pa.sin] do occur, which point to underlying stem-final /t/ being replaced by /s/. Davis and Kang (2006) provide the examples in (2), which show variation of the native forms.

(2)   *Variation for Korean word-final coronals*

UNAFFIXED	ACC		optional	LOC		optional
[pat] 'field'	[patʰ-il]	~	[pas-il]	[patʰ-ɛ]	~	[pas-ɛ]
[pit] 'debt'	[pits-il]	~	[pis-il]	[pits-ɛ]	~	[pis-ɛ]
[kʼot] 'flower'	[kʼotsʰ-il]	~	[kʼos-il]	[kʼotsʰ-ɛ]	~	[kʼos-ɛ]

The adaptation of French word-final coronal plosives is highly similar to the adaptation of English word-final coronal plosives, which has received considerable attention in the literature. Kenstowicz (2005) assumes different phonologies/OT grammars for loan and native phonology. Kim (2010, and to appear), concentrating on both French and English loanwords, argues that cases like these show that, besides perception and production, knowledge of lexical forms also plays a determining role in the adaptation of loanwords. Adaptation as /s/ is explained by the fact that Korean words in the lexical representations are more likely to end with /s/ (308 nouns) rather than with any of the other coronal plosives /t, tʰ, tʼ/. No Korean word ends in /tʼ/ and there are only a few words that end in /t/ (5, of which 2 are nouns) or/tʰ/(116 nouns). Within OT, different views, but all based on anti-correspondence, have been proposed to analyze both the loanword adaptation as in (1) and the native analogical leveling as in (2) (most noticeably Kang 2003, Davis and Kang 2006, and Boersma and Hamann 2010). This paper purports to examine these different ways of formally modeling lexical knowledge in OT and proposes an account for both the loanword adaptation and the native leveling that does not rely on anti-correspondence. This paper is organized as follows. In Section 2, we critically discuss the OT-account proposed by Boersma and Hamann

(2010). We will argue that their account of the adaptation of word-final English coronal plosives as underlying /s/ seems unrelated to the release of the plosive in the donor language and that the native analogical leveling seems to be formally unrelated to loanword adaptation. The French data are crucial in this respect. French final coronal plosives are consistently released, but it is not the case that all French coronal-final loans are adapted with a final vowel. Section 3 critically discusses the anti-correspondence based proposals by Kang (2003) and Davis and Kang (2006). In Section 4 we will argue that the lexical knowledge involved in both the native leveling and the loanword adaptation is based on a markedness hierarchy that is derived on the basis of frequency.

2. Adaptation of word-final coronals in lexical recognition

Boersma and Hamann (2010) propose a bidirectional OT model of perception and production that allows them to dispense with loanword-specific phonology. In perception, the interaction of cue constraints and markedness constraints relate a phonetic form (marked [ ]) to a perceived surface form (marked//), which in recognition, by the further inspection of faithfulness constraints, leads to an underlying form (marked | |). In production, the underlying form is inspected by the interaction of markedness and faithfulness constraints and yields a surface form, which by the cue constraints receives phonetic implementation and surfaces as a phonetic form. Adjustments can take place in perception, going from phonetic to surface perceived form, for instance *shot* [ʃʊt] analyzed by Korean speakers as surface /.sjat./ or [dɛk] *deck* and [tʰæg] *tag* perceived as /.tɛ.kʰɨ/ and /.tʰæ.kɨ/. Adjustments can also take place in recognition, that is, when going from perceived surface form to underlying form, such as, perceived surface /.sjat./ being recognized as underlying |sjas|. Before turning to this adjustment in recognition, let us first illustrate how adjustment works in perception.[1]

Korean has a three-way contrast among lenis [-tense, -asp], aspirated [+tense, +asp] and fortis [+tense, -asp] voiceless stops, but lacks a voicing contrast in obstruents. The cue constraints in (3) are used.

(3) *Korean Cue constraints*
  *[burst]/C(.): auditory release burst should not be perceived as a consonant in coda.
  *[h] / -asp/:   aspiration noise should not be perceived as -aspirated.
  *[] / ɨ/: absence of vocalic cues should not be perceived as the vowel /ɨ/.
  *[no voice] /V -tense V/: a voiceless silence should not be perceived as a lenis plosive.

---

1. For a full and complete understanding, we urge the reader to consult the original source. For reasons of space we have simplified their account to some extent.

*[no noise] /+asp/: absence of aspiration noise should not be perceived as +aspirated.

*[_] /C(.)/:   voiced closure should not be perceived as a coda consonant.

*[_] /+tense/: voiced closure should not be perceived as a fortis/tense or aspirated.

The perception of English *deck* as surface /.tɛ.kʰɨ./ is illustrated in (4) (simplified from Boersma and Hamann 2010), where superscript [ᵏ] and [ᵍ] stand for the velar plosive release burst, [ʰ] for aspiration noise, [_] for voicing during the closure of the plosive, and, [ ] for the absence of vocalic cues.

(4)   *Perception of English deck [dɛkᵏʰ] as /.tɛ.kʰɨ./*

[dɛkᵏʰ]	*[burst] /C(.)/	*[ʰ] /-asp/	*[no noise] /+asp/	*[_] /C(.)/	*[_] /+tense/	*[no voice] /V -tense V/	*[ ] /ɨ/
/.tɛk./	*!	*					
/.tɛkʰ./	*!						
/.tɛ.kɨ./		*!				*	*
/.tɛ.kʼɨ./		*!					*
☞ /.tɛ.kʰɨ./							*

The cue constraint *[burst] / C(.), an auditory release burst must not be perceived as a coda consonant, rules out the first two perception candidates where the final consonant is perceived as a syllable-final one. Perception of the final consonant as [-aspirated] is ruled out by the second cue constraint, which leaves the Korean listeners no choice but to perceive a final vowel. The cue constraint *[no voice] /V -tense V/ (a voiceless silence should not be perceived as a lenis, a [-tense], plosive) is not directly relevant in (4), but will be of relevance in the Korean production. The Korean perception of English *tag* is illustrated in (5).

(5)   *Perception of English tag [tʰægᵍ] as /.tʰæ.kɨ./.*

[tʰægᵍ]	*[burst] /C(.)/	*[ʰ] /-asp/	*[no noise] /+asp/	*[_] /C(.)/	*[_] /+tense/	*[no voice] /V -tense V/	*[ ] /ɨ/
/.tʰæk./	*!			*			
/. tʰækʰ./	*!		*	*	*		
☞ /.tʰæ.kɨ./							*
/. tʰæ.kʼɨ./					*!		*
/. tʰæ.kʰɨ./			*!		*		*

The first two candidates are ruled out by the cue constraint demanding that an audible velar release should not be perceived as a syllable-final consonant. Perception of the voiced velar as either aspirated or tense is ruled out by the cue constraint demanding that a voiced closure must not be perceived as [+tense], but rather as either aspirated [kʰ] or tense [kʼ]. Again, the low ranking of the cue constraint demanding that the absence of vocalic cues should not be perceived as a vowel, leaves the Korean listeners no choice but to perceive a vowel and causes the insertion of 'illusory' vowels in perception.

In Korean phonological production, that is when faithfulness and structural constraints interact, nothing happens: |tʰæki| surfaces as /.tʰæ.ki./ and |tɛkʰi| as /.tɛ.kʰi./. However, in phonetic implementation, the cue constraint *[no voice] /V -tense V/, which in (4) and (5) prevented a voiceless silence to be perceived as a lenis plosive, in phonetic implementation reads as follows: a lenis intervocalic plosive should not be voiceless and will take care of intervocalic voicing of native and non-native lenis plosives, such that /.tʰæ.ki./ will be realized as [tʰæ.gi].[2]

In the Korean adaptation of word-final English plosives, there is variation between adaptation with vowel insertion (*pipe* as [pʰai.pʰi]) and without vowel insertion (*type* as [tʰaip]), and sometimes both forms occur (*jeep* as [tsip] or [tsi.pʰi]) (cf., among others, Kang 2003). Following Kang (2003), Boersma and Hamann attribute this variation to the variability of the release burst in English. Without audible velar release and concomitant aspiration noise, the first two cue constraints in (4) are mute and no vowel insertion will take place, that is, modified input [dɛk] when passed through (4) will surface as perceived /.tɛk./. In order to account for the same variation

---

2. The 'illusory' vowel in the account proposed by Boersma and Hamann is in perception really there in the sense that for the relevant part of the grammar the word-final English plosive is no longer final, but intervocalic. Without that assumption the constraint *[no voice] /V -tense V/ would be evaluated differently in (4). It is questionable, however, whether the vowel is really present in pre-lexical recognition. Cutler (2011: 195 and 431) discusses a number of experiments that shed some light on this issue. In manipulated items of pronounced nonce words like [abuno], [ebuze] in which the vowel duration of [u] was step-wise reduced to zero, Japanese listeners (cf. Dupoux e.a. 1999) continued to perceive the vowel most of the time even when it was completely removed, whereas the French participants fairly accurately perceived no vowel in the same condition. English listeners evaluate a stop ambiguous between [t] and [k] in a neutral context 50% of the time as [t] and 50% of the time as [k]. After [s], as in *boss cop*, a [k] comes to partially resemble a [t] and after [ʃ], as in *wash tub*, a [t] comes to sound more like a [k]. English listeners compensate for this co-articulation effect in that a stop ambiguous between [t] and [k] tends to be judged more often as [t] after [ʃ], but as [k] after [s] (cf. Mann and Repp (1981). Japanese listeners, just as the English ones, adjust their responses to the ambiguous stop in the same way (Kingston et al. 2011). The latter finding suggest that the vowel they report to perceive is not really there in the pre-lexical processing.

for the voiced velar plosive (*big* and *bag* perceived as surface /.pik./ and /.pæk./) the cue constraint *[_] /C(.)/, a voiced closure must not be perceived as a coda consonant, is assumed to be optionally ranked below *[ ] /i/ (cf. Boersma & Hamann 2010 for a more detailed account). Let us next turn to the recognition of perceived final /t/ as underlying |s|.

Word-final [t] will be perceived as /t./ or as /tʰi/. If it is perceived as /t./, recognition will lead to |s|. Boersma and Hamann use a positional faithfulness constraint IDENT (stri(.)), which requires that, in coda position, the underlying and surface values of stridency should be identical. This constraint is split up into the two faithfulness constraints and the two anti-faithfulness constraints in (6).

(6)   *Faithful and anti-faithful constraints*
       faithful
       *|+stri|/-stri(.)/   underlying +strident should not correspond to surface
       −strident
       *|-stri|/+stri(.)/   underlying -strident should not correspond to surface
       +strident

       anti-faithful
       *|+stri|/+stri(.)/   underlying +strident should not correspond to surface
       +strident
       *|-stri|/-stri(.)/   underlying -strident should not correspond to surface
       -strident

Boersma and Hamann (2010) assume that underlying forms are freely generated candidates and use lexical constraints of the type *<field>|pas| "the morpheme <field> does not link to underlying |pas|". If the latter constraint dominates the anti-faithfulness constraint *|−stri|/-stri(.)/, the faithfulness constraint *|+stri|/-stri(.)/ and the lexical constraint *<field>|patʰ|, perceived surface /pat/ is correctly computed as underlying |patʰ| and the morpheme <field> is accessed. The recognition of underlying forms is assumed to run in parallel with the recognition of morphemes. The ranking *<field> |pas| > above *<field> |patʰ| expresses the fact that the morpheme <field> is more strongly connected to the candidate underlying form |patʰ| than to the candidate underlying form |pas|. This is illustrated in (7).

(7)   *Recognition of perceived Korean /.pat./ as underlying |patʰ|*

/.pat./	*< >	*<field>|pas|	*|−stri| /-stri(.)/	*|+stri| /-stri(.)/	*<field>|patʰ|
|pas| < >	*!			*	
☞ |patʰ| <field>			*		*
|pas| <field>		*!		*	

The first constraint in (7), *< >, penalizes the linking of a perceived surface form to no morpheme. That constraint becomes active if a surface form is recognized without a 'corresponding' morpheme being available in the lexicon. On the assumption that loanwords are not yet in the lexicon, lexical constraints do not play a role yet. In the adaptation of English *shot* [ʃʊt], if perceived as surface /.sjat./, the morpheme <shot> is not yet available and hence cannot be accessed. This implies that surface /.sjat./ enters the recognition part of the grammar without being able to link to a morpheme, that is, no existing morpheme can be found, which entails a violation of the constraint *< >. Perceived surface /sjat/ is then computed as underlying |sjas| because of the ranking of anti-faithful *|−stri|/-stri(.)/ above faithful *|+stri|/-stri(.)/, as illustrated in (8).

(8)   *Recognition of perceived English /.sjat./ as underlying |sjas|*

/.sjat./	*< >	*<field>|pas|	*|−stri| /-stri(.)/	*|+stri| /-stri(.)/	*<field>|patʰ|
☞ |sjas| < >	*			*	
|sjatʰ| < >	*		*!		
|sjat| < >	*		*!		

Subsequently, a new morpheme can be stored and a new lexical item |sjas|<shot > can then be created, with the relevant lexical constraints *<shot> | sjas|, *<shot> | sjatʰ | etc., so that perceived /.sjat./ can be computed as | sjas| and the new morpheme can be accessed. The ranking of anti-faithful *|-stri|/-stri(.)/ above faithful *|+stri|/-stri(.)/ is attributed to frequency: underlying final |s| is much more common than underlying final |t| or | tʰ|. As a matter of fact, as mentioned above, Kim (ms.) reports that there are no nouns ending in |t'|, 2 nouns in |t|, 116 in | tʰ| and 308 in |s|.

The account proposed by Boersma and Hamann raises a number of problems. First, it seems to imply, counter-intuitively, that for loanwords, at least initially, underlying forms are computed without available morphemes or meaning. Why start with computing an underlying form and not with storing a new morpheme? Why not the two in parallel? Second, the recognition of perceived final t as underlying s is based on the absence/presence of an audible plosive release in donor English, that is, the ranking in (4) will lead to perception without vowel insertion or with vowel insertion, depending on the absence/presence of an auditory release burst. Kang (2003) supports his claim that the release of the stop in foreign inputs correlates with vowel insertion after the stop in Korean loanwords by pointing out that loanwords from French with word-final stops are consistently adapted with vowel insertion and refers to Tranel (1987) for the observation that French word-final stops are consistently released. This means, however, that word-final French coronals should invariably be adapted with vowel insertion, given that they can never surface under the ranking in (4) without vowel insertion. Yet, as the examples in (1) above show, French word-final coronal plosives are also adapted as underlying |s|. In comparing her early 1990 and 2011 data, Kim (ms.) observes a strong decrease in forms with final vowel insertion, both in French and English, which cannot easily be related to variability in the plosive release. She also observes the same variation (with and without vowel insertion) for dorsal/labial plosives in French loans, as in the examples in (9), which renders the account relying exclusively on variable plosive release problematic.

(9)   *Variation for French word-final plosives*

Chirac	[si.ra.kʰɨ]	~	[si.rak]
chic	[swi.kʰɨ]	~	[swik]
cognac	[kʰo.njak.kʰɨ]	~	[kʰo.njak]
Lautrec	[lo.tʰɨ.rɛ.kʰɨ]	~	[lo.tʰɨ.rɛk]

Moreover, word-internal French and English syllable final plosives are treated alike (no vowel insertion is predominant in 20 out of 23 for French loans and in 462 out of 477 for English loans in Kim (ms.)), whereas they are released in French (Tranel 1987), but not in English. Some examples of French loans, taken from Kim (ms.), are provided in (10).

(10)   *Adaptation of French word-internal syllable-final plosives*

Without vowel insertion

Hector	[ɛk.t'o.lɨ]
Exupéry	[ɛk.tswi.p'ɛ.lɨ]
Victoire	[pik.t'u.a.lɨ]
observateur	[op.s'ɛ.lɨ.pa.t'ɛ.lɨ]
expressif	[ɛk.s'i.pʰɨ.lɛ.s'i.pʰɨ]

With vowel insertion

objet	[o.pɨ.tsɛ]
Vietcong	[pɛ.tʰɨ.kʰɔŋ]
Edgar	[ɛ.tɨ.ka.lɨ]

Third, Boersma and Hamann, (recall the examples in (2) above) mention that a similar replacement of word-final postvocalic coronal plosives can be observed in native Korean phonology where next to locative /.pa.tʰɛ./ alternative /.pa.sɛ./ occurs. However, this aspect of the native phonology cannot be modeled in the same way: the lexical constraints *<field> |pas| and *<field> |patʰ| in (7) would need to be re-ranked in order for /.pa.sɛ./ to surface. Loanword adaptation by anti-faithfulness and L1 analogy with re-ranking of lexical constraints are two ways of dealing with what seems to be one and the same phenomenon. In the next section, we discuss the proposals Kang (2003) and Davis and Kang (2006) that deal with native leveling.

3. Uniform treatment of leveling and loanwords: Paradigm uniformity and anti-correspondence

Kang (2003) observes that the adaptation of English postvocalic word-final voiceless stops with or without vowel insertion is partly dependent on the optional release of word-final stops in English, especially for word-final voiceless dorsal and labial stops. Also, there is more vowel insertion when the preceding vowel is tense rather than lax, and, when the final stop is voiced rather than voiceless. There is, however, more vowel insertion for English word-final coronal plosives than for dorsal or labial plosives, whereas coronals are released less frequently than dorsals or labials in English. This is described as a paradigm uniformity effect, that is, a preference for a uniform paradigm serves as an additional incentive for vowel insertion. Kang (2003) uses the constraints in (11).

(11)   *Korean t–s alternation and paradigm uniformity constraints*

T → S	When a noun ends in [t] in the citation form, change the stop to [s] before a vowel-initial suffix.
BASE-IDENTITY[CONT]	Output candidates are required to have the same value for [continuant] as the base
DEP-V	No vowel insertion

The assumption is that complete paradigms are evaluated as candidates. The analysis is illustrated in (12), where only the citation form and the locative are provided.

(12)   *Native Korean [tikɨt] 'name of letter t'*

tikɨt	T → S	DEP-V	BASE-IDENTITY
a. tikɨt, tikɨt-ɛ	*!		
☞ b. tikɨt, tikɨs-ɛ			*
c. tikɨti, tikɨti-ɛ		*!	

The ranking of the alternation between final [t] and prevocalic [s] in nouns, expressed by the constraint T → S, above BASE-IDENTITY creates non-uniform paradigms, as in (12b). For loanwords, the situation is different. Because English word-final coronal stops are variably released, there will be two forms available in perception, one with (13a) and one without vowel insertion (13b). Tableau (13) illustrates the analysis of the two possible forms for English *cut*.

(13)   *Word-final English coronal plosives and paradigm (non)-uniformity*

(a) kʰʌtʰɨ	T → S	Dep-V	Base-Identity
☞1. kʰʌtʰɨ, kʰʌtʰɨ-ɛ			
2. kʰʌt, kʰʌs-ɛ			*!
3. kʰʌt, kʰʌt-ɛ	*!		

(b) kʰʌt	T → S	Dep-V	Base-Identity
1. kʰʌtʰɨ, kʰʌtʰɨ-ɛ		*!	
☞2. kʰʌt, kʰʌs-ɛ			*
3. kʰʌt, kʰʌt-ɛ	*!		

If a vowel is inserted in the loanword, as in (13a), a uniform paradigm results (13a–1), given that the [t]~[s] alternation is no longer relevant. If no vowel is inserted, as in (13b), the paradigm will be non-uniform, as in (13b-2). The preference for a uniform paradigm thus serves as an additional incentive for vowel insertion (Kang 2003, 251), but only for word-final loans ending in coronals.

The ranking in (12), however, predicts that the T–S alternation in the native phonology is without exceptions. However, as Kang (2003, 251) notes "nouns ending in other coronal plosives, /ts, tsʰ, tʰ/, either have changed to /s/-final nouns or currently show optional variants with final [s]." The ranking in (12), however, allows only for the optional forms in (14) (repeated from (2) above), but not for the uniform ones. In a uniform *pat, patʰ-ɛ, patʰ-ɨl* paradigm, the noun ends in citation form in [t], but does not alternate with [s] in inflected forms, and, will be ruled out by the high ranked T → S constraint in (12).

(14)   *Variation for Korean word-final coronals*

UNAFFIXED	ACC	optional	LOC	optional
[pat] 'field'	[patʰ-ɨl] ~	[pas-ɨl]	[patʰ-ɛ] ~	[pas-ɛ]
[pit] 'debt'	[pitsʰ-ɨl] ~	[pis-ɨl]	[pitsʰ-ɛ] ~	[pis-ɛ]
[k'ot] 'flower'	[k'otsʰ- él] ~	[k'os- él]	[k'otsʰ-ɛ] ~	[k'os-ɛ]

A variable ranking of T → S and Base-Identity and both below Dep-V would allow for both forms in (14), as illustrated in (15a), but would incorrectly predict for loan adaptations word-final coronals to be adapted as paradigms in which the final coronal is adapted as such without alternations. In other words, both candidates (15b-2) and (15b-3), are incorrectly predicted to be possible adaptations.

(15)   *Variable ranking of t–s alternation and paradigm uniformity*

(a) patʰ	Dep-V	T → S	Base-Identity
☞1. pat, patʰ-ɛ		*	
☞2. pat, pas-ɛ			*
3. patʰɨ, patʰɨ-ɛ	*!		

(b) kʰʌt	Dᴇᴘ-V	T → S	Bᴀsᴇ-Iᴅᴇɴᴛɪᴛʏ
1. kʰʌtʰɨ, kʰʌtʰɨ-ɛ	*!		
☞2. kʰʌt, kʰʌs-ɛ			*
☞3. kʰʌt, kʰʌt-ɛ		*	

Finally, the ranking in (12) predicts vowel-insertion to become the general adaptation choice for loanwords with word-final coronals, no violation for the [t]~[s] alternations and uniform paradigms, as in (13a). However, as mentioned above, Kim (ms.) observes exactly the opposite when comparing her 1990 and 2011 corpus: a strong decrease in vowel insertion, both for English and for French. Let us next discuss the analysis proposed by Davis and Kang (2006).

Davis and Kang (2006) account for the variant forms in (14) by using the constraints in (16).

(16) *Korean t–s alternation and paradigm uniformity constraints*

Aɴᴛɪ-Cᴏʀʀᴇsᴘᴏɴᴅᴇɴᴄᴇ t]_W	A word-final [t] must alternate in conjugated forms
I-O-Fᴀɪᴛʜ	Corresponding sounds in the input and output should be identical
Aɴᴛɪ-Fᴀɪᴛʜ [-ᴄᴏɴᴛɪɴᴜᴀɴᴛ]	If two words are in an O–O relation then a correspondent of a word-final [−cont] must not be [−cont]
Pᴀʀᴀᴅɪɢᴍ Uɴɪғᴏʀᴍɪᴛʏ	Corresponding sounds in related words in a paradigm are identical
Cᴏᴅᴀ Nᴇᴜᴛʀᴀʟɪᴢᴀᴛɪᴏɴ	All coda segments are unreleased

The variation in the native phonology is accounted for by free ranking of the constraint IO-Fᴀɪᴛʜ, as illustrated in (17) and (18). Candidates are again evaluated as entire paradigm sets.

(17) *Korean uniform forms [pat, patʰ-ɛ, patʰ-il]*

patʰ	Aɴᴛɪ-Cᴏʀʀᴇsᴘᴏɴᴅᴇɴᴄᴇ	I-O Fᴀɪᴛʜ	Aɴᴛɪ-Fᴀɪᴛʜ [-ᴄᴏɴᴛ]	Pᴀʀᴀᴅɪɢᴍ Uɴɪғᴏʀᴍɪᴛʏ
☞1. pat, patʰ-ɛ, patʰ-il			*	*
2. pat, pas-ɛ, pas-il		*!		*
3. pat, pat-ɛ, pat-il	*!		*	*

The I–O Fᴀɪᴛʜ constraint abstracts away from violations due to Cᴏᴅᴀ Nᴇᴜᴛʀᴀʟɪᴢᴀᴛɪᴏɴ, that is, no violation for the citation form, the first form of the three paradigms in (17). It only indicates violations for the inflected forms and only one violation for the entire set, not two for (17-2) and (17-3). The free lower ranking of I–O Fᴀɪᴛʜ accounts for the optional forms in (14), as illustrated in (18).

(18)   *Korean optional non-uniform forms [pat, pas-ɛ, pas-il]*

patʰ	ANTI-CORRESPONDENCE	ANTI-FAITH [-CONT]	PARADIGM UNIFORMITY	I-O FAITH
1. pat, patʰ-ɛ, patʰ-il		*!	*	
☞ 2. pat, pas-ɛ, pas-il			*	*
3. pat, pat-ɛ, pat-il	*!	*		*

The same analysis is applied to loanwords ending in coronal plosives, as illustrated in (19).

(19)   *English '(inter)net'; Korean [nɛt, nɛs-ɛ, nɛs-il]*

	ANTI-CORRESPONDENCE	ANTI-FAITH [-CONT]	PARADIGM UNIFORMITY	I-O FAITH
1. nɛt, nɛt-i, nɛt-il	*!	*		
2. nɛt, nɛts-i, nɛts-il		*!	*	
☞ 3. nɛt, nɛs-i, nɛs-il			*	
4. nɛt, nɛtʰ-i, nɛtʰ-il		*!	*	

No underlying form is given for loanwords, intentionally so, following Davis and Kang's (2006, 11) claim that when the surface forms of borrowed words end with final [t], then the final [t] will come to be lexicalized as /s/ given the candidate evaluation in tableau (19). The ranking in (16) would produce the same result, given the fact that the I–O FAITH constraint is mute in the absence of an underlying form. However, it is not clear why an underlying form should be absent. Both the rankings in (17) and (18) evaluate surface forms of a paradigm, but do not select or point out which UR should be chosen. Lexicon Optimization would select /t/ instead of /s/. If (19) did contain an underlying form ending in /t/, the surface paradigm would still be the same, given the low ranking of I–O FAITH. However, if word-final coronal plosives were perceived with audible release and without vowel insertion and were borrowed with final [tʰ] and underlying /tʰ/, the ranking in (17) would, incorrectly, favor a paradigm [nɛt, nɛtʰ-ɛ, nɛtʰ-il]. That is, free ranking of I–O FAITH (as in (17) and (18)) and borrowing with a lexicalized /tʰ/ must be excluded, as illustrated in (20).

(20)   **English '(inter)net'; Korean [nɛt, nɛtʰ-ɛ, nɛtʰ-il]*

nɛtʰ	ANTI-CORRESPONDENCE	I-O FAITH	ANTI-FAITH [-CONT]	PARADIGM UNIFORMITY
a. nɛt, nɛt-ɛ, nɛt-il	*!	*	*	
b. nɛt, nɛts-ɛ, nɛts-il		*!	*	*
c. nɛt, nɛs-ɛ, nɛs-il		*!		*
☞ d. nɛt, nɛtʰ-ɛ, nɛtʰ-il			*	*

The conclusion that "the borrowing of word-final [t] as lexical /s/ is purely a matter internal to the morphophonology of Korean" (Davis & Kang 2006, 266) is therefore not well-motivated. Furthermore, if it is the paradigm candidate evaluation in (19) which selects underlying /s/ for final [t], why is underlying /s/ not selected for [t^h] in (18)? Also, the analysis does not address the variant loanword adaptations (with and without vowel insertion). Finally, in both Kang (2003) and Davis and Kang (2006) the ANTI-CORRESPONDENCE t]$_W$ constraint or the T $\rightarrow$ S constraint suggest that something happens, which is true, but only from a surface perspective. Without STRIDENT NEUTRALIZATION and CODA NEUTRALIZATION, there would be no alternations. In a way, the anti-correspondence constraints duplicate the effects of STRIDENT NEUTRALIZATION and CODA NEUTRALIZATION. In fact, before vowel-initial suffixes it is just the regular UR that surfaces normally. It is in coda position that STRIDENT NEUTRALIZATION and CODA NEUTRALIZATION change the UR. Or to put it differently, the analogical leveling displayed by the variant optional forms (14) has nothing to do with the anti-correspondence or paradigm uniformity constraints (same violations for both the *pat, pat^h-ɛ, pat^h-il* paradigm and the *pat, pas-ɛ, pas-il* paradigm), but is solely a matter of the relative ranking of ANTI-FAITH [-CONT] and I–O FAITH. It is underlying word-final /s/ which analogically is spreading through the native lexicon and replacing or doubling original underling forms. This fact is not directly expressed in the above analyses.

4. Leveling and loanwords without anti-correspondence or anti-faithfulness

Kiparsky (2003) discusses a similar case of analogical leveling in Gothic and proposes a constraint on underlying stems that challenges, as he argues, theories that define optimality only with regard to output representations. Although a direct constraint on underlying forms (such as, *-t/, a stem should not end in -t/ underlyingly) could be made to work, let us try to explore an alternative that does away with constraints on inputs.

We propose that, instead of lexical constraints and anti-faithfulness or anti-correspondence constraints, frequency and knowledge of likely inputs might be based on input-output chain evaluations. OT with Candidate Chains (OT-CC), which is a specific form of Harmonic Serialism (McCarthy 2007 and 2008), evaluates only well-formed chains connecting a given input to an output. A candidate is a chain of forms connecting input to output, where the first member of every candidate chain is a fully faithful parse, violating no faithfulness constraints. A single faithfulness violation in a specific location is a LUM (Localized Unfaithful Mapping). Successive forms in a chain are required to accumulate all of their predecessor's LUM and add only, exactly, one LUM. Moreover, every successive form has to be more harmonic than its predecessor.

The fact that no Korean nouns end in /tʼ/, that 2 nouns end in /t/, 116 in /tʰ/, and 308 in /s/ might lead the language learner to assume the language-specific markedness hierarchy in (21).[3]

(21)   *Korean coronal markedness hierarchy*
       <s/ (…) t]>   <<   <tʰ/ (…) t]>   (<<   <t/ (…) t]>)

The hierarchy in (21) expresses that a chain starting with final /s/ and ending in final [t] is the least marked state of affairs in the language and that a chain starting with final /tʰ/ and ending in [t] is more marked. Eventually, given the existence of only 2 nouns with final /t/, the last statement between parentheses might be added: a chain starting with final /t/ and ending in [t] is extremely rare. Alternatively, the markedness hierarchy in (22) could be assumed, which might be claimed to be based on sufficient input-output chain evaluations, and which, as such, expresses knowledge of lexical forms.

(22)   -s/   <<   -tʰ/   (<<   t/)

The markedness hierarchy in (22) directly expresses that underlying final /s/ is less marked than underlying final /tʰ/ and that underlying final /t/ is extremely marked. The Korean borrower may be guided by (21/22) in selecting the least marked underlying form for French and English words, no matter whether they end in a released plosive coronal or not (as invariably the case in French), that is final /s/. Similarly, the coronal markedness hierarchy in (21/22) could be seen as responsible for the analogical pressure going on in the native phonology and account for the optional forms in (14).

We assume, following the model outlined in Calabrese (2010) that in perception the perceived surface form is analyzed for an appropriate UR by running the perceived form through the grammar. For the hypothetical underlying forms surface forms are generated by the same grammar and, also, hypothetic, virtual acoustic images for these surface generated forms are produced by a synthesizer (analysis-by synthesis). This virtual image is then compared to the actually perceived form and the UR is selected that yields the best match. This could be seen within an OT-account as an output-output (O–O) constraint that compares the actually perceived form with the surface generated form in terms of matching consonants (O–O Consonant Faith).

We illustrate how this works in (23) for a French loan containing an audible release, where next to the possible underlying form the corresponding surface generated form is given.

---

3.   A markedness hierarchy is alluded to but not further developed in Davis and Kang (2006).

(23)   *Underlying form for perceived French word-final coronal [t] with release*

/Perceived surface [omɨlɛt^t]/	Surface generated form	OO-C Faith	Dep-Io
a) /omɨllɛt^h/	[.o.mɨl.lɛt.]	*	
b) /omɨllɛt^{h}ɨ/	[.o.mɨl.lɛ.t^{h}ɨ]		*
c) /omɨllɛt'ɨ/	[.o.mɨl.lɛ.t'ɨ.]		*
d) /omɨllɛs/	[.o.mɨl.lɛt.]	*	

In principle, four possible underlying forms are available. With vowel-insertion and a violation of OO-C Faith, the surface generated form will have a final consonant as close as possible to the perceived donor form (especially for word-final voiced plosives due to intervocalic voicing in Korean). Without vowel-insertion the surface form will have a less faithful consonant, but will have no violation for Dep-Io. The markedness hierarchy will favor UR (23d) over UR (23a).[4]

The borrower has thus in principle three possible underlying forms to choose from when dealing with French loans. Or to put it differently, three possible lexical items can be constructed: <omelet>/omɨllɛt^{h}ɨ/; <omelet>/omɨllɛt'ɨ/ and <omelet>/omɨllɛs/. The replacement of word-final -t] by underlying -s/ is possible both when the original plosive is released, as in French, or not, as variably in English.[5]

For the native analogy, again two possible underlying forms will emerge as possibilities, as illustrated in (24).

(24)   *Korean native perceived [pat]*

Perceived surface [pat]	Surface generated form	OO-C Faith	Dep-IO
☞/pat^h/	[.pat.]		
☞/pas/	[.pat.]		
/pat^{h}ɨ/	[.pa.t^{h}ɨ.]	*	*

Given the existence of the lexical item <field> /pat^h/, the alternative item <field> /pas/ will be added as an alternative UR, given the language-specific markedness hierarchy (21/22). This will lead to the existence of lexical allomorphs /pat^h~pas/ <field>, /pits~pis/ <debt>, and /k'ots^h~k'os/ <flower> for the forms in (14). Depending on the UR that is chosen, the two variant forms in (14) obtain. Native analogy is thus seen

---

4.   In order to exclude (23a) as a possible underlying form, the markedness hierarchy (21/22) could be included as a constraint in the constraint hierarchy of the language and would then directly rule out (23a). We will leave this option open here.

5.   Replacement of French [t] by both a tense [t'] or aspirated [t^h] is possible. We will not go into the possible preference for one or the other.

as lexical allomorphy, triggered by (21/22) (cf. Wetzels, 1986). Loanword adaptation in this respect closely mirrors native phonology. It also predicts that leveling does not take over entire paradigms at once, as would be predicted by the ranking in (17) or (18), but can affect single forms within a paradigm. Finally, the present proposal does not limit replacement of word-final [t] by underlying /s/ to loans that do contain unreleased plosives, as in the Boersma and Hamann account. It thus straightforwardly accounts for the French loanword adaptation in Korean.

5. Summary

In this paper we have considered the fact noted by Kim (2010) that, besides production and perception, lexical knowledge plays a determining role in the adaptation of loanwords. We have critically discussed Boersma and Hamann's (2010) proposal to model the adaptation of word-final English coronal plosives as ending in Korean with underlying /s/ by using positional faithfulness and anti-faithfulness IDENT (STRIDENT(.)) constraints. We have argued that with anti-correspondence and anti-faithfulness the analogical spreading of underlying stem-final /-s/ cannot adequately be described. We have then proposed to model frequency and lexical knowledge in the form of a markedness hierarchy based on chain evaluation (McCarthy 2007), which allows the same markedness hierarchy to account for both loanword adaptation of final coronal plosives as underlying |s| and for the analogical pressure observable in L1.

References

Allbright, Adam. 2002. *The Identification of Bases in Morphological Paradigms*. Ph.D. Dissertation, UCLA.

Boersma, Paul and Silke Hamann. 2010. "Loanword Adaptation as First-language Phonological Perception" In *Loan Phonology*, ed. by Andrea Calabrese, and W. Leo Wetzels,. 11–58. Amsterdam/Philadelphia: John Benjamins. DOI: 10.1075/cilt.307.02boe

Calabrese, Andrea. 2010. "Perception, Production and Acoustic Inputs in Loanword Phonology". In *Loan Phonology*, ed. by Andrea Calabrese, and W. Leo Wetzels, 59–113. Amsterdam/Philadelphia: John Benjamins. DOI: 10.1075/cilt.307.03cal

Cutler, Ann. 2011. *Native Listening*. Cambridge, MA: MIT Press.

Davis, Stuart and Hyunsook Kang. 2006. "English Loanwords and the Word-final [t] Problem in Korean." *Language Research* 42(2): 253–274.

Dupoux, Emmanuel, Kazuhiko Kakehi, Yuki Hirose, Christophe Pallier, and Jacques Mehler. 1999. "Epenthetic Vowels in Japanese: A Perceptual Illusion?" *Journal of Experimental Psychology: Human Perception and Performance* 25: 1568–1578. DOI: 10.1037/0096-1523.25.6.1568

Kang, Yoonjung. 2003. "Perceptual Similarity in Loanword Adaptation: English Postvocalic Word-final Stops in Korean." *Phonology*, 20(2): 219–273. DOI: 10.1017/S0952675703004524

Kenstowicz, Michael. 2005."The Phonetics and Phonology of Korean Loanword Adaptation." *Proceedings of the First European Conference on Korean Linguistics*. Vol. 1: 17–32.

Kim, Hyunsoon. 2010. "Korean Adaptation of English Affricates and Fricatives in a Feature-driven Model of Loanword Adaptation." In *Loan Phonology, ed. by* Andrea Calabrese, and W. Leo Wetzels, 155–180. Amsterdam/Philadelphia: John Benjamins. DOI: 10.1075/cilt.307.06kim

Kim, Hyunsoon (ms.) "An L1 Grammar Driven Model of Loanword Adaptation; Evidence from Korean."

Kingston, John, Shigeto Kawahara, Daniel Mash, and Della Chambless. 2011. "Auditory Contrast versus Compensation for Coarticulation: Data from Japanese and English Listeners." *Language and Speech* 54: 499–525. DOI: 10.1177/0023830911404959

Kiparsky, Paul. (2003). 'Analogy as optimization: 'exceptions' to Siever's Law in Gothic'. Aditi Lahiri (eds.) *Analogy, Leveling, Markedness*. 15–46. Berlin: Mouton de Gruyter.

Mann, Virginia, and Bruno Repp. 1981. "Influence of Preceding Fricative on Stop Consonant Perception." *Journal of the Acoustical Society of America* 69: 548–558. DOI: 10.1121/1.385483

McCarthy, John. 2007. *Hidden Generalizations. Phonological Opacity in Optimality Theory*. London: Equinox.

McCarthy, John. 2008. "The Serial Interaction of Stress and Syncope." *Natural Language and Linguistic Theory* 26: 499–546. DOI: 10.1007/s11049-008-9051-3

Tranel, Bernard. 1987. *The Sounds of French: An Introduction*. Cambridge, MA: Cambridge University Press. DOI: 10.1017/CBO9780511620645

Wetzels, Leo. 1986. *Analogie et lexique. Le problème de l'opacité en phonologie générative*. Dordrecht: Foris.

Affirmative polar replies in Brazilian Portuguese*

Mary A. Kato
State University of Campinas

This article analyzes affirmative polar replies in Brazilian and European Portuguese (BP/EP), which may consist of just the inflected verb or some polar item. These polar replies have been analyzed as instances of null subjects and VP-Ellipsis. This analysis is untenable for BP, as this variety has been losing categorical null referential subjects since the 19th century. The analysis that will be pursued here, for both BP and EP, is an adaptation of the one proposed in Holmberg (2001) for Finnish, according to which, in simple affirmative answers, which consists of just the inflected verb, the verb moves to a pre-sentential position, followed by Remnant TP-Ellipsis. But BP also differs from Finnish when more complex answers are at stake. With regard to the position and optionality of the affirmative polar item *sim* (yes), a comparison will be made with Japanese, a language identical to BP with regard to affirmative PRs.

1. Introduction

In recent years answers to *yes/no* questions have become a topic of intense syntactic inquiry due to their great variety exhibited in natural languages.[1] My aim in this paper is to describe and analyze affirmative polar replies (PRs) in Brazilian Portuguese (BP) and compare them to European Portuguese (EP), Finnish and Japanese.[2] It will be shown that, despite the deep differences in the grammar of the two main

* This work had the support of the CNPq grant N. 305515/2011–0.

1. See, for instance, the Workshop on the Syntax of Answers to Polar Questions, which took place in Newcastle in June 2012.

2. The first version of the paper was presented at the Newcastle Workshop on the Syntax of Answers to Polar Questions in collaboration with Sonia Cyrino, and it also contained negative polarity replies. I thank the audiences in both Newcastle and LSRL 43 for their important contributions. I also thank Marcello Marcelino for his usual help with the first version of this paper. I am responsible for the remaining inadequacies.

DOI 10.1075/rllt.9.11kat
© 2016 John Benjamins Publishing Company

varieties of Portuguese, their PRs are surprisingly alike, and can possibly be derived in the same manner. It will also be shown that Japanese, a typologically distant language from Romance, also shows some interesting similarities regarding Brazilian PRs. In Kato and Tarallo (1992), this was attributed to the fact that the three languages were positively marked with respect to the Null Subject Parameter (NSP), and to the fact that they also licensed VP-Ellipsis. However, later work (Duarte 1995; Kato 1999; Kato and Negrão 2000, a. o.) showed that BP was only a partial NS language, and distinct from languages like EP or Japanese with regard to certain contexts where the NS was obligatory.[3] The aim of this paper is to answer the following questions: (a) Considering that BP is only a partial NS language, why do PRS have categorical null subjects like EP and Japanese? (b) Can BP be compared to other partial NS languages? (c) Since the affirmative particles *sim,* in Portuguese, and *hai,* in Japanese, are optional, can the optionality be attributed to the same factor?

The paper is divided into the following sections: (a) Section 2 will present previous analyses of PRs in both Brazilian and European Portuguese; (b) Section 3 will present the TP-Ellipsis analysis combined with VP-Ellipsis in Finnish, also a partial NS language (Holmberg 2001); (c) Section 4 will present my analysis, an adaptation of the analysis in Holmberg (2001), using the cartographic approach (Rizzi 1997); (d) Section 5 will analyze the position and optionality of the particle *sim* in BP. The last section contains some final considerations.

2.   Previous studies of PRs in Portuguese

Kato and Tarallo[4] (1992) (K&T) claimed that affirmative Polar Replies (PR) are a locus of crosslinguistic variation, and that Portuguese, in its two varieties, is different from other Western languages, including the Romance languages like French and Italian, and more similar to a language like Japanese.

(1)   Q: *Did you eat the cake?*   English

(2)   A: a.   *(Yes), I did.*   English

      b.   *Oui, je l'ai   mangé.*   French
          yes   I   it=have.1PS   eaten

---

3.   Several studies have shown the differences between BP and other prototypical NS languages, concerning the restricted distribution of NSs in the former (cf. Barbosa et al. 2005, Kato 2009, a.o.).

4.   The first author had Japanese as her L1.

c. *Si, lo ho   mangiatto.*   Italian
   yes it=have.1PS eaten

c. *(Hai), tabemashita.*   Japanese
   yes   ate

d. *(Sim), comi.*   EP/ BP
   yes   ate.1PS

K&T showed that, (a) like in Japanese, in BP and EP the subject and the object are null; (b) contrary to French and Spanish, and like English and Japanese, the (Affirmative) particle, *sim*, is optional in unmarked neuter PRs.[5] K&T analyzed the PRs as consisting of a null subject and a null object, or a null VP, and the authors' proposal was that only languages positively marked for both the Null Subject (NS) and Null Object (NO) parameters could have such PRs.[6] Spanish and Italian, despite being NS languages, could not have such PRs because they were not NO languages.[7]

At that time those authors were not aware that BP was distinct from EP considering the NS parameter. Since Duarte's (1995) seminal thesis, which showed that BP is in the process of losing the "Avoid Pronoun" principle (cf. Chomsky 1981), Brazilian linguists started admitting that there existed "partial NS languages", in which referential subjects are overt in unmarked cases, while non-referential subjects are null (cf. Kato and Negrão 2000, and articles therein). Moreover, in certain contexts, BP cannot have a NS to co-refer to an antecedent, which does not c-command it, while other prototypical NS languages can have a NS with any antecedent (cf. Modesto 2000; Ferreira 2004 a. o.).

(3) *O   Pedro$_i$ disse para o   Paulo$_j$ que ec$_{i/*j}$ estava cansado.* BP
     the Peter   told to the Paulo   that ec$_{i/*j/*k}$ was   tired.

(4) a. *Pedro$_i$ le dijo a Pablo$_j$ que ec$_{i/j}$ estaba cansado*   Spanish
         Pedro 3pcl said to Pablo   that ec   was   tired

     b. *Piero$_i$ disse a Paolo$_j$ che ec$_{i/j}$ era stanco.*   Italian
         Pedro said to Paulo   that ec   was tired

In BP, in order for the embedded subject to co-refer with *Paulo* or some third party, the embedded subject has to be an overt pronoun. When the embedded subject is

---

5. K&T conducted a sociolinguistic survey in which social and linguistic variables were tested.

6. Actually, languages like Japanese and Chinese should be considered languages of a Null Variable type, as in Huang's (1984) proposal, where such type of language can have both the subject and the object null.

7. It has become clear now that not only languages of the NS type can license such PRs, as Capeverdian, which is not a NS language, but can nevertheless exhibit PRS (cf. Costa et al. 2012). I thank one of the reviewers for this information.

correferent to the matrix subject, the NS is optional. Prototypical NS languages, on the other hand, including EP, can have a NS with any antecedent.[8]

However, regarding PRs, we can observe that BP and EP are identical in having a *categorical* NS when the subject is unmarked for contrast, while necessarily expressing the subject only when it is contrastive. We would expect that BP would exhibit variation in the expression of the pronoun in (5A).

(5)   Q: *Você viu o   Pedro?*
            you saw the Pedro
            'Did you see Peter?'

      A: *Eu vi.*   EP   BP
            I   saw

      B: *EU vi, mas o   João, não.*
            I   saw, but the João not
            'I did, but John didn't.'

PRs in European Portuguese also have been analyzed as consisting of a NS plus VP-Ellipsis. Thus, Matos (1992) proposes that for a PR like (6), the structure would be as in (7):

(6)   Q: *Você quer comer bolo?*
            you want eat   cake?
            'Do you want to eat the cake?'

      A: *Quero.*
            want.1SG
            'Yes, I do.'

(7)   [$_{\text{IP}}$ *pro* quero$_{\text{V}}$ [$_{\text{VP}}$ ~~quero comer bolo~~]]

However, if BP is losing referential NSs, this representation should not be the correct one in this variety, or at least it should optionally allow an overt pronoun in subject position.

We will now see a VP-Ellipsis alternative proposal for EP without the shortcomings of having *pro* in the subject position. For Martins (2006) the absence of the subject is not due to the presence of *pro* as in Matos' analysis. Like in McCloskey's (1991) analysis for Irish, she derives PRs through VP-Ellipsis, with the VP containing the subject in its original position (cf. 9).[9]

---

8.   I thank Paco Ordoñez and Marilza de Oliveira for the confirmation of my assumption.

9.   In Irish, a similar type of minimal answer is found, and McCloskey (1991) was the first to analyze it as a phenomenon independent of the NS Parameters , but concerning only VP-Ellipsis, after the finite verb moves to T.

(8) Q: *O   João   comprou   um   carro   vermelho?*
the J   bought   a   car   red
'Did John buy a red car?'

A: *Comprou.*
bought
'Yes, he did.'

(9) [$_{\Sigma P}$ [$_{\Sigma}'$ comprou [$_{TP}$ T′ ~~comprou~~ [$_{VP}$ ~~O João comprou um carro~~
~~vermelho~~)]]]]   (apud Martins 2006)

V moves to Σ, the highest IP category, and licenses VP-Ellipsis.[10] EP does not have to comply with the EPP feature in TP, and the subjects can stay inside VP. In EP when there is a preverbal subject, it occupies Spec ΣP, as an unmarked Topic. Moreover, VP-Ellipsis correlates with enclisis in EP, as shown by Martins (1994).

(10) Q1: **Lhe   deste   o   livro?*   Proclisis
him   gave   the   book
'Did you give him the book?'

Q2: *Deste-lhe   o   livro?*   Enclisis
gave him   the   book

A: *Sim, dei (lho).*   VP-deletion
Yes gave
'Yes, I did.'

In Spanish, a language with generalized proclisis, there are no PRs.

(11) Q1: *Le   diste   el   libro?*   Proclisis
him   gave   the   book

Q2: **Diste-le el libro?*   Enclisis
A1: **Sí, di.*   VP-deletion
A2: *Sí, se lo di.*   Proclisis

BP, on the other hand, is a counter-example to the correlation between enclisis and VP-Ellipsis, since it has generalized proclisis like Spanish, but it has PRs like EP. What we want to show is that BP has PRs, but they cannot be derived by VP-Ellipsis. Moreover, BP does not license VS order (except with unaccusative verbs) because it has to comply with the EPP feature in T. Subjects of non-unaccusative verbs are, therefore, always pre-verbally positioned in Spec,TP (cf. Kato 2000).

---

10. The difference between Martins and McCloskey is that in the former the verb raises to Σ to stay higher than the clitics.

(12)   Q: *O   João   comprou   um   carro   vermelho?*
            the   John   bought   a   car   red
            'Did John buy a red car?'

A1: *Comprou.*
A2: **Ele comprou.*
A3: **Comprou ele.*

Notice that if we follow Martins' analysis we get A3, the wrong output in BP, as in this variety pronouns are normally expressed, but in pre-verbal position:[11]

(13) $[_{\Sigma P} [_{\Sigma'}$ comprou $[_{TP}$ ele$_i$ T'~~comprou~~ [$_{vP}$ ~~ele$_i$~~ [~~comprou um carro vermelho~~)]]]] = A3   *BP

We will see below, in Section 4, that we may figure out an analysis for PRs that accounts for both EP and BP.

3.   PRs in Finnish, a partial NS language

Analyzing Finnish, a partial NS language, Holmberg (2001) shows that it can also have PRs for an answer.[12]

(14)   Q: *Puhuu-ko   Joni   ranskaa?*
            speaks-Q   John   French
            'Does John speak French?'

A: *Puhuu.*
            speaks

For Holmberg, PRs in Finnish are proposed to derive from PolP-Ellipsis, as seen in (15).[13] However, in his analysis, the verb first moves to Pol, and the subject to SpecPol, after which the verb moves to C.

(15)   puhuu+ C [PolP Joni[Pol' puhuu [TP puhuu [VP Joni puhuu ranskaa]]]]

But Holmberg proposes VP-Ellipsis for complex replies with more than the inflected verb, which, according to him, contradict an assertion (cf. (16)):

---

11.   As BP started loosing referential NSs, it also changed with regard to free inversion, a property of NS languages (Rizzi 1982). It only retains the VS order with unaccusative verbs.

12.   See Holmberg (2005).

13.   Holmberg uses both TP-Ellipsis and PolP-Ellipsis.

(16) *Joni ei   puhuu ranskaa.*
      John not speaks French
      'John doesn't speak French.'

    A1. – *#Puhuu.*
          speaks

    A2. – *Puhuu se.*
          speaks he
          'Yes he does.'

(17) A2: [$_{\Sigma P}$ Puhuu [TP se (puhuu) [VP se ⟨puhu⟩ ranskaa]

Notice that in Finnish, affirmative complex replies can express postposed overt subjects. And if the subject is overt, everything else can be overt.

    Notice again that VP-Ellipsis cannot account for BP, as this variety of Portuguese does not license the VS order with most verbs. But we will show below that the analysis is not adequate for EP either.

    In the next section we will present our analysis for BP and EP, which will consist of an adaptation of Holmberg (2001) in simple PRs and an adaptation of Martins (2006) for complex replies.

4.   Types of affirmative replies in EP and BP

4.1   Simple PRs with just the inflected verb

Let us start with a direct adaptation of Holmberg's TP-Ellipsis analysis for simple PRs for EP and BP. Recall that in unmarked contexts EP normally has *pro* while BP has an overt pronoun.

(18) Q: *O   João   fala   francês?*
           the John speaks French
           'Does John speak French?'

    A: *Fala.*   EP BP
        Speaks
        'Yes, he does.'

(19) [$_{\Sigma P}$ [$_{\Sigma'}$ fala [$_{TP}$ ~~ele/pro fala francês~~]]]

The advantages of the TP-Ellipsis analysis are the following:[14]

---

14. TP-Ellipsis has been shown to be relevant elsewhere in Portuguese syntax: in "stripping" constructions in EP (Matos 1992), and in the derivation of semi-clefts in BP and EP (cf. Kato 2010).

- If both EP and BP can derive polar replies through TP-Ellipsis; the difference between *pro* in EP and the overt pronoun in BP is irrelevant in the output;
- the mystery of the apparent categorical occurrence of null subjects in BP is solved.

4.2   Simple PRs consisting of an "affective" operator

In Portuguese, if the question contains an "affective" element, the PR can consist of just this element, and not the verb. Affective elements belong to a mixed category which has the property of triggering proclisis in EP (negative operators, focalizing adverbs, aspectual adverbs, a sub-class of quantifiers).[15]

(20) a. *João convidou-me para ir à   festa.*   Enclisis EP
        John invited me   to go to the party

     b. *João me convidou para ir à festa.*   Proclisis BP

     c. *João já   me convidou para ir a   festa.* Proclisis EP BP
        John already me invited   to   go to the party
        'John has already invited me to go to the party.'

(21) a. *A   Maria beijou-me.*   Enclisis EP
        the Mary kissed me
        'Mary has kissed me.'

     b. *A Maria me beijou.*   Proclisis BP

     c. *A Maria não me beijou.*   Proclisis EP BP
        the Maria not me kissed
        'Maria didn't kiss me.'

These affective elements can appear as the sole element in a PR.

(22) Q: *Você já   foi   à   Bahia?*
        you already went to Bahia
        'Have you ever been to Bahia?'

     A: *Já.*   EP BP
        already
        'Yes, I have.'

(23) Q: *Você sempre vê   filmes de terror?*
        you always see films of horror
        'Do you always watch horror films?'

     A: *Sempre.*   EP BP
        always
        'Always.'

---

15.   See Raposo (1994).

(24) Q: *Você **só** fala inglês?*
you only speak English
'Do you speak only Englsih?'

     A: *Só.*   EP BP
only
'Yes, only English.'

(25) Q: *Você **nunca** fala inglês?*
you never speak English
'Don't you ever speak English?'

     A: ***Nunca.***   EP BP
never
'Never.'

Notice that this sort of PRs is also subject to cross-linguistic variation.

Aspectual adverbs like a*lways* and *never* seem to be licensed as PRs more generally. But the *already* type, for instance, does not seem to be frequently found.

(26) A: **Oui, dejà.*
A: **Yes, already.*

(27) A. *Oui, toujours.*
A: *Yes, always.*

We will see, in Section 6, that we also derive these affective element responses through TP-Ellipsis.

4.3 Simple PRS consisting of just the copula

Another more recent type of PR in BP is the single inflected copula, which has existed in BP since the 19th century, according to Oliveira (2000). Notice that in the answer to (28Q), instead of the main verb *ter* in the question, what appears as the PR is the single copula, which does not appear in the question.[16]

(28) Q: *Mas você ainda tem que passar tôda esta roupa?*
but you still have to iron all these clothes?
'But do you still have to iron all these clothes?'

     A: *É. Mas isto eu passo num instante.*   (Oliveira 2000, Chap. 3))
is but this I iron in an instant
'Yes, but I'll do it in an instant.'

---

16. One of the reviewer calls my attention to the fact that it is also possible to have an ordinary PR as an answer with the inflected auxiliary: (i) Tenho.

Oliveira (2000) claims that the copula is generally used when the question contains a verbal complex, in order to avoid the use of the whole verbal complex in the answer.

Sell (2003), on the other hand, claims that, rather than a *yes/no* answer, the copula is mostly used as a confirmation response, possibly like complex replies in Finnish.

(29) Q: *Ele chegou dizendo que estava cansado?*
          he   arrived saying   that was   tired
          'Did he arrive saying that he was tired?'

      A: *É. Ele disse.*
          is he said
          'Yes, he did.'

It is interesting to observe that when the question contains an affective element in the subject, followed by a complementizer *que*, the answer can be the affective element or the copula, but not the main verb *ir* 'go', which seems to support Sell's analysis.

(30) Q: *Só   vocês **que** vão   à   festa?*
          only you   that go.3PL to-the party
          'Is it just you that are going to the party?'

      A1: *É.*
           is

      A2: *Só.*
           only

      A3: **Vamos.*
           Go.1PL

For Kato (2010, 2014) the complementizer *que*, in this case, is part of a reduced cleft sentence, where the copula is missing. The copula starts to be dropped when it becomes grammaticalized, taking an invariable form, no longer exhibiting *person agreement* or *consecutio temporum*, as in BP.

(31) Q1: ***São** só   vocês que foram   à   festa?* EP
           are only you   that went.3PL to-the party

      Q2: *(É) só   vocês **que** foram   à   festa?* BP
           is only you   that went.3PL to-the party

      A2: *É.*   BP
           is

After the deletion of the copula in these reduced clefts, sometimes the complementizer can also be left out:[17]

(32) Q: *Só vocês vão à festa?*
         only you go.3PL to the party

  A1: *Só.*

  A2: *É.*

  A3: **Vamos*
         go.1PL

Other cases where the copula acts as an answer may deserve a hidden cleft analysis.

4.4 Complex PRs

Complex replies in EP and BP, namely replies that consist of more than one item, have different forms and derivations from Finnish. In Finnish these complex PRs are proposed to be derived through VP-Ellipsis (Holmberg 2001), with the verb raising to Σ and the subject to Spec,TP (see (17)). But in EP and BP this form is not licensed, even in EP, which allows VS order. What we have is the following:

(33) *O João não comprou o carro.*
        the J. not bought the car
       'John didn't buy the car.'

(34) A1: *Comprou ele.*   *EP *BP
           bought he

  A2: *Comprou, comprou.*   EP *BP
           bought bought
           'Yes, he did.'

  A3: *Comprou, sim.*   EP BP
           bought yes
           'Yes, he did.'

Martins (2006, 9) derives the reduplication type in (34A2) as an instance of phonetic realization of multiple links of the verbal chain (cf. Nunes 2004). However, this construction does not exist in BP, which shows that BP cannot have these two phonetic realizations at least in this case.

---

17. Kato (2014) shows that the variation in reduced clefts can also be found in *wh*-questions.

  (i) *É onde **que** você mora?* (ii) *Onde **que** você mora?* (iii) *Onde você mora?*
       is where that you live

(35) A2: [TopP [comprou$_i$]k [Top′ [CP [C′ [C comprou$_i$] [ΣP [Σ′ ~~comprou~~$_i$ [TP
[T′ ~~comprou~~$_i$ [VP ~~O João comprou o carro~~]]]]]k]]]] EP *BP

For the postposed *sim* type, Martins presupposes the subject in Spec of Σ, the *sim* merged in C, and ΣP raise to Top.

(36) A3: [TopP [ΣP ele comprou$_i$ [TP ....[VP....o carro]]] [Top′ [CP sim [ΣP ~~ele~~$_j$
~~[Σ′ comprou$_i$ [TP [T′ comprou$_i$ [VP ele$_j$ comprou$_i$ o carro~~]]]]]K]]]   EP

In BP, the derivation cannot be the same, as T has EPP-features, and the subject has to move to its Spec. What we have is a shorter derivation as in (37):

(37) a. [VP ele$_j$ comprou$_i$ o carro] *V-raising to T, and ele raising to Spec,T*
      b. [TP ele [T′ comprou$_i$ [VP ~~ele$_j$ comprou~~$_i$ o carro]]] *Merging "sim" at C*
      c. [CP sim [TP ele [T′ comprou$_i$ [VP ~~ele$_j$ comprou~~$_i$ o carro]]]]
            Moving the remnant-TP to TopP
      d. [TopP [TP ele comprou$_i$ [VP..... o carro] [Top′ [CP sim$_i$ [TP ~~ele [T′~~
~~comprou~~$_i$ [VP ~~ele$_j$ comprou$_i$ o carro~~]]]]]K]]]

Thus, what we have in EP is that, after merging *sim* to C, the remnant ΣP is raised to Spec of TopP. In BP, on the other hand, after merging *sim* above TP, what moves to Spec of TopP is the remnant TP.

5. The spurious pre-sentential *sim* in Portuguese and Japanese

Differently from languages like Spanish and French, in which the polarity particles are obligatory in affirmative answers, K&T have shown that in Portuguese *sim* is optional and possibly signals formality.

Oliveira (2000) brings support to this idea, as she discovers that in the 19th century, when BP still had the informal second person *tu* and the formal address form *senhor* 'sir', the affirmative particle *sim* was used with *senhor* (*sim, senhor*), while the PR was used for *tu*, the informal address pronoun.

We can also use a cross-linguistic argument for the formal use of *sim*. Japanese is a similar language with regard to the optionality of the particle *hai*. Here again, the use of the particle is optional and also signals formality. While in Portuguese there is no overt morphology to show the stylistic role of *sim*, Japanese exhibits morphological evidence, as the use of *hai* requires politeness morphology in the verb.

(38) Q: *Kimi-wa hon-wo   yon-da?*
         you-top book-accus read-past
         'Did you read the book?'

   A1: a. *Yon-da.*   b. **Hai. Yon-da*
          read-past

> A2: *Hai, yomi-mashita.*
> yes read-polite.past.tense
> 'Yes, I did.'

In Portuguese the burden of formality is carried exclusively by the particle *sim* pre-posed to the sentence.

(39) Q: *Você leu o livro?*
You read the book
'Have you read the book?'

A1: *Li.* (neutral) EP BP
read
'Yes, I have.'

A2: *Sim, li.* (formal) EP BP
yes, read
'Yes, I have.'

6. Our analysis of BP PRs

6.1 Theoretical assumptions

In order to derive the simple and complex PRs in Portuguese, I will assume Holmberg's TP/PolP-Ellipsis analysis, but adapt it to the cartographic approach in Rizzi (1997), and will assume his higher TopicP to be the GroundP in Kayne and Pollock (2001), where the presuppositional part of the sentence is moved to.[18] I will also assume the copy theory of movement (Nunes 2004), and the possibility of "remnant movement" (cf. Kayne 1998) before ellipsis.

(40) $[_{ForceP} [_F [_{GroundP} [_G [_{FocP} [_{Foc} [_{PolP} [_{Pol} [_{TP} [_T [_{vP} \ldots v [_{vP} V \ldots]]]]]]]]]]]]$

I will also assume the classic view that adverbs are adjoined to specific verbal heads, and are not independent projections as in Cinque's (1999) cartographic approach, except the negative adverb *não,* which is assumed to merge as the head of PolP.

---

18. Holmberg shows that what is really at stake is PolP-Ellipsis, but we will continue to refer to it as TP-Ellipsis, as PolP is the highest projection of the TP domain. PolP can also be referred to as ΣP, as in Martins (2006).

6.2 Deriving simple PRs

Notice that what appears in the PR is really the Focus of the sentence. We will start with a negative answer, with the negative adverb *não*.[19]

(41) Q: *Você não viu o acidente?*   A: *Não*
      you not saw the accident   A: no
      'Didn't you see the accident?'

(41)′ a. [$_{PolP}$ você[$_{Pol}$ não [$_{TP}$ ~~você viu~~ [$_{vP}$ ~~você viu~~ [$_{VP}$ ~~viu~~ o acidente]]]]]
  – the Verb moves from V, to v, to T;
  – the subject moves from Spec,v to Spec,T;
  – PolP is projected and *não* is merged in Pol;
  – the subject moves to Spec-Pol
  – FocP is projected and *não* is moved to Foc.

(41)″ [$_{FocP}$ [$_{Foc}$ Não[$_{PolP}$ você[$_{Pol}$ ~~não~~ [$_{TP}$ ~~você viu~~ [$_{vP}$ ~~você viu~~ [$_{vP}$ ~~viu~~ o acidente]]]]]]

- GroundP is projected and PolP undergoes remnant movement to its Spec, where it is interpreted as the presupposition in LF:

(41)‴ [$_{GroundP}$[$_{PolP}$ você[$_{Pol}$ ~~não~~ [$_{TP}$ ~~você~~ viu [$_{vP}$ ~~você viu~~ [$_{vP}$ ~~viu~~ o acidente]]]][$_{G}$ [$_{FocP}$ [Não [~~PolP~~]]]
  – Erasure of PolP in FF:
      b. [$_{GroundP}$~~PolP~~ [FocP [Foc não]]]

In Holmberg's analysis, ellipsis takes place without moving PolP to GroundP. But in our analysis LF interprets what is in GroundP as the presupposition, and erasure at PF takes place outside the nuclear stress, in the left periphery, a deaccented part of the chain.

We will now see cases in which something is moved to Pol from elsewhere, after which the derivation follows the same pattern as with negation. We will also consider the possibility that the subject is overt as in BP or covert (*pro*) as in EP. We assume that the adverb *já* is merged as an adjunction to T, before being moved to Pol.[20]

(42) Q1: *Vocês/pro viram um acidente?*   A1: *Vimos.*
      You   saw   an   accident?   saw.1PL
                              'Yes, we did.'

---

19. In Northern dialects of BP negation can appear at the end of the answer (cf. Rerisson (2012)):

   (i) Q: *Você não viu o acidente?*   A: *Vi, não.*

20. Aspectual adverbs like *ainda* and *sempre* would be merged in adjunction to Asp before being moved to Pol.

> Q2: *Vocês/pro já   viram um acidente?*   A2: *Já.*
> You   already saw   an accident   already
> 'Yes, we did.'

(42)′   A1: [$_{FocP}$ [$_F$vimos [$_{PolP}$ *nós/pro* [$_{Pol}$~~vimos~~ [$_{TP}$ ~~nós/pro vimos~~ [$_{vP}$ ~~nós/pro~~vimos
...[$_{VP}$ ~~nós/pro~~   ~~vimos~~   um acidente]]]]]]]]

A2: [$_{FocP}$ [$_F$já [$_{PolP}$ *nós/pro* [$_{Pol}$já[$_{TP}$ ~~nós [já=vimos]~~[$_{vP}$ nós vimos ...[$_{VP}$ ~~nós/~~
~~pro vimos~~ um acidente]]]]]]]]

The following steps in the derivation are the same as in (41). We project GroundP and move the remnant PolP to its Spec, where it is interpreted as a presupposition at LF. At LF, PolP is erased, and what remains is what is left in FocP.

We have seen cases of PRs that consist of a head. Let us now see a case where the PR consists of an XP:

(43)   Q: *Ele viu **tudo**?*   A: ***Tudo.***
       he saw everything   everything
       'Has he seen everything?'

(43)′   [$_{FocP}$ *tudo*[$_{Foc}$[$_{PolP}$ ~~tudo~~[$_{Pol}$ [$_{TP}$ *ele/pro* viu [$_{vP}$ ~~ele viu~~ [$_{VP}$ ~~viu~~ [$_{DP}$ ~~tudo~~]]]]]]]]]

Here *tudo*, as an XP, lands first in Spec,Pol, and then in Spec,Foc.

6.2   Deriving complex PRs

In the derivation of an answer with a preposed *sim*, the derivation proceeds as in a simple PR as far as FocP. After that, *sim* is merged as the head of ForceP, where it is interpreted as a polite, or formal answer.

(44)   a. ***Sim, vi.***   b. ***Sim, já.***   c. ***Sim, tudo.***

(45)   [$_{ForceP}$[$_F$ SIM [$_{GroundP}$ [$_{PolP}$ *eu/pro* Pol [$_{Tp}$ *eu$_i$ /pro$_i$* T [$_{vP...}$DP]]] G [$_{FocP}$ [F vi
[~~PolP~~]]]]]]

As for (46), we use a modified version of Martins (2006): after we derive PolP, the particle *sim* is merged in Focus, and PolP is moved to GroundP.

(46)   *Vi, sim.*

(47)   A: [GroundP [$_{PolP}$ *eu/pro vi (o acidente)*] G [FocP *SIM* [~~PolP~~]]]]]]]]]

7.   Conclusions

The comparison of BP polar replies (PRs) with languages like EP and Finnish, which have the same pattern in simple replies, namely the inflected verb, led us to conclude that the apparent empty category in subject position does not have to do with the Null Subject, a prior assumption (K&T a.o.), but with a derivation that does not distinguish between different types of subjects. The result has to do with PolP-Ellipsis, after the verb is moved to a Focus projection in the sentence periphery. Other types of simple PRs have been analyzed in a similar fashion, with polar items moving to the FocusP position, with the subsequent movement of the remnant PolP to GroundP, where it is interpreted as the presuppositional part of the answer in LF, and later erased at PF.

The paper also offers an analysis of complex replies with the particle *sim* overt, either in sentence-initial position or after the VP.

The final conclusion is that the cartographic approach accounts for both the syntactic derivations and the semantic interpretation of PRs in a satisfactory way.

References

Barbosa, Pilar, Maria Eugênia Duarte, and Mary A. Kato. 2005. "Null Subjects in European and Brazilian Portuguese." In *Journal of Portuguese Linguistics.* 4(2): 11–52.

Chomsky, Noam. 1981. *Lectures on Government and Binding.* Dordrecht: Foris Publications.

Cinque, Guglielmo. 1999. *Adverbs and Functional Heads.* New York: Oxford University Press.

Costa, João, Ana Maria Martins, and Fernanda Pratas. 2012. "VP-Ellipsis: New Evidence from Capeverdean." In *Romance Languages and Linguistic Theory*, ed. by Irene Franco, Sara Lusini and Andrés Saab, 155–175. Amsterdam: John Benjamins. DOI: 10.1075/rllt.4.08cos

Duarte, Maria Eugênia. 2005. *A Perda do Princípio "Evite pronome" no Português Brasileiro.* Ph.D. Dissertation. UNICAMP.

Ferreira, Marcelo. 2004. "Hyperraising and Null Subjects in Brazilian Portuguese." *MIT Working Papers in Linguistics 47: Collected Papers on Romance Syntax.* 57–85.

Holmberg, Anders. 2001. "The Syntax of Yes and No in Finnish." *Studia Linguistica* 55:141–175. DOI: 10.1111/1467-9582.00077

Holmberg, Anders. 2005. "Is There a Little *pro*? Evidence from Finnish." *Linguistic Inquiry* 36: 533–564. DOI: 10.1162/002438905774464322

Holmberg, Anders. 2006. "Null Subjects and Polarity Focus." *Studia Linguistica* 61(3): 212–236. DOI: 10.1111/j.1467-9582.2007.00135.x

Huang, James C. T. 1984. "On the Distribution and Reference of Empty Pronouns." *Linguistic Inquiry* 15: 531–574.

Kato, Mary A. 1999. "Strong Pronouns and Weak Pronominals in the Null Subject Parameter." *PROBUS*, (11)1: 1–37. Berlin, Editora Mouton de Gruyter. DOI: 10.1515/prbs.1999.11.1.1

Kato, Mary A. 2000. "The Partial Pro-Drop Nature and the Restricted VS Order in Brazilian Portuguese." In *The Null Subject Parameter In Brazilian Portuguese*, ed. by Mary A. Kato and Esmeralda Negrão, 223–258.

Kato, Mary A. 2009. "O Sujeito Nulo Revisitado no Português Brasileiro." In *História do Português Paulista*, Vol. 2, ed. by M.A.Torres-Moraes and M.L. O. de Andrade, 61–82. Campinas: Editora da UNICAMP.

Kato, Mary A..2010. "Clivadas sem Operador no Português Brasileiro." *Estudos da Língua (gem).* 8(2): 61–77. Vitoria da Conquista.

Kato, Mary A. 2014. "The Role of the Copula in the Diachronic Development of Focus Constructions in Brazilian Portuguese." In *Variation within and Across Romance Languages: Selected Papers from the 41st Linguistic Symposium on Romance Languages* (LSRL), Ottawa, 5–7 May 2011, ed. by Côté, Marie-Hélène and Eric Mathieu, 297–314.

Kato, Mary A. and Esmeralda V. Negrão (eds.). 2000. *Brazilian Portuguese and the Null Subject Parameter*. Frankfurt: Vevuert/Iberoamericana.

Kato, Mary A. and Fernando Tarallo. 1992. "*Sim*: Respondendo Afirmativamente em Português." In *Linguística Aplicada: da Aplicação a Lingüística para uma Lingüística Transdisciplinar*, ed. by M.S.Z. de Paschoal and M.A.A.Celani. São Paulo: EDUC.

Kayne, Richard. 1998. "Overt vs. Covert Movement." *Syntax* 1: 128–191.

Kayne, Richard and Jean-Yves Pollock. 2001. "New Thoughts on Stylistic Inversion." In *Inversion in Romance and the Theory of Universal Grammar*, ed. by Aafke Hulk and Jean-Yves Pollock, 107–162. New York: Oxford University Press.

MacCloskey, James. 1991. "Clause Structure, Ellipsis, and Proper Government in Irish." *Lingua* 85: 259–302. DOI: 10.1016/0024-3841(91)90023-X

Martins, Ana Maria. 1994. "Enclisis, VP-Deletion and the Nature of Sigma." *PROBUS* 6. 2–3: 173–206. DOI: 10.1515/prbs.1994.6.2-3.173

Martins, Ana Maria. 2006. "Emphatic Affirmation and Polarity: Contrasting European Portuguese with Brazilian Portuguese, Spanish, Catalan and Galician." *Romance Languages and Linguistic Theory*, ed. by Jenny Doetjes and Paz Gonzalez, 197–223. Amsterdam/ Philadelphia: John Benjamins. DOI: 10.1075/cilt.278.10mar

Matos, Gabriela. 1992. *Construçoes de Elipse do Predicado em Português—SV Nulo e Despojamento*. Ph.D. Dissertation. University of Lisbon.

Modesto, Marcello. 2000. *On the Identification of Null Arguments*. Ph.D. Dissertation. University of Southern California.

Nunes, Jairo. 2004. *Linearization of Chains and Sideward Movement*. Cambridge and London: MIT Press.

Oliveira, Marilza. 2000. "The Pronominal Subject in Italian and Brazilian Portuguese." In *The Null Subject Parameter In Brazilian Portuguese*, ed. by Mary A. Kato and Esmeralda Negrão, 37–54.

Raposo, Eduardo. 1994. "Affective Operators and Clausal Structure in European Portuguese and European Spanish." Paper presented at the 24th LSRL, UCLA/USC.

Rerisson, Cavalcante. 2012. *Negação Anafórica no Português Brasileiro: Negação Sentencial, Negação Enfática e Negação de Constituinte*. USP: Ph.D. Dissertation.

Rizzi, Luigi. 1982. *Issues in Italian Syntax*. Dordrecht: Foris. DOI: 10.1515/9783110883718

Rizzi, Luigi. 1997. "The Fine Structure of the Left Periphery." In *Elements of Grammar*, ed. by Liliane Haegeman, 281–337. Dordrecht: Kluwer. DOI: 10.1007/978-94-011-5420-8_7

Sell, Fabíola Sucupira Ferreira. 2003. *As Interrogativas do Português Brasiliero: Perguntas e Respostas*. UFSC: Ph.D. Dissertation.

Participle fronting and clause structure in Old and Middle French

Marie Labelle
Universite du Quebec a Montreal

This paper is a study of over 1100 Old and Middle French sentences in which a participle has been fronted to the left of an auxiliary, in what appears at first sight to be a Stylistic Fronting construction. These sentences were extracted from the MCVF parsed corpus of Old and Middle French. The first part of the article examines the size of the fronted element. It is shown that the fronted element may contain a single head, or it may be a full VP or a partial VP. It is argued that (remnant) VP movement accounts for the set of examples. In the second part of the paper, it is shown that the fronted constituent does not target a single position. In some cases, it occupies an IP-scrambling position between the subject in its canonical position and the finite verb; in a smaller number of cases, it is scrambled to the left of the subject. The fronted constituent is also attested within the left periphery, generally in Spec,FinP, but when the participle is contrastive or otherwise focalized, it could be analyzed a occupying Spec,FocP. The French facts are discussed in a cross-linguistic perspective.

1. Introduction

In Old and Middle French, a participle could front to the left of a finite verb. The construction, observed in main and embedded clauses, is illustrated in (1) and (2).

(1) Main clause:
     Asise s'   est devant   le   lit,
     Sat REFL is   in-front-of the bed
     'She sits beside the bed,'   (1160, MARIE-DE-FRANCE,19.334)[1]

---

[1] The examples are identified with the approximate date of the text, an abbreviated name of the text, and its reference number in the French parsed corpus of Old and Middle French (Martineau et al. 2010, supplemented with texts parsed by Anthony Kroch and Beatrice Santorini, University of Pennsylvania). For a list of the texts in the corpus, see: http://www.ling.upenn.edu/~beatrice/frenchTexts.html.

DOI 10.1075/rllt.9.12lab
© 2016 John Benjamins Publishing Company

(2)   Embedded clause:
sil   fiert   en l' elme, ki <u>gemmet</u> fut   a   or;
PRT-him struck on the helm, that jewelled was at gold
'He struck him on the helm, that was ornated with gold;'

(1100, ROLAND, 170.2306)

A number of authors have argued that this construction is one of Stylistic Fronting (e.g., Dupuis 1989; Cardinaletti and Roberts 1991/2002; Roberts 1993; Mathieu 2006, 2013), a construction initially described for Icelandic by Maling (1980/1990). Stylistic Fronting has also been argued to be the source of similar constructions in other Romance languages: Old Florentine (Franco 2012), Old Catalan (Fischer 2010), Old Spanish (Fontana, 1993; Fischer 2014), Italian (Cardinaletti 2003), Sardinian (Egerland 2011). However these studies do not always agree on the properties and analysis of what is labelled Stylistic Fronting. For example, many authors claim that Stylistic Fronting does not have discourse semantic effects in Icelandic (e.g., Maling 1980/1990; Holmberg 2000, 2006); others, like Hrafnbjargarson (2004), argue that it focalizes an element. Fischer and Alexiadou (2001) suggest that Stylistic Fronting involves head movement in Old Catalan and XP movement in Icelandic, which is the opposite of what is observed by Egerland for the difference between Sardinian (VP movement) and Icelandic (V movement). Quoting Fisher and Alexiadou (2001), Benincà (2006), and Franco (2009), Egerland suggests that Old Romance is like Sardinian and unlike Icelandic in that the fronted constituent is focused, but Molnár (2010) argues against the arguments to the effect that the fronted element is focalized in Old Romance, and Mathieu (2006) claims that it corresponds to background information in Old French. There is thus room for further study. In a comparative study of non-finite verb fronting in Sardinian and Icelandic, Egerland (2011) observes important cross-linguistic differences. He argues that in Sardinian, the fronted constituent corresponds to narrow focus, and it is thus informationally heavy; this correlates with the fact that in this language VPs are fronted, and that verb complements cannot be stranded. In addition, there is no locality condition on the fronting of non-finite verb phrases. By contrast, stylistically fronting a nonfinite verb in Icelandic is strictly local and it typically fronts light elements. VPs may not be fronted, but verbal heads are fronted, stranding verb complements. In addition, the fronted element would correspond to background information, the rest of the clause falling under maximal focus. Egerland's observations point to possibly fundamental cross-linguistic differences in non-finite verb fronting that merit further exploration.

In the present paper, we address the following questions: What are the properties of Old and Middle French participle fronting? What is the size and position of the fronted participle in Old and Middle French? Does participle fronting have discourse semantic effects, and if so, which ones? After describing the corpus used for the present study, we will first discuss the size of the fronted constituent then we will turn to the position of the fronted participle. We will argue that non-finite verb fronting in Old French is neither like Sardinian nor like Icelandic (as described by Egerland).

More precisely, it shows properties of both these languages, in allowing VP fronting, V^0 fronting, as well as partial VP fronting. A remnant VP approach to what appears to be V^0 fronting allows us to maintain that in every case, there is phrasal movement. In the second part of the paper, we show that the fronted participle phrase may occupy various positions in the sentence: in some cases, it is IP internal; in other cases, it occupies the first position of a V2 clause within the left periphery. The participle may correspond to background or to new information. In some cases it may be contrastive.

2. The corpus

The corpus studied contains 1163 clauses with a participle-auxiliary word order extracted from the MCVF parsed corpus of Old and Middle French (Martineau et al. 2010, supplemented with texts parsed by Anthony Kroch and Beatrice Santorini, University of Pennsylvania, see Footnote 1). The mean percentage of participle-finite auxiliary word order out of the total number of clauses containing a participle and a finite auxiliary is 4.5%. The distribution of the construction by text is illustrated in Figure 1. It can be seen that the construction is more frequent in verse than in prose texts, and that it is productive until the middle of the 15th century.

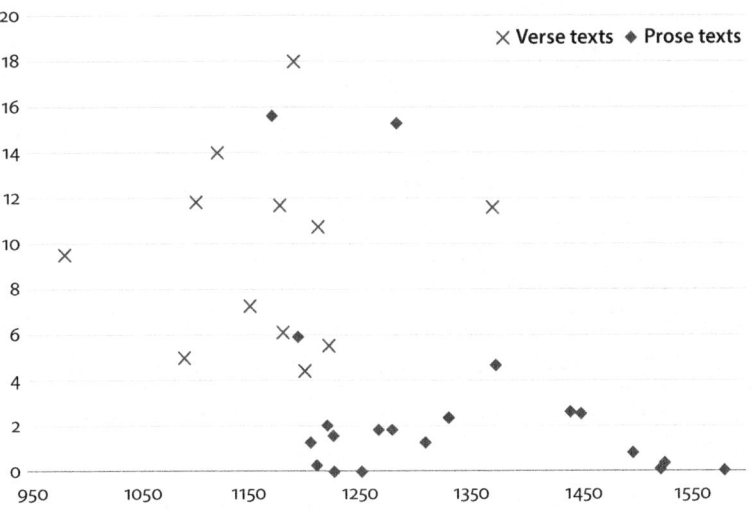

Figure 1. Rate of participle fronting per text

Fronting the participle is not specifically an embedded clause phenomenon. In our data, 57% of the clauses with a fronted participle are embedded clauses. This percentage is comparable to the 59% of embedded clauses among the total number of clauses containing an auxiliary and a participle in the corpus. The participle-auxiliary word order is found in all types of embedded clauses: Subject relatives (225), other relatives (98), other WH constructions (118), *that* complements (41), and other types of embedded clauses (55).

3. The size of the fronted constituent

In 81% of the clauses with a fronted participle, what appears to the left of the auxiliary is a verbal head V^0. In the majority of these examples (51%), a verb complement is stranded. This is illustrated in (3). In the remaining cases (30%), the VP contains only a verb, and the construction is therefore ambiguous between VP and V^0 movement.

(3) é   sálved nus ád   des   Philistiens.
     and saved us has from-the Philistians
     'and (he) saved us from the Philistians.'   (1170, QUATRELIVRE, 94.3603)

In 19% of the examples, a constituent larger than V^0 is fronted. VP fronting is illustrated in (4). In this example, the VP has an AdvVO word order. Therefore, this example cannot be analyzed as resulting from a verb final base.

(4) Einsi comme apres le sarez,   Quant bien leü ce
     just as   later it will-know, when well read this
     livre arez.
     book will-have
     'as you will know later, when you will have read this book well'
                                                      (1370, PRISE,.135)

Table 1 gives the various word orders observed when the fronted constituent is larger than V^0, including partial VP movement to be discussed below. (In the oldest texts, when the finite verb is final and the word order of the fronted constituent is OV, a verb final base cannot be excluded.)

Table 1. Numbers of clauses where the fronted constituent is larger than V^0

	VO order	OV order	Ambiguous order (V&V, advV...)
V final	20	75	44
V non final	11	24	46
	31	99	90
	(14%)	(45%)	(41%)

The construction illustrated in (3) could result from head movement, but it can also be derived by remnant VP movement (e.g., den Besten and Webelhuth 1987;

Holmberg 2006; Ott 2009; for Old French: Salvesen 2011; Zaring 2011). To account for German sentences like (5a), where a participle is fronted leaving a complement behind, den Besten and Webelhuth (1987) proposed the analysis in (5b): the object is first extracted out of the VP, and thereafter, the remnant of the VP, now containing only the non-finite verb, is moved to the left of the auxiliary. A remnant movement analysis of (3) is illustrated in (6) (using the copy and delete representation):

(5) a. Gelesen   hat Hans das Buch.
         read-PRT   has Hans the book
         'Hans has read the book.'

     b. [t$_i$ gelesen]$_j$ hat Hans [das Buch]$_i$ t$_j$

(6) a. é nus ád [des Philistiens]$_1$ [$_{VP}$ sálved [~~des Philistiens~~]$_1$]

     b. é [$_{VP}$ sálved ~~des Philistiens~~$_1$]$_2$ nus ád [des Philistiens]$_1$ [$_{VP}$ ~~sálved [des Philistiens]$_1$~~]$_2$

In our Old French data, remnant VP movement is required to account for examples with partial VP fronting, like the one illustrated in (7), which would be derived as in (8). The complement is first extracted out of the VP and the remnant of the VP, containing an adverb and the two nonfinite verbs, is fronted to the left of the auxiliary.

(7) n'   <u>onques oï   parler</u> n'   avoie de <u>chevalier</u> [...] qui
     and-not ever   heard speak NEG   have   of knight   who
     'and I have never heard of a knight who...'   (1170, YVAIN, 197.6918)

(8) a. [ne n'avoie [$_{VP}$ onques oï parler de chevalier]

     b. [ne n'avoie [de chevalier]$_1$[$_{VP}$ onques oï parler [~~de chevalier~~]$_1$]

     c. [ne [$_{VP}$ onques oï parler ~~de chevalier~~]$_2$ [n'avoie [de chevalier]$_1$
         [$_{VP}$ ~~onques oï parler [de chevalier]$_1$~~]$_2$

This example shows that there are cases of participle fronting that can only be accounted for if we assume object extraction out of the VP and remnant VP movement. Object extraction is independently attested in the following example, which has a mixed word order. The infinitival verb complement of the participle follows it, while the DP complement of the infinitival verb precedes the participle. The example can be accounted for by assuming that the VP is fronted first, and, in a second step, the object is moved to the left of the fronted VP. This derivation is given in (10).

(9) Un sydoine feit   feire avoie
     A shroud made make   had
     '(He) had caused a shroud to be made'   (1190, BORON, 55.850)

(10) a. avoie [feit feire un sydoine]

     b. [feit feire un sydoine]$_1$ avoie [~~feit feire un sydoine~~]$_1$

     c. [[un sydoine]$_2$ [feit feire ~~un sydoine$_2$~~]$_1$] avoie [~~feit feire un sydoine~~]$_1$

Extending the remnant VP movement analysis to cases like (3) where a V^0 appears to be fronted allows us to claim that in Old and Middle French the nonfinite verb always moves as an XP and never as a head.

The possibility of fronting a VP, as in (4), makes Old French like Sardinian, but unlike Icelandic (e.g. Egerland, 2011; Wood 2011, fn. 19). Interestingly, this possibility makes Old French different from Old Spanish (Fontana 1993), and Old Catalan (Fischer 2010), which have been claimed to allow only V^0 fronting. Conversely, the possibility of fronting the verb leaving complements behind is like Icelandic, Old Spanish and Old Catalan, but unlike Sardinian. Assuming a remnant VP movement analysis for all apparent V^0 fronting does not abolish the cross-linguistic differences. On the one hand, according to Egerland, Sardinian allows only movement of full VPs, and does not allow movement of remnant VPs. On the other hand, Old Spanish and Old Catalan appear to require that the moved element contain only a head. These differences are in need of an explanation. For languages that allow only full VP movement it could be that they don't allow scrambling of objects out of the VP. For languages where what is fronted is always a participle head, assuming that this head is moved as a remnant VP would have to explain why these languages must necessarily move everything except the head out of the VP before fronting the remnant. For these languages, a head movement approach is perhaps preferable. A remnant VP movement approach is particularly appropriate for languages like German and older stages of French, where there is evidence that full and partial VPs are allowed to front, and that objects are allowed to extract out of the VP.

It would be interesting if, as suggested by Egerland, size, role, and position were interrelated. Informationally weak elements would be of small size (X^0) and would occupy an unmarked position (FinP or IP internal), while informationally strong elements would be XPs and would occupy a marked, e.g., Focus, position. However, in the French data, the heavy fronted VP's are not particularly focused, as can be seen in (4), and the strongly focused participles are light, as we will see in the next sections (examples (33) and (34)). Further research is needed to better understand the facts and the cross-linguistic differences.

4.   The position of the participle

Since non-finite verb fronting is often considered a case of Stylistic Fronting, we will review here the various approaches to the position of the stylistically fronted element. In Icelandic, Stylistic Fronting is typically an embedded clause phenomenon. However, Mathieu (2006, 2013) argues that Stylistic Fronting also accounts for cases where a head—like a participle—is fronted in main clauses. In presenting the various approaches, we will abstract away from the distinction between main clause and embedded clause.

In Icelandic, Stylistic Fronting appears to move an XP or a head to the left of the finite verb when the canonical subject position is not occupied by an overt subject. Quite understandably, the construction has initially been analyzed as moving the fronted element to an empty subject position (Maling 1980/1990; Dupuis 1989; Cardinaletti and Roberts 1991/2002; Roberts 1993; for Icelandic: Platzack 1987; Holmberg 2000; Ott 2009, and others).

More recently, assuming a rich Left Periphery model like the one of Benincà and Poletto (2004), illustrated in (11), various positions within the left periphery have been proposed for the stylistically fronted element.

(11) [CP ForceP... (Frame)...(Topic)...(Focus)...FinP [IP ...]]

Some authors place the fronted element in Spec,FinP (Salvesen 2011 for fronting of infinitival VP's in Old French; Hrafnbjargarson and Wiklund 2009 for what they call *True Stylistic Fronting* in Icelandic; Franco 2009, 2012 for Old Florentine). Other authors place it in the Focus field (Hrafnbjargarson 2004; Benincà 2006). Mathieu (2006, 2013) places it in Top$^+$P, a special phrase to the right of TopP within the Topic field (for him the first element of a V2 clause is in Spec,TopP; for other authors, e.g. Holmberg 2015, it is in Spec,FinP, as we will see).

We will argue that, in our data, a leftward moved participle is observed in different positions. In some cases it occupies a position within IP, typically between the subject and the finite verb but sometimes to the left of the subject. In other cases, it occupies the left periphery, generally in Spec,FinP, but sometimes in Spec,FocP. (In the coming sections, we will use the label 'IP' to refer to the portion of the clause that excludes the left periphery; a more recent label would be TP, but we will later adopt Rizzi and Shlonsky's idea that TP is a complement of SubjP).

5. The V2 clause

Before turning to the argumentation, we need to spell out our theoretical assumptions. In Old French, main clauses are generally verb second (V2), while embedded clauses are SVO. We follow Holmberg (2015) in assuming that V2 follows from a requirement of the verb to check the low CP, that is, Fin^0, as shown in (12) (also Labelle and Hirschbühler 2005; Labelle 2007, and others). By default, some constituent comes to occupy Spec,FinP. Frey (2004, 2006), studying German V2 clauses, calls this derivation *Formal Movement*. Formal Movement has no particular semantic or pragmatic effect. Frey identifies a second type of V2 clause where the first element of the clause comes to occupy Spec,FocP through what Frey calls *True A-Bar Movement*. An element moved by True A-Bar Movement is contrastive. According to Frey, only True A-Bar Movement may move a phrase long-distance to a higher clause.

(12)

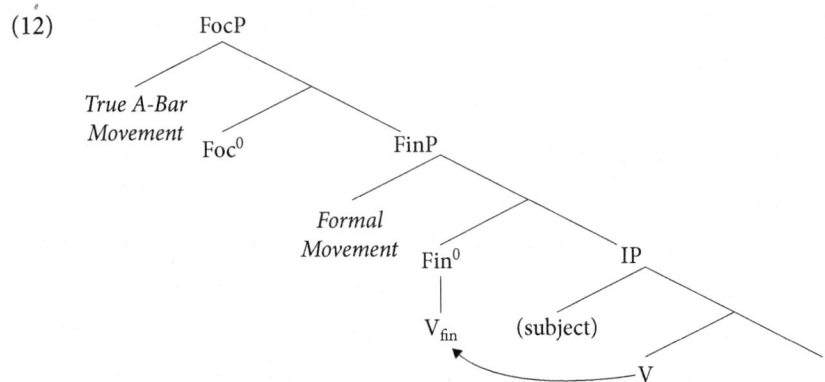

Elements in the Frame and Topic fields (to the left of Focus) are outside the core V2 clause (Benincà 2004; Benincà and Poletto 2004; Poletto 2005, 2006; Holmberg 2015); they "don't count" for V2. This is the case, for example, of left dislocated constituents, which occupy Spec,TopP.

6.   Diagnostics for determining the position of the participle

In order to determine the position of the participle, we need some diagnostics. In this section, we discuss two: *qui*, and subject inversion.

6.1   Relative *qui*

In French, the word *qui* found in subject relative clauses and in clauses with subject extraction has been analyzed by Kayne (1976) as a complementizer replacing *que* in clauses where there has been subject extraction, and by Rizzi (1990) as the agreeing variant of *que*. An Old French example of *qui* in relative clauses is illustrated in (2), repeated below in (13); *qui* in long-distance extraction of a subject is shown in (14).

(13)   sil   fiert   en l'   elme, <u>ki</u>   gemmet fut   a   or;
       PRT-him struck on the helm, that jeweled was at gold
       'He struck him on the helm, that was ornated with gold'
                                                   (1100, ROLAND, 170.2306)

(14)   Les bestes   [que tu   vois [<u>qui</u> _ monstrent felonnie]]
       The animals [that you see [that   show   violence]]
              (12th c., Roman d'Alexandre 507.3) [quoted by Kunstmann 1990, 309]

Notice that this *qui* follows the WH word in the doubly-filled COMP construction observed in some French dialects. According to Benincà and Poletto's (2004) model, the interrogative WH word occupies Spec,Foc. Since subject-extraction *qui* follows it, it cannot be higher than the low complementizer position, Fin^0.

(15) Qui$_{WH}$ ̲q̲u̲i̲ est venu?
     Who   that is come
     'Who came?'

To account for the distribution of this *qui*, Rizzi (1997) analyzes it as occupying Fin^0 (this allows it to govern the subject trace). Taraldsen (2001) proposes that the *-i* of *qui* occupies the canonical subject position; more recently Rizzi and Shlonsky (2007) propose that *-i* occupies Fin^0, allowing it to satisfy the subject criterion. In each of these analyses *qui*, or the *-i* of *qui*, occupies either the canonical subject position or the lowest position within the left periphery, to the immediate left of the subject position. Assuming this (as we do), when a fronted participle follows *qui*, as in (13), it must occupy a position within IP rather than within the left periphery. In our corpus, 42% of the fronted participles occur in subject relatives (225/537), and in that case, the participle follows *qui*. We conclude that in a large proportion of our examples, the participle is within IP.

6.2   Pronominal subjects

There is a well-known difference in French between two subject inversion constructions. Germanic inversion is observed in V2 clauses where the initial constituent is not the subject. In that case, the subject appears between the auxiliary and the participle, and in front of adverbs.

(16) Or avez ̲v̲o̲s̲ ben dit.
     now have you well said
     'You have now spoken well'   (1100, ROLAND, 277.3824)

This is accounted for by assuming that the auxiliary has raised to Fin^0 over the subject sitting in the canonical subject position. In that construction, the subject may be a weak subject pronoun.

(17)   [$_{FinP}$ XP Aux [$_{IP}$ Subject ~~Aux~~ (adv) [$_{AspP/vP}$ V ...]]]

In Romance inversion, the inverted subject follows the participle and adverbs. It is considered to be in its base position within vP.

(18) ...le poisson Que t' avera   peschié Hebron.
     ...the fish   that you will-have fished Hebron
     'the fish that Hebron will have caught for you.'   (1190, BORON,86.1387)

(19)   [$_{IP}$ ...Aux (adv) [$_{AspP}$ V [$_{vP}$ Subject ...]]]

Crucially, in that case, the subject can only be a full subject. This is accounted for by assuming that Spec,vP cannot host weak pronouns (Vance 1997; Roberts 1993), because pronominal subjects must check a feature in the canonical subject position (e.g., Cardinaletti and Roberts 1991/2002; Labelle 2007; Rizzi and Shlonsky 2007; for Germanic: Zwart 1993; Fuss 2003). As a result, weak pronominal subjects are never lower than the canonical subject position.

Recently, Rizzi (2006; see also Rizzi and Shlonsky 2006, 2007) argued that the canonical subject position is a Criterial head, which he labels Subj. In his analysis, a subject in Spec,SubjP, checking the subject criterion, is frozen in place and cannot move higher. If this analysis is correct, this means that, not only are weak pronominal subjects never lower than the canonical subject position, they are also never higher than the canonical subject position. Weak pronominal subjects constitute therefore a diagnostic for the canonical subject position. Thus, if a finite verb precedes a pronominal subject, the verb is within the CP domain, and so is any element that precedes the finite verb.

With these assumptions in mind, we can look at the data. In (20), the participle is clearly within the CP domain, since it precedes a finite auxiliary which itself precedes a pronominal subject. This is the standard V2 configuration:

(20)   <u>Oit</u>   avons nous nombre   dix manieres de pechiez de langue.
       heard have   we   enumerated ten ways   to sin   by language
       'We have heard enumerated ten ways to sin by language.'

                                            (1279, SOMME-ROYAL, 1,66.1796)

Since V2 is a main clause phenomenon, we expect this word order to be basically limited to main clauses (and to a few embedded V2 clauses complements of bridge verbs). Indeed, in our data, the configuration with a participle in clause initial position and an inverted weak pronominal subject is found only in main clauses, as shown in Table 2. Embedded clauses with a full inverted subject are cases of Romance inversion.

Table 2. Inverted subjects in main and embedded clauses with a fronted participle

	Subject Type	Totals
Main clauses	Full	100
	Pronominal	14
Embedded clauses	Full	41
	Pronominal	0

By contrast, in (21), the participle must be within IP, since it follows the weak pronominal subject:

(21) la gravance que il <u>fait</u> avoit a l' empereor ...
      the wrong   that he done had to the emperor
      'the wrong that he had done to the emperor'

(1270, CASSIDORUS, 674.4619)

To summarize, we have shown that, in our data, the participle sometimes occupies a position within IP, sometimes a position within the left periphery. In the next section, we will look at these cases in more detail.

7. Analysis

The word order *complementizer-pronominal subject-participle-verb* illustrated in (21) above has been analyzed as resulting from cliticization of the weak pronominal subject to Comp (Cardinaletti and Roberts 1991/2002), leaving the subject position empty and able to receive the participle. However, the same word order is found with full DP subjects, as shown in the second clause of (22). The fact that, in French, the participle can co-occur with a (full) subject to the left of the verb indicates that it does not occupy the subject position.

(22) Eüstaces mot n' en savoit De ço   que Dex <u>sauvé</u> avoit
      E.   word NEG GEN knew of the-fact that God saved   had

      ses effanz...
      his children

      'Eustace did not know that God had saved his children'

(1212, EUSTACE-FISHER, 31.370)

The position of the participle illustrated in (21) and (22) is not limited to participle heads, as shown in (23) and in the first clause of (22), where a DP is fronted, and in (24), where a partial VP is fronted:

(23) ... Comment il <u>le</u> <u>cors</u> leur toli Dou prophete
      ... how   he the corpse them took of-the prophet...
      '(They told him), how he took from them the corpse of the prophet'

(1190-BORON-R,68.1064)

(24) a. Ainsi Joseph <u>trestout</u> <u>feit</u> ha Ce que la vouiz
          Thus Joseph everything   done has that which the voice

          li commanda.
          him commanded

          'Thus Joseph did everything that the voice ordered him to do.'

(1190, Boron, 118.1855)

b. Li   roys […] <u>Son commandement</u> <u>fait</u>   avoit Au   noble
   The king […] His command   done had   to-the noble

   prince d' Entioche […]
   prince of Antioch

   'The king had already given orders to the noble prince of Antioch'
                                                   (1370, PRISE,.2417)

In our corpus, 11% of the clauses with a fronted participle have a preverbal subject as
shown in Table 3. In 82% of these cases, the participle follows the subject. The same
word order is documented in Italian (Cardinaletti 2003), Old English, and Old Catalan
(for these two languages, see Fischer and Alexiadou 2001; Fischer 2010). However, it
is excluded in Icelandic, where Stylistic Fronting is possible only when the canonical
subject position is not filled.

Table 3. Observed word orders in clauses with a fronted participle

Ø-PRT-V	PRT-V-Subj	Subj-PRT-V	PRT-Subj-V	Total
877	159	108	19	1163
75.4%	13.7%	9.3%	1.6%	

Martins (2005, 2011) analyzes a similar construction in Old Portuguese, which
she calls *IP scrambling*, as involving unselective movement to multiple specifiers of
TP/AgrSP. If we adopt Rizzi and Shlonsky's (2006, 2007) idea that the subject occupies
Spec,SubjP, and that the finite verb occupies T^0, we can alternatively account for the
position of the participle by assuming that the participle is merged in a freely generated functional projection FP—an IP-scrambling position—between SubjP and TP
(Labelle, 2007).[2]

(25) $[_{\text{SubjP}}$ il $[_{\text{FP}}$ PRT $[_{\text{TP}}$ V$_{\text{Fin}}$ …]]]

We assume that in embedded null subject sentences or in subject relative clauses (see
example (2)), where the canonical subject position is not overtly filled, the participle is
also merged in this IP-scrambling position.

Consider now the case where the participle surfaces to the immediate left of the
pronominal subject, as in the embedded relative clause in (26).

---

2. A reviewer asks whether the position of the participle in (22) is related to the position
observed in the Modern French construction *J'ai travaillé souvent*. 'I have worked often', where
the participle has been analyzed as being short-moved to some position to the left of the
adverb (cf. *J'ai souvent travaillé* 'I have often worked') (Pollock 1989, 417). It is difficult to
establish a relation between the two constructions. Not only is the position of the participle
different, but, for Pollock, short movement is head movement, whereas we showed that the
Old and Middle French fronting of a participle is best analyzed as (remnant) VP movement.

(26)   ... que   tout   se   departiroient de   Villevort, ou   <u>logiet</u>
          ... that   all   REFL leave   from   Villevort, where stayed

          il   estoient,
          they were

          '... that all would leave Villevort, where they were staying'
                                                     (1373, FROISSART, 308.5819)

Where is the participle in that case? Since this is not a V2 construction, Spec,FinP should not be activated, and it should not be available for the participle. The participle is not focused or contrastive, and therefore, it should not occupy Spec,FocusP. The participle is also not the topic of the clause. We tentatively assume that the participle is IP-scrambled to the left of SubjP, a word order also observed for IP-scrambling in Old Portuguese according to Martins (2011). This construction develops in the 13th century and is found mainly in Middle French, and practically exclusively with pronominal subjects. We hypothesize that, at the end of the Old French period, pronominal subjects started to be treated as phonological clitics on the verb. Speakers started to avoid separating the pronominal subject from the verb, and started to merge the participle to the left of the subject rather than to its right. (Once the construction was established it could extend to full DP subjects.)

We now turn to the cases where the participle is within the left periphery. According to Mathieu (2006, 2013), stylistically fronted elements—including non-finite verbs like participles—are fronted to a special phrase, which he labels Top⁺P. This head would be the rightmost head within the Topic field, and it would host "asserted background topics". As briefly mentioned above, for him, the first position of a V2 clause is a Topic position, where TopP precedes Top⁺P.

(27)   [TopP [Top⁺P _ [FocusP _ [FinP _V_{Fin} [IP _ $\overline{V}_{Fin}$ [vP]]]]]]

There is reason to think that this analysis is incorrect. Firstly, most current analyses of V2 place the initial constituent of V2 in a low position within the left periphery, and assume that what precedes FocusP does not count for V2 (see Holmberg 2015 for a survey). TopP hosts left-dislocated elements, which are outside of the core V2 clause. In addition, the first constituent of a V2 clause may correspond to old information, to new information, or to material that is neither a topic or a focus (e.g., an adverb), therefore, TopicP is not the correct field for it. Also, a fronted participle may be preceded by a negatively quantified subject.

(28)   nus hom <u>coronez</u> ne   sera   si cil   non qui   leiaument
          no   man   crowned   NEG will-be if the-ones not   who loyally

          se   conbatrant.
          REFL will-fight

          'no man will be crowned apart from those who will fight loyally.'
                                          (1220, PSEUDOTURPIN, 272.265)

Mathieu (2006) argues that some V3 main clauses result from applying Stylistic Front-ing to a clause where V2 topicalization has applied. Presumably, this would be the analysis he would assume for (28), the subject *nus hom* being in Spec,TopP and the participle in Top^{+0}. However, this does not seem right, since a negatively quantified subject cannot be a Topic. We propose that this sentence is not a V2 sentence, but an SVO sentence, with IP scrambling of the participle between the subject in its canonical position and the verb. If correct, this would provide support for the idea that, in V2 languages, subject-initial sentences may constitute an exception to the V2 derivation (cf. Travis 1984, 1991; Zwart 1993 for German; Vance, 1997 for OF; Hirschbühler, 1995 for MF).

In general, placing a fronted participle within the Topic field does not seem to be appropriate, since a non-finite verb does not make a good discourse topic. To consider, as does Mathieu, that the fronted participle carries "background information" (i.e., information which is part of the common ground but is not the topic of discourse) is plausible in certain cases, like in (29), but background information is not the type of information expected to be located within the Topic field, as it is informationally weak.

(29) é   distrent entre   sei: 'Mened únt   l'   arche jesque á
      and said   among themselves: 'Carried have the ark   up   to

      nus pur nus ocire...'
      us   to   us   kill...'

      'and (they) said to each other: '(They) have carried the ark up to our place
      to kill us..."   (1170, QUATRELIVRE, 13.372)

In addition, in a number of cases, the participle carries new information, and is the informational focus of the clause. This is the case in (1), repeated below with its con-text. Here again, the Topic field does not seem to be an appropriate location for an informational focus.

(30) La   dame est entrée   el   mustier   / E   cele vait al
      'The lady has entered the monastery / And she   goes to

      the chevalier / Asise s'est devant le   lit,
      knight   / She   sits   beside the bed'
                                    (1160-MARIE-DE-FRANCE, 19.334)

We have seen that the fronted participle could carry background information or new information. In addition, the participle is generally nonemphatic and noncontrastive, which suggests that it is not within the Focus field. We conclude that in V2 examples like (29) and (30), where the participle precedes the verb in main clauses, it occupies Spec,FinP, the pragmatically unmarked position hosting the first constituent of a V2 clause.

(31) [$_{FinP}$ Mened unt [$_{SubjP}$ ...

This is the unmarked case in main clauses. In a small number of examples, however, the participle appears to be strongly focalized. This is observed in what is called anaphoric anteposition focus (Benincà and Poletto 2004) exemplified in (32), and in the case of contrastive focus in (33).

(32) *Anaphoric anteposition focus:*
      car   par   le   conseil Joseph avoit il   recovree sa   terre que
      since through the advice Joseph had   he   recovered his land that

      Tholomers li   *toloit,*   et   <u>tolue</u> li   eust il   se ...
      Tholomers him was-taking, and   taken him had   he   if ...

      'since through Joseph's advice, he had recovered his land that Tholomers
      was taking from him, and he would have taken it if...'
      (1225, QUESTE, 113.2974)

(33) *Contrastive focus:*
      Se *fuït* s'   en   est   Marsilies, <u>Remés</u> i   est sis
      If fled REFL-GEN is Marsilie, remained LOC is his

      uncles Marganices,
      uncle Marganice

      'If Marsilius has fled, his uncle Marganice has stayed'
      (1100, ROLAND, 143.1937)

If these focalized participles occupy the Focus field, the structure would be as in (34), with the clitic+finite verb sequence in Fin^0 or raised higher to Foc^0:

(34) a. $[_{FocP}$ tolue [li eust $[_{SubjP}$ il ...]]
      b. $[_{FocP}$ remés [i est $[_{SubjP}$ sis uncles Marganices]]

In volitives of the type illustrated in (35), relatively frequent in main clauses, the participle is also within the left periphery, as shown by the fact that the pronominal subject follows the finite verb. It is difficult at this point to decide whether it occupies Spec,FinP or Spec,FocP.

(35) <u>Beneit</u> seies tu   de   nostre Seignur Deu
      blessed be   you from our   Lord   God
      (1150, QUATRELIVRE, 29.1034)

According to Frey (2004, 2006), movement to Spec,FinP (*Formal Movement*) is local, while movement to Spec,FocP (*True A-bar Movement*) is a possible candidate for long distance movement. Long distance movement of a fronted participle is unattested in our data. However, to find such a construction would require the combination of two rare phenomena: strongly focused participles are rare, and so is long distance movement. We cannot exclude the possibility that the construction was possible in Old French.

8.   Summary and conclusion

In this paper, we have first shown that, in Old and Middle French, a fronted participle could move as a VP and that a remnant VP movement is necessary to account for examples where a portion of the VP is fronted. Given that remnant VP movement is independently attested, the examples where a participle appears to move as a head can be analyzed as involving remnant VP movement as well. If this is correct, participle fronting in Old and Middle French involves phrasal movement, and not head movement.

In the second part of the paper, we studied the position of the participle phrase. Previous authors discussing Stylistic Fronting generally propose a single position for fronted element (an exception would be Molnár 2010). We showed that participle fronting in Old and Middle French does not target a single position: in some cases, the participle is IP-internal, in other cases, it moves to the left periphery. In the latter case, we argued that the unmarked position is Spec,FinP, the initial position of a V2 clause, where the participle may correspond to new or to background information. In a small number of cases, the participle is strongly focused, in which case, it could occupy Spec,FocP. Therefore, participle fronting is not a uniform phenomenon. Importantly, the positions where a fronted participle has been observed are independently allowed by the grammar for other types of constituents; there is no rule targeting exclusively participles. The fact that the positions where fronted participles are found are also positions where phrases are found supports our analysis in terms of (remnant) VP movement.

It was shown that participle fronting in Old and Middle French is neither like Icelandic Stylistic Fronting of a nonfinite verb nor like Sardinian nonfinite verb fronting. In French, the participle could co-occur with a subject to the left of the verb, contrary to what is the case in Icelandic Stylistic Fronting. In Icelandic, Old Spanish and Old Catalan, only verbal heads are fronted (Egerland 2011; Wood 2011 fn. 19; Fontana, 1993; Fischer, 2010); by contrast, Sardinian moves only full VPs (Egerland 2011). French may front verbal heads, full VPs and partial VPs. In Icelandic, the stylistically fronted participle corresponds to background information (according to Egerland), in Sardinian, the fronted VP is narrow focus, and in Old French, it can be either. Further research is needed to better understand these cross-linguistic differences.

Sources for the literary examples

BORON (c. 1190). Nitze, W.A., éd. 1927. *Le roman de l'estoire dou Graal.* Paris: Champion.
CASSIDORUS (1267). Palermo J., éd. 1964. *Le roman de Cassidorus.* Paris: Editions Picard.

EUSTACE-FISHER (c. 1212). Fisher, J.R., éd. 1927. *La vie de Saint Eustache par Pierre Beauvais.* Doctoral dissertation, Columbia University.

FROISSART (1373). Diller, G.T., éd. 1972. *Chroniques. Dernière rédaction du premier livre.* Genève: Droz.

MARIE-DE-FRANCE (c. 1160). Rychner, J., éd. 1973. *Les lais de Marie de France.* Paris: Champion.

PRISE (c. 1370). Mas Latrie, M.L. de, éd. 1877. *La prise d'Alexandrie, ou Chronique du roi Pierre Ier de Lusignan.* Genève: Fick.

PSEUDOTURPIN (c.1220). Auracher T., éd. 1877. *Der sogenannte poitevinische Pseudo-Turpin.* Nach den Handschriften mitgetheilt. (Extrait) Zeitschrift fur romanische Philologie 1: 262–272.

QUATRELIVRE (c. 1170). Curtius, E.R., éd. 1911. *Li quatre livre des reis.* Gesellschaft für romanische Literatur, no. 9. Dresden, Halle: Max Niemeyer.

QUESTE (c. 1225). Marchello-Nizia, Ch., éd. *La Queste del Saint Graal.* Electronic edition based on Pauphilet, A., éd. 1923. Paris: Champion.

ROLAND (c. 1100). Moignet, G., éd. 1972. *La chanson de Roland.* Paris: Bordas.

SOMME-ROYAL (c. 1269) Tysor, Ann Brooks, ed. 1949. *Somme des vices et des vertus.* M.A. thesis, University of North Carolina. 1–85.

YVAIN (c. 1170). Roques, M., éd. 1960. *Les romans de Chrétien de Troyes*, édités d'après la copie de Guiot (Bibl. nat. fr. 794). Paris: Champion.

References

Benincà, Paola. 2004. "The Left Periphery of Medieval Romance." Lecture/GURT 2004, Georgetown, 243–297. [http://www.humnet.unipi.it/slifo/2004vol2/ Beninca2004.pdf]

Benincà, Paola. 2006. "A Detailed Map of the Left Periphery of Medieval Romance." *Crosslinguistic Research in Syntax and Semantics. Negation, Tense and Clausal Architecture*, ed. by Raffaella Zanuttini, Héctor Campos, Elena Herburger, and Paul H. Portner, 53–86. Washington: Georgetown University Press.

Benincà, Paola and Cecilia Poletto. 2004. "Topic, Focus and V2: Defining the CP Sublayers." *The structure of CP and IP: The Cartography of Syntactic Structures, vol. 2*, ed. by Luigi Rizzi, 52–75. Oxford: Oxford University Press.

Cardinaletti, Anna 2003. "Stylistic Fronting in Italian." *Grammar in Focus. Festschrift for Christer Platzack*, ed. by Lars-Olof Delsing, Cecilia Falk, Gunlög Josefsson, and Halldor Armann Sigurðsson, 47–55. Department of Scandinavian Languages, Lund: Wallin and Dalholm.

Cardinaletti, Anna and Ian Roberts. 1991/2002. "Clause Structure and X-Second." *Functional Structure in DP and IP. The Cartography of Syntactic Structures, vol. 1*, ed. by Guglielmo Cinque, 123–166. Oxford: Oxford University Press. [Circulated as a manuscript since 1991]

Den Besten, Hans and Gert Webelhuth. 1987. "Remnant Topicalization and the Constituent Structure of VP in the Germanic Languages." Paper presented at the GLOW Colloquium, Venice.

Dupuis, Fernande. 1989. "L'expression du sujet dans les subordonnées en ancien français." Doctoral dissertation, Université de Montréal.

Egerland, Verner. 2011. "Fronting, Background, Focus: A Comparative Study of Sardinian and Icelandic." *Working Papers in Scandinavian Syntax* 87, 103–135.

Fischer, Susann. 2010. *Word Order Change as a Source of Grammaticalization*. Amsterdam: John Benjamins. DOI: 10.1075/la.157

Fischer, Susann. 2014. "Revisiting Stylistic Fronting in Old Spanish." *Left Sentence Peripheries in Spanish* ed. by Andreas Dufter and Álvaro S. Octavio de Toledo, 53–76. Philadelphia/ Amsterdam: John Benjamins. DOI: 10.1075/la.214.05fis

Fischer, Susann and Artemis Alexiadou. 2001. "On Stylistic Fronting: Germanic vs. Romance." *Working Papers in Scandinavian Syntax* 68: 117–145.

Fontana, Josep Maria. 1993. *Phrase Structure and the Syntax of Clitics in the History of Spanish*. Doctoal Dissertation, University of Pennsylvania.

Franco, Irene. 2009. *Verbs, Subjects and Stylistic Fronting. A comparative analysis of the interaction of CP properties with verb movement and subject positions in Icelandic and Old Italian*. Doctoral dissertation, University of Siena.

Franco, Irene. 2012. "Verbal Stylistic Fronting in Old Florentine." [http://ling.auf.net/ lingbuzz/001510].

Frey, Werner. 2004. "The Grammar-Pragmatics Interface and the German Prefield." *Sprache und Pragmatik* 52: 1–39.

Frey, Werner. 2006. "Contrast and Movement to the German Prefield." *The Architecture of Focus*, ed. by Valéria Molnár and Susanne Winkler, 235–264. Berlin: Mouton de Gruyter. DOI: 10.1515/9783110922011.235

Fuss, Eric. 2003. "On the Historical Core of V2 in Germanic." *Nordic Journal of Linguistics* 26.2: 195–231. DOI: 10.1017/S0332586503001082

Hirschbühler, Paul. 1995. "Null Subjects in V1 Embedded Clauses in Philippe de Vigneulles' Cent Nouvelles Nouvelles." *Clause Structure and Language Change*, ed. by Adrian Battye and Ian Roberts, 257–291. Oxford Studies in Comparative Syntax, Oxford University Press.

Holmberg, Anders. 2000. "Scandinavian Stylistic Fronting: How Any Category Can Become an Expletive." *Linguistic Inquiry* 31.3: 445–483. DOI: 10.1162/002438900554406

Holmberg, Anders. 2006. "Stylistic Fronting." *The Blackwell Companion to Syntax*, ed. by Martin Everaert and Henk van Riemsdijk, 532–565. Oxford: Blackwell.

Holmberg, Anders. 2015. "Verb Second." *Syntax—Theory and Analysis An International Handbook,* ed. by Tibor Kiss and Artemis Alexiadou. HSK Series. Walter de Gruyter Verlag, Berlin. [ling.auf.net/lingbuzz/001087/current.pdf]

Hrafnbjargarson, Gunnar Hrafn. 2004. "Stylistic Fronting." *Studia Linguistica* 58(2): 88–134. DOI: 10.1111/j.0039-3193.2004.00111.x

Hrafnbjargarson, Gunnar Hrafn and Anna-Lena Wiklund. 2009. "General Embedded V2: Icelandic A, B, C, etc." *Working Papers in Scandinavian Syntax* 84: 21–51.

Kayne, Richard S. 1976. "French Relative 'que'." *Current Studies in Romance Linguistics* ed. by Frederick Gerald Hensey and Marta Luján, 255–299. Washington, D.C.: Georgetown University Press.

Labelle, Marie. 2007. "Clausal Architecture in Early Old French." *Lingua* 117(1): 289–316. DOI: 10.1016/j.lingua.2006.01.004

Labelle, Marie and Paul Hirschbühler. 2005. "Changes in Clausal Organization and the Position of Clitics in Old French." *Grammaticalization and Parametric Variation*, ed. by Montserrat Batllori, Maria-Lluïsa Hernanz, Carme Picallo, and Francesc Roca, 60–71. Oxford: Oxford University Press. DOI: 10.1093/acprof:oso/9780199272129.003.0004

Maling, Joan. 1980/1990. "Inversion in Embedded Clauses in Modern Icelandic." *Modern Icelandic Syntax*, ed. by Joan Maling and Annie Zaenen, 71–91. San Diego: Academic Press. [Reedition of *Íslenskt mál*, 1980 2: 175–193.]

Martineau, France, Paul Hirschbühler, Anthony Kroch, and Yves Charles Morin. 2010. *Corpus MCVF (parsed corpus), Modéliser le changement: les voies du français*. Département de Français, Université d'Ottawa.

Martins, Anna Maria. 2005. "Clitic Placement, VP-Ellipsis and Scrambling in Romance." *Grammaticalization and Parametric Variation*, ed. by Montserrat Batllori, Maria-Lluïsa Hernanz, Carme Picallo, and Francesc Roca, 175–193. Oxford & New York: Oxford University Press. DOI: 10.1093/acprof:oso/9780199272129.003.0011

Martins, Anna Maria. 2011. "Scrambling and Information Focus in Old and Contemporary Portuguese." *Catalan Journal of Linguistics* 10: 133–158.

Mathieu, Éric 2006. "Stylistic Fronting in Old French." *Probus* 18: 219–266.
DOI: 10.1515/PROBUS.2006.008

Mathieu, Éric 2013. "The Left Periphery in Old French." *Research in Old French: The State of the Art*, ed. by Deborah L. Arteaga, 327–350. Studies in Natural Language & Linguistic Theory 88. Dordrecht: Springer. DOI: 10.1007/978-94-007-4768-5_17

Molnár, Valéria 2010. "Stylistic Fronting and Discourse." *Tampa Papers in Linguistics*, Vol. 1, 30–61.

Ott, Dennis. 2009. "Stylistic Fronting as Remnant Movement." *Working Papers in Scandinavian Syntax* 83: 141–178.

Platzack, Christer. 1987. "The Scandinavian Languages and the Null-Subject Parameter." *Natural Language & Linguistic Theory* 5(3): 377–401. DOI: 10.1007/BF00134554

Poletto, Cecilia. 2005. "Diachronic Variation in Romance." Handout of a paper presented at the Eastern Generative Grammar (EGG) Summer School, Wroclaw, Poland. [http://egg.auf.net/05/docs /handouts/Cecilia/ eggdiachronicpoletto.pdf].

Poletto, Cecilia. 2006. "Parallel Phases: a Study on the High and Low Left Periphery of Old Italian." *Phases of Interpretation*, ed. by Mara Frascarelli, 261–295. Berlin: Mouton de Gruyter.

Pollock, Jean-Yves. 1989. "Verb Movement, Universal Grammar, and the Structure of IP." Linguistic Inquiry 20(3): 365–424.

Rizzi, Luigi. 1990. *Relativized Minimality*. Cambridge: The MIT Press.

Rizzi, Luigi. 1997. "The Fine Structure of the Left Periphery." *Elements of Grammar: A Handbook of Generative Syntax*, ed. by Liliane. Haegeman, 281–337. Dordrecht: Kluwer.
DOI: 10.1515/9783110197723.4.261

Rizzi, Luigi. 2006. "On the Form of Chains: Criterial Positions and ECP Effects." *Wh Movement: Moving on*, ed. by Lisa Lai-Shen Cheng and Norbert Corver, 97–134. Cambridge: MIT Press.

Rizzi, Luigi and Ur Shlonsky. 2006. "Satisfying the Subject Criterion by a Non Subject: English Locative Inversion and Heavy NP Shift." *Phases of interpretation*, ed. by Mara Frascarelli, 341–361. Berlin: Mouton de Gruyter. DOI: 10.1515/9783110197723.5.341

Rizzi, Luigi and Ur Schlonsky. 2007. "Strategies of Subject Extraction." *Interfaces + Recursion = Language? Chomsky's Minimalism and the View from Syntax-Semantics*, ed. by Uli Sauerland and Hans-Martin Gärtner, 115–160. Berlin: Walter de Gruyter.

Roberts, Ian. 1993. *Verbs and Diachronic Syntax: A Comparative History of English and French*. Dordrecht: Kluwer.

Salvesen, Christine Meklenborg. 2011. "Stylistic Fronting and Remnant Movement in Old French." *Romance Languages and Linguistic Theory. Selected Papers from 'Going Romance' Nice 2009*, ed. by Janine Berns, Haike Jacobs, and Tobias Scheer, 323–342. Amsterdam: John Benjamins. DOI: 10.1075/rllt.3.19sal

Taraldsen, Knut Tarald. 2001. "Subject Extraction, the Distribution of Expletives and Stylistic Inversion." *Subject Inversion in Romance and the Theory of Universal Grammar*, ed. by Aafke Hulk and Jean-Yves Pollock, 163–181. NewYork: Oxford University Press.

Travis, Lisa. 1984. *Parameters and Effects of Word Order Variation*. Doctoral dissertation, MIT, Cambridge, Mass.

Travis, Lisa. 1991. "Parameters of Phrase Structure and V2 Phenomena." *Principles and Parameters in Comparative Grammar*, ed. by Robert Freidin, 339–364. Cambridge, MA.: MIT Press.

Vance, Barbara. 1997. *Syntactic Change in Medieval French: Verb Second and Null Subjects*. Dordrecht: Kluwer Academic Publishers. DOI: 10.1007/978-94-015-8843-0

Wood, Jim. 2011. "Stylistic Fronting in Spoken Icelandic Relatives." *Nordic Journal of Linguistics* 34(1): 29–60. DOI: 10.1017/S0332586511000084

Zaring, Laurie. 2011. "On the Nature of OV and VO Order in Old French." *Lingua* 121: 1831–1852. DOI: 10.1016/j.lingua.2011.07.008

Zwart, C. Jan-Wouter. 1993. *Dutch Syntax—A Minimalist Approach*. Doctoral dissertation, University of Groningen.

"Toned-up" Spanish

Stress → pitch → tone(?) in Equatorial Guinea

John M. Lipski
The Pennsylvania State University

In Equatorial Guinea Spanish is in contact with lexical tone languages of the Bantu family. The present study, based on field data, compares naturalistic Guinean Spanish with the Spanish of from Madrid, the dialect zone that served as primary input for the formation of Guinean Spanish. A preliminary analysis reveals partial convergence of a pitch accent system and lexically specified phonological tones. Guinean Spanish maintains one stress per word culminativity but expands obligatoriness by realizing a pitch accent on every syllable lexically marked for stress. The rate at which pitch accents occur is compared with the distribution of High tones in the two most prominent Guinean languages (Bubi and Fang), and it is suggested that Guineans' incomplete suppression of natively acquired F0 patterns may be facilitated by the metrical structure of Spanish, which provides for regularly occurring pitch accents whose maximum potential density is similar to that of H tones in Bubi and Fang.

1. Introduction

1.1 Contact-induced intonation in Spanish varieties

In the study of intonational patterns across Spanish dialects, current or former language contacts have frequently been implicated—with varying degrees of empirical evidence—e.g. Italian for Buenos Aires (Colantoni and Gurlekian 2004), Quechua for highland Peru (O'Rourke 2004, 2005), Guaraní for Paraguay and northeastern Argentina (Malmberg 1950), Basque for northern Spain (Elordieta 2003, Elordieta and Calleja 2005), Catalan for Majorca (Simonet 2088, 2011), and Mayan for Yucatan Spanish (Barrera Vásquez 1980, Michnowicz and Barnes 2013). All of the aforementioned adstrate languages employ stress systems characterized among other factors by some type of pitch accent on metrically prominent syllables. Less attention has been directed at contacts between Spanish and lexical tone languages, such as occurred when several million speakers of African tone languages were involuntarily resettled in Spanish America. Tone-language adstratal influence has been suggested for

DOI 10.1075/rllt.9.13lip

the intonational patterns of some contemporary Afro-Hispanic dialects, e.g., Hualde and Schwegler (2008) for the Afro-Colombian creole language Palenquero, Morton (2005) for Palenquero Spanish, and Megenney (1982) for some Afro-Dominican communities.

Pitch accents in languages such as Spanish are often perceived by speakers of lexical tone languages as High tone, and borrowings from English, Portuguese, and French into African languages amply attest to this process (cf. Lipski 2005, chap. 7). This homology is most robust in citation forms; in connected speech, which constitutes the principal input in most language contact situations, matters are not as straightforward, particularly as regards the treatment of lexically unstressed syllables (e.g., Amayo 1980; Chen and Au 2004; Deterding 1994; Griper-Friedman 1990; Gut 2005; Gut and Milde 2002; Jowitt 2000; Kenstowicz 2006; Lim 2009; Wee 2008). The present study offers data from a contact environment involving Spanish and African lexical tone languages, in Equatorial Guinea. The study has the general goal of documenting in detail the behavior of Spanish as produced by native speakers of lexical tone languages, a linguistic configuration similar to that found in much of colonial Spanish America (although in quite different sociolinguistic environments). The principal research question is whether the contact between a pitch-accent/stress language and lexical tone languages has resulted in a hybrid prosodic system for Equatorial Guinean Spanish, possibly leading to the phonologization of Spanish pitch accents (i.e., as lexical tones).

1.2   The Spanish of Equatorial Guinea

The Republic of Equatorial Guinea, formerly the colony of Spanish Guinea and an independent nation since 1968, is the only African nation in which Spanish is the official language; nearly all Guineans possess usable fluency in the language of the former metropolitan power. Equatorial Guinea consists of the island of Bioko (formerly Fernando Poo), which contains the national capital, Malabo (formerly Santa Isabel), and the continental enclave of Rio Muni (with district capital Bata), between Gabon and Cameroon, as well as tiny Annobón Island, located to the south of São Tomé. Equatorial Guinea is home to a variety of languages. The indigenous group on Bioko speaks Bubi. Nearly all residents of Malabo and other cities on Bioko also speak Pidgin English, known locally as *pichinglis* or *pichi*. The principal ethnic group in Rio Muni is Fang; the Fang have also emigrated in large numbers to Bioko. Several smaller groups (Ndowé/Combe, Bujeba, Benga, Bapuko, etc.) are found along the coast of Rio Muni. Annobón Islanders speak *Fa d'ambú*, a Portuguese-lexified creole. The indigenous Equatorial Guinean languages are lexical tone languages of the Bantu family, in which all syllables are specified for either High or Low tone.

Descriptions of Equatorial Guinean Spanish are found in Bibang-Oyee (2002), Lipski (1985, 1990, 2000, 2004, 2008) and Quilis and Casado-Fresnillo (1995). Although spoken with varying degrees of fluency by most residents, Equatorial Guinean Spanish does have common traits found in nearly all speakers that justify the postulate of Guinean dialects of Spanish (e.g. Lipski 2008). Guinean Spanish at all levels of fluency can be immediately recognized, due not only to segmental and occasional morphosyntactic traits, but also to the unique intonational patterns, which depart significantly from those found in other varieties of Spanish. Castillo Barril (1966, 16) refers to "el tono de voz elevado [...] una entonación ligeramente melosa, con el ritmo entrecortado y una variedad de tonos silábicos" [the raised tone of voice ... a slightly syrupy intonation, with a choppy rhythm and a variety of syllabic tones]. The Guinean linguist Bibang Oyee (2002,19), himself a speaker of Fang, observes that "En un hablante fang, por ejemplo, se puede observar, en términos generales, que la configuración del fundamental se mantiene en los mismos niveles frecuenciales durante el enunciado, con desviaciones acusadas entre las sílabas tónicas y átonas" [In a speaker of Fang, for example, it can be observed that in general, the fundamental frequency remains level during an utterance, with notable differences between tonic and atonic syllables]. Bibang Oyee echoes the nearly exact words of his mentor Quilis (Quilis and Casado-Fresnillo 1995, 137–8).

Throughout its colonial history, native Spanish speakers in Equatorial Guinea came almost exclusively from Spain (except for a small number of exiled Cuban revolutionaries who arrived in the 1860s). Nearly all colonial administrators came from Castile and other northern areas. The educational system was largely in the hands of the Claretian (Corazón de María) religious order, based in Catalunya, although many of the priests and nuns also came from Castile as did lay teachers. Cacao, the principal colonial enterprise, was largely in the hands of landowners from Valencia. The segmental phonetic traits of central and northern Spain, as well as Catalunya and much of Valencia are quite similar, and are reflected in Guinean Spanish:

1.3 Tone languages and pitch accent/stress languages

A comprehensive definition of tone language as opposed e.g., to pitch-accent language is elusive (e.g. Odden 1999). Yip (2002, 1) classifies languages as tone languages "if the pitch of the word can change the meaning of the word," and "A language with tone is one in which an indication of pitch enters into the lexical realization of at least some morphemes." (ibid., 4) For Hyman (2009) a language has tone if "an indication of pitch enters into the lexical realization of at least some morphemes." For Gandour (2007, 4) tone languages exploit phonologically relevant variations in pitch at the syllable level. A tone language may exhibit a higher density of pitch fluctuations than languages lacking lexically specified tones (e.g., Gauthier, Shi, and Xu 2007). For example Eady (1982) compared pitch patterns of Mandarin Chinese and American English. The speech of Mandarin subjects displayed a greater average rate of F0 change than English speakers: there were more peaks and valleys as a function of time and as a function of the number of syllables. This is consistent with the notion that F0 patterns are determined mainly by the tonal specifications of the specific lexical items in each sentence, while in English pitch peaks are normally restricted to the placement of primary stress in a predictable position and on only a few lexical items in each sentence.

A widely accepted definition of a language with stress is one in which there is an indication of word-level metrical structure meeting the following two core criteria (cf. Hyman 2006):

> OBLIGATORINESS: every lexical word has AT LEAST one syllable marked for the highest degree of metrical prominence (primary stress)
> CULMINATIVITY: every lexical word has AT MOST one syllable marked for the highest degree of metrical prominence

These two properties entail that every lexical word has ONE AND ONLY ONE primary stress. Yip (2002, 3) observes that in stress languages, what remains constant is the most prominent syllable in each morpheme, while the precise pitches associated with the prominent syllable may vary according to the embedding in a longer phrase as well as to the type of discourse (e.g., ironic, incredulous, exclamatory, doubtful, echo, etc.).

1.4   Correlates of stress in Spanish: Pitch accents

Although Spanish lexical stress has often been referred to as *acento de intensidad* 'intensity accent,' empirical research has shown that vocalic duration and rising pitch accent are the primary acoustic correlates of lexical stress, while relative intensity—including spectral tilt—is at best weakly correlated with lexical stress (e.g. Llisteri et al. 2002, 2003; Ortega-Llebaria 2006; Ortega-Llebaria and Prieto 2007; Ortega-Llebaria, Prieto, and Vanrell 2007). Spanish words may contain no more than one lexical stress; this includes prosodically stressed monosyllables such as the 2nd person singular subject pronoun *tú* 'you' as opposed to the possessive clitic *tu* 'your.' Spanish pitch accents have been extensively documented within the autosegmental-metrical ToBI framework (Beckman et al. 2002, Estebas-Vilaplana and Prieto 2008). There is considerable cross-dialectal variation in terms of the shape and alignment of both prenuclear and nuclear pitch accents, as well as the existence and typology of broad and narrow focus marking (cf. Sosa 1999, McGory and Díaz Campos 2002, and the articles in Prieto and Roseano 2010). Since the Spanish of Equatorial Guinea bears the strong imprint of Castile, especially Madrid, pitch accent patterns from this variety are the most relevant. In the Spanish of Madrid prenuclear pitch accents in broad focus typically exhibit late peak alignment, i.e., the pitch rise reaches its peak in the immediately posttonic syllable (Estebas-Vilaplana and Prieto 2010; Face 2002b, 2006; Face and Prieto 2007; Prieto et al. 1995; also Henriksen 2012). In narrow-focus constructions, the high peak may be contained within the tonic syllable (Face 2001, 2002a). Rightward high peak displacement does not usually occur across word boundaries: early high peak alignment is the norm for words ending in tonic syllables (e.g., Hualde 2002, 104). Nuclear (phrase-final) pitch accents normally exhibit early (intra-syllable) peak alignment as well, although in non-emphatic speech there is frequently no discernible phrase-final pitch accent. Initial F0 pitch as well as overall pitch patterns may also depend on overall utterance length and the number of pitch accents (Prieto et al. 2006).

From an acoustic standpoint Spanish pitch accents are characterized by a fundamental frequency (F0) trough that signals the onset of the rise defining the pitch accent (Hualde 2002:106; Prieto et al. 1995); there is usually also a pitch drop within the tonic syllable or the immediately following syllable. Pitch accent configurations observed in elicited laboratory speech bear only a partial resemblance to spontaneous speech, in which prenuclear accents exhibit a range of variability that cannot be entirely attributed to focus or emphasis (Face 2003). In the case of Equatorial Guinea, a reference to laboratory speech is not entirely irrelevant, since the bases for spoken Guinean Spanish were established principally by teachers and priests, whose declamatory didactic styles often come closer to laboratory-produced utterances than to everyday speech patterns.

2. Data collection

2.1 Participants

Data on the Spanish of Equatorial Guinea were obtained from ten female speakers and ten male speakers. Each gender group included five native speakers of Fang and five native speakers of Bubi. The age range was 25–47. None had resided outside of Equatorial Guinea, and all are sequential bilinguals who had acquired at least some of their Spanish in school. Most of the participants knew some Pidgin English, especially those residing in Malabo. As is typical in Equatorial Guinea, speakers typically use their native languages with interlocutors of the same language background and (particularly in Malabo) Pidgin English with Guineans of other language backgrounds. Spanish is spoken primarily with the small but prominent group of Spaniards and other "Europeans"; despite this relatively limited use all are fluent in Spanish, a characteristic of nearly all urban residents of this small country (Lipski 1985, Quilis and

Casado-Fresnillo 1995). The Fang speakers were interviewed in Malabo and Bata; the Bubi speakers were interviewed in Malabo, Rebola, Baney, and Luba, on the island of Bioko.

Baseline data for Bubi and Fang were obtained from two conversations recorded in Malabo, one between a male and a female Bubi speaker and the other between a male and female Fang speaker. Since the primary linguistic input for Equatorial Guinean Spanish came from central and northern Spain, Peninsular Spanish baseline data were obtained from two conversations recorded in Madrid among speakers born and raised in Madrid and its environs; one between two women and one among three men. In addition, one man and one woman from Madrid were recruited to read some of the sentences transcribed from the interviews with Guinean speakers and used in the following analyses. They were asked to speak the sentences as though they were part of a natural conversation, an obviously imperfect procedure that nonetheless provides a crude side-by-side comparison with the Guinean data.

2.2   Method

The Spanish interviews in Equatorial Guinea were conducted and recorded by the author. The format was free conversation on a variety of topics. The author also supervised the recording of the Fang and Bubi conversations, and recorded the conversations in Madrid. From each of the Guinean groups twenty complete utterances were selected at random, the criterion being that they were clearly recorded, contained a minimum of three stressable words, i.e., that could potentially receive a pitch accent (e.g., as per Harris 1983), and represented a grammatically complete sentence. All chosen utterances were declarative and none appeared to embody broad or contrastive focus. This yielded a total of 80 utterances. For the female speakers the number of potential pitch accents per utterance ranged from 3 to 9 with a mean of 5.2 (SD 1.9). For the male speakers the number of potential pitch accents per utterance ranged from 3 to 10, with a mean of 4.6 (SD 2.1). For a rudimentary comparison the male and female speakers from Madrid read the corresponding sentences as produced by Guineans. They were asked to render the transcribed utterances in as spontaneous a style as possible. Neither had listened to the Guinean recordings and both indicated that they had never heard Spanish spoken by Equatorial Guineans.

Using the same criteria applied to the Guinean recordings forty utterances each were extracted from the male and female Madrid conversations. For the female speakers from Madrid the mean number of potential pitch accents per utterance was 6 (SD 2.6) and for the male speakers the mean number of potential pitch accents per utterance was 7.3 (SD 2.3). For the Fang and Bubi baseline data a continuous sample of five minutes was extracted for each language. All utterances were imported into PRAAT software (Boersma and Weenink 1999–2005) and manually segmented into syllables. All syllables capable of receiving stress in Spanish were marked on a separate tier.

3. Data analysis

3.1 Operationalizing pitch accents and H tones

Although Spanish pitch accents as well as Fang and Bubi H and L tones are relatively easy to discern aurally and to visually identify once pitch (F0) tracks have been matched to syllables, arriving at empirically replicable definitions (e.g., automated calculation) is fraught with difficulties (e.g., Ọdẹ́lọbí 2008; Quian, Lee, and Soong 2007; Yu 2010; Zhang and Hirose 2004). These challenges are compounded when faced with the diversity of utterances and speakers, particularly for the Spanish data. With this in mind, Spanish pitch accents were first identified manually by examining the F0 tracks aligned with potentially stressable syllables on the respective text grids. F0 minima on either side of tonic syllables were marked on the text grid at "elbows" followed by pitch rises, while F0 maxima were marked at the highest value of a rising F0 slope followed by a falling gesture (e.g., as in Henriksen 2012). A pitch accent was defined as the combination of an F0 valley either in the immediately preceding syllable (for non-initial syllables) or within the tonic syllable, followed by a F0 peak either within the tonic syllable or in the immediately following syllable. Previous studies have not specified the minimum F0 peak-valley difference necessary to define a pitch accent as opposed to subphonemic F0 fluctuations (e.g., due to segmental factors; cf. Hermes 2006: 32). Most research has relied on the premise that "stressed syllables in Spanish are generally accompanied by a rise in fundamental frequency" (Face 2002c, 77) combined with measurement of relevant F0 values in the vicinity of syllables assumed to be stressed. Such an approach implicitly assumes the obviousness of pitch accents, e.g., "visible pitch rises" (Simonet 2010, 126) and "F0 points presumed to represent tonal targets" (Henriksen 2012: 547), and works backwards by measuring pitch fluctuations on syllables previously identified as stressed. Since one of the goals of the present study was to measure the total number of F0 peaks that could be regarded as instantiations of a H tone, it was necessary to identify a F0 range independently from the designation of stressed syllables. In Prieto, van Santen and Hirschberg (1995, 447) the lowest average peak range for male Mexican speakers was around 30 Hz (also Prieto 1998, 268; Prieto et al. 1996: 452 report values as low as 3 Hz), while Face (2002c, 91) reports peak ranges as low as 19 Hz for a group of 5 male and 15 female speakers from Madrid. For the present project the conservative value of 30 Hz was adopted as the minimum F0 peak range for a tonic syllable that would qualify as a pitch accent (although in reality between these values and microfluctuations of 1–2 Hz the data contain almost no clear F0 peaks with smaller peak ranges). All tonic syllables that met these criteria were manually marked on the text grid as having a pitch accent. Early vs. late peak alignment in prenuclear pitch accents was judged binarily: either the F0 peak was located within the boundaries of the tonic syllable or it occurred in the immediately posttonic syllable.

Even less information is available regarding F0 ranges responsible for H and L tones in Bantu languages, which are characterized by such phenomena as downstep (contrastive lowering of H tones following each L tone) and downdrift (gradual F0 declination). As with Spanish pitch accents most research has relied on previous knowledge of the lexical tones associated with each syllable. For the three-tone (H, M, L) language Yoruba, Ọdẹ́lọbí (2008, 32) and Connell and Ladd (1990, 14) show value of around 20 Hz separating examplars of level tones in that language. In African languages with only H and L tones values in the 20–50 Hz range have been reported, e.g., for Chichewa (Myers 1998, 379), Ibibio (Connell 2002, 126), Igbo (Liberman et al. 1993), Kipare (Herman 1996), etc. In studying the effects of Mandarin tones on English, Eady (1982, 34) adopted a threshold of 15 Hz as defining a tonal fluctuation; this corresponds closely to the data on Mandarin tones provided by Xu (1999, 71) and Yu (2010, 4). For the Bubi baseline sample the average H-L pitch range for the male speakers was 41 Hz and for the female speaker 56 Hz; for Fang the average H-L pitch range was 39 Hz (male)/51 Hz (female).

Once the pitch accents had been manually annotated on the Spanish text grids, the number and alignment patterns were recalculated by means of a PRAAT script that identified local F0 maxima and minima in each utterance and on a syllable-by-syllable basis classified as a pitch accent a rise in F0 that met or exceeded the aforementioned ratios and were followed by a fall in the same or immediately following syllable. This approach is a simplified amalgam of techniques described in Alessandro and Mertens (1995), Bagshaw (1993), Hermes (2006), Scheffers (1988), and Taylor (1994, 2000), among others. Early aligned pitch accents were defined as containing the F0 peak within the tonic syllable while in pitch accents defined as late-aligned the F0 rises throughout the syllable and reaches its peak in the following syllable. In order to further compare Equatorial Guinean Spanish intonational patterns with Fang and Bubi, additional pitch excursions not associated with stressable syllables but meeting the 30 Hz criterion were also calculated. In the (few) instances where the script produced different results from the manual classification the author and a native Spanish speaker from Madrid re-examined the pitch track before making a final determination. For purposes of comparison the same 30 Hz script was applied to the Fang and Bubi baseline data (on text grids in which only individual syllables were marked), where the corresponding F0 peaks were taken to instantiate H tones. The results from the script were compared with a visual inspection of the pitch tracks and appropriate corrections were made.

For each group of Spanish speakers the following were calculated: (1) ratio of possible stressed syllables to total number of syllables; (2) ratio of occurring pitch accents to total number of syllables; (3) ratio of occurring pitch accents to potentially stressable syllables; (4) ratio of all pitch accent-like F0 excursions to total number of syllables; (5) the mean number of syllables between F0 peaks (for both pitch accents aligned with stressable syllables and other relevant F0 peaks); (6) percentage of early-aligned prenuclear pitch accents. For the Fang and Bubi baseline data only the ratios of F0 peaks (H tones) to syllables and the mean number of syllables between F0 peaks were calculated, together with the percentage of early-aligned F0 peaks.

3.2   Results

Table 1 displays the behavior of pitch accents in the Spanish of Equatorial Guinea as compared with samples from Madrid. Since for both Equatorial Guinean and Madrid speakers' nuclear peak accents (when discernible) contained early-aligned F0 peaks, the data include both pre-nuclear and nuclear pitch accents. In this summary, words ending in tonic syllables are not calculated separately, on the premise that the proportion of such words is identical between the Spanish control and Guinean speakers and comparable among the Madrid conversational speakers.

This table shows that both male and female Guinean speakers produced pitch accents on a greater proportion of stressable Spanish syllables than speakers from Madrid, both when reading the same sentences as produced by Guineans and in spontaneous speech. These differences are systematic and significant. For the three groups of male speakers, a repeated measures ANOVA performed on the arcsine-transformed proportions of stressed to stressable syllables revealed a highly significant main effect for group: $F(2,97) = 219.9, p < .0001$. A post-hoc Tukey HSD test confirmed significant differences between male Guineans and the Madrid speaker's pronunciation of the same utterances ($p < .0001$) and between male Guineans and the conversation among male Madrid speakers ($p < .0001$), but not between the test subject from Madrid and the Madrid conversation participants ($p = .54$). These inter-group results were confirmed by Welch's t-tests: Guinea-Madrid reader: $t(55.99) = 18.56, p < .0001$; Guinea-Madrid conversation: $t(33.73) = 21.02, p < .0001$; Madrid reader-Madrid conversation: $t(57.35) = -1.07, p = .29$. For the three female categories, the ANOVA yielded a highly significant main effect for group: $F(2,97) = 25.34, p < .0001$. The Tukey HSD showed significant differences between female Guinean speakers and the female speaker who pronounced the same utterances ($p < .0001$) and between the female Guineans and the conversation among females in Madrid

Table 1. Pitch accents and F0 peaks in Equatorial Guinean and Madrid Spanish

	possible PA/syl	# syl between possible PA	occurring PA/syl	# syl between occurring PA	% occurring/ possible PA	% early aligned	all pitch peaks/syl	# syl between pitch peaks
Guinea-male	.34	2.9	.32	3.0	99%	89%	.39	2.6
Madrid-male	.34	2.9	.08	7.4	40%	5%	.20	5.0
Madrid-control-m.	.30	3.3	.13	7.5	44%	29%	.21	4.8
Guinea-female	.35	2.9	.31	3.3	90%	85%	.34	2.9
Madrid-female	.35	2.9	.24	4.5	68%	60%	.27	3.7
Madrid-control-f.	.31	3.2	.17	5.8	55%	27%	.18	5.5
Fang						98%	.42	2.4
Bubi						99%	.38	2.6

($p < .0001$). A barely significant difference was also found between the female speaker who read the Guinean utterances and the Madrid conversational data ($p = .03$). Welch's t-tests confirmed these results: Guinea-Madrid reader: $t(79.60) = 4.77$, $p < .0001$; Guinea-Madrid conversation: $t(43.64) = 8.52$, $p < .0001$; Madrid reader-Madrid conversation: $t(55.89) = 2.79$, $p = .008$. The female speaker from Madrid who read the transcribed Guinean utterances pronounced them in an exaggerated singsong intonation, despite the request to strive for a natural style; this greater intonational fluctuation is reflected in the significant difference with respect to the natural conversational data. It is probably the case that female Madrid speakers as a group exhibit more F0 fluctuations than corresponding groups of male speakers, but the data in Table 1 are skewed by the performance of the single female speaker who read the test utterances and cannot be taken as illustrative of more general tendencies. Figure 1 displays the relative proportion of pitch-accented syllables to potentially stressable syllables.

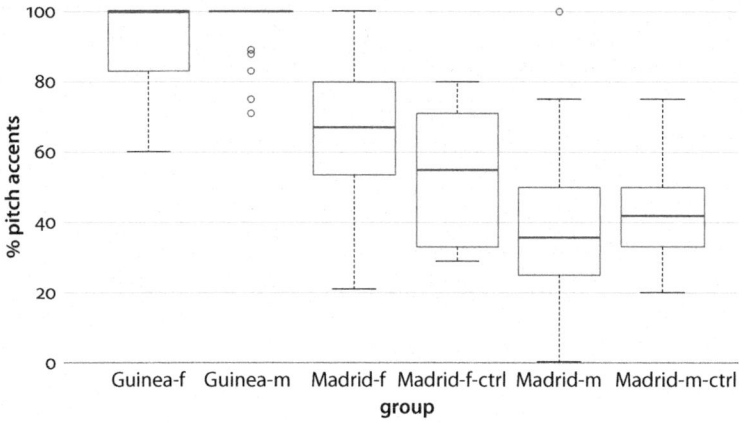

Figure 1. Proportion of pitch-accented Spanish syllables to potentially stressable syllables

Table 1 also shows that Guinean speakers early-aligned tonic pitch accents at much higher rates than the Spanish readers and Madrid conversation groups, all of which exhibited the Peninsular Spanish tendency towards late prenuclear peak alignment. Levels of significance in the proportions of early-aligned pitch accents precisely mirror the overall proportion of pitch accents: male and female Guinean speakers differed significantly from their Madrid counterparts with p-values $< .0001$, while there were no significant differences between the Spanish readers and the Madrid conversation groups. The relative proportions of early-aligned tonic syllables are displayed in Figure 2.

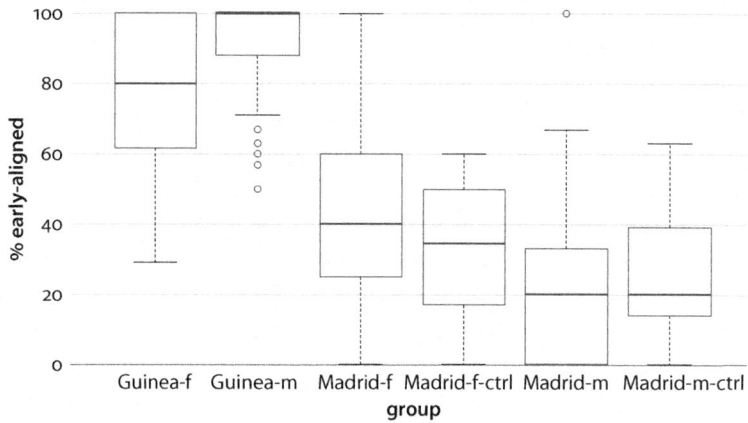

Figure 2. Proportion of Spanish early-aligned pitch accents on tonic syllables

To further illustrate the differences between Equatorial Guinean and Madrid Spanish intonation Figure 3 compares the pronunciation of a sentence by a female Bubi speaker (lower) and a female speaker from Madrid (upper). In addition to producing more pitch fluctuations than the Madrid female control group, this female Madrid speaker consistently produced late-aligned prenuclear pitch accents, as compared with the Guinean speaker's early-aligned F0 peaks. Figure 4 compares a male Bubi speaker (lower) with a male speaker from Madrid (upper); not only does the latter speaker produce late-aligned pitch accents but the inter-syllable F0 fluctuations are much smaller (both speakers had similar voice ranges).

4.   Discussion

4.1   Early peak alignment in contact situations

The Spanish of Equatorial Guinea as produced by speakers of Bubi and Fang exhibits a much higher rate of early peak alignment in prenuclear syllables than (monolingual) Peninsular Spanish varieties. In many other bilingual contact environments involving Spanish, early peak alignment is also characteristic, including in varieties stemming from previous bilingualism (e.g. Colantoni and Gurlekian 2004 for Italian in Buenos Aires; Lipski 2014 for various Afro-Hispanic varieties in Latin America). Bullock (2009. 168–169) has observed that prenuclear peak alignment "appears to occur earlier in the speech of bilinguals than in monolinguals in a range of language pairings […]," while acknowledging that early peak alignment may have emerged as a default strategy rather than being a direct consequence of L1 transfer (169–170). In the case of Spanish in contact with Basque (Elordieta 2003; Elordieta and Calleja 2005), Quechua

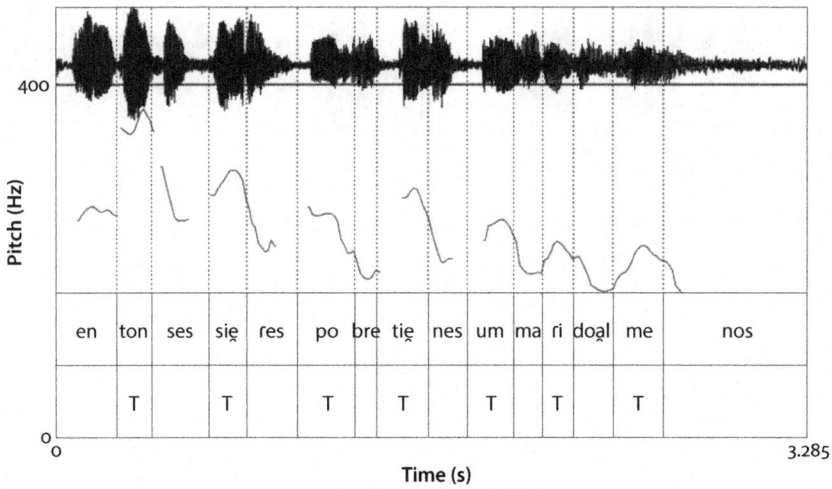

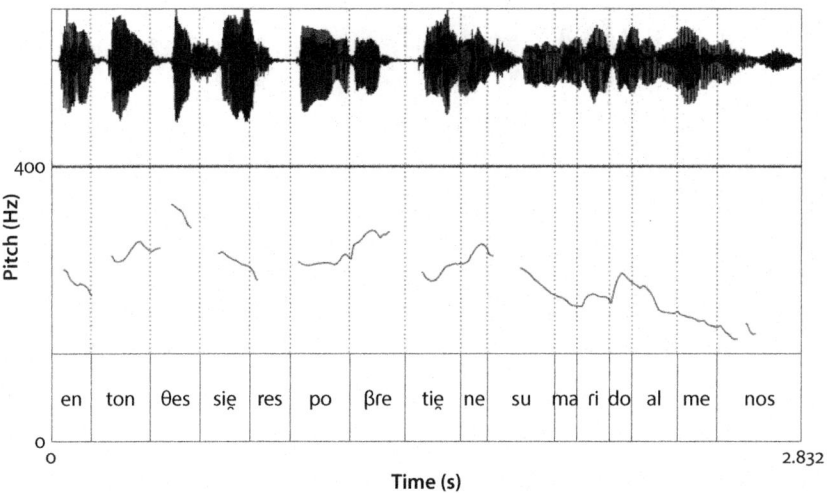

Figure 3. Female Guinean speaker (above) and female Madrid speaker (below); pitch track of *Entonces si eres pobre tienes un marido al menos* 'So if you're poor at least you have a husband.'

(O'Rourke 2004), and apparently many Italian varieties (Colantoni and Gurlekian 2004, 110), monolingual varieties of the languages in contact also exhibit early peak alignment, so direct prosodic transfer ranks high on the list of possible contributing factors. It is not clear why one pattern should prevail over the other, although prolonged Spanish-recessive bilingualism during the coalescence of a particular dialect may have been involved. Since in lexical tone languages, tones are generally aligned closely with their respective syllables, it is not unexpected that Spanish pitch accents

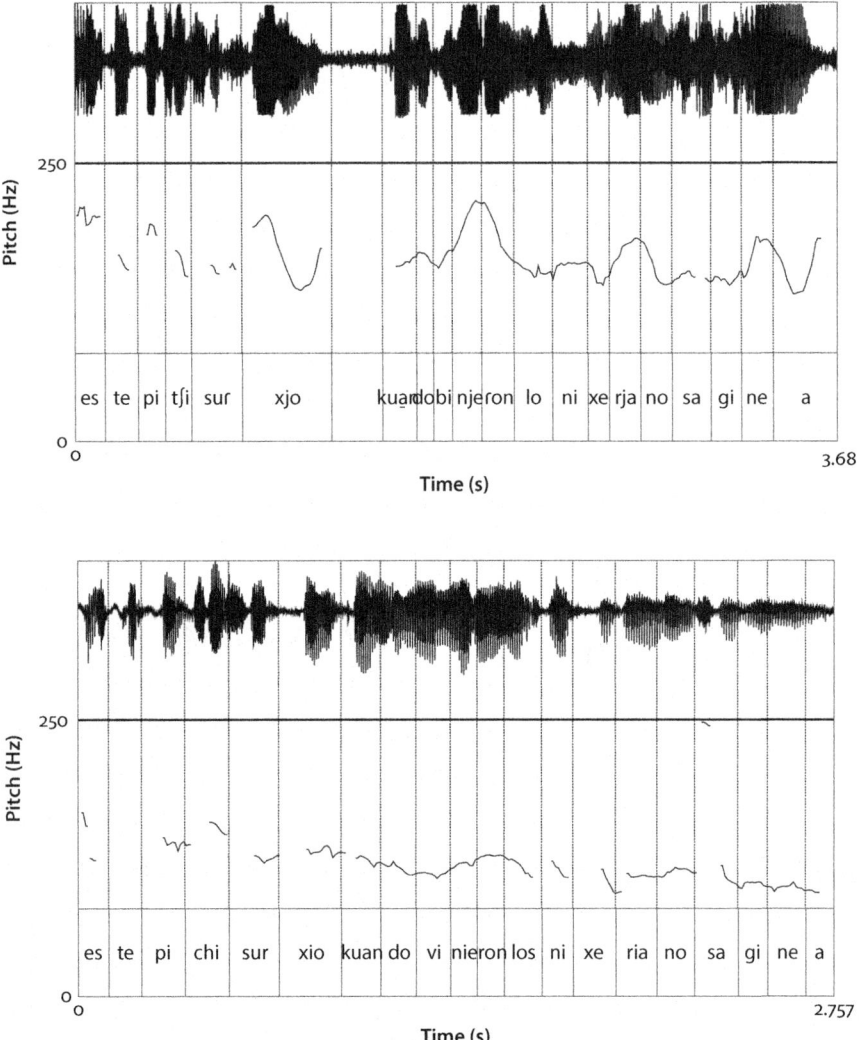

Figure 4. Male Guinean speaker (above) and Madrid speaker (below); pitch track of *Este pichi surgió cuando vinieron los nigerianos a Guinea* 'This *pichi* [Pidgin English] arose when Nigerians came to Guinea.'

(originally interpreted as H tones) would shift to an early-alignment configuration. Much the same appears to have occurred in the formation of Palenquero, which arose from contacts between colonial Spanish and Central African Bantu languages, most notably Kikongo (Hualde and Schwegler 2008). In Equatorial Guinean Spanish there is no ready explanation other than contact with lexical tone languages for the high proportion of early peak-aligned pretonic syllables combined with the comparatively high ratio of pitch-accented to potentially stressable syllables. In particular there is no clear motivation for early peak alignment as a "default strategy" when the L2 input has robust late peak alignment. This, however, does not preclude additional contributing factors, especially in view of the complex sociolinguistic and language contact situation in Equatorial Guinea. The precise circumstances under which Spanish was acquired in Equatorial Guinea are unknown, e.g., the relative contributions of spontaneous speech and classroom instruction present in the input, and the extent to which the input included the Spanish of other L2 Guinean speakers as well as Spaniards.

4.2 Tonal crowding and peak alignment

In many languages, among them Spanish, pitch accents occurring in close succession results in tonal crowding, including leftward displacement of H peaks (D'Imperio 2001; Henricksen 2012), F0 undershooting (Face 2002c), raising of the inter-peak L tones (Prieto 1998; Prieto and Shih 1995), and in some instances the suppression of a pitch accent (e.g., Levi 2002 for Turkish). In the case of Equatorial Guinean Spanish, given the shorter average expanses between tonal peaks as compared to Peninsular varieties, tonal crowding may contribute to the high rate of prenuclear early peak alignment, although in Madrid Spanish even the most extreme tonal crowding does not typically result in F0 peaks being pushed back within the boundaries of the tonic syllable (e.g., Face 2002c, 88–89). Any effect of tonal crowding is likely to be additive rather than catalytic. The relatively high number of prenuclear pitch accents per utterance—and the consequent tonal crowding—appear to result from an L1 in which lexical tones (i.e., F0 peaks and valleys) have syllable-internal anchoring points.

4.3 Possible phonologization of tone in Guinean Spanish

The data collected for the present study reveal that the Spanish of Equatorial Guinea as produced by native speakers of the lexical tone languages Fang and Bubi differs both quantitatively and qualitatively from the natively spoken Spanish of central Spain, the region that supplied most of the original input for Guinean Spanish. Male and female Equatorial Guineans' Spanish departs significantly from the Spanish of Madrid in terms of the ratio of actually occurring to potential pitch accents as well as the proportion of early-aligned pitch accents. In effect, Equatorial Guineans approach the target of one pitch accent for every lexically marked Spanish tonic syllable; by including F0 pitch accent-like peaks not associated with tonic syllables, this figure is actually reached. At the same time Guinean Spanish retains the two fundamental features normally associated with pitch-/stress-accent languages rather than lexical tone languages: obligatoriness and (usually) culminativity (each lexical word has one and only one syllable marked for prominence, i.e., pitch accent). There is no evidence that patrimonial Spanish words are consistently realized with more than one pitch accent. Another indication that pitch accents are becoming phonologized as lexical H tones would be tonal invariance for each word, i.e., not dependent on overall sentence intonational curves. This is demonstrably the case with Guinean place names used in Spanish such as Rebola (LHL), Malabo (LHL), Ureka (LHL), etc. and borrowings such as *balele* 'dance' (LHH) that retain their original tonal patterns, but also with words like *pichi* 'Pidgin English' < *pichinglis* (HH). Even patrimonial Spanish words approach tonal invariance in Guinean Spanish; unlike the varieties of Spain, in connected speech most Guinean Spanish words are pronounced with pitch accents corresponding to citation forms. This behavior is quite different from, for example, West African Englishes in contact with lexical tone languages. These contact varieties do not simply concatenate citation forms of English words, but rather have evolved innovative tonological patterns including high tone spreading, not found in Guinean Spanish. The reasons for the sharp discrepancy between Guinean and Peninsular Spanish (here exemplified by Madrid) are not entirely clear. Although in Peninsular Spanish polysyllabic words receive a pitch accent in citation forms, in connected speech the correspondence between lexical stress and H pitch accents is greatly diminished, as indicated in Table 1. Thus simple imitation of Spaniards' spontaneous speech is not likely to have been the primary source of Guineans' assignment of H pitch accents to nearly all lexically stressed syllables. For most Guineans, Spanish is learned principally in school and (until recently) was used mainly with non-Guineans. Citation forms as used in didactic classroom speech may have coalesced into retrievable exemplars around which Guineans attempted to reproduce Spanish prosodic patterns. For speakers of lexical tone languages such as Bubi and Fang, H tone placement is not optional or conditioned by discourse-level factors but rather is an integral part of each word's lexical specification. This same expectation, if extended to Spanish, would entail assigning a predictable and consistent tonal melody to each lexical item. The exemplar cloud for any Spanish lexical item pronounced by Peninsular speakers would contain both accent-less realizations as well as discernible pitch accents. The latter more closely resemble the syllable-anchored H and L tones of Guinean languages, and this salience might be sufficient to yield a "frozen" tonal pattern in connected Guinean Spanish.

In characterizing the autosegmental-metrical intonational model, Hualde (2002, 102) notes that "[…] in languages like English or Spanish only certain points in the utterance are phonologically specified for tone, the rest of the utterance being filled in by phonetic interpolation between tonally-specified points […] tonal events are associated with either stressed syllables or phrasal boundaries at the phonological level." While it is true that in Equatorial Guinean Spanish the majority of tonal events (H pitch accents) are associated with syllables marked for lexical stress, the overall density of pitch peaks (roughly every three syllables or less) suggests that rather than interpolation there is phonological alternation between H and L pitches. The regular retention of pitch accents on lexically stressed syllables together with the correspondingly lower pitch on surrounding syllables is consistent with emergent lexical tones, but further research is required before phonologization of pitch as lexical tone can be asserted for Equatorial Guinean Spanish.

4.4 Pitch accents in Guinean Spanish and H tones in Bubi and Fang

Speakers of a lexical tone language usually have no default phrase-level intonational templates (except for general tendencies such as downdrift). In addition to the homology PITCH/STRESS ACCENT ≡ HIGH TONE, whose acoustic cues are attenuated or effaced during connected speech, the only suprasegmental roadmap possessed by speakers of a lexical tone language may be an intuitive awareness of the stochastic distribution of High and Low tones in the native language. Table 1 shows that the overall density of F0 peaks in Equatorial Guinean Spanish (pitch accents aligned with tonic syllables as well as other pitch accent-like pitch rises) more closely approximates the ratio High tones/syllables found in the natively spoken lexical tone languages Fang and Bubi than the distribution of pitch accents in Peninsular Spanish. This distribution is consistent with statistical learning of probabalistic patterns in indigenous Guinean languages, including the acquisition of tonal configurations (e.g., Zamuner, Gerken, and Hammond 2005). At present this observation is merely speculative; future research may reveal demonstrable transfer of tonal distributional patterns to Spanish.

5. Conclusion

A preliminary analysis of Spanish as pronounced by speakers of two African tone languages has revealed partial convergence of a Romance-grounded pitch accent system and configurations based on lexically specified phonological tones. The naturalistic data collected for the present study do not present a clear picture of possible differences between broad and narrow focus pitch accents; given the tendency to early-align the F0 peaks of all pre-nuclear pitch accents, the most likely strategy for narrow focus would be an additional elevation of the relevant F0 peak (also employed in many African lexical tone languages: Zerbian et al. 2010). Post-focus compression (e.g., Xu et al. 2012) is another possibility: reduction of pitch range and intensity of post-focus elements. The realization of interrogatives in Guinean Spanish also bears further exploration; like Peninsular Spanish absolute interrogatives typically end in a rising tone while pronominal interrogatives do not always end in the expected L% boundary tone. Possible pre-final F0 rises in pronominal interrogatives are also worth examining. Controlled elicitation may shed additional light on the prosodic marking of information structure in Guinean Spanish. More detailed analysis of pitch accent contours in Guinean Spanish and comparison with lexical tone contours in Fang and Bubi (e.g., along the lines of Barnes et al. 2012) may reveal more subtle aspects of L1 transfer than has been revealed by counting F0 peaks and alignment patterns.

Equatorial Guineans' Spanish maintains the one stress per word culminativity but effectively expands obligatoriness by actually realizing a pitch accent on nearly every syllable lexically marked for stress. There is evidence that the acquisition and processing of lexical tone languages differs qualitatively from non-tonal languages (e.g., Harrison 2000; Mattock and Burnham 2006; Maye, Werker, and Gerken 2002; Saffran, Johnson, Aslin, and Newport 1999; Yeung, Chen, and Gerken 2013). Equatorial Guineans' incomplete suppression of natively acquired F0 patterns and expectations may be facilitated by the metrical structure of Spanish, which provides for regularly occurring pitch accents whose maximum potential density is similar to that of H tones in Bubi and Fang. Given the entry of Equatorial Guinea into the Francophone Central African economic zone and the teaching of French in Guinean schools it would be instructive to examine Guineans' acquisition of French, a language lacking the quasi-regular lexical stress patterns of Spanish. The further study of these language contact environments may contribute to the understanding of the role of typological interfaces in shaping the phonological evolution of Spanish.

References

Amayo, Airẹn. 1980. "Tone in Nigerian English." *Chicago Linguistic Society* 16: 1–9.

Bagshaw, Paul. 1993. "An Investigation of Acoustic Events Related to Sentential Stress and Pitch Accents in English." *Speech Communication* 13: 333–342.
DOI: 10.1016/0167-6393(93)90032-G

Barnes, Jonathan, Nanette Veilleux, Alejna Brugos, and Stefanie Shattuck-Hufnagel. 2010. "Tonal Center of Gravity: A Global Approach to Tonal Implementation in a Level-based Intonational Phonology." *Journal of Laboratory Phonology* 3: 337–383.

Barrera Vásquez, Alfredo. 1980. *Estudios lingüísticos.* Mérida: Fondo Editorial de Yucatán.

Beckman, Mary, Manuel Díaz-Campos, Julia Tevis McGory, and Terrell Morgan. 2002. "Intonation across Spanish, in the Tones and Break Indices Framework." *Probus* 14: 9–36.
DOI: 10.1515/prbs.2002.008

Bibang Oyee, Julián-B. 2002. *El español guineano: interferencias, guineanismo.* Malabo: n.p.

Bullock, Barbara. 2009. "Prosody in Contact in French: A Case Study from a Heritage Variety in the USA." *International Journal of Bilingualism* 13: 165–194. DOI: 10.1177/1367006909339817

Castillo Barril, Manuel. 1966. *La influencia de las lenguas nativas en el español de la Guinea Ecuatorial.* Madrid: Consejo Superior de Investigaciones Científicas.

Chen, Charles, Jr., and Ching-Pong Au. 2004. "Tone assignment in second language prosodic learning." Paper presented at Speech Prosody 2004, Nara, Japan (www.isca-speech.org/archive/sp2004/sp04_091.html)

Colantoni, Laura, and Jorge Gurlekian. 2004. "Convergence and Intonation: Historical Evidence from Buenos Aires Spanish." *Bilingualism: Language and Cognition* 7(2): 107–119.
DOI: 10.1017/S1366728904001488

Connell, Bruce. 2002. "Tone Languages and the Universality of Intrinsic F0: Evidence from Africa." *Journal of Phonetics* 30: 101–129. DOI: 10.1006/jpho.2001.0156

Connell, Bruce, and D. Robert Ladd. 1990. "Aspects of Pitch Realisation in Yoruba." *Phonology* 7: 1–29. DOI: 10.1017/S095267570000110X

D'Alessandro, Christophe, and Piet Mertens. 1995. "Automatic Pitch Contour Stylization Using a Model of Tonal Perception." *Computer Speech and Language* 9: 257–288. DOI: 10.1006/csla.1995.0013

Deterding, David. 1994. "The Intonation of Singapore English." *Journal of the International Phonetic Association* 24: 61–72. DOI: 10.1017/S0025100300005077

D'Imperio, Mariapaola. 2001. "Focus and Tonal Structure in Neapolitan Italian." *Speech Communication* 33: 339–356. DOI: 10.1016/S0167-6393(00)00064-9

Eady, Stephen. 1982. "Differences in the F_0 Patterns of Speech: Tone Language versus Stress Language." *Language and Speech* 25: 29–42.

Elordieta, Gorka. 2003. "The Spanish Intonation of Speakers of a Basque Pitch-accent Dialect." *Catalan Journal of Linguistics* 2: 67–95.

Elordieta, Gorka, and Nagore Calleja. 2005. "Microvariation in Accentual Alignment in Basque Spanish." *Language and Speech* 48: 397–439. DOI: 10.1177/00238309050480040401

Estebas-Vilaplana, Eva, and Pilar Prieto. 2008. "La notación prosódica del español: una revisión del Sp_ToBI." *Estudios de Fonética Experimental* 17: 265–283.

Estebas-Vilaplana, Eva, and Pilar Prieto. 2010. "Castilian Spanish Intonation." *Transcription of Intonation of the Spanish Language*: 17–48.

Face, Timothy. 2001. "Focus and Early Peak Alignment in Spanish Intonation." *Probus* 13: 223–246. DOI: 10.1515/prbs.2001.004

Face, Timothy. 2002a. "Local Intonational Marking of Spanish Contrastive Focus." *Probus* 14: 71–92. DOI: 10.1515/prbs.2002.006

Face, Timothy. 2002b. "Spanish Evidence for Pitch-accent Structure." *Linguistics* 40: 319–345. DOI: 10.1515/ling.2002.014

Face, Timothy. 2002c. "When Push Comes to Shove: Tonal Crowding in Madrid Spanish." *The Linguistic Association of Korean Journal* 10: 77–100.

Face, Timothy. 2003. "Intonation in Spanish Declaratives: Differences between Lab Speech and Spontaneous Speech." *Catalan Journal of Linguistics* 2: 115–131.

Face, Timothy, and Pilar Prieto. 2007. "Rising Accents in Castilian Spanish: A Revision of Sp_ToBI." *Journal of Portuguese Linguistics* 5(2): 1–32.

Gandour, Jackson. 2007. "Neutral Substrates Underlying the Perception of Linguistic Prosody." In *Tones and Tunes Volume 2: Experimental Studies in Word and Sentence Prosody,* ed. by Carlos Gussenhoven, and Tomas Riad, 3–25. Berlin: Mouton De Gruyter. DOI: 10.1515/9783110207576.1.3

Gauthier, Bruno, Rushen Shi, and Yi Xu. 2007. "Learning Phonetic Categories by Tracking Movements." *Cognition* 103: 80–106. DOI: 10.1016/j.cognition.2006.03.002

Gut, Ulrike. 2005. "Nigerian English Prosody." *English World-Wide* 26: 153–177. DOI: 10.1075/eww.26.2.03gut

Gut, Ulrike, and Jan-Torsten Milde. 2002. "The Prosody of Nigerian English." In *Proceedings of the Speech Prosody 2002 Conference,* ed. by Bernard Bel, and Isabel Marlien, 367–70. Aix-en-Provence: Laboratoire Parole et Langage.

Harris, James. 1983. *Syllable Structure and Stress in Spanish.* Cambridge, MA: MIT Press.

Harrison, Phil. 2000. "Acquiring the Phonology of Lexical Tone in Infancy." *Lingua* 110: 581–616. DOI: 10.1016/S0024-3841(00)00003-6

Herman, Rebecca. 1996. "Final Lowering in Kipare." *Phonology* 13: 171–196.
    DOI: 10.1017/S0952675700002098

Hermes, Dik. 2006. "Stylization of Pitch Contours." In *Methods in Empirical Prosody Research,*
    ed. by Stefan Sudhoff, Denisa Lenertová, Roland Meyer, Sandra Pappert, Petra Augurzky,
    Ina Mleinek, Nicole Richter, and Johannes Schließer., 29–61. Berlin and New York: Walter
    de Gruyter.

Hualde, José Ignacio. 2002. "Intonation in Spanish and the Other Ibero-Romance Languages:
    Overview and status quaestionis." In *Romance Phonology and Variation: Selected Papers
    from the* 30th *Linguistic Symposium on Romance Languages,* ed. by Caroline Wiltshire, and
    Joaquim Camps, 103–115. Amsterdam & Philadelphia: John Benjamins.
    DOI: 10.1075/cilt.217.10hua

Hualde, José Ignacio, and Armin Schwegler. 2008. "Intonation in Palenquero." *Journal of Pidgin
    and Creole Languages* 23: 1–31. DOI: 10.1075/jpcl.23.1.02hua

Hyman, Larry. 2006. "Word-prosodic Typology." *Phonology* 23: 225–257.
    DOI: 10.1017/S0952675706000893

Hyman, Larry. 2009. "How (Not) to Do Phonology: The Case of Pitch Accent." *Language Sciences* 31: 213–238. DOI: 10.1016/j.langsci.2008.12.007

Jowitt, David. 2000. "Patterns of Nigerian English Intonation." *English World Wide* 21: 63–80.
    DOI: 10.1075/eww.21.1.04jow

Kenstowicz, Michael. 2006. "Tone Loans: The Adaptation of English Loanwords into Yoruba."
    In *Selected Proceedings of the 35th Annual Conference on African Linguistics,* ed. by John
    Mugane et al., 136–146. Somerville, MA: Cascadilla Proceedings Project.

Levi, Susannah. 2002. "Limitations on Tonal Crowding in Turkish Intonation." *Proceedings of
    9th International Phonology Conference.*

Liberman, Mark, J. Michael Schultz, Soonhyun Hong, and Vincent Okeke. 1993. "The Phonetic
    Interpretation of Tone in Igbo." *Phonetica* 50: 147–160. DOI: 10.1159/000261935

Lim, Lisa. 2009. "Revisiting English Prosody: (Some) New Englishes as Tone Languages?" *English World-Wide* 30: 218–239. DOI: 10.1075/eww.30.2.06lim

Lipski, John. 1985. *The Spanish of Equatorial Guinea.* Tübingen: Max Niemeyer.
    DOI: 10.1515/9783111676890

Lipski, John. 1990. *El español de Malabo: procesos fonéticos/fonológicos e implicaciones dialec-
    tológicas.* Madrid/Malabo: Centro Cultural Hispano-Guineano.

Lipski, John. 2000. "The Spanish of Equatorial Guinea: Research on La Hispanidad's Best-kept
    Secret." *Afro-Hispanic Review* 19: 11–38.

Lipski, John. "2004. The Spanish of Equatorial Guinea." *Arizona Journal of Hispanic Cultural
    Studie/s* 8: 115–130. DOI: 10.1353/hcs.2011.0376

Lipski, John. 2005. *A History of Afro-Hispanic Language.* Cambridge: Cambridge University
    Press. DOI: 10.1017/CBO9780511627811

Lipski, John. 2008. "El español de Guinea Ecuatorial en el contexto del español mundial." In *La
    situación actual del español en África,* ed. by Gloria Nistal Rosique, and Guillermo Pié Jahn,
    79–117. Madrid: Casa de África/SIAL.

Lipski, John. 2014. "The Many Facets of Spanish Dialect Diversification in Latin America." In
    Iberian Imperialism and Language Evolution in Latin America, ed. by Salikoko Mufwene,
    38–75. Chicago: University of Chicago Press.

Llisteri, Joaquim, María Jesús Machuca, Carme de la Mota, Montserrat Riera, and Antonio Ríos.
    2002. "The Role of F0 Peaks in the Identification of Lexical Stress in Spanish." In *Phonetics*

and its Applications: Festschrift for Jens-Peter Köster on the Occasion of his 60th *birthday,* ed. by Angelika Braun, and Herbert Masthoff, 350–361. Stuttgart: Franz Steiner.

Llisteri, Joaquim, María Jesús Machuca, Carme de la Mota, Montserrat Riera, and Antonio Ríos.. 2003. "The Perception of Lexical Stress in Spanish." In *Proceedings of the* 15th *International Congress of Phonetic Sciences,* ed. by Maria Josep Solé, Daniel Recasens, and Joaquín Romero, 2023–2026. Barcelona: Causal Productions.

Malmberg, Bertil. 1950. *Etudes sur la phonétique de l'espagnol parlé en Argentine.* Lund: Alf Lombard.

Mattock, Karen, and Denis Burnham. 2006. "Chinese and English Infants' Tone Perception: Evidence for Perceptual Reorganization." *Infancy* 10: 241–265.
DOI: 10.1207/s15327078in1003_3

Maye, Jessica, Janet Werker, and LouAnn Gerken. 2002. "Infant Sensitivity to Distributional Information Can Affect Phonetic Discrimination." *Cognition* 82: B101-B111.
DOI: 10.1016/S0010-0277(01)00157-3

McGory, Julia Tevis, and Manuel Díaz-Campos. 2002. "Declarative Intonation Patterns in Multiple Varieties of Spanish." In *Structure, Meaning, and Acquisition of Spanish: Papers from the* 4th *Hispanic Linguistics Symposium,* ed. by James F. Lee, Kimberly L. Geeslin, and J. Clancy Clements, 73–92. Somerville, MA: Cascadilla Press.

Megenney, William. 1982. "Elementos subsaháricos en el español dominicano." *El español del Caribe,* ed. by Orlando Alba, 183-201. Santiago de los Caballeros: Universidad Católica Madre y Maestra.

Michnowicz, Jim, and Hillary Barnes. 2013. "A Sociolinguistic Analysis of Pre-nuclear Peak Alignment in Yucatan Spanish." In *Selected Proceedings of the* 15th *Hispanic Linguistics Symposium,* ed. by Chad Howe, Sarah Blackwell, and Margaret Lubbers Quesada, 221–235. Somerville, MA: Cascadilla Proceedings Project. www.lingref.com, document #2887.

Morton, Thomas. 2005. *Sociolinguistic variation and language change in El Palenque de San Basilio (Colombia).* Ph. D. dissertation, University of Pennsylvania.

Myers, Scott. 1998. "Underspecification of Tone in Chichewa." *Phonology* 15: 367–391.
DOI: 10.1017/S0952675799003620

Odden, David. 1999. "Typological Issues in Tone and Stress in Bantu." In *Proceedings of the Symposium Cross-linguistic Studies of Tonal Phenomena Tonogenesis, Typology, and Related Topics,* ed. by Shigeki Kaji, 187–215. Tokyo: Institute for the Study of Languages and Cultures of Asia and Africa, Tokyo University of Foreign Studies.

Ọdẹ́lọbí, Ọdẹ́tunjí Àjàdí. 2008. "Recognition of Tones in Yorùbá Speech: Experiments with Artificial Neural Networks." *Speech, Audio, Image and Biomedical Signal Processing Using Neural Networks,* ed. by Bhanu Prasad and S. R. M. Prasanna, 23–47. Berlin: Springer.
DOI: 10.1007/978-3-540-75398-8_2

O'Rourke, Erin. 2004. "Peak Placement in Two Regional Varieties of Peruvian Spanish Intonation." In *Contemporary Approaches to Romance Linguistics (LSRL 33),* ed. by Julie Auger, J. Clancy Clements, and Barbara Vance, 321–341. Amsterdam & Philadelphia: John Benjamins. DOI: 10.1075/cilt.258.17oro

O'Rourke, Erin. 2005. *Intonation and Language Contact: A Case Study of Two Varieties of Peruvian Spanish.* Ph. D. dissertation, University of Illinois Urbana-Champaign.

Ortega-Llebaria, Marta. 2006. "Phonetic Cues to Stress and Accent in Spanish." In *Selected Proceedings of the 2nd Conference on Laboratory Approaches to Spanish Phonetics and*

Phonology, ed. by Manuel Díaz-Campos, 104–118. Somerville, MA: Cascadilla Proceedings Project. www.lingref.com, document #1329.

Ortega-Llebaria, Marta, and Pilar Prieto. 2007. "Disentangling Stress from Accent in Spanish: Production Patterns of the Stress Contrast in De-accented Syllables." In *Segmental and Prosodic Issues in Romance Phonology*, ed. by Pilar Prieto, Joan Mascaró, 155–176. Amsterdam & Philadelphia: John Benjamins. DOI: 10.1075/cilt.282.11ort

Ortega-Llebaria, Marta, Pilar Prieto, and María del Mar Vanrell. 2007. "Perceptual Evidence for Direct Acoustic Correlates of Stress in Spanish." *Proceedings of the XVIth International Congress of Phonetic Sciences*, 1121–1124.

Prieto, Pilar. 1998. "The Scaling of the L Tone Line in Spanish Downstepping Contours." *Journal of Phonetics* 26: 261–282. DOI: 10.1006/jpho.1998.0074

Prieto, Pilar, Mariapaola D'Imperio, Gorka Elordieta, Sónia Frota, and Marina Vigário. 2006. "Evidence for *Soft* Preplanning in Tonal Production: Initial Scaling in Romance." *Proceedings of Speech Prosody 2006*, 803–896.

Prieto, Pilar, and Paolo Roseano (eds,). 2010. *Transcription of intonation of the Spanish language*. München: Lincom Europa.

Prieto, Pilar, and Chilin Shih. 1995. "Effects of Tonal Clash on Downstepped H* Accents in Spanish." *Proceedings of EUROSPEECH'95 Fourth EUropean Conference on Speech Communication and Technology* (Vol. 2, pp. 1307–1310).

Prieto, Pilar, Chilin Shih, and Holly Nibert. 1996. "Pitch downtrend in Spanish." *Journal of Phonetics* 24: 445–473. DOI: 10.1006/jpho.1996.0024

Prieto, Pilar, Jan van Santen, and Julia Hirschberg. 1995. "Tonal Alignment Patterns in Spanish." *Journal of Phonetics* 23: 429–451. DOI: 10.1006/jpho.1995.0032

Qian, Yao, Tan Lee, and Frank K. Soong. 2007. "Tone Recognition in Continuous Cantonese Speech Using Supratone Models." *The Journal of the Acoustical Society of America* 121: 2936–2945. DOI: 10.1121/1.2717413

Quilis, Antonio, and Celia Casado-Fresnillo. 1995. *La lengua española en Guinea Ecuatorial*. Madrid: Universidad Nacional de Educación a Distancia.

Saffran, Jenny, Elizabeth Johnson, Richard Aslin, and Elissa Newport. 1999. "Statistical Learning of Tone Sequences by Human Infants and Adults." *Cognition* 70: 27–52. DOI: 10.1016/S0010-0277(98)00075-4

Scheffers, Michael T. M. 1988. "Automatic Stylization of F0 Contours." In *Proceedings of Speech '88*, ed. by W. A. Ainsworth, and J. N. Holmes, 981–987. Edinburgh: Institute of Acoustics.

Simonet, Miquel. 2008. *Language Contact in Majorca: An Experimental Sociophonetic Approach*. Ph. D. dissertation, University of Illinois at Urbana-Champaign.

Simonet, Miquel. 2010. "A Contrastive Study of Catalan and Spanish Declarative Intonation: Focus on Majorcan Dialects." *Probus* 22: 117–148. DOI: 10.1515/prbs.2010.004

Simonet, Miquel. 2011. "Intonational Convergence in Language Contact: Utterance-final F0 Contours in Catalan-Spanish Early Bilinguals." *Journal of the International Phonetic Association* 41: 157–184. DOI: 10.1017/S0025100311000120

Sosa, Juan. 1999. *La entonación del español*. Madrid: Cátedra.

Suárez, Víctor. 1980. *El español que se habla en Yucatán*. Mérida: Universidad de Yucatán.

Taylor, Paul. 1992. "The Rise/Fall/Connection Model of Intonation." *Speech Communication* 15: 169–186. DOI: 10.1016/0167-6393(94)90050-7

Taylor, Paul. 2000. "Analysis and Synthesis of Intonation Using the Tilt Model." *Journal of the Acoustical Society of America* 107.1697–1714. DOI: 10.1121/1.428453

Wee, Lian-Hee. 2008. "Phonological Patterns in the Englishes of Singapore and Hong Kong." *World Englishes* 27: 580–501. DOI: 10.1111/j.1467-971X.2008.00580.x

Xu, Yi. "Effects of tone and focus on the formation and alignment of f_0 contours." *Journal of Phonetics* 27: 55–105. DOI: 10.1006/jpho.1999.0086

Xu, Yi, Szu-wei Chen, and Bei Wang. 2012. "Prosodic Focus with and without Post-focus Compression: A Typological Divide within the Same Language family?" *The Linguistic Review* 29: 131–147. DOI: 10.1515/tlr-2012-0006

Yeung, H. Henry, Ke Heng Chen, and Janet Werker. 2013. "When Does Native Language Input Affect Phonetic Perception? The Precocious Case of Lexical Tone." *Journal of Memory and Language* 68: 123–139. DOI: 10.1016/j.jml.2012.09.004

Yip, Moira. 2002. *Tone.* Cambridge: Cambridge University Press. DOI: 10.1017/CBO9781139164559

Yu, Kristine. 2010. "Representational Maps from the Speech Signal to Phonological Categories: A Case Study with Lexical Tones." *UCLA Working Papers in Linguistics* 15: 1–30. DOI: 10.5089/9781455202218.001

Zamuner, Tania, LouAnn Gerken, and Michael Hammond. 2005. "The Acquisition of Phonology Based on Input: A Closer Look at the Relation of Cross-linguistic and Child Language data." *Lingua* 115: 1403–1426. DOI: 10.1016/j.lingua.2004.06.005

Zerbian, Sabine, Susanne Genzel, and Frank Kügler. 2010. "Experimental Work on Prosodically-marked Information Structure in Selected African Languages (Afroasiatic and Niger-Congo)." *Proceedings of Speech Prosody 2010,* 1–4.

Zhang, Jinsong, and Keikichi Hirose. 2004. "Tone nucleus modeling for Chinese lexical tone recognition." *Speech Communication* 42: 447–466. DOI: 10.1016/j.specom.2004.01.001

On null objects and ellipses in Brazilian Portuguese*

Ruth E. V. Lopes & Sonia M. L. Cyrino
University of Campinas

Brazilian Portuguese (BP) is known to license anaphoric null objects (ANO), that is, null objects with a linguistic antecedent. It also licenses VP ellipsis (VPE), with auxiliaries, modals and main verbs, the latter a case of V-stranding VPE (V-VPE), the one with which we will be concerned. Although ANOs and V-VPE may have identical surface strings in BP, we propose that they do not have the same structure. To achieve that we examine the properties of the ANOs and compare them to V-VPE, arguing the first are cases of DP ellipsis. We present evidence for an analysis of the ANO as a base-generated empty phrase-marker that will be reconstructed in LF. We also propose that ANOs and VPE are licensed by a lexicalized aspectual head, as a consequence of the loss of generalized verb movement in BP.

1. Introduction

It is well known that Brazilian Portuguese (BP) is a null-object language:

(1) *Minha avó   fez   [sushis] porque seus filhos   queriam*
     My   grandmother made   sushi   because her children wanted

     continuar   comendo ___ depois que voltaram   da   praia.
     continue-INF eating   ___ after   that came.back from-the beach

     'My grandmother made sushi because her children wanted to keep on eating them after they came back from the beach.'

---

* Part of this research was funded by Conselho Nacional de Desenvolvimento Científico e Tecnológico (CNPq), grants #306682/2011–9 and 303006/2009–9, for each author, respectively, and FAPESP 2012/06078–9 for the second author. We thank the audience at the 43rd LSRL for their comments and suggestions as well as the generous suggestions of two anonymous reviewers. The usual disclaimer applies.

DOI 10.1075/rllt.9.14lop

(2) *Cê   tem   que   lavar   ___   antes   de   por ___.*
     You   have   that   wash-INF   ___   before   of   put-INF
     'You have to wash it before you pour it.' (talking about the rice that is being poured into the pan)

The first example illustrates the use of a null object (NO) with a linguistic anteced-ent, which we will refer to as anaphoric null objects (ANO). In this example, the DP [sushis] is recovered as the object of 'eating'. In the second example, there is a case of a pragmatically or deictically controlled NO. Our interest in this paper will be limited to the ANO cases.

The language also licenses VP ellipsis (VPE) with auxiliaries (3a), copulative verbs (3b), and main verbs (3c).

(3) a. *A   Ana   já   tinha   lido   o   livro   pra   irmã   mas   a*
         the   Ana   already   had   read   the   book   to.the   sister   but   the

         Paula   não   tinha ___.
         Paula   not   had ___

         'Ana had already read the book to her sister but Paula had not.'

     b. *O   João   é   simpático   para   todas   as   pessoas   e   a   Ana*
         the   João   is   nice   for   all   the   people   and   the   Ana

         também   é ___.
         too   is ___

         'João is nice to everybody and Ana is, too.'

     c. *A   Ana   não   leva   o   computador   para   as   aulas,*
         the   Ana   not   brings   the   computer   to   the   classes,

         porque   os   amigos   também   não   levam ___.
         because   the   friends   too   not   bring ___

         'Ana does not bring her computer to classes because her friends don't either.'

(3c) is a case of V-stranding VPE (V-VPE), the one which will concern us here.
Sometimes ANOs and V-VPE have identical surface strings in the language:

(4) *A   Ana   comprou   um   vestido   azul   e   a   Maria   também*
     the   Ana   bought   a   dress   blue   and   the   Maria   too

     comprou ___.
     bought ___

     'Ana bought a blue dress and Maria did too.'

However, we will propose that they are not the same structure. In other words, according to our proposal, BP has both ANO (5a) and V-VPE (5b) structures, irrelevant details not represented here:

(5) a. ... e [$_{TP}$ [A Maria] T [$_{AspP}$ comprou$_i$ [$_{VP}$ t$_i$ [$_{DP}$ um vestido azul]]]]
     b. ... e [$_{TP}$ [A Maria] T [$_{AspP}$ comprou$_i$ [$_{VP}$ t$_i$ [$_{DP}$ um vestido azul]]]]

Our aim in this paper is to examine the properties of the ANOs in BP and compare them to V-VPE, arguing that ANOs are cases of ellipsis as well, just not VPE, but rather, a case of DP ellipsis.

The chapter is organized as follows: in Section 2, we present the properties of ANOs in BP. In Section 3, we present the V-VPE structure in Portuguese, showing the differences between Brazilian and European Portuguese (EP). Sections 4 and 5 are devoted to exploring the null object in BP and arguing that it is a case of DP ellipsis. In Section 6, we present evidence for an analysis of the null object as a base-generated empty phrase-marker that will be reconstructed in LF. We conclude the paper with the observation that our proposal that an aspectual head has to be lexically filled to license null objects as ellipsis in BP seems to be on the right track, considering that ANOs do not occur in the absence of AspP.

2. Properties of the ANOs in BP

Unfortunately, the term "null object" has a broad use encompassing a large range of distinct properties in different languages. For that reason, we will examine the properties of the ANOs in the language, in order to unveil them.

Raposo (1986), inspired by Huang's (1984) seminal work on empty categories in Chinese, showed that EP licenses null objects as well, but precludes them from occurring inside islands, which led the author to analyze them as variables:

(6) *O   rapaz que   trouxe   ___ agora mesmo da   pastelaria
     the boy   that brought-3SG ___ now   just   of.the pastry.shop
     era teu   afilhado.
     was your godson
     'The boy that brought it just now from the pastry shop was your godson.'
                                                                    (Raposo 1986)

However, as seen in (1), and considering (6) is grammatical in BP, ANOs seem to freely occur within islands in such a variety.

They also allow strict or sloppy readings; therefore, in (7), below, *Pedro* could have kept his own money or *João's* money in the drawer:[1]

(7)   *Ontem   o   João pôs   seu   dinheiro no   cofre, mas Pedro guardou*
       yesterday the   João put   his   money   in.the safe   but Pedro kept

       ___ *na   gaveta.*
       in.the drawer

       'Yesterday, João put his money in the safe, but Pedro kept it in the drawer.'

Nevertheless, there are two restrictions for the ANOs in BP. The first one is an animacy restriction: ANOs antecedents have to be inanimate, unless they are not specific. Such a restriction seems to apply to Hebrew as well, according to Goldberg (2005):

(8)   **O   Pedro abraçou os   pais,   mas o   João beijou ___.*[2]
       the Pedro hugged   his   parents but the João kissed
       'Pedro hugged his parents but John kissed them.'

---

1.   It is interesting to note that third person clitics—when they exist in a language—may allow strict and sloppy readings (see Cyrino 2013c):

(i)   En Pere estima la   seva   mare   i   en Joan també
       the Pere loves   the poss.3 mother and the Joan also

       l'estima.   [Catalan]
       CL.FEM.3 loves

       'Pere loves his mother and Joan loves her too.' [Quer & Rosselló 2013: 357, ex. (40)]

According to the authors, there are two readings for (i): Joan loves Pere's mother (strict reading) or her own mother (sloppy reading).

In fact, Cyrino (1994/1997) assumes the neuter clitic *o*, in (ii), can also be thought of as reconstruction at LF because it allows strict/sloppy readings in European and Old Brazilian Portuguese.

(ii)   *Pedro pediu à   diretora   para ser o   professor da   turma A antes*
       Pedro asked to.the directors to   be the teacher of.the class A before

       de Jane o solicitar ao   governador.
       of Jane it solicit   to.the governor

       'Pedro asked the directors to be the teacher of class A before Jane solicited it to the governor.'

(ii) is also ambiguous: Jane asked the governor for Pedro to be the teacher of class A (strict reading), or she asked the governor for herself to be the teacher of class A (sloppy reading). Note that there is a gender mismatch that has to be reconstructed in LF in the second case.

2.   This is an example from Costa, Lobo, and Silva (2010). According to the authors it is grammatical in EP.

(9) *Rina hisi'a et Gil ha-'ira ve-horida ___ le-yad ha-bayit.*
Rina drove ACC Gil the-town and-dropped to-near the-house
'Rina drove Gil to town and dropped him near his home.'

(Goldberg 2005)

The second one is the fact that they cannot take the matrix subject as an antecedent (10), differently from Japanese (Ohara n/d) or Korean (Kim 1999), for instance.

(10) *$*O$ governador$_i$ disse que o deputado desrespeitou*
the governor said that the congressman disrespected

___ $_i$ *na convenção*
in-the caucus

'The governor said that the congressman disrespected him during the caucus.'

It could be argued that this restriction is a mere effect of the animacy one, but we will see below that it hinges on the fact that the antecedent for the ANO has to be in a complement position originally. This can be seen in (11):

(11) *A alface$_i$ murchou t$_i$ por isso os meninos não iam comer ___*
the lettuce wilted for that the boys not go eat-INF
'The lettuce wilted therefore the boys didn't want to have it.'

A last point worth mentioning is the fact that even with verbs that could get an intransitive interpretation, as cases of 'cognate complements', the favored reading in BP is always the ANO one ((12), but see also (1) and (11)), unless the sentence is somehow marked otherwise. In other words, if a linguistic antecedent is available, it will be computed for interpretive reasons:

(12) *Eu comecei a ler contos depois que o Pedro parou*
I started prep read-INF short.stories after that the Pedro quit

de ler ___.
prep read-INF

'I started reading short stories after Pedro quit reading them.'

Summing up, then, ANOs in BP have the following properties, illustrated in (13): they present strict and sloppy readings; they have inanimate antecedents; they occur in islands; and they cannot have an external argument as antecedent.[3]

---

3. One of the reviewers wondered whether the ambiguity had to do with the presence of the locatives. It does not seem to be the case. They are used in the examples as a means to tease the ANO construction apart from the V-VPE one.

(13)   *João pôs seu carro na   garagem depois que o   Pedro*
       João put his car in.the garage   after   that the Pedro

       deixou ___ na rua.
       left   in-the street

       'João parked his car in the garage after Pedro parked it in the street.'

Once again, Pedro would have parked his own car in the street or João's.

We will turn to the V-stranding VPE cases now before we can go back again to the ANO ones.

3. VP Ellipsis in Portuguese

We will explore V-VPE again once we want to show that the ANOs in BP share some of the properties found in VP ellipsis, which, as we will also see below, motivates us to propose that they are cases of ellipsis as well, just not VP ellipsis.

Both Brazilian and European Portuguese, differently from other Romance languages, license V-VPE (cf. Matos 1992; Cyrino and Matos 2002, 2005; Rouveret 2012, a.o.):

(14)   *Ninguém leu   esse livro nem admitia   que alguém   lesse ___.*
       no one   read that book nor admitted that someone read
       'No one had read that book nor admitted that someone had.'

Since there is verb movement in Portuguese, it is usually proposed that the main verb leaves vP and licenses the ellipsis from a higher functional projection. However, BP differs from EP with respect to VPE. As shown by Cyrino and Matos (2002, 2005), elided sequences receive different interpretations in these varieties. While in BP, (15) is interpreted as a case of VPE, in EP it is preferably interpreted as a sentence with an intransitive verb (i.e., he is not reading anything):[4]

(15)   *A   Maria está lendo   livros pras   crianças mas o   João não*
       the Maria is   reading books to.the children but the João not

       está lendo ___.
       is   reading

       'Maria is reading books to the children but João is not.'

---

4.   The form of the periphrasis in EP is *está a ler* (lit. 'is prep read-inf'). It is important to point out that infinitives in prepositional environments still trigger VPE in BP as can be seen in example (12).

The authors propose that the differences between EP and BP are due to the fact that VPE is licensed by the verb in different functional projections: in T in EP, and in AspP in BP. So, while (16) preserves the VPE reading in both varieties, (17) only does it in BP. As can be seen, the focal adverb *também* 'too' is lower in (17), adjoined to the aspectual category:

(16)   *Ela tem lido livros às crianças e ele **também** tem lido ___*
       she has read books to-the children and he too has read
       'She has read books to the children and he has too.'

                                                    (Cyrino and Matos 2002)

(17)   *Ela tem lido livros às crianças e ele tem **também** lido ___*
       she has read books to-the children and he has too read
       'She has read books to the children and he has too.'

Another piece of evidence for this difference comes from the adverb *sempre* 'always'. In EP *sempre* can have a non-temporal (confirmation of state of affairs) interpretation when it occurs in preverbal position—in this case it means 'indeed'. In postverbal position, it has the aspectual ('always') interpretation.

According to Brito (1999, 2001), Ambar, Gonzaga, and Negrão (2004), Gonzaga (1997), and Fiéis (2010), *sempre* as 'always' is a low adverb (i.e., adjoined to AspP), while *sempre* as 'indeed' is a high, IP-related confirmation adverb, in which case it is above TP in EP. In BP, the only possible reading for the adverb *sempre* 'always' is the aspectual reading. This fact indicates that the verb can move only as high as Asp (cf. also Cyrino 2013a, and on the absence of long verb movement in BP, see Galves 1990, 1994). (18b) represents the aspectual reading of the adverb, possible in BP, while (18c) represents the confirmative one possible only for EP, as pointed out above:

(18)   a.   *O João __sempre__   comia   batatas*
            the João always [BP/indeed (EP)] EAT.IMPERF.3SG potatoes

            no   almoço.
            in.the lunch

            'After all, João ate potatoes at lunch.'

       b. $[_{AspP}$ sempre $[_{AspP}$ comia$[_{vP}$ <comia> ...

       c. $[_{TP}$ sempre $[_{TP}$ comia $[_{AspP}$<comia> $[_{vP}$ <comia> ...

It seems, therefore, that the relevant category to license V-VPE in BP is the aspectual one, a proposal we will extend to the ANOs as well.

4.   Back to null objects in BP

Having shown that BP is a null object language, the next natural question is what is the status of the null category.

It cannot be a variable, as proposed by Raposo (1986) for EP, after Huang (1984) for Chinese, since in BP ANOs occur in islands as previously seen.

Galves (1989) and Farrell (1990), among many others, have proposed that it is a *pro*. However, if that were the case, a similar behavior is to be expected between a null object structure and its pronominal counterpart, a prediction not borne out, especially when ANO sentences which are ambiguous between a strict and a sloppy reading are examined, as will be seen in the next section. But apart from that, we have also seen that ANOs cannot have a matrix subject as antecedent. However, an overt pronoun is fine in such environments. We will repeat (10) as (19a) below to be compared with (19b) with the overt pronoun, a case easily explained by Principle B:

(19)   a.   *O   governador$_i$ disse   que   o   deputado   desrespeitou
            the governor   said   that the congressman disrespected

            ___$_i$ na   convenção
                   in.the caucus

            'The governor said that the congressman disrespected him during the caucus.'

       b.   O   governador$_i$ disse   que   o   deputado   desrespeitou   ele$_i$
            the governor   said   that the congressman disrespected   him

            na   convenção
            in.the caucus

            'The governor said that the congressman disrespected him during the caucus.'

These, and other arguments to come shortly, lead us to argue that the ANOs in BP are, in fact, a case of ellipsis. Some similar proposals have been made with respect to East-Asian languages (cf. Huang 1991; Oku 1998; Saito 2007; Takahashi 2008, 2010, among others), but we will not explore these approaches in this paper, since we assume there are other specific properties that apply to BP, but not to the other languages (see Cyrino 2011, 2013b).

5.   Null objects as ellipsis

5.1   Similarities between V-VPE and ANO

First, just as in V-VPE, the ANO in BP allows strict and sloppy readings ((20) and (22)), but notice that once an overt pronoun ((21) and (23)) is used, the sloppy reading is out, which argues against the *pro* analysis, as just pointed out.

(20) *Ontem   o   João pôs o   anel no   cofre, mas Pedro guardou*
     yesterday the João put the ring in.the safe   but Pedro kept

   _____ *na   gaveta*
         in.the drawer

   'Yesterday João put the ring in the safe, but Pedro kept it in the drawer.'

   a.   Pedro kept João's ring (strict)

   b.   Pedro kept his own ring (sloppy)

(21) *Ontem   o   João pôs o   anel no   cofre, mas Pedro guardou ele*
     yesterday the João put the ring in.the safe   but Pedro kept   it

   na   gaveta.
   in.the drawer

   'Yesterday João put the ring in the safe, but Pedro kept it in the drawer.'

   a.   Pedro kept João's ring (strict)

(22) *O   João devolveu o   livro em bom   estado   e   a   Maria*
     the João returned the book   in good condition and the Maria

   devolveu _____ estragado.
   returned   damaged

   'João returned his book in good condition and Maria returned it in bad shape.'

   a.   one and the same book

   b.   different books

(23) *O   João devolveu o   livro em bom   estado   e   a   Maria*
     the João returned the book   in good condition and the Maria

   devolveu ele estragado.
   returned it   damaged

   'João returned his book in good condition and Maria returned it in bad shape.'

   a.   one and the same book

In as much as strict/sloppy reading availability is controversial as a diagnostic test for ellipsis (see Merchant 2013), it at least seems to show that there is no parallelism between the null option and the overt pronoun option, arguing, therefore, against a *pro* analysis. In any event, controversial or not, they argue for a reconstruction effect in Logical Form (LF), a road we will take shortly.

In the second place, the ANOs in BP can only occur in parallel structures. Fiengo and May (1994) propose that ellipses are subject to a more general principle at LF, namely 'reconstruction', that is, a set of token structures, occurrences of a (sub) phrase marker in a discourse, over a given terminal vocabulary. The members of the reconstruction may or may not be (phonologically) explicit. Reconstruction is then an identity condition: it renders explicit which occurrences are the same in a phrase marker. For the reconstruction to be possible it is necessary that the members of the reconstruction preserve the grammatical category and linear relations and dominance within the grammatical category, that is, that all the occurrences are structurally composed in the same way. In other words, there is a parallelism requirement for reconstruction and ellipsis.

We have already seen that a subject cannot be the antecedent of the null object (10), repeated here as (24). We assume this is the effect of the parallelism requirement on ellipsis:

(24)   *O   governador$_i$ disse   que   o   deputado   desrespeitou
       the   governor   said   that   the   congressman   disrespected

       ___$_i$ na   convenção
              in.the   caucus

       'The governor said that the congressman disrespected him during the caucus.'

Chung (2013), among others, has claimed that the identity between the antecedent and the ellipsis site is not only semantic but also syntactic in nature; therefore, argument structure and case have to be identical. That is also the case in BP:

(25)   a.   *João   chutou   o   balde   mas   o   Pedro   bateu.
            John   kicked   the   bucket   but   the   Pedro   hit.
            'John kicked the bucket but Pedro hit it.'

       b.   João   chutou   o   balde   mas   o   Pedro   bateu   nele.
            John   kicked   the   bucket   but   the   Pedro   hit   prep-it.
            'John kicked the bucket but Pedro hit it.'

The verb *chutar* 'kick' is an accusative verb, while *bater* 'hit' is a dative one. Again, the overt pronoun saves the structure, since in order to have an overt pronoun the preposition also has to be spelled out.

In the literature on null objects in BP, the parallelism requirement has not been thoroughly explored. Bianchi and Figueiredo Silva (1994) and Ferreira (2000), for instance, point out that the following sentences are examples of animacy restrictions for the ANO in BP:[5]

---

5.   For Bianchi and Figueiredo Silva the ANO with an animate interpretation is treated as a variable, subject to Principle C, and therefore it cannot be coindexed with any argument that c-commands it (as in 26a); however, based on (26b), they assume that an inanimate ANO is a *pro*. Ferreira (2000), on the other hand, claims that ANOs in BP may be A-bound by [−human] DPs, but not by [+human] DPs.

(26) a. *O José_i impediu a esposa de matar ____i

      the José prevented the wife of kill-INF

      'José prevented his wife from killing him.'

  b. *Este tipo de garrafa_I impede as crianças de*

      this kind of bottle prevents the kids of

      abrirem ____i sozinhas

      open-inf-3PPL alone

      'This kind of bottle prevents kids from opening it on their own.'

                         (Bianchi and Figueiredo Silva 1994, 187)

(27) a. *Esse artista_i decepcionou as pessoas que*

      this actor disappointed the people who

      tentaram cumprimentar ____i

      tried to greet

      'This actor disappointed those who tried to greet him.'

  b. *Esse livro_i decepcionou as pessoas que tentaram ler ____i*

      this book disappointed the people who tried to read

      'This book disappointed those who tried to read it. (Ferreira 2000, 63)

Notice that the contrasts seen in (26) and (27) could be taken as counterevidence to the parallelism requirement we have just shown above. In both examples, the antecedent of the null object seems to be the subject of the matrix clause.

However, it has to be taken into account that the inanimate antecedents in these examples are cases of non-agentive subjects, which might as well be in a different argument structure. The following tests can be used as diagnostics for the non-agentive character of these subjects.

First, we can see a clear difference between examples (28) and (29). Only the answer in (28b) is felicitous in reply to a question that refers to an event involving an agent (28a). Notice that an inanimate subject, like the one in the example (26b) and (27b) is impossible even in the diagnostic question in (29):

(28) a. *O que o José aprontou? O que o artista aprontou?*

      what the José made-ready? what the artist made ready?

      'What was José up to?' 'What was the artist up to?'

  b. *O José impediu a esposa de matar ele. / O artista*

      the José prevented the wife of kill-inf him / the actor

      decepcionou as pessoas que tentaram cumprimentar ele.

      disappointed the people who tried to greet him

      'José prevented his wife from killing him.'/'This actor disappointed those who tried to greet him.'

(29) *O que esse tipo de garrafa apronta? *O que esse livro aprontou?*

    'What is this kind of bottle up to?' 'What was that book up to?'

Second, if we look at the possibility of forming long passives, which require the presence of an agent, we see again that only (30a) is well-formed:

(30) a. *A   esposa foi   impedida por José de matar   ele*
          the   wife   was   prevented by José of kill-INF him
          'His wife was prevented from killing him.'

      b. **As crianças foram impedidas por esse tipo de garrafa de*
          the children were   prevented by this kind of bottle   of

          abrirem ___ sozinhas.
          open-INF-3PPL alone

Likewise, if we try to contrast long (agentive) passives (31a)–(32a) with adjectival (non-agentive) passives (31b)–(32b), again, inanimate subjects are banned with agentive verbal passives (32a):

(31) a. *As pessoas que tentaram cumprimentar o   artista foram*
          the people who tried   to greet   the actor were

          decepcionadas por ele.
          disappointed by him

      b. *As pessoas que tentaram cumprimentar o   artista ficaram*
          the people who tried   to greet   the actor became

          decepcionadas com ele.
          disappointed   with him
          'People who tried to greet the actor were dissapointed by him.'

(32) a. **As pessoas que tentaram ler   esse livro foram*
          the people who tried   to read this book were

          decepcionadas por ele.
          disappointed by it

      b. *As pessoas que tentaram ler   esse livro ficaram*
          the people who tried   to read this book became

          decepcionadas com ele.
          disappointed   with it
          'People who tried to read this book were dissapointed by it.'

Causative alternations can be used as yet another test. (33a) is ungrammatical because the antecedent of the null object is the matrix subject, violating the parallelism requirement. In contrast, (33b) is grammatical because the antecedent of the null object was originally merged as the internal argument of *desligar* 'turn off':

(33) a. **João$_i$ desligou o   carrinho$_j$ antes de ele$_j$ atropelar ___$_i$*
          João   turned off the car-dim   before of it   hit-INF
          'João turned the little car off before it hit him.'

b. *O   carrinho$_i$ desligou t$_i$ antes   de a   Maria   pegar* ____$_i$
    the   car-dim   turned   off before of the Maria   catch
    'The car turned off before Maria caught it.'

The essential property seems to be the original position of the antecedent of the null
object. Crucially, if the antecedent is originally a complement, even if it raises to the
subject position, as is the case with unaccusative verbs (34), the animacy restriction
may be overridden. Therefore, merely looking at the superficial matrix position for
the animate subject antecedent for the null object may be misleading since it is just an
effect of movement:

(34) a. *João$_i$ desapareceu t$_i$ e   a   Maria não consegue achar* ____$_i$
          João   disappeared   and the Mary   not able   find-INF
          'João disappeared and Mary can't find him.'

      b. *O   livro$_i$ desapareceu t$_i$ e   a   Maria não consegue achar* ____$_i$
          the book   disappeared   and the Mary   not able   find-INF
          'The book disappeared and Mary can't find it.'

Summing up, the position of the antecedent in the argument structure seems to be
relevant for the parallelism requirement on the occurrence of null objects in BP, as
shown by the tests above.

Besides that, it is also interesting to note that languages that allow the matrix subject
as an antecedent for null objects tend to exhibit three different interpretations in such
contexts, the sloppy, the strict, and one in which the subject is interpreted as the antecedent, as illustrated in the Korean example in (35), a possibility which is not available in BP:

(35) *Mike-ka   [caki-uy ai]-lul   ttayli-ess-ta   kuleca Jeanne-to*
      Mike-nom   self-gen child-ACC   hit-PAST-IND   then   Jeanne-also,

      ttohan ____ *ttayli-ess-ta*
      too   hit-PAST-IND

      'Mike hit his child, then Jeanne hit him too.'   (Kim 1999, 265)

      a. ... and then Jeanne hit her (Jeanne's) child, too
      b. ... and then Jeanne hit his (Mike's) child, too
      c. ... and then Jeanne hit Mike, too

However, once again, a structure such as (35) could be saved by an overt pronoun in BP
(36), and, again, several of the effects we have been discussing can be entertained—the
sloppy reading, for example, will disappear. Non-local binding between the overt pronoun and the matrix subject becomes available, rendering only the (b) and (c) readings:

(36) *O   João$_i$ agrediu o   filho$_j$ e   daí   a   Ana também*
      the João   strike   his child   and then the Ana too

      agrediu ele$_{i/j}$.
      strike   him

      'John hit his child and then Ana hit him too.'

a.   ...*e a Ana agrediu o filho da Ana.
b.   ... e a Ana agrediu o filho do João.
c.   ... e a Ana agrediu o João.

Yet another similar property between ANOs and V-VPE in BP is the fact that both can occur in islands, as previously pointed out:

(37) *Pedro comprou o   livro na   FNAC depois que*
      Pedro bought   the book in.the FNAC after that

      viu ___ na   vitrine.
      saw   in.the window

      'Pedro bought the book at FNAC after he saw it in the window.'   ANO

(38) *Pedro comprou o   livro na   FNAC depois que a   Maria*
      Pedro bought   the book in.the FNAC after that the Mary

      também comprou ___.
      too   bought

      'Pedro bought the book at FNAC after Mary did too.'   VPE

Finally, Lopes (2014) shows that there is another diagnostic test that supports our claim that ANOs are ellipses. In BP, idiomatic expressions are preserved under V-VPE (39a) as they are under ANOs (39b):[6]

(39) a.   *O   João chutou o   pau da   barraca na   reunião e   o*
           the João kicked the pole of.the tent   at.the meeting and the

           Pedro também chutou ___.
           Pedro too   kicked

           'João had a fit at the meeting and Pedro did too.'

      b.   *O   João chutou o   pau da   barraca na   reunião do*
           the João kicked the pole of.the tent   at.the meeting of.the

           departamento e   o   Pedro chutou
           department   and the Pedro kicked

           ___ na reunião da   congregação.
             at.the college meeting

           'João had a fit at the departamental meeting and Pedro had one at the college meeting.'

Note, once again, that in (39a), the whole VP is ellided, whereas in (39b), only the direct object is missing.

---

6.   Gribanova (2013) shows that that is the case for V-VPE in Russian as well.

Throughout this section we have seen that characteristic elliptical behavior in VP ellipsis is reproduced in BP null object constructions. However, VPE and ANOs also have their differences, to which we turn now.

5.2 Differences between V-VPE and ANO

Since an elided sequence is allowed after a main verb, it is sometimes hard to distinguish between a V-VPE and an ANO structure, as some authors have pointed out (Matos 1992; Cyrino and Matos 2002, 2005; Goldberg 2005; Rouveret 2012), and as we have shown in the Introduction; however, Matos (1992) convincingly argues that a distinction between these constructions can be made based on the fact that ANO only involves the direct object of the verb, while VPE includes all the complements of the verb and VP adjuncts, if present.

(40) O João leu esse livro e a Ana também leu ___.
the João read that book and the Ana too read
'João read that book and Ana did too.'

(41) Ela trouxe o computador para a Universidade e ele trouxe
she brought the computer to the University and he brought
___ para o escritório.
to the office
'She brought the computer to the University and he brought it to the office.'

In BP, as seen above, ANO presents animacy restrictions (42) but V-VPE does not (43):

(42) a. João descascou a banana$_i$ e Maria comeu ___$_i$.
João peeled the banana and Maria ate
'João peeled the banana and Mary ate it.'

b. *João viu Maria$_i$ e Pedro beijou ___$_i$.
João saw Maria and Pedro kissed
'João saw Maria and Pedro kissed her.'

(43) João viu Maria na festa e Pedro também viu ___.
João saw Maria in.the party and Pedro also saw
'João saw Maria at the party and Pedro did too.'

As pointed out by Matos (1992) there is an identity requirement for the verbs in V-VPE (43) that is not obligatory for ANO (42a).

Given that V-VPE and ANO can not be rendered as a subset of each other, given the differences pointed out in this section, we will propose, based on the properties of ANOs in BP we have been discussing, that they are DP ellipsis, taken here as the reconstruction of the antecedent following licensing requirements, according to Fiengo and May (1994).

6. ANOs as empty phrase-markers

Two pieces of evidence seem to support our claim that ANOs in BP are cases of DP ellipsis, taken here as base-generated empty phrase-markers that will be reconstructed in LF, according to Fiengo and May's (1994) proposal for VP ellipsis.

As Kim (1999) has argued for Korean, Principle C should prevent (44), a grammatical sequence in Korean and BP:[7]

(44)   Eu adoro [o   carro do João$_i$], mas ele$_i$ odeia ___.
        I   love   the car   of João,   but   he   hates
        'I love João's car but he hates it.'

In fact, independent evidence shows that the language does not tolerate such a violation of Principle C:[8]

(45)   a.   *Ele$_i$ odeia o   carro do João$_i$
              he   hates the car   of João

       b.   *O   carro do João$_i$, ele$_i$ odeia ___.
              the car   of João,   he   hates

However, considering (44) is a good ANO construction, it seems plausible to assume that it gets reconstructed in LF through vehicle change.

It also seems that reconstruction makes the right predictions for cases of person mismatch between the antecedent and the ellipsis site, especially with respect to the availability of strict and sloppy readings:

---

7.   We will provide only BP examples.

8.   An anonymous reviewer has observed that Vehicle Change is not "a solution for a problem but only the name of the problem," pointing out that the phenomenon is easily circumvented in PF-deletion approaches to ellipsis. We recognize that there are different implementations for the apparent Principle C violations; however, this point is not taken here as evidence for a reconstruction versus a PF-deletion approach to ellipsis, but as another piece of evidence that ANO in BP is a case of ellipsis and, as such, we expect a uniform behavior in terms of their properties, regardless of whether they are instantiated as VPE(-V) or as ANO in BP. We acknowledge, however, that it is less of a problem to assume a reconstruction approach for the ANO, in which only the DP gets reconstructed in LF, than in the V-stranding VPE cases, in which the verb in the elliptical sentence is clearly present in the syntax. Although there are a few solutions that come to mind, it is far beyond the scope of this paper to come up with one to the V-stranding reconstruction. Nevertheless, this issue is orthogonal to the main point of our proposal.

(46) a. Pedro adora o   seu carro e   eu também adoro o
          Pedro loves the   and I   too love   the

          seu carro.
          his car

          'Pedro loves his car and I do too.'

      b. Pedro adora o   seu carro e   eu também adoro ____.
          Pedro loves the his car   and I   too   love
          'Pedro loves his car and I do too.'

In (46a) only a strict reading is available, while in (b) both a strict and a sloppy reading obtain. We will follow here Kim's (1999) arguments for Korean. If (b) were a case of PF deletion, then it had to be 'derived' from (a), and if that were the case, we should have the same interpretation in both instances, which does not obtain. Therefore, we have evidence for an analysis of the null object as a base-generated empty phrase-marker that will be reconstructed in LF.

7. Final remarks

As discussed in Section 3, when the position of adverbs and verbs were examined, we have seen that BP has lost long verb movement, keeping verb movement restricted to the aspectual head (ASP). From that position, the verb licenses the null object, its indexes being strictly reconstructed in LF, with no phonological content since this is a post-spell out operation.

We have assumed that the lexically filled ASP head is the licenser of both cases of ellipses in BP due to the loss of generalized verb movement and also due to the differences attested between BP and EP; however, no restrictions for the ANOs (or V-VPE, for that matter) occurrences in certain aspectual contexts are expected as is the case in other languages (Russian, Greek, etc.); in other words, there is no correlation between a certain aspectual realization and the occurrence of an elided construction. Nevertheless, if we claim an aspectual head has to be lexically filled to license ellipsis in BP, then we should expect that ellipsis will not occur in the absence of AspP. A proper environment to test the prediction is that with imperative sentences. Imperatives are a root phenomenon headed by MoodP only:

(47) $[_{MoodP} [_{vP/VP}]]$

In such contexts, only pragmatically controlled null objects are available. It is important to note that it is not a bidirectional restriction, as Lopes (2009) has argued. Deictic null objects can occur under an AspP, but ANOs cannot if one is not available.

Finally, another straightforward prediction of this proposal is that there will be a restriction on aspectual "parallelism", as seen in (48), which is borne out:

(48)   *??*O João estava tomando cerveja e   ontem   eu tomei ___.*
        the João was   drinking beer   and yesterday I   drank
        'João was having a beer and I had some yesterday.'

We have provided an analysis for the null object in BP that explains its peculiar behavior: we have seen that it allows strict/sloppy readings and it obeys strict parallel requirements. Both properties can be accounted for if we assume that the null object is a DP ellipsis reconstructed at LF.

References

Ambar, Manuela, Manuela Gonzaga and Esmeralda Negrão. 2004. "Tense, Quantification and Clause Structure in EP and BP. Evidence from a Comparative Study on *sempre*." *Romance Languages and Linguistic Theory 2002*. ed. by Reineke Bok-Bennema, Bart Hollebrandse, Brigitte Kampers-Manhe, and Petra Sleeman, 1–16. Amsterdam: John Benjamins. DOI: 10.1075/cilt.256.01amb

Bianchi, Valentina and Maria Cristina Figueiredo Silva. 1994. "On Some Properties of Agreement-Object in Italian and Brazilian Portuguese." *Issues and Theory in Romance Languages*. ed. by Michael Mazzola, 181–190. Washington, DC: Georgetown University Press.

Brito, Ana Maria. 1999. "Concordância, estrutura da frase e movimento do verbo no português europeu, no português brasileiro e no português de Moçambique." In *Lindley Cintra. Homenagem ao homem, ao mestre e ao cidadão*. ed. by Isabel H. Faria, 333–365. Lisboa: Cosmos/FLUL.

Brito, Ana Maria. 2001. "Clause Structure, Subject Positions and Verb Movement. About the Position of *sempre* in European Portuguese and Brazilian Portuguese." *Romance Languages and Linguistic Theory 1999*. ed. by Yves D'Hulst, Johan Rooryck, and Jan Schroten, 63–86. Amsterdam: John Benjamins. DOI: 10.1075/cilt.221.03bri

Chung, Sandra. 2013. "Syntactic Identity in Sluicing: How Much and Why." *Linguistic Inquiry* 44: 1–44. DOI: 10.1162/LING_a_00118

Costa, João, Maria Lobo, and Carolina Silva. 2010. "Which Category Replaces an Omitted Clitic? The Case of European Portuguese." *Pronouns and Clitics in Early Language*. ed. by Pilar Larranaga and Pedro Guijarro-Fuentes, 105–130. Berlin: Mouton de Gruyter.

Cyrino, Sonia. 1994. O objeto nulo no português brasileiro—um estudo sintático-diacrônico. Ph.D. Dissertation, University of Campinas.

Cyrino, Sonia. 1997. *O objeto nulo no português brasileiro—um estudo sintático-diacrônico*. Londrina: Editora da UEL.

Cyrino, Sonia. 2011. *Ensaios sobre a sintaxe do objeto nulo no português brasileiro*. University of Campinas.

Cyrino, Sonia. 2013a. "On Richness of Tense and Verb Movement in Brazilian Portuguese." *Information Structure and Agreement*. ed. by Victoria Camacho-Taboada, Ángel L. Jiménez-Fernández, Javier Martín-González, and Mariano Reyes-Tejedor, 297–318. Amsterdam and Philadelphia: John Benjamins. DOI: 10.1075/la.197.11cyr

Cyrino, Sonia. 2013b. Null Objects in Brazilian Portuguese Revisited. Paper presented at the Workshop on Brazilian Portuguese. Università Ca'Foscari Venezi. May 2–3, 2013.

Cyrino, Sonia. 2013c. Null Objects and Bare Nominals in Brazilian Portuguese. Paper presented at the Centre de Linguistica Teòrica, Universitat Autònoma de Barcelona.

Cyrino, Sonia and Gabriela Matos. 2002. "VP Ellipsis in European and Brazilian Portuguese—a Comparative Analysis." *Journal of Portuguese Linguistics* 1: 177–196.

Cyrino, Sonia and Gabriela Matos. 2005. "Local Licensers and Recovering in VP Ellipsis." *Journal of Portuguese Linguistics* 4: 79–112.

Farrell, Patrick. 1990. "Null objects in Brazilian Portuguese." *The Linguistic Review* 8: 325–346.

Ferreira, Marcelo Barra. 2000. Argumentos Nulos em Português Brasileiro. M.A. Thesis, University of Campinas.

Fiéis, Alexandra. 2010. "On the Position of *sempre* in Medieval Portuguese and in Modern European Portuguese." *The Linguistic Review* 27: 75–105. DOI: 10.1515/tlir.2010.004

Fiengo, Robert and Robert May. 1994. *Indices and Identity*. Cambridge, Mass: MIT Press.

Galves, Charlotte. 1989. "Objet nul et la structure de la proposition en Portugais Brésilien." *Review des Langues Romanes* 93: 305–336.

Galves, Charlotte. 1990. "V-Movement, Levels of Representation and the Structure of S." 13th GLOW Colloquium, University of Cambridge.

Galves, Charlotte. 1994. "V-Movement, Levels of Representation and the Structure of S." *Letras de Hoje* 96: 35–58.

Goldberg, Lotus. 2005. *Verb-Stranding VP Ellipsis: A Cross-Linguistic Study*. Ph.D. Dissertation, McGill University.

Gonzaga, Manuela. 1997. Aspectos da sintaxe do advérbio em português. Dissertação de Mestrado. University of Lisbon.

Gribanova, Vera. 2013. Verb-Stranding Verb Phrase Ellipsis and the Structure of the Russian Verbal Complex. *Natural Language and Linguistic Theory* 31: 91-136.

Huang, C.-T. J. 1984. "On the Distribution and Reference of Empty Pronouns." *Linguistic Inquiry* 15: 531–574.

Kim, Suwon. 1999. Sloppy/Strict Identity, Empty Objects, and NP Ellipsis. *Journal of East Asian Linguistics* 8: 255–284. DOI: 10.1023/A:1008354600813

Lopes, Ruth. 2014. "Null Objects and VP-Ellipsis in Brazilian Portuguese." Paper presented at the Department of Linguistics Colloquia Series, University of Chicago.

Lopes, Ruth. 2009. "Aspect and the Acquisition of Null Objects in Brazilian Portuguese." *Minimalist Inquiries into Child and Adult Language Acquisition*. ed. by Acrisio Pires and Jason Rothman, 105–128. Berlin: Mouton de Gruyter. DOI: 10.1515/9783110215359.1.105

Matos, Gabriela. 1992. Construções de Elipse de Predicado em Português—SV Nulo e Despojamento. Ph.D. Dissertation, University of Lisbon.

Merchant, Jason. 2013. "Diagnosing Ellipsis." *Diagnosing Syntax*. ed. by Lisa Lai-Shen Cheng, and Norbert Corver, 537–542. Oxford: Oxford University Press. DOI: 10.1093/acprof:oso/9780199602490.003.0026

Ohara, Masako. no date. Object Drop in English and in Japanese. http://sir.lib.shimane-u.ac.jp/metadb/up/70237860/Nullarguments.pdf.

Quer, Josep and Joana Rosselló. 2013. "On Sloppy Readings, Ellipsis and Pronouns—Missing Arguments in Catalan Sign Language (LSC) and Other Argument-Drop Languages." *Information Structure and Agreement*. ed. by Victoria Camacho-Taboada, Ángel L. Jiménez-Fernández, Javier Martín-González, and Mariano Reyes-Tejedor, 337–370. Amsterdam: John Benjamins. DOI: 10.1075/la.197.13que

Raposo, Eduardo. 1986. "On the Null Object in European Portuguese." *Studies in Romance Linguistics*. ed. by Osvaldo Jaeggli and Carmen-Silva Corvalán, 373–390. Dordrecht: Foris.

Rouveret, Alain. 2012. "VP Ellipsis, Phases and the Syntax of Morphology." *Natural Language and Linguistic Theory* 30: 897–963. DOI: 10.1007/s11049-011-9151-3

Age effects and the discrimination of consonantal and vocalic contrasts in heritage and native Spanish

Natalia Mazzaro, Alejandro Cuza & Laura Colantoni
University of Texas at El Paso / Purdue University / University of Toronto

This study explores the perception of consonantal and vocalic contrasts in two groups of Spanish-English bilingual speakers: heritage speakers and long-term immigrants. We test the discrimination of Spanish stops and mid and high vowels via an AX discrimination task with natural stimuli consisting of real Spanish words. Overall, results revealed no significant differences between heritage speakers and long-term immigrants in their discrimination of Spanish stops and vowels. Both groups were more accurate in their discrimination of vowels than of consonants. As for the discrimination of stops, positional and place effects were observed; i.e. a higher proportion of errors was found in word-initial position and with dorsals. We argue that contact with English does not necessarily affect the discrimination of the Spanish contrasts. Implications of these results for maturational approaches to final L2 attainment are discussed.

1. Introduction

To what extent does language contact affect our perception of consonantal and vocalic contrasts? We seek to answer this question by comparing the perception of Spanish stops and vowels (mid and high) by two groups of bilingual speakers (heritage speakers and long-term immigrants) and a group of Spanish monolinguals. The two bilingual groups tested here spoke Spanish from birth but differed in their age of onset of acquisition of English. Whereas the heritage speakers (HSs) were exposed to English early on and received formal education in English, the long-term immigrants (LTIs) were exposed to English after puberty and were educated in Spanish. In addition, participants within each group differ in their language proficiency, use, and self-reported degree of comfort using each of the languages. Thus, these populations allow us to test theories on the role that maturational constraints and age of exposure on the perception of segmental contrasts.

DOI 10.1075/rllt.9.15maz

Previous research shows a strong correlation between native-like attainment in a second language (L2) and age of arrival (AOA) and L2 exposure (Abrahamsson and Hyltenstam 2009; Boomershine, Birdsong, Bialystok, Mack, Sung, and Tsukada 2006; Flege, Yeni-Komshian, and Liu 1999). The argument is that after a certain age (12 to 14 for most authors) L2 learners are unable to fully acquire L2 speech patterns not present in their first language (L1) due to maturational reasons (Hyltenstam and Abrahamsson 2003). However, the extent and the sources of difficulties in the native-like attainment of phonological patterns are still not clear. Recent research documents comparable patterns of morphosyntactic (Cuza 2010; Sorace 2000) and phonetic divergence (Hopp and Schmid 2011; Major 2009) between near-native L2 learners and long-term immigrants undergoing L1 attrition, casting doubts on maturational constraints in language learning.

We contribute to existing research by comparing the effect of language contact and cross-linguistic influence (CLI) in two different types of bilingual populations largely underexplored in the literature: Spanish heritage speakers and long-term immigrants. This comparison is important for shedding light on existing proposals on the source and nature of heritage language development and for helping us understand the linguistic competence of bilingual speakers as far as phonological development is concerned. Specifically, we investigate the discrimination of segmental contrasts that have been reported to be vulnerable to CLI and L1 attrition, namely Spanish voiceless and voiced stops in initial and medial position (1a–1c) and /e/ vs. /i/ and /o/ vs. /u/ (2) in stressed and unstressed syllables, as shown in Table 1:

Table 1. Segmental contrasts under analysis

1. Initial Position	Medial Position
a. [b]ata vs. [p]ata ('robe' vs. 'foot')	a. su[β]e vs. su[p]e ('go up' vs. 'I knew')
b. [g]iso vs. [k]iso ('stew' vs. 's/he wanted')	b. pe[ɣ]ar vs. pe[k]ar ('to hit' vs. 'to sin')
c. [d]una vs. [t]una ('dune' vs. 'prickly pear')	c. me[ð]í vs. me[t]í ('I measured' vs. 'I put')
2. Stressed syllable	Unstressed syllable
a. qu[e]so vs. qu[i]so ('cheese' vs. 's/he wanted')	a. p[e]sar vs. p[i]sar ('to weigh' vs. 'to step on')
b. p[o]zo vs. p[u]so ('hole' vs. 's/he put')	b. d[o]rar vs. d[u]rar ('to tan' vs. 'to last')

If maturational approaches to final L2 attainment are correct, we would expect HSs and LTIs to behave similarly, as both groups acquired Spanish before puberty. However, if prolonged exposure to a second language before maturation affects perception, HSs might have difficulties in their discrimination of Spanish contrasts due to reduced Spanish input and use. In particular, it should prove difficult for these speakers to discriminate Spanish voiced and voiceless stops because they map onto one English phonetic category (i.e. voiced stops); these participants are also expected to confuse mid-vowels (front-vowels in particular) because the Spanish [e] overlaps with the English [i] (Bradlow 1995). LTIs, in contrast, should behave closer to the attested monolingual patterns, as they were exposed to English after maturation (MacKay, Flege, Piske, and Schirru, 2001).

In what follows, we review the background research (Section 2) necessary for supporting our hypotheses (Section 3) and motivating our methodology (Section 4). Results are reported in Section 5 followed by Sections 6 and 7, in which we evaluate our hypotheses and present our conclusions.

2. Background

2.1 English and Spanish stops and mid/high vowels

Spanish and English have a system of six stop phonemes that contrast in place and voicing. Although from a phonological point of view the systems are rather similar, the phonetic implementation of the voicing contrast is different. In Spanish, voiceless stops are not aspirated and voiced stops are prevoiced; i.e. the vocal folds keep vibrating throughout the closure. These differences have several acoustic correlates (duration of preceding vowel, duration of stop closure, F0 patterns at the offset of the closure) but the phonetic differences in voicing have been mostly analyzed in the literature in terms of the Voice Onset Time or VOT (Abramson and Lisker 1970, 1973; Lisker and Abramson 1964, 1970). VOT is the temporal relation between the release of the stop consonant and the onset of glottal pulsing (or periodicity). This acoustic parameter has been shown to capture cross-linguistic differences in stop voicing in production and perception. Both English and Spanish voiceless stops have positive VOTs. Yet, one important difference between these two languages is that English VOT is longer than Spanish VOT; i.e. the vocal folds start vibrating earlier in Spanish than in English. As for voiced stops in Spanish, VOT is negative; that is, periodicity starts before the release. Yet, in English, the VOT of /b, d, g/ is short and positive.[1] Thus, the boundaries for the perception of a given stop as voiced or voiceless are different in each language. In Spanish, the cross-over point, that is, the point at which perception of a voiced stop changes to voiceless and vice versa, has been reported to be around 14 ms (Abramson and Lisker 1973), but later studies showed that this point varies from dialect to dialect, with a reported cross-dialectal range from -10ms to -5ms (Rosner, López-Bascuas, García-Albea and Fahey 2000; Williams 1977b). In English, stops with a VOT of 25ms

---

1. Space limitations preclude our presentation of examples and spectrograms of voiced and voiceless stops. For more detailed discussion, please see Thomas (2011) for English and Hualde (2005) for Spanish.

or higher have been reported to be perceived as voiceless (Lisker and Abramson 1970). VOT differences are sensitive to place of articulation. Specifically, differences are larger for labials and dentals than for velars (Williams 1977a; Rosner et al. 2000). The above discussion, however, is relevant only for Spanish stops in absolute word-initial position. In word medial position, there is an additional manner contrast. Voiced stops are realized as approximants (for a more detailed analysis of the distribution of stop and approximant alternations, see Hualde (2005) and Perissinotto (1975), although the latter used the term 'fricative' instead of 'approximant'). Thus, VOT is not relevant here to distinguish voiced and voiceless stops; voicing and duration, instead, continue to distinguish both types of stops.

As opposed to stop consonants, Spanish and English have largely different vocalic inventories. Whereas Spanish has five phonemic vowels, general American English has been described as having a system of either 11 or 10 vowels (see Stockwell and Bowen 1965 for a comparison of both systems). In particular, English has four high vowels /i u ɪ ʊ/ whereas Spanish has only two /i u/. The mid vowels /e o/ are diphthongized in English but not in Spanish. Beyond these phonological differences, additional phonetic differences have been reported for some varieties of American English and Peninsular Spanish. In a comparative study in which only the vowels that are present in both languages were analyzed, Bradlow (1995) found that English vowels were more fronted than the corresponding vowels in Spanish. Morrison (2006) obtained similar results when comparing only English and Spanish front vowels.

2.2 Cross-linguistic speech perception: Stops and vowels

A recurrent question in L2 acquisition and bilingualism research is how bilinguals handle the different languages. Are the languages separated or integrated? Experimental studies that have looked at early bilinguals have reported evidence for and against integration (Genesee, 1989; Paradis and Genesee 1996; Volterra and Taeschner 1978).

The integration hypothesis suggests that bilinguals, albeit showing differences in performance when tested in the different language contexts, consistently differ from monolinguals, showing identification scores that are somewhere between the values obtained for the monolinguals of each of the languages. This hypothesis has been proposed by Caramazza, Yeni-Komshian, Zurif and Carbone (1973) as a result of their study of English-French bilinguals. The authors tested bilingual speakers on their ability to identify French and English voicing contrasts using synthetic CV syllables with the consonant, which could be any of the six stops, being followed by the vowel [a]. Their results revealed that French-English bilinguals showed scores that were between those reported for each monolingual group. In other words, the perception of bilinguals showed interference from one language to the other. Williams (1977b) confirmed Caramazza et al.'s results with a group of Spanish-English bilinguals. This study, which involved discrimination and identification tasks, used stimuli consisting of synthetic /pa ~ ba/ syllables. The two groups of monolingual subjects showed different perceptual crossovers with those of bilinguals occupying an intermediate position.

Elman, Diehl, and Buchwald (1977), using natural speech and CV stimuli (/ba pa/), proposed an alternative hypothesis. Three groups of subjects, monolingual English speakers, monolingual Spanish speakers, and English-Spanish bilinguals, were asked to label stimuli embedded in different language contexts according to the subjects' native language. Bilingual subjects heard the test stimuli in both English and Spanish. Their results showed that the two monolingual groups differed substantially in their identification performance, with English speakers tending to label most of the syllables as /ba/ and Spanish speakers tending to label most of them as /pa/. The bilingual subjects perceived a reliably greater number of the test items as /ba/ in the English than in the Spanish context. Based on these results, Elman et al. concluded that bilinguals vary their placement of category boundaries as a function of language context in which the stimuli were presented. These results were recently confirmed by García-Sierra, Diehl and Champlin (2009) in a similar study that used /ga/ ~ /ka/ synthetic syllables.

Differences in the results have been attributed to the use of synthetic vs. natural stimuli (i.e., Elman et al. 1977) and identification vs. discrimination tasks. This claim has been recently supported by Antoniou, Tyler and Best (2012) who argued that differences reported in the literature could be the consequence of not controlling for language mode or language dominance. Participants were tested separately on an English and Greek mode on their perception of labial and coronal stops in word-initial and intervocalic position. Stimuli were recorded by native speakers of each language and used for a categorization task (with goodness of fit ratings) and an ABX discrimination task. Results revealed that speakers behaved differently in each of the tasks. In the ABX discrimination task, bilinguals patterned with monolinguals of the same dominant language. In the categorization task bilinguals instead behaved more like monolinguals of the language that was activated during the experiment. Crucially, there was no evidence that participants mixed the phonological categories of the respective language. This study has interesting implications for our work. First, it shows that task-effects are expected and that language dominance plays a crucial role in discrimination tasks. Second, results revealed that participants were able to keep the categories apart in word initial and medial position. Finally, these results further demonstrate the flexibility of bilinguals.

Research on vowels clearly points to the influence of the L1 on the L2 even in the case of early and fluent Spanish-Catalan bilinguals (Sebastián-Gallés and Soto Franco 1999; Bosch and Sebastián-Gallés 2003). Most of the studies that have compared the perception of Spanish and English vowels have focused on English, which is not surprising given the differences described in the previous section.[2] Of those studies, the majority has explored the perception of English vowels by L2 Spanish speakers (Fox, Flege and Munro 1995). A recent exception to this tendency is the work by Boomershine (2013), where she analyzes the perceived similarity between minimal pairs of English front vowels by different bilingual groups (native English-Advanced L2 Spanish, native Spanish-Advanced L2 English and heritage Spanish speakers). An interesting finding is that Spanish heritage speakers patterned with Spanish monolingual speakers, when judging the degree of similarity between the members of a given English minimal pair. Research on L1 English-L2 Spanish speakers (Morrison 2003, 2006) reveals more confusion with front than with back Spanish vowels. In particular, Morrison reports a bi-directional confusion with front mid-high vowels, with /i/ being confused with /e/ more often than /e/ with /i/. Back vowels also showed some instances of misperceptions but only in one direction (/o/ was perceived as /u/). The number of errors in perception, however, was rather small. The roles of inventory size and language experience repeatedly occur as factors in L2 and bilingualism research. As in the case of consonants, perceptual flexibility has also been demonstrated for vowels (e.g. Fox et al. 1995).

As a whole, these studies show the importance of (i) controlling for speakers' variables, such as language proficiency, use and dominance; (ii) language modes (or context); (iii) task effects (identification vs. discrimination); and (iv) type of stimuli (natural vs. synthetic). Thus, in the present study, we controlled for participants AOA and length of residency (LOR) in the U.S.; we tested our participants in Spanish and used a discrimination task with natural stimuli. However, we departed from previous studies in the use of minimal pairs, which tested the target contrasts in a variety of phonetic environments.

3.   Research questions and hypotheses

Based on previous research on bilingualism and the existing differences between English and Spanish, we pose the following research questions:

> RQ1: Do Spanish HSs and LTIs differ in their discrimination of Spanish stops and mid and high vowels to the point of not being able to fully discriminate them?
> RQ2: If differences are found, can they be attributed to differences in language-use patterns, age of onset of bilingualism, and knowledge of Spanish (as reflected in their proficiency scores)?

---

2.   Catalan was the target language in previous research with Spanish-Catalan bilinguals, which also has a larger phonemic inventory than Spanish.

If maturational constraints play a role, we hypothesize that Spanish HSs and LTIs should behave similarly since both groups acquired Spanish before puberty. However, if contact with English plays a role, then Spanish HSs should differ from the other two groups, since they were exposed to English before puberty.

With regard to the specific contrasts under study, based on previous descriptions and on the analysis of our own perception stimuli, we pose the following hypotheses:

1. For consonants, there will be more confusion between voiced and voiceless stops in word-initial than in word-medial position. With regard to their place of articulation, there will be more confusion with dorsals than with labials and coronals.
2. For vowels, we expect more confusion with front vowels than with back vowels. In addition, we anticipate more confusion with unstressed vowels than with stressed ones.

4. The Study

4.1 Participants

A total of forty-five participants (n=45) took part in the study: 25 HSs, 6 LTIs and 14 recent arrivals serving as controls. The participants resided in West Lafayette/ Lafayette, Indiana, and in El Paso, Texas. All of them were university students enrolled in different programs at two major universities. Following previous research (Montrul 2008; Silva-Corvalán 2003), the HSs were second or first generation immigrants who acquired their native language (Mexican Spanish) during early childhood at home or in another natural context where a majority language (English) was spoken. They were either born and raised in the U.S. or immigrated permanently to the U.S. at or before the age of 12.[3] The LTIs arrived from Mexico after the age of 13 with a fully developed L1 grammar.

Participants completed an adult language background questionnaire, which elicited information on place of birth, primary language of schooling, and patterns of language use. This questionnaire also elicited a self-proficiency judgment in both English and Spanish in the four linguistic skills via a Likert scale, ranging from basic/limited (1) to excellent/native (4). In addition to the self-proficiency measure, participants completed an independent proficiency task, adapted from the *Diploma de Español*

---

3. For the purpose of this study, we took the age of 12 as the cut-off point to differentiate HSs from LTIs. This classification is based on previous research in the L2 acquisition of phonology, which suggests significant long-term effects in the lack of native-like attainment past this age (Long 1990; Scovel 1988).

como Lengua Segunda (DELE). Following previous research using the same methodology, participants were grouped as advanced (scores between 40 and 50 points), intermediate (scores between 30 and 39), and beginners (scores between 0 and 29) (Cuza, Pérez-Leroux and Sánchez 2013).

The HSs were divided into two groups based on their proficiency score in the DELE test (see Table 2): advanced HSs (n=19; DELE score, 44/50) and intermediate HSs (n=6; DELE score 35/50). The advanced group included participants born and raised in the U.S. and participants who came to the U.S. at an early age (Table 2). Of those participants not born in the U.S., all of them except for one came from the state of Chihuahua, Mexico. Table 2 shows their self-proficiency ratings and language use.

LTIs (n=6) included first generation immigrants from the state of Chihuahua, Mexico (age at testing, *M*= 39; AOA, *M*=26; LOR, *M*=15), except from one participant who came from Mexico City.[4] Participants were tested in El Paso, Texas. See Table 2.

The control group consisted of fourteen (n=14) recent arrivals to El Paso, Texas, from the state of Chihuahua, Mexico. They were all university students enrolled in an ESL program (age at testing, *M*= 21; AOA, M=21; LOR, *M*=9 months). See Table 2.

4.2　Stimuli

Stimuli consisted of real Spanish words. For the voiced and voiceless stops, 43 minimal pairs were used, which were controlled for place of articulation (/b/ vs. /p/, /d/ vs. /t/, /g/ vs. /k/), position in the word (initial vs. medial), following vowel (/a, e, i, o u/) and stress (tonic vs. post-tonic). For vowels, 36 minimal pairs were used, controlled for type of vowel (/e/ vs. /i/, /o/ vs. /u/) and stress (tonic vs. post-tonic). Stimuli are included in Appendix A.

Stimuli were recorded twice by a native Spanish speaker from Ciudad Juárez, Chihuahua, Mexico. All stimuli, with the exception of those for stop consonants in initial position (which were recorded using a list form) were produced in a carrier phrase: *Digo X para ti* ('*I say X again*'). Stimuli were extracted from the list of isolated words or from the carrier phrase and presented in pairs to participants. Below, we summarize the acoustic characteristics of the stimuli.

4.2.1　*Acoustic analysis of our own perception stimuli*
The stimuli used to design the experiment were acoustically analyzed with PRAAT (Boersma 2001) to ensure that the voiced and voiceless stops were sufficiently different.

4.　The higher number of HSs compared to LTIs stems from the fact that recruitment took place in Spanish courses attended mostly by HSs who wanted to increase their knowledge of Spanish.

Table 2. Participants' demographic information

	Advanced HSs (n=19)			Intermediate HSs (n=6)			LTIs (n=6)			Controls (n=14)		
Mean age at testing (SD)		22 (2.33)			24 (7.4)			32(13.19)			21 (6.85)	
Place of birth	US		Mexico	US		Mexico		Mexico			Mexico	
Mean AOA	–		10	–		6		23			21	
Mean LOR	–		14	–		20		10			0;9	
DELE score		44/50			35/50			44/50			44	
	SPAN	ENG	BOTH	SPAN	ENG	BOTH	SPAN	ENG	BOTH	SPAN	ENG	BOTH
Language use												
Home	80%	10%	10%	38%	38%	24%	83%	17%	0%	93%	0%	7%
School	15%	70%	15%	0%	88%	12%	50%	17%	33%	71%	7%	22%
Work	6%	59%	35%	0%	86%	14%	25%	50%	25%	100%	0%	0%
Social situations	30%	30%	40%	0%	100%	0%	80%	0%	20%	85%	0%	15%
	SPAN	ENG	BOTH	SPAN	ENG	BOTH	SPAN	ENG	BOTH	SPAN	ENG	BOTH
More comfortable language	15%	15%	70%	0%	63%	38%	80%	0%	20%	93%	0%	7%

The acoustic parameters analyzed were Voice Onset Time (VOT) and Percentage Voicing (%V). The results are summarized in Table 3.

Table 3. Summary of the acoustic analysis of voiced and voiceless stops used in the perception stimuli

	/p/	/t/	/k/	/b/	/d/	/g/
VOT (ms) word initial	10.49	15.57	21.95	−55.72	−85.70	−63.36
VOT (ms) word medial	7.01	16.26	37.59	–	−16.79[5]	−7.89
%V word initial	24.92	20.02	12.83	96.58	98.78	78.83
%V word medial	4.67	3.06	2.51	90.26	72.62	93.25

These results show that the stimuli used for our perception experiment displayed a clear difference between voiced and voiceless stops at each place of articulation. As in previous studies, voiced stops are fully voiced and have a long negative VOT. Voiceless stops have a short positive VOT (Abramson and Lisker 1973). The values for voiceless stops in initial position are similar to those reported for Castilian Spanish (Rosner et al. 2000), but our voiced stops in initial position had shorter voicing lead than in Castilian Spanish (/b/ −91.5, /d/ −91.6, /g/ −73.7). Yet, as stated by Williams (1977a) and confirmed by the results reported by Rosner et al. (2000), Spanish VOT values seem to vary across dialects. The values for stops in intervocalic position are also consistent with results previously reported for other Spanish dialects (Lewis 2000). In particular, these results are similar to those obtained by Lewis for the Colombian speakers in his study (VOT: /p/ 12.77; /t/ 18.72; /k/ 30.4), although the values for percentage voicing obtained here are slightly higher than Lewis' (/p/ 14%; /t/ 15%; /k/ 6.8%). Finally, although dorsals do not show the smallest difference in VOT in our corpus, the values obtained for percentage voicing motivate our hypothesis. In summary, as stated earlier, the values presented in Table 3 show clear voicing contrasts between voiced and voiceless stops.

The F1 and F2 of the vowels used to test the discrimination of /e/ vs. /i/ and /o/ vs. /u/ were measured in Bark. The average values for the vowels in stressed (S) and unstressed (U) positions are listed in Table 4:

---

5.   VOT in medial position was measured when relevant (i.e. with stops in absolute initial position). In the variety under investigation this included the realization of /d/ in *ardo* 'burn' and /g/ in *rasgo* 'tear', which are realized as stops, as opposed to the most frequent approximant realization observed in other dialects. All cases of /b/ in medial position were realized as approximants; thus VOT was not measured.

Table 4. Mean F1-F2 values (in Bark) for the vowels [e, i, o, u] in the perception stimuli

	[e]		[i]		[o]		[u]	
	S	U	S	U	S	U	S	U
F1	5.5±0.15	5.3±0.21	3.7±0.30	3.4±0.22	5.6±0.23	5.4±0.18	3.7±0.70	4.5±0.26
F2	13.2±0.41	13.2±0.47	14±0.26	14.2±0.26	8.4±0.21	8.7±0.45	7.3±0.74	7.6±0.94

The F1-F2 values displayed in Table 4 are very close to those reported by Morrison and Escudero (2007) for Peruvian Spanish, yet our F1 for [i] and [u] are slightly lower (Peruvian [i] and [u] are 4.2). Table 4 shows that the vowels used in our perceptual experiment were distinctively produced and that the differences in formant values were slightly lower in post-tonic than in tonic positions.[6]

4.3 Procedure

An AX discrimination task was used to test our hypotheses, where 'X' was either different or similar to 'A'.[7] Members of the pair were separated by a 4s ISI (inter-stimulus interval). After hearing the second item, the participant had to decide whether the two items were the same or different by pressing either a red or a green button on a response pad connected to the computer running Superlab Pro 4.1. After selecting a response, a one second pause was inserted, and the next pair was presented.

The experiment was conducted in two sessions (one for consonants and the other one for vowels); participants sat in a quiet room, wearing headphones. Both sessions were conducted completely in Spanish. The first session had a total of 129 pairs. There was a break after 45 trials, for a total of 2 breaks. The second session included a total of 108 pairs. A break was provided after 40 trials, for a total of 2 breaks.

For every pair of stimuli the following information was recorded by Superlab: Contrast (either /b, p/, /g, k/, /d, t/, /e, i/, /o, u/), the actual words used in each item of the pair (this was used later to retrieve the position, stress and context), whether the words were the same or different, the participant's response, and the response time of the participant (from the end of the second item in the pair to the moment the participant pressed a key).

---

6. The authors reported formant values in Hz, so we converted their values to Bark in order to compare them with our data.

7. The number of stimuli where X was different from A was 79 and where X was similar to A was 162.

5.   Results

This section presents the results for each of the hypotheses tested. First, we analyze group performance; second, we discuss the results for consonants according to place of articulation and position; and third, we present the results for vowels according to stress and their position on the front-back axis.

5.1   Differences between groups

Performances between groups were compared based on overall errors and then further investigated for influence of linguistic variables included in the present study. First, a one-way ANOVA was conducted to compare performance per group, where vowels and consonants were collapsed in a single error score per speaker. Overall, controls had the lowest percentage of errors (6.75%) followed by intermediate HSs (9.8%), Advanced HSs (10.2%), and LTIs (13.6%).[8] Results showed a significant difference between groups (F (32, 41) = 4.01, p=0.014). A Tukey post-hoc test showed that the control group was significantly different from the LTIs. There were no significant differences in error scores between HSs and LTIs. The similarity between the bilingual groups suggests that contact with English may have an impact on their perception of segmental contrasts.

We investigated these results further by analyzing the performance of groups in each linguistic context. In every case we performed a one-way ANOVA, and when a significant difference was found, a Tukey post-hoc test was performed. For the discrimination of consonants (see Appendix B), there was a significant difference (F (3, 41) = 4.58, p=0.007) between controls (7.09%) and LTIs (16.9%), with the performance of HSs somewhere in between, but not significantly different from the other two groups. These results match the ones obtained for overall performance. For the discrimination of vowels, no significant differences were found between groups (F (3, 41) = 1.07, p=.37), although the pattern is similar to the one observed in consonants (see Appendix B).

Two further analyses were performed in order to determine whether there were further differences between groups. First, we analyzed the reaction times to explore whether the relative differences in accuracy between groups were due to differences in speed. Thus, we conducted a one-way ANOVA on the logarithms of the response time[9]

---

8.   We also tested other groupings of the subjects based on DELE scores, most comfortable language and percentage of language use. In none of those cases significant differences between the groups were found.

9.   We used the natural log of the response time measured in ms., because the distribution of the logarithms is closer to a Gaussian (normal) distribution than the actual response times.

to compare the performance between groups (Table 5). The only significant difference was found in the performance of the intermediate HS group, which had the slowest response time (F (3, 10402) = 22.66, p < 0.001).

Table 5. Logarithm of response time per group

Group	N	Mean	SD	Equivalent Resp. Time (ms.)
Advanced HSs	4401	6.38	0.82	590 ms
LTIs	1374	6.39	0.81	593 ms
Controls	3229	6.40	0.81	603 ms
Intermediate HSs	1402	6.58	0.74	719 ms

The second type of analysis was a comparison of the directionality of errors per group in order to determine whether participants presented more errors in similar pairs, suggesting some kind of task-effects, or in different pairs. Thus, a one-way ANOVA was conducted to explore the type of error by group, that is, whether similar stimuli were perceived as different (= false alarm) or whether different stimuli were perceived as the same (= miss). A score of error directionality was calculated per speaker as the difference between the 'miss' and 'false alarm' rates. The differences between groups were not significant (F (3, 41) = 0.25, p = 0.86). Table 6 shows the averages per group.

Table 6. Score of error directionality per group

Group	N	False Alarm	Miss	Difference[10]	St.Dev.
Advanced HSs	19	10.6%	9.4%	−1.22%	7.79%
Controls	14	7.4%	5.4%	−1.99%	2.56%
Intermediate HSs	6	9.9%	9.7%	−0.20%	4.40%
LTIs	6	13.4%	13.9%	0.55%	10.06%

We noticed that both heritage groups had a higher rate of false alarms than misses, which mirrors the performance of the control group. HSs also had a lower rate of discrimination errors than LTIs.

---

10. A negative number indicates a higher proportion of false alarms (same stimuli detected as different) and a positive number indicates a higher proportion of misses (different stimuli detected as same).

5.2   Differences between groups: Consonants vs. vowels

Performance between groups varied depending on consonant place of articulation. There was significant difference (F (3, 41) = 6.32, p=.001) between groups in the discrimination of labials, with advanced HSs (5.51%) and controls (4.25%) having a better performance than LTIs (16.41%). Also, a significant difference (F (3, 41) = 3.95, p=0.015) was found in the discrimination of dorsals, with controls (10.71%) performing better than advanced HSs (18.63%) and LTIs (20.35%). No significant differences were found between groups for coronals (F (3, 41) = 2.28, p=0.04). See table in Appendix C.

With regard to the discrimination of vowels by the different groups, no significant differences were found either for front vowels (/e, i/) (F(3, 41) = 1.05, p=0.38) or back vowels (/o, u/) (F (3, 41) = 0.62, p=0.6). Although differences were not significant, again controls had the lowest error rates and LTIs the highest. See table in Appendix D.

5.3   Stop consonants by position and place of articulation

For this part of the analysis all bilingual groups were collapsed. A total of 6 error scores per speaker were calculated (3 places of articulation x 2 positions). The mean and SD values are shown in Table 7. The high values of SD are due to high inter-speaker differences. To analyze the significance of the differences due to consonants' position and place of articulation, a repeated measures ANOVA was conducted to mitigate the effect of the high inter speaker variation.

Results support our hypotheses for consonants. There were more discrimination errors in word-initial than in word-medial position. Consonants in initial position had a mean error score of 17.8%, compared to 8% in medial position (F (1, 149) = 48.0, p<0.001). With regard to place of articulation, there were more discrimination errors with dorsals (19.70%) than with coronals and labials (11.5% and 7.6%, respectively) (F (2, 148) = 25.31, p<0.001). A Tukey post-hoc test revealed significant difference between dorsals and the other two types of consonants.

Table 7. Consonants by position and stress

Consonant by position				Consonant by place of articulation			
Position	N	Mean	St.Dev.	Contrast	N	Mean	St.Dev.
Initial	90	17.87%	12.80%	/b/ vs. /p/	60	7.60%	9.10%
Medial	90	8.01%	8.09%	/d/ vs. /t/	60	11.51%	10.25%
				/g/ vs. /k/	60	19.70%	12.43%

5.4   Vowel by front-back dimension and stress

An ANOVA was conducted to compare vowels according to stress and their position in the front-back axis. Front vowels were not more difficult to discriminate than back vowels. In fact, front vowels had a lower mean error score than back vowels (8.5% and 9.1%, respectively), but these differences were not significant (F (1, 89) = 0.30, p=0.585). As predicted, unstressed vowels were significantly more difficult to discriminate than stressed vowels (10.4% and 7.1%, respectively) (F (1, 89) = 12.22, p=0.001).

Table 8. Vowels by stress and type (front vs. back)

Vowel by stress				Front vs. back vowels			
Stress	N	Mean	St.Dev.	Contrast	N	Mean	St.Dev.
Stressed	60	7.12%	4.87%	/e/ vs. /i/	60	8.50%	7.38%
Unstressed	60	10.40%	8.00%	/o/vs. /u/	60	9.06%	6.31%

6. Discussion and conclusions

6.1 Research questions and hypotheses

Controls significantly differed from LTIs in their discrimination performance, yet there were no significant differences in the overall performance of advanced HSs and LTI. This includes the number and directionality of errors and the response time. Some differences were found for consonants, with advanced HSs patterning with controls in the perception of labial contrasts and with LTIs in the perception of dorsals. Taken together, these results are consistent with maturational approaches to language acquisition, since they suggest that being exposed to Spanish at an early age allows bilinguals to discriminate native contrasts.

As stated earlier, the fact that LTIs patterned significantly differently from controls is intriguing and it needs further investigation before we can draw any conclusions, especially because the LTI group was smaller than the other groups (see our discussion in §6.2). Keeping this in mind, we suggest that these results could be an indication that exposure to an L2 later in life affects native speech perception (Flege 1995). Language acquisition studies suggest that the L1 phonological system acts as a filter that accommodates new linguistic input to its structure (Trubetzkoy 1969; Wode 1978). Adult L2 learners already have a phonological system in place when they incorporate new speech categories from the L2. Thus, the native phonological system may be affected as new sounds are integrated into an already established system (Flege 1995). As opposed to LTIs, HSs are exposed to both languages since early childhood; thus, their native phonological system could still be developing when the L2 is being acquired. Since speech categories from both languages are acquired almost simultaneously, there is no phonological system formed a priori to which new categories will be added (Antoniou et al. 2012).

With regard to the specific contrasts under study, the hypotheses for stop consonants involving position and place were supported. Stops in word-initial position were more difficult to discriminate than those in word-medial position. This was expected given the acoustic differences (VOT and percentage voicing) between voiced stops in initial and word-medial positions. In addition to these acoustic differences, /b, d, g/ are realized as approximants in word medial intervocalic position. This makes it easier to distinguish these consonants from voiceless stops in the same environment (e.g. 'ro[t]ar' *to rotate* vs. 'ro[ð]ar' *to roll*). Concerning the discrimination of consonants according to place of articulation, dorsal stops were more difficult to discriminate than coronals and labials. As explained earlier, this could be due to smaller differences in percentage voicing between voiced and voiceless dorsals.

Concerning vowels, we confirmed the hypothesis that unstressed vowels are more difficult to discriminate than stressed ones. Yet, the hypothesis about front vowels being more difficult to discriminate than back vowels was not supported. These results are consistent with Morrison's (2003) perceptual analysis of Spanish vowels by native Spanish and English speakers. In his study, Spanish listeners (L2 learners of English) had slightly higher misidentification rates for back vowels compared to front vowels (9% vs. 7%, respectively). English listeners (L2 learners of Spanish) showed the opposite pattern in their identification of Spanish vowels; they had higher rates of misidentification in front than in back vowels (16% vs. 9%, respectively). This would suggest that our subjects were using the Spanish mode of perception to discriminate relevant contrasts.

6.2 Experimental conditions and our bilingual groups

The difference in performance between the LTIs and the control group may be attributed to potential task-effects. Previous studies suggest that bilinguals do not behave similarly in discrimination vs. labelling tasks. For instance, in Antoniou et al.'s (2012) study, bilinguals behaved like monolinguals in discrimination tasks. Similarly, in Boomershine's (2013) study, Spanish heritage speakers patterned with Spanish monolinguals when judging the degree of similarity between the members of a minimal pair. However, Stevens, Liberman, Studdert-Kennedy and Ohman's (1969) study, which used two types of tests (labeling and discrimination), found that participants did not behave similarly. In the identification task with synthetic stimuli, American English and Swedish listeners behaved significantly different (i.e., the vowels identified were related to the vowel inventory of the listeners' L1); yet, in the ABX discrimination task, their performance was similar. Stevens et al. (1969) claim that these differences could be due to more universal auditory factors used by the participants in the discrimination task. Although in our study we used an AX discrimination task, we believe that similar tasks effects could have been at play, which made HSs behave like monolinguals in the discrimination test.

With regard to the testing condition, the experiments were conducted completely in Spanish by researchers who are native Spanish speakers. We predicted this would have a positive effect on our participants' discrimination of Spanish sounds. Consistent with Antoniou et al.'s (2012) finding, we would expect to find differences in bilinguals' performance if the language mode were shifted from Spanish to English. In the future, we would like to test our participants in English to determine whether their performance in one language can be correlated to their performance in the other.

It is also important to point out that bilinguals from El Paso have continuous exposure to both Spanish and English daily. This is the case in most environments: home, social, and work. Other bilinguals who live in more monolingual (English) environments may not have such intensive contact with both languages.

To summarize, the present study has offered a perceptual analysis of consonants and vowels in different populations of bilingual Spanish-English speakers: HSs and LTIs. The results do not provide evidence in support of the claim that there is phonological-perceptual attrition in HSs. On the contrary, HSs performed better than LTIs in the discrimination test. The results should be taken with caution given the low number of LTIs vis-à-vis HSs. We are currently supplementing this research with data from more speakers. In addition, we plan to incorporate other variables including language dominance to examine more closely the potential correlation between bilinguals' performance and their linguistic ability in both languages.

References

Abrahamsson, Niclas, and Kenneth Hyltenstam. 2009. "Age of Onset and Native-likeness in a Second Language: Listener Perception versus Linguistic Scrutiny." *Language Learning* 59(2):, 249–306. DOI: 10.1111/j.1467-9922.2009.00507.x

Abramson, Arthur S., and Leigh Lisker. 1970. "Discriminability along the Voicing Continuum: Cross Language Tests." *Proceedings of the* 6th *International Congress of Phonetic Sciences, Prague:* 569–573.

Abramson, Arthur S., and Leigh Lisker. 1973. "Voice Timing Perception in Spanish Word-initial Stops." *Journal of Phonetics* 1: 1–8.

Antoniou, Mark, Michael D. Tyler, and Catherine T. Best. 2012. "Two Ways to Listen: Do L2-Dominant Bilinguals Perceive Stop Voicing according to Language Mode?" *Journal of Phonetics* 40: 582–594. DOI: 10.1016/j.wocn.2012.05.005

Boersma, Paul. 2001. "Praat, a System for Doing Phonetics by Computer." *Glot International* 5(9/10): 341–345.

Boomershine, Amanda. 2013. "The Perception of English Vowels by Monolingual, Bilingual, and Heritage Speakers of Spanish and English." *Selected Proceedings of the* 15th *Hispanic*

Linguistics Symposium, ed. by Chad Howe et al., 103–118. Somerville, MA: Cascadilla Proceedings Project.

Bosch, Laura, and Núria Sebastián-Gallés. 2003. "Simultaneous Bilingualism and the Perception of a Language-specific Vowel Contrast in the First Year of Life." *Language and Speech* 46: 217–243. DOI: 10.1177/00238309030460020801

Bradlow, Ann R. 1995. "A Comparative Acoustic Study of Spanish and English Vowels." *Journal of the Acoustical Society of America* 97: 1916–1924. DOI: 10.1121/1.412064

Caramazza, Alfenso, Grace H. Yeni-Komshian, Edgar. B. Zurif, and Ettore Carbone. 1973. "The Acquisition of a New Phonological Contrast: The Case of Stop Consonants in French-English Bilinguals." *Journal of the Acoustical Society of America* 54: 421–428. DOI: 10.1121/1.1913594

Cuza, Alejandro, Ana T. Pérez-Leroux, and Liliana Sánchez. 2013. "The Role of Semantic Transfer in Clitic-drop among Simultaneous and Sequential Chinese-Spanish Bilinguals." *Studies in Second Language Acquisition*, 35(1): 93–125. DOI: 10.1017/S0272263112000691

Cuza, Alejandro. 2010. "The L2 Acquisition of Aspectual Properties in Spanish." *Canadian Journal of Linguistics*, 55(2): 1001–1028. DOI: 10.1353/cjl.2010.0007

Elman, Jeffrey. L., Randy. L. Diehl, and Susan Buchwald. E. 1977. "Perceptual Switching in Bilinguals." *Journal of the Acoustical Society of America* 62: 971–974. DOI: 10.1121/1.381591

Flege, James. E. 1995. "Second-language Speech Learning: Theory, Findings, and Problems." In *Speech Perception and Linguistic Experience: Issues in Cross-Language Research*, ed. by Winifred Strange, 233–277. Timonium, MD: York Press.

Flege, James, Grace H. Yeni-Komshian, and Serena Liu. 1999. "Age Constraints on Second Language Acquisition." *Journal of Memory and Language*, 41: 78–104. DOI: 10.1006/jmla.1999.2638

Fox, Robert A., James E. Flege, and Murray J. Munro. 1995. "The Perception of English and Spanish Vowels by Native English and Spanish Listeners: A Multidimensional Scaling Analysis." *Journal of the Acoustical Society of America* 97 (4): 2540–2551. DOI: 10.1121/1.411974

Garcia-Sierra, Adrian, Randy L. Diehl, and Craig Champlin. 2009. "Testing the Double Phonemic Boundary in Bilinguals." *Speech Communication* 51: 369–378. DOI: 10.1016/j.specom.2008.11.005

Genesee, Fred. 1989. "Early Bilingual Development: One Language or Two." *Journal of Child Language*, 16: 161–179. DOI: 10.1017/S0305000900013490

Hopp, Holger, and Monika S. Schmidt. 2011. "Perceived Foreign Accent in First Language Attrition and Second Language Acquisition: The Impact of Age of Acquisition and Bilingualism." *Applied Psycholinguistics*: 1–34.

Hualde, José. 2005. *The Sounds of Spanish*. New York: Cambridge UP.

Hyltenstam, Kenneth, and Niclas Abrahamsson. 2003. "Age of Onset and Ultimate Attainment in Near-native Speakers of Swedish." In *Selected Papers from the 8th Nordic Conference on Bilingualism. Multilingualism in Global and Local Perspectives 2001*, ed. by Fraurud Kary and Kenneth Hyltenstam, 319–340. Stockholm: Centre for Research on Bilingualism, Stockholm University, and Rinkeby Institute of Multilingual Research.

Lisker, Leigh, and Arthur S. Abramson. 1964. "A Cross-language Study of Voicing in Initial Stops: Acoustical Measurements." *Word*, 20: 384–422.

Lisker, Leigh, and Arthur S. Abramson. 1970. "The Voicing Dimension: Some Experiments in Comparative Phonetics." *Proceedings of the 6th International Congress of Phonetic Sciences, Prague*, 1967: 563–567.

Long, Michael H. 1990. "Maturational Constraints in Language Development." *Studies in Second Language Acquisition*, 12: 251–285. DOI: 10.1017/S0272263100009165

Lewis, Anthony. 2000. "Acoustic Variability of Intervocalic Voiceless Stop Consonants in Three Spanish Dialects". In *Hispanic Linguistics at the Turn of the Millennium* ed. by Héctor Campos, Elena Herburger, Alfonso Morales-Front, and Thomas J. Walsh, Somerville, MA: Cascadilla Press.

MacKay, Ian R. A., James E. Flege, Thorsten Piske, and Carlo Schirru. 2001. "Category Restructuring during Second-language Speech Acquisition." *The Journal of the Acoustical Society of America*, 110(1): 516–528. DOI: 10.1121/1.1377287

Major, Roy C. 2009. *Sociolinguistic Factors in Loss & Acquisition of Phonology*. CUP.

Morrison, Geoffrey S. 2003. "Perception and production of Spanish vowels by English speakers." *Proceedings of the* 15th *International Congress of Phonetic Sciences: Barcelona 2003*, ed. by Maria-Josep Solé, Daniel Recansens, and Joaquín Romero, 1533–1536. Adelaide, South Australia: Causal Productions.

Morrison, Geoffrey S. 2006. *L1 & L2 Production and Perception of English and Spanish Vowels: A Statistical Modelling Approach*. Doctoral dissertation, University of Alberta, Edmonton, Alberta, Canada.

Morrison, Geoffrey, and Paola Escudero. 2007. "A Cross-dialect Comparison of Peninsular- and Peruvian-Spanish Vowels." *Proceedings of the* 16th *International Congress of Phonetic Sciences*, 1505–1508.

Montrul, Silvina. 2008. "Incomplete Acquisition in Spanish Heritage Speakers: Chronological Age or Interface Vulnerability?" *Proceedings of the* 32nd *Annual Boston University Conference on Language Development*: 299–310.

Paradis, Johanne, and Fred Genesee. 1996. "Syntactic Acquisition: Autonomous or Interdependent?" *Studies in Second Language Acquisition, 18*: 1–25. DOI: 10.1017/S0272263100014662

Perissinotto, Antonio. 1975. *Fonología del español hablado en la Ciudad de México. Ensayo de un método sociolingüístico*. México: El Colegio de México.

Rosner Burton. S., Luis E. López-Bascuas, José E. García-Albea, and Richard P. Fahey. 2000. "Voice-onset Times for Castilian Spanish Initial Stops." *Journal of Phonetics* 28: 217–224. DOI: 10.1006/jpho.2000.0113

Sebastián Gallés, Núria, and Salvador Soto-Franco. 1999. "Online Processing of Native and Non-native Phonemic Contrasts in Early Bilinguals." *Cognition* 72:111–123. DOI: 10.1016/S0010-0277(99)00024-4

Silva-Corvalán, Carmen. 2003. "Linguistic Consequences of Reduced Input in Bilingual First Language Acquisition". In *Linguistic Theory and Language Development in Hispanic Languages*, ed. by Silvina Montrul, and Francisco Ordóñez, 375–397. Somerville, MA: Cascadilla Press.

Sorace, Antonella. 2000. "Differential Effects of Attrition in the L1 Syntax of Near-Native L2 Speakers." *Proceedings of the* 24th *Boston University Conference on Language Development,* ed. by Catherine Howell, Sarah Fish, and Thea Keith-Lucas. Somerville: Cascadilla Press.

Stevens Kenneth, Alvin Liberman, Michael Studdert-Kennedy, and Sven Ohman. 1969. "Cross Language Study of Vowel Perception." *Language & Speech* 12: 1–23.

Scovel, Thomas. 1988. *A Time to Speak. A Psycholinguistic Inquiry into the Critical Period for Human Speech*. New York, NY: Newbury House Publishers.

Stockwell, Robert, and Donald Bowen. 1965. *The Sounds of English and Spanish*. Chicago: The University of Chicago Press.

Thomas, Erik R. 2011. *Sociophonetics: An Introduction.* Basingstoke, U.K./New York: Palgrave.

Trubetzkoy, Nikolai. 1969. *Principles of Phonology.* Berkeley, CA: University of California Press.

Volterra, Virginia, and Traute Taeschner. 1978. "The Acquisition and Development of Language by Bilingual Children." *Journal of Child Language* 5: 311–326. DOI: 10.1017/S0305000900007492

Williams, Lee. 1977a. "The Voicing Contrast in Spanish." *Journal of Phonetics* 5: 169–184.

Williams, Lee. 1977b. "The Perception of Stop Consonant Voicing by Spanish-English Bilinguals." *Perception and Psychophysics* 21: 289–297. DOI: 10.3758/BF03199477

Wode, Henning. 1978. "The Beginning of Non-school Room L2 Phonological Acquisition." *International Review of Applied Linguistics* 16:109–25. DOI: 10.1515/iral.1978.16.1-4.109

Appendix A

Table A1. Stimuli used in the discrimination task

Consonants

Initial Tonic

/b/	/p/	/d/	/t/	/g/	/k/
Bata	Pata	Dales	Tales	Gana	Cana
Beso	Peso	Dejo	Tejo	Guiso	Quiso
Vino	Pino	Dilo	Tilo	Goce	Cose
Boca	Poca	Doce	Tose	Guste	Custe (last name)
Buzo	Puso	Duna	Tuna		

Initial Atonic

/b/	/p/	/d/	/t/	/g/	/k/
Bazar	Pasar	Dañó	Tañó	Garita	Carita
Becar	Pecar	Dejado	Tejado	Gordura	Cordura
Visar	Pisar	Diré	Tiré		
Volar	Polar	Domar	Tomar		

Medial Tonic

/b/	/p/	/d/	/t/	/g/	/k/
Subimos	Supimos	Rodar	Rotar	Pegar	Pecar
		Medí	Metí	Pegué	Pequé
		Cardón	Cartón	Seguía	Sequía
				Rasgó	Rascó
				Agudas	Acudas

Medial Atonic

/b/	/p/	/d/	/t/	/g/	/k/
Taba	Tapa	Falda	Falta	Vaga	Vaca
Sube	Supe	Arde	Arte	Pegue	Peque
Rubia[11]	Rupia	Ardo	Harto	Ego	Eco
Cabo	Capo				

Vowels

Initial Tonic

/e/	/i/	/o/	/u/
Peso	Piso	Poso	Puso
Tero	Tiro	Toco	Tuco
Queso	Quiso	Copo	Cupo
Ves	Bis	Modo	Mudo
Dejo	Dijo	Sopla	Supla
Zeta	Cita	Fondo	Fundo
Dele	Dile	Oso	Uso
Dejo	Dijo	Rombo	Rumbo
Mesa	Misa	Locas	Lucas
		Boda	Buda
		Dona	Duna

Initial Atonic

/e/	/i/	/o/	/u/
Pesar	Pisar	Acosado	Acusado
		Osaba	Usaba
		Sociedad	Suciedad
		Dorar	Durar

Medial Tonic

/e/	/i/	/o/	/u/
Senté	Sentí	Agosto	Agusto
Bebé	Bebí		
Medea	Medía		

---

11.   The contrast 'rubia ~ rupia' was later excluded from the analysis, because at this point we were only testing the influence of pure vowels on the discrimination of the sounds in question.

Medial Atonic

/e/	/i/	/o/	/u/
Pepe	Pepi	Hago	Agu[13]
Ante	Anti		
Roque	Rocky		
Cebe_	Sebi[12]		
Ande	Andi_		
Drogue	Drogui		

Appendix B

Table B1. Percentage of errors per group for consonants and vowels. A one-way ANOVA showed a significant difference in the discrimination of consonants but not vowels. A Tukey post-hoc test showed that the difference is significant between controls and LTIs (long term immigrants). IHS stands for 'intermediate heritage speakers' and AHS stands for 'advanced heritage speakers'

Group	N	Vowels		Consonants		Tukey's Grouping
		Mean	St.Dev.	Mean	St.Dev.	
LTI	6	9.72%	6.14%	16.87%	8.92%	A
IHS	6	6.96%	4.18%	12.27%	2.22%	AB
AHS	19	8.04%	4.14%	12.05%	6.54%	AB
CTRL	14	6.35%	3.06%	7.09%	3.42%	B

Appendix C

Table C1. Percentage of errors per group for labial, dorsal and coronal consonants. Significant differences were found in the discrimination of labials and dorsals.

Group	N	/b, p/		Tukey's Grouping	/t, d/		/g, k/		Tukey's Grouping
		Mean	St.Dev.		Mean	St.Dev.	Mean	St.Dev	
LTI	6	16.41%	11.56%	A	14.07%	10.86%	20.35%	7.45%	A
IHS	6	9.12%	3.50%	AB	11.11%	5.80%	16.67%	6.90%	AB
AHS	19	5.51%	6.15%	B	12.05%	7.85%	18.63%	8.72%	A
CTRL	14	4.25%	2.98%	B	6.35%	5.00%	10.71%	5.01%	B

---

12. Nickname for 'Sebastian'

13. Nickname for 'Agustina'

Appendix D

Table D1

Percentage of errors per group per vowel contrast. No significant differences were found.

Group	N	/e, i/ Mean	/e, i/ St.Dev.	/o, u/ Mean	/o, u/ St.Dev.
LTI	6	9.81%	5.82%	9.65%	7.43%
IHS	6	6.10%	5.13%	7.95%	4.59%
AHS	19	7.65%	5.06%	8.46%	4.34%
CTRL	14	5.89%	4.16%	6.86%	3.05%

The linguistic competence of second-generation bilinguals

A critique of "incomplete acquisition"

Ricardo Otheguy
Graduate Center CUNY

This paper discusses the native linguistic competence of second-generation bilinguals born of immigrant, refugee, expatriate, or otherwise dislocated parents, concentrating on the grammars of second-generation Hispanics in the U.S. Scholarly opinion has gravitated toward the position that the Spanish of these speakers reflects a process of incomplete acquisition. This paper invites examination of the alternative view, namely: what we observe in second-generation bilingual Latinos is not errors, as they are frequently described in the literature, but rather points of divergence between their Spanish and that of the previous generation, due to normal intergenerational language change accelerated by conditions of language contact. The notion of incomplete acquisition rests on an incorrect view of child language acquisition as a process of perfect reproduction of parental grammars. But the process is one where children engage in grammar construction through hypothesis testing. Consequently, all next-generation grammars end up somewhat different from parental ones, paving the way for language change. The grammars of U.S.-born Latinos are thus, like all next-generation grammars, different, not incomplete. Examining the use of subjunctives for a brief illustration, grammarians regularly note variability in cases like *Quizás venga* (subjunctive) ~ *Quizás viene* (indicative) but obligatoriness in *Quiero que lo llames* (subjunctive), with the indicative alternative occurring seldom or never, and analyzable as ungrammatical, **Quiero que lo llamas* (indicative). Second generation bilinguals have extended variability, so that for them the latter is usable, and analyzable as grammatical, a fact that disables these bilinguals from successful participation in experiments centered on somebody else's grammaticality judgments, leading to conclusions of incompleteness.

1. Introduction

This paper discusses the native linguistic competence of second-generation bilinguals born of immigrant, refugee, expatriate, or otherwise dislocated parents worldwide.

DOI 10.1075/rllt.9.16oth
© 2016 John Benjamins Publishing Company

It concentrates on what is probably one of the most studied of these competences, that of second-generation Hispanic bilinguals in the United States.[1] Based on both the absence of certain grammatical forms in sociolinguistic corpora and on what are said to be incorrect responses in psycholinguistic experiments, scholarly opinion has gravitated toward the position that the Spanish of second-generation bilinguals in the U.S. is a case of "incomplete acquisition" (Benmamoun, Montrul and Polinsky 2010; Montrul 2008, 2009, 2013; Zapata, Sánchez and Toribio 2005, Silva-Corvalán 2003). The term indicates that the process that in monolinguals follows a normal trajectory, culminating in a fully and successfully developed grammar, follows in these bilinguals a deviant course leading to an unsuccessful outcome. This paper invites examination of the alternative view, that what we observe in both the natural and experimental linguistic behavior of second-generation bilingual U.S. Latinos is not errors, as they are frequently described in the literature, but rather points of divergence, dialectal differences if you will, between their Spanish and that of the previous generation, due to normal intergenerational language change accelerated by conditions of language contact.[2] While the focus in this paper will be on Spanish and on the U.S., the same point can be made about second-generation bilinguals everywhere, including, for example, the children of Russian immigrants in the U.S. and of Turkish immigrants in Germany. About these, I would also argue that what we are faced with is not unsuccessfully acquired languages, but rather normal, successfully acquired versions of Russian and Turkish that are simply different from what the parents brought to their new settings from Russia and Turkey.

Two themes run through the present critique. The first is that the flawed concepts and methods embraced by the language acquisition proposal render it of little empirical value. The second is that the level of incoherence afflicting the proposal makes it highly unlikely that it can ever be salvaged by means of conceptual refinement or methodological improvement.

---

1.   Following standard practice in linguistics and sociology, we use the term *second generation* for those born in the U.S. of parents born abroad (Veltman 2000; Portes and Rumbaut 2001). For ease of reading, we use the term adult to refer to both adults and late adolescents, distinguishing between them only when necessary.

2.   Incomplete acquisition has been briefly criticized in Carreira and Potowski (2011, 150n); a chapter-length critique is in Otheguy and Zentella (2012, Chapter 10). Some skepticism regarding details, combined with general acceptance of the proposal, is in Putnam and Sánchez (2013).

2.   A clarification regarding social dialects

A clarification is in order before proceeding. Throughout the world, speech produced by people of low socioeconomic status and little formal education is often regarded as incorrect and made the object of social reproof. In many settings worldwide, poor, uneducated monolingual native speakers of many languages are said to speak incorrectly and to produce speech marred by errors. In North American linguistics, beginning in the times of Boas and Sapir, and continuing in subsequent decades in such widely read works as Hall (1950), linguists have taken the position, eloquently restated in the following generation by Labov (1969), that such ways of speaking constitute structurally systematic varieties of their languages. Consequently, many linguists hold that these forms of speech should be the object of documentation, analysis and social support, and that the right of their users to them should be forcefully affirmed. In this understanding of popular speech, the reasonableness of which strikes me as undiminished, second-generation bilingual Latinos would be considered speakers of a socially disfavored variety of Spanish. Such a perspective would offer a substantively different conception of the Spanish competence of these bilinguals from the one advanced in works on "incomplete acquisition." It would be a conception that would hold parallels with, for example, the current understanding of the Englishes of many African-Americans in the U.S. And yet, and to avoid confusion, it is important to stress that the question taken up in this paper is not whether or not the speech of second-generation U.S. Latinos is deserving of sympathetic appreciation, nor is it whether they have a right to it. Without in any way diminishing the importance of those questions, it should be kept in mind that they are not at the center of the present discussion. The alternative to the notion of incomplete acquisition of which we urge consideration here (that of a differently evolved rather than an incomplete grammar) is of a linguistic-psychological rather than a social-political character, focusing on empirical adequacy and theoretical coherence rather than social amelioration.

3.   Popular forms of Spanish and the grammars of second-generation bilinguals

With this in mind, it will be clear that the term *grammar* is being used here in the sense familiar in theoretical linguistics of mental grammar, a sense that is psychological and non-prescriptive. The vast majority of second-generation Latinos in the U.S. grow up in communities that are outside the mainstream of formally standardized Spanish usage, and receive little or no education in, or about, Spanish (Menken and

Kleyn 2010). There is thus little point in debating the obvious fact that their familiarity with standardized features of Spanish tends to be very weak. Instead, the debate must be about the grammars underlying the informal registers that tend to predominate in the vernacular Spanishes of the U.S.[3]

Given that these popular forms of speech constitute the only reasonable path to an understanding of these speakers' underlying linguistic competence, one must regard with concern the research design implemented in much of the literature on incomplete acquisition (especially in the comparative-experimental branch of the literature, but in the corpus-based branch as well). For these designs do not sufficiently guard against the very strong possibility that the Spanishes in circulation in the communities where second-generation bilinguals developed their grammars during early childhood differ, at many points, from the Spanish reflected in the research items.

For example, Montrul's (2009) study of incomplete acquisition deals with Spanish preterit and imperfect verbs, apparently assuming that the standardized usage of the tenses that is reflected in the test items matches the normative usage of the parents and the communities where second-generation bilinguals were exposed to Spanish. Similarly, Zapata, Sánchez, and Toribio (2005) study word order, again assuming that the standardized usage reflected in the test items is normative in the communities of birth of second-generation bilinguals. My concern, in other words, is that second-generation bilinguals may be, to an indeterminate extent, sitting for experimental tasks in a language quite different from the one that they acquired. When experimental subjects are tested on the basis of items belonging to somebody else's grammar, their lack of success (which leads to the conclusion of incompleteness) is preordained and unavoidable, and therefore unrevealing. A brief illustration of second-generation Spanish will provide us with a specific instance of this problem.

4.   A brief illustration of second-generation Spanish

Sentences like (1a) and (2a) are usually described in grammars of standardized Spanish as obligatory subjunctives, with (1b) and (2b) constituting unacceptable alternatives in the indicative. In contrast, (3a) and (4a) are said to be optional subjunctives, with (3b) and (4b) constituting valid indicative alternatives.

---

3.   While our investigation is of considerable relevance to the growing interest in American high schools and universities in teaching Spanish to second-generation bilinguals (cf. Fairclough 2005), our purpose here is not to engage directly with these educational initiatives that (quite properly perhaps) revolve around standard Spanish. Rather, the present paper is about the foundational linguistic competence, reflected in popular speech, on which those efforts depend.

(1)   a.   Quiero que lo <u>llames.</u>
           'I want you to call him.'

       b.   *Quiero que lo <u>llamas.</u>
           'I want you to call him.'

(2)   a.   Dudo mucho que <u>venga.</u>
           'I doubt very much that he will come.'

       b.   *Dudo mucho que <u>viene.</u>
           'I doubt very much that he will come.'

(3)   a.   Quizás <u>venga.</u>
           'Perhaps she will come.'

       b.   Quizás <u>viene.</u>
           'Perhaps she will come.'

(4)   a.   Busco uno que <u>tenga</u> tapa.
           'I'm looking for one with a cover.'

       b.   Busco uno que <u>tiene</u> tapa.
           'I'm looking for one with a cover.'

But studies of Spanish in the U.S. have consistently shown that indicatives found in volitional contexts such as (1b) and commentary contexts such as (2b) are common among second-generation bilinguals (Gutiérrez 1990; Lantolf 1978; Lynch 1999; Merino 1983; Ocampo 1990; Silva-Corvalán 1994; Torres 2009). A fuller illustration of these types of verbal mood choices in Spanish in the U.S. helps to make the point.

Bookhamer (2013) uses transcribed interviews to describe the difference between 26 first-generation Latin American newcomers to New York City and 26 second-generation bilingual New Yorkers. The author isolated ten environments or context types that are said to require or favor the subjunctive. For each such environment, Bookhamer observed the percentage of cases where speakers from both immigrant generations in fact chose the subjunctive. First-generation speakers displayed categorical or near-categorical choice of subjunctives in only five of these context types; these included causative clauses (*hizo que vinieran* 'he made them come') and purpose clauses (*para que vengan* 'so that they will come'). In the other five context types, the first generations displayed variable behavior, that is, they alternated between moods. For example, in contexts like (1) and (2), the subjunctive percentage fell short of 100, to 99 percent and 88 percent subjunctives respectively. And in utterances of the type 'if I could I would go with them' the proportion of subjunctives versus indicatives (*si pudiera <u>fuera</u>/iba con ellos*) dropped to 77 percent.

Second-generation speakers in Bookhamer's corpus resembled first-generation ones in choosing subjunctives in the same context types, but differed as to where these choices were categorical or variable. For second-generation speakers, only causative contexts were categorical. The other categorical choices of the first generation have become variable in the second. For example, purposive environments, which showed 100 percent subjunctive for the Latin Americans, showed 90 percent subjunctive among the New Yorkers. For some contexts, the generational differences were considerable; for example, for future contexts such as 'we will talk when they come', first-generation speakers chose subjunctives (*hablaremos cuando vengan*) in 97 percent of cases, whereas second-generation ones did so in only 76 percent of cases, resorting to indicatives (*hablaremos cuando vienen*) for the rest. Some of the contexts that are variable in Latin America and Spain also showed large intergenerational differences. For example, in indefinite contexts such as 'I'm looking for one who will come', first-generation speakers used subjunctives (*busco uno que venga*) in 84 percent of cases, but second-generation speakers did so in only 64 percent of cases, choosing indicatives (*busco uno que viene*) for the rest.

The peculiarities of indicative and subjunctive usage of second-generation bilinguals documented by Bookhamer are susceptible to two very different kinds of interpretations. As we have seen, second-generation mood choices can be seen as errors, supporting the "incomplete acquisition" position (Montrul 2007, 2008, 2009). My alternative interpretation is as follows. The direction of mood choices is the same in both generations. The contexts that strongly favor the subjunctive in the first generations are also subjunctive-favoring in the second, but less so. In some cases, contexts that are categorically subjunctive in the first generation become variable in the second (e.g. purpose clauses). In others, variable contexts where the subjunctive is highly preferred in the first generation continue as variable in the second, but with the subjunctive being only moderately preferred (e.g. future clauses). Rather than a sharp distinction between correct usage and errors, research like Bookhamer's uncovers a different pattern of variability, a pattern that, if Spanish were to persist in the U.S. for several generations, may simply be the normal prelude to eventual categorical change (Otheguy and Zentella 2012, Chapter 10). With respect to mood choice, second-generation speakers have successfully acquired a natural and systematic Spanish grammar, one that differs from that of the first generation in having moved a few notches the line between obligatory and variable environments, as well as in having yielded more space to the indicative in those environments where previous generations had already been making room for it. Similar lines of analyses should be applicable to the other features that distinguish the Spanish of second-generation bilinguals.

5.   Misapprehensions related to claims of "incomplete acquisition"

The claim regarding incomplete acquisition is weakened by more than unwarranted conclusions of incompleteness reached on the basis of mere quantitative intergenerational differences such as the ones just illustrated; and by more than insufficient appreciation, as discussed above, of the importance of socio-dialectal differences between the standardized features of the language of the researcher and the popular features of the language of the informant. In addition, the claim of incompleteness relies crucially on misapprehensions regarding four highly problematic notions: the *native monolingual control*, the *experimental subject*, the *heritage speaker*, and the *Spanish language*. Once the flaws in these concepts are exposed, the underlying proposal regarding incomplete acquisition loses much of its appeal.

5.1 The problem of native speaker monolingual controls

Studies purporting to establish incomplete acquisition of Spanish and other minority languages in the U.S and other settings have relied heavily on comparisons between second-generation bilinguals and native monolingual controls. These controls are usually well-educated residents of the native countries of the parents of the second-generation bilinguals under study. For example, in Martínez Mira (2009), the controls were monolingual Spanish-speakers in Mexico, and in Polinsky (2010) the controls were Russian-speaking residents of Moscow. In other instances, perhaps most, the controls are international students in short stays in U.S. colleges and universities. In the literature under discussion, the shortcomings of comparisons with monolingual home-country controls tend to undermine research of all types, but they present especially serious problems for studies based on experimental or comparative designs.

The central problem is that home-country controls differ from second-generation U.S. bilinguals in ways that render the comparison uninformative. The differences include the type of environment where they first acquire the language, the amount of exposure to schooling in it, the frequency of its use with siblings and same-age friends, and the extent of experience speaking it in a majority setting. These differences inevitably produce an apples-and-oranges effect that weakens the validity of conclusions regarding incomplete acquisition. In these studies, the initial differences between home-country controls and second-generation U.S. bilinguals raise the question of what exactly the Latin American home-country controls share with the second-generation Latino experimental subjects, other than the fact that the same word is used to name their native linguistic competences (in other words, what is it that grants them the status of legitimate controls other than the fact that they, like the experimental subjects, are native speakers of something called Spanish).

The concern has already been expressed that many linguistic features found in the standardized language of the home-country controls may not be part of the popular language of experimental subjects. To cite just two examples, Rothman and Pires (2009) show that inflected infinitives are found in literate but not popular Brazilian speech. And as noted above, Bookhamer found that contexts like (1) and (2) which, if the standard grammars are to be believed, constitute categorical subjunctive contexts for educated Latin Americans, were actually *not* categorical in the popular usage of

Latin American newcomers to New York (thus very likely not categorical in popular usage in the home countries either). Portuguese inflected infinitives and categorical Spanish subjunctives are the sort of usages that are readily available to provide the comparative basis for conclusions of incompleteness in second-generation Brazilians and Hispanics in the U.S. But given the actual popular speech of first-generation U.S. speakers that constitutes the model for the second generation, such conclusions would have to be received with considerable skepticism.

The problem with home-country controls, then, is that they are likely to have grammars that are comparable neither to those of the second-generation experimental subjects nor to those of the first-generation speakers who were the second generation's models during early acquisition. These inappropriate comparisons make the poor performance of second-generation bilinguals in research tests foreordained and inescapable, tainting the conclusion of "incompleteness" with the character of a necessary result, rather than endowing it with the required quality of a contingent outcome.

The incommensurability between home-country controls and second-generation bilinguals is also related to the lack of Spanish literacy already noted for the latter. Much of the research leading to conclusions of incompleteness relies on metalinguistic judgments of grammaticality, felicity, logic, etc. These studies are undermined by the strong possibility that, quite independently of the feature under investigation, literacy itself may be a prerequisite for the accurate production of such judgments (Bialystok and Ryan 1985; Birdsong 1989). Particularly relevant is the greater ability by literates to objectify language (Bialystok 1986) and the strong possibility that this, and not anything related to actual speech or underlying mental grammar, is the explanation for the much greater success of literate home-country controls in metalinguistic tasks.

More important, from the perspective of the language-change alternative to incomplete acquisition being urged here, the differences of usage and judgment between home-country controls and second-generation bilinguals that are turned up by researchers are of little consequence. The position maintained in this paper *expects* differences between experimental U.S. second-generation subjects and Latin American controls. The alternative understanding proposed here already grants, indeed it presses, the point that, with respect to many features, second-generation bilinguals will *not* have the same grammar as their U.S.-based parents, let alone the Latin American-based home-country controls. The relevant question is not whether there are areas of the grammars of second-generation speakers that are different from the analogous areas of educated Latin Americans. The question, with respect to these grammatical features, is whether the second-generation grammars were acquired on the basis of standardized Latin American models (not very likely), or were instead grown on the basis of models of popular speech prevalent in U.S. barrios (much more likely) that do not get factored into the design of research studies. And be that as it may, the question is also whether the expectably new second-generation grammars have ended up, through the process of partial replication and innovation, as normal human grammars (that are however different from those of the home countries and of the first generation); or as grammars that are in some way fractured, imperfect or "incomplete."

5.2   The problem of selection of experimental subjects

Research inspired by the assumption of incomplete acquisition suffers not only from inappropriate home-country controls but also from less than ideal U.S. experimental subjects. Since the goal is to settle, in a theoretically sound manner, the question of the correct characterization of second-generation Spanish grammars, our focus must be on those U.S.-born Latinos whose early childhood created favorable conditions for the formation of such a grammar. People who sincerely claim a strongly felt Latino identity, but whose early childhood experiences are such that it is very unlikely that a Spanish grammar would have formed, do not qualify for research investigating second-generation bilingual Spanish competence.

Such disqualifying experiences would include, for example, the case of informants with Latin American-born, but long U.S.-settled, bilingual parents who speak to each other in Spanish but to their children in English; or cases where the father speaks Spanish (and often provides the research subject's last name) but the mother is a monolingual Anglophone, creating in the home a predominantly English surround. Many such conditions are found in U.S. Latino society, negating the possibility of first-language acquisition of Spanish by many Hispanics. When early childhood circumstances for grammar formation have not obtained, findings of "incompleteness" are of no theoretical relevance, because they hold true ipso facto, in ways essentially parallel to the incompleteness of languages learned through brief travel or occasional lessons; and because such findings follow necessarily, and therefore uninterestingly, from the fact that the conditions for development of biculturalism often exist in homes that lack the conditions for the development of bilingualism.

5.3   The problem of the concept "heritage speaker"

A major contributor to the problem just described is the notion of the heritage speaker. Originating in pedagogical circles (Fishman 2001), the term heritage speaker is acknowledged to be of vague and uncertain applicability (Carreira 2004; Valdés 2000, 2003, 2005), and to be used only for lack of a better word (Benmamoun, Montrul, and Polinsky 2010). The heritage speaker has thus been established as a type by simply asserting that it exists, without ever saying how one is to distinguish it from other types. The ill-defined term contributes to the unfounded initial legitimacy of the incomplete acquisition hypothesis, for it serves to naturalize the position that heritage speakers, whatever they are, *are not native speakers*. This removal of second-generation bilinguals from the group of native speakers makes it possible for linguists to overcome what would otherwise be a reluctance to view anyone's native language in deficit terms. In addition, the term makes it acceptable to dispense with the common assumption among linguists that, when confronted with unfamiliar items in speakers who have used a language from earliest infancy, what we are witnessing is dialectal differences among natives rather than incompleteness.

Remove the term heritage speaker, set aside the Hispanics we have discussed above who are bicultural but not bilingual, and linguists would be placed in the awkward position of assuming incompleteness for speakers who were Spanish mono-lingual until the start of their school years; who well into their fifth or sixth birthday deployed their Spanish mental grammars (in many cases deploying no other) to speak with mothers, and often relied on it too when speaking with fathers; who typically rely on this grammar as adults when talking with many first-generation speakers in the U.S. (including their grandparents), as well as when talking with relatives of all ages when they travel to Latin America or Spain; who often use this grammar with siblings and friends; who in many cases crank it up in a revival of Hispanic speech practices in early adulthood in the vast Spanish-medium U.S. labor market; and who engage in all these grammar-supported speech interactions in what appear to be interpersonally successful ways.

The fact that, in the eyes of many Spanish-speaking researchers, these speech ways are in fact anything but successful is quite another story. The postulation of a separate category of heritage speaker may be, one suspects, ultimately inspired by informal per-ceptions that native second-generation bilinguals have inadequate Spanish communi-cative skills. But this perception has not been the object of theoretical articulation or empirical demonstration, as researchers have trained their sights narrowly, and based their conclusions of "incompleteness" solely, on grammatical rather than communica-tive features. To be sure, the literature on incomplete acquisition does report on what are called proficiency differences between heritage speakers (cf. Polinsky and Kagan 2007). But to my knowledge, no one has demonstrated that second-generation bilin-guals are unsuccessful users of Spanish *when situated in natural habitats and engaged in conversations with culturally sanctioned interlocutors*. Yet it is precisely such a dem-onstration that would be required to establish the distinctness of a heritage (and non-native) speaker type, as well as the validity of the initial step toward a conclusion of underlying incompleteness. As matters stand now, a well-articulated theory of native-language communicative abilities that would properly single out second-generation bilinguals as ineffective communicators belonging in a separate category of heritage (non-native) speakers remains beyond the horizon.

The absence of any definition of heritage speaker suggests that the only reason-able way to deal with second-generation Latinos who during early childhood grew up under conditions leading to the construction of Spanish grammars is to re-insert them into the class of native Spanish speakers. Once this insertion is accomplished, their speech peculiarities will lead to analyses of a very different cast than do the ones related to "incomplete acquisition."[4]

6. Problems of coherence related to incomplete acquisition

The incomplete acquisition hypothesis labors under serious problems of coherence, caused by shortfalls related to the idea of the "target," the notion of "Spanish," and the concept of "incompleteness" itself. Each is taken up in the following sections.

6.1 The incoherence of incomplete acquisition: The problem of the "target"

The coherence of the proposal about "incomplete acquisition" is weakened, first, by the simplistic stance taken with regard to the process of language acquisition. In the acquisition of natural languages everywhere, monolingual environments included, grammars are not simply handed down and installed as wholes in the minds of the members of the next generation. Rather, all children, monolinguals included, acquire grammars through a process of hypothesis formation and testing (Lust 2006). This is never a copying process of perfect cross-generational reproduction. Rather, the testing of hypotheses necessarily leads children to eventually settle on grammars that, with regard to several features, will differ from the grammars of the previous generation (Lightfoot 2010). The imperfect replication of parental grammars underlies the universally acknowledged fact of long-range language change, which builds up out of the gradual accumulation of short-range, intergenerational change. And it is the recognition of the pervasiveness of intergenerational language change that motivates my position that even though the native speech of second-generation bilinguals is admittedly not the same as that of their parents, it is very likely underpinned by grammars that are natural and fully developed rather than incomplete.

---

4. The reinsertion of second-generation bilinguals into the class of native speakers is advisable given the current understanding of the matter prevailing in most linguistics circles. But the suggestion is hedged by reservations. As a number of critics have pointed out (cf. Bonfiglio 2010), the native speaker, and the distinction between natives and non-natives, are, for all their acceptance in most areas of academic linguistics, deeply flawed categories, resting on socio-political power assertions rather than on research-based linguistic conclusions. The contents of this literature, seldom or never addressed by research on "heritage speakers," contribute to the uphill climb involved in the attempt to establish the validity of incomplete acquisition.

In the literature on incomplete acquisition, the facts of imperfect cross-generational replication and consequent change are ignored, replaced by the notions of *target* and *non-target attainment*, with non-target attainment systematically equated with incompleteness (cf. Montrul 2009). But if the theoretical understanding of second-generation bilinguals is to accommodate, as it must, the fact of language change, then it is not helpful to think in terms of targets. Models, yes, but not targets. The concept of a target makes sense when talking about students in a foreign-language class who aim to master, through explicit study, a stable set of standardized features on the basis of explicitly spelled out rules; but targets cease to make sense when talking about children in natural settings aiming subconsciously to build up a grammar. In such cases, children will always miss some of the lexical and grammatical targets, that is, they will always innovate on the model; otherwise languages would never change.

Second-generation bilingual acquirers in the U.S., then, build grammars that differ partially from those of the previous generation. On this account, they are the same as monolingual children acquiring Spanish in Latin America and Spain, for these children too end up with grammars that differ at specific points from those of the previous generation. The construct of "incomplete acquisition" is thus not useful as a unique characterization of second-generation bilinguals. If the construct were to have any meaning at all, it would have to be applied to *all* acquisition, since all acquisition, in monolingual and bilingual environments alike, is always "incomplete" with respect to many features of the model.

The innovative, imperfectly replicated Spanish grammars assembled by children in the U.S. under conditions of bilingualism and language contact may well show more divergence from the previous generation's model than do the also imperfectly replicated ones assembled in monolingual settings in Spain and Latin America. But to my knowledge, the literature has offered no criteria warranting the conclusion that the process of innovative grammatical construction in Latin America and Spain leads to grammars that are systematic and "complete," underwriting the production of appropriate utterances, whereas the equally innovative process in the U.S. leads to grammars that are deficient or "incomplete," leading to the production of errors. In other words, since the intergenerational transmission of all languages involves children repeatedly "missing the target," the field needs a theory that would tell us why misses by second-generation bilinguals in the U.S., unlike misses by monolinguals in the home countries, amount to incompleteness. We know that in cross-generational linguistic transmission the proverb is reversed: the apple *always* falls far from the tree. Supporters of the notion of incomplete acquisition claim that second-generation bilingual apples in the U.S. have fallen *too* far, but without telling us what criteria they used to measure, making it impossible to evaluate whether the claim makes any sense.

6.2   The incoherence of incomplete acquisition: The problem of "Spanish"

Linguists have long recognized that terms like Spanish, English, Arabic, Quechua, Swahili, etc., make reference to socio-cultural entities, not to mental grammars. The terms that designate discrete, enumerable languages are useful because members of social groups so regard them. But they lose much of their validity when they are reified as the names of distinct grammars, for the simple reason that they inevitably corral under the same rubric highly heterogeneous collections of linguistic systems. As is well known, the striking differences found among people who are claimed by society as speakers of the same language, as well as the compelling similarities found among those that are said to be speakers of different ones, tend to negate any objective effort to justify which individual grammars properly belong under a particular language label and which do not, or which belong more and which less. The point is old in linguistics. It was already sketched out by the scholars who compiled the course notes published as Saussure (1916); it is well articulated and grounded in theoretical considerations in Diver (1995); and is rearticulated and extended in the elaborations by several of the authors in Makoni and Pennycook (2007). The idea that language names are not grammar names fits well with the distinction in Chomsky (1971) between I-language and E-language. In this formulation, Spanish, English, Quechua, etc. are E-language labels designating social entities, not I-language ones designating grammars.

Now, "incomplete acquisition," from all appearances, is a claim about I-language, that is, a claim about the incomplete state of a mental grammar. Yet, contradictorily, this I-language claim rests squarely on the E-language term *Spanish*. Experimental subjects in the incomplete acquisition literature are given Spanish proficiency tests; and the conclusion of incompleteness depends in every case, as we have seen, on stacking up the performance of "heritage speakers" of Spanish against that of Spanish monolingual controls (Martínez Mira 2007; Montrul 2009).

This exercise of coming to systemic, I-language conclusions on the basis of social, E-language categories injects into the literature on incomplete acquisition a large dose of incoherence. For it turns out under scrutiny that it is not simple incompleteness that is being identified, but incompleteness with respect to the complete social whole sponsored by the E-language notion of Spanish. No data or theoretical reasoning has been offered that the speech of second-generation bilinguals is reflective of something that fails to meet the requirements for a human grammar to be complete. That is, these speakers have not been shown to produce speech on the basis of something that falls short of being a possible I-language system; they have only been shown to produce speech on the basis of something that falls short of being the researcher's familiar E-language Spanish. With reference to our examples above, the incomplete acquisition assumption rests on the claim that utterances such as (1b) and (2b), with indicatives, reflect incompleteness of acquisition because, in order to be grammatical in something called Spanish, (1) and (2) need subjunctives, as in (1a) and (2a). Plainly, this is an E-language appeal, and no effort has been made to show that, in some strictly systemic sense, the use of an indicative to communicate 'I want you to call him' cannot reflect I-language wholeness, systematicity, and "completeness." If the claim were different, and all four sentences in (1) and (2) were to be admitted, in a different social exercise of E-language adjudication, into what is called Spanish, incompleteness with respect to this feature would evaporate.

The point is worth repeating in a different way. The incomplete acquisition claim, if it is to make any sense at all, cannot be that the entity that is incompletely acquired is a socio-cultural one, and that the errors described in experiments are failures to comply with social conventions of correctness. Those would be the prescriptive evaluations of a schoolteacher, not the descriptive or explanatory hypotheses of a scientist. The notion of incomplete acquisition is, undoubtedly, a proposal related to mental grammar put forth within the science of linguistics (including psycholinguistics and sociolinguistics). And yet, disturbingly, the argument for the incomplete condition of the mental grammar of a second-generation bilingual depends crucially on the social category "Spanish," since the errors of informants are detectable only by comparison with the linguistic behavior of other speakers, who also fall under the social label Spanish.

In order to sustain "incomplete acquisition" as a hypothesis freed from social, E-language considerations, proponents would have to argue about (1) and (2) above that no possible language can subsist when the watershed between categorical and variable mood choices is located where second-generation bilinguals have it, that completeness requires that it be located exactly where (some forms of) Latin American Spanish show it. No arguments for such a claim have been put forth.

In other words, proponents of incomplete acquisition have not answered why, for example, sentence (5) below, with a finite verb and no pronoun, and (6), with an infinitive and a pronoun, are both widely regarded as part of "complete" Spanish, whereas (1b) and (2b) are not.

(5)   La tarjeta es para que <u>llames</u>.
      'The card is for you to call.'

(6)   La tarjeta es para tú <u>llamar</u>.
      'The card is for you to call.'

The utterance in (5) is usually described as belonging to Spanish, period. The alternative in (6) is described as Spanish, but regional (more specifically, Caribbean, a geographical claim whose accuracy, or lack thereof, is beside the point here). The case for incomplete acquisition would have to work out an E-language-independent, I-language-centered argument that would justify the claim that speakers who consistently use (6) have successfully reached the stage of a complete, if regional, Spanish, whereas those who use (1b) and (2b) have not. Similarly, proponents of incomplete acquisition would need to explain why speakers who only have (7), and who lack the distinction between familiar and formal in the plural in the manner of speakers who have both (8a) and (8b), are nevertheless within the confines of completeness, whereas speakers who lack the subjunctives above are relegated to the territory of incompleteness.

(7) Los espero mañana.
     'I am expecting you tomorrow.'   [plural, familiar and formal]

(8) a. Os espero mañana.
         'I am expecting you tomorrow.'   [plural, familiar only]

     b. Los espero mañana.
         'I am expecting you tomorrow.'   [plural, formal only]

The unmet challenge of the incomplete acquisition hypothesis is thus enormous. The conclusion of incompleteness enjoys a measure of success only because its I-language claim is invalidly amalgamated with the E-language notion of Spanish, thus allowing differences to be turned into errors. Under a critical look, what the "incomplete acquisition" studies really show is that (1b) and (2b), and countless other U.S-utterances like them, are not Spanish as spoken by the researcher; or as spoken in the Latin American home countries; or presumably (for this is unlikely and has not been demonstrated) as spoken by the first-generation parents of second-generation bilinguals. That is, it would appear that proponents of incomplete acquisition have so far pressed their point mostly by socially supported assertion, deciding to bestow the E-language term Spanish on certain productions, as in (1a), (2a), and (3) through (8), while denying it to others, as in (1b) and (2b), and then turning this act of social name-giving into a claim about I-language grammar.

6.3 The incoherence of incomplete acquisition: The problem of "completeness"

The notion of incomplete acquisition has its origins in the analysis of the learning of second languages, usually in school environments, in the context of late bilingualism (Bley-Vroman 1989; Schachter 1990; Sorace 1993). In those contexts, it seems reasonable to speak of a second language that in many cases is only partially mastered. But conceptual difficulties start to creep in the moment the assumption of incompleteness is extended to the analysis of the acquisition of first languages in contexts of early bilingualism. Such a notion, in the context of home-based acquisition of a first language from earliest infancy, would require, in order for it to make sense, the articulation of a counterpart notion of "completeness".

But to my knowledge, no structural criteria exist on the basis of which we can tell whether a first grammar acquired by normal children during early childhood is complete. Until the criteria for completeness are spelled out, the concept of incompleteness remains exceedingly difficult to understand. In the absence of system-focused, I-language-centered criteria that are free of E-language and social considerations, "incomplete" in the study of second-generation bilinguals runs the risk of being no more than another term for unusual, or unattested in the home countries, or unfamiliar to the researcher.

7.   Summary and conclusion

The assumption of "incomplete acquisition" as a characterization of the grammars of second-generation bilinguals appears unsupported. Empirically, the assumption is undermined by still-unsolved problems regarding:

– the definition and isolation of a heritage speaker type that is properly distinguishable from the native-speaker type;
– the identification of the "control" speakers with whom second-generation bilinguals can be properly compared;
– the lack of cogency of the E-language foundation on which research on incomplete acquisition has been built.

More generally, the assumption of incomplete acquisition is jeopardized by the large role played in its adoption by a number of unsupported assertions. These include:

– that the conceptual apparatus used for analyzing the acquisition of second languages makes sense for the study of first languages;
– that second-generation speakers are not native speakers, of whom it thus makes sense to predicate that they have incomplete rather than differently evolved grammars;
– that there is no intergenerational language change, that is, that the general norm is for the speech of children to reach parental targets, and that failure to do so should be deemed reflective of grammatical incompleteness;
– that proficiency tests and comparative and experimental procedures relying on standardized features can tap the grammar of speakers who have had little or no natural early exposure to such features;
– that informants participating in tests and experiments in Spanish, which they usually neither read nor write, can be reasonably compared to informants for whom Spanish is the first, and main, language of literacy;

- that the cultural rubric "Hispanic" or "Latino" warrants the supposition of the existence of a true period of Spanish grammar formation in the lives of any individual claiming the label;
- that there is, out there, ready to be acquired, a unique, monolithic I-language entity called Spanish whose grammatical contours are commensurate with those of the sociocultural, E-language category Spanish; and
- that there is such a thing as a complete first-language grammar in comparison to which an incomplete one can be readily identified.

With regard to all these points, the need arises to sound a cautionary note, to urge skepticism, and to conclude that an empirically corroborated and theoretically tenable claim regarding the incomplete acquisition of the first language of second-generation bilinguals has not yet been put forth, leading to the concern that such a claim is ultimately incoherent and may prove impossible to sustain.

References

Benmamoun, Elabbas, Silvina Montrul, and Maria Polinsky. 2010. *White paper: Prolegomena to Heritage Linguistics*. Harvard University. Retrieved from http://scholar.harvard.edu/mpo-linsky/files/hl_white_paper_june_12.pdf

Bley-Vroman, Robert. 1989. "What is the logical problem of foreign language learning?" In *Linguistic Perspectives on Second Language Acquisition*, ed. by Susan M. Gass and Jacquelyn Schachter, 41–68. New York: Cambridge University Press. DOI: 10.1017/CBO9781139524544.005

Bonfiglio, Thomas Paul. 2010. *Mother Tongue and Nations: The Invention of the Native Speaker*. New York: Walter de Gruyter, Inc. DOI: 10.1515/9781934078266

Bookhamer, Kevin. 2013. *The Variable Grammar of the Spanish Subjunctive in Second-generation Bilinguals in New York City*. City University of New York, Ph.D. dissertation.

Carreira, María, and Kim Potowski. 2011. "Commentary: Pedagogical Implications of Experimental SNS research." *Heritage Language Journal* 8 (1): 134–151.

Chambers, J.K. 2009. "Cognition and the Linguistic Continuum from Vernacular to Standard." In *Vernacular Universals and Language Contacts: Evidence from Varieties of English and Beyond*, ed. by Markku Filppula, Juhani Klemola, and Heli Paulasto, 19–32. New York: Routlege.

Chomsky, Noam. 1971. *Problems of Knowledge and Freedom*. London: Pantheon.

Diver, William. 1995. "Theory." In *Language: Communication and Human Behavior. The Linguistic Essays of William Diver*, ed. by Alan Huffman and Joseph Davis, 445–552. Leiden: Brill.

Fairclough, Marta. 2005. *Spanish and Heritage Language Education in the United States: Struggling with Hypotheticals*. Lengua y Sociedad en el Mundo Hispánico [Language and Society in the Hispanic World], Vol. 12. Madrid: Iberoamericana.

Gutiérrez, Manuel. 1990. "Sobre el mantenimiento de las cláusulas subordinadas en el español de Los Ángeles." In *Spanish in the United States: Sociolinguistic Issues*, ed. by John Bergen, 31–38. Washington DC: Georgetown University Press.

Hall, Robert A. 1950. *Leave Your Language Alone!* Ithaca, NY: Linguistica.

Labov, William. 1969. "The Logic of Nonstandard English." In *Georgetown Monograph on Language and Linguistics*, Vol. 22, ed. by James Alatis, 1–44. Washington, DC: Georgetown University Press.

Lightfoot, David. 2010. "Language Acquisition and Language Change." *WIREs Cognitive Science* 1 (5): 677–684. DOI: 10.1002/wcs.39

Lynch, Andrew. 1999. *The Subjunctive in Miami Cuban Spanish: Bilingualism, Contact, and Language Variability*. University of Minnesota, Ph. D. dissertation.

Lantolf, James. 1978. "The Variable Constraints on Mood in Puerto Rican-American Spanish." In *Contemporary Studies in Romance Linguistics*, ed. by Margarita Suñer, 193–217. Washington DC: Georgetown University Press.

Lust, Barbara. 2006. *Child Language Acquisition and Growth*. Cambridge: Cambridge University Press. DOI: 10.1017/CBO9780511803413

Makoni, Sinfree and Alistair Pennycook. 2007. *Disinventing and Reconstituting Languages*. Bristol: Multilingual Matters, Ltd.

Martínez Mira, María Isabel. 2009. "Spanish Heritage Speakers in the Southwest: Factors Contributing to the Maintenance of the Subjunctive in Concessive Clauses." *Spanish in Context* 6: 105–26. DOI: 10.1075/sic.6.1.07mar

Menken, Kate, and Tatiana Kleyn. 2010. "The Long-term Impact of Subtractive Schooling in the Educational Experiences of Secondary English Language Learners." *International Journal of Bilingual Education and Bilingualism* 13: 399–417. DOI: 10.1080/13670050903370143

Merino, Barbara J. 1983. "Language Loss in Bilingual Chicano Children. *Journal of Applied Developmental Pschology* 4: 277–294. DOI: 10.1016/0193-3973(83)90023-0

Montrul, Silvina. 2007. "Interpreting Mood Distinctions in Spanish as a Heritage Language." In *Spanish Contact, Policy, Social and Linguistic Inquiries*, ed. by Kim Potowski and Richard Cameron, 23–40. Amsterdam: John Benjamins. DOI: 10.1075/impact.22.04mon

Montrul, Silvina. 2008. "Incomplete Acquisition in Spanish Heritage Speakers: Chronological Age or Interfaces Vulnerability." In *BUCLD 32 Proceedings*, ed. by Harvey Chan, Heather Jacob and Enkeleida Kapia, 299–310. Somerville, MA: Cascadilla Press.

Montrul, Silvina. 2009. "Knowledge of Tense-Aspect and Mood in Spanish Heritage Speakers." *International Journal of Bilingualism* 13: 239–269. DOI: 10.1177/1367006909339816

Montrul, Silvina. 2013. "Bilingualism and the Heritage Language Speaker. In *The Handbook of Bilingualism and Multilingualism* (2nd ed.), ed. by Tej K. Bhatia and William C. Ritchie, 168–189. Oxford: Blackwell Publishing, Ltd.

Ocampo, Francisco. 1990. "El subjuntivo en tres generaciones de hablantes bilingües." In *Spanish in the United States: Sociolinguistic Issues*, ed. by John Bergen, 39–48. Washington DC: Georgetown University Press.

Otheguy, Ricardo, and Ana Celia Zentella. 2012. *Spanish in New York: Language Contact, Dialectal Leveling and Structural Continuity*. New York: Oxford University Press. DOI: 10.1093/acprof:oso/9780199737406.001.0001

Portes, Alejandro, and Rubén G. Rumbaut. 2001. *Legacies: The Story of the Immigrant Second Generation*. Berkeley: University of California Press.

Putnam, Michael, and Liliana Sánchez. 2013. "What's So Incomplete About Incomplete Acquisition?" *Linguistic Approaches to Bilingualism* 3: 478–508. DOI: 10.1075/lab.3.4.04put

Schachter, Jacquelyn. 1990. "On the Issue of Completeness in Second Language Acquisition." *Second Language Research* 6: 93–124. DOI: 10.1177/026765839000600201

Silva-Corvalán, Carmen. 1994. "The Gradual Loss of Mood Distinctions in Los Angeles Spanish." *Language Variation and Change* 6: 255–272. DOI: 10.1017/S095439450000168X

Silva-Corvalán, Carmen. 2003. "Linguistic Consequences of Reduced Input in Bilingual First Language Acquisition." In *Linguistic Theory and Language Development in Hispanic Languages,* ed. by Silvina Montrul and Francisco Ordóñez, 375–397. Somerville, MA: Cascadilla Press.

Valdés, Guadalupe. 2000. "Introduction: Spanish for native speakers." In *AATSP Professional Development Series: Handbook for Teachers K-16,* Vol. 1, ed. by N. Anderson, 1–20. Fort Worth, TX: Harcourt College Publishers.

Valdés, Guadalupe. 2001. "Heritage Language Students: Profiles and Possibilities." In *Heritage Languages in America: Preserving a National Resource,* ed. by Joy K. Peyton, Donald A. Ranard, and Scott McGinnis, 37–80. McHenry, IL: Delta Systems.

Valdés, Guadalupe. 2005. "Bilingualism, Heritage Language Learners, and SLA Research: Opportunities Lost or Seized?" *Modern Language Journal* 89: 410–426.
DOI: 10.1111/j.1540-4781.2005.00314.x

Veltman, Calvin. 2000. "The American Linguistic Mosaic: Understanding Language Shift in the United States." In *New Immigrants in the United States,* ed. by Sandra McKay and Sau-ling Cynthia Wong, 58–95. Cambridge: Cambridge University Press.

Zapata, Gabriela C., Liliana Sánchez, and Almeida Jacqueline Toribio. 2005. "Contact and Contracting Spanish." *International Journal of Bilingualism* 9: 377–395.
DOI: 10.1177/13670069050090030501

The X⁰ syntax of "dative" clitics and the make-up of clitic combinations in Gallo-Romance

Diego Pescarini
Universität Zürich

This contribution focuses on the morphosyntax of third person dative clitics in Gallo-Romance. The first part addresses the morphology of clitic elements: in Gallo-Romance, third person datives can be expressed by an etymological form *li(s)* deriving from Lat *illi(s)* or by various kinds of non-etymological formatives, e.g. sg. *lui, y, lou*; pl. *leur, yz, lous, lous-y, les-y*, etc. I hypothesize that the above forms lexicalize different portions of the same functional hierarchy. The second part of the chapter focuses on the behaviour of third person dative clitics when combined with another third person clitic. In this context, (Gallo-)Romance varieties exhibit a number of irregularities and two possible orders: accusative > datives (as in both old and modern French), or dative > accusative (as in many French vernaculars). Moreover, in both medieval and present-day dialects, the accusative clitic is frequently dropped when clustered with a third person dative clitic. I wonder about a possible correlation between the morphology of the dative clitic and the make-up of clitic combinations.

1. Introduction

This contribution focuses on the morphosyntax of third person dative clitics with the intent of establishing a link between their morphology and their interaction with other third person clitics.

First of all, I will deal with the morphology of clitic elements in Gallo-Romance, where third person dative clitics can be expressed by an etymological form deriving either from Lat ILLI (as in old French (1a)), by a formative identical to non-clitic forms such as mod.Fr. *lui/leur* (1b), or by an invariable form *i/y* corresponding to the so-called locative clitic, as in many French dialects and in the so-called *français populaire* "popular French" (1c):

(1) a. Et   il   **li**   dit...   (Old French)
         And he   to.him/her   says
         'and he says to him/her...'

DOI 10.1075/rllt.9.17pes
© 2016 John Benjamins Publishing Company

b. Et   il **lui**   dit...   (Modern French)
    And he to.him/her says
    'and he says to him/her...'

c. j'   **y**   donne.   (Popular French)
    I= to.him/her/them= give
    'I give it to him/her/them.'

Occitan dialects (Ronjat 1937; Rohlfs 1970 on Gascon) exhibit cases of *loísmo*,[1] i.e. the dative clitic is expressed by an etymologically accusative form, as in (2a). Furthermore, plural dative clitics may be expressed by compound forms in which a reflex of ILLIS/ILLOS is followed by the clitic *y/i* as in (2b) and (2c), respectively; lastly, it is worth noticing that in some dialects *i* becomes *is* when plural, as in (2d).

(2) a. et   pay   **lou**   ditz...
         the dad to.him/her= says
         'Dad says to him/her...'

     b. que **lez y**   dic...
         que to.them= he/she.says
         'He/she says to them...'

     c. **lous y**   cousinabo de bounos càusos.
         to.them= I.cooked   of good   things
         'I cooked them good things.'

     d. que **is**   parlo.
         que to.them= speak
         'I speak to them.'

In what follows, I hypothesize that the above forms correspond to different chunks of the same functional hierarchy. Cross-linguistic differences in the morphological realization of dative clitics depend on which portion of the functional hierarchy is expressed.

In the second part of the paper I will focus on the behaviour of the dative clitic when combined with another third person clitic. These combinations exhibit various possible realizations: in old French the combination had the order accusative dative, e.g. *la li, les li*, etc., but the accusative clitic was frequently dropped (Foulet 1919: §201–202). The same pattern of clitic drop is attested in many of the dialects

---

1. The term *loísmo* normally refers to a pattern of syncretism found in Ibero-Romance dialects in which the reflex of ILLU(M) references (animate) datives. This pattern is rather common in other Romance areas such as southern Gallo- and Italo-Romance. To the best of my knowledge, in the terminological tradition of French and Italian descriptive grammars there is no specific term to refer to the phenomenon. This led Romanists such as Ledgeway (2000) to extend the terms *loísmo/laísmo* to non-Iberian vernaculars.

surveyed by the *Atlas Linguistique de la France* (ALF), where the sequence meaning 'it/him/her/them to her/him/them' is usually expressed by an invariable form *y* or *li*. In standard French, clitic drop is usually avoided and the cluster exhibits the same order as old French, although the morphology of the dative clitic has changed, e.g. *le li* → *le lui*. Lastly, in southern France we find attestations of the opposite order, e.g. *li lu, lui le*.

One may argue that these aspects—namely, the polymorphism of third person dative clitics and the variability in the formation of clitic combinations—are somehow related and, in the following sections, I will try to establish a link between the internal make-up of dative clitics and their behaviour in clusters.

The structure of the paper is as follows: Section 2 deals with the morphology of dative clitics in Romance; Section 3 accounts for the internal structure of the clitic forms attested in Gallo-Romance varieties; Section 4 introduces some hypotheses concerning the make-up of clitic combinations; Section 5 summarizes some data regarding clitic sequences and Section 6 explores a possible correlation between the morphology of dative clitics and their realization in clitic clusters.

2.   A typology of dative clitics

Third person dative clitics exhibit a number of variants, some of which cannot originate from regular phonological changes. What follows is a tentative typology.

In several languages, the third person dative clitic is expressed by a regular reflex of Lat. ILLI(S) (with various degrees of palatalization), which was originally inflected only for number.

A few languages have developed a non-etymological dative feminine pronoun. Italian, for instance, exhibits an opposition between *gli* 'to him' and *le* 'to her', possibly by analogy with the opposition *li/le* ('them.M/F') in the accusative series.

In other areas, the original distinction between the dative *li(s) and the accusative forms *lo(s)/la(s) has been obliterated. This gave rise to *laísta* and *loísta* patterns in which feminine and/or masculine datives are pronominalized by means of an etymologically accusative form. In Madrileño, for instance, the dative form *le(s)* references masculine individuals, while feminine datives are pronominalized by the accusative clitic *la(s)*, as shown in the following example:

(3)   A   ella,   **la**=   dolía   la   cabeza.   (Mad., Quilis 1985 a.o.)
      To her,   to.her= was hurting the head
      'She had a headache.'

In various Gascon dialects (see Rohlfs 1970, a.o.) the pronoun *lou* < ILLUM is used as a dative form regardless of the gender feature of the pronominalized constituent.

Consequently, the form *lou* pronominalizes masculine elements when accusative and both feminine/masculine elements when dative.

(4)   et   pay   **lou**=   ditz...   (Gsc., Rohlfs 1970)
      the   dad   to.him/her=   says
      'Dad says to him/her...'

Various languages exhibit compound forms, i.e., clitic pronouns which are formed by the combination of two clitic items. In Occitan (Ronjat 1937, §505–6; Rohlfs 1970, 182), the dative clitic is often formed by combining the accusative clitic with *i*, e.g. *lou-i*. The same holds for the Catalan dialect spoken in Barcelona, where the third person dative clitic /əlzi/ 'to them' is a combination of the clitic əlz—which corresponds to the accusative plural clitic—with an oblique marker -i, identical to the so-called locative clitic (written *hi* 'there'; Bonet 1991).[2] The hypothesis of a compound is confirmed by the fact that in the same dialect the genitive/partitive clitic *(ə)n* occurs between the formatives əlz and *i* giving rise to the sequence əlz-ən-i 'to them of it' (Bonet 1991).

Notice that—leaving orthographic issues aside—the formative *y/i* of compound forms cannot be a reflex of the dative formative -*i* of Latin ILL-I. In fact, as shown in (5) the dative -*i* precedes the number formative -*s* in languages that have preserved the original morphology, while in languages exhibiting *loísmo*, such as Catalan and Occitan dialects, -*i* follows -*s*:

(5)   a.   l i   s   (Sard., Jones 1993, a.o.)
      b.   l ou s i   (Gasc.)

One might wonder whether the same analysis holds for singular forms of the type *li*, which, instead of being a regular reflex of ILLI, may result from a previous accusative-pro-dative clitic (e.g., *l(o)*) combined with the oblique clitic *y* (hence, *l'y* rather than *li*). In other words, Catalan and Occitan *li* does not necessary have the same X^0 structure as the homophonous *li* in a language like Sardinian, since the former might result from a previous stage of *loísmo*, as illustrated in (6b):

(6)   a.   l i   (Sard.)
      b.   l (ou) i (Gasc.)

In many Romance varieties the third person dative clitic is expressed by a morphological exponent deriving from a locative particle (e.g. Lat. HINC(E), HIC, IBI, etc.) or the third person reflexive element (Lat. SE). As a result, in these varieties the third person clitic is syncretic with another clitic form and is expressed by an invariable formative

---

2.   The plural dative clitic əlzi is often written *els hi*.

which does not display gender and number morphology (on Italo-Romance, see Rohlfs 1969; Calabrese 1994; Loporcaro 2002).

The syncretism due to the substitution of the third person dative clitic with a locative form is particularly frequent in French, Italian and Catalan varieties (i.e. in all the areas in which the locative clitic is attested).

(7) díse   =y...   (Gsc.)
     he/she.say =to.him/her/them
     'he/she says to him/her...'

Foulet (1919, §436) notes that the use of *i* for *lui* has been attested since old French, as in (8):

(8) Mes ge la   vi   e   s' i   parlai.   (o.Fr.)
     but I= her= saw and so to.her= spoke
     'but I saw her and spoke to her.'

One might wonder whether the above syncretism is a consequence of palatalization, which, in a previous chronological stage, made the regular reflex of ILLI become opaque and, in various dialects, homophonous with the "locative" clitic. In various Romance vernaculars palatalized determiners originate in prevocalic contexts where li#V > lj#V > (ʎ)j#V and successively are extended to preconsonantal contexts. The nature of the dative/locative syncretism, however, is much more controversial and cannot result only from regular morphophonological processes. Manzini and Savoia (2002) and Rezac (2010) argue that in many languages the cause of the syncretism is syntactic in nature rather than phonological (for a principled explanation, I refer the interested reader to these works and references therein.)

Lastly, in French we observe the evolution from the etymological form *li* (< Lat. ILLI) to the modern one *lui*.

(9) a. Et   il   li   dit...   (o.Fr.)
          And he   to.him/her says
          'and he says to him/her...'

     b. Et   il   **lui**   dit...   (mod.Fr.)
          And he   to.him/her says
          'and he says to him/her...'

This might be considered another compound form due to the combination of an accusative clitic *lu < ILLU(M) with an oblique marker -*i*. However, the form *lui* (and its feminine counterpart *lei*) are widely attested in other Romance languages, including old French, as strong pronouns. This means that Fr. *lui* (and possibly pl. *leur*) was originally used as a strong pronoun and, later, acquired a clitic status making *li* "fall out of use."

The above data are summarised as follows:

(10)   Lat. ILLI
$$\begin{cases} \text{Sp. } le(s) & \text{etymological forms} \\ \text{It. } le \text{ 'to her'} & \text{analogical forms} \\ \text{Fr. dial. } y & \text{suppletive forms with loc. etymology} \\ \text{Campidanese Sard. } si & \text{suppletive forms with refl. etymology} \\ \text{Madr. } la, \text{ Gasc. } lou & laísmo \text{ and } loísmo \\ \text{Occ. } loui; \text{ Cat. } elsi & \text{compound forms} \\ \text{Fr. } lui/leur & \text{apparent strong forms} \end{cases}$$

The crucial point of the above discussion concerns the status of the formative /i/, which may derive from either the dative pronoun ILLI(s) or a locative particle, e.g. HIC/IBI. Arguably, the latter gives rise to compound forms such as Occ. lou-s-i 'to them'.

2.1   An aside on animacy

In many Romance languages, the distribution of dative clitics is sensitive to animacy distinctions.

This holds for vernaculars with patterns of loísmo/laísmo as the accusative clitic may pronominalize a dative complement if and only if it references a human individual. In Neapolitan, for instance, human datives may be expressed by either the dative/locative clitic ncə or by an accusative form such as 'o/'a/'e ('him/her/them', see Ledgeway 2000, a.o.).[3] Non-human datives, conversely, do not admit any alternation; see (11b).

(11)   a.   ncə/'a=   rispunneteno,   a   Maria.   (Neapolitan)
            to.her=   they.replied   to   Maria
            'They replied to her (Maria).'

       b.   ncə/*'a=   rispunneteno   â   lettera.   (Neapolitan)
            to.it=   they.replied   to.the   letter
            'They replied to it (the letter).'

Animacy effects are present also in languages without traces of loísmo/laísmo. In Italian, French and Catalan, for instance, reflexes of ILLI are usually replaced by the locative clitic (Fr. y, It. ci, Cat. hi) when denoting a non-human entity, see (12)–(14) (Rigau 1982).

---

3.   In many dialects of Italy (upper-southern and Ligurian dialects), Gallo-Romance vernaculars (see below) and Portuguese, 3p clitics have undergone aphaeresis of l. For space limits, I cannot address this issue here. However, it seems to me that, given its geographical distribution, this phenomenon is orthogonal to the one at issue.

(12) a. A   la   meva filla,   li=   dedico molt de temps. (Cat.)
          To the my   daughter, to.her= I.devote lot   of time
          'As for my daughter, I devote lots of time to her.'

      b. A   això, hi=   dedico molt de temps.
          To this, there=   I.devote lot   of time
          'As for this, I devote lots of time to it.'

(13) a. A   mia figlia,   le=   dedico molto tempo.   (It.)
          To my   daughter,   to.her= I.devote lot.of time
          'As for my daughter, I devote lots of time to her.'

      b. A   questo, ci=   dedico molto tempo.
          To this,   there=   I.devote lot.of time
          'As for this, I devote lots of time to it.'

(14) a. Luc lui   est fidèle (à sa femme).   (Fr.)
          Luc to.her= is   faithful
          'Luc is faithful to her (his wife).'

      b. Luc y   est fidèle (à ceci).
          Luc to.them= is   faithful
          'Luc is faithful to them (his principles).'

Furthermore, it is worth noting that speakers allow the locative clitic *ci/hi/y* to reference a human entity in those contexts in which the presence of a third person dative form would cause a violation of the so-called Person Case Constraint, namely the restriction preventing third person dative clitic from co-occurring with a first/second person accusative clitic. The following examples (from Bonet 1991; Pescarini 2010, and Rezac 2010, respectively) show that the substitution of the dative clitic with the locative one may avoid a PCC violation:

(15) a. A   en Pere m'   *li→√hi va   recomanar en Josep. (Cat.)
          To the Pere me= to.him= goes   recommend the Josep
          'Josep recommended me to him (Pere).'

      b. ti   *gli→√ci presento io.   (It.)
          you   to.him=   introduce I
          'I'll introduce you to him.'

      c. Pierre me *lui→√y présentra,   à   son oncle.   (Fr.)
          Pierre me to.him   will.introduce to his uncle
          'Pierre will introduce me to him, his uncle.'

Building on the idea that the PCC is a restriction on pronouns encoding animate entities capable of mental experience (Bianchi 2006; Adger & Harbour 2007, a.o.), one may suggest that the above fact show that "locative" clitics such as *hi/y/ci* are in fact dative clitics deprived of features encoding "animacy" or related concepts.

3.   Morphology as X^0 Syntax

Functional elements are the morphological realization of layers of syntactic structure. Hence, if the difference between strong and clitic elements follows from the presence vs absence of certain layers (Cardinaletti & Starke 1999 among others), we arrive at the hypothesis that the evolution from strong to clitic forms results from a process of pruning. This analysis, in turn, opens the door to the possibility that, among clitics, differences may arise as a consequence of the number of pruned layers i.e., some clitics are "more clitic" than others inasmuch as a bigger portion of their original functional layer has been pruned (see Bonet 1991 for a morphological view; see also Martin 2009).

In what follows I will try to draw a possible structure that captures the above variation in the morphological realization of dative forms. As all clitic forms have a X^0 status, all the projections I am going to illustrate are X^n with $n < 0$.

As for the category X^0, one might wonder whether X is a D projection or not. The answer, in my opinion, is far from straightforward. In fact, if we limit ourselves to the analysis of 3p dative clitics, I would assume a D analysis for all clitic forms having a *li*-type exponent, i.e. a formative identical to other determiners. However, what about syncretic formatives like *y, bi, ncə, ndə*, etc. which in a number of Romance varieties pronominalize both 3p dative clitics and so-called locative or partitive clitics? The latter, in fact, cannot be considered clitic counterparts of DPs, but rather pro-PP (Kayne 1975), namely clitic particles standing for prepositional phrases such as locatives, instrumentals, comitatives, genitives, etc. Hence, in the latter case we can neither conclude nor exclude that the clitic has a D^0 status; this is why in the remainder of the paper I will not commit myself regarding the categorical nature of X^0.

The analysis proposed here is reminiscent of accounts based on feature geometries (see Harley & Ritter 2002; Heap 2002, on clitics), according to which pronouns and functional elements in general are viewed as morphological realizations of hierarchical arrays of φ-features. The nature of such geometries, which may correspond to either syntactic nodes or morphological (namely: non-syntactic) trees (see Bonet 1991 on clitics) is debatable, but due to space limitations I cannot discuss the issue here.

Let us start with a possible structure for etymological forms such as Spanish *le(s)*, Sardinian *li(s)* in which the formative *l* of 3rd person clitics is followed by a Thematic Vowel (Harris 1994, among many others) which is in turn followed by the number exponent:

(16) $[[[\; l\;]\; i\;]\; s\;]$

Following Baker's *mirror principle*, a structure like (16) might be due to the movement of the root $\sqrt{l}$ along the structure in (17): the root moves across the higher layers picking up gender and number agreement features which, at the Syntax/PF interface are mapped into morphophonological endings (Halle & Marantz 1993). The above variation in the morphological realization of dative clitics might therefore follow from the parametrization of the movement of √ in the structure of X^0.

(17)

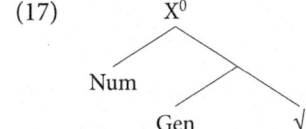

Under the analysis in (17), one may wonder about the nature of the formative -i/e- in etymological forms such as *li(s)/le(s)*. If we compare dative and accusative clitics (e.g. *lo(s)/la(s)*), we may observe that in the morphological realization of datives, gender is always neutralized. We can therefore consider -i- as a default Thematic Vowel inserted once gender features are obliterated in the context of a dative X^0. This therefore leads us to wonder which kind of features do characterize dative clitics.

Let us suppose that dative clitics differ from accusative ones in having a further functional layer encoding case morphosyntax as shown in (18). The assumption that the K layer is more external is consistent with typological observations on the order of nominal morphemes such as Greenberg's universal 39. If √*l* reaches dative K, the gender feature is impoverished, namely deleted. As a result, a default Thematic Vowel -i/e- is inserted instead of -o-, -a- which express masculine and feminine agreement, respectively.

(18)

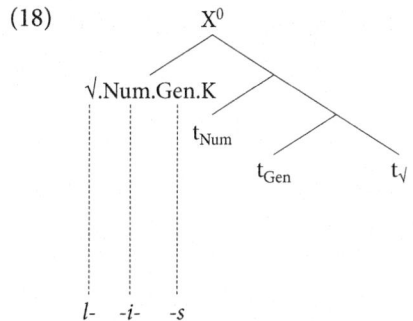

In *laísta* and *loísta* dialects, conversely, gender is not neutralized and the dative clitic ends up being expressed by what looks like an accusative form. We can however distinguish at least two patterns of accusative-pro-dative clitics: one in which the accusative clitic, when used as a dative form, maintains its gender feature, e.g. *lo* 'to him' vs *la* 'to her' and another system in which a single form, say *lo*, becomes a dative clitic referencing both masculine and feminine individuals.

In the former case, I claim that the dative/accusative syncretism and the absence of gender neutralization are obtained when the root √*l* fails to reach K.

In the latter case, the accusative/dative syncretism combines with gender neutralization as the same form, e.g. *lou*, stands for both masculine and feminine datives. If we assume that gender neutralization takes place when the root √*l* reaches K, this means that in these varieties √*l* does incorporate on K and that the accusative/dative syncretism takes place in Morphology, following from the fact that in these dialects the default Thematic Vowel coincides with the one expressing masculine agreement.

The analysis in (18) can in turn shed light on the morphology of so-called compound forms, i.e. dative forms which are due to the combination of an accusative form (e.g. *lou(s)*) followed by an oblique element *i/y*. Under the above analysis, I *i/y* is the overt lexicalization of K. The proposed structure is therefore as follows:

(19) $[_K [_{Num} [_{Gen} [_√$ *l* $]$ *ou* $]$ *s* $]$ *y* $]$

As for dialects in which *i/y* is the only possible dative form, the above proposal offers two possible analyses: (a) in these dialects the lower layers of the X^0 structure are silent or empty and only the K feature is expressed by an invariable, non-agreeing exponent (see (20)); or (b) we might think that the monomorphemic element *i* is a palatalized reflex of *li* and as such, it may lexicalize other layers of X^0, as shown in (21).

(20) $[_K [_{Num} [_{Gen} [_√$ _ $]$ _ $]$ _ $]$ *y* $]$

(21) $[_K [_{Num} [_{Gen} [_√$ *y* $]$ _ $]$ _ $]$ $]$

We cannot exclude either option *a priori*. Evidence for the latter analysis comes from Gascon varieties, where /i/ can combine with the plural formative -*s*, e.g. *i* 'to him/her' vs *is* 'to them':

(22) $[_K [_{Num} [_{Gen} [_√$ *i-* $]$ _ $]$ -*s* $]$ $]$

Evidence in favor of the former option comes from the analysis of compound forms in (19), where *i* occupies the outer layer of the X^0 structure.

Lastly, let us turn to French *lui/leur*. What is of interest here is that they behave like clitics although they do not look like clitic pronouns. Diachronically, it is worth recalling that the etymological singular dative *li* has been replaced by the present-day form *lui*, which already existed as a non-clitic form.

(23)   a.   Et   il   **li**   dit...   (Old French)
                And   he   to.him/her   says
                'and he says to him/her...'

        b.   Et   il   **lui**   dit...   (Modern French)
                And   he   to.him/her   says
                'and he says to him/her...'

We have already seen that in some Gallo-Romance varieties compound forms have been introduced to compensate the loss of √ movement to the higher layers of X⁰. In particular, I submitted the hypothesis that a formative *i/y* is inserted in K to lexicalize case features, which, otherwise, would remain silent. What we observe in French is an alternative strategy for realizing the same feature: instead of building a compound structure bottom up—as in Occitan dialects—standard French seems to pick up a form which is already attested in the pronominal system an "fit" it into the structure of X⁰. What we obtain is in fact a structure similar to the one of a compound form—in which a *i/y* formative follows a reflex of Lat. ILLU(M)—but with an important difference: in French the form *lui* comes as a single unit "borrowed" from the functional inventory of strong pronouns and does not result from √ movement across the layers of X⁰.

The above proposal is summarized in the trees below, showing the base-generation position and the morphological realization of each element: (24) illustrates the Occitan pattern, in which *lui* results from the incorporation of √ on *i/y* lexicalizing K; (25) shows the French pattern, in which *lui* is base-generated in K.

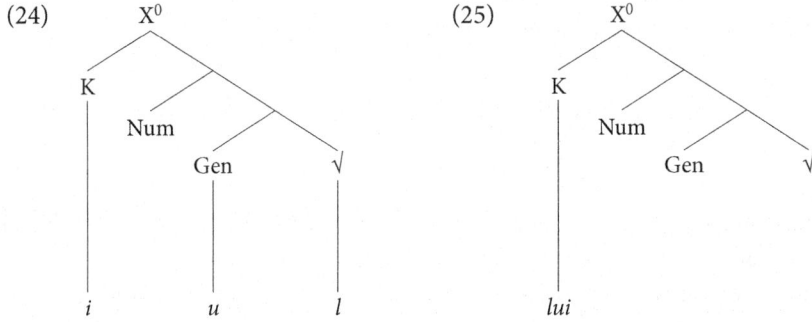

This state of affairs is due to the different historical evolution of the two forms. Although homophonous, the former originates from a previous pattern of *loísmo*, attested in present day-dialects of the same area), while the latter has a completely different origin. Analogously to the dative plural clitic *leur* (< ILLLORUM), *lui* is already attested as a non-clitic form in old French and, later on (around the 16th century), *lui* began to replace *li* with the function of singular dative clitic.

4. An account of cluster formation

In this section I consider whether the morphology—namely, X⁰-syntax—of dative clitics has consequences for the make-up of clitic combinations.

Kayne (1994, 19–21) argues that clitic combinations may be either split or clustered: in the former case, the two (or more) clitics occupy different syntactic positions as shown in (26a); in the latter case one clitic is left-adjoined to the other as in (26b).

(26) a   [cl ... [cl ...]]   split
      b. [[cl [cl]] ...]   cluster

Ordóñez 2002 proposed that in some Romance varieties certain clitics are not rigidly ordered insofar split and cluster structures are in free variation. Pescarini (2014, in press a,b) argued that many Romance languages—including Italian and French—evolved from split to cluster configurations. In origin, cf (27a) and (28a), the order is accusative > dative and later on it turns to dative > accusative, as shown in (27b) and (28b):

(27) a.   che [...] voi   **la** **mi**   concediate   (Boccaccio, Filocolo 212)
           that [...] you.PL it.f= to.me= grant.SUBJ
           'that you grant it to me'

      b.   se Egli **me** **la** concede   (Boccaccio, Filocolo 72
           if He   to.me it.f grants   = mod. It.)
           'if He grants it to me'

(28) a.   Je **le** **te**   comande.   (old Fr.)
           I   it   to.you order
           'I order you to do it.'

      b.   Je **te**   **le**   comande.   (mod. Fr.)
           I   to.you it   order
           'I order you to do it.'

As a consequence of the incorporation of the dative clitic on the accusative one, the former is targeted by suppletion. In particular, third person clitics—namely, reflexes of ILLI—are often replaced by another clitic exponent which may be either a reflexive clitic (e.g. Sp. *se*) or a locative one (e.g. Sard. *bi*).

(29) a.   Juan *le → $^{\sqrt{}}$se   lo   comprò.   (Sp.)
           Juan to.him/her= it= bought
           'Juan bought it for him/her/them.'

      b.   *li → $^{\sqrt{}}$bi   l'   appo   datu. (Log. Sardinian, Jones 1993:220)
           to.him/her/them= it= I.have given
           'I gave it to him/her/them.'

Pescarini (2014, 2015, in press) argued that the above opacity arises because 3p dative clitics (e.g. Sp. *le* 'to him/her') are bimorphemic (Kayne 2000; see also Cardinaletti 2008) and only a sub-component of the clitic (its "root" $\sqrt{}$) is incorporated, leaving its agreement features behind. As a consequence, with monomorphemic datives (e.g. *me* 'to me', *te* 'to you', etc.), incorporation does not produce any anomaly. Bimorphemic elements, conversely, are subject to further restrictions, due to their composite structure. The example in (30) shows that, while monomorphemic clitics are free to incorporate on the higher clitic, the third person dative *l-e-(s)* fails to incorporate because its agreement features (Φ) remain stranded in the lower position. This prevents the *l* formative from being inserted after root incorporation and causes the retreat to the unmarked exponent *se*.

(30)　$[_{Acc^0}\ \sqrt{}_{Dat}\ [\sqrt{}+\Phi]]$　　$[_{Dat^0}\ \sqrt{}+\Phi]$

me	lo	'it/him to me'
te	lo	'it/him to you'
se	lo	'it/him to himself/herself/themselves'
* l	lo	'it/him to him/her/them'

As we will see in the next sections, Gallo-Romance differs from this picture in several respects.

5.　Data from the *Atlas Linguistique de la France*

This section focuses on the morphology of clitic combinations in Gallo-Romance on the basis of data from the *Atlas Linguistique de la France* (ALF).

The following data do not provide an exhaustive representation of Gallo-Romance clitic clusters, nor are they meant to illustrate most "representative" or statistically frequent patterns. Rather, the following sample aims to introduce various possible patterns to show whether and how the ALF data challenge the above hypotheses on cluster formation.

I will consider few ALF datapoints. Recall that the data represent French vernaculars spoken more than a century ago: this means that what observed in the ALF may not correspond any longer to the usage of the corresponding present-day dialects. Second, as atlases report data on a restricted number of contexts, we cannot exclude that the forms illustrated below were subject to further variation, depending on orthogonal conditions. What matters here is that certain forms have been attested and still call for a principled analysis.

I take into consideration eight dialects, which have been selected in order to illustrate different patterns. The list of localities is the following: 271 Maurois; 525 Cabariot; 902 Souvigny; 610 Chazelles; 724 Rieupeyroux; 698 Tramesagues; 866 Orpierre; 855 Nyons.

The maps I have scrutinized are the following:

- n. 785 (et que nous **lui** rendions son argent;
- n. 1650 (Je n'ai pas osé **le lui** dire);[4]
- n. 761 (j'ai eu de la peine à **le leur** faire comprendre).

4.　Map 1650 represents only the southern half of France, so it does not report any data for point 271 (Maurois).

First of all, I will compare the morphology of the third person singular dative clitic (Fr. *lui*) as represented in map 785 with the morphology of the cluster in map 1650, which is formed by two singular clitics. If relevant, I will take into consideration the data in map 761, which contain a plural dative clitic (Fr. *leur*).

The parameters I will observe are the following:

- the morphology of the dative clitic, which can be
  - an etymological form *li*
  - an invariable form *i*
  - an etymologically accusative form *lou*
  - a compound form *les-i, lou-i*
- the morphology of the cluster, which can show:
  - clitic drop, e.g. *le lui* → *li*
  - accusative > dative ordering
  - dative > accusative ordering

The following table shows the forms of the third person singular dative clitic (map 785):

(31) Point: 271 525 902 610 724 698 855 866
      Fr. *lui* 'to him/her' i   li   lɥi lɥi li   li   li   u

When we turn to clusters, map 1650 shows that many dialects (including Occitan vernaculars) exhibit clitic drop, i.e. the accusative clitic is never pronounced. In my sample, this happens in two localities:

(32) Point: 271   525
      Fr. *lui* 'to him/her'   i   li
      Fr. *le lui* 'it/him to him/her'   i   li
      Fr. *le leur* 'it/him to them'   jœ   lœ

One locality (902 Souvigny) exhibits a rather peculiar pattern as it shows clitic drop, but the form of the dative clitic changes from *lɥi* (corresponding to Fr. *lui* 'to him/her') to *li* (corresponding to Fr. *le lui* 'it/him to him/her'). The plural dative form, regardless of the presence of an accusative clitic, is expressed by a compound form transcribed as *jœzi* in which one can individuate a plural formative *-z-* followed by the exponent *i*.

(33) Point: 902
      Fr. *lui* 'to him/her'   lɥi
      Fr. *le lui* 'it/him to him/her'   li
      Fr. *le leur* 'it/him to them'   jœzi

Some vernaculars display the order accusative > dative, which is the only possible order in both medieval and modern French.

(34) Point: 724
     Fr. *lui* 'to him/her'   li
     Fr. *le lui* 'it/him to him/her'   u li
     Fr. *le leur* 'it/him to them'   (z)u lur

Three dialects of my sample feature the opposite order (namely, dative > accusative):

(35) Point: 698   866   855
     Fr. *lui* 'to him/her'   li   u   li
     Fr. *le lui* 'it/him to him/her' l ok   li u   lu
     Fr. *le leur* 'it/him to them' euz u   lur u   li lu

In 698 we observe the form *ok* which is the so-called neuter clitic *oc* (< HOC 'this'), sometimes *ac*, used in Occitan dialects to refer to mass nouns or events as in the following example:

(36) Pròbo   m   **oc.**   (Gsc., from Rohlfs 1970)
     prove.IMP =to.me   =it
     'Prove it to me.'

In 866 we can observe a puzzling interaction between *loismo* and cluster formation: the *loista* form *u* (with a dative interpretation) is in fact turned to *li* in combination with a 'true' accusative form, e.g. *li u* instead of **u u* 'it to him/her'. In 855 the dative form *li* seems to disappear when co-occurring with an accusative clitic as we find *lu* instead of the expected *li lu*. This might be due to a rule deleting the lateral of the accusative clitic (in the neighboring dialect, 866, the accusative form is always *u*), and consequent elision of *-i*: *li lu > li u > l'u*. The deletion of *l* with the plural dative, conversely, might be blocked because of the presence of an underlying plural formative: *li(z) lu > *l'u*.

Lastly, in some dialects we observe that the dative singular and plural clitics seem to have opposite orders with respect to the third person accusative clitic. In the dialect of Chazelles, for instance, the order is clearly accusative > dative with the plural clitic *lur*, but things are a bit more complicated with the singular dative clitic as the outcome of the cluster is the form *l u*.

(37) Point: 610
     Fr. *lui* 'to him/her'   lᵾi
     Fr. *le lui* 'it/him to him/her'   l u
     Fr. *le leur* 'it/him to them'   lu lur

6.   Some preliminary remarks on cluster formation

In Section 4 I argued, following Kayne (1994), that clitic sequences occur in either a split or cluster configuration. In particular, I proposed that the order dative > accusative is due to a cluster structure derived via left-adjunction of a clitic to the other (see also Pescarini 2014, 2015, in press).

According to this analysis, medieval and modern (standard) French, which exhibit the order accusative > dative, have split combinations, i.e. clitics occur in separate positions. As noticed for other Romance dialects, the combinations with this order are normally transparent, i.e. they do not display any irregularity:[5]

(38)		mod.Fr.	o.Fr	Rieupeyroux (724)
	'to him/her'	lui	li	li
	'it/him to him/her'	le lui	le li	u li
	'it/him to them'	le leur	le lor	(z)u lur

Conversely, sequences with the opposite order (dative > accusative) are often characterized by several irregularities, in particular when the dative clitic is singular. As shown in (39), the formative -*i*- of the singular dative clitic is dropped, which may be deemed a clue of incorporation. In 866, the -*i*- formative is not dropped. However, we observe another anomaly: the form *li* is used only in clusters, while in the absence of another clitic this dialect shows *loismo*. Plural datives, by contrast, are free to co-occur to the left of the accusative clitic. However, it is worth recalling that such forms, which arguably coincide with strong forms (*eux, leur*), are directly inserted in K as monomorphemic formatives and, as monomorphemic elements they are not expected to undergo suppletion.

(39)	Point:	698	866	855
	Fr. *lui* 'to him/her'	li	u	li
	Fr. *le lui* 'it/him to him/her'	l ok	li u	lu
	Fr. *le leur* 'it/him to them'	euz u	lur u	li lu

It is worth noting that the loista clitic *u* in 866 turns into *li* once clustered. This might be due to a surface constraint against combinations of identical exponents (Pescarini 2010, a.o.) which triggers the retreat to an alternative dative exponent *li* taken as an

---

5.   Ordóñez (2002) argued that the split/cluster divide can account for the variability in clitic combination in enclisis in imperatives, e.g. *donne-le-moi* vs *donne-moi-le*. In particular, Ordóñez (2002) argues that one of the clitics must be a weak pronoun. One might therefore argue that the same holds in Old French and dialects such as Rieupeyroux. Space limits prevent me from exploring further this hypothesis.

indivisible unit from the functional lexicon (this in turn may account for the presence of the -*i*- formative).

We can now turn to clitic drop. "Central" Romance, i.e. Gallo-Romance, Catalan, and—according to an anonymous reviewer—Basque Spanish, differ from the other Romance languages in allowing systematic clitic drop in clusters formed by two third person clitics. When two third person clitics combine—but the same happens in combinations of a third person dative and a partitive clitic—the output is what looks like as a single clitic form, in which no clear morphological boundary between accusative and dative formatives can be drawn (see Bonet 1991 for an in-depth analysis of Barcelonan Catalan). One might hypothesize that clitic drop is allowed in those dialects in which the accusative clitic may occur before the dative one, which amounts to saying that clitic drop is allowed with split combinations.

7. Conclusions

This contribution has dealt with the morphology of third person clitics in Gallo-Romance. I have focused on the form of clitics in old French, modern French and in a series of vernaculars, Gascon dialects in particular.

In Gallo-Romance, the third person dative clitic is expressed by an etymological formative, e.g. *li(s)*, by an element identical to the accusative clitic, e.g. *lu*; by a compound form, in particular when plural, e.g. *louzi, lezi*; by a form coinciding with a strong pronoun, e.g. *lui, leur*; by a monomorphemic form /i/.

The monomorphemic /i/ can be either a reflex of a locative particle or a reflex of *li* due to palatalization or aphaeresis. I argued that both types of /i/ are attested in present-day dialects. In some dialects, /i/ can precede the plural formative -*s*, while in so called compound forms /i/ follows /s/: this amounts to saying that in the former case /i/ is a reflex of ILLI, while in the latter it is a monomorphemic element occurring "outside" the structure derived from ILLE.

In the last part of the paper I focused on the behaviour of the dative clitic in clitic sequences containing another third person element. French dialects exhibit three main patterns: clitic drop (i.e. sequences in which the accusative clitic is deleted), sequences with the order dative > accusative and sequences with the order accusative > dative, as in old and modern (standard) French. I noticed that sequences with the order dative > accusative tend to be morphologically irregular, which is consistent with the morphological behaviour of clitic clusters in other Romance areas, although the patterns displayed by Gallo-Romance vernaculars posit a series of challenges to previous accounts of cluster formation.

References

Adger David, and Daniel Harbour. 2007. "Syntax and Syncretisms of the Person Case Constraint." *Syntax* 10.1: 2–37. DOI: 10.1111/j.1467-9612.2007.00095.x

Baker, Mark. 1985. "The Mirror Principle and Morphosyntactic Explanation." *Linguistic Inquiry* 16: 373–416.

Bianchi, Valentina. 2006. "On the Syntax of Pronominal Arguments." *Lingua* 116: 2023–2067. DOI: 10.1016/j.lingua.2005.05.002

Bonet, Eulalia. 1991. *Morphology after Syntax: Pronominal Clitics in Romance*. MIT, doctoral dissertation.

Calabrese, Andrea. 1994. "Syncretism Phenomena in the Clitic systems of Italian and Sardinian Dialects and the Notion of Morphological Change." In *Proceedings of NELS 25.2*, ed. by Jill Beckman, 151–174. Amherst (Mass.): GLSA.

Cardinaletti, Anna. 2008. "On Different Types of Clitic Clusters." In *The Bantu-Romance Connection*, ed. by Cécile De Cat and Katherine Demuth, 41–82. Amsterdam: Benjamins. DOI: 10.1075/la.131.06car

Cardinaletti, Anna, and Michal Starke. 1999. "The Typology of Structural Deficiency: A Case Study of the Three Classes of Pronouns." In *Clitics in the Languages of Europe*, ed. by Henk van Riemsdijk, 145–233. Berlin and New York: De Gruyter.

Foulet, Lucien. 1919. *Petite syntaxe de l'ancien francais*. Paris: Champion.

Halle, Morris, and Alec Marantz. 1993. "Distributed Morphology and the Pieces of Inflection." In *The View from Building 20*, ed. by Kenneth Hale and Samuel Jay Keyser, 111–176. Cambridge: MIT Press.

Harley Heidi, and Nancy Ritter. 2002. "Person and Number in Pronouns: A Feature-Geometric Analysis." *Language* 78.3: 482–526. DOI: 10.1353/lan.2002.0158

Harris, James 1994. "The Syntax-Phonology Mapping in Catalan and Spanish Clitics." In *MIT-WPL 21, Papers on Phonology and Morphology*, ed. by Andrew Carnie and Heidi Harley, 321–353.

Heap, David 2002. "Split Subject Pronoun Paradigms: Feature Geometry and Underspecification." In *Current Issues in Romance Languages: Selected Papers from the* 29th *Linguistic Symposium on Romance Languages (LSRL29)*, ed. by Teresa Satterfield, Christina M. Tortora, and Diana Cresti, 129–144. Amsterdam: Benjamins. DOI: 10.1075/cilt.220.10hea

Jones, Michael Allan. 1993. *Sardinian Syntax*. London: Routledge.

Kayne, Richard. 1975. *French Syntax: The Transformational Cycle*. Cambridge, MA: MIT Press.

Kayne, Richard. 1994. *The Antisymmetry of Syntax*. Cambridge, MA: MIT Press.

Kayne, Richard. 2000. *Parameters and Universals*. New York: Oxford University Press.

Ledgeway, Adam. 2000. *A Comparative Syntax of the Dialects of Southern Italy: A Minimalist Approach*. Oxford: Blackwell.

Loporcaro, Michele. 2002. "External and Internal Causation in Morphological Change: Evidence from Italo-Romance Dialects." In *Morphology 2000*, ed. by Sabrina Bendjaballah, Wolfgang U. Dressler, Oskar E. Pfeiffer, and Maria D. Voeikova, 227–240. Amsterdam: Benjamins. DOI: 10.1075/cilt.218.19lop

Manzini, Maria Rita, and Leonardo Savoia. 2002. "Clitics: Lexicalization Patterns of the So-called 3rd Person Dative." *Catalan Journal of Linguistics* 1: 117–155.

Martin, Txuss. 2009. "Deconstructing Dative Clitics." In *NYU Working Papers in Linguistics 2*, ed. by Patricia Irwin and Violeta Vázquez Rojas Maldonado.

Ordóñez, Francisco. 2002. "Some Clitic Combinations in the Syntax of Romance." *Catalan Journal of Linguistics* 1: 201–224.

Pescarini, Diego. 2010. "*Elsewhere* in Romance: Evidence from Clitic Clusters," *Linguistic Inquiry* 41.3: 427–444. DOI: 10.1162/LING_a_00003

Pescarini, Diego. 2014. "Prosodic Restructuring and Morphological Opacity. The Evolution of Italo-Romance Clitic Clusters." In *Diachrony and Dialects: Grammatical Change in the Dialects of Italy*, ed. by Adam Ledgeway, Paola Benincà, and Nigel Vincent, 155–176. Oxford: Oxford University Press.

Pescarini, Diego. 2015. "The Emergence of Two Classes of Clitic Clusters in (Italo)Romance." In *Romance Linguistics 2012: Selected papers from the 42nd Linguistic Symposium on Romance Languages*, ed. by Jason Smith and Tabea Ihsane, 171-183. Amsterdam: Benjamins.

Pescarini, Diego. In press. "Clitic Clusters". In *The Blackwell Companion to Syntax* (2nd ed.), ed. by Martin Everaert and Henk Van Riemsdijk. London: Wiley-Blackwell.

Quilis, Antonio. 1985. *Los pronombres le, la, lo y sus plurales en la lengua española hablada en Madrid*. Madrid: Consejo Superior de Investigaciones Científicas.

Rigau, Gemma. 1982. "Inanimate Indirect Object in Catalan." *Linguistic Inquiry* 13: 146–150.

Rohlfs, Gerhard. 1969. *Grammatica storica della lingua italiana e dei suoi dialetti*, Vol II: Morfologia. Torino: Einaudi.

Ronjat Jules. 1937. *Grammaire istorique des parlers provençaux modernes*. Montpellier: Société des Langues Romanes.

Rezac, Milan. 2010. "Ineffability through Modularity: Gaps in the French Clitic Cluster." In *Defective Paradigms: Missing Forms and What They Tell Us*, ed. by Matthew Baerman, Greville G. Corbett, and Dunstan Brown, 151–180. Oxford: Oxford University Press.

Rohlfs, Gerhard. 1970. *Le gascon*. Tübingen: Niemeyer.

Some notes on *falloir, devoir,* and the theory of control*

Lisa A. Reed
The Pennsylvania State University

This article sheds new light on the structure and meaning of sentences containing the French modal verbs *devoir* and *falloir*, as well as on the syntax and semantics of Control generally. Well-known and previously unnoticed empirical facts are examined that support the author's novel contention that *falloir* and *devoir* are syntactically and semantically ambiguous. These data are also argued to offer indirect support for the analysis of Control clauses recently developed in Reed (2014: Ch. 6 and 7), according to which there is a theoretical primitive (PRO) and it is associated with a "minimal" feature bundle consisting of just [−expletive] and [+N] syntactic features, with a separate, post-syntactic Theory of Control determining its understood phi-features.

1. Introduction

This paper examines some well-known and previously unnoticed properties of deontic and epistemic uses of the French modal verbs *falloir* 'to be necessary' and *devoir* 'must', arguing for the novel position that both verbs are three-way syntactically and semantically ambiguous. I focus here on these two modals, leaving aside, e.g., verbs like *vouloir* 'to want' and *pouvoir* 'to be able', because only they exhibit surprising properties that hold important implications for theories of control. Namely, specific facts involving *falloir* and *devoir* will be argued below to be amenable to analysis in terms of a theory that recognizes the existence of PRO and assumes that its reference is determined at LF by the application of a syntactically guided Bare Output Condition (BOC). More specifically, the data discussed below will be shown to follow from the analysis of Control developed in Reed (2014: Ch. 6 and 7), according to which PRO is licensed neither by

---

* I wish to thank Marc Authier, Julia Herschensohn, the audience at *LSRL 43*, and two anonymous reviewers for insightful comments and suggestions. Sincere thanks as well to Christina Tortora, Marcel den Dikken, Ignacio Montoya, and Teresa O'Neill for bringing this work to press. All remaining errors and omissions are my own.

DOI 10.1075/rllt.9.18ree

the need to check an EPP feature that is morphologically [−finite] (as in Chomsky and Lasnik 1995) semantically [+tense] I/T (Martin 2001; Bošković 2007), nor by an I/T associated with an uninterpretable [−R] feature (as in Landau 2004). Instead, I follow Bowers (2002: 206–207) in treating PRO as a truly "minimal" NP, licensed by similarly "minimal" functional and lexical heads, namely, those semantically associated with thematic roles, but uninvolved in Case and phi-feature valuation. Thus, this article can also be seen as an indirect argument against approaches to Control couched in terms of NP-movement (as in, e.g., Hornstein 1999), implicit arguments (cf. Jackendoff 1990; Sag and Pollard 1991), or Agreement (see, e.g., Landau 2004), although space constraints preclude a detailed discussion of exactly why these alternative theories cannot currently accommodate these data.

The contributions of this article are, therefore, two-fold. It improves upon on our understanding of the syntax and semantics of French epistemic and deontic modals and on the nature of Control.

The discussion is organized into three sections. Section 2 provides a brief overview of the theoretical assumptions being adopted from previous literature on Control, as well as on the novel proposals made here with respect to *devoir* and *falloir*. Section 3 then shows how a wide range of empirical facts associated with these modals falls out of the resulting analysis. Final conclusions are drawn in Section 4.

2.   Theoretical assumptions and proposals

In this section, I will briefly lay out the theoretical mechanisms needed to account for the empirical facts to be introduced in Section 3. These assumptions are of two distinct types. The first relate to Control Theory generally, and the second to the novel lexical entries that are being proposed here for *devoir* and *falloir*. I begin with the former, making seven key assumptions.

First, I will assume that Control clauses do contain the phonetically non-overt pronominal known as PRO, as argued, in more recent minimalist terms, in Chomsky and Lasnik (1995), Martin (2001), Landau (2004), and Bošković (2007), among others. Space considerations preclude a defense here of this particular approach to Control over competing analyses in terms of either Movement or implicit arguments. The reader is referred to Reed (2014: Ch. 5) for detailed argumentation to this effect.

Second, I assume, following work dating back to the government-binding (GB) era, specifically, Safir (1985: 33–38) and Lasnik (1992: 242–247), that PRO is an inherently non-expletive pronominal, a view that is supported by their data in (1a–c) where PRO is shown to be licensed only in the subject position of a thematically-associated verbal head, cf. (1a) and (1b,c).

(1) a. [*Before* PRO *making such an important decision*], *every option should first be considered.*

  b. [**PRO/It being obvious that John won't be returning*], *we can now leave.*

  c. *I wanted* [*for it/*PRO to seem that Mary is crazy*].

Third, I assume, as originally suggested in Chomsky (1981:324), that Arbitrary PRO differs from obligatorily controlled PRO in referring only to [+human] entities, much like the French pronoun *on* 'one'. For example, in (2a,b), the obligatorily controlled PRO is clearly [−human], but the Arbitrary PRO in (2c) disallows any reading in which it is co-referential with the [−human] NP *the device*. I also follow Williams (1992) in assuming this fact to be due to the logophoric determination of Arbitrary PRO's reference.

(2) a. *A little ice would serve/help/suffice* [PRO *to chill the beer*]. Kajita (1967)

  b. *The device arrived* [*while* PRO *still spewing forth sparks*]. Williams (1992)

  c. ***[*While* PRO *still spewing forth sparks*], *the device arrived.*

I next follow Grinder (1970), Epstein (1984), and Landau (2000: Ch. 2) in assuming that PRO is subject to Obligatory, not Arbitrary, Control in contexts like (3). While in (3a), PRO takes as its antecedent the explicit or implicit *for* NP; the indicated reading in (3b) (*It's fun for Bill or some implicit individual when other arbitrary individual(s) play baseball*) is unavailable. This suggests that (3a) is a case of Obligatory Control.

(3) a. *It's fun/difficult/necessary (for Bill$_x$)* [PRO$_x$ *to play baseball*].

  b. **It's fun/difficult/necessary (for Bill$_x$)* [PRO$_{arb}$ *to play baseball*].

Fifth, I assume, with Bowers (2002) and Reed (2014: Ch.6), that PRO is associated with a "minimal" bundle of features consisting of just a [+N] categorial feature and a [−expletive] semantic feature.[1] As for the phi-features that PRO is ultimately understood to bear, I assume (cf. Reed 2014:302), that these are due to the application of a BOC at LF. Thus, PRO enters and exits the syntactic component devoid of phi-features, acquiring them only at LF in a fashion to be made clear momentarily. The convergent application of a BOC is, therefore, what accounts for the fact, first observed in Postal (1970), that PRO must be plural in *They want to become millionaires*, but singular in *She wants to become a millionaire*.

---

1. An anonymous reviewer offers the alternative, more minimalist, suggestion that PRO be associated with just a [+N] feature, attributing the non-expletive requirement to a general underspecification of certain pronouns for this feature.

Sixth, following Reed (2014) and contra Bowers (2002), I adopt the view that PRO does not check an EPP feature on I/T.[2] As a consequence, PRO is taken to not undergo movement to Spec I/T unless this movement satisfies the need to obey other principles (e.g., Binding Theory). In short, I assume that a configuration of Obligatory Control like (2a) has the structure in (4), where PRO remains in its initial merge position in Spec vP (a.k.a. PrP, cf. Bowers 2002).

(4)   *A little ice would serve/help/suffice* [$_{FinP}$ *to* [$_{vP/PrP}$ PRO *chill the beer*]].

Finally, I assume, following Reed (2014: Ch. 7), that the reference of PRO is established at LF by the BOC in (5).

(5)   a.   Control Theory
By default, PRO must take as its antecedent a c-commanding implicit or explicit argument within the superordinate clausal domain that immediately dominates the clause in which it appears, with lexical specifications of the type discussed in e.g., Sag and Pollard (1991), Jackendoff and Culicover (2003), Rooryck (2000: Ch. 3, 2007), and Landau (2013: Ch. 5) ruling out potential antecedents and ForceP constituting a phase that "closes off" the search space. If there are no c- commanding potential antecedents or the search space is closed off by ForceP, PRO is assigned the index *arb* and its phi-feature specifications are logophorically determined.

b.   C-command domain of implicit arguments
An implicit argument c-commands X if the lexeme of which it is an implicit argument c-commands X.   Williams (1985: 303)

The empirical effects of (5) will become clear in the next section. For now, it is worth pointing out that (5) argues against antecedent determination in Control clauses reducing to NP-Movement, as suggested in Hornstein (1999), to Agree, as argued in Landau (2000, 2004), or to meaning postulates/lexical semantic factors, as proposed, e.g., in Bach (1979) and Jackendoff and Culicover (2003). An in-depth discussion of the problems associated with Hornstein's movement approach can be found in Reed (2014: 149–171, 217–218, 228–229, 242–244, 246, 250–251, 253, 329–330). Reed (2014: 136–138, 217–218, 224–228, 232–239, 329–330) also points out various problems faced by Landau's Agreement analysis; and Reed (2014: 182–184, 188–189, 196–201, 211, 217–218, 229, 241–242, 246–254, 329–330) discusses some of the difficulties encountered by implicit argument approaches.

---

2.   See Reed (2014: 120–123) for an enumeration of the problems associated with this aspect of Bowers' (2002) analysis.

Finally, I introduce, in (6) and (7), the novel lexical entries for the deontic and epistemic uses of the two modals *falloir* and *devoir*. These include redundant "GB"-style specifications for argument structure (i.e., theta-roles). This is purely for expository purposes, however, since, in line with much of minimalist literature (cf., e.g., Harley 2011), I assume that grammaticality effects related to theta-roles obtain at LF via the Principle of Full Interpretation (PFI). Under this view, if an argument merges in the Spec of a thematic *v* that merges with a VP headed by a verb like *seem*, this results in a PFI violation at LF and the same is true if such an argument fails to merge in the Spec of a *v* that merges with a VP headed by a verb like *play*.

(6) a. *falloir₁* = deontic *falloir* + subjunctive
         c-selection: _____ForceP
         s-selection: <_____, Proposition>
         Meaning: *It deontically must be the case that p.*

         Illustrative example:
         Il faut [$_{ForceP}$ *qu'elle   travaille*].
         it is-necessary that she work
         'She must work.'

     b. *falloir₂* = deontic *falloir* + infinitive
         c-selection: _____(Indirect Object Clitic), _____FinP
         s-selection: <_____, Deontic Obligation, Proposition>
         Meaning: *It is deontically required of NP that p.*

         Illustrative example:
         Il (lui)   faut [$_{FinP}$ PRO *travailler*].
         it her-DAT is-necessary   to-work
         'She must work.' (*lui* variant)/'One must work.'

     c. *falloir₃* = simplex deontic *falloir*
         c-selection: _____(Indirect Object Clitic), _____DP
         s-selection: <_____, Deontic Necessity, Theme>
         Meaning: *X deontically must have Y.*

         Illustrative example:
         Il (lui)   faut   une autorisation   spéciale pour avoir
         it her-DAT is-necessary an   authorization special for to-have

         accès à ces   documents.
         access to these documents

         'She must have special authorization in order to have access to these documents.' (*lui* variant)
         /'Access to these documents requires special authorization.'

(7) a. *devoir₁* = epistemic *devoir* + infinitive
      c-selection: _____TP
      s-selection: <_____, Proposition>
      Meaning: *It epistemically must be the case that p.*

      Illustrative example:
      Ton pneu est dégonflé. Un clou doit [$_{TP}$ *(un clou) l'avoir*
      your tire is flat   a   nail must   a   nail it-to-have

      (un clou) pénétré].
      (a nail) punctured

      'Your tire's flat. A nail must have punctured it.'

  b. *devoir₂* = Non-external-theta-role associated deontic *devoir* + infinitive
      c-selection: _____Non-Thematic vP
      s-selection: <_____, Proposition>
      Meaning: *It deontically must be the case that p.*

      Illustrative example:
      Il doit [$_{Non\text{-}Thematic\ vP}$ *y   avoir   du   savon dans toutes les*
      it must   there to-have of-the soap in   all   the

      toilettes publiques].
      restrooms public

      '(By law) There must be soap in all public restrooms.'

  c. *devoir₃* = External-theta-role associated (Control) deontic *devoir* +
      infinitive
      c-selection:_____FinP
      s-selection:<Subject NP, Proposition>
      Meaning: *NP deontically must p.*

      Illustrative example:
      Marie, tu dois [$_{FinP}$ PRO *travailler plus dur].*
      Marie you must   to-work   more hard
      'Marie, you must work harder.'

The empirical effects of these entries are the topic of the next section, so I will not elaborate on them further here. Two brief comments are, however, in order.

First, note that (6b,c) specify that deontic *falloir* selects for an indirect object that can only surface as a clitic, never a full DP. This is intended to account for contrasts in grammaticality that exist between examples like (6b,c) and ones like, **Il fallait à Marie travailler* 'Marie had to work' and ?**Il faut à ton père des lunettes pour lire* 'Your father needs glasses to read.' In (6b,c), this is treated in terms of a lexical restriction. Alternatively, it could be assumed that *falloir* belongs to a class of verbs that selects for a defective AgrO, one that fails to undergo Agree with any phi-associated NP initially merged in the VP-internal object position. Object clitics could then be seen as undergoing initial Merge in AgrO, which would enable them to agree with it directly.

Second, it also bears emphasizing that the preceding entries are indeed novel. According to the "classic" view, developed with respect to French in Dubois (1969:119) Kayne (1969, 1975:259), and Huot (1974:171–172), epistemic modality in infinitival contexts correlates with Raising, whereas deontic modality is associated with Control.[3] I clearly depart from this view, since the entry in (7b) associates deontic *devoir* with a non-Control structure. Further, given that (7c) associates deontic *devoir* with a Control entry, my proposals also contrast with "non-classic" analyses that treat both epistemic and deontic *devoir* as a Raising verb (e.g., Ruwet 1972: Ch. 2; Zubizarreta 1983:214–215).[4] While the present approach is clearly less parsimonious than its predecessors, the complexity of the data to be introduced in the next section will be shown to justify it.

3. Enumeration and account of the empirical facts

In this section, seven distinct empirical facts associated with *falloir* and *devoir* will be introduced, the entirety of which will be shown to fall out under the theoretical assumptions made in Section 2, but only portions of which follow under previous analyses.

First, traditional grammars, such as *Harper's Grammar of French*, have long observed that *falloir* and *devoir* contrast in their ability to select for both an inflected (subjunctive) complement clause and an infinitival one. Only *falloir* allows both options:

(8) a. *Marie, il faut₂* [$_{\text{FinP}}$ *travailler plus dur*].
Marie it is-necessary   to-work   more hard
'Marie, you must work harder.'

   b. *Marie, il faut₁* [$_{\text{ForceP}}$ *que tu travailles plus dur*].
Marie it is-necessary   that you work   more hard
'Marie, you must work harder.'

(9) a. *De par la loi, il doit₂* [$_{\text{Non-Thematic vP}}$ *y avoir du*
as per the law it must   there to-have of-the

savon dans toutes les toilettes publiques].
soap in all the toilets public

'By law, there must be soap in all public restrooms.'

---

3. The "classic" view has been argued for with respect to English in, e.g., Ross (1969) and Perlmutter (1970:1150).

4. See Barbiers (1995:161–162) for a similar Raising approach to Dutch modals and Eide (2006:140–143) for critical discussion of that analysis.

b. *J'ai   entendu quelque chose! Il **doit**₁ [_TP y avoir   quelqu'un*
   I have heard   some   thing it must there to-have someone

   dans la   maison]!
   in   the house

   'I heard something! There (epistemically) must be someone in the house!'

c. **De par la   loi, il **doit** [_ForceP qu'il y **ait**   du   savon*
   as per the law it must   that it there have of-the soap

   dans toutes les toilettes publiques].
   in   all   the toilets   public

   'By law, there must be soap in all public restrooms.'

Under any analysis of *devoir* and *falloir*, including the present one, this is accounted for in terms of arbitrary lexical specifications for tensed and/or infinitival complement clauses, cf. the lexical entries in (6)–(7). It would be preferable to derive this difference from some deeper grammatical principle, but such an account, if it is even possible, has not yet been developed.

Second, traditional grammars have also observed that both *falloir* and *devoir* can be productively used to encode deontic modality (cf. (8) and (9a)). However, (10a,b) show that only *devoir* can also be productively used to encode epistemic modality.[5]

(10)   Speaker A:
       On dit   que Patrick sort   avec une fille qui
       one says that Patrick is-going-out with a   girl who

       s'appelle   Cécile.
       herself-is-called Cécile

       'They say that Patrick is going out now with a girl named Cecile.'

   a. Speaker B:
       *#Comme je le   connais, il **faut**   qu'elle soit blonde*
       as   I him-ACC know   it is-necessary that she be blond

       aux   yeux bleus.
       with-the eyes blue

       #'Knowing him, she (**deontically**) must be blonde-haired and blue-eyed.'

   b. Speaker B:
       *Comme je le   connais, elle **doit** être   blonde aux*
       as   I him-ACC know   she must to-be be blond with-the

       yeux bleus.
       eyes blue

       'Knowing him, she (**epistemically**) must be blonde-haired and blue-eyed.'

---

5. This is not to say that *falloir* precludes bouletic or teleological uses, only that it does not productively encode epistemic modality.

In interest of brevity, this difference will be treated as a matter of lexical semantics, although this assumption warrants further research in light of Kratzer (1981, 1991). Namely, the truth conditions associated with each of the uses of *falloir* and *devoir* in (6) and (7) are assumed to involve universal quantification over sets of accessible worlds, with the sets of worlds selected differing in each case. More specifically, the deontic uses of these modals involve universal quantification over sets of worlds consistent with certain norms, laws, moral principles, and so forth, whereas the epistemic use of *devoir* (*devoir₁*) involves worlds consistent with some individual's beliefs or knowledge.

Third, these modals are also well known to allow expletive subjects, as evidenced by the examples above in (8a,b) and (9a,b). (See e.g., *Harper's Grammar of French*; Zubizarreta 1983:213; Authier and Reed 2009:44–45.)

This fact follows from the proposed analysis, expressed, for ease of exposition, in terms of s-selection frames. Namely, in each of *falloir*'s lexical entries in (6a–c) there is a blank indicating that this verb is unassociated with a thematic subject. The same is true of epistemic *devoir* in (7a), as well as in the entry of deontic *devoir* in (7b).[6]

As observed in Zubizarreta (1983:213), the grammaticality of expletive matrix subjects in deontic *devoir* examples of the type in (9a) is problematic for the "classic"

---

6. *Falloir* and *devoir₁ & 2* are being analyzed here as verbs unassociated with an external argument. An anonymous reviewer notes that the proposed analysis leaves unexplained the fact that *falloir* contrasts with *devoir₁* and, especially, *devoir₂* in clearly allowing expletive *il* 'it' drop in examples like the following:

(i) *(Il) faut   pas sortir.*
     it   is-necessary not to-leave
     'It is forbidden to leave.'

(ii) ?*(Il) doit₁ bien y   avoir   des   solutions.*
      it   must well there to-have of-the solutions
      'There (epistemically) must be a solution.'

(iii) *(De par la loi) *(Il) doit₂ y   avoir   du   savon dans toutes les*
      as per the law   it   must there to-have of-the soap   in   all   the
      toilettes publiques.
      toilets   public
      'By law, there (deontically) must be soap in all public restrooms.'

This gap is not necessarily problematic, however, since *il*-drop is well known to be subject to poorly understood restrictions related to frequency of use, the expletive/quasi-expletive nature of the *il* associated with a given verb, verb class type (e.g., modal versus non-modal, existential, etc.), and so on. See Culbertson and Legendre (2014) and Zimmerman and Kaiser (2014) for distinct proposals, neither of which is able to predict, on theoretical grounds, when expletive *il* can or cannot drop.

analyses of this modal developed, e.g., by Dubois (1969: 119), Kayne (1969, 1975: 259), and Huot (1974: 171–172). As mentioned earlier, these authors have argued that deontic *devoir* is always associated with a Control structure; i.e., it must be associated with an argument that initially merges in thematic subject position, whereas epistemic *devoir* is a Raising verb, unassociated with an external argument. The example in (9a) shows that this cannot be true. Deontic *devoir* must be associated with a Raising verb entry of the type in (7b).

While Zubizarreta (1983: 214–215) concludes from this that *devoir* on all of its uses is unambiguously a Raising verb, a position originally developed in Ruwet (1972: Ch. 2), certain data observed in Authier and Reed (2009: 44–45) prove problematic for this view. Specifically, Authier and Reed note that in those contexts in which the matrix NP is expletive, only *falloir* + subjunctive places no restrictions on the type of predicate that may appear in the complement clause, as illustrated in (11).

(11) a. *De par la   loi, il faut₁*   [$_{ForceP}$ *qu'il   y   ait   du*
          as per the law   it is-necessary   that-it there have of-the

          savon dans toutes les   toilettes publiques].
          soap   in   all   the   toilets   public

          'By law, there must be soap in all public restrooms.'

     b. *Il faut₁*   [$_{ForceP}$ *qu'elle/Marie travaille]*.
          it is-necessary   that she/Marie work

          'She/Marie must work.'

Falloir + infinitive, in contrast, accepts only complement clauses headed by a verb that is itself theta-associated, as made clear by (12).

(12) a. **De par la   loi, il faut₂*   [$_{FinP}$ *y avoir   du   savon*
          as per the law   it is-necessary   there to-have of-the soap

          dans toutes les   toilettes publiques].
          in   all   the   toilets   public

          *'By law, it is required of anyone to have soap in all public restrooms.'

     b. *Il faut₂*   [$_{FinP}$ PRO *travailler]*.
          it is-necessary   to-work

          'One must work.'

Finally, in these same contexts, *devoir* only accepts complement clauses headed by a verbal element that is not theta-associated, as evidenced by (13).

(13) a. *De par la   loi, il doit₂* [$_{Non\text{-}Thematic\ vP}$ *y   avoir   du*
          as per the law   it must   there to-have of-the

          savon dans toutes les   toilettes publiques].
          soap   in   all   the   toilets   public

'By law, there (deontically) must be soap in all public restrooms.'

b. *J'ai   entendu   quelque   chose!   Il   doit₁   [TP y   avoir   quelqu'un*
    I have   heard   some   thing   it   must   there   to-have   someone

    dans   la   maison]!
    in   the   house

    'I heard something! There (epistemically) must be someone in the house!'

c. **Marie, il doit₂* [Non-Thematic vP PRO *travailler plus dur*].
    Marie   it   must   to-work   more   hard
    'Marie, you (deontically) must work harder.'
    (Grammatical on the irrelevant reading of *devoir₃* 'He must work harder.')

d. *Il   y   a   beaucoup   de   livres   ici.   *Il   doit₁/₂*
    it   there   have   many   of   books   here   it   must

    [TP/Non-Thematic vP PRO *lire   beaucoup*].
                          to-read   a-lot

    'There are a lot of books here. There (epistemically) must be a lot of reading going on.'
    (Grammatical on the irrelevant reading of *devoir₃* 'He must read a lot.')

The fact that examples like (13c,d) are ungrammatical is not predicted by the structurally unambiguous Raising approach to *devoir* advanced in Ruwet (1972: Ch. 2) and Zubizarreta (1983:214–215). They are incorrectly predicted to be as acceptable as those in (13a,b). The full range of data does, however, fall out under the analysis advocated in Section 2. To see how, notice first that these contrasts only emerge when the matrix subject is expletive. Given this, we are not dealing with *devoir₃*—a verb that is associated with a subject theta-role—so that entry can be set aside.

Looking more closely at the data, the lexical entry for *falloir₁* in (6a) specifies that it s-selects for a proposition-denoting, inflected ForceP complement clause, resulting in the structures provided above in (11a,b). Given these structures, one correctly predicts that no thematically based restrictions are imposed on the NP that appears in the subject position of the complement clause. Turning to (12a,b), the lexical entry for *falloir₂* in (6b) interacts with the version of Control Theory outlined in Section 2 to produce the indicated structures. The entry for *falloir₂* specifies that this modal must be thematically associated with an internal argument that refers to an individual or set of individuals who are deontically obligated to ensure the realization of the embedded predicate. However, this argument is only optionally c-selected, so it may remain syntactically implicit, as it does in (12a,b). However, its obligatory presence in the argument structure of *falloir₂* renders an example like (12a) semantically deviant, because the absurd assertion is made that it is deontically required of any arbitrary individual that soap be in every public restroom. When the embedded verb is replaced with one that is associated with a thematic subject, as in (12b), the result is well formed because PRO must now be projected in order for the embedded verb's theta-requirements to be met, and, by the BOC in (5a), PRO is obligatorily controlled by the implicit argument of *falloir*, making the plausible assertion that everyone must work.

Looking now at the *devoir* data in (13a–d), the lexical entries for epistemic and deontic *devoir* in (7a,b) interact with Control Theory to produce the indicated structures. According to (7a,b), neither epistemic *devoir* nor deontic *devoir$_2$* must be thematically associated with an internal argument beyond the complement clause. In other words, there is no implicit argument that is understood to either bear a deontic obligation or hold a belief with respect to the embedded proposition. Thus, both of these uses of *devoir* tolerate embedded clauses headed by verbs that are not associated with an external argument, accounting for the grammaticality of (13a,b). In contrast, if the embedded clause is headed by a verb that is associated with such a theta-role, as in (13c,d), then PRO is projected and assigned that thematic role. By the BOC in (5a), it will be obligatorily controlled by the only NP that c-commands it in the relevant domain. This being the expletive NP *il*, the result is semantic ill-formedness. (PRO is inherently non-expletive.)

Consider next a previously unnoticed set of facts that show that the various uses of *falloir* and *devoir* also contrast with respect to the exact types of thematic subjects that are permitted in the complement clause. Specifically, *falloir* + subjunctive tolerates both inanimate and weather expletive subjects in the embedded clause, as illustrated in (14):

(14)   a.   *Dans cette station,   il faut$_1$*   [$_{ForceP}$ *qu'il   s'arrête   de*
in   this   ski-station   it   is-necessary   that   it   it-self   stop   of

neiger]   avant   qu'on   puisse   légalement   utiliser
to-snow   before   that   one   can   legally   to-use

des   dameuses.
of-the   snow-groomers

'At this ski station, it must stop snowing before snow groomers are permitted.'

b.   *Pour qu'il   soit légal   de pêcher   dans cette rivière,   il*
for   that it   be   legal   of to-fish   in   this   river   it

faut$_1$ [$_{ForceP}$ *que le   niveau   de l'eau   soit au*
is-necessary   that   the   level   of the water   be   at-the

moins   de 2 mètres].
least   of 2 meters

'The water level of this river must stand at a minimum of 2 meters before fishing is allowed.'

In contrast, *falloir* + infinitive does not allow the understood subject to be either of these NP types, as (15) shows.

(15) a. **Dans cette station, il (nous) faut$_2$* [$_{\text{FinP}}$ PRO
in   this ski-station it us   is-necessary

s'arrêter   de neiger] avant qu'on   puisse légalement
oneself to-stop of to-snow before that one can   legally

utiliser des   dameuses.
to-use of-the snow-groomers

*'At this ski station, it is legally required of the weather/us that it/we stop snowing before snow groomers are permitted.'

b. **Pour qu'il soit légal de pêcher dans cette rivière, il (nous)*
for   that it be legal of to-fish in   this river   it (us-DAT)

faut$_2$ [$_{\text{FinP}}$ PRO être   au   moins de 2 mètres].
is-necessary   to-be at-the least of 2 meters

*'The law requires of this river/us that it/we stand at a minimum of 2 meters before fishing is permitted.'

With respect to *devoir*, one finds, by and large, a split in behavior with respect to its deontic and epistemic uses. The facts in (16) show that epistemic *devoir* freely accepts inanimate and weather expletive embedded subjects. However, the data in (17) indicate that deontic *devoir* is generally intolerant of both NP subject types, with a few notable exceptions in the case of inanimate NPs given in (18).

(16) a. *Ton pneu est dégonflé. Un clou doit$_1$* [$_{\text{TP}}$ *(un clou) l'avoir*
your tire is flat   a   nail must   (a   nail) it-to-have

(un clou) pénétré].
(a   nail) punctured

'Your tire's flat. A nail (epistemically) must have punctured it.'

b. *Regarde ces   gros nuages noirs sur le pic là-bas.   Il*
look-at those big   clouds black on the peak over-there it

doit$_1$ [$_{\text{TP}}$ *(il) y   pleuvoir].*
must   (it) there to-rain

'Look at the big black clouds over that mountaintop. It (epistemically) must be raining up there.'

(17) a. **Pour qu'il soit légal de pêcher dans cette rivière, le niveau*
for   that it be legal of to-fish in   this river   the level

de l'eau   doit$_3$ impérativement [$_{\text{FinP}}$ PRO *atteindre au*
of the water must imperatively   to-reach at-the

moins de 2 mètres].
least of 2 meters

*'Before one can fish in this river, the law strictly requires of the water level that it reach a minimum of 2 meters.'

b.   *Dans cette station,   il doit₃ impérativement [FinP PRO
in   this ski-station it must imperatively

s'arrêter   de neiger] pour qu'on   puisse légalement
oneself to-stop of to-snow for that one can   legally

utiliser des   dameuses.
to-use of-the snow-groomers

*'At this ski station, the weather is strictly required to stop snowing
before snow groomers are permitted.'

(18) a. *De par la   loi, un litre de lait   doit₃ [FinP PRO contenir*
as per the law a   liter of milk must   to-contain

au   moins 5% de crème].
at-the least 5% of cream

'By law, a liter of milk is legally required to contain at least 5% cream.'

b. *Pour être   exportable, un vin   doit₃ [FinP PRO faire   au*
for to-be exportable a   wine must   to-make at-the

moins 11 degrés].
least 11 percent

'Wines produced for export are legally required to contain at least 11%
alcohol.'

While the ungrammaticality of examples like (17a,b) is unexpected under the Raising approaches to deontic *devoir* developed in Ruwet (1972) and Zubizarreta (1983), it and the other facts follow from the analysis developed in Section 2, an analysis that results in the structural configurations indicated above. Consider first the two "tolerant" constructions, namely, *falloir* + subjunctive in (14) and epistemic *devoir* in (16). In these examples, the inanimate or quasi-expletive initially merges in a thematically compatible position and then undergoes licit movement to its surface position for feature valuation purposes, resulting in a grammatical output.

Contrast this with the "intolerant" constructions, given in (15) and (17). In these cases, syntactic considerations force the projection of PRO. That is, PRO is the only NP that is licensed in the subject position of the embedded clause because it is the only referential NP that has no Case or phi-features requiring valuation. By the BOC in (5a), PRO, by default, must take as its antecedent a c-commanding NP in the matrix clause and it is this requirement that accounts for the attested restrictions. Namely, in (15a), only expletive *il* 'it' and *nous* 'us' are candidate antecedents for PRO. Since PRO is inherently non-expletive, any co-reference with expletive *il* will result in semantic deviance. Co-reference with *nous* 'us' is equally unacceptable because *nous* cannot be understood to be co-referential with the thematic subject of *neiger* 'to snow.' Thus, we account for the fact that the understood subject of *falloir* + infinitive constructions cannot be interpreted as a weather expletive. Turning to (15b), once again, if expletive *il* is selected as the antecedent of [–expletive] PRO, deviance results, a line of reasoning that applies equally to (17b). If, on the other hand, *nous* is selected in (15b), we obtain an irrelevant (and strange) reading in which the referent of *nous* 'us' must attain a given water level. In any event, we account for the fact that inanimate understood subjects are also unattested with *falloir* + infinitive. Looking next at (17a), here, the only potential antecedent for PRO is a water level. Thus, the deviant claim is made that a level of water bears a deontic obligation ("is obliged/ legally required") to attain a certain level.[7] Consider, finally, those few cases in which deontic *devoir* tolerates an inanimate subject. In (18a,b), we have rare situations in which an inanimate entity *is* required to exhibit certain properties. For example, in (18a), a liter of milk is deontically—legally—required to contain a certain percentage of cream.

The sixth group of facts to be considered here involves NPs that form part of an idiom in the complement clause. As made clear in (19), *falloir* + subjunctive quite freely accepts idioms in the complement clause. In contrast, the novel data in (20) show that *falloir* + infinitive rejects them.

---

7.   An anonymous reviewer notes that s/he at least marginally tolerates embedded weather predicates in examples like (i), a type of sentence that initially appears to be parallel to ungrammatical examples like (17b):

(i)   ?*Dans cette station,   il   doit   s'arrêter   de   neiger   pour   qu'on*
        in   this   ski-station   it   must   oneself-to-stop   of   to-snow   for   that one

       puisse   légalement   utiliser   des   dameuses.
       can   legally   to-use   of-the   snow-groomers

       'At this ski station, it must stop snowing before snow groomers are permitted.'

There is, however, an important semantic difference between the two examples. Sentence (17b) involves deontic modality—quantification over sets of worlds where laws/rules are respected—whereas (i) expresses a different type of circumstantial modality— quantification over sets of worlds in which certain physical facts hold. As explained in the text, weather expletives are unacceptable with deontic *devoir* in examples like (17b) because we cannot legislate/dictate what the weather must do. The adverb *impérativement* 'strictly' in (17b) serves to single out this reading. We can, however, impose legal requirements on what *people* can do under particular weather conditions. This is the case in (i), in which *impérativement* 'strictly' is absent. No claims have been made in this article with respect to the syntax of non-deontic/non-epistemic *devoir* and *falloir*, although the subject certainly warrants attention.

(19)   a.   *Pour que notre chef de département prenne au   sérieux ce*
            for   that our   head of department take   to-the serious this

            genre de plainte,   les   plumes, il faudrait₁   vraiment
            type of complaint the feathers it would-be-necessary really

            [_ForceP *qu'elles   volent*].
                      that they fly

            'In order for our department head to take this type of complaint
            seriously, the fur would (deontically) really have to fly.'

   b.   *Il faut₁   [_ForceP que justice soit rendue   (justice)].*
        it is-necesssary   that justice be   rendered (justice)
        'Justice (deontically) must be served.'

(20)   a.   **Pour que notre chef de département prenne au   sérieux ce*
            for   that our   head of department take   to-the serious this

            genre de plainte,   les   plumes, il faudrait₂   [_FinP PRO
            type of complaint the feathers it would-be-necessary

            vraiment voler].
            really   to-fly

            'In order for our department head to take this type of complaint
            seriously, the fur would (deontically) really have to fly.'

   b.   **Justice, il faut₂   [_FinP être   rendue PRO].*
        justice it is-necessary   to-be rendered
        'Justice, it (deontically) must be served.'

The novel facts in (21) show that while epistemic *devoir* accepts idioms, those in (22)
and (23) demonstrate that deontic *devoir*, surprisingly, only accepts idiomatic NPs
that are initially merged in thematic object, never thematic subject, position. In other
words, deontic *devoir* tolerates only VP, not sentential, idioms.

(21)   a.   *Quand ils   ne   sont pas   d'accord   sur quelque chose,*
            when   they NEG are   not of agreement on   some   thing

            les   plumes doivent₁ [_TP (les   plumes) voler].
            the feathers must   (the feathers) to-fly

            'When they don't agree on something, the fur (epistemically) must
            really fly.'

   b.   *Un tel   apaisement après des   mois   d'émeute! Justice doit₁*
        a such peace   after some months of rioting justice must

        [_TP *(justice), avoir   été   rendue (justice), d'une façon ou*
             (justice), to-have been served (justice) of one way   or

        d'une autre.
        of an other

        'Such peace after months of rioting! Justice (epistemically) must have
        been served in one way or another.'

(22) a. *Quand je leur   dis qu'ils   ne   valent   rien   en
        when   I   them-DAT tell that they NEG are-worth nothing in

        tant   qu'équipe, les plumes   doivent$_2$ [$_{\text{Non-Thematic vP}}$ *voler*].
        terms that team the feathers must   to-fly

        'When I tell them that they're a nowhere team, the fur (deontically)
        must fly.'

    b. *Justice doit$_2$* [$_{\text{Non-Thematic vP}}$ *(justice) être rendue   (justice)*].
        justice must   (justice) to-be rendered (justice)
        'Justice (deontically) must be served.'   (Ruwet 1972:72)

(23) *Quand je leur   dis qu'ils   ne   valent   rien   en tant
      when   I   them-DAT tell that they NEG are-worth nothing in terms

      qu'équipe, les plumes   doivent$_3$ [$_{\text{FinP}}$ PRO *voler*].
      that team the feathers must   to-fly

      'When I tell them that they're a nowhere team, the fur (deontically)
      must fly.'

This range of facts is also problematic for previous analyses. Namely, if one assumes with Dubois (1969:119), Kayne (1969, 1975:259), and Huot (1974:171–172) that deontic *devoir* is associated only with a Control structure parallel to (23), then the grammaticality of examples like (22b) remains unexplained. Conversely, if one follows Ruwet (1972: Ch. 2) and Zubizarreta (1983:214–215) in assuming that deontic *devoir* is unambiguously a Raising verb, as in (22b), then we have no account of the ungrammaticality of sentences like (23). Under the analysis in Section 2, however, the full range of data follows. Namely, given the structures in (19) and (21), we would expect idioms to quite freely appear with *falloir* + subjunctive and epistemic *devoir*. There is no reason why they shouldn't. In contrast, the *falloir* + infinitive examples in (20) are ungrammatical because PRO obligatorily takes as its antecedent the implicit argument of *falloir$_2$*, the individual on whom a deontic obligation is imposed with respect to the complement clause, destroying the idiomatic readings. Sentence (20a), for example, can be paraphrased as *In order for our department head to take this type of complaint seriously, the fur, one would really have to fly*. As concerns the *devoir$_2$* facts in (22), here *devoir* c-selects for a non-thematic vP; that is, a vP headed by the type of v or Pr head that does not assign a subject theta-role. Because of this c-selection frame, *devoir$_2$* tolerates only VP idioms. That is, in an example like (22a) the embedded external theta-role remains unassigned, resulting in a violation of the Principle of Full Interpretation. On the other hand, in passive idioms like (22b), passivization absorbs the external theta-role, rendering the structure interpretable at LF as all theta-roles that must be discharged in the syntax are discharged. Finally, in (23) we find a derivation involving *devoir$_3$*. Such examples are ruled out because this modal assigns a thematic role of obligation to the NP in matrix subject position, destroying the idiomatic readings. For this reason, (23) has the bizarre meaning *When I tell them that they're a nowhere team, the fur will be required to fly.*

For completeness' sake, a seventh and final fact concerning propositional *falloir* and *devoir* deserves mention, namely, these modals also diverge in their selection—or lack of selection—for an internal argument beyond the complement clause. As (24)– (26) make clear, *falloir*$_1$ and *devoir* both differ from *falloir* + infinitive in that only the latter selects for an internal argument beyond the complement clause.[8]

(24)   *Il **lui**   fallait   qu'elle/son fils   travaille.
       it her-DAT was-necessary that she/her   son   work
       'It was deontically required **of her** that she/her son work.'

(25)   Il **(lui)**   faut   travailler.
       it her-DAT is-necessary to-work
       'It is necessary **(for her)** to work.' (*lui* variant)/'One must work.'

(26)   a.   *De par la loi, il **lui**   doit   y   avoir   du   savon
            as per the law it her-DAT must there to-have of-the soap

            dans toutes les   toilettes publiques.
            in   all   the   toilets   public

            'By law, it is (deontically) required **of her** that there be soap in all public restrooms.'

       b.   *Son fils **lui**   doit   travailler.
            her son her-DAT must to-work
            'It (epistemically) must be true **of her** that her son work.'

This contrast is captured in the lexical entries proposed in Section 2. Only in the lexical entry for *falloir*$_2$ does one find an indirect object optionally c-selected by the modal.

4.   Summary

In conclusion, Reed (2014: Ch. 6 and 7) has developed a novel analysis of Control that recognizes the existence of PRO and analyzes it as a truly "minimal" NP, associated with just an [N] categorial feature and a [−expletive] semantic feature. Having no inherent phi-features of its own, PRO is assumed to obtain them at LF, via a BOC that, by default,

---

8.   An anonymous reviewer notes that certain non-deontic uses of *falloir* + subjunctive differ from the deontic use in this respect:

(i)   Il **(lui)**   fallait   que je lui   dise tout.
      it to-her was-necessary that I to-her tell all
      'She (bouletically) needed me to tell her everything.'

selects as its antecedent any c-commanding NP within the domain of the superordinate clause. In this paper, I have explored some interesting properties of the French modals *falloir* and *devoir* in order to not only better understand their syntactic and semantic properties, but also to demonstrate that an account of them offers interesting indirect support for this particular approach to Control.

References

Authier, J.-Marc and Lisa Reed. 2009. "French *Tough*-Movement Revisited." *Probus* 21 (1): 1–21. DOI: 10.1515/prbs.2009.001

Bach, Emmon. 1979. "Control in Montague Grammar." *Linguistic Inquiry* 10 (4): 515–531.

Barbiers, Sjef. 1995. *The Syntax of Interpretation*. The Netherlands: Holland Institute of Generative Linguistics.

Bošković, Željko. 2007. "The Syntax of Nonfinite Complementation: An Economy Approach." *Minimalist Syntax: The Essential Readings* ed. by Željko Bošković and Howard Lasnik, 86–111. Oxford: Blackwell Publishers.

Bowers, John. 2002. "Transitivity." *Linguistic Inquiry* 33 (2): 183–224. DOI: 10.1162/002438902317406696

Chomsky, Noam. 1981. *Lectures on Government and Binding*. Dordrecht: Foris.

Chomsky, Noam and Howard Lasnik. 1995. "The Theory of Principles and Parameters." *The Minimalist Program*, Noam Chomsky, 13–127. Cambridge, Mass.: MIT Press.

Culbertson, Jennifer and Géraldine Legendre. 2014. "Prefixal Agreement and Impersonal *il* in Spoken French: Experimental Evidence." *Journal of French Language Studies* 24 (1): 83–105. DOI: 10.1017/S0959269513000380

Dubois, Jean. 1969. *Grammaire structurale du français: La phrase et les transformations*. Paris: Larousse.

Eide, Kristin. 2006. *Norwegian Modals*. Berlin: De Gruyter. DOI: 10.1515/9783110899634

Epstein, Samuel. 1984. "Quantifier-pro and the LF Representation of PRO." *Linguistic Inquiry* 15 (3): 499–505.

Grinder, John. 1970. "Super Equi-NP Deletion." *Papers from the Sixth Regional Meeting of the Chicago Linguistic Society*, 297–317. Chicago, Illinois: University of Chicago.

Harley, Heidi. 2011. "A Minimalist Approach to Argument Structure." *The Oxford Handbook of Linguistic Minimalism* ed. by Cedric Boeckx, 427–448. Oxford University Press: Oxford.

Hornstein, Norbert. 1999. "Movement and Control." *Linguistic Inquiry* 30 (1): 69–96. DOI: 10.1162/002438999553968

Huot, Hélène. 1974. *Le verbe* devoir: *étude synchronique et diachronique*. Paris: Klincksieck.

Jackendoff, Ray. 1990. *Semantic Structures*. Cambridge, Mass.: MIT Press.

Jackendoff, Ray, and Peter Culicover. 2003. "The Semantic Basis of Control in English." *Language* 79 (3): 517–556. DOI: 10.1353/lan.2003.0166

Kajita, Masaru. 1967. *A Generative-Transformational Study of Semi-Auxiliaries in Present-Day American English*. Ph.D. dissertation, Princeton University, Princeton, NJ.

Kayne, Richard. 1969. *The Transformational Cycle in French*. Ph.D. dissertation, MIT, Cambridge, MA.

Kayne, Richard. 1975. *French Syntax: The Transformational Cycle*. Cambridge, Mass.: MIT Press.

Kratzer, Angelika. 1981. "The Notional Category of Modality." *Words, Worlds, and Contexts. New Approaches in Word Semantics* ed. by Hans-Jürgen Eikmeyer and Hannes Rieser, 38–74. Berlin: de Gruyter.

Kratzer, Angelika. 1991. "Modality." *Semantics: An International Handbook of Contemporary Research* ed. by Arnim von Stechow and Dieter Wunderlich, 639–650. Berlin: de Gruyter.

Landau, Idan. 2000. *Elements of Control: Structure and Meaning in Infinitival Constructions.* Dordrecht: Kluwer Academic Publishers.

Landau, Idan. 2004. "The Scale of Finiteness and the Calculus of Control." *Natural Language and Linguistic Theory* 22 (4): 811–877. DOI: 10.1007/s11049-004-4265-5

Landau, Idan. 2013. *Control in Generative Grammar: A Research Companion.* Cambridge: Cambridge University Press. DOI: 10.1017/CBO9781139061858

Lasnik, Howard. 1992. "Two Notes on Control and Binding." *Control and Grammar* ed. by Richard Larson, Sabine Iatridou, Utpal Lahiri, and James Higginbotham, 235–251. Dordrecht: Kluwer Academic Publishers. DOI: 10.1007/978-94-015-7959-9_7

Martin, Roger. 2001. "Null Case and the Distribution of PRO." *Linguistic Inquiry* 32 (1): 141–166. DOI: 10.1162/002438901554612

Perlmutter, David. 1970. "The Two Verbs *Begin.*" *Readings in English Transformational Grammar* ed. by Roderick Jacobs and Peter Rosenbaum, 107–277. Waltham, Mass: Ginn and Company.

Postal, Paul. 1970. "On Coreferential Complement Subject Deletion." *Linguistic Inquiry* 1 (4): 439–500.

Reed, Lisa. 2014. *Strengthening the PRO Hypothesis.* Berlin: de Gruyter.

Rooryck, Johan. 2000. *Configurations of Sentential Complementation.* London: Routledge. DOI: 10.4324/9780203187654

Rooryck, Johan. 2007. "Control via Selection." *New Horizons in the Analysis of Raising and Control* ed. by William Davies and Stanley Dubinsky, 281–292. Dordrecht: Springer. DOI: 10.1007/978-1-4020-6176-9_13

Ross, John. 1969. "Auxiliaries as Main Verbs." *Studies in Philosophical Linguistics Series I* ed. by William Todd, 77–102. Evanston: Great Expectations Press.

Ruwet, Nicolas. 1972. *Théorie syntaxique et syntaxe du français.* Paris: Editions du Seuil.

Safir, Kenneth. 1985. *Syntactic Chains.* Cambridge: Cambridge University Press.

Sag, Ivan, and Carl Pollard. 1991. "An Integrated Theory of Complement Control." *Language* 67 (1): 63–113. DOI: 10.2307/415539

Williams, Edwin. 1985. "PRO and Subject of NP." *Natural Language and Linguistic Theory* 3 (3): 297–315. DOI: 10.1007/BF00154265

Williams, Edwin. 1992. "Adjunct Control." *Control and Grammar* ed. by Richard Larson, Sabine Iatridou, Utpal Lahiri, and James Higginbotham, 297–322. Dordrecht: Kluwer Academic Publishers. DOI: 10.1007/978-94-015-7959-9_9

Zimmermann, Michael and Georg Kaiser. 2014. "On Expletive Subject Pronoun Drop in Colloquial French." *Journal of French Language Studies* 24 (1): 107–126. DOI: 10.1017/S0959269513000392

Zubizarreta, Maria Luisa. 1983. "On the Notion 'Adjunct Subject' and a Class of Raising Predicates." *MIT Working Papers in Linguistics* 5: 195–232.

The phonology of postverbal pronouns in Romance languages*

Lori Repetti

Department of Linguistics, Stony Brook University (SUNY)

In many Romance varieties, the verb in imperative verb + (postverbal) pronoun phrases retains primary stress: Italian/Spanish: [kómpra]/[kómpra-melo] 'buy!'/'buy me it!'. However, in others varieties, stress in these phrases may be realized on a different syllable: [kompra-meló], [kompra-mélo], [kompra-mélozo]. In this paper, I address questions that have puzzled linguists for some time: Why is there a stress shift when enclitic pronouns are added to the imperative verb? How is the position of the stressed syllable determined? I propose that many factors are involved, including morpho-syntactic factors (the presence of a weak or a clitic pronoun, which are prosodized differently), phonological processes (the mapping of syntactic to prosodic structure), and phonetic processes (tonal association to metrically prominent syllables).

1. Introduction

In Italian and Spanish imperative verb + (postverbal) pronoun phrases, the verb retains primary stress.

(1)   Italian/Spanish: [kómpra]/[kómpra-melo] 'buy!'/'buy me it!'[1]

---

* This paper reports on collaborative work conducted with Francisco Ordóñez (Stony Brook University), Miran Kim (Korea University), and Emily Romanello (Stony Brook University). I would like to thank them, the audience at LSRL 43, two anonymous reviewers, and the NSF for grant #0617471 awarded to Lori Repetti and Francisco Ordóñez which allowed us to conduct the field research and build the database (Repetti & Ordóñez 2011) upon which much of this research is based.

1. All imperative verbs presented in this paper are 2sg, unless otherwise noted, and all third person pronouns are masculine, unless otherwise noted. Furthermore, I indicate the boundary between a verb and pronoun, or between two pronouns, with a dash.

2. Numbers after a word or phrase, such as (31_23) for Massa di Maratea, indicates the speaker number (#31) and utterance number (#23) found in the *Clitics of Romance Languages* database (Repetti & Ordóñez 2011).

DOI 10.1075/rllt.9.19rep

In other Romance varieties, stress in these phrases may be realized on the antepenultimate syllable (3b), the penultimate syllable (2)–(3a), or the final syllable (4).

Penultimate stress shift is common in Catalonia, southern Italy, and Sardinia (2).

(2)　stress shift to penultimate syllable:
　　a.　Massa di Maratea (Basilicata): [vénni]/[venn-íllʊ] (31_23)[2] 'sell!'/'sell it!'
　　b.　Anzi (Basilicata): [dá]/[da-mmíɖɖə] (32_13a) 'give!'/'give me them'
　　c.　Formentera (Balearic Islands): [púrtə]/[purtə-mə́lə] (50_2)
　　　　'bring!'/'bring me it'
　　d.　Siliqua (Sardinia): [bɛɳɖéj]/[bɛɳɖej-míɖɖʊ] (21_59) 'sell.2PL!'/'sell.2PL
　　　　me it!'

In some Sardinian varieties, we find stress realized on the antepenultimate or penultimate syllable in these constructions. If there is a final epenthetic (copy) vowel (underlined in the examples) added to avoid a word-final consonant, such as the plural /s/ marker, stress is realized on the antepenultimate syllable. If there is not a final epenthetic vowel, stress is realized on the penultimate syllable (Kim and Repetti 2013).

(3)　stress shift to (ante)penultimate syllable (Siliqua, Sardinia):
　　a.　penultimate stress:
　　　　[bɛɳɖej-míɖɖu] (21_59) 'sell.2PL me it!' (=2d)
　　b.　antepenultimate stress with final epenthetic (copy) vowel:
　　　　[bɛɳɖej-míɖuzu̱] (21_56) 'sell.2PL me them!'

Another stress pattern involves stress shift to the final syllable, attested in some varieties of Catalan, Ligurian, and Gascon (4).

(4)　stress shift to final syllable:
　　a.　Majorca (Balearic Islands): [ómpli]/[ompli-lozmə́] (56_26) 'fill!'/'fill
　　　　them for me!'
　　b.　Pigna (Liguria): [dá]/[da-umé] (93_1b) 'give!'/'give it to me!'
　　c.　Vallée d'Ossau (Pyrénés-Atlantiques): [baja-uzí] (82_33) 'give it to them!'

These data raise a number of questions: Why is there a stress shift when enclitic pronouns are added to the imperative verb? How is the position of the stressed syllable determined? These questions have long intrigued linguists and have been addressed within many theoretical frameworks. In this paper, I propose that no single module of the grammar (just the phonology, just the syntax, etc.) can be responsible for the stress patterns observed. Instead, they are the result of various interacting processes: phonological processes, morpho-syntactic processes, and phonetic processes.

This paper is organized as follows. I begin by discussing the segmentation of these phrases (Section 2), and I then review the phonological approaches that have been proposed to account for the data (Section 3). I show that a purely phonological approach is untenable since morpho-syntactic factors are at play (Section 4). A model incorporating different types of pronouns (weak and clitic) is adopted to account for the morpho-syntactic facts: some pronouns traditionally referred to as "clitics" are, in fact, "weak." I present a prosodic analysis of these two types of pronouns that can account for the phonological patterns (Section 5). I conclude the paper in Section 6.

2. Segmentation

Before we proceed with an analysis of stress shift, the topic of segmentation needs to be addressed. In the data examined in this paper, it is not always clear whether a particular segment belongs to one pronoun or the adjacent one (5a), or where the verb ends and the clitic begins (5b).

(5) a. Siliqua (Sardinia): [bɛɳɖej-míɖɖu] 'sell.2PL me it!'
        i. /bɛɳɖej-mí-ɖɖu/
        ii. /bɛɳɖej-m-íɖɖu/
    b. Massa di Maratea (Basilicata): [venníllu] 'sell it!'
        i. /venní-llu/
        ii. /venn-íllu/

Segmentation varies from variety to variety, and some research has been done on Neapolitan segmentation with regard to structures similar to (5a). In Neapolitan phrases like [pɔrtatíllə] 'bring yourself it', is the /í/ part of the first pronoun (/pɔrta-tí-llə/) or the second pronoun (/pɔrta-t-íllə/)? Vowel quality and historical evidence support the latter. Bafile (1993, 1994) points out that the quality of the stressed vowel depends on the gender of the accusative pronoun: [pɔrtatíllə] 'bring yourself it.MAS' ~ [pɔrtatéllə] 'bring yourself it.FEM': we find /í/ if the pronoun is MAS, and /é/ if it is FEM. The quality of the stressed vowel in these structures is determined by the quality of the historical final vowel (final /u/ and /i/ for MAS; final /a/ and /e/ for FEM). A final high vowel triggered raising of the stressed vowel in a type of vowel harmony called *metaphony*. If the original unstressed final vowel of the pronoun was [-high] (i. e., /a/ FEM.SG or /e/ FEM. PL) the preceding stressed vowel evolved in the usual way without raising; i. e., Latin *ĭ* > [e], so pronoun *illa* > [élla]. If, instead, the final vowel was [+high] (i. e., /u/ MAS. SG or /i/ MAS.PL), the preceding stressed vowel underwent metaphony and was raised: *ĭlli* > */élli/ > [ílli]. Since this process is no longer productive, we can assume that the stressed vowel is now part of the accusative pronouns: /íllə/ MAS.SG/PL and /éllə/ FEM. SG/PL. A second piece of evidence supporting the segmentation /pɔrta-t-íllə/ comes from the history of these forms (Bafile 1993, 1994), which derive from Late Latin structures like *tē+ ĭllu*, with elision of /e/: *t' ĭllu*. (Note that historically Latin stressed *ē* and *ĭ* both evolved to /e/). These two observations support the segmentation in (5aii).

    To the best of my knowledge, the segmentation of the structure in (5b) has not been addressed in the literature. If we examine the quality of the vowel in question, i.e., the /í/ in (5b), we find that in some cases it is of the same quality as the theme vowel of the verb.

(6)

	theme vowel: /a/	theme vowel: /e/~/i/
a. Cagliari (Sardinia)	[pettinádus] (3_42) 'comb them!'	[bɛɳdídus] (3_20) 'sell them!'
b. Milis (Sardinia)	[kompɔrádusu] (14_22a) 'buy them!'	[bɛɳdíduzu] (14_10) 'sell them!'
c. Massa di Maratea (Basilicata)	[piʎʎállʊ] (31_27b) 'take it!' [akkattállʊ] (31_28) 'buy it!'	[venníllʊ] (31_23) 'sell it!' [vennílla] (31_25) 'sell it.FEM!'

In (6a) the stressed /á/ of [pettinádus] and the stressed /í/ of [bɛɳdídus] cannot both be associated with the pronoun (i.e., /ádus/ and /ídus/), since the pronoun is the same in the two examples: MAS.PL.ACC. In the former, the theme vowel of the verb is /a/, supporting the analysis of the stressed /á/ as part of the verb, and in the latter, the theme vowel is unstressed /e/~/i/, supporting the analysis of the stressed /í/ as part of the verb, as in (5bi). Further support for this analysis comes from data in which the vowel in question is not the theme vowel, but part of the inflectional suffix of the verb. For example, in Massa di Maratea (Basilicata), first person plural imperatives end in /mu/, and in stress shift contexts, the /u/ is stressed, regardless of the nature of the following pronoun: [vennemúllʊ] (31_34) 'let's sell it.MAS!', [vennemúlla] (31_36) 'let's sell it.FEM!', [vennemúlli] (31_35) 'let's sell them.MAS!', [vennemúlli] (31_37) 'let's sell them.FEM!'. These phrases must be segmented as /vennemu-llu/, /vennemu-lla/, and /vennemu-lli/.

In other dialects, the patterns are more complicated. In San Leucio del Sannio (Campania) the quality of the stressed vowel at the boundary of the verb and the pronoun may depend on two factors: the quality of the theme vowel (as in (6)) and the gender of the pronoun (as in the Neapolitan data above). If the theme vowel is /a/, that vowel surfaces regardless of the pronoun that follows: [telefonálla] (33_67) 'call her!', [telefonállu] (33_68) 'call him!'. If the theme vowel is not /a/, the quality of the stressed vowel varies depending on the gender of the accusative pronoun. A masculine pronoun (either singular or plural) has /í/ in this context ([vənníllə] (33_28b) 'sell it.MAS!', [vənnílli] (33_29b) 'sell them.MAS!'), while a feminine pronoun (either singular or plural) has /é/ in this context ([vənnélla] (33_30b) 'sell it.FEM!', [vənnéllə] (33_31b) 'sell them.FEM!). The reason for this difference in vowel quality has to do with metaphony, as with the Neapolitan data discussed above.

The San Leucio data suggest that there are two different segmentations possible—/telefoná-lla/ and /vənn-élla/—and the choice between the two is determined by an implicational hierarchy. If the theme vowel is /a/, it is stressed (/telefoná-lla/); if it is not /a/, the stressed vowel is part of the pronoun (/vənn-élla/). How can we incorporate this observation into a unified analysis of segmentation? We can posit for the pronoun a lexical form with an initial vowel (for example, /ella/), and for the verb a lexical form with a final vowel. In the verb + pronoun phrase, the initial vowel of the pronoun is adjacent to the final vowel of the verb: /telefona/ + /ella/, /venni/ + /ella/. In hiatus contexts, a series of phonological and morphological factors decide which (if any) vowel is deleted (see Garrapa 2011). In San Leucio /a/ + vowel, or /u/ + vowel sequences, the /a/ and /u/ are retained, and the initial vowel of the pronoun is elided: /telefona/ + /ella/ > [telefona-lla]; however, in /i/ + vowel, or /e/ + vowel sequences, the final vowel of the verb is elided, and the initial vowel of the pronoun realized: /venni/ + /ella/ > [vənn-ella]. For clarification purposes, the elided vowel may be indicated as "*v*": /telefona-*v*lla/, /vənn*v*-ella/.

3. Phonological Approaches

The phonological motivation for the patterns described in (2), i.e., stress shift to the penult, has been discussed widely in the Romance literature, analyzed within many theoretical frameworks (rule-based, Lexical Phonology, Prosodic Phonology, Optimality Theory, etc.), and can be summarized as follows: the stress shifts to the penultimate syllable to repair a suboptimal metrical structure (Anderson 2005; Bafile 1993, 1994; Bonet 2009; Kenstowicz 1991; Klavans 1995; Loporcaro 2000; Monachesi 1996; Nespor and Vogel 1986; Peperkamp 1997; Torres-Tamarit 2010; Vogel 2009). The argument roughly goes as follows. Many Romance languages have what is called the "three-syllable window" of stress assignment (i.e., stress falls on one of the final three syllables of the word), and the stressed syllable in forms like /kómpra-melo/ falls outside of the "three-syllable window". Languages like Spanish and Italian tolerate this suboptimal structure (1), but others use a repaired form with stress on the penultimate syllable: /kompra-mélo/ (2). (Note that the repair does not result in a form with antepenultimate stress, except in those Sardinian cases in (3b) discussed in §1.) The languages that repair suboptimal forms fall into two groups: those that tolerate antepenultimate stress in these structures, and those that do not. The latter includes varieties like San Leucio del Sannio (Campania), in which antepenultimate stress is (optionally) banned in verb + enclitic structures: if the addition of a single enclitic or an enclitic cluster would result in antepenultimate stress (or pre-antepenultimate stress), a form with stress on the penult is instead used (7)–(9). (Note, however, that antepenultimate stress is tolerated lexically as in (8a).)[3]

---

3.   *Raddoppiamento sintattico* (*RS*), or the gemination of an initial consonant when preceded by a stressed vowel across certain morpho-syntactic boundaries, has been invoked to account for the geminate consonant; however, Bafile (1993, 1994) shows that the consonant length

(7)   San Leucio del Sannio (Campania) (Repetti and Ordóñez 2011; Iannace 1983)
    a.   [vínnə]   'sell!'
    b.   *[vínnə-lə]; [vənn-íllə]   'sell it!'
    c.   *[vínnə-mələ]; [vənnə-míllə] 'sell me it!'

(8)   San Leucio del Sannio (Campania) (Repetti and Ordóñez 2011; Iannace 1983)
    a.   [péttəna]   'comb!'
    b.   *[péttəna-lə]; [pəttəna-íllo]   'comb him!'
    c.   *[péttəna-məla]; [pəttəna-mmélla] 'comb her for me!'

(9)   San Leucio del Sannio (Campania) (Repetti and Ordóñez 2011; Iannace 1983)
    a.   [dá]   'give!'
    b.   [dá-mmə]   'give me!'
    c.   *[dá-mmələ]; [da-mmíllə]   'give me it!'

Other Romance varieties, such as Neapolitan, allow antepenultimate stress in these contexts (10b), but not pre-antepenultimate stress (10c).

(10)   Neapolitan (Campania)   (Bafile 1993, 1994)
    a.   [pórta]   'bring!'
    b.   [pórta-lə][4]   'bring it!'
    c.   *[pórta-tələ]; [pɔrta-tíllə]   'bring yourself it!'

While this explanation accounts neatly for the San Leucio data and the Neapolitan data in (10), it only works for Neapolitan if the verb has penultimate stress. If, instead, we examine a verb with final stress or antepenultimate stress, the explanation breaks down. We expect antepenultimate stress to be tolerated in these phrases in Neapolitan, as in (10b); however, this is not always what we find. Neapolitan does not tolerate antepenultimate stress in these phrases if the verb is monosyllabic (i.e., it has final stress) (11) (Bafile 1993, 1994; Kenstowicz 1991; Peperkamp 1997).

(11)   Neapolitan (Campania)   (Bafile 1993, 1994; Peperkamp 1997)
    a.   [fá]   'do!'
    b.   [fá-llə]   'do it!'
    c.   *[fá-tələ]; [fa-ttíllə]   'do yourself it!'

---

of the clitic in Neapolitan is not the result of a productive phonological process (see also Peperkamp 1997). There is strong evidence that this claim also holds for most other varieties considered in this paper (Loporcaro 1997). We will not address consonant length in this paper.

4.   Optional stress shift in this context is also attested: /astúta/ + /la/ > [astúta-la]~[astutá-lla] 'turn it off!' (Ledgeway 2009, 34). See §6 for discussion.

Equally unexpected, Neapolitan allows pre-antepenultimate stress in phrases containing a verb with antepenultimate stress followed by a pronoun (12b) (Bafile 1993, 1994; Kenstowicz 1991; Peperkamp 1997).

(12) Neapolitan (Campania)   (Bafile 1993, 1994; Peperkamp 1997)
     a.   [péttina]   'comb!'
     b.   [péttina-lə]⁵   'comb them!'
     c.   *[péttina-tələ]; [pettina-tíllə]   'comb yourself them!'

In order to account for the ungrammaticality of the form in (11c) with antepenultimate stress, and the surprising acceptability in the form in (12b) with pre-antepenultimate stress, it has been proposed that these forms are in some way exceptional and are marked in the lexicon (Bafile 1993, 1994; Kenstowicz 1991; Peperkamp 1997). Others have noticed that stress assignment is sensitive to the number of enclitics, whereby in varieties like Neapolitan stress shift takes place with two enclitics but not with one, and have accommodated this fact within the frameworks of metrical and prosodic phonology (Monachesi 1996; Peperkamp 1997). We will see in the next section that a purely phonological approach, even with ad hoc accommodations, cannot handle the facts once all of the data are considered. But first we will briefly examine stress shift to the antepenultimate and final syllables.

The analysis of stress shift to the antepenultimate syllable in Sardinian can be accounted for in the same way as stress shift to the penultimate syllable, modulo the paragogic vowel found after a phrase-final consonant. The epenthetic final vowel is not involved in stress assignment either because it is invisible to metrical processes, or because it is inserted after metrical structure has been established (3) (Kim and Repetti 2013).

Stress shift to the final syllable in imperative phrases is problematic for any phonological approach since final stress is not the unmarked stress patterns in these languages (4). This type of stress shift has been addressed in Argentinian Spanish, in which imperatives are optionally pronounced either with stress on the verb or with stress on the final vowel of the enclitic(s): [dámelo] ~ [dameló] (Colantoni, Cuervo, and Hualde 2010; Moyna 1999; Huidobro 2005). Given the optionality of the phenomenon, most researchers have addressed the question of the semantic motivation for stress shift, but some phonological issues have also been raised, including the prosodic constraints involved, the type of stress (whether the shifted stress is primary or secondary), and why the stress shifts to the final vowel. As with the exceptional Neapolitan cases discussed above, ad hoc constraints resulting in final stress are invoked.

---

5. Forms with the expected stress shift are also attested: /frávəka/ + /lə/ > [frávəka-lə]~[fravəká-llə] 'build it!' (Ledgeway 2009, 34). See Section 6 for discussion.

4. Morpho-Syntactic Factors

Despite the attempts to account for these cases of stress shift within a phonological framework, when the full range of data is taken into consideration, we see that a purely phonological approach is untenable (Ordóñez and Repetti 2006, 2008). For example, the type of pronoun may affect stress shift: in Lucanian a single 3rd person postverbal pronoun is involved in stress shift, but a single 1st/2nd person pronoun is (optionally) not (Gioscio 1985; Lüdke 1979; Ruggieri and Batinti 1992). In Cabras (Sardinia) we find 3rd person pronouns involved in penultimate shift ([tɛlɛfɔná-ɖi] 'call him/her/them!' 2_27), and 1st/2nd person pronouns involved in final shift ([tɛlɛfɔna-zí] 'call us!' 2_28).

The relative order of the pronouns in a cluster may be correlated with the type of stress shift (i.e., penultimate or final stress shift). With ACC-DAT order of enclitics, we never find penultimate stress shift, only final stress shift.

(13) (=(4)) ACC-DAT order of enclitics and final stress
    a. Majorca (Balearic Islands): [ómpli]/[ompli-lozmə́] (56_26) 'fill!'/'fill them for me!'
    b. Pigna (Liguria): [dá]/[da-umé] (93_1b) 'give!'/'give it to me!'
    c. Vallée d'Ossau (Pyrénés-Atlantiques): [baja-uzí] (82_33) 'give it to them!'

The number of enclitics may correlate with the presence/absence of stress shift. A single postverbal pronoun in Neapolitan does not affect the position of stress, regardless of how far the stressed syllable is from the end of the word: [fá-llə] 'do it!', [pɔ́rta-lə] 'bring it!', [péttina-lə] 'comb them!'. However, a postverbal pronoun cluster always triggers stress shift: [fa-ttíllə] 'do yourself it!', [pɔrta-tíllə] 'bring yourself it!', [pettina-tíllə] 'comb yourself them!'.

Additionally, the verb form may be correlated with the presence/absence of stress shift: in many varieties, 2SG imperatives with enclitics undergo stress shift, while 1PL imperatives do not. For example, in the dialect of Albano di Lucania (Basilicata), a 2SG imperative verb + MAS.SG.ACC enclitic undergoes stress shift, while a 1PL imperative verb + MAS.SG.ACC enclitic does not (Romanello and Repetti 2014).[6]

(14) Albano di Lucania (Basilicata)   (Manzini and Savoia 2005)
    [cáma] ~ [cam-íllə] 'call him!'
    [camámmə] ~ [camámmə-lə] 'call.1PL him!

---

6. The verb form is correlated not only with the presence/absence of stress shift, but also with the lexical form of the enclitic pronoun. For example, in Anzi (Basilicata) the MAS.PL.ACC enclitic is realized either as [íddə] or as [lə]. The former is used with 2SG imperatives ([vənn-íddə] 'sell.2SG them!'), while the latter is found with 1PL imperatives ([vənní:mə-lə] 'let's sell them!') (Romanello and Repetti 2014).

The constraints on stress shift outlined above are not phonological, but instead are morpho-syntactic in nature: the type of pronouns, the order of pronouns in a cluster, the number of pronouns, the form of the verb. A purely phonological approach cannot handle these data. The phonology should not care if a syllable is associated with the 1st vs. 2nd/3rd person form of the pronoun, or the 2sg vs. 1pl form of the verb, nor should it care if a syllable is associated with a DAT vs. ACC pronoun, or indeed a pronoun vs. verb suffix.

It has been proposed that two different types of morpho-syntactically distinct pronouns are involved in these encliticization processes: true clitics and weak pronouns (Ordóñez and Repetti 2006, 2008, 2014). A number of diagnostics has been proposed for distinguishing between clitic and weak pronouns. These diagnostics are syntactic, morphological, and phonological in nature. Syntactically, weak pronouns are described as syntactically lower than clitic pronouns, and they land in a Spec position while clitics land in a head position. Weak pronouns are morphologically more complex than clitic pronouns, and weak pronouns can be stressed, while clitics cannot (Cardinaletti and Starke 1999; Cardinaletti and Repetti 2008; Ordóñez and Repetti 2006, 2008, 2014). Based on these studies, I adopt the following morpho-syntactic tests for a pronoun's status as a clitic or weak pronoun.

(15) diagnostics for clitic pronoun vs. weak pronoun
    a. In a mixed pronoun cluster, a weak pronoun will not precede a clitic pronoun.
    b. Weak pronouns land in a Spec position, while clitics land in a head position.
    c. Weak pronouns are morphologically more complex than clitic pronouns.

As shown elsewhere (Ordóñez and Repetti 2006, 2008, 2014), some Romance postverbal pronouns (including the partitive, but also the locative) meet the criteria of weak elements. The morpho-syntactic evidence has be detailed in Ordóñez and Repetti (2006, 2008, 2014), namely, in mixed clusters, the order of pronouns is clitic + weak, some postverbal pronouns land in a Spec position while others are in a head position, and those that land in Spec are morphologically more complex. Crucially, these are precisely the pronouns that can be stressed, as predicted by the phonological diagnostic of weak pronouns proposed by Cardinaletti and Starke (1999).

How can we accommodate the morpho-syntactic factors involved in stress shift with the weak vs. clitic pronoun proposal? The type of pronoun may affect stress shift because two types of pronouns are involved: weak pronouns affect stress shift (they consist of a foot), while clitics do not (they do not consist of a foot). The number of postverbal pronouns may affect stress shift because in some dialects imperatives can attract at most one clitic, so when two pronouns are used, the lower probe attracts a weak pronoun (Ordóñez & Repetti 2014). The verb form may affect whether or not there will be stress shift because certain verb forms (i.e. inflectional projections) host weak pronouns while others host clitics (Ordóñez and Repetti 2014).[7]

In the next section I investigate how weak pronouns vs. clitics are incorporated into prosodic structure, accounting for the stress shift facts.

5.   Prosodic Analysis of Verb + Clitic/Weak Pronoun(s)

How can clitic and weak pronouns be incorporated into a prosodic analysis? The constraints regulating the syntax to prosody mapping proposed by Selkirk (1995) include alignment constraints on prosodic words (PWs) and lexical words (i.e., syntactic units). Since clitics are function words, not lexical words, those alignment constraints do not apply to them. Weak pronouns are also function words, but they have not yet received as thorough a prosodic investigation as clitics. We will assume that weak pronouns, as opposed to clitics, have prosodic structure associated with them lexically, namely, a foot. While a full constraint-based analysis is beyond the scope of this paper, the approach using alignment constraints is easily captured in the representations below. In the following paragraphs, we will see how function words that consist only of a segment (or segments) but no metrical structure (i.e., clitic pronouns) are mapped to prosodic structure, and how function words that consist of segments *and* foot structure (i.e., weak pronouns) are incorporated into prosodic structure. In neither case is the foot structure of the verb altered, thanks to output-output correspondence constraints; in other words, in both cases the pronoun is incorporated into prosodic structure above the level of the verb's foot structure.

We begin with clitics. Since clitics are usually defined as *unstressed* elements (Halpern 1998), we can assume they are not incorporated into a foot. This means that clitics are adjoined to prosodic structure at a higher level than the foot, either the Prosodic Word (PW) level or the Phonological Phrase (PP) level. (I do not consider a representation with a recursive PW since I have found no evidence supporting that structure.) In the data under consideration here, this means that clitics are incorporated into the verb phrase as in (16a) or (16b).[8]

---

7.   The role of clitic order (ACC-DAT vs. DAT-ACC) in stress shift is currently being investigated in Ordóñez and Repetti (in progress).

8.   Preverbal object pronouns are always clitics, i.e., they are never weak pronouns. What is the evidence for this claim? Proclitics are never stressed and are not involved in any type of stress shift, and, to the best of my knowledge, the morpho-syntactic form of the verb never correlates with different forms of proclitics. Proclitics may be identical to non-stress shifting postverbal pronouns: Italian: *mi parla/parlami* 's/he speaks to me'/'speak to me!'; Northern Italian dialects: [ət-bev]/[bev-ət] 'you.SG drink'/'do you.SG drink?'. In each case, the preverbal

(16)   a. PP   b. PP

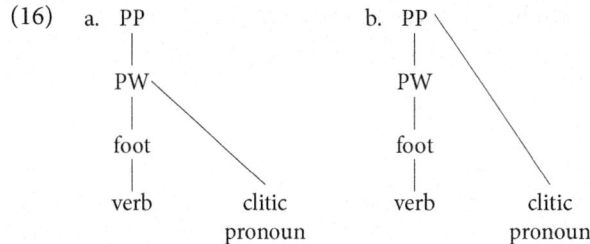

The main difference between these two structures is that the clitic pronoun is in the same PW as the verb in the former, but is outside of the verb's PW in the latter. In other words, in the structure in (16a) the lexical word (i.e., the verb) is not right-aligned with the PW, while in (16b) it is. Crucially, in both cases, the clitic lies outside of foot structure as it does not interact with stress assignment.

The prosodic analysis of Romance imperative verb + pronoun phrases in Loporcaro (2000) and Bonet and Lloret (2005) assumes the structure in (16a). (Loporcaro 2000 assumes the same prosodic structure in stress-shifting and non stress-shifting contexts, the difference being that postlexical stress reassignment is permitted in the former but not the latter.) Peperkamp (1997) suggests the structure in (16b) for non-stress shifting enclitics.

We will see below that some of the pronouns that meet the criteria for clitics must be analyzed as in (16a). Further support for this model (over (16b)) comes from the fact that no other PWs (only another clitic pronoun) can intervene between the verb and the clitic.[9]

We have already noted that weak pronouns can be stressed, and I have proposed that they have a foot as part of their lexical representation. The foot associated with the weak pronoun is part of the same PP as the imperative verb, but how is that foot incorporated into the PP? There are many possible analyses. The foot of the weak pronoun can be part of the same PW as the verb (17a), or it can be its own Prosodic Word separate from the verb (17b), or it can adjoin recursively to the Prosodic Word (17c). (A fourth possibility is that the foot skips the PW and adjoins directly to the

---

and postverbal pronouns are analyzed as the same lexical item realized in different syntactic positions (Cardinaletti and Repetti 2008), and they can be represented as in (16), modulo the position of the pronoun relative to the verb. For similarities and differences between proclitics and enclitics, see Benincà and Cinque (1993), Cardinaletti (2010), Cardinaletti and Repetti (2008), Ordóñez and Repetti (2014), Peperkamp (1997).

9.   This does not necessarily apply to all verb + clitic structures. For example, indicative verb + postverbal subject clitic pronouns in interrogative structures in northern Italian dialects are argued to have the structure in (16b) since the subject clitic pronoun cannot be analyzed as part of the same PW as the verb (Cardinaletti and Repetti 2008).

PP. That option is not discussed here as there appears to be no evidence supporting it.)

(17)

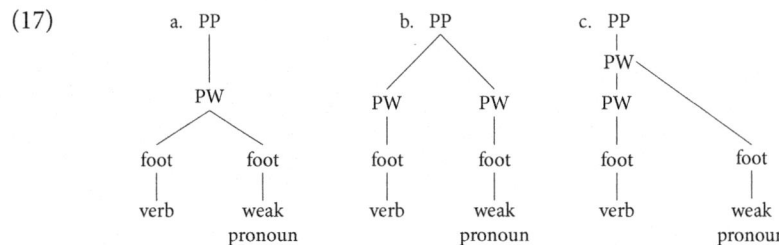

Note that the structure in (17a) is comparable to the structure in (16a), the difference being that in (16a) the pronoun is not part of a foot, while in (17a) it is, and, therefore, it is involved in stress assignment. Monachesi (1996) proposes a structure similar to (17b) for verb + enclitic pronoun clusters, and Peperkamp (1997) adopts the structure in (17c) for grammars like Neapolitan, which have stress stability with one enclitic and stress shift with two. Note also that the outer PW in (17c) is similar to the Clitic Group or Composite Group (Nespor & Vogel 1986; Vogel 2009).

An important difference among the various structures in (16) and (17) is that the verb + enclitic pronoun(s) form a single PW in (16a), (17a), and (the outer PW of) (17c) (i.e., the lexical word is not aligned with the PW), but there is a PW boundary between the verb and pronoun in (16b), (17b), and (17c) (i.e., the lexical word is aligned with the PW). We can use this difference to help select the best representations to account for the data. In the next paragraphs we will see that in at least one of the languages under investigation, verb + postverbal pronoun phrases consist of two words (thereby supporting the models in (17b) and (17c)), and in another there is PW boundary between the verb and the postverbal pronouns (thereby supporting the models in (16b), (17b), and (17c)).

Bafile (1993, 1994) analyzes the Neapolitan phrase in (10c) as containing two primary stressed syllables, and, therefore, for our purposes, two PWs. Her analysis proceeds as follows: the penultimate syllable (i.e., the postverbal pronoun) of the phrase [pɔrta-tillə] is perceived as having primary stress, but the lexically stressed vowel of the verb stem must also be analyzed as being stressed since it can have a quality which is only found in primary stressed syllables, such as /ɔ/. (Note that stressed /ɔ/ raises to /u/ when stress is shifted, but this is not what is found in phrases like (10c): *[purta-tíllə].) This analysis of Neapolitan supports the models in (17b)-(17c), i.e., the verb + pronoun phrase consists of two PWs.

Sardinian offers another test case that also supports the representations in (17b)-(17c). A diagnostic for PW boundaries in some Sardinian dialects suggests that there is a PW boundary between the verb and some postverbal pronouns. A paragogic vowel is found after the final stressed vowel of monosyllabic words in some Sardinian dialects: /dá/ > [dá*i*] 'give!' (18a) (Bolognesi 1998, 66; Lai 2002, 2004; Pittau 1972, 18–19). (I use a bold italicized *i* to represent the paragogic vowel.) It may also be found after a monosyllabic verb that is followed by an enclitic pronoun cluster, suggesting that the verb is aligned with the right edge of a PW (18b). However, when only one pronoun follows the verb, the paragogic vowel is not present, suggesting that the verb is not right-aligned with a PW (18c). (See Kim and Repetti 2013, 292–293.)

(18)   Nuorese Sardinian
    a.   /dá/ > [dá*i*]   'give!'
    b.   /dá/ + /mi + ilu/ > [da*i*-mílu], *[dá-milu]   'give me it!'   (16_4)
    c.   /dá/ + /mi/ > [dá-mi], *[dá*i*-mi]   'give me!'   (16_1)

We can analyze these facts as follows: /mi/ is a clitic and /ilu/ is weak. The 1SG pronoun in (18c) should be analyzed as a clitic since it meets the morpho-syntactic criteria for clitics outlined in (15): it is morphologically less complex than weak pronouns (clitic /mi/ 1SG vs. weak /ilu/ 3SG.MAS.ACC), and it precedes a weak pronoun in a cluster (/mi/ + /ilu/, */ilu/ + /mi/). Crucially, it does not trigger stress shift ([teléfɔna-mi] (16_26) 'telephone me!', [kɔ́mpɔra-mi] (16_3) 'buy me!', [píka-mi] (16_17) 'get me!'). If it is a clitic, it is represented by one of the structures in (16). Since there is not a paragogic vowel *i* after the verb in (18c), signaling a PW boundary, we can assume that the pronoun is part of the same PW as the verb, as in (16a).

The cluster /milu/ (18b) should be analyzed as consisting of a clitic /mi/ plus a weak pronoun /ilu/.[10] The pronoun /ilu/ meets the morpho-syntactic criteria for weak pronouns: it follows the clitic /mi/, it is morphologically more complex than clitics (weak /ilu/ vs. clitic /lu/, see Footnote 10), and it is involved in stress shift. Therefore, it is represented by one of the structures in (17). We know that the clitic pronoun clusters prosodically with the weak pronoun and not with the verb, because there is an epenthetic *i* between the verb and the clitic pronoun in (18b), marking a PW boundary (as in (17b) or (17c)). And we know that object pronouns can enter a cluster configuration syntactically with each other (Cardinaletti 2008; Cattaneo 2009; Pescarini 2013).

---

10.   There are two 3SG.MAS.ACC pronouns in Nuorese Sardinian: clitic /lu/ and weak /ilu/. In preverbal position and as a single postverbal pronoun, the 3SG.MAS.ACC pronoun is clitic /lu/: [lu̲ pottu fákɛɾe] (16_51) 'I can do it', [péttɛna-lu̲] (16_32) 'comb him!'. These forms cannot be analyzed as deriving from /ilu/ via initial vowel deletion since there is no independent evidence of /i/ deletion in these contexts: we find phrase initial /i/ ([inu ɛ́ maría] (16_74) 'where is Maria?'), as well as /ail/ sequences at the boundary of verb + enclitic pronoun units ([mannikái-lu̲] (16_42) 'eat.2PL it!'). In postverbal clusters, the 3SG.MAS.ACC pronoun is analyzed as weak /ilu/, as in (18b), and not as clitic /lu/ (as in */mi + lu/) for the reasons discussed above.

While the cluster in (18b) is represented as a clitic + weak pronoun, it is not the case that every pronoun cluster consists of a clitic + weak pronoun: in standard Italian or Spanish single pronouns and pronouns in clusters appear to be true clitics. Similarly, while the single enclitic in (18c) is analyzed as a clitic, it is not the case that all single postverbal pronouns are clitics. There are Sardinian dialects, such as the dialect of Laconi, which have single postverbal pronouns that are stressed ([beɳḍe-mía] (7_16) 'sell me.DAT!'), suggesting they are weak pronouns. In addition, in these dialects we find a paragogic *i* between a monosyllabic verb and a single postverbal pronoun: [dʒai-mía] (7_1) 'give me.DAT!', signaling a word boundary between the two elements.[11] The preverbal 1SG.DAT pronoun is not stressed and is lexically different from the postverbal one: [mi-práʃi] (7_112) 'I like it (it pleases me)'. Given these facts, the postverbal pronoun in Laconi is best analyzed as a weak pronoun and represented with the structure in (17b) or (17c), while the preverbal one is a clitic. It has been argued elsewhere (Ordóñez and Repetti 2014) that the choice of a single clitic vs. weak pronoun in postverbal position, or the choice of elements that make up postverbal clusters (such as clitic + weak, or clitic + clitic) depends on the inflectional projection that hosts them.

Since penultimate stress is considered the default stress pattern in these varieties (i.e., stress is assigned by the formation of a right-aligned trochaic feet), this model allows us to account for both penultimate and antepenultimate stress (in which the final vowel is epenthetic) in these structures. However, final stress shift is problematic since an iambic foot is not the foot structure in those varieties with final stress shift. Therefore, the motivation for final stress must be sought elsewhere.

Although it is beyond the scope of this paper to analyze the cases of final stress shift, a possible approach can be found in Kim and Repetti (2013) in which (ante)penultimate stress shift in Sardinian is analyzed *not* as a shift in stress, but as the association of each tone of a bitonal pitch accent (HL*) with a metrically prominent syllable, resulting in the perception of a stress shift: the leading H tone is associated with the lexically stressed syllable of the verb, and the starred L tone with the rightmost metrically prominent syllable, i.e., the (ante)penultimate syllable belonging to the weak pronoun. The final stress shift data might be analyzed along these lines: the pitch accent is associated with a metrically prominent position, but its secondary association is with the right edge of the verb + enclitic pronoun phrase, resulting in a change of tone at the right edge of the word which is perceived as a final stress shift. (See also Grice 1995; Grice, Ladd, and Arvanit 2000; Pierrehumbert and Beckman 1988; Prieto, D'Imperio, and Fivela Gili 2005.)

---

11.   In Laconi, paragogic *i* is also present between monosyllabic verbs and enclitic clusters: [dʒai-míḍu] (7_4) 'give me it!', [dʒai-zíḍu] (7_8) 'give him it'.

Using the representations in (16) and (17), we can make a number of predictions. For example, we would *not* expect to find a language that prosodizes clitics as in (16b) (i.e., clitics are not part the same PW as the verb, suggesting that the constraint enforcing the alignment of PWs and lexical words is high ranked) and weak pronouns as in (17a) (i.e., weak pronouns are part of the same PW as the verb, suggesting that the constraint enforcing the alignment of PWs and lexical words in low ranked). I have not found any data that falsify these predictions.

6. Conclusions

We have seen that so-called stress shift in imperative phrases is the result of many factors, including morpho-syntactic factors, such as the presence of a weak vs. clitic pronoun. The presence of one vs. the other has phonological implications. A weak pronoun consists of a foot, which affects the metrical structure of the phrase by adding a metrically prominent syllable to the right of the lexically stressed syllable of the verb, which, however, retains its metrical structure. On the other hand, a clitic has no metrical structure associated with it, and is prosodized as part of the same PP as the verb, although outside of the verb's foot structure.

There is another factor affecting stress assignment in imperative verb + enclitic pronoun phrases (and also other phrases with enclitics, such as locatives, partitives, and possessives). The original phonological analyses of this phenomenon (see §3) were correct: stress shift can be a strategy to repair metrical violations. Those original analyses were wrong only in over-generalizing their claims. We have seen that weak pronouns are involved in stress shift because they consist of a foot, but clitics can (optionally) also be involved in stress shift if certain high ranked metrical constraints are violated (19).

(19) Nuorese (Pittau 1972: 20–21, 82–83)
     a.   /nára/ + /lu/ > [nára-lu]   'say it!'
     b.   /bókina/ + /lu/ > [bókina-lu], [bokiná-lu]   'call him!'

In these varieties, stress is not shifted with one enclitic, *unless* the resulting structure would have pre-antepenultimate stress, in which case it is optionally shifted to the penult. These data can be accounted for in the following way: the single enclitic is a true clitic and is not expected to be involved in stress shift. However, when stress is in an illegal pre-antepenultimate position, it is (optionally) reassigned to the "default" penultimate position, if the grammar allows for postlexical stress reassignment (Loporcaro 2000) or the formation of phrase-level syllables (Cardinaletti and Repetti 2009). (See also footnotes 4–5.)

The realization of metrical prominence in imperative verb + pronoun phrases involves the complex interaction of morpho-syntactic, prosodic, phonetic, and other factors. Only by studying this phenomenon from various perspectives can we have a complete and accurate understanding of it.

References

Anderson, Stephen. 2005. *Aspects of the Theory of Clitics*. Oxford: Oxford University Press. DOI: 10.1093/acprof:oso/9780199279906.001.0001

Bafile, Laura. 1993. *Fonologia prosodica e teoria metrica*. Ph.D. dissertation, University of Florence.

Bafile, Laura. 1994. "La riassegnazione postlessicale dell'accento nel napoletano." *Quaderni del dipartimento di linguistica dell'università degli studi di Firenze* 5: 1–23.

Benincà, Paola and Guglielmo Cinque. 1993. "Su alcune differenze tra enclisi e proclisi." *Omaggio a Gianfranco Folena*, 2313–2326. Padova: Editoriale Programma.

Bolognesi, Roberto. 1998. *The Phonology of Campidanian Sardinian: A Unitary Account of a Self-organizing Structure*. Dordrecht: ICG Printing.

Bonet, Eulàlia. 2009. "Stem Extensions in Catalan Encliticized Imperatives." Manuscript.

Bonet, Eulália and Maria-Rosa Lloret. 2005. "More on Alignment as an Alternative to Domains: The Syllabification of Catalan Clitics." *Probus* 17: 37–78. DOI: 10.1515/prbs.2005.17.1.37

Cardinaletti, Anna. 2008. "On Different Types of Clitic Clusters." In *The Bantu -Romance Connection*, ed. by Cécile De Cat, and Katherine Demuth, 41–82. Amsterdam: John Benjamins. DOI: 10.1075/la.131.06car

Cardinaletti, Anna. 2010. "Morphologically Complex Clitic Pronouns and Spurious *se* Once Again." In *Movement and Clitics: Adult and Child Grammar*, ed. by V. Torrens, et al., 238–259. Newcastle: Cambridge Scholars Publishing.

Cardinaletti, Anna and Lori Repetti. 2008. The Phonology and Syntax of Preverbal and Postverbal Subject Clitics in Northern Italian Dialects. *Linguistic Inquiry* 39: 523–563. DOI: 10.1162/ling.2008.39.4.523

Cardinaletti, Anna and Lori Repetti. 2009. "Phrase-level and Word-level Syllables: Resyllabification and Prosodization of Clitics." In *Phonological Domains: Universals and Derivations*, ed. by Janet Grijzenhout, and Baris Kabak, 79–104. Berlin: Mouton de Gruyter. DOI: 10.1515/9783110219234.2.79

Cardinaletti, Anna and Michael Starke. 1999. "The Typology of Structural Deficiency: A Case Study of the Three Classes of Pronouns." In *Clitics in the Languages of Europe*, ed. by Henk van Riemsdijk, 145–233. Berlin: Mouton de Gruyter.

Cattaneo, Andrea. 2009. *It Is All About Clitics: The Case of a Northern Italian Dialect Like Bellinzonese*. Ph.D. dissertation, NYU.

Colantoni, Laura, María Cristina Cuervo and José Ignacio Hualde. 2010. "Stress as a Symptom." Paper presented at LSRL 40, University of Washington, March 26–28, 2010.

Garrapa, Luigia. 2011. *Vowel Elision in Florentine Italian*. Bern: Peter Lang.

Gioscio, Joseph. 1985. *Il dialetto lucano di Calvello*. Stuttgart: Steiner.

Grice, Martine. 1995. *The Intonation of Palermo Italian: Implications for Intonation Theory*. Tübingen: Niemeyer.

Grice, Martine, D. Robert Ladd and Amalia Arvaniti. 2000. "On the Place of Phrase Accents in Intonational Phonology." *Phonology* 17: 143–185. DOI: 10.1017/S0952675700003924

Halpern, Aaron L. 1998. Clitics. In (eds.), *Handbook of Morphology*, ed. by Andrew Spencer, and Arnold M. Zwicky, 101–122. Oxford: Blackwell.

Huidobro, Susana. 2005. "Phonological Constraints on Verum Focus in Argentinian Spanish." Manuscript.

Iannace, Gaetano. 1983. *Interferenza linguistica ai confini fra stato e regno: Il dialetto di San Leucio del Sannio*. Ravenna: Longo.

Kenstowicz, Michael. 1991. "Base-Identity and Uniform Exponence: Alternative to Cyclicity." In *Current Trends in Phonology: Models and Methods (vol. 1)*, ed. by J. Durand and B. Laks, 363–393. Manchester: ESRI.

Kim, Miran and Lori Repetti. 2013. "Bitonal Pitch Accent and Phonological Alignment in Sardinian." *Probus* 25: 267–300.

Klavans, Judith. 1995. *On Clitics and Cliticization: The Interaction of Morphology, Phonology, and Syntax*. New York: Garland.

Lai, Jean-Pierre. 2002. *L'intonation du parler de Nuoro (Sardaigne)*. Ph.D. dissertation, Université Stendhal (Grenoble).

Lai, Jean-Pierre. 2004. "Le sarde de Nuoro au sein du nouvel Atlas Multimédia Prosodique de l'Espace Roman (AMPER)." *Gólinguistique* 9: 145–187.

Ledgeway, Adam. 2009. *Grammatica diacronica del napoletano*. Tübingen: Max Niemeyer. DOI: 10.1515/9783484971288

Loporcaro, Michele. 1997. *L'origine del raddoppiamento fonosintattico: saggio di fonologia diacronica romanza*. Tübingen: Francke.

Loporcaro, Michele. 2000. "Stress Stability under Cliticization and the Prosodic Status of Romance clitics." In *Phonological Theory and the Dialects of Italy*, ed. by Lori Repetti, 137–168. Amsterdam: John Benjamins. DOI: 10.1075/cilt.212.09lop

Lüdke, Helmut. 1979. *Lucania*. Pisa: Pacini.

Manzini, Maria R., and Leonardo M. Savoia (2005). *I dialetti italiani e romanci: Morfosintassi generative (3 volumes)*. Alessandria: Edizioni dell'Orso.

Monachesi, Paola. 1996. "On the Representation of Italian Clitics." In *Interfaces in Phonology*, ed. by U. Kleinhenz, 83–101. Berlin: Akademie Verlag.

Moyna, María Irene. 1999. "Pronominal Clitic Stress in Rio de la Plata Spainish: An Optimality Account." *The SECOL Review* 23: 15–44.

Nespor, Marina and Irene Vogel. 1986. *Prosodic Phonology*. Dordrecht: Foris.

Ordóñez, Francisco and Lori Repetti. 2006. "Stressed Enclitics?" In *New analyses in Romance linguistics*, ed. by Jean-Pierre Montreuil, and Chiyo Nishida, 167–181. Amsterdam: John Benjamins. DOI: 10.1075/cilt.276.13ord

Ordóñez, Francisco and Lori Repetti. 2008. "Morphology, Phonology and Syntax of Stressed Enclitics in Romance." Paper presented at NYU Workshop on Clitics, New York, May 2–3. Manuscript.

Ordonez, Francisco and Lori Repetti. 2014. "On the Morphological Restriction of Hosting Clitics in Italian and Sardinian Dialects." *Italia dialettale* 75: 173–199.

Ordóñez, Francisco and Lori Repetti. in progress. "Clitic Order and Stress Shift."

Peperkamp, Sharon. 1997. *Prosodic Words*. The Hague: HAG.

Pescarini, Diego. 2013. "The make-up of clitic clusters in the history of (Gallo-)Romance." Talk presented at LSRL 43.

Pierrehumbert, Janet and Mary Beckman. 1988. *Japanese tone structure*. Cambridge, Massachusetts: MIT Press.

Pittau, Massimo. 1972. *Grammatica del sardo-nuorese: Il più conservativo ei parlari neolatini.* Bologna: Pàtron.

Prieto, Pilar, Mariapaola D'Imperio and Barbara Fivela Gili. 2005. "Pitch Accent Alignment in Romance: Primary and Secondary Associations with Metrical Structure." *Language and Speech* 48: 359–396. DOI: 10.1177/00238309050480040301

Repetti, Lori and Francisco Ordóñez. 2011. *Clitics of Romance Languages (CRL).* http://crl.linguistics.stonybrook.edu/.

Romanello, Emily and Lori Repetti. 2014. "Special Characteristics Involving Imperatives in Romance Varieties Spoken in Italy." *Italian Journal of Linguistics* 26: 135–163.

Ruggieri, Donato and Antonio Batinti. 1992. *Lingua e dialetto ad Anzi: Potenza.* Potenza: Il Salice.

Selkirk, Elisabeth. 1995. "The Prosodic Structure of Function Words." In *Papers in OT (UMOP 18),* ed. by Jill N. Beckman, Laura Walsh Dickey, and Suzanne Urbanczyk, 439–469. Amherst: GLSA.

Torres-Tamarit, Francesc. 2010. "Stress Shift under Encliticization in Formenteran Catalan: A Case of an Unmarked Stress Pattern." Manuscript.

Vogel, Irene. 2009. "The Status of the Clitic Group." In *Phonological Domains: Universals and Deviations,* ed. by Janet Grijzenhout and Baris Kabak,15–46. Berlin: Mouton de Gruyter. DOI: 10.1515/9783110219234.1.15

From N to particle

Prepositionless *home* in the dialects of Northern Italy*

Silvia Rossi
University of Padua

The paper addresses the distribution of preposition-drop with the noun *casa* 'home' in the spatial adpositions of some Northern Italian varieties. It is shown that in these varieties P-less *home* behaves syntactically as a locative adverb, which under specific circumstances, becomes a *particle*. It is suggested that P-less *home* is not a special noun but a proper member of the category P generated in a specific projection in the fine-grained PP (Cinque 2010), hosting *viewpoint* modifiers of the silent head PLACE. The adverb vs. particle nature of P-less *home* derives from motivated movements inside and outside the PP triggered by a directional context. The same analysis is extended to Modern (and Old) English *home*.

1. Introduction

Preposition-drop (P-drop; Ioannidou and den Dikken 2009) in spatial adpositions is a rather infrequent phenomenon cross-linguistically (Gehrke and Lekakou 2013), exhibiting moreover no systematic behavior either across or within the languages allowing it (Ioannidou and den Dikken 2009; Terzi 2010; Gehrke and Lekakou 2013 on Modern Greek; Collins 2007 on English; Myler 2011 on some Northern British varieties; Longobardi 2001; Penello 2003 and Cattaneo 2009 on Northern Italian

* Many thanks to Davide Bertocci, Jacopo Garzonio, Diego Pescarini, Cecilia Poletto and two anonymous reviewers for comments and suggestions. I also thank the audiences at the 39th IGG (University of Modena-Reggio Emilia, 21–23 February 2013), and at LSRL 43 (CUNY Graduate Center, 17–19 April 2013), at which parts of this paper were presented. The usual disclaimers apply.

DOI 10.1075/rllt.9.20ros

dialects, NIDs). In these languages, null Ps have lexical and syntactic restrictions regarding: (i) their optional or mandatory occurrence; (ii) the argument vs. adjunct status of the PP they head; and (iii) the type, number and semantic characterisation of the nominals they select. All the above languages, however, share one striking characteristic: null Ps always—and in some languages only—occur with the noun *home*.

The present paper investigates the *synchronic* distribution of P(reposition)less *home* in the spatial adpositions of some Northern Italian dialects, integrating the data from the existing literature (Penello 2003; Cattaneo 2009) with examples from the ASIt database (Atlante Sintattico d'Italia, 'Syntactic Atlas of Italy', http://asit.maldura. unipd.it/). It will be shown that P-drop in the database is mostly attested in the Veneto region, while it is rarely found in the other NIDs. Subsequently, I consider the behaviour of P-less *home* with regard to the above restrictions, for which I put forward a syntactic account in light of the Split-PP hypothesis (Koopman 2000; Tortora 2008; Cinque 2010; Svenonius 2010; Terzi 2008 a.m.o.). Specifically, I argue that P-less *home* in the NIDs is not a special noun, but a proper member of the category P hosted in a dedicated projection inside the fine-grained structure of prepositional phrases (PP). P-less *home* is treated as a P-item (an intuition already present in Longobardi 2001), which in some varieties (Venetan and Borgomanero, Novara) and under specific conditions, has the syntactic status of a *particle*. The two different syntactic shapes of P-less *home* are derived from the same underlying structure to which motivated internal (and external) movements apply.

The paper is organised as follows: Section 2 briefly presents the phenomenon and its formal accounts in the above languages. The NIDs data from the ASIt database are discussed in Section 3. In Section 4, I introduce the theoretical assumptions behind my proposal and I examine the evidence for the adverbial/particle nature of P-less *home* in Borgomanerese (Tortora 2002, 2014), Old and Modern English (Rossi 2012), and Venetan. The details of my proposal in the light of the Split–PP Hypothesis are outlined in Section 5. Section 6 concludes.

2.   P-less *home* cross-linguistically.

In this section, I briefly review the major formal accounts of P-less *home* for English (Section 2.1), Modern Greek (Section 2.2), and for the NIDs (Section 2.3).

2.1   Modern English P-drop

Modern English (ModE) restrictions on P-less *home* are very well-known: P-drop is mandatory when *home* is in a PP argument of a V of motion, i.e., in directional

contexts (1a); it is impossible in locative adjuncts (1b), while it is optional in PP arguments of stative Vs like "stay" or "be," (1c).

(1) a. I went (*to) home/I took Mary (*to) home.
     b. I ate *(at) home.
     c. I stayed/was (at) home

On the basis of these oppositions, Collins (2007) proposes that ModE *home* has a peculiar status as it comes in three forms: (i) a *fully-fledged DP*, (2a); (ii) a *bare noun*, with no
functional structure between D^0 and N^0 (it cannot be modified/pluralized etc, and must
present a P), (2b); and (iii), a *light bare noun* with no functional structure at all, (2c).

(2) a. He found a new home.
     b. He worked at home.
     c. I go home/I stay home.

Having no functional heads intervening between N^0 and P^0, light bare *home* moves to
the Spec of its selecting P^0, satisfying in this way its lexicalization requirement. Collins
(2007) formalizes this requirement as Edge(X), a revisited version of the Doubly-Filled
COMP Filter, by which the Edge of a given head X must be phonetically overt, by spell-
ing out either the head or its Spec, but not both. Ps then remain silent as long as their
Edge receives phonetic content either by lexicalizing the P head, or in the case of light
bare *home,* by movement to SpecPP:

(3) [$_{PP}$ home AT/TO [~~home~~]]

Once in SpecPP, light bare *home* moves as a light PP into PredP, a projection hosting
arguments other than direct objects (DOs), thus accounting for the unavailability of
null Ps in adjunct PPs.

2.2 Modern Greek P-less *home.*

In stark contrast to ModE, Modern Greek allows P-drop with many place names
(*school, gym, office,* etc.) and with many city names (*Athens, Thessaloniki,* etc.). Nevertheless, just like ModE, Modern Greek P-drop is fully grammatical only when the null
P is directional, while its grammaticality degrades in stative argument PPs, becoming
ungrammatical in adjuncts (Terzi 2010).

Yet again, even Modern Greek P-less *spiti* 'home' is special since it is grammatical
in all spatial adpositions irrespective of their argument vs. adjunct nature (examples
from Terzi 2010):

(4) a. Emina (sto) spiti mexri arga.
         stayed-1s (se.the) home until late
         'I stayed home until late.'

b.   Sinithos magirevo/troo (sto) spiti
     usually cook-1s/eat-1s (se.the) home
     'I usually cook/eat at home.'

Ioannidou and den Dikken (2009) offer the first formal account of these facts, arguing
that Modern Greek allows null Ps because these incorporate onto V. In the absence of
an overt P, *spiti* moves to SpecDP in order to check D^0's EPP feature and to have its
case valued. Ioannidou and den Dikken (2009) consider *spiti* as a fully-fledged nominal with a complete set of functional heads in the complement position of a null P
incorporated onto V.

    In accordance with Ioannidou and den Dikken (2009), Terzi (2010) maintains
that Greek null Ps are syntactically present but phonologically silent. Her account,
based on the recent developments on the rich internal architecture of PPs, establishes a direct connection between the availability of null Ps and the nature of
their nominal arguments as places/locations. Terzi (2010) translates this semantic
property into syntax by considering these nominals as lexicalizations of the null
PLACE head, which is embedded under $PLoc^0$ and $PGoal^0$ encoding stativity and
directionality:

(5) $[_{PPGoal} PGoal^0 \, \emptyset \, [_{PPLoc} PLoc^0 \, \emptyset \, [_{DP/NP} PLACE \, [_{DP} DP \text{ argument}]]]]$

$PGoal^0$ and $PLoc^0$ are generally lexicalized by the simple P *se* "to, at" and the DP argument of *se* is in a possessor relation with the PLACE head (see Section 4.1). Yet, in the
case of locational nouns like *spiti*, these are not possessors of PLACE but are themselves instantiations of PLACE. This special nature allows *spiti* to move to $SpecPGoal^0$/
$PLoc^0$, thus satisfying the lexicalization requirement of the Edge of these heads (cf.
Collins 2007), which remain silent by Edge(X):

(6)   a.   V $[_{PPLoc} \text{spiti } PLoc^0 \, \emptyset \, [_{DP/NP} \text{~~spiti~~}]]$
      b.   V $[_{PPGoal} \text{spiti } PGoal^0 \, \emptyset \, [_{PPStat} \text{~~spiti~~} PStat^0 \, \emptyset \, [_{DP/NP} \text{~~spiti~~}]]]]$ [1]

Recently, Gehrke and Lekakou (2013) have proposed a different analysis capitalising
on the fact that Greek null Ps are possible only with D-less nouns, i.e., with *bare* nouns
denoting stereotypical locations. Their syntactic analysis does away with the idea
that P-drop involves syntactically present but phonologically null heads and propose

---

1.   P-drop in Modern Greek is always optional. The P variant has the full DP *spiti* as the
possessor of the null PLACE head (Terzi 2010):

(ii)   Pao $[_{PPdir} \text{se } [_{PPstat} \text{~~se~~} [_{DP/NP} PLACE \, [_{DP} \text{to spiti}]]]]$

instead that Greek P-drop is an instance of pseudo-incorporation, i.e., an NP which adjoins and incorporates onto VP at LF:

(7) $[_{IP}$ I $[_{VP}$ $[_{NP}$ beach] go]]

2.3   P-less *home* in the Northern Italian Dialects

Cases of P-less *home* in the Italo-Romance domain were already noted in Rohlfs (1969, §819, 215–6), who comments "[i]l sostantivo *casa* è decaduto alla funzione di preposizione" ('the noun *casa* has decayed to the function of a preposition'), as in *casa la madre*, lit. "home the mother" meaning "at the mother's place", from Boccaccio Old Italian).

The first syntactic account of P-less *home* in cases like (8) below is offered in Longobardi (2001):

(8)   Vago casa   (Paduan)
      Go.1sg home
      "I go home"

Longobardi (2001 and previous work) claims that Italo-Romance D-less *casa* derives from movement of N^0 to D^0, thus making *home* a *construct case* noun (cf. the Semitic construction). He formalizes this in the following generalization:

(9)   Movement of a noun to (an empty) D is licensed only if an overt or
      understood genitive argument is realized.

Thus, when *casa* 'home' appears without a determiner it must be interpreted as "home of/to someone."

For the Venetan case in (8), Longobardi (2001) proposes that these varieties legitimate a null locative P only if it is incorporated into a placename. Structurally, this is possible only with nouns moving to D^0:

(10) $[_{PP}$ N–D^0–P$_{zero}$-loc $[_{DP}$ N̶–D̶^{0} ... $[_{NP}$ N̶]]]

Venetan P-less *home* is investigated more in detail by Penello (2003), who shows that the phenomenon is possible in directional, stative and adjunct PPs:

(11)   a.   Vo (*a) casa   (Gazzolo d'Arcole, Verona)[2]
           Go.1sg home
           'I'm going home.'

---

2.   The Venetan examples are from the author's native variety of Gazzolo d'Arcole (Verona). All examples have been checked with speakers of the same variety, and with speakers of varieties with the same system.

    b.   So stà (*a) casa
        Am.1SG stayed home
        'I stayed in/home.'

    c.   Go fato i compiti (*a) casa
        Have.1SG done the homework home
        'I did my homework at home.'

This situation however is not true of all Venetan dialects as there is much speaker-variation in the obligatory, optional or impossible omission of Ps depending on the syntactic context, whether argument or adjunct, stative or directional. Penello (2003) captures this rather complex picture in the following generalization:

(12)   Generalization for locative *a* 'to, at':
      a.   if a dialect omits stative *a* it also omits directional *a*
      b.   if a dialect has P-less *school* it also has P-less *home*

The Ns allowing P-drop are different for each variety,[3] but are all semantically characterized as [+habitual], i.e., relevant for a linguistic community ("familiar"). Syntactically, Penello attributes the differences among the dialects and between the dialects and Italian to the possibility/impossibility to legitimate a null P, P_{zero}-loc, the derivation of P-drop remaining essentially the same as in Longobardi (2001).

   More recently, Cattaneo (2009) considers P-drop in Bellinzonese (Switzerland) and Paduan, to which he applies an analysis in terms of Collins (2007). Unlike Paduan, which has obligatory P-less *home* in all contexts (as in [11] above), Bellinzonese P-drop is optional, and occurs only in argument PPs (Cattaneo 2009):

(13) a.   Te ste (a) cà/ Te ve (a) cà.
        You stay home/You go home

      b.   Te cüsina *(a) cà.
        You cook at home

For Cattaneo (2009), the differences between Bellinzonese and Paduan rely on the availability in the former of both a light bare *home* and a bare *home*, while the latter has only a light bare *home,* see Section 2.1.

---

3.   Venetan and Bellinzonese P-drop occurs with several other nouns (*scola* 'school', *messa* 'mass', *militare* 'army' and a few more) and with "familiar" cities names. The analysis proposed here for P-less *casa* may be extended to these nominals: they might be considered items merged as absolute viewpoint markers in a PP (see Section 4.1), as they are absolute for a given language community (this is why they are different from variety to variety, thus difficult to characterise semantically apart from "familiar, habitual").

2.4 Concluding remarks

Though different in their formal mechanisms and in their theoretical assumptions, most of the above syntactic approaches to P-less *home* maintain that *home* is originated as an N/D argument inside a PP. P-drop with this noun occurs because of the special syntactic nature of *home* as either a *bare* noun or as an instantiation of the PLACE head, which allows it to scramble PP-internally.

In the following sections, I will put forward an alternative analysis in which P-less *home* is not the argument of a P with a special syntax, but is itself a P,[4] at least in English and in the NIDs I consider. Its peculiar behavior is dependent on its nature as a locative adverb, which becomes a *particle* under specific circumstances in those languages allowing verb-particle combinations. Oversimplifying my proposal for the sake of clarity, I claim that in the languages considered P-less *home* is not a noun synchronically, but a proper adverb with a fully-fledged PP structure, to which, in specific contexts, some motivated movements apply deriving the *particle* form. My proposal is then an attempt to translate and adjust Longobardi's (2001) intuition in a new theoretical perspective, the Split-PP, where many heads intervene between D^0 and P^0, also trying to give a uniform account for some problematic facts of Venetan P-less *home*, as the possibility for it to be a modifier in a bigger PP (see Section 4.4).

In the next section, I present the distribution of P-less *home* in the NIDs of the ASIt database.

3. P-less home in the ASIt database

The ASIt: database developed at the University of Padua is a collection of written questionnaires with sentences which speakers of various Italo-Romance varieties were asked to translate into their native dialect. The sentences are syntactically annotated and the database can be searched for various syntactic phenomena.

I searched for locative PPs with *home* in the NIDs of the database, focussing on the Gallo-Italic area (Piedmont, Lombardy, Emilia-Romagna, Liguria) and on the Veneto region. The results are summarised in Table 1.

---

4. As pointed out by an anonymous reviewer, my proposal is not very far from Terzi's (2010), who considers P-less nominals in Greek akin to adverbials like as *here* and *there* (Terzi 2010: 185). The only difference regards the fact that Greek has no particle counterpart of *home*, since Modern Greek does not have particles.

Table 1. P-drop with home in Gallo-Italic and Venetan (B = Borgomanero, T = Trecate)

	Gallo-Italic		Venetan	
DIRECTIONAL CONTEXTS	P-drop	P	P-drop	P
Il tuo amico è andato a casa ieri... (ASIt 1,18) "Your friend went home yesterday..."	2 (B, T)	46	12	6
Lo devo portare a casa (ASIt 1,51) "I have to take it home"	1 (B)	47	5	12
Crede di poterci portare a casa (ASIt 1, 94) "He thinks he can take us home"	2 (B, T)	46	7	11
Vado a casa (ASIt 2, 14) "I'm going home"	1 (B)	79	18	26
STATIVE CONTEXTS	P-drop	P	P-drop	P
Maria se li è visti arrivare a casa... (ASIt 1, 44) "Mary saw them getting into her house..."	0	48	6	11
... sono costretta a restare a casa (ASIt 1,86) "... I'm forced to stay (at) home"	1 (T)	46	5	12

Table 1 shows a clear asymmetry between Venetan and Gallo-Italic: on a total of ca. 45 Gallo-Italic varieties, only the following examples of P-less *home* were found:

(14) a.   L to amis l'è naci **cà** jarsera e ...   (Borgomanero, NO)
          the your fried CL.is gone home yesterday.night

    b.   A to amis l'è indai **ca** jer, e ...   (Trecate, NO)
          The your friend CL.is gone home yesterday
          'Your friend went home yesterday and ...'

(15) J devi purtè **callu**.   (Borgomanero, NO)
      I must take home=it
      'I have to take it home.'

(16) a.   'L crodda da pudì purte **canni**.   (Borgomanero, NO)
          He thinks from can take home=us

    b.   A croda da pudi' purte **cana**.   (Trecate, NO)
          he thinks from can take home=us
          'He thinks he can take us home.'

(17) J' vaghi **cà**.   (Borgomanero, NO)
      'I'm going home.'

P-less *home* is attested only in Borgomanero, near Novara, Piedmont (Tortora 2014). (Trecate has a similar system to Borgomanero).[5] Moreover, the above examples indicate

---

5. The Bellinzonese facts may constitute a second exception in Gallo-Italic, but, unlike Borgomanerese *cà*, Bellinzonese P-less *home* is always optional (similar systems are found also

that the canonical context for Borgomanerese P-less *home* is in argument directional PPs (cf. Tortora 2014, Section 4.2), since in stative contexts, only the P-variant is attested:

(18)   Maria l'a vustij rivè tucci 'n ca 'ntun mumentu.   (Borgomanero, NO)
        'Mary saw them arriving[6] at her house all at once.'

(19)   ... son stacia ubligà a stè 'n cà.   (Borgomanero, NO)
        '... I have to stay home.'

By contrast, the numbers in Table 1 for Venetan show that, P-less *home* is more attested in this region than in the whole of Gallo-Italic, although the overt P cases are roughly twice as many as the P-drop cases. The occurrences of an overt P with *home* are consistent with the results of Penello (2003), who showed that some Venetan varieties have a system similar to Bellinzonese (in [13] above). In this respect, however, I tentatively suggest that the relative low numbers for Venetan P-less *home* in the ASIt database may be due to the fact that speakers were asked to translate and write their dialect (a task which may have favored the 'prestigious' P variant, which these dialects share with Italian, over the possible P-less variant).

4. The particle nature of P-less home in NIDs and English

4.1 The Split PP Hypothesis

Many recent studies have argued for the presence of a rich functional layering above the lexical projection of P. Studies on single languages like Koopman (2000) on Dutch, Tortora (2008) on Italian and Spanish, Svenonius (2010) on English, Terzi (2008) on Greek a.m.o., and cross-linguistic studies (Cinque 2010) have identified the following projections (structure from Cinque 2010):

(20)   [PPdir [PPstat [DPplace [DegP   [ModeDirP
       from/to   *AT*   *2 inches*   *diagonally*
       [AbsViewP [RelViewP [RelViewP [DeicticP
       north   *up/down*   *in/out*   *here/there*
       [AxPartP   [KP/PP K^0/P^0 [NPplace *Ground* [PLACE]...]
       under/behind

---

in Venetan, Penello 2003). In the Venetan varieties I consider P-less *home* is mandatory (when asked, informants judged the P-variants as more "Italian"). A possible analysis for systems like Bellinzonese is sketched in Section 5.2, though some problematic aspects remain, cf. fn. 16. As to the reason why P-less *home* is attested only in Borgomanerese (and Trecate), I have no real satisfactory explanation yet.

6.   'To arrive' selects a stative argument, cf. ModE. *arrive in London/at the station* (**to London/*to*). Italian and NID *a* introduces both Goals and Locations.

A significant result of these studies is the idea that "phrases composed of spatial prepositions, adverbs, particles, and DPs do not instantiate different structures but merely spell out different portions of one and the same articulated configuration" (Cinque 2010, 3).[7]

The structure in (20) presents two functional heads, PPdir and PPstat, for directionality and stativity respectively, which take a DPplace projected by a null PLACE head as their complement. This DPplace contains a series of ordered modifier projections, hosting deictic elements, various adverb/particle items and lexical Ps (or AxPartP; Svenonius 2007). The DP object of a P, which offers the reference point, the Ground, is in a possessive relation with PLACE; the K^0 head between AxPartP and the Ground is a case head (Svenonius 2007), which, following some recent work (Garzonio and Rossi 2013), I consider to be lexicalised by the dative marker/simple P *a* 'to, at' in both Italian and the NIDs.

Anticipating the analysis in Section 5.1, I take Venetan and ModE *home* to be hosted in one of the modifiers projections in the DPplace. This position, typical of modifiers like adverbs and/or adjectives, is motivated semantically by the lexical features of P-less *home* which match one of the specific values of the functional modifiers of PLACE, and syntactically by its similar behaviour as other locative items hosted in the same projection. Before turning to the analysis proper, I present now the evidence for the *particle* nature of P-less *home* in Borgomanero, ModE and Venetan.

4.2 *Borgomanerese* cà.

Borgomanerese (Tortora 2002, 2014) shows a peculiar pattern of clitic placement: object and benefactive clitics appear encliticalliy on non-finite verbs and on certain lower aspectual adverbs. Tortora (2002, 2014) argues that Borgomanerese enclitics are hosted in a Z^0 head in the functional domain of the clause (between $T_{anterior}$ and $AspP_{terminative}$ in Cinque's 1999 hierarchy):

(21) ... [$_{XP}$ *mija* "not" [$_{YP}$ *già* "already" [$_{ZP}$ *piö* "anymore" CL-Z^0
      [$_{WP}$ *sempri* "always" [$_{UP}$ *bei* "well" [$_{VP}$ ...] ...]

The set of "adverbial" hosts for enclitics includes also some locative adverbs, but only when these are directional arguments of a V of motion. These P hosts are *denti* 'in', *fö* 'out', *sö* 'up', *sgiö* 'down', *vi* 'away' and the R-pronouns *inò* 'there' and *scià* 'here'.

---

7. This result follows from the important conclusion already established in the first generative studies on PPs (Jackendoff 1973 and van Riemsdijk 1978) that adverbs and particles are of the same category, P.

Interestingly, also *cà*[8] 'home' is among these hosts (examples from Tortora 2002, see also Section 3):

(22) i porti cà-tti.   vs.   *i porta-ti cà.
      I=bring.1sg home=you   I=bring.1sg=you home
      'I'm taking you home.'

Tortora (2002, 2014) argues that these P-items have no functional structure, and as such, they can move out of their PP into an "aspectual" projection in the clause where adverbs encoding a [bound] feature are hosted:

(23)   mija > già > *DENTI /CA*> piö—CLs > sempi > bej

This structural possibility is available only when these P-items are directional arguments of a V of motion, a structural configuration I suggest is to be captured in terms of a verb-particle combination. Borgomanerese then allows enclisis on P-items that are directional *particles*, and directional Borgomanerese P-less *cà* is then to be considered a particle.[9]

4.3   *Home* in Old and Modern English

The Borgomanerese P hosts for enclisis form a coherent group from a morphosyntactic perspective also in other languages, in particular in Germanic. German for instance has separable prefix counterparts for all of Borgomanerese P-hosts (also for R-pronouns, cf. distal *hin-* and proximal *her-*), while Old High German allowed allative, locative and ablative morphemes only on adverbs like *in/out, up/down north/east/ west/south* and on the R-pronouns *here/there/where* (Mackenzie 1978, 133, his table [4]). Interestingly, *heim* "home" was part of this group, with the same morphological endings as *up/down, in/out.*[10] OHG *heim*, like Modern German *heim-*, was used as a separable prefix, the closest counterpart of a *particle*.

A separable prefix *home* is found also in Old English. Rossi (2012) shows that in Ælfric's *Lives of Saints* (10th cent.), *ham* 'home' was the usual form in directional

---

8.   Borgomanerese *cà* is a phonologically reduced form of Lat. casa(m), which is not restricted to locative uses as the noun has the same form. Indeed, *cà* is the most attested form for "home" in Gallo-Italic, which, unlike Venetan, has undergone a massive loss of unstressed syllables in the evolution from Latin. A reduced form *cà* is also attested in Venetan, but in highly restricted contexts, such as place names (cf. *Cadidavid*, near Verona, lit. "House of the Davi").

9.   Borgomanerese P-less *cà* is only a particle when directional, with no full adverb counterpart since in stative and adjunct contexts *cà* is always embedded under an overt P.

10.   The OHG forms were *heim-e* 'at home', *heim* 'home', *heimana* 'from home', the morphologically simplest form being the directional one.

contexts, with the exact same distribution as particles/separable prefixes *in, ut* and *up*. In stative contexts, however, OE presented the PP *æt ham*:

(24)   and þæt halige heafod **ham feredon** mid him (ALS Edmund, 158)
       and the holy head home took with them
       'And they took the holy head home with them.'

In the light of the OE data, the ModE P-less *home* looks suspiciously like a relic of a previous stage, with the only difference that *home* has now become a particle. Indeed, ModE P-less *home* presents the same syntactic possibilities as particles of phrasal verbs:

   (a)   *Locative Inversion*   (Jackendoff 2002)
(25)   Home we go!   (cf. Off we go)

   (b)   *Prt-with construction*   (Jackendoff 2002)
(26)   Home with you lot!   (cf. Off with their heads)

(27)   a.   Let someone home   (cf. Let someone out/in)
       b.   He danced home   (cf. He danced in)

   (c)   *Right Modification*   (Collins 2007)
(28)   a.   He went right home   (cf. He went right off/in)
       b.   *He stayed right home   (cf. *He stayed right in) [11]

   (d)   *Particle Shift and no Right-modification in the shifted position*
(29)   a.   Take home the children!
       b.   Take the children home!
       c.   Take the children right home
       d.   *Take right home the children

Thus, ModE P-less *home* can be considered a particle.

4.4   Back to NIDs: Particle home in Venetan

Venetan P-less *casa* "home" behaves like particles *fora* 'out', *su* 'up' etc, which modify PPs and form transparent verb particle combinations (cf. Benincà and Poletto 2006): P-less *casa* can be used in isolation (30a), and can be focalized (30b). Yet, most importantly, P-less *casa* can modify other PPs (31a), its modifier nature being supported by the fact that no intonational break occurs between particle and PP, and by the ungrammaticality of the reversed order (31b), (all examples from Gazzolo d'Arcole, VR).

---

11.   Stative argument P-less *home* depends on the same reasons (still unclear to me), allowing *in* and *out* to occur with stative Vs. This was not possible in OE, where particles/separable prefixes were only directional, stative contexts requiring more complex forms (directional *ut/ham* vs. stative *beutan, wiðutan/æt ham*; Rossi 2012).

(30) a. A. Ndo veto?   B. Casa/Fora.
          Where go=you?   Home/Out
          'Where are you going?'

      b. CASA vo!/FORA vo!
          Home go.1SG/out go.1SG
          'I'm going HOME/OUT.'

(31) a. So/Vo/Lo porto casa (in leto)/fora (in giardin) Am.1SG/go.1SG/
          It=take.1SG home (in bed) /out (in garden)
          'I am/I'm going/I'm taking it home (to bed)/out
          (in the garden)'

      b. *So/Vo/Lo porto in leto casa/ in giardin fora

The unmarked position for directional *home* is immediately post-verbal, while adjunct
P-less *home* occurs preferably after the V and its object, cf. (32a) vs. (33a), that is, in the
typical position of ordinary PPs. The opposite orders (32b) and (33b), though grammatical, are somehow marked:

(32) a. Porto *casa* [i toseti]
          Take.1SG home the children
          'I'm taking home the children.'

      b. Porto [i toseti] *casa*
          Take.1SG the childrem home.
          (*casa* is focalized; 'I take them home, not somewhere else.')

(33) a. Go cusinà [i funghi] *casa*
          have.1SG cooked the mushrooms home
          'I cooked the mushrooms at home.'

      b. Go cusinà *casa* [i funghi]
          have.1SG cooked the mushrooms home
          (*i funghi* is focalized)

Yet, when directional *home* is modified by a possessive adjective or by another PP. its
unmarked position is sentence-final, just like adjunct *home*:

(34) a. Porto [i toseti] *casa sua/casa in leto*. (unmarked)
          Take.1SG the children home their/home in bed
          'Take the children to their home/home in bed.'

      b. Porto *casa sua/casa in leto* [i toseti]
          Take.1SG home their/home in bed the children
          (*i toseti* is focalized)

These examples indicate then that Venetan P-less *home*:

i.   behaves like a locative adverb, as it can be used alone or focalized, but it can also modify another PP;

ii. may occupy different positions in the sentence according to its "complex" or "bare" nature: it is "bare" when directional in immediate post-V position, while it is a full form when modified or in an adjunct position.

In the next section, these facts are accounted for by proposing that P-less *home* may come in two forms: as an adverb, with a full arrange of functional projections and the PLACE head (with a *pro* Ground), and as a particle, which I take to be a *weak* adverb, instantiating purely functional features in a PP without a lexical restrictor. In other words, I claim that P-less *home* is a P-item in Venetan (and in English), which may surface with a more or less complex structure (a proper adverb vs. a particle) because of PP-internal movements triggered by a specific condition, i.e., under a V of motion.

5.   *Home* and other particles in the fine-grained PP

The data in Section 4 indicate rather clearly that Borgomanerese, English and Venetan P-less *home* can be considered a proper locative item rather than a special noun, which exhibits particle behavior in directional contexts. I now turn to the structural analysis of adverbial *home* in the light of the Split-PP hypothesis sketched in Section 4.1 focusing first on the position particles occupy within the fine-grained PP (Section 5.1), and then on the structural derivation of adverb and particle *home* (Section 5.2).

5.1   Particles as Viewpoint modifiers

In the fine structure of PPs, Cinque (2010, 9–10) identifies three modifier positions within the DPplace which "host particles that indicate how the ground (plus axial part) is located with respect to (a) an absolute (geographical)viewpoint ('north/south', 'seaward/inland', etc.) and to (b) two relative viewpoints, a 'vertical' one ('up/down') and an interior/exterior one ('in/out')."

(35)   [PPdir [PPstat [DPplace [DegP [ModeDirP
        [AbsViewP *north* [RelviewP *up* [RelviewP *in* [DeicticP
        [AxPartP   [KP/PP K⁰/P⁰ [NPplace [PLACE]…]

These *viewpoint* modifiers indicate that the Ground is located higher/lower/inside/ outside or in absolute terms with regard to a certain viewpoint which may be the speaker's, the subject's, or that of a linguistic community.

Cinque (2010) places *up/down*, *in/out*, i.e., particle material in one of these *viewpoint* projections (RelViewP). Given its morpho-syntactic affinities with *up/down/in/*

out particles, I take P-less *home* to be a *viewpoint* marker, encoding, the speaker's/subject's relation with the Ground in absolute terms (like *seaward, inland*; in a sense, *home* is the absolute counterpart of "in").

(36)   [PPdir [PPstat [DPplace ... [AbsViewP *home* [DeicticP [AxPartP [KP/PP
        K^0/P^0 [NPplace [PLACE]...]

Under such proposal, the fact that Venetan P-less *home* can appear as a modifier in a bigger PP (see the examples in [31a]) is straightforwardly accounted for. Moreover, (36) represents also a structural motivation of the semantic characterizations identified in Penello (2003) that nouns under null Ps must be "familiar"; the familiar interpretation obtains because the "holder" of the *absolute viewpoint* marked by *home* is that of the speaker/subject, or that of the language community.

With (36) in mind, let us now turn to the derivation of the different sentential positions P-less *home* occupies in Venetan, (and in ModE).

5.2   P-less home: Particle and adverb

Borgomanerese (Section 4.1) and ModE (Section 4.2) P-less *home* is to be treated as a particle in directional contexts. The distributional properties of Venetan (Section 4.3) P-less *home*, however, are rather more complex, indicating that it can be both a particle in directional contexts, and a full adverbial form when stative, modified, or in adjunct position. One may conclude then that Venetan presents two homophonous P-less *home*, a particle and an adverb.

However, this is not the view I want to take: instead, I maintain that the lexical entry is always the same, and that the two syntactic shapes it assumes depend on motivated movements, deriving the particle from the fully-fledged adverb. In other words, the syntactic difference between adverbial *home* and particle *home* is to be understood in terms of "structural deficiency" differentiating a strong form (the adverb) from a *weak* form (the particle).

Let us start by considering the internal structure of adverbial *home*, i.e., when it is an adjunct. In this context, P-less *home* has a fully-fledged structure, i.e., it is inside a spatial PP with a phonetically null Ground (*pro*).

(37)   [PPdir [PPstat AT [DPplace ... [Abs/RelViewP *home* [DeicticP [AxPartP [KP/PP K^0/P^0
        [NPplace *pro* [PLACE] ...]

P-less *home* has this fully-fledged structure also when it is used as a directional P-item in isolation, topicalized/focalized, or modified by other PPs or by possessives (recall that in this last case the preferred position in Venetan is after the V and the DO, the same positions as ordinary PPs).[12]

---

12.   This is the structure I also assume for ModE particles when in the non-shifted position, where they can also admit *right*-modification.

By contrast, P-less *home* is a particle when it is used as a *bare* directional P. In accordance with Koopman (2000), Collins (2007) and Terzi (2010), I assume that directional contexts involve movement of an item from inside the DPPlace into SpecP-Pdir, which has been activated/selected by a V of motion. My account of directional P-less *home* however does not involve scrambling of *home*. Instead, I propose that it is the *pro* Ground that moves to SpecPPdir by a process of *feature stripping*, first proposed by Poletto (2006) for deriving cases of "doubling" of functional elements like clitics or *wh*-items. In particular, I propose that *feature stripping* applies "stripping" the DPplace of its lexical restrictor, i.e., the PLACE head plus the *pro* Ground, moving it to SpecPPdir. This is the same movement which derives ordinary cases of directional PPs headed by *a* 'to, at' in Italian, (38a) structurally represented in (38b), with the only difference that in particle *home* it applies with a *pro* Ground:

(38) a. Vado a casa   (Italian)
          Go.1SG to home
          'I go home.'

     b. Vado $[_{PPdir}$ *a casa* $[_{PPstat} [_{DPplace} \cdots [_{AxPartP} [_{KP} \text{a} [_{NPplace}$ *casa* PLACE]] ....]^{13}

This movement then voids the directional PP of its restrictor, leaving *home* inside the PP to lexicalize a bundle of functional features (*viewpoint* maker). *Home* ends up with little structure and can move via remnant into the functional domain, to a dedicated projection for structurally deficient elements (cf. both Collins 2007 and Tortora 2014 on structureless *home*/light PPs moving into PredP or AspP):

(39) [TP ... [FP **home** .... $[_{PPdir}$ *pro* $[_{PPstat}$ AT $[_{DPplace} [_{Abs/RelViewP}$ *home* $[_{DeicticP}$ $[_{AxPartP} [_{KP/PP}$ K$^{\theta}$/P^{0} $[_{NPplace}$ *pro* [PLACE] ...]

In these terms, structural deficiency does not regard absence of functional structure (as in Cardinaletti and Starke 1999); the structurally deficient element lexicalizes only part of the functional structure of a lexical category that has been voided of its restrt-ictor. Structural deficient items must move to dedicated projections in the clause (cf. clitic positions, see Poletto 2006, *Wackernagel* positions for weak elements, or particle positions in the aspectual domain).

A final remark on optional P-less *home* of Bellinzonese seems in order. It may be the case that in this variety (as well as in others with a similar system), two structures are available: P-less *home* may have the same structure as proposed above, i.e., it may be an adverb or a particle merged as a *viewpoint* marker in the PP, while the overt

---

13. See Garzonio and Rossi (2013) for a similar proposal for Italian (and dialectal) complex PPs.

P-variants may have the same underlying representation as Italian, here repeated in (40), where *home* is the Ground in a PP, i.e. a proper noun:

(40) $[_{PPdir} [_{PPstat} AT [_{DPplace} \cdots [_{Abs/RelViewP} [_{DeicticP} [_{AxPartP}$
      $[_{KP/PP} K^0/P^0 a [_{NPplace}$ *casa* [PLACE] ...]^{14}

In this case, *casa* is a construct-state noun, that is, a DP where movement of N^0 to D^0 has occurred (Longobardi 2001). [15]

6. Conclusions

In this contribution, I showed that there is syntactic evidence that in some NIDs, P-less *home* can be treated as a proper member of the category P, as it can surface either as a full adverb or as a particle: P-less *casa* 'home' is an adverb when it is in adjunct position or when it is modified, while it is a particle when it occurs in immediate post-verbal position as a *bare* (unmodifiable) item in directional contexts.

As a P-item, Venetan P-less *home* is merged in a dedicated projection inside the fine-grained PP (Cinque 2010), which, on the basis of morphosyntactic affinities with other particles, I identified as that of *viewpoint* modifiers like *up/down* etc. and *north/south* etc. *Home* is a *viewpoint* marker in the PP indicating how the silent Ground (*pro*) is to be located with respect to a specific viewpoint (the speaker's, the subject's or that of the linguistic community).

---

14. I would like to add here just some very tentative speculations on how the noun *casa* might have become or be synchronically reinterpreted as a P-item. A key step in this process is, I think, the construct-state nature of Romance *casa*, which presents an implicit genitive argument (see Longobardi's 2001 generalization in [9]). This implicit genitive could make it a good candidate for the modifier projections of the PP domain. For instance, construct-case *casa* may be a good candidate for the AxPart projection (Svenonius 2007), which hosts "relational nouns" like body parts, inalienable *possessa*, appearing in complex Ps like *in front of* (complex Ps with *home* are attested in the Italo-Romance domain, cf. *akk'u miéreche* "lit. at home the doctor, at the doctor's", Monte di Procida and Forio d'Ischia, Naples, Rohlfs 1969, §819). Notice incidentally that AxPart nouns and construct-state nouns display the same syntactic restrictions (lack of a determiner; impossibility to be modified, pluralized; Svenonius 2007). Moreover, the interpretation of the implicit genitive argument of *home*—usually as the subject but not only—may also be the trigger for its reanalysis (or grammaticalization?) into a *viewpoint* marker. These claims clearly need to be further supported by a careful diachronic investigation, which I intend to tackle in the next future.

15. I have no real satisfactory answer for the reason why in varieties similar to Bellinzonese adverb *casa* cannot be used as an adjunct. I must leave this potentially problematic aspect open.

The adverb vs. particle status of Venetan P-less *home* is derived from the same structure, that of a fully-fledged adverb (a PP), which undergoes *feature stripping* when it is the argument of a V of motion. In this process, the lexical restrictor of the adverb—PLACE plus the *pro* Ground—moves to SpecPPdir leaving the modifier *home* without a restrictor and capable of moving as a *weak* element into the functional domain of the clause. An analysis in these terms straightforwardly accounts also for cases in which Venetan P-less *casa* modifies another PP, a phenomenon that is not easily accommodated in previous accounts.

References

Benincà, Paola, and Cecilia Poletto. 2006. "Phrasal Verbs in Venetan and Regional Italian." *Language Variation-European Perspective,* ed. by Frans Hinskens, 9–22. Amsterdam: John Benjamins. DOI: 10.1075/silv.1.02ben

Cardinaletti, Anna, and Michal Starke. 1999. "The Typology of Structural Deficiency: A Case Study of Three Classes of Pronouns." *Clitics in the Languages of Europe,* ed. by Henk van Riemsdijk, 145–233. Berlin: Mouton.

Cattaneo, Andrea. 2009. *It Is All About Clitics: The Case of a Northern Italian Dialect Like Bellinzonese.* Ph.D. dissertation, New York University.

Cinque, Guglielmo. 1999. *Adverbs and Functional Head. A Cross-linguistic perspective.* Oxford: Oxford University Press.

Cinque, Guglielmo. 2010. "Mapping Spatial PPs: An Introduction." *Mapping Spatial PPs. The Cartography of Syntactic Structures,* ed. by Guglielmo Cinque, and Luigi Rizzi, vol. 6, 3–25. Oxford-New York: Oxford University Press.
DOI: 10.1093/acprof:oso/9780195393675.003.0001

Collins, Chris. 2007. "Home Sweet Home." *NYU Working Papers in Linguistics* 1: 1–34.

Garzonio, Jacopo, and Silvia Rossi. 2013. "Case and Subordination in Italian Complex Ps." Manusript. University Ca'Foscari, Venice.

Gehrke, Berit, and Marika Lekakou. 2013. "How to miss your preposition." *Studies in Greek Linguistics* 33: 92–106.

Ioannidou, Alexandra, and Marcel den Dikken. 2009. "P-drop, D-drop, D-spread." *Proceedings of the 2007. Workshop in Greek Syntax and Semantics,* ed. by C. Halpert, J. Hartman, and D. Hill, 393–408. Cambridge, Mass.: MIT Press.

Jackendoff, Ray. 1973. "The base rules for prepositional phrases." *A festschrift for Morris Hale,* ed. by S. R. Anderson & P. Kiparsky, 345–356. New York, NY: Holt, Rinehart and Winston.

Jackendoff, Ray. 2002. "English particle construction, the lexicon, and the autonomy of syntax.". In *Verb-Particle Explorations,* ed. by Nicole Dehè, Ray Jackendoff, Andrew McIntyre, and Silke Urban, 67–94. Berlin: Mouton de Gruyter. DOI: 10.1515/9783110902341

Koopman, Hilda. 2000. "Prepositions, Postpositions, Circumpositions and Particles: The Structure of Dutch PPs." *The Syntax of Specifiers and Heads. Collected Essays of Hilda J. Koopman,* ed. by Hilda Koopman. London: Routledge.

Longobardi, Giuseppe. 2001. "Formal Syntax, Diachronic Minimalism and Etymology: The History of French *Chez.*" *Linguistic Inquiry* 32: 275–302. DOI: 10.1162/00243890152001771

Mackenzie, J. Lachlan. 1978. "Ablative-locative transfers and their relevance for the theory of case-grammar." *Journal of Linguistics* 14: 129–156. DOI: 10.1017/S0022226700005831

Myler, Neil. 2011. "Come the pub with me: Silent TO in a Dialect of British English." *NYU Working Papers in Linguistics (NYUWPL)* 3, 120–35.

Penello, Nicoletta. 2003. *Capitoli di morfologia e sintassi del dialetto di Carmignano di Brenta.* Ph.D. dissertation. University of Padua.

Poletto, Cecilia. 2006. "Doubling as Economy." *University of Venice Working Papers in Linguistics* 16: 211–235 (http://lear.unive.it/bitstream/10278/209/1/2006-7s-Poletto.pdf).

van Riemsdijk, Henk. 1978. *A case study in syntactic markedness: The binding nature of prepositional phrases.* Lisse: The Peter de Ridder Press.

Rohlfs, Gerhard. 1969. *Grammatica storica dell'italiano e dei suoi dialetti. Sintassi e formazione delle parole,* vol. III. Turin: Einaudi.

Rossi, Silvia. 2012. *P in Old English. P-Stranding, Post-positions and Particles in a Cartographic Perspective.* Ph.D. dissertation, University of Padua.

Svenonius, Peter..2007. "The Emergence of Axial Parts." *Adpositions. Special issue of Nordlyd: Tromsø Working Papers in Linguistics, 33.1,* ed. by Peter Svenonius, and Marina Pantcheva,, 49–77. (http://www.ub.uit.no/munin/nordlyd/).

Svenonius, Peter. 2010. "Spatial P in English." *Mapping Spatial PPs. The Cartography of Syntactic Structures, vol. 6,* ed. by Guglielmo Cinque, and Luigi Rizzi, 127–160. Oxford-New York: Oxford University Press.

Terzi, Arhonto. 2008. "Locative Prepositions as Modifiers of an unpronounced Noun." *Proceedings of WCCFL* 26: 471–480.

Terzi, Arhonto. 2010. "On null spatial Ps and their arguments." *Journal of Catalan Linguistics* 9: 167–187.

Tortora, Christina. 2002. "Romance Enclisis, Prepositions and Aspect." *Natural Language and Linguistic Theory* 20: 725–758. DOI: 10.1023/A:1020455332427

Tortora, Christina. 2008. "Aspect inside Place PPs." *Syntax and Semantics of Spatial P,* ed. by Anna Asbury, Jakub Dotlačil, Berit Gehrke, and Rick Nouwen, 273–301. Amsterdam: John Benjamins. (http://www.let.uu.nl/~Anna.Asbury/personal/Tortora.pdf). DOI: 10.1075/la.120.14tor

Tortora, Christina. 2014. *A Comparative Grammar of Borgomanerese.* Oxford: Oxford University Press. DOI: 10.1093/acprof:oso/9780199945627.001.0001

Marsican deixis and the nature of indexical syntax

Mario Saltarelli

Marsican demonstratives show evidence of an extended deixis beyond nominals, adverbial phrases, and sentential clause types, including the realization of Speaker time and aspect of the event. Typological considerations and the quest for universals make a case for the covalence of deixis and indexicality. This human language scenario exceeds the descriptive power of narrow syntax (Chomsky 2008), hence inviting the encoding of indexical elements in the functional phase of syntax CP (Giorgi 2010). This paper proposes an operator-variable binding theory of 'the deictic hypothesis' (DH), where the human context (i.e. the intentional Speaker) is encoded as an operator in the (functional) CP phase, binding the deictic variable in the (content) vP phase. DH assumes a human cognitive foundation of the deictic act as a conceptual necessity. Under DH the person category in morpho-syntax is derived, while accounting for covalent indexicality. The empirical feasibility of DH is explored for Marsican's Latin origin and its cognitive relevance projected for further research in the acquisition of deictic elements in similar language types (e.g. Basque, Korean).

0. From a human perspective

Demonstrative deictic elements in nominal phrases like 'I want *this* book, not *that* one' receive independent attention in philosophy and in linguistics with an apparently consensual division of labor. On the one hand, philosophers like Kaplan (1989:528) propose a context (direct reference) theory of the demonstrative element, while the content (syntax) phrase in which it is uttered is of no immediate concern. On the other hand, generative syntactic analyses of a similar deictic expression are couched under the Determiner Phrase (DP) hypothesis (Abney 1986), in which the deictic element is the determiner of the nominal phrase and the (referential) context in which the deictic element is uttered is of no immediate concern.

DOI 10.1075/rllt.9.21sal

More recently, however, descriptively recalcitrant interface phenomena raise compelling arguments for encoding properties of the context in syntax judging from the perspective of an optimal syntactic theory of human language (Chomsky 2005, 2008). Pursuing this general line are Bernstein (2008), encoding person features in NP; Zanuttini (2008), encoding the Addressee as a Jussive Phrase projection; Giordano and Longobardi (2008), encoding person licensing; Giorgi (2010), encoding the Speaker in the left periphery; Saltarelli (2011), encoding parallel domains; and Alcázar and Saltarelli (2014), encoding the Speaker > Addressee relation. It seems appropriate to attribute the interface evolution in the design of the syntactic theory of language to the influence of the philosopher's theory of speech acts (Austin 1962).

Along these conceptual lines, the general goal of this paper is toward a unified account of the philosopher's context-semantics and the linguist's content-syntax of demonstratives and other aspects of deixis in its indexical character. The narrower empirical goal is a minimalist account by derivation of Marsican (M) deictic demonstratives. I will argue that a descriptively adequate analysis requires a unified approach to the (context(content)) interface. Towards this goal I propose in Section 5 an implementation of the functional split-CP domain for the derivation of the Marsican demonstrative system. If substantiated, a generalized approach is expected to offer a more adequate understanding of the interdependence between the indexical nature of the context of a deictic utterance and the morpho-syntactic form of its narrow syntax.

I will assume a treatment of the philosopher's "context of utterance" as the syntactitian's (function(content)) CP(vP) under a strong minimalist thesis in a theory of phases (Chomsky 2008).

The empirical evidence for a uniform treatment of demonstratives under the more general topic of deixis comes from the singular evidence of the Marsican vernacular of Pescasseroli (P) (in the province of L'Aquila), in western Abruzzo.[1] The descriptive inspiration comes from the textbook analysis of the Latin system of demonstratives *hic, iste, ille* in Allen and Greenough's *New Latin Grammar* (Greenough et al., §297). The Marsican system of spatial demonstratives appears to be a faithful diachronic evolution of Latin in contact with its Italic substratum (see Section 7). In this respect, initial scholarly credit is due to the Romanists on whose shoulders we stand, for example

---

1. The deictic data presented here is surprisingly undocumented in the Romanistic literature (Saltarelli 2011), considering the eminent tradition in Italian (including Abruzzan) dialectology. Only unconfirmed scholarly notes are available (Devoto 1974, 203). Yet, Pescasseroli's variety shows a unique situation of gender diglossia (Neri and Saltarelli 2005), which remains unaddressed by sociolinguistics, ethnography, and variation genetics. Textual analysis is, of course, impossible, due to hegemonic policy in the public schools (cf. Saltarelli 2014). In diachrony, reconstruction suggests a new path of development (cf. Section 7 below) for Romance deixis.

Rohlfs (1968, §491–496) and Lausberg (1971, §738–742), among many others, who in a long tradition in Romance and beyond contributed to this language-in-context issue.

On evidence from Marsican (P), this paper seeks to confirm the following factors. First, the syntax of demonstratives encodes properties of the context of utterance, which are compatible with those of indexical pronouns (*I, you, he/she*). Second, deixis spans over parallel domains of nominal, temporal/aspectual, and adverbial phrases, in a morpho-syntactic behavior overlapping with that of indexicals. If this conceptual argument is sustained, then a unified account of deixis would appear to exceed the descriptive capacity of narrow syntax (as we know it so far), thus inviting a new look at the ontology of (demonstrative) deixis and considering the prospect of an indexical syntax at the conceptual-intentional interface, toward a closer perspective of human language and cognition (cf. Alcázar and Saltarelli 2014, ch.4).

1. The Marsican paradigm and the indexical nature of syntax

Deictic elements in the Marsican (M) variety of Pescasseroli (P) encode the three-term indexical context system of Latin (cf. Greenough et al.). The three-value/three-term contrast is observed in parallel phrasal domains irrespective of hierarchical structural relations (i.e., nominal phrases and adverbial phrases: place (def./indef.), manner). The deictic contrast in indexicality is also observed in clausal speech acts such as exclamatives and imperatives (Alcázar and Saltarelli 2014). In addition we note that deixis is context-sensitive to the temporality of the event. Finally the indexical blueprint of deixis is obviously observed in the person morphology of the verb in this richly inflected language. It is to be noted that, except for structural subject-verb agreement, current narrow syntax computation falls short of an optimal account of Marsican's deixis in the absence of the philosopher's indexical "context of utterance". This paper offers a cognitive understanding of deixis as observed in Marsican and an account within the theory of narrow syntax coherent with parallel domain phenomena (cf. Section 5).

Figure 1 below displays the Marsican paradigm of ad-nominal demonstratives. The three-way ad-nominal contrast is observed in the second column: *quíste/quísse/ quìse*, "pointing to" (referencing) deictically the masculine, singular, count noun *cane* 'dog'. The deictic demonstrative is understood as the linguistic function for the identification of the object noun (via the context of utterance) at the time, place, and world of the intended speech act (Figure 1, first column). Cognitively, it is strictly an indexical direction which requires a measurement (quantization; see Section 5) to locate a referent via distance or proximity (Anderson and Keenan 1985) to the participant(s) of the speech act.

Coordinate	Count N (m.)	Count N (f.)	-Count N (m.)	Num
(a) Speaker P1	*(quí)ste* ['kwistə] *cane* 'this dog'	*(qué)sta*['kwésta] *mane* 'this hand'	*quéste* ['kwestə] *pane* 'this bread'	Sing.
	(quí)šche ['kwiʃkə] *cane* 'these dogs'	*(qué)ste* ['kwestə] *mane* 'these hands'	**********	Plur.
(b) Hearer P2	*(quí)sse* ['kwissə] *cane* 'that dog'	*(qué)ssa*['kwes:a] *mane* 'that hand'	*quésse* ['kwessə] *pane* 'that bread'	Sing.
	(quí)šše ['kwiʃʃə] *cane* 'those dogs'	*(qué)sse* ['kwes:ə] *mane* 'those hands'	**********	Plur.
(c) (¬SH) P3	*quìse* ['kwɨsə] *cane* 'that dog'	*quéla* ['kwela] *mane* 'that hand'	*quéle* ['kwele] *pane* 'that bread'	Sing.

Figure 1. Ad-nominal deictic demonstratives[2]

Ad-nominal demonstratives in M vary morpho-phonologically in agreement with the categories of the head noun: αCount, βGender, γNumber. Their unstressed prosody (a,b) is limited to essential indexicals. Incidentally, the paradigm in Figure 1 is the demonstrative system of M's gender diglossia, robustly preserved in the vernacular of women in P (Neri and Saltarelli 2005).

The context of utterance in Figure 1 (first column) is articulated as a cognitive property of the human speech act. It is anchored on two conceptually known variables in the situation, namely the Speaker (Person1) and the Hearer (Person2, Addressee), thus confirming the "essential" indexicality (*I, you*) of deictic demonstratives (Perry 1997; Hockett 1966, 4; 21). The third term (Person3) is the default or unknown value in the deictic context. It is empirically relevant to note the P1,2 vs. 3 categorical contrast, with respect to prosody. Only essential indexicals P1(a), P2(b) can be unstressed, namely *'ste, 'sse* (hence pro-cliticized on the noun). In addition, the person contrast P1,2/3 is syntax-sensitive elsewhere in Marsican, such as in the distribution of auxiliary verbs *èsse/avì* 'be/have'. Namely, 'be'(*èsse*) is used for 1p (*so*) and 2p (*si*) while 'have' (*avì*) is used for 3p (*ha*), as illustrated in following paradigm examples: *so_magnate* (be.p1) 'I have eaten', *si magnate* (be.p2) 'you have eaten', *ha/*è magnate* (have.p3) 'he has eaten'. The same contrast 1p,2p/3p is observed in the prosodic distribution of kinship enclitic genitives: *patre-me, patre-te, patre-*se* 'my/your/*his father'.[3] A general

---

2. This reflex of the evolution from the Latin demonstrative system, complete with the third person *quìse* ['kwɨsə] (¬SH P3), is uniquely instantiated in the Marsican diglossia of Pescasseroli (P), previously undocumented, hence its empirical relevance unaddressed in the literature regarding the description (see Section 6) and diachrony (see Section 7) of Romance deixis.

3. The evidence from P regarding the context-sensitivity of enclitic (kinship) possessives was discussed in Saltarelli (2014).

account of these and other context phenomena reveal the indexical nature of language and reclaim its necessary role in narrow syntax.

1.1   Marsican in the typology of deictics

A typological assessment of the three-values/three-terms demonstrative system emerges from a cross-linguistic survey of the world's languages. We note in Figure 2 below that Marsican, along with Basque and Korean (among many other languages in the survey) observes transparency at the C–I interface with morpho-syntax, in regards to the full exploitation of the deictic system. Note also that the highest percentage of the languages surveyed encodes a reduced two-term demonstrative contrast out of the conceptual three-values on a speech act hypothesis, thus increasing the load of syntactic homophony. In an analytical perspective, contrastively reduced demonstrative systems like English *this/that* (as opposed to Marsican three-terms *quíste, quísse, quìse*) under-define the conceptual system verbally, hence requiring gestural context as a last resort: pointing or gazing generalized as the philosopher's concept of "demonstration" or "ostension" (Kaplan 1989).

Speaker, Hearer coordinate*	% of types	Languages (234)
Three values/one term		German, *French (7)
Three values/two terms	54.3%	English, Romanian (127)
Three values/-three terms	37.6%	Basque, Korean, **Marsican** (88)
Three values/four (five**) terms		Hausa (8), (4**)

*French contiguous *ce-ci/là* and discontiguous *cet-homme-ci/là* may support two-term.
**Not considered.

Figure 2. Classification of demonstrative systems (after Diessel 1999)

This paper claims, however, a wider view of deixis, conveyed in language beyond the demonstrative phrase in concordance with a restrictive nominal modifier (relative) clause (a) or (b) an adverbial phrase: "lend me *this/that* book (that) you are reading vs. over there on the shelf". The indexical nature of a ubiquitous deixis calls for the design of a context-sensitive theory of syntax from a descriptively comprehensive perspective of human language. Apparent demonstrative outliers in Figure 2, like German and French, fall under the ad-verbially enhanced narrow syntax of deixis by encoding their common ontology with indexicals.

2.   Ad-verbial deixis: Beyond the syntactic domain demonstratives

Note in Figure 3 below that Marsican exhibits a functionally parallel three-term adverbial phrase deixis along the same indexical speech act coordinates and beyond the syntactic domain of ad-nominals (Figure 1). This is specifically observed in space (3.1) and manner (3.2) ad-verbials. We note further that Marsican develops a homologous three-way deictic contrast under definiteness. Conceptually, the extended (adverbial) distribution confirms the necessity of indexical reference for a generalized syntax of deixis, not only in demonstrative nominal phrases but also in their parallel agreement with the adverbial phrases. This extended empirical factor raises again the descriptive question on more solid grounds: how to formalize a generalized account of the concord of both ad-nominal and ad-verbal domains of deixis in a uniform syntactic description.

One of the descriptive issued at hand is a syntactic account of '(a) temporal, (b) spatial compatibility' in the parallel selection of ad-verbal (a) and ad-nominal (b) deixis. Observe, the grammaticality requirement in the following sentences: (a) "Peter is sleeping now,*yesterday", (b) "give me that/*this book over there/*here". Encoding cross-clausal concord in the deictic system suggests on inspection a higher order access to the epistemics of the Speaker and a deeper understanding of the human language faculty, the theory of grammar and the act of speech.

	3.1 Space		3.2 Manner
	Def	Indef	
(a) Speaker P1	*ècche* 'here'	*dècqueta* '(around) here'	*acquescí* 'like this'
(b) Hearer P2	*èsse* 'there'	*dèsta* '(around) there'	*ascí* 'like that'
(c) P3	*lóche* 'there'	*dèlleta* '(around) there'	*allescí* 'like that'

Figure 3. Space, Manner

3. Clausal deixis: Beyond phrase structure

Deixis, in its indexical context distribution, is observed in Marsican not only across phrasal domains (Figures 1 and 3) but also as a higher order speech act phenomenon across sentential types, such as exclamatives (4.1) and imperatives (4.2), in Figure 4. The exclamative or presentative clause (4.1) is construed in Marsican with a "light" imperative-like verb *vì* 'look'. The imperative (4.2) is literally "*leva-te èsse* 'get yourself out of there-P2."

	4.1 Exclamative	4.2 Imperative
(a) Speaker P1	*ècchese, vì!* 'here he is, look!'	
(b) Hearer P2	*èssese, vì!* 'there he is, look!'	*lèvat'èsse!* 'go away'
	èllese, vì! 'there he is, look!'	

Figure 4. Imperative

4. Speaker time: The conceptual origin of indexical deixis

Observe in Figure 5 the role of the temporal variable in the selection of deictic elements. The system of Marsican deixis described so far is homogeneously respected within Speaker's time (the ultimate indexical property) at the Conceptual-Intentional interface. Note that while the deictic system is transparent in the present (E,S) it is restricted to the type (c) beyond Speaker's time.

	Speaker's time E,S present	E_S past and *S
(a) Speaker P1	'ste càne che ténghe ne mócceca' 'this dog I have doesn't bite'	*(quì)ste càne che tenìva ne meccechìva *'this dog I had didn't bite'
(b) Hearer P2	'sse càne che tì ne mócceca' 'that dog you have doesn't bite'	*(quì)sse càne che tenìve ne meccechìva 'that dog you had didn't bite'
(c) ¬SH P3	'se càne che tè ne mócceca' 'that dog he/she has doesn't bite'	quìse càne che tenìva ne meccechìva 'that dog he/she had didn't bite'

Figure 5. Speaker time: The ultimate corollary of indexical deixis

Note further that what is observed in Figure 5 is that the realization of a full deictic system (i.e. three values/ three terms) is grammatically transparent only under Speaker time coordinates, that is, present time (not in the past or future, where the distal demonstrative only is observed).

An example from Spanish confirms beyond Marsican the required congruity of the deictic system with the indexicality of the utterance:

(1) a. esta/*esa/*aquella camisa que llevo ahora/*ayer es de algodón.
     b. *esta, esa, aquella camisa que llevaba *ahora/ayer era de seda pura.

The syntactic restrictions in the computation of deixis across domains are likely to turn out to be an invariant property of human language.

5. Deixis as a cognitive quantization of the speech act

The pervasive role that deixis plays in languages, such as Marsican, appears to exceed a characterization in terms of lexical (DemP), phrasal (DP), or clausal categories. The only factor common to the contrastive deictic forms are the speech act referential coordinates (Speaker, Hearer).

Under this scenario, deixis is not a categorical entity, but rather the quantization of a measurement (arguably tri-laterality (see Section 5.1) based on the two known (C-bound) variables to determine the referential location of an intended free variable in the speech act. Accordingly, an adequate syntactic derivation requires access to the indexical coordinates of the context as a conceptual necessity. In what follows a sketch of the proposed syntactic hypothesis of a generalized deixis is outlined.

5.1 An operator-variable binding hypothesis

I lay out here my operator-variable binding hypothesis:

a. Deixis enters as an endowed (or acquired) cognitive factor at the conceptual-intentional interface
b. Deictic elements are variables x^1, y^2, z^3 in $(_{CP}$ context $(_{vP}$ content)) syntax (heads, adjuncts)
c. Operator(-variable) binding: (Speaker (x^1) = P1, Hearer (y^2) = P2, z^3 ($\neg$SH) = P3
d. D-values: x^1, y^2 fixed (C-bound); z^3 unknown (free) (Bijection Principle: Koopman&Sportiche 1982)
e. Morpho-syntactic Person-categories are not syntactic primitives, but rather derived D-values

I provide here a possible geometry of the deictic theorem:

quìse (z)

S ————— H

quíste (x) > *quísse (y)* (Marsican (P))

5.2 Deixis across languages overlapping with indexicality

Figure 6 below presents a sample of the distribution of pronominals, adnominals and adverbial deictic elements showing their overlap with indexicals. Note, in particular, the *non-occurrence of indexicals. Latin, Basque, and Turkish do not exhibit a third person (default) indexical, a term which is substituted by the demonstrative *ille, hura*, and *o*, respectively. It is reasonable to conjecture that these facts suggest the overlapping indexicality of demonstrative and essential indexical pronouns. Furthermore, the systemic indexical invariance observed across the languages of the world surveyed strongly confirms its universal nature and narrows the ontological basis of human language.

It may be analytically instructive to inquire into the inception and order of acquisition of deixis. In the case of two-term English first in order of acquisition is the term *that* (West 2011), while *this* follows significantly later. To further the human perspective advocated in this paper, it would be relevant as a cognitive phenomenon to investigate the inception of the demonstrative *this/that* in contrast with pronominal *I/you*, in search of a diagnostic on the inception of human self-idenitification. Studies on the acquisition of three-term demonstrative like Turkish *bu, şu, o* (Küntay and Özyürek 2006) report that the acquisition of the term *şu* is delayed until six years of age, raising questions about the cognitive nature of deixis, its evolution, and development.

Speaker	Hearer	(¬SH)	Indexicals	speech act operator
x^1	y^2	(z^3)	Variable	bound (free)
I ego ni ben	you tu hi, zu sen	s/he *0 (ille) *0 (hura) *0 (o)	English C. Latin Basque Turkish	1, 2, 3 *pronominals* 1, 2, *3 1, 2, *3 1, 2, *3
			Deictics	bound (free)
this hic hau bu i	that iste hori şu ku	*0 (that) is, ille, ipse hura o ce	English C. Latin Basque Turkish Korean	1, 2, *3 *adnominals* 1, 2, 3 (Greenough et al.) 1, 2, 3 (Saltarelli 1988) 1, 2, 3 (Küntay and Özyürek) 1, 2, 3 (Diessel 1999)
here ècche hemen yeki honela acquescí	there èsse hor keki horrela asscí	(there) lóche han ceki hala allescí	English Marsican Basque Korean Basque Marsican	1, 2, *3 *adverbials* 1, 2, 3 place (Saltarelli 1988) 1, 2, 3 place (de Rijk 2008) 1, 2, 3 place (Diessel 1999) 1, 2, 3 manner (de Rijk 2008) 1, 2, 3 manner (Saltarelli)

Figure 6. The indexical distribution of deictics

6. Deriving Marsican adnominal demonstratives at the morpho-syntactic interface

Assuming a phase-theoretic syntax where the CP layer encodes as operators the indexical context and the content DP(Dem) phrase, where deictic elements are A'-bound variables (see 5.1), the morpho-syntax of spatial demonstratives in Marsican is derived as in Figure 7, through the operation Merge.

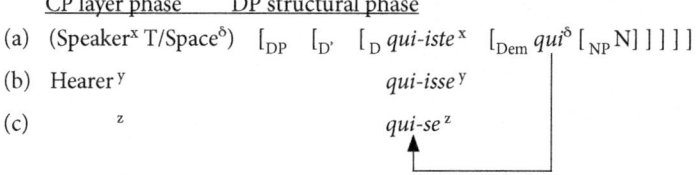

       CP layer phase   DP structural phase

(a) (Speaker^x T/Space$^\delta$) $[_{DP}$ $[_{D'}$ $[_D$ *qui-iste*^{x} $[_{Dem}$ *qui*$^\delta$ $[_{NP}$ N$]$ $]$ $]$ $]$ $]$

(b) Hearer^y *qui-isse*^{y}

(c)   z   *qui-se*^{z}

Figure 7. The Morpho-Syyntax of Marsican Demonstratives

An understanding of the evolutionary diachronic process is discussed in Section 7. The derivation in Figure 7 considers the demonstrative variable morpheme *qui-* (<*lat. *hic*) merging with the determiner. For M the hypothesis is supported by the morphological shape of the determiner *-se* (< lat. *ipse*), the recognized etymological source of the masculine definite article in Marsican diglotic Pescasseroli and 18th century Pelignian Scanno, along with Sardinian and Mallorquí.

7.   Excursus on the evolution and development of Marsican deixis

While preserving the three-value/three-term deictic system, Marsican undergoes a shift in demonstrative terms following the arguable demise of the first person *hic* in Latin. The conjecture is that *hic* is preserved in the development through diachronic merge as stated in Figure 8.1(a) and synchronically derived as proposed in Section 6.

		Latin		*P	Marsican (P)
S	1p	hic[1]		†	
H	2p	iste	1p	eccu+istu	*quíste*
	3p	ipse, ille[2]	2p	eccu+issu	*quísse*
		is[3]	3p	eccu+is	*quìse*

Figure 8.1(a). From Latin to Marsican

Notes to Figure 7.1(a)

i.   *hic* used 'near the speaker' (in time, place, or thought). It is hence called the 'demonstrative of the first person' (Greenough et al.1983, §297); Apparently lost in the dynamics of Romance grammaticalization.

ii. *ipse* and *ille* were in competition in the first millennium in southern Italian dialects for the formation of the definite articles (Tekavčić 1980, §4.2; Rohlfs 1968, §494). Marsican invites another path (cf. fn 3).

iii. *is* is a weaker P3 demonstrative in Latin and is especially common as a [third] person pronoun (Greenough et al. 1983, §297). In the dynamics of the shift in the three-term value system, Latin *is* survives in Marsican (P3) as masculine definite article *se* and demonstrative *quì-se*, uniquely in the (XX) diglossia of Pescasseroli.

		Latin		*	
S	I	hic		†	
H	II	iste	I,II	istu	rom. *ăst*, o.fr. *est*
				eccu+istu	rom. *acest, cest*
				ecce+istu	o.fr. *icest*, pr. *cest*, m.fr. *cet*
	III	ille	III	illu	rom. *ăl*
				eccu+illu	rom. *acel, cel*
				ecce+ille	eng. *tschel*, o.fr. *icel, cel*

Figure 8.1(b). Reduction from three- to two-terms (cf. Lausberg 1971, 139)

Notes to Figure 7.1.(b)

iv. In three-to-two term reduction, the value II of toscano †*codesto* is assumed by *quello* (II,III) (the C-free default term), rather than *questo* (the C-bound P1 term). The same goes with two-term languages like English.: *this* I, *that* I,II. Lausberg's I,II (rather than II,III) reduction needs empirical confirmation.

v. The higher number of two-term system (54%) vs. three-term grammatical systems (34%) reported in the typological survey (Figure 2) may indicate the "pure" essence of effects of the C–I binding opposition P1,2/3 (cf 5.1(e)). The tendency to a reduction of 3 > 2 may indicate the "pure" essence of indexicality (Kaplan 1989; Perry 1977; Hockett 1996) and the necessity of the speech act hypothesis (Austin 1962). Computationally, the shift may be favored by an optimal binarity constraint at PF interface. The same indexical split (1,2/3) surfaces elsewhere in Marsican morpho-syntax (cf. Section 1). The indexicality scenario offered in Figure 6, is supported by these evolutionary factors and their development across time, strictly within morpho-syntactic paradigm assumptions implicating access to the cognitive context of the speech act.

8. The deictic system in flux: Italian dialects and Romance

Beyond the historical evolution from Latin to Marsican proposed in Section 7, the deictic system of demonstratives in other Italian and Romance varieties is developing along the general typology presented in Figure 2, namely, from a three-term toward a two-term deictic system.[4] This reduction could be viewed to be in line with the indexical nature of deixis, encoding essentially Speaker > Hearer, the philosoper's "pure" indexicals (Perry 1997). The 1,2/3 person split is evidenced in syntactic behavior in Marsican.

In Figure 9 below, where the items in bold are in competition, we can observe a microshift in the E-language of Romance optimally defined by an I-lamguage binarity condition. For example *quello* is taking over the deictic function of *codesto*. This could describe the evolutionary status of the deictic system in Italian and Romanian (and English). In

---

4. The morpho-syntactic paradigm theory of the development of Romance demonstratives is not theoretically inconsistent nor in agreement with pragmatic grammaticalization proposals such as "subjectivization" (Stavinschi 2012). Rather, for either hypothesis the puzzle is in exploring why in Romance (and beyond) the alternation falls between a binary and a ternary system and back (Figure 2). Encoding in syntax the Speaker > Addressee irreflexive relation (Alcázar and Saltarelli 2014, 106) in the I-language of human speech acts provides formal boundary posts for the design of observable E-language. Accordingly, diachronic (and synchronic; cf. Section 6) shift is attributable to the general "polysemy of I–E language interface," specifically and arguably created by the demise of (Figure 6.1) or restructuring of Lat. hic† as suggested for Marsican (Section 6).

other neo-Latin varieties, however, the deictic term reduction involves either the generalization of the P1-term in Catalan, or the P2-term over the P1-term in Neapolitan, Barese, Brasilian Portuguese. While the term-reduction can be expected (cf. Figure 2.), we have also seen the Latin to Romance term-shift (cf. Figure 8.1) arguably attributed to the demise of the P1-*hic* to locative Root+proximity to Speaker, Adddressee, or neither.

	S	H	(-SH)	
Tuscan	questo	codesto/**quello**	**quello**	
Abruzzese	quištə	quissə	quillə	
Marsican (P, XX)	*quíste*	*quísse*	*quìse*	*/kʷ+iste, ipse, is/*
Neapolitan	chistə/**chissə**	**chissə**	chillə	
Calabrian	chistu	chissu	chillu	
Barese	**cussu**	**cussu**	cuddə	
Sicilian	chistu	chissu	chiḍḍu	
Catalan	**aquest**	**aquest**	aquell	
Portuguese (B)	este/**esse**	**esse**	aquele	
Portuguese	este	esse	aquele	
Spanish	este	ese	aquel	
Romanian	acest	**acel**	**acel**	
Italian	questo	**quello**	**quello**	

Figure 9. Pure indexicality, polysemy, and deictic shift

9. Conclusions[5]

The analysis of Marsican demonstratives presented here leads to a transparent account into the extended indexical nature of deixis at the Coonceptual-Intentional interface.

---

5.   The ontology of the proposed operator-variable binding hypothesis for encoding essential indexicals in syntax matured as a "performative hypothesis of imperative clauses" in Chapter 4 of Alcázar and Saltarelli (2014). The hypothesis, within a strong minimalist thesis (Chomsky 2005, 2008), was preceded by extensive empirical review of "imperatives across languages" (Ch. 2), and a critical analysis of extant proposals (including Speas and Tenny 2003; Sigurðsson 2004; Poletto& Zanuttini 2003; and Zanuttini 2008). While all achieved their defined goal, empirical phenomena such as the formal accountability of the philosopher reference shifting indexicals (Schlenker 2003) did not resolve crucial aspects of imperative deixis, such as logical irreflexivity of Speaker > Addressee (Alcázar and Saltarelli 2014, ch. 4), or an account of allocutivity in languages like Basque (Alcázar and Saltarelli 2014, ch.5). Such empirical issues of deictic syntax implicate essential indexicals' temporal concord ('Peter is sleeping now, *yesterday'), or person compatibiility ('give me that/*this book over there/*here'). It is argued that access to indexicals in the functional phase (CP) binding variables in the content phase (vP,nP) is a way to resolve inadequacies in the computation of narrow syntax, in addition promoting a philosophy/linguistics consensual connubium.

The pervasive role of deixis in parallel domains of syntax supports encoding indexical (prototype) categories (Speaker, Hearer) in syntax as a virtual conceptual necessity. Arguably, deixis falls under a variable binding hypothesis where Person 1 and Person 2 are fixed variables (i.e., bound by null operators in C, namely the prototype values of *Speaker* and *Hearer* respectively. Person 3 is a free variable).

This account of Marsican deixis is sustained by common properties of indexicality across parallel domains of deixis. Moreover the analysis is in accord with typological, historical, evolutionary, and independent studies of collateral morpho-syntactic phenomena. Research on allocutivity in Basque (Alcázar and Saltarelli 2014, ch.5) and indexical shift across languages of the world reach similar conclusions on the general conceptual necessity of encoding *Speaker* (and *Hearer)* in the syntactic computation of Human Language.

References

Abney, Steven. 1987. *The English Noun Phrase in Its Sentential Aspect*. Ph.D dissertation, MIT.

Alcázar, Asier, and Mario Saltarelli. 2014. *The Syntax of Imperatives*. Cambridge: Cambridge University Press.

Anderson, John, and Edward Keenan. 1985. "Deixis." In *Language Typology and Syntactic Description*, ed. by Timothy Shopen, 259–308. Cambridge: Cambridge University Press.

Austin, J.L. 1962. *How to do Things with Words*. Cambridge, MA: Harvard University Press.

Bernstein, Judy. 2008. "Reformulating the Determiner Phrase Analysis." *Language and Linguistics Compass* 2.6: 1246–1270. DOI: 10.1111/j.1749-818X.2008.00091.x

Berwick, Robert C., and Noam Chomsky 2011. "The Biolinguistic Program: The Current State of Its Development." In *The Biolinguistic Enterprise*, ed. by Anna Maria Di Sciullo and Cedric Boeckx, 19–41. Oxford: Oxford U. Press.

Chomsky, Noam. 2005. "Three Factors in Language Design." *Linguitic Inquiry* 36: 1–22. DOI: 10.1162/0024389052993655

Chomsky, Noam. 2008. "On Phases." In *Foundational Issues in Linguistic Theory. In Honor of Jean-Roger Vergnaud*, ed. by Robert Freidin, Carlos P. Otero, and Maria Luisa Zubizarreta, 133–166. Cambridge, MA: MIT Press.

de Rijk, Rudolf P.G. 2008. *Standard Basque. A Progressive Grammar*. Cambridge, MA: MIT Press.

Devoto, Giacomo. 1974. *Il linguaggio d'Italia*. Milano: Rizzoli Editore.

Diessel, Holger. 1999. *Demonstratives. Form, Function and Grammaticalization*. Amsterdam: John Benjamins. DOI: 10.1075/tsl.42

Diessel, Holger. 2013. "Distance Contrasts in Demonstratives." In *The World Atlas of Language Structures Online*, ed. by Matthew S. Dryer and Martin Haspelmath. Leipzig: Max Planck Institute for Evolutionary Anthropology. (Available online at http://wals.info/chapter/41)

Giorgi, Alessandra. 2010. *About the Speaker: Towards a Syntax of Indexicality*. Oxford: Oxford University Press.

Greenough, J.B., G.L. Kittredge, A.A. Howard, and Benj. L. D'Ooge. 1983. *Allen and Greenough's New Latin Grammar*. New Rochelle, New York: Aristide D. Caratzas.

Guardiano, Cristina, and Giuseppe Longobardi. 2008.*The Syntax of Demonstratives: A Parametric Analysis*. Ms.

Hockett, Charles F. 1966. "The Problem of Universals in Language." In *Universals of Language*, ed. by Joseph H. Greenberg, 1–22. Cambridge, MA: MIT Press.

Kaplan, David. 1977. "Demonstratives." In *Themes From Kaplan*, ed. by Joseph Almog, John Perry, and Howard Wettstein, 481–563. Oxford: Oxford University Press.

King, Jeffrey C. 2001. *Complex Demonstratives. A Quantificational Account*. Cambridge, MA: MIT Press.

Koopman, Hilda, and Dominique Sportiche. 1982. "Variables and the Bijection Principle." *The Linguistic Review* 2: 139–160. DOI: 10.1515/tlir.1982.2.2.139

Küntay, Aylin C., and Asli Özyürek, 2006. "Learning To Use Demonstratives in Conversation: What Do Language Specific Strategies in Turkish Reveal?" *Journal of Child Language* 33 (2): 303–320. DOI: 10.1017/S0305000906007380

Lausberg, Heinrich. 1971. *Linguistica Romanza*, Vol. II (Morfologia). Milano: Feltrinelli.

Liao, Wei-wen Roger, and Jean Roger Vergnaud. 2010. "Phases and DP." Talk given at the GLOW in Asia 8, August, 2010, Beijing Language and Culture University.

Neri, A.T., and Mario Saltarelli 2005. *Genere e identità linguistica*. Pescasseroli: Istituto B. Croce.

Nunberg, Geoffrey. 1993. "Indexicality and Deixis." *Linguitics and Philosophy* 16.1: 1–43. DOI: 10.1007/BF00984721

Perry, John. 1999. "Indexicals and demonstratives." In *A Companion to Philosophy of language*, ed. by Robert Hale and Crispin Wright, 586–612. Oxford: Blackwell.

Poletto, Cecilia, and Raffaella Zanuttini. 2003. "Making imperatives. Evidence from Central Rhaeto-Romance." In *The Syntax of Italian Dialects*, ed. by Christina Tortora, 175–207. New York: Oxford University Press.

Rohlfs, G. 1968. *Grammatica storica della lingua italiana e dei suoi dialetti. Morfologia*. Torino: Einaudi.

Saltarelli, Mario. 1988. *Basque*. (*Croom Helm Descriptive Grammars*.) London: Croom Helm.

Saltarelli, Mario. 1999. "Sull'identità linguistica dei Marsi: L'articolo determinativo." *Argomenti* 19: 36–46.

Saltarelli, Mario. 2011. "Spatial Demonstratives in Marsican: Towards a Grammaticalization of Indexical Reference." Talk given at the Sixth Cambridge Italian Dialect Syntax Meeting (CIDSM6), June 16–17, 2011, University of Cambridge, Cambridge, U.K.

Saltarelli, Mario. 2014. "On Language Unity and Disunity." *Forum Italicum* 48.2: 188–201. [Special Issue: *Linguistic Identities of Italian in Italy and North America*, ed. by Lori Repetti and Hermann Haller.]

Saltarelli, Mario. 2014. "The Context-sensitivitiy of Enclitic Possessives. Evidence from Abruzzan, Salentino, and Grico." Talk given at the Eighth Cambridge Italian Dialect Syntax Meeting (CIDSM8), June 20–22, 2014, Universities of Padua and Venice, Italy.

Schlenker, Philippe. 2003. "A Plea for Monsters." *Linguistics and Philosophy* 26: 29–120. DOI: 10.1023/A:1022225203544

Sigurðsson. Halldór Á. 2004. "The Syntax of Person, Tense, and Speech Features." *Rivista di Linguistica* 16.1: 219–251. [Special Issue ed. by Valentina Bianchi and Ken Safir.]

Speas, Margaret, and Carol Tenny. 2003. "Configurational Properties of Point of View Roles." In *Asymmetry in Grammar*, ed. by Anna Maria Di Sciullo, 315–343. Amsterdam: Benjamins. DOI: 10.1075/la.57.15spe

Stavinschi, Alexandra. 2012. "On the Development of the Romance Demonstrative Sytems. Historical Remarks and Theoretical Conclusions." *Diachronica* 29.1: 72–97. DOI: 10.1075/dia.29.1.03sta

Tekavčić. Pavao. 1980. *Grammatica storica dell'italiano.* Vol. II. Bologna: Il Mulino.

West, Donna E. 2011. "Deixis As A Symbolic Phenomenon." *Linguistik Online* 50.

Zanuttini, Raffaella. 2008. "Encoding the Addressee in the Syntax: Evidence from English Imperative Subjects." *Natural Language and Linguistic Theory* 26 (1): 185–218. DOI: 10.1007/s11049-007-9029-6

Index